Baptists and Revivals

MERCER UNIVERSITY PRESS

Endowed by

TOM WATSON BROWN
and
THE WATSON-BROWN FOUNDATION, INC.

Baptists and Revivals

Papers from the Seventh International

Conference on Baptist Studies

Edited by William L. Pitts Jr.

Foreword by *David Bebbington*

MERCER UNIVERSITY PRESS | *Macon, Georgia*
2018

MUP/ P574

© 2018 by Mercer University Press
Published by Mercer University Press
1501 Mercer University Drive
Macon, Georgia 31207
All rights reserved

9 8 7 6 5 4 3 2 1

Books published by Mercer University Press are printed on acid-free paper that meets the requirements of the American National Standard for Information Sciences—Permanence of Paper for Printed Library Materials.

Printed and bound in the United States.

This book is set in Adobe Caslon

ISBN   978-0-88146-683-6

Cataloging-in-Publication Data is available from the Library of Congress

Contents

Contributors	ix
Foreword by David Bebbington	xi
Introduction by Bill Pitts	1

PART 1: BAPTISTS AND REVIVAL IN NORTH AMERICA

1. Jonathan Edwards, Revival, and the Baptists,
   by Chris Chun   11

2. The Holy Spirit and Right Living: Separate Baptists and
   the Southern Revival,
   by Rosalie Beck   32

3. Baptist in South Carolina During the Second Great Awakening,
   by Kim Kellison   44

4. Baptists and Early Pentecostal Revivalism,
   by C. Douglas Weaver   64

5. Convert Every Tight-Wad You Can: Revivalism as Fundraising
   among the Southern Baptists,
   by Andrew Smith   88

6. University and Revival: The Baylor Youth-Led Revival 1945–46,
   by William L. Pitts Jr.   98

7. "O how many things brot tears from my eyes": Sympathetic Reading
   in Nineteenth-Century Baptist Piety,
   by Keith Grant   113

8. The Mission of Isabel Crawford: Applying the Pattern of Revival,
   by Marilyn Färdig Whiteley   129

PART 2: BAPTISTS AND REVIVAL IN EUROPE

9. Andrew Fuller and the Revival of Eighteenth-Century Particular Baptist Life,
   by Peter Morden   141

10. "Useful Learning": Theological Training and the Particular Baptist Revival in the Long Eighteenth Century,
    by Anthony R. Cross   160

11. John Ryland, Jr. (1753-1825), Evangelical Calvinism, and the Evangelical Revival,
    by Christopher W. Crocker   181

12. The Hymns of Anne Steele in John Rippon's Selection of Hymns: The Sung Theology of the English Particular Baptist Revival,
    by Joseph V. Carmichael   200

13. Baptists and the Second Great Awakening in England, 1859-65,
    by Terry Carter   214

14. "A Larger Outpouring of the Spirit of God": Baptists in Scotland and the 1859 Revival,
    by Brian Talbot   227

15. Baptist Revivals in Nineteenth-Century Scotland,
    by Harry Sprange   242

16. Revival among Scottish Baptists in the Early Twentieth Century,
    by Kenneth B. E. Roxburgh   252

17. British Baptist Revival at the Front during the First World War,
    by Neil E. Allison   274

18. "Dumb Dogs that Cannot Bark": The Puritan Origins of Preaching Revival,
    by Jan Martijn Abrahamse   288

19. Revival Among the Aliens: The Case of Lithuanian Baptists,
    by Lina Toth (Andronoviene)   304

20. Three Romanian Baptist Evangelists: Pitt Popovici,
    Liviu Olah and Iosif Ton,
    by George Hancock-Stefan   324

PART 3: BAPTISTS AND REVIVAL IN THE MAJORITY WORLD

21. New Zealand Baptists and the Cultural Restraint of Revival,
    by Martin Sutherland   339

22. Joseph Kemp, Revivalism, and the New Zealand Baptist Movement,
    by John Tucker   355

23. German Baptist Churches of Southeast Queensland and Revival,
    by David Parker   369

24. A Hundred Years of Baptist Ministry in Bangladesh,
    by Dennis Dilip Datta   382

25. Baptists and Revival in Africa through Changing Scenes: The
    Nigerian Baptist Experience, 1850-2014,
    by Simon Ademola Ajayi   393

Index   409

The James N. Griffith Series in Baptist Studies

This series on Baptist life and thought explores and investigates Baptist history, offers analyses of Baptist theologies, provides studies in hymnody, and examines the role of Baptists in societies and cultures around the world. The series also includes classics of Baptist literature, letters, diaries, and other writings. For a complete list of titles in the series, visit www.mupress.org and visit the series page.

—C. Douglas Weaver, Series Editor

Contributors

Jan Martijn Abrahamse, Tutor Systematic Theology and Ethics, Dept. of Theology, Christelijke Hogeschool Ede and Research Fellow Dutch Baptist Seminary, Amsterdam, The Netherlands

Simon Ademola Ajayi, Professor of History, University of Ibadan, Ibadan, Nigeria

Neil E. Allison, Pastor of Helensburgh Baptist Church and the "Official Historian of the United Navy, Army and Air Force Board," Helensburg, Scotland

David Bebbington, Professor of History, University of Stirling, Stirling, Scotland, UK

Rosalie Beck, Associate Professor, History of Christianity, Dept. of Religion, Baylor University, Waco, Texas, USA

Joseph V. Carmichael, Teaching Elder, Presbyterian Church in America, Professor, Birmingham Theological Seminary, Montgomery, Alabama, USA

Terry Carter, Professor of History of Christianity, Pruet School of Christian Studies, Ouachita Baptist University, Arkadelphia, Arkansas, USA

Chris Chun, Associate Professor of Church History, Gateway Seminary, Ontario, California, USA

Christopher W. Crocker, Graduate Student, Bristol Baptist College, Bristol, UK

Anthony R. Cross, Member of the Faculty of Theology and Religion, Oxford University, Oxford, UK

Dennis Dilip Datta, Bangladesh Baptist Church Fellowship

Keith Grant, PhD Candidate, Dept. of History, University of New Brunswick, Fredericton, New Brunswick, Canada

George Hancock-Stefan, Palmer Theological Seminary, Philadelphia, Pennsylvania, USA

Kim Kellison, Chair, Department of History, Baylor University, Waco, Texas, USA

Peter Morden, Vice Principal and Tutor in Church History and Spirituality, Spurgeon's College, London, UK

David Parker, Baptist Church Archives, Queensland, Gaythorne, Queensland, Australia

William L. Pitts Jr., Professor of History of Christianity, Dept. of Religion, Baylor University, Waco, Texas, USA

Kenneth B. E. Roxburgh, S. Louis and Ann W. Armstrong Professor of Religion, Samford University, Birmingham, Alabama, USA

Andrew C. Smith, Assistant Professor of Religion; Director, Center for Baptist Studies, Department of Religion, Carson-Newman University, Jefferson City, Tennessee, USA

Harry Sprange, Pastor Bathgate Baptist Church, Bathgate, Scotland, UK

Martin Sutherland, Academic Dean, Laidlaw College, Auckland, New Zealand.

Brian R. Talbot, Minister of Broughty Ferry Baptist Church, Dundee, and Extraordinary Professor, North West University Faculty of Theology, South Africa

Lina Toth (Andronoviene), Assistant Principal and Lecturer in Practical Theology, Scottish Baptist College, University of the West of Scotland, Paisley, Scotland, UK

John Tucker, Lecturer in History and Homiletics, Carey Baptist College, Auckland, New Zealand

C. Douglas Weaver, Professor of History of Christianity, Dept. of Religion, Baylor University, Waco, Texas, USA

Marilyn Färdig Whiteley, Independent Scholar, Guelph, Ontario, Canada

Foreword

In the aftermath of the First World War, in 1919, the small Baptist community of the southern region of Mizoram in the hill territory of northeastern India was transformed by "a wave of Revival." A delighted missionary was able to report that "companies of joyful, Spirit-filled young men and women" were "going up and down the land proclaiming by word and song the Gospel of the Cross."[1] Dancing, the spontaneous use of drums, and the composition of original hymns accompanied the singing. There were many conversions. The whole area caught what seemed like spiritual fire. The expectation of revival had been present since the arrival from Britain of two representatives of the Baptist Missionary Society in 1903. Four years later a flame of revival burned briefly among the Mizo Baptists through influences coming from the north of the territory, where Welsh Calvinistic Methodists had established a mission. The Welsh Revival of 1904–5, a movement that naturally swayed the Calvinistic Methodist missionaries, was behind the sparks kindled among the Baptists. Prayer meetings were held four or more times a week and entire villages professed conversion. But the events of 1907 were eclipsed by what happened from 1919 onward. Between that year and 1924 church membership mushroomed by over 300 percent. It was the most striking instance of church growth on any field of the Baptist Missionary Society during the twentieth century.

The phenomenon of revival, an intensification of spiritual life accompanied by a significant number of conversions, had been known since at least the early seventeenth century, when it sprang up among some of the Presbyterians of Scotland. The Congregationalists of New England experienced comparable awakenings in the later seventeenth and early eighteenth centuries even before their most eminent theologian, Jonathan Edwards, gave revivals wide publicity in the 1730s and 1740s. Baptists tended to copy the pattern of the Congregationalists, not least because many of the Baptists committed to revivalism in the eighteenth-century colonies of America had begun as Congregationalists. But Baptists were soon touched by the less restrained ways of the Methodists, who allowed more lay initiative and more emotional expression. Like the Methodists, the Baptists grew by revival, especially in the American

---

[1] Baptist Missionary Society Annual Report, 18–19, quoted by Brian Stanley, *The History of the Baptist Missionary Society, 1792–1992* (Edinburgh: T&T Clark, 1992), 275.

South, during the nineteenth century. By the opening of the twentieth century Baptists were contributing to the early stages of Pentecostal revivalism. The tradition of revivals lived on among the Baptists themselves long into the twentieth century, merging with charismatic renewal in many lands.

Consequently, there was no one style of Baptist revival. Baptists participated in many different approaches over the centuries. In particular, they were involved in awakenings that were largely spontaneous and missions that were carefully planned though equally termed "revivals." The spontaneous variety could affect a single church but could also rouse a whole nation. Thus the Welsh Revival of 1904–5, in which one of the leading figures was the Baptist minister R. B. Jones, percolated into virtually every corner of the land. Of the planned variety, the greatest exponent was Billy Graham, himself a Southern Baptist minister. The missions arranged by the Billy Graham Evangelistic Association throughout the world during the later twentieth century were organized with punctilious efficiency. Baptists had no monopoly on any of the patterns of revival but played a prominent part in most of them.[2]

The variety of revivals is reflected in the essays in this volume. All the papers were delivered at the seventh International Conference on Baptist Studies held at Luther King House in Manchester, England, in July 2015. The sequence of conferences, which have been held every three years since 1997, is designed to throw light on the history of Baptists of all types in any country over the whole period of their existence. The seventh took up the topic of revival because, as so many papers in this volume demonstrate, it has often (though not always) been such a prominent feature of Baptist life, and especially Baptist growth. There are papers on America, where the phenomenon put down deep roots, and Canada, but also on Britain, continental Europe, New Zealand, Australia, Bangladesh, and Nigeria. The book shows that the stirring experience of the Baptists of Mizoram in 1919 was far from unique.

David Bebbington, University of Stirling
January 2016

---

[2] There is discussion of the trajectory and interpretation of revivals in David Bebbington, *Victorian Religious Revivals: Culture and Piety in Local and Global Contexts* (Oxford: Oxford University Press, 2012), chaps. 1 and 2.

Introduction

William L. Pitts Jr.

Since their notable influence during the mid-eighteenth century, revivals have been a key element in the Baptist story. Many Baptist churches have welcomed revivals as a source of renewal in their churches and as a major strategy of their evangelism. Survey histories of Baptists often discuss the impact of the First and Second Great Awakenings on Baptist growth during the eighteenth and early nineteenth centuries. But following those initial revivals the Baptist narratives often shift to other important subjects and neglect later revivals. Yet revivals have remained a significant means to Baptist growth. This book addresses the larger story of revivals in Baptist life from the Great Awakening to the present day and across the globe. Each chapter is devoted to a revival or a set of revivals or to some dimension of the practice of revivalism.

These chapters address major issues in the study of revivals, including definition, characteristics, and influence. The definition of revival depends on context of place and time. The authors of these chapters include a variety of expressions of religious vitality, including Pentecostalism, missions, church renewal, and personal deepening of religious emotion and spirituality. Often described as periods of intensified religious experience, revivals frequently produce noticeably higher levels of emotional intensity. Explanations for revival have been variously traced to changing theological understandings, evangelists' effectiveness, extended prayer meetings, the presence of the Spirit of God, adverse social circumstances such as impoverishment or war, or favorable cultural contexts such as a sense of community. Equally intriguing is the question of why revivals end; recognizing their limited duration, participants often speak of "seasons of revival." Another notable characteristic is the way revivals tend to influence additional churches throughout a region or even spread to other nations, creating historically recognized eras of revival such as the Lay Revivals of 1857–62, the Welsh Revival, and the Billy Graham revivals and its imitators. Historians are also interested in trying to explain why revivals do not occur in some regions at all. The influence of revivals is often measured in terms of conversions and church growth, but interpreters also identify a variety of additional outcomes. The studies presented here address these and other related dimensions of revivalism among Baptists.

By the mid-eighteenth century Protestantism was well established in Germany and the northern European Continent, in Britain, and in the American colonies. In all three of these areas Protestant churches experienced important new forms of renewal, respectively labeled Pietism, Methodism, and Revivalism, and collectively often called "The Evangelical Awakening." All three movements shifted the focus of becoming Christian from baptism to the experience of personal conversion and individual profession of faith. The quest for conversions provided the ethos that nurtured revivalism.

The studies in this volume are arranged by geographical regions. Part 1 is devoted to Baptist revivals in North America. Revivals have been a recurrent influence contributing to Baptist growth in the United States from the eighteenth century to the present. Many observers doubt the continued viability of revivals in North America in the future, but there is little doubt of their central role in the past. Part 2 explores the Baptist revivals in Europe, beginning in England and influencing all of Britain, with chapters on Scotland, Wales, and Ireland. In the nineteenth century, Baptists experienced revivals on the Continent, including the eastern European countries of Lithuania and Romania, both represented here. Part 3 examines Baptist revival experiences outside of North America and Europe, in what is now often called the "Majority World." Baptists have succeeded in planting churches in both New Zealand and Australia. In Bangladesh they have struggled, but they have managed to establish a small presence there, whereas in Nigeria their rapid growth puts them among the largest Baptist constituencies in the world.

Part 1 explores the Baptist revival experience in the United States and Canada. Among the North American colonies that would become the United States, the series of revival meetings in the eighteenth century, later called The Great Awakening, influenced Baptist growth directly. Whereas the English evangelist George Whitefield was the face and voice of revival, the American pastor Jonathan Edwards was the theologian of revival—affirming the necessity of engaging the heart and the will in conversion. Historians now emphasize the transatlantic character of the revival. Chris Chun documents Edwards's influence on Baptists and their revivals in both Britain and North America. Chun traces Edwards's direct impact on Andrew Fuller and William Carey through their reading of Edwards's *Freedom of the Will* and his *Humble Attempt*. He shows that Edwards also influenced Baptist leaders in America, especially in the way he articulated a theology of revival.

Rosalie Beck traces the paths of the eighteenth-century Baptist revival from New England to the southern United States through the efforts of Shubal Stearns

INTRODUCTION

and Daniel and Martha Stearns Marshall. Reared in Connecticut as Congregationalists, they converted to the Separate Baptist position. These three preachers migrated to North Carolina in 1754 where they engaged in an effective style of revival preaching, and where they established Sandy Creek Baptist Association, which was a powerful influence on Baptists in the southern United States for generations to come.

Due in no little part to the tradition of revivalism, Baptists eventually grew to become the largest Protestant denomination in the United States. A key turning point in this development was the Baptist appropriation of revival patterns of the Second Great Awakening during the early years of the nineteenth century. Baptist revival preachers learned to connect with masses of ordinary citizens, leading to the conversion of thousands of people. Kim Kellison examines the impact of the Second Awakening revivals on Baptists in South Carolina during the 1830s. Led by W. B. Johnson, Furman student preachers and other evangelists, and prompted by a widely reported astronomical phenomenon described as a darkening of the sun, revivals occurred frequently at mass associational meetings and also at individual local Baptist churches. Revivals of this era were formative in establishing Baptist life in South Carolina.

Many modern studies of revivalism now include Pentecostalism as a form of Christian renewal akin to traditional revivalism. Doug Weaver studies the intersection of early Pentecostal revivalism with Baptists, pointing out that numerous Pentecostal leaders were former Baptists. He focuses especially on Adolphus Spalding Worrell (1831–1908), who "was the best known Baptist to observe and interact with the early Pentecostal movement." Already age sixty when he testified to a "life-changing experience" of being "filled by the Holy Spirit," Worrell had support from some circles, but also experienced strong negative reaction from Holiness, Fundamentalist, and Baptist critics.

During the 1920s the rapidly growing Southern Baptist Convention (SBC) created its first coordinated fundraising campaign. Andrew Smith notes several ways Baptist leaders sought to employ the successful techniques of evangelistic revivalism in order to persuade church members to support the causes of the denomination with their financial resources. In the end they modeled the new Cooperative Program on the already well-established systematic giving to missions pioneered by the Woman's Missionary Union.

A university-based revival is the subject of Bill Pitts's study. Nurtured by the religious ethos of a Baptist university and led by energetic youth in the context of World War II, the 1945–46 campus revivals proved highly successful. Baptist leaders asked the students to take the revival format to larger outdoor gatherings in major cities across the south. Again, the revivals were a success. In its third iteration local pastors asked for this university style revival to be adjusted to local Baptist youth revivals held in smaller towns across the southern region of the United States. The results were notable in church growth and especially in recruiting a generation of ministers who served Baptists for the following half century.

Accounts of two religious figures represent nineteenth- and twentieth-century Canadian Baptist piety. Keith Grant describes Edward Manning's devotion to reading religious literature, especially missionary publications. His *Diary* from the 1820s and 1830s reveals the intensity of his feelings—"I am melted to tears," he wrote. Grant sees weeping as a common expression of deep emotion in Baptist piety in this era. Insights of studies of emotion are brought to bear in understanding religious sensibilities experienced in revivals.

Marilyn Färdig Whiteley recounts the Baptist missionary life of Canadian Isabel Crawford. Crawford was converted as a child, but her baptism was delayed so that deacons could observe the quality of her Christian life; after an interim she was baptized and began to engage in "Christian activity." She was deeply impressed when she attended revival services led by Dwight L. Moody and later those led by Billy Sunday. Crawford devoted her life to working among Native Americans in the states of Oklahoma, Washington, and New York. Whiteley shows how Crawford sought to replicate her own personal religious experience of conversion, nurturing before baptism, and service as the model for shaping the spirituality of Native Americans.

The chapters in Part 2 address Baptist revivals in Europe. A recurring question in historiography is the cause of revival. Interpreters have considered fear, prayer, singing, emotion, gender, class, and charisma among other possible causes. Revival participants and historians often note personal and spiritual qualities of individual preachers as a key factor in the success of revivals, while notice of their education has been neglected. Anthony Cross explores the establishment of Baptist training centers in Britain beginning in the eighteenth century. He demonstrates their significance for training of ministers in Bible, in languages, and in the practice of preaching. The goal was to train the young ministers so that they would be "useful" in their calling by combining religious zeal with a high quality education.

Chris Crocker observes John Ryland Jr.'s first-hand experiences of the Great Evangelical Revival. Ryland's acquaintance with leading preachers of the Awakening, his own conversion experience in 1767, his attendance at revival meetings, and the influence of mentors all shaped his ministry. Crocker shows how the experience of revival influenced Ryland's doctrinal stance as a Particular Baptist who combined Calvinism with experiential religion.

Andrew Fuller, long recognized as instrumental in Baptist evangelical efforts in England and beyond, reshaped theology in a way that accommodated and encouraged revival and missions. Peter Morden focuses on Fuller's spirituality, arguing that in the 1780s he was influenced by Puritan patterns, including lack of assurance of salvation, but that after 1792 he became more confident and joyful, due in part to his evangelical activity, especially his work for the new overseas mission.

Congregational singing has been a central part of revival culture. Joseph Carmichael examines the importance of Baptist hymn writer Anne Steele for revivals in England. Her hymns appeared in John Rippon's *Selection of Hymns* and were widely used during the revivals of the 1780s–1830s era. Congregational singing took its place in revival services from the eighteenth century to the present, helping to foster among the laity the vital dimension of a feeling of participation in the revival meetings.

Terry Carter devotes much of his chapter to defining characteristics of revivals and comparing these markers with the record of events described as revival in England during the period 1859–65. This was a principal era of awakening according to pioneer revival historian J. Edwin Orr. Carter challenges Orr's methods and conclusions; nevertheless, with Orr, he finds evidence to support Baptist desire for religious awakening during this era.

Three chapters focus on Baptist revivals in Scotland during the nineteenth and twentieth centuries. Brian Talbot analyzes the 1859 British revival, with particular emphasis on Scotland. He traces the revival from its genesis in America (1857), to its spread to Ulster, and finally to mainland Britain. This revival, like its American progenitor, is noted for its lay leadership and emphasis on united prayer meetings. Talbot concedes that the increases in church attendance and converts were very modest in Ulster, Scotland, and England. However, he points to other important outcomes: the revivals helped prompt the Baptists to organize the Association of Baptist Churches in Ireland and the Baptist Union in England and Scotland.

Harry Sprange offers a general survey of revivals in Scotland during the nineteenth century. Following the founding work of the Haldane brothers, revivals continued throughout the century. Sprange touches on numerous regions of revival in Scotland, leading evangelists, churches affected by revivals, and descriptions of hearers' feelings and responses. He describes the of Dwight L. Moody and Ira D. Sankey 1874 mission to Scotland as a second wave of revival which influenced Scottish churches down to the end of the century.

Ken Roxburgh's chapter explores the far-reaching Scottish revival of the early twentieth century, and he argues that the chief catalyst was the Welsh Revival of 1904–5. He traces revival influence in four major regions of Scotland and includes discussion of leadership roles by women, interactions with early phases of Pentecostalism, and hopes for revival during the Great War. Following the war, revival came again in 1921–1922 to the Fisher Folk of northeast Scotland. However, Baptists in Scotland overall declined numerically, from 21,175 in 1920 to just over 14,000 in 2000. Roxburgh concludes that revival was not the answer for Baptists in Scotland during the twentieth century.

War brought new challenges to churches. Neil Allison examines the work of the chaplaincy of Baptist ministers from the United Kingdom during World War I, citing evidence of their efforts to bring about revival. He includes an account of the work of John Howard Shakespeare, leader of the Society of the Baptist Union of Great Britain and Ireland, who sought and secured formal recognition of Baptist ministers as military chaplains. Allison discusses the work of these chaplains from England, Scotland, and Wales, and as far afield as Australia and New Zealand. The chaplains reported local revivals among soldiers during the war years, but loss of life to war and pneumonia was so high that the total numerical results of the revivals of the war era cannot be measured accurately.

Critical to the success of revivals is the preaching style of evangelists. Jan Martijn Abrahamse compares the Puritan style of preaching with the preaching of Charles Haddon Spurgeon. Abrahamse cites Spurgeon's *Autobiography*, in which he declared, "my gratitude most of all is due to God, not for books, but for the preached Word…. The revealed Word awakened me, but it was the preached Word that saved me." The centrality of effective preaching is clear in Spurgeon's ministry. Abrahamse finds the requisite qualities of revivalist preaching articulated and practiced already among the Puritans, especially noting the shift from instruction to exhortation. He thereby links nineteenth-century revivalism to seventeenth-century Protestantism.

Turning to Eastern Europe, Lina Toth analyzes the Baptist experience in Lithuania and shows how cultural context decisively affected religious experience there. In the nineteenth century Lithuania was divided into Prussian Lithuania and Lithuania Proper. The Prussian region was dominated by German Lutheran culture, and in that region Pietism provided context for nurturing Baptist growth. Pietism emphasized the importance of a personal conversion experience, and this emphasis was conducive to Baptist success among Lithuanian speakers in Prussia.

INTRODUCTION

By contrast, the Lithuanian homeland has long embraced Roman Catholicism as part of its national identity. Roman Catholic culture resisted Pietistic-Baptist practice, and Baptist influence here was severely limited. In fact, Toth concludes that there was "no revival whatsoever" in Lithuania Proper.

Finally in Europe, George Hancock-Stefan recounts the ministry of three effective Baptist ministers in twentieth-century Romania. Despite suffering persecution by the state and eventually exile from their own country, these evangelistic ministers led their churches openly and offered leadership for Baptists despite opposition by authorities. The author gives special attention to the several qualities which place these ministers in the tradition of earlier revivalists.

Part 3 of the book reaches far beyond accounts of transatlantic revivals in Europe and North America to the Majority World, including examples of the Baptist experience in New Zealand, Australia, Asia, and Africa. Martin Sutherland asserts that New Zealand Baptists did not enjoy a strong tradition of revival, and he searches for an explanation. He notes that New Zealand was a late British colony, established without infrastructure of religious community found in other parts of the British Empire. Drawing on cultural studies, he believes that revivals are communal. He notes that the Maori, who enjoyed a common cultural cohesiveness, experienced a significant revival. However, a dominant image among New Zealand immigrants was "the man alone," and no sufficient cultural community existed on which to build a Baptist revival ethos.

John Tucker offers a revised perspective on evangelist John Kemp. Kemp was an internationally known revivalist whose ministry in New Zealand during the 1920s had a profound influence on Baptists of that country. Tucker argues that whereas Kemp is usually interpreted in terms of his Fundamentalism, a more adequate lens for understanding the man is his revivalism. According to Tucker, Kemp subordinated everything else to his desire to establish among his hearers "the necessary conditions for revival."

David Parker recounts the experience of the German Baptist immigrants in southeast Queensland, Australia. Noting that revival is a much-debated topic in Australian Christianity, he identifies key characteristics in the usual definitions of revival, and concludes that revival sentiment did in fact play a significant role in the establishment of this Baptist community.

Baptist missionaries have planted Baptist churches throughout much of the world. Dennis Dilap Datta describes efforts to establish Baptist churches in Bangladesh. Several missionary societies planted churches during the past century, but they failed to consult with local church members or to include them in leadership positions. Growth was slow until around 1970 when a new evangelical thrust inspired by Billy Graham and evangelical conferences held in Europe produced vision for new forms of evangelism in Bangladesh and accounted for much more rapid growth of Baptist churches. In this predominantly Muslim culture traditional public revivalism was not a viable option; conversions had to proceed one by one, based on individual personal contacts. Baptist churches in Bangladesh today face serious challenges, including limited resources and legal restrictions. Nevertheless, in his study Datta celebrates the centennial of Baptist presence in his country.

In contrast to Bangladesh, the final chapter describes the phenomenal Baptist success in Nigeria, which now has one of the largest Baptist populations in the world. Ademola Ajayi recounts the introduction of Baptists into the nation in the nineteenth century and describes four critical periods of transformation and revitalization, including the Nigerian Baptist Schism (1888), Reunion and Formation of a Convention (1914), Post-World War II success (1945–80), and finally, the explosive growth during and since the Charismatic Revival of the 1980s and 1990s. Ajayi finds expressions of spiritual vitality, revival, and renewal in each of the major stages of Nigerian Baptist history.

These studies demonstrate the powerful influence of revivals among Baptists. The remarkable two-and-a-half centuries of revivalism and its global adaptability have made the practice of revivalism an enduring paradigm in Baptist life. It gives me pleasure to express my deep gratitude to the contributors who have recorded their accounts of Baptists and their revivals. I would also like to recognize and express my deepest thanks to my graduate assistant, Scott Prather, for his excellent assistance in producing this volume.

Part 1

North America

1

Jonathan Edwards, Revival, and the Baptists

Chris Chun

The eighteenth century ushered in a novel and optimistic way of thinking about human capacities. The Age of Enlightenment, or Age of Reason, saw external authority, such as religion, as bondage that hampered people's ability to reach their full human potential. As these streams of ideas began to dominate mainstream culture on both sides of the Atlantic, ecclesiastical institutions declined into worldliness and unbelief on the eve of the Evangelical Revival in England as well as the Great Awakening in America. Although the overall situation looked bleak, it could be seen as an opportune time for revivals. After a period of moral decline, revivals are series of spiritual renewals that restore the church to a more fervent relationship with God. The revival, therefore, could be accompanied by mass conversions and produce positive moral influence in the life of the church.[1] Among all the great Christian thinkers who lived in the Enlightenment epoch, said Harry Stout, "No eighteenth-century figure thought more about revivals than Jonathan Edwards."[2] His influence and the reception of his corpus on worldwide revivals are far beyond the scope of this paper. Yet, the indebtedness that we, as Baptists, have in this New England divine within selected transatlantic revivals is its intended scope.

First, this essay will survey Edwards's influence on the Particular Baptist revival in England vis-à-vis Bristol Academy and Northamptonshire Association. The significant Baptist admirers of Edwards from those two networks

---

[1] For precondition of the renewal and its impact on gospel in the church and culture, see Richard Lovelace, *The Dynamics of Spiritual Life: An Evangelical Theology of Renewal* (Downers Grove: InterVarsity Press, 1979) 75, 81–94, 145–200.

[2] Harry S. Stout, "Edwards and Revival," in *Understanding Jonathan Edwards: An Introduction to America's Theologian*, ed. Gerald R. McDermott (New York: Oxford University Press, 2009) 37.

will be mentioned. The second part will examine Edwards's impact on Baptists in America. It will highlight early Regular and Separate Baptist movements as well as Charleston and Sandy Creek traditions, and underscore how these groups have interacted with America's premier theologian. Last, it will examine Edwards's influence on Baptists in the twentieth and twenty-first centuries by noticing the recent New Calvinist movement, otherwise known as "Young, Restless, and Reformed," and the present-day Baptist scholarship on Edwards.

Jonathan Edwards's Influence on Baptists in Britain

In the autumn of 1733, the twenty-nine-year-old Northampton pastor preached *A Divine and Supernatural Light*. Four months later, his sermon was published; thereafter, a revival sparked in the Connecticut Valley, which became the basis for what came to be known as the first Great Awakening in America. These fervent activities were heightened further by George Whitefield (1714–1770),[3] who stirred up the revivals in the transatlantic evangelical network in England and New England. "America's Theologian,"[4] however, was not the great itinerate preacher, nor were any others members of the Holy Club at Oxford,[5] but that reputation, as Harry Stout and Robert Jenson have recognized, belongs to Jonathan Edwards.

The Age of Reason grabbed hold of English Baptists. The effects of Socinianism, Unitarianism, Latitudinarianism, and Deism were sapping the life out of General Baptists, causing the denomination to decline rapidly. The person who contributed the most in helping to revive the situation was Dan Taylor (1738–1816). By confronting the Socinians, Taylor was able to draw out many members of the sects; that is, many discouraged with the Old General Baptists came out and joined The New Connection of General Baptists. The new connection brought new piety and life into the denomination. Meanwhile, in the eighteenth century, their Particular Baptists counterpart

---

[3] For an academic biography of George Whitefield, see Thomas S. Kidd, *George Whitefield: America's Spiritual Founding Father* (New Haven: Yale University Press, 2014); for a confessional perspective, see also Arnold Dallimore, *George Whitefield: God's Anointed Servant in the Great Revival of the Eighteenth Century* (Wheaton, IL: Crossway Books, 1990).

[4] The Holy Club was an organization in Oxford, formed in 1729 by brothers John and Charles Wesley.

[5] Robert W. Jenson, *American's Theologian: A Recommendation of Jonathan Edwards* (New York: Oxford University Press, 1988) and Stout, "Edwards and Revival."

was not doing much better than the Old General Baptists.

Many of the Particular Baptists, with their sceptical attitudes towards religious fervency, sat out from the broader Evangelical revivals led by the Wesley brothers and Whitefield. Just as the Enlightenment eroded historical orthodoxy in the Old General Baptists, Particular counterparts held these sound Protestant doctrines so tightly that, ironically, they became less orthodox by pressing the doctrines to logical extremity. By the mid-eighteenth century, Hyper-Calvinism, Antinomianism, and Sandemanianism were sending Particular Baptists into disarray. Renewal among the Particular was not so simplistic,[6] but it was in such a predicament that Edwardsean Calvinism stalled the decline and stirred in the revivals. Edwards's idea not only provided sound theology for the life of the mind, but his piety for the heart brought warmth to calloused Particular Baptists. The New England divine's mantle largely continued in the British Isles by two Baptist networks in this era; namely, Bristol Baptist Academy and Northamptonshire Association. Indeed, Particular Baptists were paralyzed by and large, but these interdependent groups were an exception to this broader norm. Under the leadership of Barnard Foskett, Hugh and Caleb Evans (1737–1791),[7] as well as John Ryland Jr. (1753–1825), Bristol Academy became the intellectual bedrock for vibrant orthodoxy with passion for revivals.[8] President Foskett introduced the writings of Jonathan Edwards to his impressive pupil John Sutcliff (1752–1814), as Foskett was reading Edwards in the 1760s.[9] Caleb Evans, in 1767, indicated his early commitment to Edwardsean Calvinism. In fact, he recom-

---

[6] Peter Morden has documented this complexity in detail in *The Life and Thought of Andrew Fuller (1754–1815)* Studies in Evangelical History and Thought (Buckinghamshire: Paternoster, 2015) 15–28.

[7] Caleb Evans was born in November 1737, in Bristol, and was a Particular Baptist minister and college head. Roger Hayden notes that it was Sutcliff who introduced Fuller to Edwards in Evans's *An Address to the Serious and Candid Professors of Christianity* (1772) in which Evans employed the thinking of Edwards to explain the distinction between natural and moral ability. Fuller's *Gospel Worthy*, 1st ed., which "quoted pages 11–13 of Evans's book verbatim, provided the theological key to liberating English Baptists from a sterile High Calvinism into a vibrant, worldwide, missionary community"; Roger Hayden, "Evans, Caleb (1737–1791)" in *Oxford Dictionary of National Biography* http://www.oxforddnb.com/view/article/40192.

[8] For history of Bristol College, see F. E. Robinson, "Bristol Baptist College—The 250th Anniversary," *Baptist Quarterly* 4, no. 7 (July 1929): 292–99.

[9] Michael Haykin, *One Heart and One Soul: John Sutcliff of Olney, His Friends and his Times* (Durham: Evangelical Press, 1994) 55.

mended the writings of the New England pastor to all Evans's students, including Sutcliff and Ryland Jr. Following the Evans presidency, Ryland, who was also an avid reader of Edwards's work, popularized America's theologian among English Baptists.

When Andrew Fuller's church in Soham joined neighbouring Northamptonshire Association in 1775, he became friends with these graduates of Bristol Academy who were also members of this association and had been taught the Edwards version of evangelical Calvinism with robust piety. Near the end of his life, Fuller nostalgically looked back on his initial encounters with those who later became his colleagues and friends:

> In 1776 I became acquainted with Mr. Sutcliff, who had latterly come to Olney; and soon after with Mr. John Ryland, jun. then of Northampton. In them I found *familiar and faithful brethren*; and who, partly by reflection, and partly by reading the writings of Edwards, Bellamy, Brainerd, &c. had begun to doubt of the system of *False Calvinism*.[10]

Fuller, along with his kindred spirited connections with "familiar and faithful brethren," certainly shared their esteem for the New England divine. For example, in 1814, a few weeks before the death of Sutcliff, Fuller wrote to, by this time, his long-time friend Ryland Jr.: "We have heard some who have been giving out, of late, that 'if Sutcliff and some others [that is, the Northamptonshire Association] had preached more of Christ, and less of Jonathan Edwards, they would have been more useful.'"[11] To these rather mocking remarks—without denying the allegation of "preaching Jonathan Edwards"—Fuller unashamedly replied with the following witty comment: "If those who talked thus, preached Christ half as much as Jonathan Edwards did, and were half as useful as he was, their usefulness would be double what

---

[10] Andrew Fuller, "Letter to My Dear Friend [John Ryland Jr.?]," February 1815, Typewritten. Fuller's Letters, Box 4/5/2, Angus Library, University of Oxford. Italics mine.

[11] Andrew Fuller, *The Complete Works of the Rev. Andrew Fuller: With a Memoir of His Life by the Rev. Andrew Gunton Fuller*, 3 vols. (Harrisonburg: Sprinkle Publications, 1988); henceforth *WAF*. "Correspondence with Friends" *WAF*, 1:101. According to Haykin, what "initially attracted" Fuller and Ryland to one another was the discovery that they shared a strong "predilection" for same authors, "in particular, Jonathan Edwards." Michael Haykin, ed., *The Armies of the Lamb: The Spirituality of Andrew Fuller* (Dundas: Joshua Press, 2001) 43.

it is."[12] The "False Calvinism," according to Fuller, was referring to an unpleasant experience that he knew all too well. His own doctrinal quandary stemmed from personal struggles with the shackles of a Hyper-Calvinistic background in which the "subjective warrant" was considered necessary for a person to approach God for salvation.[13] However, since Fuller could not find sufficient basis to conclude definitively that he was one of the elect, during the three-year period between 1766 and 1769—when he believed he was not qualified to come to Christ—he suffered intense agony. Fuller understood in retrospect that this painful and delayed conversion experience was unnecessary. In 1755, having recognized Fuller's struggles with Hyper-Calvinism, Robert Hall, another Bristol alumnus who was a part of Northamptonshire Association, recommended Fuller to read "Edwards on the Will." However, at the age of twenty-one, and not being very well acquainted with Jonathan Edwards's corpus, Fuller mistakenly read John Edwards's[14] work entitled *Veritas Redux* in thinking that it was *Freedom of the Will*. Amusingly enough, Fuller thought that John Edwards had actually written a "pretty good book," yet he oddly wondered about it since it "did not seem exactly to answer Mr. Hall's recommendation"[15] about divine sovereignty and human responsibility. Thus, it was not until two years later, in 1777, that Fuller realized his mistake and finally got hold of the right book! Fuller's review *Freedom of the Will* is in the preface of his *Gospel of Christ Worthy of All Acceptation*: "I had read and considered, as well as I could, Mr. Jonathan Edwards' *Enquiry into the Freedom of the Will*...on the distinction of *natural and moral ability, and inability*. I always

---

[12] Fuller, "Correspondence with Friends," 1:101. This statement is yet another example of Sutcliff and Fuller's esteem for Edwards.

[13] Peter J. Morden, *Offering Christ to the World: Andrew Fuller (1754–1815) and the Revival of Eighteenth Century Particular Baptist Life*, vol. 8, Studies in Baptist History and Thought (Carlisle: Paternoster, 2003) 27–29, 161. For a helpful discussion regarding Hyper-Calvinism among the Particular Baptists see P. Naylor, "Andrew Fuller," in *Calvinism, Communion and the Baptists: A Study of English Calvinistic Baptists from the Late 1600s to the Early 1800s*, Studies in Baptist History and Thought (Carlisle: Paternoster, 2003) 7:164–82. For a comprehensive survey of Hyper-Calvinism, see Peter Toon, *The Emergence of Hyper Calvinism in English Nonconformity 1689–1765* (London: Olive Tree, 1967).

[14] For a secondary source on "true John Edwards," see Jeongmo Yoo, *John Edwards (1637–1716) on Human Free Choice and Divine Necessity: The Debate on the Relation Between Divine Necessity and Human Freedom in Late Seventeenth-Century and Early Eighteenth-Century England* (Bristol, CT: Vandenhoeck & Ruprecht, 2013).

[15] Andrew Fuller, "Ordained Pastor," *WAF*, 1:15.

found great pleasure in this distinction."[16]

Fuller may have found "great pleasure" in Edwards's distinctions, for he not only saw them as central in unlocking the evangelistic restraint of Hyper-Calvinism, but he also describes the Edwardsean logic as "nothing better calculated to destroy"[17] Arminianism. Fuller was enormously successful in revitalizing the denomination. Based on a close reading of "Edwards on the Will," Fuller not only provided the doctrinal underpinning for a revival among Baptist denomination, but also became the foremost theologian in the Modern Missionary Movement. Hence, among many evaluations of Edwards's impact on England, it is no wonder that David Bebbington concludes, "probably most important in the reception of Edwards by the English Baptists was the impact on Andrew Fuller."[18]

The most celebrated friend of Fuller in this endeavour was a shoe cobbler from Northampton, England: William Carey. *The Gospel Worthy* laid an important foundation for the Father of Modern Mission's perennial work, *An Enquiry Into the Obligations of Christians to Use Means for the Conversion of the Heathens* (1792), a work that Ralph Winter refers to as the "Magna Carta of the Protestant mission movement."[19] If Carey's *Enquiry* was the ethical catalyst for the movement, then Fuller's *Gospel Worthy* provided the theological underpinning for it. In other words, Fuller was the theologian and Carey the activist and visionary of the missionary awakening.

Freedom of the Will was not the only book in Edwards's corpus that was particularly influential to Particular Baptist revivals. His *Humble Attempt* also helped spark the missionary movement when John Ryland Jr. received a parcel of books from John Erskine in 1784. Ryland, fully aware of the esteem in

---

[16] Andrew Fuller, *The Gospel of Christ Worthy of All Acceptation*, 1st ed. (Northampton: Dicey, 1785) v.

[17] Fuller, *Gospel Worthy*, 1st ed., 192.

[18] David W. Bebbington, "Remembered Around the World: The International Scope of Edwards's Legacy," *Jonathan Edwards at Home and Abroad: Historical Memories, Cultural Movements, Global Horizons*, ed. D. W. Kling and D. A. Sweeney (Columbia: University of South Carolina Press, 2003) 184. For supplementary discussions, see Mark Noll, "Freedom of the Will Abroad," in *Jonathan Edwards at 300: Essays on the Tercentenary of His Birth*, ed., Harry Stout, Kenneth Minkema, and Caleb Maskell (Lanham, MD: University Press of America, 2005) 89–108.

[19] Ralph Winter, "Four Men, Three Eras, Two Transitions: Modern Missions," in *Perspectives: On the World Christian Movement*, ed. Steve Hawthorne and Ralph Winter (Pasadena: William Carey Library, 1999) 254.

which Fuller and Sutcliff held Edwards, swiftly sent them the books, thereby changing mission history. The secondary literature has recognized the influence of *Humble Attempt* on the Prayer Call of 1784, but few have acknowledged the role that Edwards's eschatological optimism played in driving the British missionary enterprise. Edwards's thinking about the end of the world depended on his interpretation of the slaying of the witnesses in Revelation 11. Some thought this implied a coming catastrophe for the church, but Edwards argued for the exact opposite to promote the Concert of Prayer.[20] Edwards feared that if the slaying of the witnesses were a future event yet to be fulfilled, it would be a great "hindrance" for the Concert. Instead, Edwards argued for an unprecedented outpouring of the Spirit of God, and a time when the whole world would embrace the light of the gospel, with Christ's kingdom victorious against the dark world. Fuller also saw the ransacked days of the church as a thing of the past, for he interpreted the French Revolution as a crucial sign that it had shook the "papal world to its centre."[21]

The fact that *Humble Attempt* was reprinted in 1789, when the Revolution began, seemed to confirm the optimistic eschatology that Fuller adopted from Edwards. Although Fuller did not stress immediacy in the way Edwards did, both believed the latter days would be publicly discernible, and that the current ascendancy of Protestantism, coupled with diminishing papal authority in Europe and America, were evidence of fulfilment of apocalyptic forecasts in the book of Revelation. This optimistic eschatological outlook encouraged Fuller and motivated those in Northamptonshire to pray more fervently. This became the groundwork for courage to engage in rigorous foreign missions. In describing the 1789 edition of the *Humble Attempt*, Fuller spoke about "how much this publication contributed to that tone of feeling" and gave the confidence to "venture," and face their "fear" in taking on a missionary task of "such magnitude." He added, "I cannot say; but it doubtless had a very considerable influence on [BMS]."[22] In such a setting, it is not sur-

---

[20] The Concert of Prayer refers to agreements by ministers in the UK and the American colonies to pray on the first Monday of each month for the advancement of Christ's Kingdom.

[21] Fuller, *WAF*, 3:252–53. See also, J. W. Morris, *Memoirs of the Life and Writings of the Rev. Andrew Fuller* (London: Wrightman and Cramp, 1826) 206–9.

[22] Andrew Fuller, "Principle and Prospects of a Servant of Christ," *WAF*, 1:351. BMS apparently refers to Baptist Missionary Society.

prising that William Carey was able to find confident expectation in propagating the success of the Great Commission to the church, and thus coined his famous phrase, "Attempt great things; expect great things."[23] For good or ill, it is in this eschatological climate that BMS and the Modern Missionary Movement were born. Having been influenced by Edwards, the conclusions that were drawn from Fuller's *Gospel Worthy* and Carey's *Inquiry* and Prayer Call of 1784 provided new expressions for Edwardsean Calvinism in the British context, instilled vitality into Particular Baptists, and stimulated prayer movements for the heathen and foreign missions.

Edwards's Influence on Baptists in America

Baptist beginnings in America can be traced to two main sources: Regular Baptists and Separate Baptists. Both traditions have been influenced by Edwards in different ways. The "Regular" label includes the earliest Baptists who arrived in Rhode Island, as well as a larger group who settled in the Middle colonies; most of the latter were Particular Baptists from England. On July 27, 1707, some of these Regular churches united to form the Philadelphia Association, which turned out to be the first Baptist association in America. This association adopted the revised 1689 version of the Second London Confession to draft the Philadelphia Baptist Confession of Faith (1742). Out of this tradition arose the famous Charleston Association in 1751, and the Charleston tradition adopted two previous Calvinistic confessions, thereby continuing to emphasize confessionalism, strong support for education, and quasi-liturgical worship and order, so much so that Walter Shurden dubbed Charleston members as "semipresbyterians." [24] This association, from Charleston, South Carolina, during the eighteenth century, was the center of Baptist activities in America. Southern Baptists and this tradition had a long heritage in holding on to Edwards's reformed thoughts. For example, a notable figure like Richard Furman (1755–1825), a pastor of First Baptist Church in Charleston and first president of the Triennial Convention, was from the

---

[23] For further discussions on this phrase, see Timothy George, "Let It Go: Lessons from the Life of William Carey," in *Expect Great Things, Attempt Great Things: William Carey and Adoniram Judson, Mission Pioneers*, ed. Allen Yeh and Chris Chun (Eugene, OR: Wipf & Stock, 2013) 6.

[24] Walter B. Shurden, *Not an Easy Journey: Some Transitions in Baptist Life* (Macon, GA: Mercer University Press, 2005) 204.

Charleston tradition. In addition, the leadership of the early years of the Convention, such as Basil Manly Sr. (1798–1868) and William B. Johnson (1782–1862), as well as the country's first systematic Baptist theologian, John L. Dagg (1794–1884), may be classified as representing the Charleston tradition and influenced by Edwards's theology.[25] Long-time Southern Baptist historian Tom Nettles has this to say about his own denominational heritage:

> Present day Baptist life cannot be understood apart from being aware of the massive influence he [Edwards] exerted. It might safely be contended that the Southern Baptist Convention was born, theologically, out of the energy of the writings of Jonathan Edwards.[26]

While Baptist development that took place through this Regular Baptist movement and Charleston tradition were substantial, at these early stages there was another movement occurring simultaneously with the Great Awakening that showed even more rapid growth. This is what was called the Separate Baptists, because they separated from Congregationalist parishes. Soon after the itinerate preacher Whitefield visited Edwards at the Northampton parish across the pond, the Great Awakening began sweeping across many of the separate Congregationalists of the eastern seaboard. Many of these New Light Congregationalists ironically came to adopt believer's baptism under the preaching ministry of Whitefield, an infant baptizing, Anglican-Methodist preacher. The great evangelist was less than thrilled with these unintended side effects. These revivals were gaining ground, particularly among the New Light congregations in Massachusetts, New Hampshire, and Connecticut. In conjunction with this movement, Separate Baptists also gained over a hundred new churches, about which Whitefield lamented, "Behold all my chickens have become ducks!"[27] William McLoughlin has described these New Light Congregational churches as "halfway houses on the road to becoming Bap-

---

[25] See E. Brooks Holifield, *Theology in America: Christian Thought from the Age of the Puritans to the Civil War* (New Haven: Yale University Press, 2003) 278–86; Walter Shurden, *Not an Easy Journey*, 202–4. See also Tom J. Nettles, "Edwards and His Impact on Baptists," *Founders Journal* (Summer 2003): 1–18.

[26] Tom J. Nettles, "Jonathan Edwards: An Appreciation" *Founders Journal* (Summer 2003): http://founders.org/fj53/jonathan-edwards-an-appreciation.

[27] George Whitefield as quoted in Derek H. Davis, *Religion and the Continental Congress 1774–1789: Contributions to Original Intent* (New York: Oxford University Press, 2000) 125.

tists"; moreover, David Benedict called these separate folks "nurseries of Baptists."[28]

It is not surprising, in such a broader context, that the conversion of Isaac Backus (1724–1806) came about in 1741 in the heat of the revival, and he eventually became a Separate Baptist in 1756. As the young colonies transitioned from Colonial America to the newly established country of the United States, Backus was poised to be one the most pivotal Baptists in American history. Whitefield was not the only one who engaged these Separates. There is evidence that Edwards was quite sympathetic to, or even had a congenial attitude toward, these separatists. For instance, on August 4, 1750, about a month and a half after his dismissal from Northampton, in his preface to Joseph Bellamy's *True Religion Delineated* (1750), Edwards praised his prized pupil for "having also had much acquaintance and frequent long conversation with many of the people called Separatists."[29]

In any case, Backus lived in a generation immediately following that of Edwards, which could be seen as an era of New England theologians,[30] yet Backus did not see himself as part of the New Divinity School. In fact, he was quick to distance himself: "I am much better acquainted with Edwards's writing than they [the New Divinity] are."[31] As a Baptist in the Puritan tradition,[32] Backus saw himself as a more legitimate heir of the Edwards's legacy. As a Baptist historian, I have been tempted to read Edwards as one who could have

---

[28] William G. McLoughlin and David Benedict as quoted in H. Leon McBeth, *The Baptist Heritage: Four Centuries of Baptist Witness* (Nashville: Broadman, 1987) 205.

[29] Jonathan Edwards, "Preface to True Religion" in *The Works of Jonathan Edwards*, ed. C. C. Goen (New Haven: Yale University Press, 1972) 4:572. *The Works of Jonathan Edwards*, 26 vols. (New Haven Yale University Press, 1957–2008) is henceforth abbreviated as *WJE*. Moreover, Goen actually labels them as "Separate Baptist." See C. C. Goen "Editor's Footnote," *WJE* 4:572n2.

[30] Insofar as interpretation of the New Divinity School is concerned, Foster produced the most influential work. While commenting that Edwards Amasa Park articulated the "most perfect system" in New England theology, Foster believed that if this theology was to be "consistently carried out, [it] must in the end disrupt the system of Calvinism." Frank Foster, *A Genetic History of the New England Theology* (Chicago: University of Chicago Press, 1907) 471, 452.

[31] Isaac Backus, A *History of New England with Particular Reference to the Denomination of Christians Called Baptists*, with notes by David Weston, vol. 2 (Newton, WA: Backus Historical Society, 1871) 252.

[32] See Stanley Grenz, *Isaac Backus—Puritan and Baptist: His Place in History, His Thoughts and Their Implications for Modern Baptist Theology*, Dissertation Series, no. 4 (Macon: Mercer University Press, 1983).

been an advocate for the believer's church, but not in his public persona.[33] This, of course, is an assumption based on how Edwards fenced the table in his Northampton parish; however, Brandon O'Brien's recent PhD dissertation, written under the tutelage of Douglas Sweeney (supervisor) and Kenneth Minkema (external examiner), has demonstrated the postulation that I have cautiously held for quite some time, namely, the historical position of Backus's reading on Edwards's view on baptism. O'Brien argues, "In one of his more surprising uses of Edwards, Backus appealed to the Northampton's pastor in his defence of believer's baptism."[34] He adds, "as far as Backus was concerned, whatever he said in print, Edwards was a Baptist at heart. His rejection of the Half-Way Covenant 'naturally leads to the exclusion of infant sprinkling.'"[35] At this juncture, recounting Backus's own story might be a helpful window into why he was convinced of such thinking. Backus was first persuaded to believe in regenerate church membership in 1749 when two of his church members adopted believer's baptism, but for the next two years, he vacillated on the issue of infant baptism. As a Congregationalist pastor, Backus observed that practicing infant baptism tended to diminish fervency of people about conversion. For this reason, Backus appealed to Edwards, as Backus had the same qualms that Edwards had concerning Solomon Stoddard's view (his grandfather's policy allowing unconverted people in the Half-Way Covenant to take part in the Lord's Supper). This, of course, is a minor step away from full-blown regenerate membership marked by believers-only baptism. Backus's congregation officially became a Baptist church in Middleboro in

---

[33] In October 2011 I delivered a cheeky essay that was never intended for publication. As a former Presbyterian, I had many close paedobaptist friends and the essay was mainly to "stir the pots" among them. It was entitled "Interdenominational Dialogue: Jonathan Edwards as Proto-Baptist" delivered at Jonathan Edwards Society, at The First Churches, Northampton, MA. For an opinion contrary to mine, especially regarding Edwards's ecclesiology, see Rhys S. Bezzant, *Jonathan Edwards and the Church* (Oxford: Oxford University Press, 2014) 174–79.

[34] Brandon J. O'Brien, "The Edwardsean Isaac Backus: The Significance of Jonathan Edwards in Backus's "Theology, History, and Defense of Religious Liberty" (PhD diss., Trinity International University, 2013) 69.

[35] O'Brien, "The Edwardsean Isaac Backus," 70. O'Brien points to Edwards's *An Humble Inquiry into the Rules of the Word of God, Concerning the Qualifications Requisite to a Complete Standing and Full Communion in the Visible Christian Church*, in WJE 12:196, as it was quoted by Backus. It makes his point that Edwards might be "Baptist at Heart." See Isaac Backus, *The Substance of an Address to an Assembly in Bridgewater, March 10, 1779, Previous to the Administration of Baptism* (Providence: John Carter, 1779) 5–6.

1756.

The effect the Great Awakening had on the genesis of Separate Baptists like Backus is an intriguing narrative that, I am convinced, should not be overlooked. Many who later altered their views on paedobaptism were converted during the revival led by Edwards, Whitefield, Theodore Frelinghuysen, Gilbert Tennent, and others. Another example of a revival leader is none other than fervent Separate Baptist preacher Shubal Stearns (1706–1771), a revival preacher capable of inspiring the most powerful emotions in his congregation. Stearns was from the New Light Congregationalists. Stearns's church, around the same time as Backus's parish, became involved in a 1751 controversy over the proper subjects of baptism. Several years later in 1755, Stearns relocated to Sandy Creek, North Carolina, to build a new church. That separatist congregation, in the words of Thomas Kidd and Barry Hankins, "grew like wildfire."[36] From there, Separate Baptists spread in the South, and the church quickly grew from sixteen members to 606, which showed more substantial growth than did its Regular Baptist counterpart. Morgan Edwards, a Baptist minister who visited Sandy Creek the year after Stearns's death, recorded, "in 17 years, [Sandy Creek] has spread its branches westward as far as the great river Mississippi; southward as far as Georgia; eastward to the sea and Chesopeck [sic] Bay; and northward to the waters of the Pottowmack [sic]; it, in 17 years, is become mother, grandmother, and great grandmother to 42 churches, from which sprang 125 ministers."[37]

Shubal Stearns apparently was small in stature, but according to Earl Waggoner, he was a "giant in the pulpit." Through his warm voice accompanied by strong gestures, Stearns would move his hearers to tears in his singular tone.[38] Unfortunately, historical evidence that can directly link Stearns to Edwards's legacy is lacking, as most of Stearns's writings did not survive. However, the role that the Great Awakening and Whitefield played in the formation of Separate Baptists like Stearns and Backus cannot be overstated.

---

[36] Thomas Kidd and Barry Hankins, *Baptists in America: A History* (New York: Oxford University Press, 2015) 36.

[37] Morgan Edwards, *Materials towards a History of the Baptists* (1770/1792) prepared for publication by Eve B. Weeks and Mary B. Warren in 2 vols. (Danielsiville, GA: Heritage Papers, 1984) 2:93.

[38] See Earl Waggoner, "Shubal Stearns 1706–1771" in *A Noble Company: Biographical Essay on Notable Particular-Regular Baptists in America*, ed. Terry Wolever (Springfield, MO, Particular Baptist Press, 2013) 3, 7–8.

There is no doubt Backus was an Edwardsean Calvinist, but would Stearns be classified as such? Robert Caldwell, in *Theologies of the American Revivalists*,[39] pointed out, The Sandy Creek Church covenant (1757), which probably had been written by Stearns, has an explicitly Calvinistic articulation of what can only been construed as Reformed theology:

> [Holding…] particular election of grace by the predestination of God in Christ…free justification through the imputed righteousness of Christ…progressive sanctification through God's grace and truth; the finial perseverance, or continuance of the saints in grace.[40]

Following the mid-eighteenth century, as E. Holifield points out, in spite of an "undercurrent of internal Arminian protest," the Baptists generally "gravitated towards the Calvinism of Westminster and Philadelphia confessions or towards Edwardsean version of it."[41] The latter[42] seems historically plausible in Stearns's case, given how widespread the Separate Baptist revivalist ethos was. Even Jessie Mercer (1769–1841), who in some sense embodied the best parts of both the Charleston and Sandy Creek traditions in antebellum southern Baptist history, touted the Edwardsean and Fullerite distinction between natural and moral ability and inability.[43]

Perhaps no one captures Baptist imagination quite like Ann Judson,[44]

---

[39] I am grateful to have read Robert W. Caldwell III's Edwards chapter from his *Theologies of the American Revivalists: The Theology of the Great Awakenings from Whitefield to Finney* (Downer's Grove: InterVarsity Press, 2017).

[40] For this excerpt from Sandy Creek Church covenant, see William L. Lumpkin, *Baptist Foundations in the South: Tracing through the Separates the Influence of the Great Awakening* (Eugene, OR: Wipf & Stock, 2006) 62. Lumpkin likewise states that if he wrote this covenant, "Shubal Stearns, too, must be classed as a Calvinist." If Stearns did not, I suspect, based on lack of evidence, the verdict can be viewed as still up for grabs.

[41] Holifield, *Theology in America*, 278.

[42] Paul Helm makes distinction between "older forms" of Calvinism and Edwardsean Calvinism. Helm writes, "Jonathan Edwards was certainly a Calvinist, though one of a rather different kind." See Paul Helm, "A Different Kind of Calvinism? Edwardseanism Compared with Older Forms of Reformed Thought" in *After Jonathan Edwards*, 103.

[43] Holifield, *Theology in America*, 284. For Mercer's use of Edwards's distinction between natural and moral ability, see Anthony Chute, *A Piety above a Common Standard: Jesse Mercer and Evangelistic Calvinism* (Macon, GA: Mercer University Press, 2004) 76. For Edwards's and Fuller's rendering, see Chris Chun, "A Mainspring of Missionary Thought: Andrew Fuller on Natural and Moral Inability," *American Baptist Quarterly* 25, no. 4 (Winter 2006): 335-55.

[44] For a well-illustrated and brief biographical sketch of Ann Judson see Dana Robert, "The Mother of Modern Missions," *Christian History and Biography* (Spring 2006): 24. See also,

who wrote to her dear friends while in a vessel en route to India as the first intercontinental missionary commissioned in the United States. Ann wrote, "we are confirmed Baptists, not because we wished to be, but because truth compelled us to be.... We anticipate the loss of reputation, and of the affection and esteem of many of our American friends."[45] Ann and her celebrated husband, Adoniram Judson, along with Luther Rice, left America as Congregationalists but arrived on the mission field as Baptists, somewhat under the influence of William Carey. This iconic event in mission history became a major turning point, as Baptists needed to get their act together to support these missionaries newly converted to Baptist beliefs. The event united Baptists at the national level and launched the Triennial Convention in 1814.

After some time had passed, the Baptists in the United States wanted a confession of faith around which they could organize a missionary society under the Triennial Convention. John Newton Brown drew up The New Hampshire Confession of Faith (1833), and this confession was widely accepted by Baptists. Many considered the New Hampshire Confession of Faith a milder form of the doctrines of older confessions, which expressed the Calvinistic Baptist tenets. Even though the New Hampshire articulation was shorter than the Philadelphia and Charleston versions, the verbiage of the New Hampshire appears to include both predestination and free will without negating election. The New Hampshire Confession borrows heavily from Andrew Fuller's language of natural and moral inability, which we now know derives from Jonathan Edwards's *Freedom of the Will*. The confession is stated deliberately to make Calvinism more palatable to non-Calvinistic Baptists. The New Hampshire Confession articulates that "[Humans] by voluntary [free will] transgression fell from the holy and happy state [in which they were created]" and that "We believe that Election [predestination] is the eternal purpose of God, according to which he graciously regenerates, sanctifies, and saves sinners." With such nuanced wordings, many saw the New Hampshire Confession as accepting free will, and as result, the Free Will Baptists in the

---

Sharon James, *My Heart in His Hands: Ann Judson of Burma* (Durham: Evangelical Press, 1998). For her contemporary biography, see James D. Knowles, *Memoir of Mrs. Ann H. Judson, Wife of the Rev. Adoniram Judson Missionary to Burmah*, 2nd ed. (London: Printed for Wightman and Cramp, 1829).

[45]Ann Judson, "Letter to a friend about becoming a Baptist" (1812) in *A Sourcebook for Baptist Heritage*, ed. H. Leon McBeth (Nashville: Broadman, 1990) 208.

Northeast and West accepted the confession. Interestingly, Calvinistic Baptists in the South rejected the confession preferring the older confessions, yet remained in the Triennial Convention. In nineteenth-century America, Calvinistic Baptists in the South embraced Edwards's theology regarding God's sovereignty and human responsibility, but many were concerned about Fuller's view of the atonement as some sort of moral governmental theory of the New Divinity School. Nonetheless, the New Hampshire Confession served as an important guide for Southern Baptists as they drafted their own version, known as the Baptist Faith and Message. This confession was first approved in 1925, but it can trace its lineage from The New Hampshire Confession.

At any rate, coming back to the story of Ann Judson, her well-known Baptist conversion narrative from Congregational upbringing to Baptist persuasion appears in almost every Baptist textbook. What is less familiar, however, is that Edwards and his successors influenced Ann Judson. In her early years, Ann received a thorough education in Bradford Academy and was not timid in thinking about weighty theological matters. Her contemporary biographer, James Knowles, describes her as one who "thirsted for the knowledge of gospel truth, in all its relations and dependencies," and emphasized how she practiced "daily study of the Scripture."[46] Ann also drank deeply from the piety of *David Brainerd*, Edwards's most popular work.[47] Furthermore, Ann engaged scholarly minds of her generation and read their work "with deep interests." Among these authors were Edwards's pupil Joseph Bellamy, Samuel Hopkins, and of course, their revered mentor himself. Knowles fondly recounted his first-hand encounter with Ann when she drafted her theological reflection and finally finished her transcription of Edwards's magnum opus, *A History of the Work of Redemption*:

> With Edwards on Redemption, she was instructed, quickened, strengthened. Well do I remember the elevated smile, which beamed on [Ann's] countenance, when she first spoke to me of its precious content. She had transcribed, with her own hand, Edwards' leading and most striking remarks on this great subject.[48]

---

[46] Knowles, *Memoir of Mrs. Ann H. Judson*, 20.

[47] Joseph Conforti, "Jonathan Edwards's Most Popular Work: 'The Life of David Brainerd' and Nineteenth-Century Evangelical Culture," *Church History* 54 (June 1985): 188–201.

[48] Knowles, *Memoir of Mrs. Ann H. Judson*, 20.

Robert Caldwell recently put forth compelling historical evidence in locating Adoniram Judson's family background and linking his upbringing to the wider nineteenth-century context, where New England divines were portrayed as influential forces with which the Judsons had to wrestle. The new missionary revival began in the United States, but as Caldwell argued, "Edwardsean leaders, institutions, and ideals were central to it."[49] I concur with seeing the Judsons' ministry as part of the macro New Divinity period.

With this type of learned Edwardsean background, it is no wonder Ann was able to produce a catechism in Burmese to instruct the young converts as well as to engage in translation work with her husband in 1819. About eight years into the missionary work, in 1822, Ann became so ill that she needed to return to America for a rest, but she also capitalized on this window of time to write a book entitled *An Account of the American Baptist Mission to the Burman Empire*. When the manuscript was published in 1823, her book immediately became a bestseller and proved to be a significant impetus for missions by way of recruiting churches to support missionary enterprises with their finances and prayers. As David Bebbington writes, "The couple became missionary icons, inspiring the extension of missionary enterprise into Assam, Siam, southern India, China, and Liberia."[50]

Edwards's Influence on Baptists in the Twentieth and Twenty-First Centuries

The late nineteenth and early twentieth centuries were not so kind to Puritanism in general, and Edwards was no exception to these trends. Through radio broadcast, this was the era of progressivism and the jazz age. This milieu saw Puritanism as antiquated, judgmental, and prudish. *The Scarlet Letter* (1850), Salem Witchcraft Trials (1692), and Edwards's "Sinners in the Hand of an Angry God" (c. 1741) were all viewed as the same genre and were taught in most high schools in America. A popular outlook on Puritan forebears from this time is well captured in H. L. Mencken's cynicism found

---

[49] Robert Caldwell, "New England's New Divinity and the Age of Judson's Preparation," *Adoniram Judson: A Bicentennial Appreciation of the Pioneer American Missionary* ed., Jason Duesing (Nashville: B&H Academic, 2012) 41.

[50] David W. Bebbington, *Baptists through the Centuries: A History of a Global People* (Waco: Baylor University Press, 2010) 220.

in his famous 1916 quote "Puritanism: the haunting fear that someone, somewhere, may be happy."[51] But he was not alone. Mark Twain, in 1902, after having read *Freedom of the Will*, commented that Edwards was a "drunken lunatic…a resplendent intellect gone mad."[52] With such modern cultural ethos, it is not too surprising to find that many would turn their attention away from this supposedly irrelevant character; that is, until Harvard's Perry Miller referred to Edwards as "the greatest philosopher-theologian yet to grace the American scene."[53] When Miller's intellectual biography on Edwards was released in 1949,[54] it landed like a bombshell in the halls of many ivory towers. Since Miller's work, there has been academic revival in Edwards studies. The number of PhD dissertations is doubling every decade.

By far the most famous (or shall I dare say "infamous") sermon from Edwards's pen is "Sinners in the Hands of an Angry God," preached at Enfield, Massachusetts on July 8, 1741. But it is fascinating to note that the most renowned evangelist in the twentieth century delivered this particular sermon almost two centuries later. In late 1949, thirty-one-year-old Billy Graham, at the height of his revival in Los Angeles, delivered America's most well known sermon. At this juncture, one may question Graham's Baptist credentials. Graham, unlike his lifelong associate Grady Wilson, who showed his Baptist colors more clearly,[55] did not make the denomination a focal point of his ministry. Nevertheless, as Grant Wacker admits, "The Southern Baptist ordained him when he was twenty-one"[56] and Billy remained a Baptist in spite of being raised by Presbyterian parents, and his wife Ruth persisted in being Presbyterian until her passing. In any case, why did this twentieth-century Baptist legend preach Edwards's message so many generations later? Billy Graham makes his intentions plainly known:

> What has been considered one of the greatest sermons ever preached by

---

[51] H. L. Mencken, *A Mencken Chrestomathy: His Own Selection of His Choicest Writing* (New York: Vintage, 1982) 624.

[52] Mark Twain, "Letter to Rev. Joseph H. Twichell, February 1902," *Reading Jonathan Edwards: An Annotated Bibliography in Three Parts, 1729–2005*, ed. M. X. Lesser (Grand Rapids: Eerdmans, 2008) 152.

[53] Perry Miller, "General Editor's Note," *Freedom of the Will*, ed. Paul Ramsey, *WJE*, 1:viii.

[54] Perry Miller, *Jonathan Edwards* (New York: William Sloane Associates, 1949).

[55] Evidently when a reporter asked Grady Wilson what he would be if he were not a Baptist, Wilson fired back saying, "I'd be ashamed." See Grant Wacker, "Billy Graham's America," *Church History* 78, no. 3 (September, 2009): 505.

[56] Wacker, "Billy Graham's America," 505.

a man since the days of Pentecost, was one sermon that was used of God to shake New England in that day and age. The sermon was entitled "Sinners in the hands of an angry God." Jonathan Edwards stood before the crowd of people, hardly an eyelash moved, hardly a person moved a hand, and before he was through preaching, people gripped the front of the benches in front of them and screamed in mercy, and revival broke out that night. Tonight, in the very strange providence of God, I'm doing something I've never done before in my ministry. I'm bringing to you that message that was preached 200 years ago by Jonathan Edwards, the president of Princeton University. I'm going to do as he did. He stepped to the platform, and with gestures he preached, but he read every word of it. It's a very brief sermon, it's not too long. I'm going to read it, and extemporize part of it, but I want you to feel the grip, I want you to feel the language. I'm asking tonight the same blessed Holy Ghost that moved in that day to move again tonight in 1949 and shake us out of our lethargy as Christians and convict sinners that we might come to repentance.[57]

In Wacker's colossal work, *America's Pastor* (2014), he documents Graham's indebtedness to eighteenth-century evangelicals. He writes, "Like John Wesley and Jonathan Edwards before him, he addressed disparate subjects in disparate settings as they arose" and his messages "drew from deep-running tradition in American evangelicalism" as he captures from the "impulses in the Great Awakenings."[58] Throughout the twentieth century, whether it is in the academic tradition of Perry Miller or the revivalist tradition of Billy Graham, Jonathan Edwards continues to have towering influence in the church and academy. That said, in 1983 Mark Noll summarized the situation in this manner:

> Edwards's piety continued on in the revivalist tradition, his theology continued on in academic Calvinism, but there were no successors to his

---

[57] "Billy Graham & Sinners in the Hands of an Angry God: A Digital Exhibit," accessed on December 17, 2014, http://edwards.yale.edu/education/billy-graham#one. However, Billy Graham was not the only well-known Baptist who preached this sermon. Mark Dever, senior pastor of Capitol Hill Baptist Church in Washington, DC, also delivered "Sinners in the Hands of an Angry God" to his congregation on October 5, 2003.

[58] Wacker, *America's Pastor*, 51, 65.

God-entranced world-view.... The disappearance of Edwards's perspective in American Christian history has been a tragedy.[59]

Since Noll's lament in the early 1980s on this "disappearance," there has been a significant shift in the dawn of the twenty-first century. To celebrate the tercentennial anniversary of Edwards's birth, overwhelming numbers of publications and conferences on Edwards were held all over the world, but there were two major conferences worthy of mention here. The first commenced October 3 and ended October 4, 2003, at the Library of Congress in Washington, DC. The Pew Charitable Trusts, the Lilly Endowment, the Henry Luce Foundation, and Yale University sponsored this academic conference. George Marsden was their keynote speaker, as he timely released his definitive biography of Edwards that set new standards in Edwards studies for the early twenty-first century.[60] The conference proceedings were then published as *Edwards at 300*.[61] The second conference had more confessional characteristics than the former, and it took place in Minneapolis just several days later on October 10, 2003, in the form of the National Conference for Desiring God, which also had a significant impact on Baptist churches and their pastors. During the conference, J. I. Packer and Iain Murray delivered their presentations on the New England divine. John Piper, then pastor of Bethlehem Baptist Church, borrowed the phrase "God-entranced world-view" from Noll to host this epic pastors' event with thousands of attendees. Following the conference, *A God Entranced Vision of All Things: The Legacy of Jonathan Edwards* was published as their conference proceedings.[62]

Due largely to his tercentennial anniversary, Edwards's legacy continues to make a significant impact on Baptists into the twenty-first century. The latest influence on a revival movement is known as the New Calvinism. In 2009, *Time* Magazine published an article entitled "10 Ideas Changing the World Right Now," and among those ten influential ideas New Calvinism

---

[59] Mark Noll, "Jonathan Edwards, Moral Philosophy, and the Secularization of American Christian Thought," *Reformed Journal* (February 1983): 26. For Noll's extensive research to validate his claim on "tragedy," see Mark Noll, *America's God: From Jonathan Edwards to Abraham Lincoln* (Oxford: Oxford University Press, 2002).

[60] George Marsden, *Jonathan Edwards: A Life* (New Haven: Yale University Press, 2003).

[61] Stout, Minkema, and Maskell, *Jonathan Edwards at 300*.

[62] *A God-Entranced Vision of All Things: The Legacy of Jonathan Edwards*, ed. John Piper and Justin Taylor (Wheaton, IL: Crossway, 2004).

was identified.⁶³ This new revival of Calvinism, of course, is much broader than purely Baptist, but some of the key leaders in the movement are Baptists. Some of the influential names are John Piper, Albert Mohler, Mark Dever, and David Platt. Likewise, *Christianity Today* underscored this revival as the cover story for the September 2006 issue, which featured a hip youngster wearing a t-shirt bearing the words "Jonathan Edwards is My Homeboy" tucked into his blue jeans. The cover story, written by Collin Hansen, is entitled "Young, Restless, Reformed, Calvinism is making a comeback—and shaking up the church."⁶⁴ Piper, one of the movement's leaders and arguably the greatest popularizer of Edwards in this generation, has characterized the New Calvinism as interdenominational with a "strong Baptistic element."⁶⁵ This movement, according to Piper, places an emphasis on piety in an Edwardsean Puritan vein, with affections for Christian living, while maintaining life of the mind through serious scholarship.

In the twentieth century and onward, Miller's intellectual biography ushered in the new era and in some way, "revival" in Edwards studies, but scholarship particularly produced by Baptist historians is no exception to this norm. By way of very small sample, in North America, Michael Haykin,⁶⁶ Robert

---

⁶³ The following are the ten ideas: (1) "Jobs Are The New Assets; (2) "Recycling the Suburbs"; (3) "The New Calvinism" (4) "Reinstating the Interstate"; (5) "Amortality"; (6) "Africa, Business Destination"; (7) "The Rent-A-Country"; (8) "Biobanks"; (9) "Survival Stores"; (10) "Ecological Intelligence."

⁶⁴ For his entire documentation on the subject see Collin Hansen, *Young, Restless, Reformed: A Journalist's Journey with the New Calvinists* (Wheaton, IL: Crossway Books, 2008); for further discussions, see also D. G. Hart, "Before the Young, Restless, and Reformed: Edwards's Appeal to Post World War II Evangelicals," in *After Jonathan Edwards: The Courses of the New England Theology*, ed. Oliver D. Crisp and Douglas A. Sweeney (New York: Oxford University Press, 2012) 237–53.

⁶⁵ Piper delivered the Gaffin Lecture Westminster Seminary on April 13, 2014, where he outlined twelve features of the New Calvinism.

⁶⁶ Michael A. G. Haykin, "Great Admirers of the Transatlantic Divinity: Some Chapters in the Story of Baptist Edwardseanism" in *After Jonathan Edwards*, ed. Crisp and Sweeny, 197–206; Michael Haykin, *Jonathan Edwards: The Holy Spirit in Revival* (Webster: Evangelical Press, 2005); Michael Haykin ed., *A Sweet Flame: Piety in the Letters of Jonathan Edwards*, Profiles in Reformed Spirituality (Grand Rapids: Reformation Heritage Books, 2007).

Caldwell,[67] Josh Moody,[68] as well as I, too, have written on the New England divine.[69] In the British Isles, Paternoster Press, with their Studies in Baptist History and Thought series and *The Reformation Today* magazine, which adheres to the 1689 London Baptist Confession of Faith, have given their attention to America's theologian. Scholarly contributions of British Baptists like David Bebbington,[70] Stephen Holmes,[71] and Peter Morden[72] firmly located Edwards in Baptist historiography in the United Kingdom. From way back in the eighteenth century, Baptists have been rather enamored with Jonathan Edwards, particularly with respect to his theology of revivals. Needless to say, there is no sign of slowing down.

---

[67] Robert W. Caldwell III, *Communion in the Spirit: The Holy Spirit as the Bond of Union in the Theology of Jonathan Edwards*, Studies in Evangelical History and Thought (Carlisle: Paternoster, 2006); Steven M. Studebaker and Robert W. Caldwell III, *The Trinitarian Theology of Jonathan Edwards: Text, Context, and Application* (Farnham, UK: Ashgate, 2012).

[68] Josh Moody, ed., *Jonathan Edwards and Justification* (Wheaton, IL: Crossway, 2012); Josh Moody, *The God-Centered Life: Insights from Jonathan Edwards for Today* (Vancouver, BC: Regent College Publishing, 2007); Josh Moody, *Jonathan Edwards and the Enlightenment: Knowing the Presence of God* (Lanham, MD: University Press of America, 2005).

[69] Chris Chun, *The Legacy of Jonathan Edwards in the Theology of Andrew Fuller*, Studies in the History of Christian Traditions (Leiden: Brill, 2012); Chris Chun, "The Legacy of Jonathan Edwards: Eighteenth Century Catalysts for the Revivals among Presbyterians and Baptists in Scotland," in *Jonathan Edwards in Scotland*, ed. Kenneth Minkema, Adriaan Neele, and Kelly Van Andel (Edinburgh: Dunedin Academic Press, 2011) 63–74; Chris Chun, "Alternative Viewpoint: Jonathan Edwards's Life and Career," in *Understanding Jonathan Edwards: An Introduction to America's Theologian*, ed. Gerald R. McDermott (New York: Oxford University Press, 2009).

[70] David W. Bebbington, "The Reputation of Edwards Abroad," in *Cambridge Companion to Jonathan Edwards*, ed. Stephen J. Stein (Cambridge: Cambridge University Press, 2007) 239–61. David W. Bebbington, "Remembered Around the World," in *Jonathan Edwards at Home and Abroad*, 177–200.

[71] Stephen R. Holmes, *God of Grace and God of Glory: An Account of the Theology of Jonathan Edwards* (Grand Rapids: Eerdmans, 2001); Stephen R. Holmes, "Does Edwards Use a Dispositional Ontology?" in *Jonathan Edwards: Philosophical Theologian*, ed. Paul Helm and Oliver D. Crisp (Aldershot: Ashgate, 2003) 99–114. Stephen R. Holmes, "Religious Affections by Jonathan Edwards," in *The Devoted Life*, ed. Kelly M. Kapic and Randall C. Gleason (Downers Grove: InterVarsity Press, 2004) 285–97. Stephen R. Holmes, "Strange Voices: Edwards on the Will," in *Listening to the Past: The Place of Tradition in Theology* (Grand Rapids: Baker Academic, 2002) 86–107.

[72] Morden, *Offering Christ to the World*, 38–51; Morden, *The Life and Thought of Andrew Fuller*, 47–68.

2

The Holy Spirit and Right Living: Separate Baptists and the Southern Revival

Rosalie Beck

For more than 150 years, historians of American religion and of colonial America marked a spiritual movement in the 1730s and '40s, called the First Great Awakening, as a watershed for the colonies.[1] The accepted knowledge held that leaders like Jonathan Edwards, George Whitefield, and Theodore Freylinghuysen guided the colonies into a shared religious experience that laid the foundation for an American identity: a common identity that pulled the colonists together during the Revolutionary War. Most research on this era focused on stirrings in New England and the Middle Colonies, and on George Whitefield's preaching tours from Georgia to Maine, which tied the movement together. Baptists had only a small place in the story of the First Great Awakening because their numbers were few, and only from the 1750s to the 1780s did they experience surprising growth, mostly in the South. Because their "revival" was late and misplaced, in the least educated and poorest part of colonial America, little research focused on Baptists and revival in colonial America outside of New England.

In 1982, historian of American religion Jon Butler challenged the idea that the First Great Awakening had a substantive impact on the American

---

[1] William Warren Sweet, *Revivalism in America* (New York: Charles Scribner's Sons, 1944) 31. For example, in New England between 1740 and 1760, 150 new Congregational churches were founded and between 30,000 and 40,000 people were added to the state churches; the period of the First Great Awakening is usually cited as between 1726 and 1756; Howard Dorgan, "Separate Baptists of Central Appalachia: Followers of Shubal Stearns," *Journal of the Appalachian Studies Association* 5 (1993): 110.

psyche. He defined revival as an awakening that created lasting socio-economic and political effects.[2] For example, Butler held that the colonial religious movement in the South was not a true revival because the born-again Christians did not abolish slavery. With Butler's new definition of revival, American colonial historians began to re-examine the First Great Awakening, Southern religion, and the role of Baptists in the South. From this re-examination came interesting insight into how the First Great Awakening spread south from New England and the role of Separate Baptists in extending the movement through the South. Moreover, the research highlighted the work of individual Separate Baptist preachers who contributed to the Great Southern Revival in the eighteenth century. While Butler currently maintains his position on "no revival" in the South, contemporary scholarship affirms that something revolutionary took place between 1755 and 1785 that planted Baptists throughout the South and brought thousands of ordinary folks into organized Christianity.[3]

The story of the Great Southern Revival began with an Anglican evangelist named George Whitefield preaching in the colonies. Whitefield tied together the First Great Awakening as he traveled through each colony on the trips he made to America. In his sermons, he demanded that the auditors make a personal commitment to God, experience a new birth, and live a righteous life.[4] For Whitefield, there was nothing half-hearted about a real commitment to God. Emotions and the power of the Holy Spirit worked together to bring people to the Lord and to live a godly life. Although a staunch Calvinist, Whitefield taught that both the heart and the mind must be involved

---

[2]Jon Butler, "Enthusiasm Described and Decried: The Great Awakening as Interpretive Fiction," *Journal of American History* 69 (September 1982): 310–13. Butler wrote, "Revivalism never was the key to the expansion of the colonial churches." He asserted that growth came from population increase, not religious renewal.

[3]Jon Butler, "Religion and Eighteenth-Century Revivalism," the Gilder Lehrman Institute of American History, accessed June 27, 2015, http://www.gilderlehrman.org/history-be-era/religion-and-eighteenth-century-revivalism/essays/religion-eighteenth-century-rev.

[4]Matthew W. Cook, "The Impact of Revivalism on Baptist Faith and Practice," (PhD diss., Baylor University, 2009) 72; J. Timothy Allen, "Shubal Stearns (1706–1771)" accessed June 25, 2015, http://www.northcarolinahistory.org/encyclopedia/143/entry.

in commitment to God, and he expected an emotional response to his preaching if he was being effective.[5] His message and style of preaching attracted many adherents, several of whom left their Congregational-Presbyterian roots in New England and became Separate Baptists.[6]

The crucial years for the beginning of the Baptist revival in the South were 1740-1745, and the location was eastern Connecticut. During those years, Whitefield preached at least twice in Connecticut and attracted followers to his understanding of conversion. During one of Whitefield's trips, Shubal Stearns (1706–1771) and Daniel Marshall (1706–1784) experienced the New Birth.[7] Both men grew up attending the established church and both experienced conversion and baptism in that church as young adults. They both left the state church after a new birth experience during a Whitefield meeting. Stearns' and Marshall's lives took different paths for several years, but they were drawn eventually to the southern colonies as evangelists. And when they began to work together, revival occurred.

Shubal Stearns grew up in Tolland, Connecticut, as part of a farming family. The eldest of eleven children, when his father died Stearns assumed family leadership.[8] When Whitefield came to Tolland in 1745 the entire Stearns family attended his preachings and all embraced Whitefield's message of salvation through the new birth. Stearns realized he could not remain in the established church because he believed that only those who experienced the new birth should be members of a church, and many within the established

---

[5] David T. Morgan, "The Great Awakening in North Carolina: The Baptist Phase," *North Carolina Historical Review* 45 (July 1968): 264. Morgan explains the role of German pietism in adding "vital piety, the mystic union of the believer with God, the enthronement of emotion upon its rightful seat, and a thoroughgoing reformation of morals" to Whitefield's message of conversion. The Separate Baptists emphasized the union with God through the work of the Holy Spirit and the reformation of morals as evidence of the Spirit's presence; Cook, "Impact," 70.

[6] Robert Baylor Semple, *A History of the Rise and Progress of Baptists in Virginia* (Richmond, VA, 1810) n.p. Semple explained on p. 12, "None were admitted who did not profess vital religion. Having thus separated themselves from the established churches, they were denominated *Separates*." Semple, 13, also described the Separates as having a strong faith in the immediate teachings of the Spirit and believing that they were led by the Spirit to the glory of God and the salvation of the lost.

[7] Morgan, "Great Awakening," 267.

[8] David T. Morgan, "Stearns, Shubal Jr.," in *Dictionary of North Carolina Biography*, ed. William S. Powell (1994) 430. Stearns married Sarah Johnston in 1726. While they had no children, they raised several of his siblings as their children.

congregation had not embraced this concept, nor did their lives reflect an association with Christ. He became a Separate Congregationalist. This separated congregation was paedobaptist, but did not reject anyone who was immersed.[9] For five years Stearns led a group of like-minded Separates in the study of Scripture and in theological discussions about the relationship of conversion to lifestyle and the work of the Holy Spirit in a believer's life.

During this time, the Stearns family came into contact with Waitstill Palmer, a Baptist minister in Stonington, Connecticut, and Palmer explained how Baptists understood conversion, baptism and living a godly life. Stearns and his family embraced Palmer's position and were baptized as Separate Baptists in 1751 in the Willamantic River.[10] The family founded a Separate Baptist Church in Tolland, and Stearns led the congregation until 1754 when he had a vision of God calling him to a great ministry southwest of Connecticut. With only a rudimentary education and no theological training, Shubal Stearns and several of his siblings and their families set out, traveling southwest, following the leadership of the Holy Spirit to a new work.[11] Waitstill Palmer and John Morse, the Baptist pastor in New London, Connecticut, ordained Stearns to the gospel ministry before he began his journey to the southwest, to Virginia.[12]

Born and raised in Windsor, Connecticut, not too far from Tolland, Daniel Marshall embraced Whitefield's message in 1745, and like Stearns, he separated from the established church because unrepentant members were acceptable to it. The break was perhaps more difficult for Marshall because he had served as a deacon in his local congregation for more than twenty years

---

[9] Josh Powell, "Shubal Stearns and the Separate Baptist Tradition," *Founders Journal* 44 (Spring 2001) accessed June 23, 2015, http://founders.org/fj44/shubal-stearns-and-the-separate-baptist-tradition, separation was based on II Corinthians 6:17 which called on true believers to "Come out from among them and be ye separate"; Semple, *Rise and Progress*, 12; Morgan, "Great Awakening," 268.

[10] John Sparks, *The Roots of Appalachian Christianity* (Lexington: University of Kentucky Press, 2001) 43; James H. Sightler, "The Separate Baptist Revival and Its Influence in the South," accessed April 3, 2015, http://www.sightlerpublications.com/history/SeparateBaptistRevival.htm.

[11] Sweet, *Revivalism in America*, 37. Neither Stearns nor Marshall had much formal education or any theological training for the ministry.

[12] Sparks, *Roots*, 43.

before he left. After the death of his first wife, Hannah Drake Marshall, during the birth of their son Daniel in 1744, Marshall met and married Martha Stearns, Shubal's younger sister, in 1747.[13] Both embraced the Separated position. They affirmed the demand for a new birth and godly living, and they agreed with Shubal Stearns that the immediate leadership of the Holy Spirit had to be followed.

Shortly after their marriage, the Marshalls sold all their possessions and moved to the Susquehanna River valley in Pennsylvania to work with the Mohawk tribe at the settlement of Onnaquaggy.[14] When inter-tribal warfare and the French and Indian War made their work dangerous, they crossed the border into Winchester, Virginia, in 1754.[15] Through conversations with local Baptists, the Marshalls embraced the Baptist faith and were baptized. Affiliated with the Philadelphia Baptist Association, the church the Marshalls joined in western Virginia was a Regular Baptist church that accepted the Philadelphia Confession of 1742, which was a revision of the Second London Confession (1677).[16] As Calvinists who were committed to affiliating with other Baptists beyond the local church, the Virginia Regular Baptists nurtured the Marshalls for three years.

Stearns and Marshall merged ministries when their paths came together in 1754 in Virginia. Unable to find a ministry niche in the sparsely populated area around Winchester, and unwilling to embrace what they saw as restrictions on the work of the Holy Spirit imposed by the Philadelphia Confession, especially in worship, the Stearns and the Marshalls moved to North Carolina. A friend had written Stearns a letter stating that in that colony it

---

[13] Robert G. Gardner, "Daniel Marshall (1706–1784)" accessed 30 April 2015, http://www.georgiaencyclopedia.org/articles/arts-culture/daniel-marshall-1706–1784; Sparks, *Roots*, 13. Martha was twenty years younger than Daniel but they worked together well and had nine children of their own; Sightler, "The Separate Baptist Revival and Its Influence in the South," accessed April 3, 2015,http://www.sightlerpublications.com/history/SeparateBaptistRevival.htm.

[14] William B. Sprague, *Annals of the American Pulpit*, vol. 6: *Baptists* (New York, NY: Robert Carter & Bros., 1860) 59.

[15] Jesse Harrison Campbell, *Georgia Baptists: Historical and Biographical* (Richmond, GA: H. K. Ellyson, 1847) 15. Marshall was in his mid-forties when his family moved into First People (Native American) territory. The Virginia Baptist church licensed Marshall to preach, but did not ordain him.

[16] James B. Taylor, *Lives of Virginia Baptist Ministers*, 2nd ed. (Richmond, VA: Yale & Wyatt, 1838) 16; Sparks, *Roots*, 11.

was not unusual for someone to travel fifty miles by horseback or wagon in order to hear a preacher.[17] The decision by Stearns and Marshall to move some two-hundred miles further south, in order to do something great for God, set off events that culminated in the Great Southern Revival that embraced Virginia, the Carolinas, Georgia, and stretched into Kentucky and Tennessee.

The travelers settled in an area called Sandy Creek in 1755. Immediately, Marshall and Stearns began itinerating in the area,[18] preaching a call to experience the new birth, to live a godly life, to respond to the leadership of the Holy Spirit.[19] Morgan Edwards, a Baptist historian from Philadelphia who made notes on the story of the Separate Baptists in the late 1700s, described this part of North Carolina as barbaric, peopled with folks who had been raised in the state church but had no real understanding of true faith. Low morality characterized the lives of those who lived in this region, and although the colony was officially Anglican, the state did not care about this backwoods section and little religious persecution occurred.[20] Robert Semple in 1810 and David Benedict in 1848 repeated the assessment made by Edwards. The area into which Stearns and Marshall brought the gospel was a land of spiritual darkness.[21]

People came from miles around to hear Stearns preach at Sandy Creek and to hear Marshall preach wherever he went.[22] Within fifteen years of the founding of the Sandy Creek Baptist Church in 1755 by sixteen people,

---

[17] Semple, *Rise and Progress*, 13.

[18] Cook, "Impact," 80.

[19] Morgan, "Great Awakening," 283. Morgan wrote that the establishment of the work at Sandy Creek was "undeniably one of the greatest landmarks in the history of Baptists, North Carolina, and the South."

[20] David Morgan noted that the areas surrounding Sandy Creek had Quaker, Moravian, Lutheran, and Presbyterian communities when the Separate Baptists arrived; Morgan, "Great Awakening," 271.

[21] David Benedict, *A General History of the Baptist Denomination in America and Other Parts of the World* (New York: Lewis Colby and Co., 1848) 683; Mark Sidwell, "The Sandy Creek Revival: The South's Great Awakening," in *Faith of Our Fathers*, ed. Mark Sidwell (Greenville, SC: BJU Press, 1991) accessed May 20, 2015, http://greatawakeningdocumentary.com/items/show/30; Governor Samuel Johnston labeled the people in the Sandy Creek area as "wild and barbarous" in 1750. See G. W. Paschal, "Early Baptists in Eastern North Carolina," *Biblical Recorder* 21 (November 1934): 1.

[22] Morgan, "Great Awakening," 274.

mostly members of the Stearns and Marshall families, the church grew to a membership of more than six hundred people, with multiple churches growing in areas where Marshall itinerated.[23] While Jon Butler might not think increasing in membership from sixteen to more than six hundred constitutes a revival, Stearns, Marshall and the twelve preacher/missionaries they nurtured in the work, did understand that they were part of a mighty work of God.[24] In 1758, the Sandy Creek Baptist Association, the third Baptist association formed in the American colonies, consisted of seven churches.[25] And the growth continued. Within seventeen years, forty-two churches populated the area, hundreds of members did the work of the church, and more than 125 missionaries had been sent by these Separate Baptists to work in Virginia, Tennessee, Kentucky, the Carolinas and Georgia.[26] While growth of church membership and activity is not the only mark of a revival, growth is a clear sign that something important is occurring.

Relying on the notes of Morgan Edwards, historians from Robert Semple in the early 1800s to John Sparks in the early 2000s have tried to explain the attraction of the Separate Baptist message for frontier audiences. Separate Baptist meetings were often held in the open because of the large number of participants and lasted between one and six weeks, with daily preaching and Bible study.[27] Open to all persons interested in attending, the worship services provided great entertainment for people on the frontier. Emotions ran high during the worship services, with people crying, shouting in joy, trembling, becoming unconscious, and weeping.[28] Edwards wrote: "It was not uncommon for the brethren and…the sisters to give expression to their feelings in outbursts of joy and praise, but it appears that they were free from those wild

---

[23]Morgan, "Stearns," 430.
[24] Cook, "Impact," 85–87.
[25]Morgan, "Stearns," 430.
[26]James E. Tull, *Shapers of Baptist Thought* (Macon, GA: Mercer University Press, 1984) 74; Sightler stated that within fifty years, some one hundred daughter congregations existed in Kentucky, Virginia, the Carolinas, and Georgia.
[27] Guion Griffis Johnson, "Revival Movements in Ante-Bellum North Carolina," *North Carolina Historical Review* 10 (January 1933): 23; Sweet, *Revivalism in America*, 37–40.
[28]George Washington Paschal, *History of North Carolina Baptists*. Vol. 1:1663–1805 (Raleigh, NC: General Board, North Carolina Baptist Convention, 1930) 298–99. Drawing from Morgan Edwards's notes, Paschal told of the way in which preachers left the pulpit and entered the crowd to shake hands during a hymn of invitation. To some people, the preacher would extend a personal invitation and offer to pray with them.

and fantastic exercises which prevailed in other places."[29] The preaching was powerful, directed at the hearts of people, demanding the new birth, godly living, and openness to the leadership of the Holy Spirit. Most Separate Baptists preachers emulated the style of Shubal Stearns. Edwards described that style as follows:[30]

> His voice was musical and strong, which he managed in such a manner as, one while, to make soft impression on the heart, and fetch tears from the eyes in a mechanical way; and anon, to shake the very nerves and throw the animal system into tumults and perturbations. All the Separate ministers copy after him in tones of voice and actions of body; and some few exceed him.... In his eyes was something very penetrating, seemed to have a meaning in every glance....[31]

Stearns himself, although a man of small stature, had a gaze and delivery that riveted listeners and drew a response from them. Tidence Lane and Elnathan Davis became Separate Baptist ministers and Morgan Edwards recorded their conversion stories.[32] Tidence Lane attended a service led by Stearns out of curiosity, but he felt Stearns' gaze drawing him toward the place of decision, the altar. Wherever he walked, he felt Stearns was staring at him and talking to him. At one point he lost consciousness, and when he awoke, he could no longer resist the call to the altar, and he embraced the new birth. Elnathan Davis attended a service led by Stearns because Stearns was baptizing a man named John Stewart who was very large. Stearns was small, and Davis figured he would lose his grip on Stewart, and provide great entertainment as Stewart floated down the river. He underestimated the grip of a Baptist pastor. After the baptismal service, Stearns began to preach; people trembled and wept, and Davis became scared. He left the campground but was drawn back by Stearns' voice. Eventually, Davis experienced the new birth and became a Separate Baptist preacher. Drawn by novelty, both Lane and Davis were overwhelmed

---

[29]Quoted in Robert I. Devin, *A History of the Grassy Creek Baptist Church* (Raleigh, NC: Edwards, Broughton & Co., 1880) 70.

[30]A. H. Newman wrote of Stearns: "It is doubtful whether any evangelist but Whitefield surpassed Stearns in magnetic power over audiences." See A. H. Newman, *A History of the Baptist Churches in the United States*, rev. ed. (Philadelphia, PA: American Baptist Publication Society, 1898) 293; also Sweet, *Revivalism in America*, 15.

[31]G. W. Paschal, "Morgan Edwards' Materials Towards a History of the Baptists in the Province of North Carolina," *North Carolina Historical Review* 7 (July 1930): 386.

[32] Thomas Kidd, *The Great Awakening* (Boston: Bedford/St. Martin's, 2008) 261.

by the power of Stearns' message and delivery. Revival for the Separate Baptists came with the power of the Holy Spirit to draw people to God's self. Separate Baptist preachers believed the presence of the Holy Spirit was essential for a worship service to be effective, and that presence was indicated by an emotional response to the preaching.[33] Separate Baptist meetings were spontaneous and experiential.

While Stearns itinerated occasionally, he stayed close to Sandy Creek and became known as "Old Father Shubal" to the many preachers he trained. Before his death in 1771, Stearns grew increasingly autocratic and created tension among the churches in the association.[34] Even so, at his death, the Sandy Creek Church was, as Morgan Edwards wrote, the mother and grandmother of active Baptist work in North Carolina, and had sent Separate Baptist preachers as far west as Kentucky and Tennessee, as far north as Virginia and as far south as Georgia.[35]

From the time of their arrival in the backwoods of North Carolina, Daniel and Martha Marshall traveled extensively throughout the region.[36] They journeyed to the coastal area, suffered imprisonment for "disturbing the peace,"[37] worked with a church at Abbot's Creek, North Carolina, and finally moved to Horse Creek, South Carolina, in 1770, where they established a Separate Baptist congregation.[38] Sharing preaching and teaching responsibilities, Daniel and Martha led the fledgling church for a few years before moving further South to found the Kiokee Baptist Church in Georgia in 1771,

---

[33]David C. McCollum, "A Study of Evangelicals and Revival Exercises from 1730–1805" (PhD diss., Southeastern Baptist Theological Seminary, 2009) 185–88. Stearns and Marshall believed a preacher should be "exercised" while preaching in order to express their own lost state.

[34]Allen, "Shubal Stearns (1706–1771)" accessed June 25, 2015, http://www.northcarolinahistory.org/encyclopedia/143/entry.

[35]Paschal, "Morgan Edwards," 385.

[36]John Broadus, "The American Baptist Ministry of One Hundred Years Ago," *Baptist Quarterly* 11 (1875): 10. Broadus noted that Martha was "wonderfully impressive" in her preaching and praying.

[37]In June 1768, Virginia officials arrested Separate Baptist ministers John Waller, Lewis Craig, and James Child. During their trial for being disturbers of the peace, the prosecutor noted, "May it please your worships, these men are great disturbers of the peace, they cannot meet a man upon the road, but they must run a text of Scripture down his throat." See Sweet, *Revivalism in America*, 29–30.

[38]Campbell, *Georgia Baptists*, 16.

the first Separate Baptist church in that state.[39] They stayed with the Kiokee congregation until their deaths. Daniel Marshall died in 1784.

After twenty years of preaching, teaching and worshipping in the South, the Separate Baptists grew into the largest evangelical denomination on the American frontier. The drive of Shubal Stearns and the itineration of Daniel Marshall firmly planted this new approach to Baptist life in the poorer regions of the southern colonies, and created tension with other Baptist groups in the South, particularly the Regular Baptists. Even close relatives do not always welcome revival. The Regular Baptists adhered to the Philadelphia Confession and discipline documents.[40] From the beginning of Separate Baptist work on the frontier, Regular Baptists criticized the Separates for the emotional content and spontaneity of their meetings and for the role of women in public worship. They also criticized the Separates for having nine ordinances rather than two.[41]

In response, the Separate Baptists saw the Regulars as stiff and formal, i.e., the Regular Baptists blocked the work of the Holy Spirit by demanding conformity in worship, a high level of education for ministers, and by denying the public display of spiritual gifts by both men and women.[42] The tension between the two groups was strong enough that when Shubal Stearns planned to ordain Daniel Marshall to the ministry no Regular Baptist ministers would participate. Two Separate Baptist pastors, Stearns and Henry Ledbetter, ordained Marshall as pastor of the Abbots Creek church with no input from

---

[39]*A History of the Baptist Denomination in Georgia* (Atlanta, GA: Jas. P. Harrison & Co., 1881) 13. Marshall was sixty-five when he began the work in Georgia. He was seen as "a man of pure faith, fervent spirit, holy zeal, indefatigable in religious labors, and possessed of the highest moral courage" (14); Samuel Boykin, *History of the Baptist Denomination in Georgia* (Atlanta, GA: Index Publishing, 1881) 1:13.

[40]Sparks, *Roots*, 39.

[41]The nine ordinances were immersion, communion, laying on of hands for repentance and healing, foot washing, love feasts, anointing the sick, embracing and shaking the hands of members, the kiss of charity, and offering the right hand of fellowship to new members. Allen, "Shubal Stearns (1706–1771)" accessed June 25, 2015, http://www.northcarolinahistory.org/encyclopedia/143/entry; Kidd, *Grat Awakening*, 250; Cook, "Impact," 17, 79.

[42]Powell, "Shubal Stearns and the Separate Baptist Tradition," *Founders Journal* 44 (Spring 2001) accessed June 23, 2015, http://founders.org/fj44/shubal-stearns-and-the-separate-baptist-tradition; Sparks, *Roots*, 48. Sparks noted that Separate Baptists "set great store by what they perceived as direct impressions of the Holy Spirit on their consciences… …" and for the Regular Baptists this belief was too disorderly.

Regular Baptist pastors.⁴³ Later, John Gano, a missionary minister for the Philadelphia Association, visited Sandy Creek to assess whether or not the Separate Baptists were doctrinally orthodox. He was received cautiously and he wrote to Philadelphia that although the Separates were "immethodical" in their meetings, they grasped the "root of the matter" and were true Baptists.⁴⁴

More problematic for the Regular Baptists was the role of women in Separate Baptist life. Morgan Edwards commented on the public nature of women's ministry among the Separates by describing the work of Martha Stearns Marshall. Mother of nine children and stepmother of one, she exhorted and preached in public regularly, and she was effective at what she did.⁴⁵ Edwards described her style as compelling and fervent. One episode he related took place when a local official arrested Daniel Marshall for disturbing the peace and Martha challenged the official by quoting Scripture and speaking with "force and pertinency." Her words convicted "many to their hearts." She so impressed the officer that he later became a Baptist.⁴⁶ Although Martha was singularly gifted, any public preaching and praying by a woman was not acceptable to the Philadelphia Association. But for the Separates, the role of the Holy Spirit in guiding and empowering believers as the Spirit chose was so crucial that gender was a less relevant category for them in the areas of leadership and public worship.

Conclusion

Something happened in the southern colonies between 1755 and 1785 that altered the religious life of thousands of people, and that altered their civic and moral lives, too. William Warren Sweet wrote that the Separate Baptists' emphasis on individual responsibility and the work of the Holy Spirit created "something new and aggressive and distinctly American."⁴⁷

Stearns and Marshall influenced more than Baptist churches during the Great Southern Revival. Methodist Churches adopted some of the worship

---

⁴³ Sprague, *Annals 6: Baptists*, 60. Marshall was fifty-two when he was ordained.
⁴⁴Semple, *Rise and Progress*, 66.
⁴⁵Dan White, "Martha Stearns Marshall: Pioneer Woman Preacher, accessed 28 May 2015, http://www.faithwriters.com/article-details.php?id=166671.
⁴⁶*A History of the Baptist Denomination in Georgia*, 14.
⁴⁷Sweet, *Revivalism in America*, xii, 35.

practices and message of the Separate Baptist churches and grew rapidly, especially after the beginning of the Second Great Awakening in 1800.[48] Thus, the work of the Separate Baptists provided a bridge for the message and emotion found in the frontier phase of the Second Great Awakening.[49]

---

[48]Sparks, *Roots*, xii. Loyal Jones affirmed that Stearns preached a populist religion that was available to all people, regardless of age, gender or socioeconomic stratum. He influenced folks throughout the Appalachian region, far beyond the boundaries of the Separate Baptists. Loyal Jones, "Forward," in Sparks, *Roots*, xiii.

[49]Johnson, "Revival Movements," 22.

3

Baptists in South Carolina in the Second Great Awakening

Kim Kellison

In the early 1830s in South Carolina, Baptists experienced an amazing, refreshing season of revival. Pastors gave thanks that the "the Lord has been pleased...in a wonderful manner to pour out his Spirit in many quarters of his vineyard." Many people had "been brought to the knowledge of the truth as it is in Jesus."[1] Baptist minister James C. Furman remembered that the "years 1831 and 1832 were memorable years in the history of the denomination, the gracious outpouring of the Spirit was witnessed by a widespread awakening." The resulting "ingathering into the churches was unprecedented," he attested.[2] The revival was strongest in the northern and western portions of South Carolina, in the upper districts known as the Up-country and along the western districts close to the Savannah River. It led to major Baptist growth in these areas, changing the lives of converts and increasing the already strong presence of Baptists in the region. Yet this revival has generated relatively little scholarly attention, even though contemporary observers and participants noted its widespread impact, marking it as a great event in their lives. How and why did this revival originate? How long did it last? What were its effects? Finally, how does it enhance our understanding of revivalism in the South?

---

[1] Minutes of the Saluda Baptist Association, August 11, 1832, Baptist Historical Collection, Furman University.

[2] Harvey Toliver Cook, *The Life Work of James Clement Furman* (Greenville, SC: published by Alester G. Furman, 1926) 16. For scholarship on Up-Country South Carolina, see particularly Lacy K. Ford, *Origins of Southern Radicalism: The South Carolina Up-Country, 1800–1860* (New York: Oxford University Press, 1988) 1–95, and Orville Vernon Burton, *In My Father's House are Many Mansions: Family and Community in Edgefield, South Carolina* (Chapel Hill: University of North Carolina Press, 1985) 3–103.

BAPTISTS IN SOUTH CAROLINA IN THE SECOND GREAT AWAKENING

Two Streams of Baptists in South Carolina

Baptists in the South Carolina Up-country (called in the colonial period the Backcountry) experienced three major revivals in the years before the Civil War. Separate Baptists settled in the region in the 1760s, and despite the American Revolution, grew dramatically in number in the 1770s and 1780s. A second major awakening, this one widely interdenominational, spread through the Up-country in the early 1800s. A third Baptist revival occurred in the early 1830s, a product of deliberate attempts by coastal Baptists to create a stronger denominational presence throughout the state.[3] While all three revivals had a profound effect on Baptist growth in the state, and while South Carolina preachers played a fundamental part in initiating and sustaining the revival, the awakenings followed significantly different paths. Both the Separate Baptist Revival and the Great Revival of the early 1800s spread to South Carolina from other southern states, resulted in widespread conversions, and were largely shunned by Baptist leaders in the coastal, or Low Country, region.[4] As a result, both awakenings reinforced, rather than unite, a divided Baptist presence South Carolina. Occurring a generation later, much of the impetus for the Revival of the early 1830s came not from outside of the state, but from the Low Country, where Baptists aggressively worked to spread a denominational presence by emphasizing extra-congregational organization, education, and missionary work. The gentrification of Baptist culture, by the spread and acceptance of Low Country Baptist views to the Up-country, blurred the lines between the two groups of Baptists. Although the change would not be completed for decades (as the Primitive-Missionary schism of the 1820s and 1830s revealed), the revival of the early 1830s represented the

---

[3] The terms "First Great Awakening" and "Second Great Awakening" prove to be helpful categories, but significant questions about the nature and time span of southern revivalism remain. How, for instance, does one determine when the Second Great Awakening ended? Was the Second Great Awakening, as experienced by South Carolina Baptists, comprised of one or two major revivals? As Tommy Kidd and Barry Hankins suggest, perhaps a better way to view American Baptist revivals is to see them as a sequence of awakenings without fixed categorical boundaries. Thomas Kidd and Barry Hankins, *Baptists in America: A History* (New York: Oxford University Press, 2015) 84–85.

[4] Low Country as well as Up-country churches saw strong numerical increases in the 1780s, but church growth does not seem to have stemmed from one particular source of revivalism. Leah Townsend, *South Carolina Baptists, 1670–1805* (Florence, SC: Florence Printing, 1935) 105–66.

transformation of South Carolina away from a "two-Baptist" state and toward a "one-Baptist" entity, from a regionally divided Baptist culture to a more unified state-wide Baptist presence guided by denominational concerns.[5]

In the colonial period, Baptists divided into two loose groups, those centered in the Charleston, or Low Country, area and those cantered in the Up-country. From the very start, their character and perspective were different, just as the two regions, economically and socially, diverged. While both groups stressed the importance of congregational authority, Low Country Baptists also developed an organizational culture to propagate their beliefs. The first Baptists to come to Charleston—and to South Carolina—came from England and from Piscataway, Maine, in the 1680s, and by the 1690s had organized Charleston Baptist Church.[6] By the mid-1700s, Baptist churches in the Charleston area communicated with similar-minded Baptist congregations throughout the colonies, particularly Baptists in Philadelphia. In 1751, under the leadership of Oliver Hart, Charleston Baptists organized South Carolina's first Baptist association, the Charleston Baptist Association, to foster communication between member churches. Through the Charleston Baptist Association, the Pennsylvania-born Hart and his successor, Richard Furman, coordinated funds contributed from individual churches in support of missionary work and clergy education, with Furman organizing, by the 1790s, a General Committee of the Charleston Association to oversee such functions. This commitment to organizational, extra-congregational efforts to spread the Kingdom of God made Charleston Baptist leaders crucial participants in the creation of state and national denominational organizations in the 1810s and 1820s.[7]

Up-country Baptists, by contrast, remained congregational in outlook, viewing organizational connections with suspicion. The first Baptists to settle in the Up-country were Separate Baptists from Sandy Creek, North Carolina.

---

[5] Kimberly R. Kellison, "South Carolina Baptists, the Primitive-Missionary Schism, and the Revival of the Early 1830s," *South Carolina Historical Magazine* 110 (July-October 2009): 154–79; James R. Mathis, *The Making of the Primitive Baptists: A Cultural and Intellectual History of the Antimission Movement* (New York: Routledge, 2004).

[6] The Life and Works of Morgan Edwards, quoted in David Benedict, *A General History of the Baptist Denomination in America and Other Parts of the World* (New York: Lewis Colby, 1849) 701–2; Townsend, *South Carolina Baptists*, 7–12; Joe M. King, *A History of South Carolina Baptists* (Columbia, SC: R. L. Bryan, 1964) 10–16.

[7] Townsend, *South Carolina Baptists*, 7–75, 165–78; King, *History of South Carolina Baptists*, 10–25, 62–68, 156–79.

Unconcerned about educational training, emotional in their preaching, and fiercely dedicated to the rebirth of the soul, Separates followed the Bible with fervor. Their leaders, products of the Great Awakening in New England, were Shubal Stearns and Daniel Marshall. Along with Phillip Mulkey, who founded the first Separate church in South Carolina in 1759 or 1760, Stearns and Marshall established numerous Separate congregations in the Up-country. Prone to allowing women participation in religious services and given to periods of profuse emotion, the Separate Baptist brand of evangelism differed markedly from that of Low Country Baptists, whose leaders emphasized an educated clergy and a sense of social decorum. Low Country Baptists voiced great distrust of Separates (as did colonial authorities).[8] The pastor of Welsh Neck Church refused to participate in the ordination of Separate Baptist Daniel Marshall under the claim "that he held no fellowship with [Shubal] Stearns's party, that he believed them to be a disorderly set, suffering women to pray in public, and permitting every ignorant man to preach that chose, and that they encouraged noise & confusion in their meetings."[9] In the years after the American Revolution, Separates modified some of their more radical beliefs. According to David Benedict, starting in the 1790s "the name of Separate began to be disused, and was soon entirely laid aside, so that the [Baptists] in South Carolina, from whatever source they originated, have for many years been united in their external order and doctrinal statements."[10] This modification process was a gradual one, however, especially in churches far removed from the Low Country, where Baptists remained suspicious of extra-congregational authority.[11] Only as plantation agriculture created a new social order in the Up-country—one tied more directly to that of the Low Country—would the Separate heritage fade, a process that took generations.

Despite some moderating tendencies, then, at the turn of the century South Carolina Baptists remained religiously and culturally bifurcated, their

---

[8] Townsend, *South Carolina Baptists*, 76–99; King, *History of South Carolina Baptists*, 69--99; Benedict, *General History*, 706-707-7; Kidd and Hankins, *Baptists in America*, 35–38.

[9] Townsend, *South Carolina Baptists*, 78.

[10] Benedict, *General History*, 712.

[11] Townsend, *South Carolina Baptists*, 178–79. Denominational organizer and leader Richard Furman was baptized by Separate Baptist Joseph Reese in 1770; Thomas S. Kidd argues that "no person did more to bridge the divide between the Separate and Regular Baptists in South Carolina" than Furman. Thomas S. Kidd, *The Great Awakening: The Roots of Evangelical Christianity in Colonial America* (New Haven: Yale University Press, 2007) 263–64.

values shaped by differing social orders and religious outlooks. Eighteenth-century revivalism affected both groups of Baptists before and after the American Revolution, with Charleston churches experiencing periods of significant increase but with Up-country churches growing most rapidly. By the late 1790s, many parts of South Carolina, as well as Baptists throughout the South, worried about declining spiritual interest. They prayed ardently for revival. In the early 1800s, their prayers were answered with the "Great Revival" that swept through key regions of the southern states.[12]

The Second Great Awakening

Fueled by Presbyterian James McGready's phenomenal revival in Kentucky in the late 1700s, Baptists, Methodists, and Presbyterians worked together at the turn of the century to foster interdenominational camp meetings throughout the southeast. Religious interest increased through the Up-country as news spread of the camp meetings. The 1800 annual meeting of the Up-country Bethel Association drew almost 3,500 people to hear ministers preach and exhort.[13] The first major interdenominational camp meeting in South Carolina occurred at the Waxhaws settlement of Lancaster district in May 1802. A total of twenty-one preachers (five Methodists, five Baptists, and eleven Presbyterians) attended the meeting. Ministers took turns preaching at the two main stands; in between sermons, they also traveled from tent to tent praying and exhorting. The preaching was electric. Estimates of crowd attendance ranged from three to eight thousand people.[14]

Other camp meetings followed in Up-country South Carolina. Presbyterians initiated, and Baptist and Methodists joined, a camp meeting at Nazareth Church in Spartanburg district that attracted between five and six thousand people. Individual churches and associations experienced revival as well. A reported two thousand people gathered at Woodruff Church in Greenville district in the summer of 1802, where thirty-six people were baptized in one

---

[12] John B. Boles, *The Great Revival, 1787–1805: The Origins of the Southern Evangelical Mind* (Lexington: University Press of Kentucky, 1972) 78–81; Townsend, *South Carolina Baptists*, 181–86; Rogers, *James A. Furman*, 102–3.

[13] Townsend, South Carolina Baptists, 181–86.

[14] Baptists did not commune with non-Baptist converts. See Townsend, *South Carolina Baptists*, 183. John Boles lists eighteen ministers, eleven Presbyterian, four Baptist, and three Methodist preachers at the meeting. Boles, *The Great Revival*, 79.

day.[15] The years 1802 and 1803 proved particularly fruitful, with additions by baptism in some churches ranging from one hundred to four hundred. The Bethel Association grew so rapidly that new associations, including the Saluda Association, were created to administer the many new churches. South Carolina Baptist historian Leah Townsend estimates that by 1803 roughly ten thousand whites and blacks belonged to South Carolina Baptist churches, representing an 80 percent increase in membership over a three-year period.[16]

Although the Great Revival primarily affected Up-country churches, camp meetings drew onlookers from other parts of the state. At the Waxhaws meeting, one Baptist observer noted many people "from the lower part of this state" in attendance, some of whom "came under...impressions."[17] Stories about the camp meetings no doubt created religious excitement in some Low Country churches; in the Low Country Beaufort district, located along the Georgia border, public meetings led to large scale revivalism. At Black Swamp Church, roughly twelve hundred people participated in a three-day camp meeting in December 1803.[18] Nearby Beaufort church, originally an arm of Black Swamp Church, experienced revival the following year. More formal in decorum, the Beaufort revival lacked some of the more excessive emotional aspects of the Up-country revival. At the age of twenty-two, future Baptist leader William Bullein Johnson accepted Christ at this revival, his spiritual mentor an English woman who had earlier converted to the Baptist faith in Savannah.[19]

The Great Revival energized its participants. Highly emotional camp meetings frequently evoked physical reactions from participants, with reports of swooning, fainting, dancing, and even barking like dogs coming out of

---

[15] Townsend, *South Carolina Baptists*, 184.
[16] Townsend, *South Carolina Baptists*, 185–86.
[17] Townsend, *South Carolina Baptists*, 183.
[18] George Howe, *History of the Presbyterian Church in South Carolina* (Columbia: W. J. Duffie, 1883) 2:112; Stephanie McCurry, *Masters of Small Worlds: Yeomen Households, Gender Relations, and the Political Culture of the Antebellum South Carolina Low Country* (New York: Oxford University Press, 1997) 148.
[19] Hortense Woodson, *Giant in the Land: A Biography of William Bullein Johnson, First President of the Southern Baptist Convention, 1845–1851* (Nashville: Broadman, 1950) 7–11; McCurry, *Master of Small Worlds*, 148–50.

some meetings.[20] Such behavior did not fit into the more refined culture of educated Low Country Baptists. Charleston leader Richard Furman, underscoring an emphasis upon propriety and order, worried about the "enthusiasm" of the camp meeting and voiced concern as well about the "too free intercourse between the sexes in such an encampment."[21] Ironically, decades earlier, at the age of sixteen, Furman had been converted at a revival in the South Carolina interior led by Separate Baptist Joseph Reese.[22]

As such, aside from the Beaufort awakening, which had a very different emotional tenor than meetings in the Up-country, the Great Revival remained a regional revival in South Carolina. Richard Furman and other leaders chose not to capitalize on or cultivate interdenominational revivalism in the Low Country. Dismissing the emotionalism of the awakenings, Charleston Baptists poured resources and energy into their specific vision of evangelism, one centered not upon interdenominational revivalism but upon training new clergy and sending missionaries into destitute portions of the state. The Great Revival generated tremendous religious excitement and growth in the Up-country, but it did not forge a unified white Baptist culture in South Carolina. Indeed, God's work went on in distinctively different ways for these two groupings of Baptist believers.

The denominational emphasis of Charleston Baptists soon began to blur and ultimately shift these regional identities, as did economic and social transformations taking place in the Up-country. By the early 1810s, Low Country Baptists, who had been energized by missionary endeavors since the mid-1700s and who in the early 1810s embraced eagerly the budding foreign missionary movement, proved highly instrumental in forming the "General Missionary Convention of the Baptist Denomination in the United States of America for Foreign Missions," more commonly called the Triennial Convention because the organization met every three years. The first meeting occurred in May 1814 in Philadelphia, where delegates voted Richard Furman, the leading figure among South Carolina Baptists and an advocate of missions

---

[20] James Jenkins, Experiences, *Labours, and Sufferings of the Reverend James Jenkins, of the South Carolina Conference*, quoted in Townsend, *South Carolina Baptists*, 183. See also Townsend, *South Carolina Baptists*, 181–85.

[21] Townsend, *South Carolina Baptists*, 183–84.

[22] Townsend, *South Carolina Baptists*, 90–91; Rogers, *Furman*, 17–19; Kidd, *Great Awakening*, 263–64.

and education, as their first president.[23] Drawing on the excitement of the Triennial Convention, mission-minded Baptists throughout the South established state organizations to coordinate their commitment to foreign and domestic evangelization. In 1820, Furman and other Baptist leaders proposed a South Carolina convention comprised of representatives from regional Baptist associations. Up-country Baptists, wary of the missionary and educational goals of the convention, declined the invitation. Charleston Baptists believed in the idea so strongly, though, that in 1821 they formed the Convention anyway, and then requested other associations to join. In addition to six delegates from the Charleston Association, two from Edgefield and one from Savannah River Association came together in a meeting in Columbia to create the organization. Delegates chose Richard Furman as president of the convention, which pledged to promote "the evangelical & useful knowledge, by means of religious education; the support of missionary service among the destitute; & the cultivation of measures promotive to the true interest of the churches of Christ in general, & of their union, love, & harmony in particular."[24] The delegates were quite energetic. They embraced the missions cause with vigor, worked to convince doubting congregations that education and missionary societies were part of God's word, and, before the decade was over, had founded the Furman Academy and Theological Institution, named after the esteemed Richard Furman, who died in 1825.[25]

The 1810s and particularly the 1820s, then, proved to be dynamic, transitional years of growth for Charleston Baptists, whose organizational activity now could now be carried out on both national and state-wide levels. Driven by these gains, Low Country Baptists also expanded their presence into new parts of the Up-country, sending trained missionaries and educated preachers into areas without a strong Baptist presence, or where existing Baptists had little connection to the State Baptist Convention. Their greatest immediate success occurred in Edgefield district in the western part of the state. The Baptist State Convention paid the twenty-four-year old Baptist minister Basil

---

[23] Woodson, *Giant*, 32–39; King, *History of South Carolina Baptists*, 167–68.

[24] Minutes of the South Carolina State Convention of the Baptist Denomination in South Carolina, 1821, Baptist Historical Collection, Furman University.

[25] King, *History of South Carolina Baptists,* 170–73. William Bullein Johnson succeeded Furman as president of the State Baptist Convention. See Woodson, *Giant,* 49.

Manly eight hundred dollars to evangelize the area in 1822. Joining Big Stephen's Creek Church, Manly was ordained in March of 1822. The following month, he helped establish a Baptist congregation in Edgefield Village.[26] As he surveyed the territory the year before, Manly informed his close friend Iveson Brookes that of the roughly thirty-seven or thirty-eight churches in the district (most of which had a great deal of wealth) fewer than ten ministers existed, "and not one of those ministers can write a sentence fit to appear even in the minutes." Manly counted at least three churches worth "at least $500,000," with others boasting lesser, but still significant wealth. Such possibilities for pastoral support, and the need for educated Baptist ministers, provided a fertile ground for Low Country Baptists to send additional preachers into the area for explicitly denominational reasons, "not to undo them and make Methodists and Presbyterians out of them, but to build them up and rescue the sinking Baptist name."[27]

Basil Manly represented what Low Country Baptists were learning to do well: reshaping Up-country Baptist culture along Low Country lines, in the process forging a state-wide denominational structure. Under Manly's leadership, Edgefield experienced a revival between 1822 and 1824 that led to nearly five hundred additions to nearby churches. In a district that by the 1820s had grown in status and wealth, the educated young minister introduced a more refined Baptist style, one that fit much more easily with Low Country objectives and organization. Soon after the revival, the Baptist State Convention chose Edgefield as the initial home of Furman Academy and Theological Institution, which opened in 1827.[28] Although the institution was moved to a different location two years later due to financial strains, Edgefield district, with its wealth and religious growth, had become a hot spot for organizational Baptists. In January 1831, William Bullein Johnson, who became the most prominent Baptist leader in the state following the death of Richard Furman, accepted the pastorate of Edgefield Village Church.[29] Johnson advocated ed-

---

[26] A. James Fuller, *Chaplain to the Confederacy: Basil Manly and Baptist Life in the Old South* (Baton Rouge: Louisiana State University Press, 2000) 43–44.

[27] Basil Manly to Iveson Brookes, September 24, 1831, quoted in Fuller, *Chaplain to the Confederacy*, 44.

[28] Woodson, *Giant*, 56–67; King, *History of South Carolina Baptists*, 180–207.

[29] At the same time that he became the pastor of Edgefield Village Church, Johnson also assumed leadership of the Edgefield Female Academy. See Woodson, *Giant*, 61–67.

ucation and missionary work as fiercely as his predecessor Furman, and Johnson, perhaps even more than Furman, was an adept denominational organizer and administrator. Although Charleston and other Low Country churches continued to be the center of the Charleston tradition, with Manly's and later Johnson's presence in Edgefield the nexus of Baptist influence expanded to include a more central part of the state. Organizational Baptists were poised for revival, which came in the early 1830s and quickly spread in two directions: further into the Up-country, and southward, along the Savannah River, toward Beaufort.

The Revival of the Early 1830s in South Carolina

In July of 1831, a magnificent revival began at Sardis Church in Edgefield district. The power of this particular revival was so overwhelming that William Bullein Johnson, who had only recently moved from Greenville to Edgefield, wrote to his friend and fellow South Carolina Baptist William Brantly, who now supplied the Baptist Church in Philadelphia and who edited the *Christian Index*, about the refreshing news of the event. "It pleased God," Johnson noted, "to grant us a spiritual revival, accompanied with the addition of many redeemed souls to the church." Brantly quickly published Johnson's revival story, called, appropriately, "Animating Scenes in Zion."[30]

The revival, Johnson stated, began in 1831, when Baptists of the Edgefield Association, learning the news of a camp meeting in Virginia the previous year, decided to turn the July 1831 union meeting at Sardis into a camp meeting. The meeting drew at least five hundred people, and sparked revivalism in the local region. Twenty-eight people confessed their sins and asked for salvation; ministers baptized eight people at the meeting.[31]

Johnson and others asked the Sardis leaders to visit Edgefield Village Church, to spread the revival fervor. "To our surprize [sic] and joy," wrote Johnson, "several of them came to see us in the evening of the day on which they left the camping ground." When the revivalists came to the church, the church bell was rung, alerting the town residents of a religious meeting. Johnson most likely gave the first sermon, after which "the church with all Christians present were requested to approach the area in front of the pulpit, and

---

[30] William Bullein Johnson, "Reminiscences," in Woodson, *Giant*, 74.
[31] Bullein, "Reminiscences," 74.

kneeling, united in prayer for the blessing of God upon the coming of his servants."[32] Public meetings followed for ten days. The young revivalists joined Johnson and other elders each morning for a sunrise meeting, which "ushered in the duties and delights of the day." Meetings followed at 10:00 a.m., 4:00 p.m., and in the evening, where ministers preached and exhorted. Preachers met with anxious sinners to talk and pray, and with Baptist leaders, "directing them [the sinners] to the Lamb of God who teeth [taketh] away the sin of the world." In between the morning and afternoon public meetings, participants also met at private houses—Johnson lived close by, as did others—so that "prayer, praise, and exhortations were constantly going on." The church itself was seldom empty. People hurried to find seating in the crowded meeting house during the public services. "Long before the bell would announce the arrival of the hour for preaching," Johnson recounted, "the streets and ways leading to the meeting house would be covered with those who were hastening to obtain seats." Crowds filled the church "from sunrise to ten or eleven o'clock at night." One night, Johnson stated, "one poor stricken soul" remained in the church until the early hours of the morning, well after the evening service had ended.[33]

News of the revival, "of these amazing scenes," spread to nearby regions, motivating crowds of people to "come and see the Lord's doing, so marvelous in our eyes." Edgefield residents hosted guests from surrounding locales. Some businesses closed for part of the day, and the male and female academies, consisting of a total of one hundred pupils, "were at first partially suspended, and finally dismissed" so that teachers and students could attend the services.[34]

The revival, then, had become a community event. The baptismal process reinforced this sacred communal bond. Some of the earliest converts were young men and women, "mostly in the bloom of life." After relating "the dealing of God with their souls," the first candidates prepared for baptism, which took place on a Monday afternoon. The baptismal scene, replicated in other southern revivals, began with an orchestrated, elaborate procession designed

---

[32] Bullein, "Reminiscences," 74.
[33] Bullein, "Reminiscences," 74–75.
[34] Bullein, "Reminiscences," 75.

to be, in the words of Johnson, "imposing."[35] Large crowds gathered to observe the sacred event. "For the accommodation of the multitude in attendance, those who rode in carriages were requested to leave the house in the first place and to take their stations on the opposite side of the stream convenient for witnessing the solemn ceremony." Johnson, who referred to himself as "the administrator," then led the delegation of ministers ("five or six deep") and the baptismal candidates, dressed in white, with women walking first and males following behind. The church members came next in the procession, followed by the congregation. At the church, the ministers and attendees began to sing a hymn, so that "the air resounded with the praises of the most High God, while we passed through the streets of our town to the baptismal wave." Upon arriving at the baptismal stream, Johnson, "in the presence of a thousand spectators," had "the exquisite delight of immersing into the liquid grave, twenty-one immortal beings in token of their death to sin, and resurrection to a newness of life." Later in the week, "the same scene was renewed," with ten baptisms on Wednesday and fourteen on Friday, "making in the whole forty-five immortal beings, who, within the short space of ten days, were translated as we trust, from the kingdom of darkness into the kingdom of God's dear Son, and publicly professed their allegiance to their new Sovereign." Johnson also tallied those who had "professed to have received comfort at the meeting" (twenty-five), some of whom were later baptized at nearby Baptist churches in the weeks following the Edgefield Church awakening, and others who planned to join the Episcopal, Presbyterian, or Methodist church.[36]

Of the Baptists who helped with the revival, students from the Furman Theological Institution played a vital role. James C. Furman, son of the late Richard Furman and a ministerial student, noted "Edgefield district shared largely in [the] gracious awakening." Deluged by "constant and pressing calls for labor," local preachers asked for ministerial help from the school. Professor Jesse Hartwell, principal and teacher, and two unidentified students traveled to Edgefield to assist with services; James Furman later participated in at least one revival in Edgefield district, as well as in other parts of the state. "Everywhere immense congregations gathered, and through the day meetings were

---

[35] Bullein, "Reminiscences," 75; David Bebbington, *Victorian Religious Revivals: Culture and Piety in Local and Global Contexts* (New York: Oxford University Press, 2012) 53–81, esp. 58–60.

[36] Bullein, "Reminiscences," 75–76.

held in the open air," the young minister proclaimed.[37] William Johnson noted that the presence of such youthful leaders appealed to the young converts, particularly. Though young themselves—"destitute of the advantages of human learning," as Johnson put it, "they spoke well for their Master," displaying both zeal and ability in preaching and exhorting.[38]

After the public meetings ceased at Edgefield Village, ministers moved next to nearby churches in the district, preaching and holding public services for five- and six-day periods. Had more preachers been available to assist with such services, Johnson felt, even more conversions would have occurred.[39] Regardless, revivalism had a profound impact on the residents of Edgefield district. Edgefield Baptist Church baptized seventy-four people by October 1831; the year before, only seventy-nine members belonged to the church. Little Stephen's Creek, with 250 on its roll, baptized sixty-six converts. The twenty-five members of Mt. Moriah witnessed the baptism of eighty-six people in 1831. And Sardis Church, where the revival began, experienced fifty baptisms, its membership surging 115 members.[40] In August 1832, reports continued to bring cheering news. Edgefield witnessed 130 baptisms; Big Stephen's Creek 75, and Little Stephen's Creek 113, surging the already heavy membership in that latter church from 256 to 365.[41] By 1833, numbers began to wane in most churches—Edgefield baptized only five people that church year, although Mountain Creek church, located northwest of Edgefield, experienced revival late, with 150 people baptized between August 1832 and August 1833.[42]

Membership in the Edgefield Baptist Association also increased dramatically. Baptisms escalated from 361 in 1830 to 1,062 in 1831. The following year, 1832, brought even more spiritual accessions: 1,643 people were baptized, followed by 878 in 1833. Baptisms declined more sharply after 1833,

---

[37] Cook, *James Clement Furman*, 15–35, quote at 17. Students from Furman also assisted in the revival efforts at Black Swamp Church and Beaufort Church, both in Beaufort district. See Cook, *James Clement Furman*, 16.

[38] "Bullein, "Reminiscences," 76–77.

[39] "Bullein, "Reminiscences," 77.

[40] Minutes of the Edgefield Baptist Association, August 1831, Baptist Historical Collection, Furman University.

[41] Minutes of the Edgefield Baptist Association, August 1832.

[42] Minutes of the Edgefield Baptist Association, August 1833; also Bullein, "Reminiscences," 77.

dropping to a decade-low number of thirty-seven in 1837. In the early 1840s another spurt of revivalism occurred, due largely to the association's employment of additional domestic missionaries, with 537 baptisms in 1842 and 439 in 1843. Still, revivals in the 1840s and 1850s could not match what transpired in the early 1830s.[43] To many participants, the awakenings of the 1830s truly seemed to be, in the words of William Johnson, "indications of the rapid approach of the kingdom."[44]

Much farther north of Edgefield district lay Brushy Creek Baptist Church, in Greenville district. Constituted in 1795, Brushy Creek had experienced some growth during the Great Revival of the early 1800s, although not to the extent of other churches.[45] In 1830, roughly forty members belonged to the rural church, mostly small farmers, a handful of slaves, and a small number of wealthier residents of nearby Greenville Village.[46] Low Country Baptist William Bullein Johnson, who had moved to Greenville to take charge of its male and female academies, preached at Brushy Creek on a regular basis between 1822 and late 1830. At Brushy Creek and nearby churches, Johnson noted there existed "good and substantial members" led by ministers who were "destitute of scholastic education" but who were sincere, laborious, and earnest in their labors."[47] One such minister who emerged in the 1820s was Lemuel J. Hudson, who had joined Brushy Creek in 1821. The following year, he was granted authority to "sing & pray & exhort or to lecture from any passage of Scriptures as he might feel his mind imprinted."[48] In 1826, elders ordained him to the ministry, but in 1827, they voiced division over which pastor to call, not doing so until February of 1828.[49] William B. Johnson continued to preach at the church as well, although not in the formal capacity as regular supply.

It was during Brother Hudson's tenure that the "Great Revival" in the

---

[43] Minutes of the Edgefield Baptist Association, 1830–60.

[44] Minutes of the Edgefield Baptist Association, 1831.

[45] King, *History of South Carolina Baptists*, 111.

[46] Bullein, "Reminiscences," 51; Susan Frazier Kahl, *The Bicentennial History of Brushy Creek Baptist Church: Taylors, South Carolina, 1794–1994* (n.p.: published by Brushy Creek Baptist Church, 1994) 37.

[47] Bullein, "Reminiscences," 51; Kahl, *Bicentennial History*, 25–26.

[48] Kahl, *Bicentennial History*, 35–36, Minutes of Brushy Creek Baptist Church, February, 1828, Baptist Historical Collection, Furman University.

[49] Kahl, *Bicentennial History*, 35–36.

Brushy Creek community occurred. No one recorded the number of attendees present when the annual meeting of the Saluda Association began in August of 1831, but surely the crowd numbered in the thousands. In the preceding year, when the association assembled at Neal's Creek Church in Anderson district, an estimated four to five thousand people turned out for the annual event.[50] The religious anticipation and social excitement must have been palpable. Most likely, ministers had heard reports of the Sardis camp meeting in Edgefield district. The presence of two ministers from Georgia, Jonathan and James Davis, who had participated in sweeping revivals in Georgia in the late 1820s, added to the sense of enthusiasm. These events alone might have been enough to start an awakening, but another phenomenon, this one coming from the sky, stirred people's emotions mightily. The church clerk, who normally recorded church business in a perfunctory manner, clearly felt moved by the magnitude of the revival. "It is here worthy to notice," he wrote in the church book, "that the Saluda Association commenced at the plain on the Saturday before the second Sunday in this month." At that time, "a number of preachers from a distance attended and preached to a numerous and serious congregation, with great effect." During the meeting, the clerk noted, the "sun wore such a glowing & unnatural appearance, that of a greenish pale colour which was observed through-out the united States and has not been satisfactorily accounted for."[51]

Lewis Rector, a former pastor of Brushy Creek, had prophesied about a coming revival shortly before his death in 1830. Recounting the event more than fifty years later, Baptist minister H. P. Griffith also remembered the supernatural events that characterized the revival of 1831. Griffith noted that there occurred also "a strange phenomenon in nature" where "the rays of the sun were dimmed by a dark spot on his disk." The eclipse cast a "pale, somber hue" on "the whole face of creation," causing men to be either alarmed or humbled, "as under the finger of God." The preachers at the Saluda meeting at Brushy Creek, "eager to lay hold of every means adapted to the awakening and humbling of sinners, made happy and forcible allusions to the surrounding scene," pointing to the mysterious greenish light of the sun as a sign of the

---

[50] Minutes of the Saluda Baptist Association, 1830, Baptist Historical Collection, Furman University.

[51] Minutes of Brushy Creek Baptist Church, August 1831, Baptist Historical Collection, Furman University.

supernatural. Additionally, the Davis brothers from Georgia, "who had recently been in a great revival at home," brought a sense of excitement. With "all things being seemingly ready," the association meeting and accompanying revival began, lasting for four days and bringing large numbers of converts.[52]

Similar to reports of other awakenings, Griffith described the way that the Brushy Creek Revival involved the entire group of participants. The Holy Spirit moved through the crowd "not definitely at first, but vaguely and mysteriously." Converts experienced a sense of presentiment, "that unaccountable feeling, which sometimes weighs heavily upon the heart and which, men say, heralds the approach of mighty events." Audiences initially seemed anxious and restless; soon, entire communities became connected by a sense of "deep solemnity" that occurred internally, with no sign of "any outward circumstances or condition." It was, Griffith reported, "the troubling of the waters of the pool of Bethesda by the angel of God."[53]

In the summer of 1832, recounting events of the past year in the annual letter to the Saluda Association, the clerk of Brushy Creek described the results of the revival. The associational meeting of 1831 was "a meeting long to be remembered," one leading to an "almost [Pentecostal] season ever since." People of all ages, from "the old, the middle aged and young yea little boys and girls of ten and Twelve years," joined the church. Members had not seen "such a general and great revival" in their lifetime—a telling description, since some would have remembered the Great Revival of the early 1800s. Nor had the revival ended. "The Redeemer is still adding to his Church," explained the clerk, writing that "the earthly tabernacles of the Lord have become both [solemn] and delightful." Many "have been brought to rejoice in a Saviour's name, and many more have been cut to heart and made to crie for mercy." How wonderful, the clerk noted, to see "the rebellious sinner abowing at the foot of the cross and crying for mercy."[54]

The revival had a major impact on Brushy Creek, surging membership almost sixfold. In July 1831, the month before revival hit, roughly forty members belonged to the church. By 1832, 190 members names appeared on the church roll. The spring of 1832 proved a particularly fruitful season. Men,

---

[52] H. P. Griffith, *The Life and Times of John G. Landrum* (Philadelphia: H. B. Garner, 1885) 66–68.

[53] Griffith, *Landrum*, 79.

[54] Minutes of Brushy Creek Baptist Church, August 1832.

women, and their slaves crowded into the meeting house. After preaching, Brother Hudson invited anxious mourners to come to the front of the church, where he prayed for their salvation. Conversion and baptisms continued in the fall of 1832 and spring of 1833. By 1833, 225 members belonged to Brushy Creek Church.[55]

As with the Edgefield revival, the Brushy Creek revival served as a hub from which other awakenings in nearby churches took hold. The Saluda Baptist Association, the home association of Brushy Creek Church, saw its membership increase almost fourfold. Most of this growth came between 1831 and 1833, but in some cases, congregants continued to manifest religious interest into 1834 and later. H. P. Griffith claimed that the revival lasted in some places "with little or no abatement for three years." Men and women traveled far distances to hear the gospel preached. Ministers "went from house to house" and preached from stands in brush arbors or even "under the spreading oak by the roadside," their message "'reasoned of righteousness, temperance, and judgment to come.'" Within a twenty-five-mile radius of Brushy Creek Church, Griffith estimated that thirteen new churches were established, while older ones "were filled to overflowing." Between "two and three thousand souls" joined churches in the Brushy Creek region, with all classes of people, not just the "ignorant and excitable," among the elect. Indeed, "the best material in the country was gathered into the folds of the church," so that "a new era dawned upon the Baptists of Upper Carolina."[56]

While the Second Wave Revival lit fires throughout Up-country, it also affected churches in the Low Country Beaufort district. The revival in this area came from two directions: it was assisted by Furman students and no doubt inspired by the Edgefield revivals, but another major force came out of Savannah, Georgia, in the form of Presbyterian Daniel J. Baker. Following a successful interdenominational revival in Savannah, Baker accepted invitations to preach in surrounding locations. In the fall of 1831 he traveled to several towns in Beaufort district, where crowds welcomed his dynamic, energetic preaching. Baker effected about sixty conversions in Gillisonville and "marked results" in Grahamville, and the town of Beaufort saw the most dramatic results. Unconcerned about denominational affiliation (Presbyterian

---

[55] Kahl, *Bicentennial*, 37–38; Minutes of the Brushy Creek Baptist Church, July 1831–December 1833.

[56] Griffith, *Landrum*, 68.

historian George Howe lamented that of all the converts of the Beaufort revival, "not one became a Presbyterian"),[57] Baker worked with the local Baptist and Episcopal ministers (their's were the only two churches in the town), holding revival services two and three times a day. "A holy atmosphere pervaded the town, and affected the entire population to a degree unparalleled, save in the revival described by President Edwards, at Northampton, in 1735," remembered Baker.[58] Up to three hundred people were converted during the revival, including prominent men and women in the community. Baptist leader Richard Fuller, South Carolina radical politician Robert Barnwell Rhett, and future Episcopal bishop Stephen Elliott comprised only some of the well-known converts.[59] Rather than replace an older Baptist style with a new one, the revival helped solidify an evangelical culture in Beaufort, a culture that was already controlled by the elite. In both its origins and its results, the Beaufort awakening differed in important respects from the revivals in the Up-country.

Conclusion

What, then, do we make of the Second Wave Revival? Four main points follow. First, the awakening strengthened the Baptist framework in South Carolina, substantially increasing the Baptist population by rejuvenating existing churches and creating a network of new congregations. The most dramatic growth occurred in the upper and western portions of the state, within the boundaries of the Saluda, Edgefield, and Savannah River Associations. Meeting in 1833, the Baptist State Convention estimated that the state had witnessed 7,456 baptisms between 1832 and 1833, bringing the total number

---

[57] Howe, *History of the Presbyterian Church*, 2: 556–57; McCurry, *Masters of Small Worlds*, 150–53.

[58] William M. Baker, *The Life and Labours of the Rev. Daniel Baker, D. D., Pastor and Evangelist* (Philadelphia: Presbyterian Board of Publication, 1858) 145–59, quote at 152. Fuller, *Chaplain to the Confederacy*, 110.

[59] McCurry, *Masters of Small Worlds*, 150–58. During the early 1830s, in a reflection of the nation's increasing sectional tensions, white South Carolinians fiercely divided over the explosive question of whether the state should nullify the federal tariffs of 1828 and 1832. Politician Robert Barnwell Rhett, a convert of the 1831 Beaufort revival, employed revivalistic techniques and language in his arguments for nullification; other prominent Low Country politicians followed suit. In the Up-country, where unionist support was stronger, churches argued and sometimes fractured over this heated topic.

of church members to 28,255.⁶⁰ If Townsend's estimate that the revival of the early 1800s led to ten thousand new Baptist church members is correct, and if baptisms for 1831 and 1833 are added to the 1832 figures reported by the Baptist State Convention, the revival of the 1830s produced numerical growth comparable to, and most likely in excess of, the Great Revival of the early 1800s.

Second, the awakening changed peoples' lives in momentous ways. Men and women, girls and boys, slave and free, stepped out of their everyday routines to participate in a sacred event, one shared with others but also profoundly personal. As they gathered together as mourners or as they celebrated conversion, Baptists momentarily suspended the differences of race, class, gender, or age that normally defined them.⁶¹ The profundity of the revival was not lost on its participants. Years later, references to the revival still appeared in church minutes and in personal memoirs. To a whole generation of South Carolinians, the "great" revival occurred in the early 1830s, not years before.

Third, the Second Wave Revival signified a crucial religious-cultural shift occurring in the Up-country, one which saw a Low Country denominational culture become increasingly influential in the region. Local pastors worked with ministerial students from the Furman Academy and Theological Institution and with traveling preachers from Georgia to spread revival. This collaboration of forces represented a blending of older Baptist traditions with newer ones. Such movement among ministers surely provided a platform for Up-country converts to hear a range of Baptist perspectives about missionary endeavors and educational work, leading some toward a stronger embrace of (and some toward a stronger resistance to) this encroaching culture. By the 1850s, the decision to relocate the Furman Academy and Theological Institution (which became Furman University in 1851) to Greenville further transformed the region, as more and more trained, missionary-style ministers now supplied churches in upper portions of the state. Ironically, as the state became more denominationally integrated, national Baptist missionary boards fractured, resulting in the 1845 formation of the Southern Baptist Convention, with William B. Johnson serving as the chief organizer and president in the

---

⁶⁰ Minutes of the State Convention of the Baptist Denomination in South Carolina, 1833, Baptist Historical Collection, Furman University.

⁶¹ Reminders of gender and especially of racial difference nevertheless remained, reflected in segregated seating and other spatial arrangements in churches and on meeting grounds.

inaugural years of the convention's history.[62] The passion of Low Country denominational leaders for educating, evangelizing, and converting now took place within a distinctly southern framework, providing Up-country and Low Country Baptists a regionalized cultural mooring with far-reaching implications.

Finally, South Carolina's revival of the early 1830s illustrates the need for more research on revivalism in the South, particularly in terms of the patterns of southern awakenings. Georgia Baptists engineered a pronounced revival in the late 1820s that, as in South Carolina, showed the territorial expansion of convention-minded Baptists.[63] Did Baptists in other southern states experience similar revivals? Were these revivals explicitly connected to denominational growth, or did political factors such as the Nullification Crisis and reactions to abolitionism also contribute to the Second Wave revivals? How did race factor into these revivals, not to mention gender, class, and age? While many of these questions require further elucidation, it is clear that in South Carolina, the revival of the early 1830s proved a defining moment for Baptists as a people and as a denomination.

Ironically, three Northerners, in the persons of Daniel and Martha Stearns Marshall and Shubal Stearns, led a movement that reordered religious life in the uplands of the Southern colonies and established a strong Baptist presence in areas that previously lacked any organized religion. Their demand that auditors experience the New Birth, live a holy life, and respond to the leadership of the Holy Spirit struck a chord in the lives of the backwoods population. And the frontier people responded by the hundreds and thousands. Revival captured the Southern frontier because of the committed lives and ministry of the Separate Baptists.

---

[62] Woodson, *Giant*, 911–139, King, *History of South Carolina Baptists*, 216–19.

[63] Jared Burch, *Adiel Sherwood: Baptist Antebellum Pioneer in Georgia* (Macon: Mercer University Press, 2003) 50–63; Jesse Harrison Campbell, *Georgia Baptists: Historical and Biographical* (Richmond: H. K. Ellyson, 1847) 193–94, 237, 248–49. Also see Bebbington, *Victorian Religious Revivals*, 131–58, esp. 136–39.

4

Baptists and Early Pentecostal Revivalism

C. Douglas Weaver

In his personal testimony about becoming a Pentecostal, Ansel Howard Post related that he was a Baptist minister for thirty years but then desired a "deeper fullness of God's love." About the time the Azusa Street Revival in Los Angeles began in April 1906, Post traveled to Pasadena and engaged in tent evangelism. According to Post, the Holy Spirit led him to visit Azusa and he received the baptism "without an overflow of joy or emotion." However, two days later the emotion erupted. Without seeking the gift of speaking in tongues, Post declared that "The Holy Spirit fell on me and filled me literally as it seemed to lift me up, indeed, I was in the air in an instant, shouting, praise God, and instantly I began to speak in another language."[1]

Post had left the Baptists and become a pastor in the "Household of God." His tent meetings were punctuated with shouts of glory and hallelujah, and he was even arrested for disorderly conduct.[2] As his revival ministry unfolded, Post described the Pentecostal revival, as "this is that, 'the restoration of the biblical Day of Pentecost in Acts 2 and the gift of the Holy Spirit baptism signaled by tongues to fulfill the prophesied imminent end-time' latter rain." Post declared, "This is only the beginning of the gracious latter rain…he will fully restore all the gifts."[3]

Nineteen years later in 1925, J. N. Hoover, Baptist pastor in Santa Cruz, California, attended services at a full gospel Baptist church in San Jose, and

---

[1] A. H. Post, "Testimony of a Minister," *Apostolic Faith* (January 1907): 4.

[2] "Head of Sect is Disturber," *Pasadena Daily News* (July 13, 1906) 12.

[3] A. H. Post, "Testimony of a Minister," *Apostolic Faith* (January 1907): 4. Eventually Post traveled internationally, desiring to spread revival fires across the world. See "The Gospel in Foreign Lands: In Memoriam," *Pentecostal Evangel* (August 15, 1931): 8. On Post's story, see Cecil M. Robeck Jr., *Azusa Street Mission and Revival: The Birth of the Global Pentecostal Movement* (Nashville: Thomas Nelson, 2006) 205–9.

responded to the invitation. As ministers gathered around him, Hoover testified that "the power of God was upon me and I shook from head to foot like a leaf in the wind. Such an experience I had never known. A light more glorious than the noon-day sun fell upon me, and a power went thru me like a consuming fire while from my lips went forth with the heavenly language as the Spirit gave utterance." God had given him an experience like those who received the Spirit in the Upper Room at Pentecost, Hoover testified, and the experience was as "glorious as conversion" many years before.[4]

David Bebbington has offered a definition of revival from an 1849 American Methodist periodical as "outpourings of the Spirit, which result in the quickening of the church and the conversion of sinners." He elaborated that the revival impulse soon "coalesced with the novel phenomenon of Pentecostalism, marked by speaking in tongues." The Pentecostals, "in their early days, stressed that theirs was a revival movement. They looked for unprompted visitations by the Spirit, but before long they settled down to more organized ways."[5] The revival testimonies of A. H. Post and J. N. Hoover reflect the nature of revivalism in early Pentecostalism, the early years of Azusa, and later more local-church-sponsored revival campaigns. Scholars suggest that Pentecostal revivalism waned after the initial Azusa years before experiencing a sort of comeback in the 1920s.[6] However, Pentecostals never stopped desiring that their movement be a continuous Holy Spirit revival.

The elements described in the Post and Hoover stories were some of the most essential found in the Pentecostal narrative. The full gospel, often called the fourfold gospel or later the foursquare gospel, consisted of conversion, Holy Spirit baptism with its initial evidence of speaking in tongues, divine healing, and an imminent second coming of Christ. Restoration of biblical miracles was part of a "latter rain" revival. Holy Spirit baptism was often, though not always, accompanied by strong emotional outbursts or what came to be called being "slain in the Spirit."

At the risk of not giving enough basic definition, or too much, let me

---

[4] J. N. Hoover, "The Baptism and Ministry of the Holy Spirit," *Latter Rain Evangel* (July 1930) 7, 21. J. N. Hoover, "A Baptist Preacher's Testimony," *Pentecostal Evangel* (March 13, 1926) 5.

[5] David W. Bebbington, "Revivals, Revivalism and the Baptists," *Baptistic Theologies* (Spring 2009): 1, 11.

[6] Robert Mapes Anderson, *Vision of the Disinherited: The Making of American Pentecostalism* (New York: Oxford University Press, 1979) 66.

provide a bit more backstory. During the late nineteenth century, Wesleyans spoke of Holy Spirit baptism as a purification of sin and equated it with sanctification. The Keswick holiness influence from England and Americans like D. L. Moody and R. A. Torrey said the second baptism was considered an enduement of power for gospel witnessing. For both perspectives, no particular sign of Spirit baptism was claimed—the experience might be instantaneous or progressive depending on the group—but the language of Pentecost was used to describe it.

At the outset of the twentieth century, evangelicals, especially those with ties to the Holiness movement, earnestly hoped for a Holy Spirit revival. In 1901, the holiness healer Charles Parham and the students in his Topeka, Kansas, Bible school declared that they had discovered and experienced the biblical meaning of the Spirit baptism of Acts 2. Its sign or "Bible evidence" was speaking in tongues, or xenolalia, the miraculous speaking of a foreign language without having learned it, to spread the gospel at the end-time. After Parham resettled in Houston, Texas, William J. Seymour, an African-American holiness preacher, accepted Parham's teaching and then left for Los Angeles, California, where he preached the new Pentecostal message. As the story goes, speaking in tongues occurred in prayer services, Seymour formed the Azusa Street Mission, and revival erupted in April 1906. The revival has been described as a three-year continuous overflow of the Holy Spirit, witnessed in Holy Spirit baptism via tongues and accompanied by the practice of other miraculous spiritual gifts.

This chapter examines how Baptists interacted with, participated in, and opposed the Pentecostal revival experience. Ian Randall has done excellent work on Baptists and Pentecostals, with concentration on English Baptists.[7] I will focus on Baptists in America, primarily on the earliest years of seemingly unprompted Pentecostal revival known as the famous Azusa Street Revival, but with some attention on later revivalists in the 1920s.

Pentecostal Precursor: The Welsh Revival of 1904

When the Welsh Revival of 1904 erupted, many Holiness evangelicals

---

[7] Ian M. Randall, "'Days of Pentecostal Overflowing': Baptists and the Shaping of Pentecostalism," in *The Gospel in the World*, ed. David Bebbington (Waynesboro, GA: Paternoster, 2002).

were ecstatic and believed the revival was the anticipated outpouring of the Holy Spirit. A few Baptists were heavily involved in the revival, particularly F. B. Meyer of England.[8] In 1905, Meyer traveled to Los Angeles, spoke about the movement of the Spirit, and as scholars have noted, contributed to the environment for the Pentecostal revival.[9]

Baptists in America heard positive reports about the Welsh Revival. *The Watchman*, a publication in Boston, received an eyewitness testimony from York King. He said that he experienced the "marvelous manifestations of the Holy Spirit's presence and God's power, expressing itself through every available channel" in this "Acts of the Apostles up to date."[10] The *Baptist Argus* of Kentucky also provided thorough coverage of the Welsh Revival though reports rarely were tied to any end-time "latter rain" of the Spirit.[11] Those who did so like Joseph Smale were important links between the Welsh Revival and the Pentecostal revival on Azusa Street.

Joseph Smale

Timothy Welch has recently given extensive attention to the role of Joseph Smale in early Pentecostalism. Early Pentecostal evangelist Frank Bartleman described Smale as the "Moses" of Pentecostalism, greatly contributing to its origins but not entering into the Promised Land as a full-fledged participant. Welch concurs and doubly emphasizes Smale's link to the Welsh Revival.[12]

---

[8] Ian M. Randall, "F. B. Meyer: Baptist Ambassador for Keswick Holiness Spirituality," *Baptist History and Heritage* (Spring 2002): 44-60. Ian M. Randall, *Spirituality and Social Change: The Contribution of F. B. Meyer (1847-1929)* (Milton Keynes, UK: Paternoster, 2003).

[9] Anderson, Vision of the Disinherited, 64, 78. Edith Blumhofer, *The Assemblies of God: A Chapter in the Story of American Pentecostalism*, vol. 1, To 1941 (Springfield: Gospel Publishing House, 1989) 99-103. Robeck, *Azusa Street Mission and Revival*, 58-60. Timothy Bernard Welch, "'God Found His Moses,' A Biographical and Theological Analysis of the Life of Joseph Smale (1867-1926)" (PhD diss., University of Birmingham, 2009) 152-55.

[10] York A. King, "Another View of the Welsh Revival," *Watchman* (March 8, 1906) 9.

[11] For example, Rev. T. Shankland, "The Great Welsh Revival: A New Outpouring of the Spirit," *Baptist Argus* (January 12, 1905): 4. Rev. G. Campbell Morgan, "It is Pentecost Continued: The Great Welsh Revival. But One Explanation—God," *Baptist Argus* (February 16, 1905): 1, 13, 16. Rev. T. Shankland, "Baptist Union of Wales: Revival Breaks Out—Notable Scenes," *Baptist Argus* (September 7, 1905): 2. "Our Welsh Letter: The Revival is Yet On," *Baptist Argus* (January 25, 1906): 1, 16.

[12] Welch, "God Found His Moses," 2. Blumhofer, *Assemblies of God*, 99-103.

English native Joseph Smale attended C. H. Spurgeon's Pastor's College. Welch contended that Spurgeon's teachings provided an atmosphere that nurtured the desire for the power of the Holy Spirit without affirming a second experience of Spirit-baptism. Smale pastored Baptist churches in Isle of Wight and Arizona in the USA before an eight-year ministry at First Baptist Church, Los Angeles, California (1897–1905).[13]

From the outset, Smale's ministry in Los Angeles revealed emphases of the Holiness revival. At least by 1902, he was advocating a Keswick holiness belief in the baptism of the Spirit as an enduement of power. In 1904, he attended the Welsh Revival and the experience intensified his focus on a Spirit-filled ministry.[14] From May to September 1905 Smale held fifteen weeks of daily prayer meetings at his church to further the Welsh Revival. Church members testified that they experienced "manifestations" and were "filled with the Spirit."[15] As the protracted prayer meetings for Holy Spirit revival reached week nine, the church advertised itself to the public as "a fellowship for evangelical preaching, evangelical teaching, Pentecostal life and Pentecostal service."[16] Smale advocated a three-prong restoration: conversion of sinners, baptism of the Holy Spirit for all, and the restoration of the church to being a New Testament church, meaning, having "Holy Ghost administration."[17]

Smale's application of Holy Spirit revivalism away from traditional notions of Baptist polity led to trouble with some church members. His shift from congregational polity to a "Spirit-led" autocratic style led to the firing of the music director so the Holy Spirit could lead worship. His sudden Independent baptist-like constant criticisms of Baptist mission boards was also highly controversial. Conflict ensued and Smale resigned on September 19, 1905.[18]

Almost immediately Smale formed a new non-denominational church

---

[13] Welch, "God Found His Moses," 63–94.

[14] Welch, "God Found His Moses," 99, 104, 129, 132–41.

[15] Welch, "God Found His Moses," 152–55. Welch considered the parallels of events at First Baptist Church, Los Angeles to the Welsh Revival to be striking. On Smale and the Welsh Revival, see also Robeck, *Azusa Street Mission and Revival*, 58–60.

[16] Welch, "God Found His Moses," 165.

[17] Welch, "God Found His Moses," 165–67.

[18] "Baptist Boil Still 'Biling,'" *Los Angeles Times*, September 12, 1905, II10. See also Welch, "God Found His Moses," 174–90.

to continue the revival. The First New Testament Church of Los Angeles soon had about 200 ex-members of First Baptist Church, as well as forty other Spirit-seeking members.[19] While non-denominational, Smale told the public he still held the Baptist principles, which followed the New Testament. However, denominational boards, immersion as a requirement for membership and man-made traditions had become barriers to revival.[20]

Historians of Pentecostalism have increasingly taken note of the pivotal role of Smale's First New Testament Church in the formative days of the Azusa Street Revival. The church reported an atmosphere of "perpetual revival" in January 1906—four months after the church's formation and one month before Azusa leader, William Seymour, came to Los Angeles. As Robert Mapes Anderson noted, Los Angeles was certainly in an expectant mood for an end-time revival when Seymour arrived.[21] When revival fires were unleashed at the Azusa Street Mission, a parallel revival was being sustained at First New Testament Church.[22]

Smale was initially ecstatic at the eruption of Pentecostal revivalism at his church and at Azusa. "We are nearing a great Pentecost" and "the simplicity of New Testament life," Smale wrote a city newspaper. Church members not surprisingly believed that they were emulating the success of the Welsh Revival and felt vindicated that they had been pushed out of First Baptist Church because Smale "had the (Spirit's) power."[23]

As the Azusa Revival increased in popularity, however, Smale's support decreased. He was no doubt worried when some of his congregation began attending the Azusa Mission and at first he promised full "liberty" of Spirit-filled worship for them to return. However, he most likely shifted his views because he never spoke in tongues himself. In July 1906, Smale announced that tongues was not a gift to be sought by every believer—a view contrary to Azusa Street. By September 1906, the First New Testament Church had split as Smale accused the Pentecostal revival of excessive emphasis on tongues and

---

[19] Welch, "God Found His Moses," 190–92.

[20] "New Church is Organized," *Los Angeles Express*, September 25, 1905, 3. Smale's rejection of missionary boards sounds like Landmarkism or the Gospel Mission Movement in nineteenth-century Baptist life. "Immersion Unessential," *Los Angeles Times*, October 28, 1905, I16.

[21] Anderson, *Vision of the Disinherited*, 64.

[22] Robeck, *Azusa Street Mission and Revival*, 74–75. Welch, "God Found His Moses," 202–8.

[23] "Rolling on Floor in Smale's Church," *Los Angeles Times*, July 14, 1906, I11.

extreme emotionalism.[24]

One of the members who left the church was Elmer Kirk Fisher, Smale's associate pastor. After reading holiness advocate R. A. Torrey on the Holy Spirit, Fisher, a Northern Baptist pastor in Glendale, California, had to leave his church under pressure from deacon leadership after he preached sermons about receiving the Holy Spirit and some in the congregation had emotional outbursts.[25] Fisher then joined the staff of Smale's New Testament congregation and received the Holy Spirit baptism before leaving in the split over the need for more freedom of emotional expression. He then started his own independent mission and worked closely with the Azusa Revival efforts.[26]

Smale never ceased to emphasize his Keswick perspective or to speak of the need for Holy Spirit baptism, but he remained convinced that Pentecostals had ruined the revival with too much focus on tongues. After a return to his native England for three years of independent ministry, Smale returned to Los Angeles and perhaps not surprisingly pastored a Baptist church again.[27]

A. S. Worrell

A study of Baptist interaction with early Pentecostal revival could mention many names or stories after Joseph Smale. Robert Mapes Anderson did a study of early Pentecostal leadership and found 10 of 45 to be former Baptists.[28] While unlikely, some have said William Seymour was a former Baptist. However, the small group of African-American believers that responded to Seymour's preaching and became the base of the Azusa Mission had been recently excluded from a Baptist church because of their holiness beliefs. Minor figures in the Azusa story like A.H. Post and Elmer Fisher who have already been mentioned were Baptists. Others traveled to Azusa and became

---

[24] Welch, "God Found His Moses," 210–11.

[25] Robeck, *Azusa Street Mission and Revival*, 66–67, 190, 198–204. Robeck speculated that Fisher's opponents in Glendale knew about Smale's experience at First Baptist Church, Los Angeles, and did not want the Pentecostal-type emphasis repeated at their church.

[26] Fisher was pastor of the Baptist church in Camarillo, CA (1903–1905) and Calvary Baptist Church, Glendale, CA (1905–1906). Robeck, *Azusa Street Mission and Revival*, 66–67, 190, 198–204. See also Welch, "God Found His Moses," 302–3. S. M. Horton, "Elmer Kirk Fisher," in *Dictionary of Pentecostal and Charismatic Movements*, ed. Stanley M. Burgess and Gary B. McGee (Grand Rapids: Zondervan, 1988) 310.

[27] Welch, "God Found His Moses," 250, 311, 322.

[28] Anderson, *Vision of the Disinherited*, 98–103.

Pentecostal. The more prominent names include C. H. Mason, founder of the largest African-American Pentecostal group, the Church of God in Christ, and William H. Durham, key Pentecostal leader in Chicago. The Assemblies of God, which formed in 1914, had key early leaders like E. N. Bell and Arch Collins. Those stories provide the larger Baptist-Pentecostal picture. However, the Baptist who most closely reported on the Azusa Revival was Adolphus Spalding Worrell (1831–1908).

Worrell was the best-known Baptist to observe and interact with the early Pentecostal movement. He was a Greek scholar and had served as president of several Baptist schools and as editor of numerous Baptist newspapers. Worrell was a widely traveled evangelist very active in Kentucky Baptist life.[29]

On August 10, 1891, at the age of sixty, Worrell testified to a life-changing experience in which he was "infilled by the Holy Spirit." He had been a Christian for forty-seven years and a Baptist preacher for thirty-three, and affirmed that he had already experienced the Holy Spirit, in his words, "on me and blessedly with me." With this distinct new experience, Worrell said that he knew the Spirit was "far more mightily and blessedly IN me... the opening up of the well of living water IN me, whose blissful flow has never since subsided." In other words, he had been born of the Spirit at conversion, but he now had the second experience of baptism in the Holy Spirit.[30] Subsequently, Worrell began publishing the *Gospel Witness* journal as well as several books and a New Testament translation that gave focus to this new experience of the Spirit.[31] His extensive itinerant evangelistic ministry also gave him a platform to spread his views.

Worrell expressed the goal of the Spirit-filled life in terms compatible

---

[29] Michael Kuykendall, "A. S. Worrell's New Testament: A Landmark Baptist-Pentecostal Bible Translation from the Early Twentieth Century," *Pneuma* 29 (2007): 255. William Cathcart, "Worrall, A. S.D.D.," *Baptist Encyclopedia* (Philadelphia: Louis H. Everts, 1881; rpt., Baptist Standard Bearer) 1279. See Kuykendall "A. S. Worrell's New Testament," for a complete list of Worrell's publications, including his Landmark Baptist works.

[30] A. S. Worrell, *Full Gospel Textbook* (Louisville: Pentecostal Publishing Co., 1901) 54. See also A. S. Worrell, *Full Gospel Teachings* (Louisville: Charles T. Dearing, 1900) 38, 70–73.

[31] A. S. Worrell, *The New Testament, revised and translated by A. S. Worrell, With Notes and Instructions designed to aid the earnest Reader in obtaining a clear Understanding of the doctrines, Ordinances, and primitive Assemblies as revealed in these Scriptures* (Louisville: A. S. Worrell, 1904). A. S. Worrell, *Didactic and Devotional Poems* (Louisville: A. S. Worrell, 1906) as well as *Full Gospel Textbook* and *Full Gospel Teachings*.

with the Higher Life/Keswick teaching on being filled with the Holy Spirit for service and witnessing power. Like R. A. Torrey, he did not connect being Spirit-filled with any particular sign, but argued that those who obeyed Christ's commands could ask for the Holy Spirit.[32] On some occasions, he combined traditional Baptist language with the new holiness focus on Pentecost and spoke of being immersed in the Holy Spirit.[33] Worrell lamented that many believers never had a second experience of the Spirit and even boldly concluded that preachers, evangelists and missionaries should cease their ministries until they were "endued with power from on high."[34] In a comment that foreshadowed why he would be open to the Pentecostal revival, Worrell wrote, "The revival of a full Gospel ecclesia would include the restoration of the "gifts of the Spirit."[35]

Of course most Baptist leaders did not agree with Worrell's new emphasis on the necessity of a separate experience of the Holy Spirit after conversion. In 1901, when he published a book with the provocative title for most Baptists—*Full Gospel Text-Book*—one Baptist reviewer said he always enjoyed hearing Worrell preach, but it was "well-nigh impossible for some of us to agree with the good Doctor in all that he says."[36]

In 1906, when the Azusa Street Revival broke out, sympathetic friends told Worrell to go and examine it. The previous year he had spoken to Joseph Smale's Baptist church on the topic of the Holy Spirit during its fifteen-week prayer meeting for revival. This time Worrell traveled to Los Angeles and stayed four months.[37] The *Apostolic Faith* magazine of the Azusa Street Mission noted in its December 1906 issue that Worrell had attended the revival and had been tarrying for the Holy Spirit baptism but did not report that he

---

[32] Worrell, *Full Gospel Textbook*, 108, 115.

[33] Worrell, *The New Testament*, revised, 164.

[34] Worrell, *Full Gospel Teachings*, 44, 291.

[35] Worrell, *Full Gospel Textbook*, 180.

[36] Wm. Lunsford, "Full Gospel Teachings," *Baptist Argus* (January 31, 1901) 4.

[37] Rev. A. S. Worrell, "The Modern Pentecostal Movement," *Baptist Argus* (June 6, 1907): 7. Worrell's language of equipment was later seen in Alvin L. Branch, "A Pentecostal Baptism," 22–23. In his testimony about leaving Baptists for the Pentecostal experience, Branch said that he wanted the "best that God has in the way of equipment for His servants." For an example of how this language was used for the apostles in Acts 2, see J. A. McCord, "Thoughts on Pentecost," *Western Recorder* (February 27, 1908): 5.

had claimed the experience.[38]

In the fall of 1906, however, Worrell published reports of the revival that were very positive: "One might as well try to sweep back the waters of the Pacific, as to attempt to check this mighty display of God's power."[39] He said the revival was surely from God because of the evidence: tongues and other spiritual gifts were present; the Word of God was honored and the blood of Christ was exalted, Worrell said, "as I have rarely known it."[40] However, Worrell cautioned that at Azusa there were two movements, one of God and one of Satan. The Devil was at work counterfeiting spiritual gifts. All instances of tongues were certainly not demonic, Worrell asserted, since the Devil "can't counterfeit unless the real is there."[41]

Worrell was also positive in subsequent assessments of the Azusa Revival and he was especially complimentary toward its leadership; thus, there is no surprise that Azusa's *Apostolic Faith* journal printed Worrell's thoughts. "The writer has not a single doubt but that Brother Seymour has more power with God, and more power from God, than all his critics in and out of the city."[42]

In May 1907, the *Baptist Argus*, published in Louisville, Kentucky where Worrell lived, first reported Worrell's views of the revival. In contrast, the *Western Recorder* of Kentucky was silent about Worrell. As was his custom, Worrell attended the local minister's conference in Louisville in May and reported on his travels. On this occasion, he described the Azusa revival and remarked that at first he was prejudiced about it—something contrary to his other published accounts—but found "genuine evidence of Pentecostal times" there. He reiterated that he found both genuine and counterfeit expressions of tongues but said "love reigns supreme" and Christ was magnified. He concluded, "Brethren, we are in a marvelous time. We need to open our eyes and see what is happening. What is coming I do not know, but something strange and wonderful is breaking loose upon us."[43]

A month later, the *Baptist Argus* published a more extensive assessment

---

[38] Untitled article, *Apostolic Faith* (December 1906): 2.
[39] A. S. Worrell, "Wonderful Works Going on in Los Angeles," *Gospel Witness* 16 (September 1906): 30.
[40] A. S. Worrell, "The Movements in Los Angeles, California," *Triumphs of Faith* 26, no. 12 (December 1906): 256.
[41] Worrell, "Movements in Los Angeles," 256.
[42] A. S. Worrell, "Work Increasing," *Apostolic Faith* (February-March 1907): 5.
[43] A. S. Worrell, "Louisville and Vicinity," *Baptist Argus* (May 30, 1907): 8.

of Azusa from Worrell. For the first time he noted that at least some of the speaking in tongues was xenolalia, the miraculous speaking of a foreign language, and that some conversions had resulted from some missionaries having this gift. However, Worrell moved beyond earlier assessments to say that while some of the tongues evidence was genuine, the Azusa participants had over-emphasized tongues, the position that Joseph Smale also developed.

Worrell admitted that practically everyone who was receiving the "Pentecostal blessing" spoke in tongues; at the same time, since the Devil could counterfeit tongues, he hoped—most likely because he did not speak in tongues himself—that Azusa participants would view tongues only as a sign, not the sign of Spirit baptism, since it was only one of nine biblical spiritual gifts. Worrell again acknowledged that some fanaticism was present at the Azusa Revival but he was still captivated by it. He told his fellow Baptists that the "latter rain," that last great revival of saving souls, was underway and would "hasten the preparation for the pre-tribulational rapture."[44]

Journals read by Pentecostals continued to publish Worrell's thoughts as the revival persisted into 1907. He still found authentic and counterfeit tongues in the Pentecostal revival. However, more space was given to explaining the errors of focusing on tongues. For example, tongues speakers were prone to pride and acted superior to those who had more valuable spiritual gifts. Tongues speakers also were unfortunately not willing to be taught by anyone who had not spoken in tongues.[45]

Worrell had not ceased his support of the revival, however. In an "open letter to opposers of the Pentecostal Movement," he re-affirmed his support of those testifying to a Pentecostal experience as believers whose love of Christ and the Word of God was the most intense he had ever seen. Satan had gained a foothold in some of the movement but it was blasphemy against the Holy Spirit to ascribe the working of the Spirit among Pentecostals to the Devil.[46] Worrell also defended Pentecostal revivalism from one of the most prevalent

---

[44] Worrell, "Modern Pentecostal Movement," 7.

[45] A. S. Worrell, "The Pentecostal Movement in Los Angeles," *Triumphs of Faith* (August 1907): 179–81. Like other Worrell articles, this was reprinted from his *Gospel Witness*.

[46] A. S. Worrell, "An Open Letter to the Opposers of the Pentecostal Movement," *Triumphs of Faith* (November, 1907): 246–49; published in *Assemblies of God Heritage* 12, no. 1 (Spring 1992): 16–18. Quotation at 16.

charges against it—the excessive emotionalism of the slain in the Spirit phenomenon, especially among the lower classes. The class argument did not faze him. Worrell reminded readers that revivals always had expressions of strong emotion—it was a common experience of the preaching of prominent evangelists like Wesley, Whitefield, Peter Cartwright, Finney and others. The end-time revival seen in Wales and now in America, which also was reaching the "lowly humble type," should expect the same emotion.[47]

Worrell died in 1908. Consistent with his beliefs in divine healing, he had refused medical attention. The public newspaper in Louisville acknowledged his prominence as an evangelist and as an "eccentric but Godly man."[48] He was, as Michael Kuykendall has suggested, a "seeker of tongues" but as one who already claimed the Spirit.[49] While Joseph Smale ceased being Baptist for a time, Worrell never did. Both were heavily involved in Pentecostal matters, had praise for the revival, but the praise was tempered by their own personal experience.

Holiness-Fundamentalist Baptist Critics: William B. Riley and A. C. Dixon

To describe the Baptist role in early Pentecostal revivalism is not to obscure the fact that most Baptists were opposed to it. Those influenced by the Holiness movement had more at stake with their own Spirit-focus. Scholars of the Holiness and Pentecostal traditions have described two types of holiness-fundamentalists. One type leaned on religious experience, supported by correct doctrine; the other type leaned on doctrinal orthodoxy, supported by religious experience.[50] Baptist doctrinaire holiness-fundamentalists included

---

[47] Worrell, "An Open Letter," 18. A. S. Worrell, "Wonderful Times Coming," *The Bridegroom's Messenger* (March 1, 1908) 4.

[48] "Divine Healer To The Last," *Louisville Courier Journal*, August 1, 1908, 4.

[49] Kuykendall, "Worrell's New Testament," 270. Grant Wacker called him a "sympathetic onlooker" who most likely did not join the movement because he did not speak in tongues. Grant Wacker, *Heaven Below: Early Pentecostals and American Culture* (Cambridge: Harvard University Press, 2001) 148.

[50] Grant Wacker, "Travail of a Broken Family: Radical Evangelical Responses to the Emergence of Pentecostalism in America, 1906–16," in *Pentecostal Currents in American Pentecostalism*, ed. Edith Blumhofer, Russell Spittler, and Grant Wacker (Chicago: University of Illinois Press, 1999) 25. Anderson, *Vision of the Disinherited*, 142.

William B. Riley and A. C. Dixon, best known for their roles in fundamentalist-modernist conflicts.

In 1907, soon after the Azusa Street revival had broken out, William B. Riley of Minnesota published a small book entitled *Speaking in Tongues*. He characterized his era as "an age of religious novelties... every month makes for a new religious movement." After rebuking the Pentecostal precursor, divine healer Alexander Dowie of Zion City, Illinois, Riley got to the point: "The Pacific coast, not to be out-done by the Eastern sea-board.... (has) the honor of starting a revival of "Unknown tongues."[51]

Riley belittled the Azusa Revival in a number of ways. He deemed newspaper reports that compared the revival to the Biblical Pentecost of Acts 2 to be "ludicrous."[52] He refuted Seymour's Apostolic Mission for connecting tongues with an end-time revival and for its insistence that tongues was the initial evidence of Holy Spirit baptism. Riley questioned the emotionalism of revival services and the ecstatic nature of the tongues experience, suggesting that tongues was more often due to a "psychical temperament, than of Scriptural teaching." He confessed impatience with people who did not communicate in "plain speech" and simply rejected trances as unchristian.[53] Despite these criticisms, Riley remained the Keswick influenced holiness-fundamentalist who stopped short of claiming the cessation of miracles in the present age.

In 1909, A. C. Dixon was pastor of the Moody Church in Chicago but pastored Baptist churches before and afterward. Like Riley, Dixon attacked the Pentecostal revival with a small book entitled *Speaking with Tongues*.[54] Dixon rebuked the Pentecostal contention that speaking in tongues spread revival. He asserted that the correct focus of the Pentecost story in Acts 2 was that the growth of the early church was the result of Peter's preaching, not from any focus on tongues.[55] In contrast, he charged that tongues speakers were so obsessed with their experience that they ceased to be soul winners.

---

[51] W. B. Riley, *Speaking in Tongues* (Minneapolis: Hall, Black & Co. 1907) 3.
[52] Riley, *Speaking in Tongues*, 9.
[53] Riley, *Speaking in Tongues*, 4, 7, 10, 11, 13. Quotations at 4 and 10.
[54] A. C. Dixon, *Speaking with Tongues* (Chicago: Bible Institute Colportage Association, 1909).
[55] Dixon, *Speaking with Tongues*, 11.

The obsession with tongues had especially damaged evangelism on the mission field, Dixon argued. The illusion of the quick fix of xenolalia, claiming a miracle tongue to preach the gospel to those in foreign lands, meant that missionaries were not "counting the cost." Expecting a revival of tongues on the mission field gave mission work a false charm yet ended with humiliation and left the disappointed missionaries vulnerable to losing their belief in the supernatural.[56]

Dixon also attacked the excessive emotion of the revival as unbiblical. Pentecostal worship produced "nervous spasms and muscular contortions, crowing like roosters, hissing like serpents, shrieking like madmen, barking like dogs, and talking baby talk in church." Like other opponents of the emotional excesses associated with revivals of the First and Second Great Awakenings, Dixon said that some misguided believers wanted to judge the Spirit's presence by the amount of noise that could be conjured up. While male Pentecostals were certainly included in Dixon's criticism, he added a sexual element. Women prostrated on the floor or leaping into the air were simply not biblically appropriate.[57]

Dixon offered several possible explanations for the tongues phenomena, including physical stress, psychological (i.e., excitable or hysterical temperaments), hypnosis, and Satanic delusion.[58] In explaining the manifestation of physical jerks that were reported on the frontier during the Second Great Awakening, Dixon leaned toward a psychological answer: the jerks "seemed to be a purely nervous disorder, which was short-lived."[59] The history of revivalism proved his point, he thought. According to Dixon, both Jonathan Edwards and John Wesley had first approved of emotional outbursts in their revivals but then regarded them as delusions. D. L. Moody had evangelistic services with hundreds of thousands of converts but which were always "free from extravagances."[60] Echoing Keswick, Dixon concluded that a special sign of the Spirit's baptism was not needed. If a believer was testifying of Christ

---

[56] Dixon, *Speaking with Tongues*, 12–15.

[57] Dixon, *Speaking with Tongues*, 4–12. Quotation at 11. Radical evangelicals (like higher life fundamentalists) thought Pentecostalism and its "hysterical" tendencies were more successful among women. See Wacker, "Travail of a Broken Family," 30.

[58] Dixon, *Speaking with Tongues*, 16–20.

[59] Dixon, *Speaking with Tongues*, 26.

[60] Dixon, *Speaking with Tongues*, 26.

and souls were being saved, that was enough evidence.[61] Of course, Pentecostals were quick to express disappointment in Dixon. His book particularly bothered the former Baptist and key early leader, William Durham, who retorted, what about the times he had spoken in tongues when he was not emotional but just had a burden for the lost.[62] Not surprisingly, Dixon did not stop criticizing the Pentecostals.[63]

Baptist Critics of the Azusa Revival: Newspapers

The Watchman

Baptist newspapers also gave some attention to early Pentecostal revivalism. *The Watchman* of Boston was the friendliest, actually being cautiously positive. Even before reporting on Azusa Street, *The Watchman* offered extensive coverage from September 1906 to March 1908 of reports of the Baptist-led Pentecostal-like revival at Nellore, India. *The Watchman* editors[64] said that they trusted the eyewitnesses, missionaries Mrs. and Dr. David Downie, the latter having been the treasurer of the American Baptist Telugu Mission for many years. Without efforts to artificially "work up" a revival, the editors noted, revival came "like a flash of lightening out of a clear sky" with "unusual and remarkable exhibitions" of the Spirit like the apostolic Pentecost. The Indian revival reportedly included visions and trances where participants were slain in the Spirit. Dr. Downie described it as being "dumb in the Spirit" as young women either "fairly writhed in agony for about two hours" or were motionless and "prone to the ground."[65] In a rebuke toward those who touted a cessation of miracles, the editors said that ever since the Welsh Revival, a belief that episodes of Pentecost could occur elsewhere had been revived.[66]

It is not surprising, then, for *The Watchman* to offer a cautiously positive assessment of the Azusa revival occurring at the same time. In June 1907, *The*

---

[61] Dixon, *Speaking with Tongues*, 28.

[62] William Durham, "Doctor Dixon Answered," *Pentecostal Testimony* (July 1, 1910): 12–14.

[63] In 1914, for example, he continued to criticize speaking in tongues while pastor of the Spurgeon Tabernacle in London. Ian M. Randall, "'Days of Pentecostal Overflowing,'" 94.

[64] The editors were Edmund F. Merriam and Joseph S. Swaim.

[65] "The Descent of the Holy Spirit," *Watchman* (September 6, 1906): 7. Mrs. D. Downie, "Revival at Nellore, India," *Watchman* (September 6, 1906): 10–11.

[66] "Descent of the Holy Spirit," 7. The editors referenced the revival led by Pundita Ramabai near Poona, India.

Watchman's editors said there was no reason to doubt the sincerity of the worshippers who claimed to be following the lead of the Holy Spirit. For forty years Bible expositors had been trying to eliminate the supernatural from Scripture. Healings and trances might have natural explanations, they conceded, but the presence of xenolalia was surely a miracle. *The Watchman's* assessment was so positive that *Word and Work*, a journal dedicated to Pentecostal "latter rain truths," printed the article verbatim two years later, conveniently it appears, without the conclusion of *The Watchman*'s evaluation. The Baptist editors, despite their sympathy for Pentecostal experience, ended with a caution the Pentecostals obviously chose to omit. The ability to speak in tongues as a "mere wonder," *The Watchman* concluded, contradicted Scripture's decree that tongues was not the most important spiritual gift and its exaltation was hampering the revival in Los Angeles.[67]

In 1909, *The Watchman* offered a brief analysis of "The New Revival" that revealed the newspaper's ultimate judgment of cautious approval. The editors wrote—as historians still do—that the era was characterized by a variety of restorationist movements that desired to usher in a revival of primitive New Testament Christianity. On the cautious side, the editors acknowledged that most restorationist movements had been defective in over-emphasizing one particular external feature of early Christianity. Nevertheless, they remained steadfast in their appreciation for the sincerity of the adherents of the "New Revival": a "devotion and readiness for self-sacrifice for their ideas which is not to be paralleled in the regular denominational churches." Tongues and healings were not simply dismissed as the editors concluded that whatever the errors were, there was a "revival of that spirit of life which was the distinguishing characteristic of the early disciples of Christ...."[68]

Baptist Argus

The *Baptist Argus* of Kentucky was willing to include write-ups about the Azusa revival from A. S. Worrell. Respect for the aged journalist/evangelist,

---

[67] "Speaking With Tongues," *Watchman* (June 20, 1907): 7–8. "The Judgment of an Impartial Observer. By the Editor of the Baptist "Watchman." (Boston)" *Word and Work*, 31, 10 (October 1909): 221. The journal was affiliated with the nondenominational Christian Worker's Union; its subtitle was *"Issued Monthly for the dissemination of Pentecostal Latter Rain Truths."*

[68] "The New Revival," *Watchman* (September 9, 1909) 7.

however, did not really mean support for the emerging Pentecostal revival experience. In August 1907, the newspaper included an extensive article that questioned the purpose of the revival, which, in good Baptist fashion, should be missions and evangelism. Tongues, however, was being sought "as a spiritual experience and proof of closeness to God."[69] The *Baptist Argus* claimed no desire to accuse Pentecostals with deception and cited Worrell, suggesting "his report seemed to settle all question as to the genuineness of some of the experiences." Seemingly in an attempt at fairness, the newspaper then cited a positive assessment from *The Watchman*, which included reference to the recent Pentecostal-like revival in Nellore, India.

However, the *Baptist Argus*, while expressing some caution against second-hand speculation, ultimately sided against the Pentecostal revival. The newspaper concluded with a strongly negative review from a leading Swedish Baptist, C. E. Benander, who reported on the spread of the Azusa revival to Sweden. Benander offered the typical warning about the excessive emotion of the "slain in the Spirit" phenomenon: "Persons who once get hypnotized through the strange influence or power propagated by the agent of the movement seem to lose all their power of sound judgment. It is in vain to try and reason with them. Some of our ministers have been ensnared, and I fear a number of churches will go under the most extravagant noise and disorder at the meeting." The *Baptist Argus* concluded, "This is the most serious report we have heard from the movement. It is well for our churches to be ready to deal wisely, tenderly, strongly with the matter."[70]

The newspaper included two more critical assessments in the next six months. One was a front page "cover story" that declared, similar to A. C. Dixon, how the Pentecostal revival had led to failures in evangelism and missions. The article was actually written by a missionary of the Bible Missionary Society. He reported on numerous Pentecostal missionaries in China, Japan and India who claimed tongues for witnessing only to fail even in speaking a

---

[69] "Speaking with Tongues," *Baptist Argus* (August 8, 1907): 17. The article was unsigned but the editor was J. N. Prestridge. *Baptist Argus* started in 1897 when supporters of W. H. Whitsitt at Southern Baptist Theological Seminary wanted a different view than that of T. T. Eaton, Whitsitt's opponent and editor of the long-time Kentucky paper, *Western Recorder*. See T. T. Eaton, "American Baptist Newspaper and Periodical Press, Part 2: Southern and Southwestern," in A. H. Newman, ed. *A Century of Baptist Achievement* (Philadelphia: American Baptist Publication Society, 1901) 277.

[70] "Speaking with Tongues," 17.

foreign language "in the simplest affairs of life."[71] They had been duped by the alleged glow of xenolalia. God might give the miracle of speaking in other languages, the article exhorted, but God was not doing so now.[72] On the other hand, Pentecostal literature, as should be expected, declared that some missionaries claimed greater success after being rejected by Baptists.[73]

Western Recorder and the Biblical Recorder

The *Western Recorder* of Kentucky and the *Biblical Recorder* of North Carolina both emphasized themes found in other critics: Pentecostals ironically hurt missions and were really anti-revival as tongues, most likely meaningless gibberish, had become an obsession, an end in itself. Pentecostal revival was excessively emotional and thus fanatical. Sounding like the rationalists who opposed the First Great Awakening, Baptist critics said that Pentecostal revival needed sanctified reason and less feeling because "the heat of the heart burns into fever in the brain."[74] These two newspapers, while not exclusively, often followed a cessationist perspective against the "so-called Pentecostal revival."[75]

The *Western Recorder*, for example, included an article that utilized the opinions of several Baptist cessationists. New York leader, Thomas Armitage, was cited to contend that no authentic cases of tongues had occurred since the New Testament and thus modern efforts were fanaticism. J. B. Jeter of Virginia was also a cessationist who cited the dominant view that the baptism of the Holy Spirit had only been for the apostles so they "might infallibly bear witness unto Christ" in the growth of the early church.[76] In the *Biblical Recorder*, J. H. Fontane declared that Pentecostal claims of healing were in reality

---

[71] S. C. Todd, "Some Sad Failures of Tongues in Mission Fields," *Baptist Argus* (January 23, 1908): 1.

[72] Todd, "Some Sad Failures," 1.

[73] "Baptism of the Spirit Transforms a Baptist Missionary," *Latter Rain Evangel* 13, no. 7 (April 1921): 2–7.

[74] Rev. Thomas Parry, "Errors of the Feelings," *Western Recorder*, March 26, 1908, 2.

[75] "Editorial: The So-Called Pentecostal Movement," *Western Recorder*, September 12, 1907, 5. T. T. Eaton was incapacitated on June 27, 1907, so subsequent editorials like this one would have been by C. M. Thompson, the next editor, or perhaps by the associate editor, J. G. Bow.

[76] "Questions Answered by Senex," *Western Recorder*, January 24, 1907, 2. C. R. W. Dobbs, "Baptized with the Spirit," *Western Recorder*, January 31, 1907, 3.

the use of psychic power to hypnotize. So-called healings were temporary and only pertained to certain diseases. But divine miraculous healing power could heal anyone and that gift had ceased with the apostles. Pentecostal healing evangelism was thus inauthentic.[77] In typical fashion Veteran North Carolinian minister, J. J. Landsell, offered a cessationist response based on the "tongues shall cease" passage of I Corinthians 13. But Landsell did more: he questioned the role of African-Americans in leadership. When error was unleashed, there was no telling how far it could go, Landsell declared: "I have heard of some ignorant negroes who claimed to have received the baptism of the spirit and professed to speak in unknown tongues, and would babble out a string of sounds that neither they nor those who heard understood.... And there is as much sense in their ejaculations as there is in praying that the baby about to be sprinkled with water might also be baptized with the Holy Ghost."[78]

One issue that particularly bothered the *Western Recorder* was the question of alleged new revelation in the revival. Pentecostals who had a "harsh spirit of judging" bothered the editor.[79] Sounding his cessationist alarm, the editor noted that biblical tongues were always accompanied by miraculous power and new revelation from God, but that the Scriptures had pronounced a curse on any subsequent attempts at revelation beyond the divine message in its pages. Tongues speakers who claimed to be the only full possessors of the Holy Spirit were thus claiming to speak infallibly.[80] The editor was aghast that a Baptist pastor claimed the Spirit baptism and acted like he had infallible authority over his congregation by licensing both men and women to preach without the approval of the congregation and allowing only them to speak in worship—a violation of Baptist congregation polity and the priesthood of believers. A revival of Holy Spirit baptism, the editor concluded, was an unbiblical tyranny of authoritarian leadership.[81]

---

[77] Rev. P. H. Fontane, "Can Miracles Be Wrought Today," *Biblical Recorder*, May 12, 1909, 5.

[78] Elder J. J. Lansdell, "The Baptism of the Spirit," *Biblical Recorder*, March 11, 1908, 5.

[79] "Editorial: The So-Called Pentecostal Movement," 5.

[80] "Questions Answered," *Western Recorder*, January 2, 1908, 2.

[81] "Questions Answered By Senex," *Western Recorder*, January 16, 1908, 8.

Pentecostal Revival in the 1920s

Pentecostals admitted that revival fires waned amid theological conflict in the second decade of the twentieth century. But they cited an upsurge in revival in the 1920s in planned revival campaigns. Baptists argued with faith healing evangelists like F. F. Bosworth[82] but I want to finish briefly with two woman evangelists, Eleanor Mae Frey and Aimee Semple McPherson.

Eleanor Mae Frey.
Historians of Pentecostalism have taken note of Eleanor Mae Frey, an extremely active Pentecostal evangelist whose earliest ministry was in a Northern Baptist context. Frey married an evangelist, assisted his work and took classes at Baptist related Rochester Theological Seminary.[83] When the Northern Baptist Convention was formed in 1905, the Freys affiliated and worked as evangelists and Baptists in western New York ordained her.[84]

During these Baptist years, Frey was an example of a Northern Baptist significantly influenced by the Holiness movement. She said that she was healed of tuberculosis in 1907 after prayer from a Christian and Missionary Alliance minister and she tarried unsuccessfully for the baptism of the Holy Spirit at a CMA convention.[85] While pastoring a Baptist church in New Jersey in 1918, Frey, again unsettled about receiving the Spirit baptism, attended a small Pentecostal mission and finally received the blessing. She later testified that the Lord told her to quit "rattling dry bones" in the pulpit and tarry for the Spirit.[86]

By 1921, Frey had become an evangelist with the Assemblies of God. However, she still did not completely leave her Baptist past. She often held revival campaigns among Baptists who affirmed the full gospel. Services often

---

[82] Christopher Richmann, "Living in Bible Times: F. F. Bosworth and the Pentecostal Pursuit of the Supernatural," (PhD diss., Baylor University, 2015).

[83] For biographical information on Frey, see Gerald W. King, "Mae Eleanor Frey: Pentecostal Evangelist and Novelist," *Assemblies of God Heritage* 29 (2009): 57–62.

[84] Mae Eleanor Frey, "An Evangelist's Story," *Pentecostal Evangel* (May 15, 1926): 9, and idem (May 22, 1926) 8. Edith Blumhofer, "Selected Letters of Mae Eleanore Frey," *Pneuma* 17, no. 1 (Spring 1998): 67. King, "Mae Eleanor Frey," 57.

[85] Frey, "An Evangelist's Story," (May 22, 1926): 8.

[86] Frey, "An Evangelist's Story," (June 5, 1926): 8.

included the full gospel of healings, tongues, Holy Spirit baptism and preaching about the imminent return of Christ. Sometimes her audiences included believers with experiences similar to hers: former Baptists who had left Baptists because of their belief in the full gospel.[87]

One of Frey's biggest fans was William Towner, the Baptist pastor from San Jose, California. The San Jose church helped spread the Pentecostal revival to four other Baptist churches in the Bay area. Historian Gerald King notes that Towner thought Frey was the best evangelist around except for Aimee Semple McPherson.[88] Frey sometimes complained that she had more freedom among Northern Baptist leaders who ignored her, especially when she considered being a Pentecostal pastor rather than an evangelist, but she remained Pentecostal because she believed that only with the full gospel could she genuinely reach souls for God.[89]

Aimee Semple McPherson

Baptist interaction with Pentecostals in the 1920s offered the same criticisms found in the reactions to Azusa Street. One matter was added—the role of women revivalists—or to be more specific, the identification of Pentecostalism with a charismatic Sister Aimee and thus its repudiation.

Aimee Semple McPherson, one of the most famous evangelists in American history, embarked on a preaching ministry in 1913 and by the end of the decade had become a popular evangelist who often dramatized biblical stories that captivated her audiences. Coming from Salvation Army roots, she joined the fledgling Assemblies of God in 1919 but soon sought a broader revivalist-evangelical tent. Her re-alignment included Baptist ordination in 1921 by First Baptist San Jose. McPherson said she was tired of the "extravagances and fanaticisms" of Pentecostalism and sought to connect with the fundamentalist spirit of the Baptists she had met in her revivals.[90] The dissenting moderator

---

[87] "Hungry Audiences," *Pentecostal Evangel* (May 8, 1926): 12.

[88] King, "Mae Eleanor Frey," 62. William K Towner, "'Pentecost' in a Baptist Church," *Pentecostal Evangel* (August 16, 1924): 9. Uldine Utley and Virginia Lee Berg also preached at First Baptist Church, San Jose, by Towner's invitation.

[89] "To: J. R. Evans, From: Kitchener, Ontario, October 31, 1928," cited in Blumhofer, "Selected Letters of Mae Eleanore Frey," 80. Frey remained active in ministry until 1950 and died in 1954.

[90] Matthew A. Sutton, "Between the Refrigerator and the Wildfire": Aimee Semple McPherson, Pentecostalism, and the Fundamentalist-Modernist Controversy," *Church History*

of the church's association emphasized that McPherson's ordination was the decision of First Baptist Church's right as an autonomous local Baptist church and was not necessarily endorsed by other Baptists.[91]

Scholars have identified Clifton Fowler, the Baptist head of the Denver Bible Institute, as one of Sister Aimee's chief critics. He attended her Denver revival campaign in 1921 and concluded she was a dangerous heretic to his dispensationalist cessationist ears. He admitted, however, that she had a personal magnetism, a personality that charmed the crowds. The pages of Fowler's *Grace and Truth* journal were filled frequently over the next several months about the dangers of McPhersonism and the "high priestess" of Pentecostalism."[92] McPhersonism and Pentecostalism became synonymous.

In 1926, Sister Aimee disappeared for months from her mega-church, the Angelus Temple in Los Angeles. Supporters believed her story that she was kidnapped; critics were sure she had run away in a sexual affair. John Roach Stratton of New York, who had become a supporter of divine healing, was the most prominent Baptist supporter of McPherson. He called McPherson a "poor, persecuted woman preacher."[93] Other Baptists were not so generous but they too played on the theme of gender. Clifton Fowler epitomized their attack and said women did not belong in the pulpit per biblical prescriptions. Sister Aimee the Amorous, Fowler called her, had built a following based on sex appeal and now the sexual affair was her disgusting downfall. Fowler remarked, "I hear her talk amorously in supposed prayer to Him who is the Savior of the world, and marvel at the gullibility of the thousands who seemed to relish her trashy dramatics and mushy love scenes with her "Jesus dear." It is reported that… she dropped her head on her pulpit and mournfully called to heaven, saying, "Dear Jesus, I'm so tired, so very, very tired. Oh Jesus dear, won't you come and put your great strong arms around me and love me? I'm so tired, so tired." The words themselves were bad enough, Flower exclaimed, but the "theatrical "rendition" of the prayer" was "subverting to the

---

72, no. 1 (March 2003): 174. Sutton cited "J. H. Sparks to E. N. Bell, March 28, 1922," Ministerial File of Aimee Semple McPherson, Flower Pentecostal Heritage Center, which is no longer available to the public.

[91] "Baptists Split on Ordination of Faith Curer," *San Francisco Chronicle*, April 2, 1922, G11.

[92] P. W. Philpott, "Pentecostalism Arraigned," *Grace and Truth* (January 1929): 19.

[93] "Noted Pastor in Defense of Mrs. M'Pherson," *Los Angeles Record*, September 30, 1926.

souls of her listeners. It is inescapably suggestive."[94] For most Baptists, with McPherson as their example, Pentecostal revivalism had been demonically duped or seduced to its most unbiblical level with its acceptance of women revivalists.

Concluding Thoughts

After studying Baptist-Pentecostal interactions, I'll never again say as I used to, that Baptists have had a shy member of the Trinity. Certainly, Baptists have loved Jesus but have not forgotten the Spirit. In addition, my study has revealed that the influence of the Holiness movement on Baptists, at least in America, is a story rarely told. When it comes to Baptists and early Pentecostal revivalism, I have found it revealing that the interaction of Baptists and the Holiness-Pentecostal revival tradition is substantive if not extensive. Grant Wacker has said that before 1950, most Americans had not heard of Pentecostals.[95] The prominent historian was perhaps engaging in intended exaggeration but Baptist sources, particularly newspapers, tell a different story.

Why the Baptist reactions found in this presentation? While there surely are multiple suggestions, it is good to remember that Baptists drawn to Pentecostal revival came from a Baptist background warmed by revival and a quest for direct personal encounter with God. Seeking a more intense tangible experience of the Holy Spirit was a logical progression for some believers like Elmer Fisher, Joseph Smale and A. S. Worrell. But tarrying for the Spirit was also a pivotal reason why others could see in a more emotionally demonstrative full gospel a negative assessment of their own religious experience. It was too much of a good thing, too disorderly, and thus became unwarranted.

More importantly, both groups were versions of restorationism. The Baptist story often emphasized that Baptists were the New Testament church, not simply a restored version. With the growth of Pentecostalism's full gospel restorationism, the two faiths had similar agendas: faithfulness to a literal reading of the New Testament and personal experience its confirmation.

This restorationist perspective was why Baptists, especially fundamentalist ones, had significant tension with Pentecostals. Whose attempt to re-

---

[94] Clifton Fowler, "As the Editor Sees It: Aimee the Amorous," *Grace and Truth* (February 1927): 33.

[95] Wacker, "Travail of a Broken Family," 23.

store or duplicate the New Testament church was most biblical? Fundamentalist Baptist dispensational exegesis might be employed to adopt cessationism and read the return of miracles to a future age. But conflict came when revival—usually considered a good thing—contended that a literal application of Acts 2 via Holy Spirit baptism and tongues were necessities to really accept the gospel fully. And the discovery involved leadership of African-Americans, no less.

By the 1920s, McPhersonism represented an issue in full gospel restorationism, which seemed to most scare and attract/repel the Baptists: women preachers. Baptists accused McPherson for sexualizing the ministry. They certainly sound like they did. Baptist interaction with Pentecostal revivalism became part of a biblical hermeneutic wrestling match and a culture war—then and now.

5

"Convert Every Tight-Wad You Can": Revivalism as Fundraising during the Southern Baptist Seventy-Five Million Campaign, 1919–1925

Andrew Smith

In the heady days following the end of World War I, Southern Baptist leaders began to wonder aloud whether the people of the Southern Baptist Convention (SBC) should frame a grand program of fundraising that would put the denomination in a position to help shape the post-war world. Eventually, at the 1919 Southern Baptist Convention, the denomination did adopt such a program, the five-year Seventy-Five Million Campaign. For the first time ever, Southern Baptists projected a plan that would allow all the objects of Southern Baptist support, such as the home and foreign mission boards, colleges, and seminaries, to be supported through a single fundraising effort projected to raise fifteen million dollars a year for five years, from 1919 to 1924.

While those churches and pastors that orbited their denomination closely tended to embrace the campaign, there seems to have been a large number of churches in rural areas that failed to participate closely in the campaign out of suspicion, ignorance, or both. Southern Baptist leaders seemed anxious that the pastors of these churches, holding as they did the keys to these small congregations, failed to enlist their churches in the campaign.[1] As a result, Southern Baptist leaders sought ways to appeal directly to laypeople for their support.

Although leaders expressed hope that laypeople would take an increased interest in their various state Baptist newspapers, influential Baptists seem to have identified annual Southern Baptist summertime revivals as the single most promising opportunity for reaching rank-and-file rural Baptists. As a

---

[1] Jeff D. Ray, "The Country Church and Millions for the Master," *Baptist and Reflector*, November 6, 1919, 3–4.

result, denominational officials wrote several pieces for Southern Baptist state newspapers suggesting that time be set aside during these regularly scheduled events for the campaign to be promoted to those present. Additionally, some suggested that a new sort of revival, the "enlistment revival" or "stewardship revival," be created with an eye towards converting Christians to greater dedication to denominational activities. As one observer exhorted, "We should be 'fishers of men.' Work hard after the big ones. Little fish can be caught easily. Convert every tight-wad you can."[2] All of this was justified by casting "stewardship" as a hitherto neglected element of Christian doctrine, plainly taught in Scripture, but questions remained as to how quickly rank-and-file Southern Baptists were to accept this claim. In the end, revivalism was not to remain as an important Southern Baptist denominational fundraising strategy long after the end of the campaign, giving way instead to methods pioneered by the denomination's women.

Almost from the beginning of the campaign, leaders noticed and subtly articulated that many pastors and churches seemed to be cooling towards the campaign as the initial flush of "victory week," when pledges were originally collected, wore off. B. J. W. Graham, having recently resigned as the editor of the Georgia Baptist newspaper, *Christian Index*, and returned to the pastorate, wrote:

> To a plain pastor who has no official connection with any of our Baptist institutions, there seems to be a reaction. It is harder to collect the subscriptions than it was to secure them. It is not as easy to get co-operation now as it was then. There is not as much talk about collecting the money as there was about getting it subscribed. I do not hear so much praying for the success of collecting the money as I heard during the campaign to get it subscribed. Many churches oversubscribed their quotas but I have heard of very few which have overpaid their subscriptions. It looks like there has been a general let-up along the line of Baptist activities.[3]

Graham believed that the solution lay in a reinvigorated practice of revivalism among Southern Baptists:

> It seems to me, also, that the proposed Southwide evangelistic campaign has been postponed too long. Southern Baptists need a new objective, one that will challenge the very best that is in them. That objective

---

[2] A. G. Melton, "A Little Sermon on Revival of Tithing," *Biblical Recorder*, March 15, 1922, 9.

[3] B. J. W. Graham, "Signs of Reaction," *Biblical Recorder*, April 28, 1920, 7.

should be spiritual and not material. Too many material resources with too little spirituality will mean our undoing. Such a state of affairs will breed faultfinding in administration, which will result in shrinkage in the collection of subscriptions. Revivals and evangelistic campaigns in the churches will obscure blunders in administration and increase the spirit of liberality. Such revivals and evangelistic campaigns will prevent the disasters of reaction.[4]

Graham was initially reluctant to imagine the revival as a platform for explicit fundraising activities. Instead, Graham simply believed that raising the spiritual temperature of the denomination would help people forgive the manifold administrative errors that had accompanied the emergence of the campaign and prepare people to give generously. Another author, however, was more than willing to suggest speaking to revival audiences about the campaign directly in 1919, even before the campaign began to show signs of stress. In August of that year, J. B. Tidwell wrote about his own revival strategies:

> I would spend five or ten nights, according to the nature and size of my congregation and length of my meeting, stating our doctrines, so as to reach our program of 75 Million as a climax. I would then take a day for it, or at least one full service, and lay out the program to the church and call them to the task. I'd make the best speech I could on it and would commit the church fully to it. It will then appear to be an effort on our part to give the world the doctrines which had been discussed and which were dear to us.[5]

Even at this early date, a Baptist leader was willing to offer as the "climax" of Baptist doctrine a denominational fundraising program that had first been imagined in the wake of the Great War. Other Baptist leaders, such as L. R. Scarborough, the director of the Seventy-Five Million Campaign and the president of Southwestern Baptist Theological Seminary, would similarly discuss stewardship as one of the doctrines to be discussed at revivals along with any treatment of Christian doctrine.[6] In other words, its creators never imagined the Seventy-Five Million Campaign as a mere fundraising effort. Instead, in those heady days following the armistice, Southern Baptist leaders

---

[4] Graham, "Signs of Reaction," 7.
[5] J. B. Tidwell, "Getting the 75 Million Drive into Our Revival Meetings," *Baptist Standard,* August 7, 1919, 12.
[6] L. R. Scarborough, "Southern Baptists in for a Great Campaign for Souls, *Religious Herald,* June 22, 1924, 5–6.

imagined the campaign as the final step in the evolution of the Baptist denomination, showing that Southern Baptists had finally come into their own. "The Campaign was not a revolution; it was more than that, it was something better.... The Campaign was an evolution.... At last as a denomination we are awake; at last we have authorized leadership and plans definite and adequate."[7] In the same way that a Roman Catholic would include the authority of the bishop of Rome in her account of the gospel, Southern Baptists would now have to include the Seventy-Five Million Campaign in their explanations of God's offer of salvation to humankind. After all, the campaign had been no mere human creation. One editorial expressed a typical attitude: "no human being may fairly claim to have "started" this campaign. That honor solely belongs to him for whose glory Southern Baptists are laying their lives and their all on the altar in these strenuous days."[8]

As the five-year campaign wore on, it became increasingly obvious that the ninety-two million dollars pledged would not materialize; in fact, it seemed as if the original $75,000,000 goal would not be reached. As the campaign fell farther and farther behind, leaders began placing increasing stress on the importance of reaching revival crowds with the news of the campaign. Writing in 1924, for instance, L. R. Scarborough noted:

> The pastors will hold most of the revival meetings this summer and the pastors will attend in the largest numbers the associational meetings; and these constitute the two occasions on which we will have our best chance to reach our people.... Most of our great mass of unreached Baptists will attend the Baptist revivals of this summer. Many of them know but little about the 75 Million Campaign.... The cause can be greatly advanced if the pastors aided by their helping evangelists will adopt the following simple method of reaching the great unreached mass of our people at these meetings.[9]

That Scarborough himself insisted on attention to the campaign at annual revivals shows that this strategy was far from idiosyncratic.

Other pastors and leaders, however, took the idea of using revivalism as

---

[7] W. H. Barton, "The 1919 Campaign, What It Should Mean to the Veteran Pastor," *Baptist Message*, January 15, 1920, 5.

[8] J. W. C[ammack], "Who 'Started' It and What For?," *Religious Herald*, October 9, 1919, 10.

[9] L. R. Scarborough, "The Pastors and Two Momentous Chances," *Baptist Courier*, July 24, 1924, 15.

a fundraising tool to an even higher level of refinement. Rather than simply tacking the goals of the campaign on to existing revivals, some leaders suggested using "enlistment revivals" or "stewardship revivals" in which Southern Baptists would be enlisted into greater church involvement through revivalist methods. Gaines Dobbins, for instance, very early in the campaign period asserted that a special "enlistment revival" would prove to be the best method of drawing inactive church members into more frequent church participation:

The evening services during this "Enlistment Revival" should be so planned as to reach the entire community.... Each evening should be devoted to some special phase of the work and at the close of the services effort made to clinch the matter by having those present actually enroll in the activities of the church.... The series of services may well close with a great "Dedication Day," for "calling out of the called," and the rededication of the lives of professing Christians to the service of the Master.[10]

Later, in 1924, as the campaign was winding down and leaders had begun to put stress on local church budgeting as a means of guaranteeing that the denomination would receive a share of a congregation's income, T. V. Herndon suggested that a church's budgeting process include a "stewardship revival," warning that "We should back up any sort of a program with evangelism. People will give through any church that is saving souls. It is hard to interest them in any sort of a program that is not linked directly with the winning of souls."[11] Herndon's words may suggest pushback from rank-and-file Baptists who were uninterested in seeing the traditional evangelistic emphases of revivals supplanted by appeals for increased denominational support.

Southern Baptist leaders, however, having identified the Seventy-Five Million Campaign as an object worthy of attention at revival meetings, occasionally tied divine judgment to non-participation in the campaign in ways reminiscent of a revivalist's vivid depictions of the damnation of the unrepentant. George W. Truett, writing in 1919, told the story of a "very wealthy woman...who had used her great wealth for her own self. Never was it known for her to give a cent to the relief of anybody. She never made a contribution for God's causes." When a doctor told her that she would be dead by the time

---

[10] G. S. Dobbins, "Enlisting the Whole Church," *Baptist and Reflector*, October 9, 1919, 3.

[11] T. V. Herndon, "The Place of Stewardship in the Fall Campaign," *Baptist Standard*, September 18, 1924, 11.

the sun had set, she "drew the sheets about her face and screamed, 'Oh, how I dread to meet God to account for the way I have lived!'" Truett was unafraid to turn the knife: "And may well she dread that meeting! She will have to give an account to him for the use of all she had, including her time, money, and talents."[12] George Truett, one of the most influential leaders among Southern Baptists during the campaign period and remembered today as a "moderate," was absolutely willing to dangle baptized Christians over the possibility of eternal damnation when talking about stewardship. Writing later in the campaign period, J. F. Love, the corresponding secretary of the Foreign Mission Board, posed a number of questions about the Seventy-Five Million Campaign to Southern Baptists in an op-ed column. Rather pointedly, Love asked,

> What shall the answer be at the Judgment? Since the 75 Million Campaign was started in 1919, thousands of our brethren and sisters have laid down their armor, been released from the engagement, and have passed on towards the Judgment. The years are not many when three million Southern Baptists will stand before the White Throne to give account of the deeds done in the body. I fancy that among the deeds for which we shall give answer or there receive encomiums of heaven, will be the deed of paying our campaign pledge, of giving or not giving to Christ in this great world-hour to help Him minister to the needs of a distressed world and to save the lost for whom He died.

Like Truett, Love left little to the imagination; if Southern Baptists failed to answer this and other questions adequately, "they will answer themselves to our condemnation."[13]

At least some Southern Baptists seem to have been skeptical about much of what their leaders were telling them. Some of this resistance found its way into the Southern Baptist press. C. C. Brown, writing in the Tennessee *Baptist and Reflector* in 1924, expressed doubt that Southern Baptist leaders were right when they suggested that an increase in emphasis on giving would necessarily bring about an increase in spiritual temperature:

> As far as I have been able to learn, there is no great spiritual revival at work among the churches. There is a financial revival in the churches, and a revival of the spirit of Voltaire and Hume without.

---

[12] George W. Truett, "Dr. Truett Says," *Maryland Baptist Church Life*, December, 1919, 3.

[13] J. F. Love, "What Shall the Answer Be?," *Baptist Record*, December 20, 1923, 6.

> We have pulled down the bars too low, and made it too easy to get into the Baptist church. Our doctrine of a converted membership is all a hoax. We are following the teaching of Sam Jones-"Quit your meanness and join the church." In this way the world gets into the church, and church discipline is an impossibility, for Satan will not cast out Satan.[14]

Although many insisted that emphasis on the campaign should be an inseparable part of Southern Baptist revival preaching during this period, others believed that the emphasis on money had obscured evangelistic aims. In the end, even L. R. Scarborough had to admit, "We let up on evangelism. We pressed enlistment, campaigns for money, paying pledges, and took the emphasis off missions and soul-winning…and in the meantime forgot, as we should not have done, to put the emphasis on winning men to Christ."[15]

Scarborough's words may well represent that Southern Baptist leaders felt themselves chastised at having bitten off more than they could chew during the Seventy-Five Million Campaign. Poor planning, a post-war economic slump, an uncomfortable Fundamentalist movement among Baptists to the North, and a row over evolution among Baptists in the South all conspired to hobble the campaign. Despite this, leaders decided to model a new 1925 campaign on the Seventy-Five Million Campaign, retaining the plan of funding a variety of denominational institutions through a single fundraising program. Although the subscription goal would be grossly reduced from the fifteen million dollars expected annually from the Seventy-Five Million campaign, the 1925 campaign proved that the methods of the original campaign could be adopted as a permanent method of denominational funding, today known as the Cooperative Program.

As the Cooperative Program has grown in importance over the last ninety years, it seems that Southern Baptist leaders achieved by mid-century some of the aims that were apparent in their use of revivalism to promote the original Seventy-Five Million Campaign: they convinced many Southern Baptists that contribution to the Cooperative Program was a *required* part of Christian discipleship, and even if they failed to create a denominational culture in which persons would be *converted* to stewardship, they did succeed in injecting the Cooperative Program into Southern Baptist theology as a non-

---

[14] C. C. Brown, "Standing in Doubt," *Baptist and Reflector*, September 16, 1920, 6–7.

[15] L. R. Scarborough, "A Matter of Supreme Primacy," *Western Recorder*, February 19, 1925, 3–4.

negotiable part of our own peculiar doctrine of sanctification.¹⁶ At the same time, Southern Baptists also realized that revivalistic methods were not particularly effective as a method of fundraising. One observer notably remarked:

> We need large sums to sustain our present programs. And we need these sums coming in a steady stream into the treasuries of all the objects we foster. It is demonstrated that the old method of drives, both periodic and sporadic, will not yield the sums we need and must have. It is also demonstrated that dependence upon these methods produces embarrassment in the form of large debts and enormous interest bills. It appears now that the only possible way to get the large sums we need, and to obviate the embarrassments we have suffered is to get our people into the habit of making their contributions from week to week perennially.¹⁷

---

¹⁶ Historians of the Southern Baptist tradition have puzzled over the decline of church discipline during the late nineteenth and early twentieth centuries. Some evidence exists that Southern Baptists moved away from corrective systems of church discipline during this time because they sought instead to retain members who gave generously and helped to build the church and denomination as institutions, even if some of their private behaviors were questionable. E. Y. Mullins, for instance, suggested that "those who might afterwards become useful Christians are cut off by a discipline that is too peremptory." Instead, Mullins recommended "a patient but persevering effort to reclaim the dancer[s] and lead them to a higher ideal of Christian life." E. Y. Mullins to J. E. Lucas, March 25 1903, Letter, Southern Baptist Theological Seminary, Edgar Young Mullins Papers. Quoted in Paul Harvey, *Redeeming the South: Religious Cultures and Racial Identities among Southern Baptists* (Chapel Hill: University of North Carolina Press, 1997) 84. During the Seventy-Five Million Campaign, however, some leaders began seeking to use traditional methods of church discipline against members failing to give appropriately to the campaign. A. T. Robertson, for instance, pushed for churches to discipline greedy members: "I have asked many audiences at Northfield, at Winona, at Montreat, and in many pulpits of various denominations if any one had ever known a church member excluded from church on the charge of covetousness. I have yet to receive one affirmative answer...we let pass the idolatrous covetousness of "Deacon Skinflint," which cries to heaven.... One needs tact, to be sure, in handling the covetous church member, but he also needs courage.... Judgment must begin at the Throne of God, but it should begin. Thank God, a new day has come." A. T. Robertson, "Covetousness and Church Discipline," *Biblical Recorder*, January 7, 1920, 1. These shifts in church disciplinary attitudes and practices indicate that Southern Baptists were developing a new theology of sanctification, one in which Christians were thought to grow in grace as they gave more money to and worked more closely with their church and denomination to meet organizational goals. For another perspective on this shift, see Gregory A. Wills, *Democratic Religion: Freedom, Authority and Church Discipline in the Baptist South, 1785–1900* (New York: Oxford University Press, 1997) 131–38.

¹⁷ J. R. Hobbs, "Convention Notes," *Alabama Baptist*, May 31, 1923, 6.

Interestingly, it was the Woman's Missionary Union (WMU) that provided the model for just this sort of fundraising. While male leaders sought to raise funds through what came to be derided by one editor as the "whoop-em-up" method of fundraising, Southern Baptist women raised money systematically by encouraging members to lay a little money aside each week.[18] In the process, the WMU became the only constituency within the SBC to raise its assigned quota: a whopping fifteen million dollars. As Scarborough himself observed, Southern Baptist women

> won by systematic, and in many cases sacrificial, regular, persistent, constant giving. As far as I know, they have not secured many large sums. But my, how they have constantly and systematically gone after regular, moderate, and smaller gifts! Women are not known especially as moneymakers, but Southern Baptist women are known for their ability as money-givers.... In literally thousands of cases this fifteen million dollars that they have given represents sacrificial, self-denying gifts.[19]

More pungently, V. I. Masters of the Kentucky *Western Recorder* suggested "Our women are more quiet about their work than the men, but they always get results...which the men do not always do with their masculine methods."[20]

Given the evolution of Southern Baptist fundraising over the course of the twentieth century, it is safe to say that the leaders of the Southern Baptist Convention abandoned their "masculine methods" of revivalist fundraising, emphasizing instead the WMU's more effective method of encouraging steady, moderate giving. Ultimately, the Cooperative Program evolved into a method of funding directed not at individuals but at churches, which were requested to set aside a certain percentage of their members' undesignated contributions for the work of their local associations, state conventions, and the Southern Baptist Convention. In the process, with the exception of two offerings decorously collected by the Women's Missionary Union annually for the sake of home and foreign missions and a handful of special offerings col-

---

[18] L. L. Gwaltney, "Baptists and Democratic Movements," *Alabama Baptist*, March 22, 1923, 3.

[19] L. R. Scarborough, "A Marvelous Achievement and an Inspiring Example," *Baptist Standard*, July 24, 1924, 7.

[20] V. I. Masters, "Baptist Women, Baptist Pastors, and Baptist Paper," *Western Recorder*, May 15, 1924, 11.

A Student-Initiated Revival: Reiji Hoshizaki

The BSU regularly sponsored an annual pre-school retreat at Latham Springs, a Baptist encampment about twenty miles from Waco. In the fall of 1944 four hundred students attended.[8] The impetus for the revival among Baylor students began during this brief retreat. Baylor students M. D. Oates, a future missionary to Peru, and Reiji Hoshizaki, a Japanese American and future missionary to Japan, had attended a Youth for Christ rally in Chicago during the summer. The speaker was Billy Graham.[9] Many young Baptist ministers sought to imitate Graham, and he made a strong impression on these two Baylor students. At the Latham Springs retreat Oates and Hoshizaki described to a small circle of students their experience and their dream of bringing a similar event to Baylor and Waco. When they returned to campus, students continued to pray for revival. Dick Baker pointed out the big step the students were proposing. He recalled, "We did have strong youth programs, but we had not seen...big rallies such as the Chicago meeting attended by Oates and Hoshizaki."[10] The Baylor students were fortunate to have Bob Denny as their BSU director. He was an independent thinker and was willing to support the students' bold idea.[11] When they asked him who could preach for them, he essentially told them to "do it yourselves."[12] The students, not the BSU director, conceived the idea and carried out the revival.[13] The leaders of the movement later credited Reiji Hoshizaki with the idea of organizing a

---

[8] Bruce McIver, *Riding the Wind of God: A Personal History of the Youth Revival Movement* (Macon, GA: Smyth and Helwys, 2002) 13. McIver was a student leader and preacher in this revival, and he wrote a full narrative account of the revival.

[9] See Grant Wacker, *America's Pastor: Billy Graham and the Shaping of a Nation* (Cambridge: Belknap Press, 2014) 8–9.

[10] Richard Dee Baker, "Oral Memoirs," interview by Daniel B. McGee, Katy Jennings Stokes, and Thomas L. Charlton, 24 August 1982, transcript, Institute for Oral History, Baylor University, Waco, Texas, interview 1: 15.

[11] McIver, *Riding the Wind of God*, 14. Denny later became the executive director of the Baptist World Alliance.

[12] McIver, *Riding the Wind of God*, 25.

[13] W. F. Howard, "Oral Memoirs of Wilbur Forrester Howard," interviews by L. Katherine Cook and Katy Jennings Stokes, 8–9 May 1982, transcript, Institute for Oral History, Baylor University, Waco, Texas, interview 2:23. Howard, the Director of Student Work for the Baptist General Convention of Texas, was skeptical about the revival at first. His active involvement and support came later, in organizing subsequent revivals led by students.

large-scale revival at Baylor.[14]

A Student-Organized Revival

Students took full responsibility for organizing the revivals. Most of the three hundred students who worked behind the scenes are unsung and unknown volunteers who organized virtually all major aspects of the revival.[15] The students arranged for professional publicity to promote the revivals: they contacted the local newspapers and radio stations to advertise the meeting; they printed brochures featuring pictures and biographical notes on the speakers for the week and raised money to pay for all of these essentials; they contacted local pastors, asking them to make announcements to their church members about the forthcoming meeting. Finally, they organized door-to-door personal visits throughout the city to invite people to the meetings.

The students wanted a unique setting for the revivals. They believed the meeting needed to be conducted away from the familiar setting of any local church sanctuary or campus building. They rented a large tent to accommodate the event and set it up in downtown Waco. This was to be a university based revival, but the audience was to include the wider community. Two additional arrangements essential to the success of this revival were the organization of sustained student prayer meetings and the selection of speakers for the week. Again, students took the initiative in both vital areas.

The students organized a protracted period of prayer that extended for several weeks. The prayer meetings began with a small number of participants, but eventually involved scores of students. In their later reflections, the student leaders regularly attributed the success of the revivals to the work of God, but they believed that these extended prayer meetings served as a vital instrument in the process.[16] These prayer sessions were marked by their intensity. They served not only as the central focus to petition for revival, but also became the occasion for confessions of sin by some students. Ron Hill recalled how his

---

[14] See the comment of Howard Butt in "Oral Memoirs of Howard E. Butt Jr. and Katy Jennings Stokes," interview 1:25.

[15] McIver, *Riding the Wind of God*, 89.

[16] Robert Jackson Robinson, "Oral Memoirs of Robert Jackson Robinson," interview by Katherine L. Cook, 20 May 1982, transcript, Institute for Oral History, Baylor University, Waco, Texas, interview 1:43.

spirit was broken and restored during one of the prayer meetings.[17] Moreover, some conversions occurred at the prayer meetings, well before the opening of the revival meeting proper. Active supporters of the revival bonded in prayer. They formed a community within the larger university, and their gatherings created significant support for revival.

The highest profile prayer meeting conversion was the transformation of Charles Wellborn, one of the university's most gifted students. He won two national debate championships for Baylor and emerged as a key leader in the revivals. He was a little older than most of the other youth revival preachers, having left Baylor to enter military service during the war. He returned from military duty, finished his degree, taught political science, and was accepted to Harvard Law School. However, he was deeply impressed by the sincerity he observed in fellow student Jackie Robinson's commitment to Christianity. Wellborn also attended Friday Night Missions and observed how students devoted themselves to working with the poor. He recalled that at this point in his life he was not hostile to religion, but rather indifferent.[18] He attended revival prayer meetings in the basement of Seventh and James Baptist Church and there experienced his own conversion during the week preceding the revival. Wellborn described his conversion experience, reporting that it produced "a total reorientation of my values, [and it] gave me driving purpose."[19] The word spread rapidly throughout the campus: the brightest man they knew had been converted. The prayer meetings thus served multiple vital functions in the revival. They doubtless created hope for and expectation of revival among many students, while others experienced recommitment or personal conversion experience before the formal meetings began.

The most striking feature of the Baylor youth-led revival was the presence of student preachers. Their leadership was unique for a major revival, and the idea of having twenty-year-olds preach succeeded spectacularly.[20] Without formal seminary training and relying on their very limited experience, six

---

[17] Ron Hill made this point emphatically in his recollection of the revival. See McIver, *Riding the Wind of God*, 182.

[18] Wellborn, "Oral Memoirs," 7, 10.

[19] Wellborn, "Oral Memoirs," 9.

[20] For a study of leadership dimensions of this revival see William L. Pitts Jr., "Leadership in the Youth-Led Revival Movement," *Journal of Texas Baptist History* 32 (2012): 39–68.

students were selected to preach at the revival services.[21] Apparently, they had all spoken at a Baylor Religious Hour service or at some public venue. The talent he observed in the speakers struck Howard Butt. He recalled, "The first time I ever was at BRH, I heard Jess Moody speak, and...he was so colorful. And then one after another of the [BRH speakers] were remarkably inspiring.... But boy I was impressed with the remarkable people who were here at Baylor during that time."[22] And Jackie Robinson, in turn, was overwhelmed with Howard Butt's speaking ability. He said that Butt had the ability 'to communicate with somebody on the last row of a crowd of twenty thousand.... He could out-preach [Billy] Graham—my soul!'[23] Moreover, Robinson reported that on one occasion when Butt needed a sermon to preach he simply read James Stewart's "Why Be Christian?" and quoted the sermon word for word. Robinson concluded that Butt had "a photographic mind and was very able to communicate from the very first."[24] Buckner Fanning's experience was similar: "it was the caliber and quality of those people that really impressed me. The Lord really used those individuals."[25] The young men were gifted speakers and aspired to become ministers. Their skill had been observed. Some had preached in their home churches or at Friday Night Missions or a Baylor Religious Hour service. According to Bruce McIver, the BSU student leadership came to a consensus in electing preachers for the event.[26] Doubtless, BSU director Bob Denny also was influential in coordinating selection of the six students who would be featured in the revival services.

---

[21] The services would be conducted in the evenings, Monday through Saturday. The students were careful not to schedule any revival services that would conflict with regularly scheduled Sunday services.

[22] Howard E. Butt, "Oral Memoirs of Howard E. Butt Jr. and Katy Jennings Stokes," interview 1:6–7.

[23] Robinson, "Oral Memoirs," interview 1:21.

[24] Robinson, "Oral Memoirs," interview 1:23. James Stewart rapidly became one of the young preachers' favorite preachers. Several of them traveled to Edinburgh, Scotland, to study with him.

[25] Charles Buckner Fanning and Richard D. Baker, "Oral Memoirs," interview by Thomas Charlton and Katy Jennings Stokes, 24 August 1982, transcript, Institute for Oral History, Waco, Texas, interview 2:5.

[26] McIver, *Riding the Wind of God*, 32.

Two Baylor Revival Events: April 16–21, 1945, and April 1–6, 1946

The first campus revival meeting took place during the week of April 16–21, 1945. Each evening during that meeting five to six hundred students formed a mass procession and sang as they walked some twenty blocks from the campus through the city to the revival tent site. The revival theme in 1945 was "Waco Youth for Christ."[27] When Baylor students gathered in this era to talk about religion, a favorite theme was "What is God's will for my life?" The revivalists' response was to call students first to devote themselves fully to Christ. They emphasized this message with revival mottos or themes such as "I'd Rather Have Jesus," "Try Jesus," or "Christ for Me."[28] The initial revival was so successful that the students planned another for the following year. Howard Butt recalled that the first revival was described as "the big event of the school year. And there was a sense of anticipation about repeating revival during the following spring."[29] The second and even more impressive revival was held April 1–6, 1946.

Youth culture was a critically important feature of these two campus revivals. The target audience for the sermons was the Waco high school-age youth. Ralph Langley recalled that Dick Haverton, his BSU director in North Carolina, had told him that college age students who were only a year or two older could have a powerful influence on underclassmen and on high school students. Langley was persuaded by this analysis of the workings of social psychology. He declared that implementing this insight was "one of the ingenious contributions of the youth revival movement."[30] The Baylor BSU director Bob Denny echoed Haverton, recognizing that the young preachers' "testimony to those of their own age is more effective than that of adults."[31] The revival au-

---

[27] Students created large banners with revival themes and displayed them across streets and behind the pulpit and choir at the meetings.

[28] John D. Pierce, "Revival Movement Expands to the Southeast," in Bruce McIver *Riding the Wind of God,* 260–61. McIver died before the book was published. However, he did live to complete the manuscript, and Pierce, executive editor of *Baptists Today,* added an essay on how the revival movement soon spread throughout the southeastern United States.

[29] Butt, "Oral Memoirs," interview 1:25.

[30] See "Oral Memoirs of Ralph Henderson Langley," interviews by Thomas L. Charlton, L. Katherine Cook, and Daniel McGee, 27–28 July 1982, transcript for Oral History, Baylor University, Waco, Texas, interview 1:7.

[31] Robert Denny, "Youth Evangelism," *Baptist Standard* 31, no. 8 (May 1952): 30.

dience in fact included many college students and older adults who also supported the young preachers and responded to their messages.[32]

Youthful university students did all the preaching for the revivals. This was the most striking feature of the university revival. Their lack of formal training was likely a decided advantage. People knew what to expect of a traditional Baptist minister, but here were unconventional proclaimers of the gospel.[33] The students delivered simple messages with catchy titles, unencumbered by technical language.[34] The message they delivered seemed fresh not only to high school students but also to all ages. Additional students offered personal testimonies. An orchestra and a chorus of 150 performed each evening. Despite costs, the students determined to take no offering during the service. They conducted no protracted begging for people to respond during the invitation following the sermon. Robinson's observation that this revival "was not the same old sevens and sixes" is pertinent.[35] Langley asserted that part of the success of the revival was because the messengers were so young.[36] He thought it was not so much a new message as a fresh delivery that elicited enthusiastic response to the university based revival.

Most of the young preachers recalled how frightened they were to assume the task of proclamation. Bruce McIver later said that he was so weak in the knees before preaching his revival sermon that he had to have help getting to the pulpit.[37] Howard Butt said that fear almost immobilized him.[38]

---

[32] Langley, "Oral Memoirs." interview 1:9; McIver, "Oral Memoirs," interview 1:9; Jimmy Allen, "Oral Memoirs of Jimmy Raymond Allen," a series of interviews conducted by Susie Valentine and Robert Parham, 13 March 1980–24 June 1983, transcript, Institute for Oral History, Baylor University, Waco, Texas, interview 1:17.

[33] The preachers for April 1945 were Angel Martinez, BO Baker, Reiji Hoshizaki, Le Ray Fowler, M.D. Oates, and Ralph Langley. McIver, *Riding the Wind of God*, 30–31.

[34] Charles Wellborn published a collection of these sermons in *Youth Speaks* (Nashville: Broadman, 1949). In his introduction to the volume Wellborn wrote, "Neither the young preachers nor the compiler suffer under the illusion that they are great sermons. These are very largely the products of immature and inexperienced minds. But they are messages which have been gloriously used in the reaching of young people for Christ."

[35] Robinson, "Oral Memoirs," interview 1:29.

[36] Langley noted, "it was mighty good to bring peer pressure into divine operation…the whole youth revival movement was peer pressure par excellence." Pierce, "Revival Movement Expands," in McIver, *Riding the Wind of God*, 263.

[37] McIver, *Riding the Wind of God*, 106.

[38] Butt, "Oral Memoirs," interview 1:11.

Recognition of their near failure caused the young preachers readily to give God the credit for the success of the revivals. This view appears again and again in their oral histories. They feared failure, but did not fail. As they saw it, God must have intervened. For them there was no other explanation.[39] The revivals were indeed successful. Some three thousand people attended each service of the 1945 meeting, and 281 made public commitments.[40] The United States dropped atomic bombs to end World War II in August. General Douglas MacArthur called for a thousand missionaries, and during the following year students again prepared for revival. Leading to the 1946 revival, they organized ninety consecutive days of prayer (January–March) and selected speakers for the week.[41] Their theme for the second revival was "Use Me" or "Make Me Usable."[42] This time the revival was held nearer the campus at Fifth Street and Clay and drew four thousand in attendance with five hundred decisions. The external cultural milieu for this campus revival was unique. From a national perspective the most important fact was that the war had ended, and veterans returned to campus, many with serious purpose about life. Baylor had lost 122 people in the war. Many returning students had made vows during the war that they meant to keep, and the majority of decisions were recommitments.[43] The change in the student body was dramatic and evident to all. Baylor enrolled 1,370 in 1944, 1,660 in 1945, and 3,655 in 1946, which included 1,900 veterans.[44] Forty percent of the campus in 1946 was returned military personnel. Observers later suggested that the returners were "more mature emotionally and lent 'stability' to the revivals."[45] At the same time some struggled with the scars of war. Buckner Fanning later recalled his

---

[39] McIver, *Riding the Wind of God*, x; McIver, "Oral Memoirs," interview 1: 16; Fanning, "Oral Memoirs," interview 2:13; BO Baker, "Oral Memoirs," interview 1:29. Wellborn, in McIver, *Riding the Wind of God*, 73. Bill Cody and Leta Woodfin expressed similar views; see McIver, *Riding the Wind of God*, 193 and 195.

[40] Denny, "Youth Evangelism," 29.

[41] The speakers for the 1946 revival were Jess Moody, Jack Robinson, BO Baker, Mark Moore, Howard Butt, and Bruce McIver. McIver, *Riding the Wind of God*, 63, 65, 68. The revival theme song was "He Lives."

[42] McIver, *Riding the Wind of God*, 68.

[43] Robinson, "Oral Memoirs," interview 1:15–17.

[44] These numbers are reported each year in the September issues of *Baylor Lariat*. See the Digital Collection database of the 1944–46 *Baylor Lariat*, http://bit.ly/1BTbA6x, accessed 26 June 2015.

[45] Butt, "Oral Memoirs," interview 1:23.

spiritual distress: "I landed in Nagasaki…and…our responsibility was to find people who'd been burned by the bomb—women, children, others—but who had not received adequate medical treatment. And this began to tear me up inside…. I was hungry for some spiritual interpretation of life."[46] Awareness of these attitudes and feelings helps to explain receptivity to the campus revival. These two revival meetings were unique in the school's history. Stories of "The Baylor Revival" circulated during the following decade along with talk on campus of reprising revival, but this hope was never realized. Within a short time, the week of revival at Baylor had been replaced by the routine of an annually scheduled Religious Emphasis Week, featuring preaching by a successful Baptist minister.

Beyond the Campus Revivals: New Forms of Youth-Led Revivals

The impact of this Baptist university revival was far-reaching. Building on the model of the Baylor experience, two additional Baptist revival movements enjoyed much success: citywide crusades and youth-led summer revivals in local churches.

City-Wide Crusades

The citywide revivals took the Waco format to much larger venues. This development represented the second wave of youth revivals. Pastors and denominational leaders in Texas wanted the students to preach to thousands in Houston, Fort Worth, and Dallas, and made preparation for revivals led by the young university preachers. The meeting held outdoors at Cole Park in Dallas was one of the most successful of these meetings, drawing as many as ten thousand people at one service.[47] *The Dallas Morning News* reported that the vast majority present were school-age young people.[48] Interpreted by size, publicity, and public response, these meetings imitated the feel of Graham's

---

[46] Fanning, "Oral Memoirs," interview 2:4.

[47] McIver states 10,000 (McIver, *Riding the Wind of God,* 113); Brymer mentions 15,000. Jack Brymer, "Youth Revivalists of Late 1940s" *Baptist Press* May 25, 1999, http://www.bpnews.net/1055/youth-revivalists-of-late-1940s-to-convene-for-public-symposium, accessed 28 August, 2015.

[48] "Bobby Soxers Flock to Mammoth Revival," *Dallas Morning News,* August 2, 1946. The paper included a picture of the large crowd. The article declared that "the response was something that hasn't been seen in Dallas in a long time."

much larger crusades. Interest in the revivals spread quickly.

For many years Baptist students gathered each summer at the North Carolina Ridgecrest Baptist Assembly for a week=long program focused on university student interests. In June 1946, Baptist students from across the South who attended Student Week at Ridgecrest learned about the Texas revivals. This meeting provided the critical link by which the idea spread to other states.[49] Soon students on campuses in several states formed teams to lead revivals, imitating the Baylor model. These crusade-type revivals were conducted in major cities of the South, including Birmingham, Knoxville, and Nashville, as well as Honolulu, Hawaii. Out of this latter movement grew an important new initiative for the Baptist missionary enterprise—the Student Summer Mission Program.[50]

At the Birmingham citywide meeting in 1949, an estimated five thousand attended the final evening to hear the Texas Youth Revival team. Jack Robinson, Charles Wellborn, and Howard Butt shared preaching assignments, and Frank Boggs was the song leader for the week.[51] At a personal level, future Southern Baptist Convention leaders Arthur Walker and Bill Hull, then students at Samford University were profoundly influenced by the Alabama revival. Walker, later Executive Director of the Education Commission of the Southern Baptist Convention, noted, "Many of us had been involved in World War II and were seeking for answers …. During the war many lost all sight of what it was to be sober, sincere, and moral."[52] Hull, later a distinguished New Testament professor, preacher, and administrator, recalled "these young men, who were articulate and were thrilling to listen to, created a legitimacy for the young preacher…. They made a profound impression on me."[53] Large cities could accommodate the citywide revival concept, but most Baptists were located in small population areas.

---

[49] John Pierce, "Revival Movement Expands to Southeast," in McIver, *Riding the Wind of God*, chap 19.

[50] Marv Knox, "Youth Revivalists Shaped a Generation," *Baptist Standard*, June 30, 1999. This was a vital program in recruiting students for lifetime service for Baptist mission programs.

[51] Brymer, "Youth Revivalists of Late 1940s."

[52] Brymer, "Youth Revivalists of Late 1940s."

[53] Brymer, "Youth Revivalists of Late 1940s."

Summer Youth-Led Revivals for Local Churches

The third wave and final form of the youth revivals proved the most durable and most influential. Soon Baptist pastors in small cities and towns of the American South sought university students to conduct youth-led revivals in their local churches. Now the Texas BSU, led by W. F. Howard, became deeply involved. Howard had attended the 1946 revival and was convinced of its value. His office interviewed university students and created teams of four—two preachers, a musician, and a social leader—usually a woman—who conducted after-church seminars and fellowship meetings.[54] What is implicit, but seldom noted, is the reception of the idea of these revivals. The meetings were often billed as youth revivals rather than youth-led, creating the perception among the young in a local church that this was an event designed by their church especially for them. The young people seldom received so much direct attention in Baptist churches as they did during this week. It is of course impossible to measure the level of influence these revivals had on retaining loyalty to the church among the young, but it seems a likely contributing factor. Once again university students provided a special appeal, contributing to the success of these revivals. They were selected from many universities and led revivals in many churches in Texas and beyond. The key to selection according to Howard was that the youth revival leader must have a "tremendous ability to express himself…[and]…the fervor and the spirit and the excitement that could turn youth on."[55] Howard's office prepared instruction booklets for revival teams, providing guidance for appropriate behavior. They also published brochures with guidelines for preparing for revival meetings in local churches.[56]

The student teams conducted up to twelve one-week revival meetings in local churches during the summer months. Again, the unique appeal was their youth. Parents wanted their children involved in church, and supported these revivals. Young people were drawn to the youthful team leadership.[57] It was a

---

[54] McIver, *Riding the Wind of God*, 199.

[55] Howard, "Oral Memoirs," interview 3:76.

[56] *A Pictorial History of the Baylor Youth Revival Movement*, 52–54. This is a scrapbook album with a few selected quotations from revival participants. No editor and no publication data are listed. The book is housed in the Truett Heritage Room at Baylor University.

[57] Jimmy Allen, "Oral Memoirs of Jimmy Allen," interview by Susie Valentine, 13 March 1980, transcript, Institute for Oral History, Baylor University, Waco, Texas, interview 1:21.

popular concept and remained effective in Baptist churches for the next seventeen years. These youth-led revivals gave up several of the original and unique features of the campus revival, but they gained a natural home in the local church where the revival was readily adapted to a week of services. The young preachers polished their sermons, spent time visiting in the community, and found time to be with the young people. The music director led the congregational singing and often sang a solo or played the trumpet. Favorite topics for after church fellowship included sex, dating, and understanding God's will. This phase of the youth-led revival influenced by far the largest number of people. The Texas Baptist Department of Student Work kept records of these summer youth revivals for the seventeen-year period of 1946 through 1962. During this era the department booked 1,560 revivals, an average of about ninety-two per year. These records report 54,916 public Christian commitments, 10,224 of which were professions of faith and also 3,681 commitments to professional ministry.[58] Moreover, these were only the revivals sponsored by the Baptist Student Department. Many students not selected for these teams organized on their own. Participant Jimmy Allen recalled, "The youth revival movement was far broader than what the student division itself was sponsoring."[59] Bruce McIver, who spent the remainder of his career as a leading Baptist minister observed that in the years following World War II "youth buildings, youth activities, youth directors, youth choirs, youth days, youth weeks, and youth conferences became familiar terms in many of our growing [Baptist] churches."[60] The revivals were a natural complement to the emphasis on the religious formation of young people in the churches. The Baylor youth revivals thus had three iterations: (1) the two original on-campus revivals (2) city-wide crusades using a similar format for larger city audiences, and (3) a seventeen-year run of summer youth revivals adapted to local Baptist churches. This chapter has focused primarily on the first phase, but all three phases of these Baptist revivals owe a common debt to a Baptist university.

Conclusion

Baptist churches in the American South experienced a variety of revivals in the era following World War II, contributing to their vitality and explosive

---

[58] See McIver, *Riding the Wind of God*, 158, for statistics relating to these revivals.
[59] Allen, "Oral Memoirs," 2:17.
[60] McIver, *Riding the Wind of God*, 161.

growth during the 1950s. Revivals in churches located in Texas, Oklahoma, Arkansas, and Louisiana regularly experienced invigorating meetings during this era, including youth-led revivals. Many of the older Baptists of this region today remember these revivals. Some made life-changing decisions during these meetings. The BSU statistics indicate a ratio of about four recommitments to one conversion. This suggests that the revivals were chiefly a source of renewed commitments for church members.

Revivals also provided an important impetus for many young people to devote all their lives to ministry. If the commitments they made were kept, these revivals added an average of 216 people per year to the ranks of the ministry. These revivals clearly produced many future leaders for the denomination. Hundreds of young people identified their religious vocation during these revivals and went on to serve churches for the remainder of their lives.

General Baptist church histories are often careful to describe the organizational structure of denominations, theological developments and controversies, and statistics relating to membership, building programs, and finances. Curiously, after discussing Baptists in the two Great Awakenings, they have given sparse attention to the nature of week by week preaching and the special revival meetings that sustained Baptist growth during eras of rapid growth such as the 1950s. Yet this dimension of the life of the church is integral to the story of Baptists, and it deserves more attention in future Baptist histories.

The youth revival movement spread throughout much of the South. These revivals were set in motion at a university, and university students led all three expressions of the revival. The days of the campus revival soon passed, and later efforts to replicate it failed miserably. Nevertheless, it is noteworthy that a university managed to nurture a series of revivals, which affected Baptist life in the Southern United States for a half century. University students organized the Baylor revivals, and they were directed at young people. The university revival at Baylor and the revivals it inspired thus form a unique and significant chapter in the long and diverse history of Baptist revivalism.

Chapter 7

"O how many things brot tears from my eyes":
Sympathetic Reading in
Nineteenth-Century Baptist Piety

Keith S. Grant

Reading was an intensely emotional experience for Edward Manning (1766–1851) of Nova Scotia.¹ In January of 1821, for example, he confided to his diary, "Reading the Intelligence from Burmah: the death of the King, the conversion of Maung Nau, the Death of Mr. Wheelock, etc., etc., all tend to excite various immotions." And later the same day, "Have been reading the Magazine this day…. Many pieces have struck my mind and moved my affections. But when I read of James Talmage, Jessy Jones, Maxwell, and Winchell my heart hath quite overflowed. Various have been my immotions."² In November 1830, he and his wife discussed missionary developments in Burma and the death of Ann Judson. He wrote, "I was so overcome that it was with much difficulty that I could keep from crying out loud; from tears I could not. My heart hath been rather soft ever since…. Spent an hour reading the American B[aptist] M[issionary] Magazine."³ Of the memoirs of Ensign Lincoln,

---

¹ An earlier version of this chapter was read at the International Conference on Baptist Studies at Manchester, England, July 17, 2015. Related material was also presented at the Canadian Historical Association, Ottawa, Ontario, on June 3, 2015. I am grateful for the conversations, questions, and suggestions of Gord Heath, Hannah Lane, Elizabeth Mancke, Bonnie Huskins, Gwen Davies, Martin Sutherland, Derek Murray, Neil Allison, and Linda Wilson.
² Edward Manning Diary, January 2, 1821, Edward Manning Collection, Esther Clarke Wright Archives, Acadia University (Wolfville, Nova Scotia); hereafter cited as Manning Diary. A typed transcript of the diary, prepared by Freeman Fenerty, has been generously made available to me by the Esther Clarke Wright Archives. Like many nineteenth-century writers, Manning's spelling was idiosyncratic; rather than clutter the text with *sic*, quotations in this chapter will retain those misspellings, correcting them only when the meaning would otherwise be unclear.
³ Manning Diary, November 6, 1830.

he recorded, "I am melted to tears."[4] And of that quintessential evangelical biography, Jonathan Edwards's *Life of David Brainerd*, "O how many things brot tears from my eyes, and blushing in my face, and groans from my heart...."[5] Only a few volumes of Manning's library are extant, but one strongly suspects that were more to be found, many of them would be tear-stained.

What to do with all those tears? Such intense emotional responses to texts seem almost unthinkable to modern readers. Yet the frequency of Manning's tears suggests that feelings were not incidental to his reading, and a case can be made that neither was his experience merely idiosyncratic. Manning's tears, that is, have a history. Though it may be tempting to ignore them (to wipe them away, as it were), by making them comprehensible a story can be told that is at the intersection of the history of religion, the history of reading, and the history of emotions. Manning's tears are rendered less strange by observing that he was reading at an important juncture in the print and Protestantism; he experienced both the reading revolution and the expansion of evangelical missions, and his tears underline the emotional as well as the intellectual import of these changes.[6]

Two features of these overlapping stories of print and Protestantism contextualize Manning's demonstrative reading. First, with the proliferation of

---

[4] Manning Diary, April 22, 1834.

[5] Manning Diary, March 26, 1835.

[6] Tears have not been ignored by historians. See, for example, Anne Vincent-Buffault, *The History of Tears: Sensibility and Sentimentality in France*, trans. Teresa Bridgeman (New York: St. Martin's Press, 1991); Julie Ellison, *Cato's Tears and the Making of Anglo-American Emotion* (Chicago: University of Chicago Press, 1999); Thomas Dixon, "Weeping in Space: Tears, Feelings, and Enthusiasm in Eighteenth-Century Britain," in *Spaces for Feeling: Emotions and Sociabilities in Britain, 1650–1850*, ed. Susan Broomhall (New York: Routledge, 2015) 137–58; and Thomas Dixon, *Weeping Britannia: Portrait of a Nation in Tears* (Oxford: Oxford University Press, 2015); Bernard Capp, "'Jesus Wept' but Did the Englishman? Masculinity and Emotion in Early Modern England," *Past and Present* 224, no. 1 (2014): 75–108. On the changing vocabularies of "emotion" and allied concepts, see Thomas Dixon, *From Passions to Emotions: The Creation of a Secular Psychological Category* (Cambridge: Cambridge University Press, 2003) and Nicole Eustace, *Passion is the Gale: Emotion, Power, and the Coming of the American Revolution* (Chapel Hill: University of North Carolina Press, 2008) especially the appendix. On evangelicalism and emotion, see especially Phyllis Mack, *Heart Religion in the British Enlightenment: Gender and Emotion in Early Methodism* (Cambridge: Cambridge University Press, 2008).

new narrative genres during the later eighteenth and early nineteenth centuries, sentiment and sympathy in reading were, by turns, promoted and feared. This was as true of religious memoirs as it was of other kinds of "useful" biographies or sentimental novels. Second, the explosion of print media (especially periodicals) and the global expansion of the missionary movement were both overwhelmingly new experiences for nineteenth-century evangelical readers. The ascription of unparalleled eschatological significance to expanding missions and religious print freighted these experiences with powerful feelings.

A third context is suggested by Manning's location in British North America. Manning's teary reading of missionary biographies and news from colonial settings may offer hints about the emotional experience of the British Empire, of the feelings—such as attachment, sympathy, or difference—that structured what Emma Rothschild has called in another context, the "inner life of Empire."[7] Manning may also help us consider how subjects in white settler colonies, rather than the metropole, felt about colonization and empire.

Rather than focus on particular revivals, this chapter explores adjustments to the sentimental culture of Baptist churches, and evangelicalism more broadly, during their renewal and expansion in the early nineteenth century. Recent works by Abram Van Engen and Claudia Stokes have argued, respectively, that sentimental culture had deep roots in Puritan fellow-feeling, as well as in the more immediate religious transformations of Second Great Awakening revivalism.[8] This, then, is a study of the piety—the textual affections—shaped by revivalism and a revolution in reading. Attending to the lachrymose reading of Edward Manning of early nineteenth-century Cornwallis, Nova Scotia, is an attempt to render the history of ideas and the history of reading from the perspective of personal, deeply felt experience.

Edward Manning, the Reader

An analysis of Manning's reading is possible because his almost-daily

---

[7] Emma Rothschild, *The Inner Life of Empires: An Eighteenth-Century History* (Princeton: Princeton University Press, 2011).

[8] Abram C. Van Engen, *Sympathetic Puritans: Calvinist Fellow Feeling in Early New England* (Oxford: Oxford University Press, 2015); Claudia Stokes, *The Altar at Home: Sentimental Literature and Nineteenth-Century American Religion* (Philadelphia: University of Pennsylvania Press, 2014).

diary is extant for the second half of his long life, about 1810 to 1846.[9] There are approaching seven hundred diary entries about his reading, almost two hundred individual book titles, and hundreds of references to issues of at least thirty different periodicals. Though the Manning of his diary is an extensive reader, he was not always so. He was converted as a young man to the populist New Light Congregationalism of Henry Alline (1748–1784), that self-described "anti-traditionalist."[10] Manning's radical evangelical piety was made more so in the early 1790s, when some New Lights in the Maritime Provinces entered a hyper-subjective antinomian phase, decrying all outward forms. Manning himself declared that even "the Bible was a dead letter" and he would "preach without it."[11] As an itinerant in Maine in 1796, then thirty years old, a layman charged him with being an enthusiast whose preaching was "a jumble of words, not half articulated." Though his critic urged him to improve his gifts "by reading and study," one of Manning's peers bluntly countered, "No minister ever went to heaven that...received a liberal Education."[12]

Remarkably, by the time the diary picks up in 1810, Manning had undergone a series of linked transformations, embracing moderate Calvinist theology, a concern with order, and the necessity of a more learned ministry. He became the pastor of the Baptist church in the large, rural Cornwallis Township, where he would serve the rest of his life. Manning also participated in an extensive correspondence network throughout New England and the Maritime Provinces, including authors and publishers; he contributed regularly to

---

[9] On Manning, see Barry M. Moody, "Manning, Edward," in *Dictionary of Canadian Biography* (1985); and "From Itinerant to Pastor: The Case of Edward Manning (1767–1851)" *Historical Papers: Canadian Society of Church History* (1981); George A. Rawlyk, *The Canada Fire: Radical Evangelicalism in British North America, 1775–1812* (Montreal: McGill-Queen's University Press, 1994); Daniel C. Goodwin, *Into Deep Waters: Evangelical Spirituality and Maritime Calvinistic Baptist Ministers, 1790–1855* (Montreal: McGill-Queen's University Press, 2010); Julian Gwyn, "The King's County World of the Reverend Edward Manning to 1846," *Journal of the Royal Nova Scotia Historical Society* 16 (2013): 1–18.

[10] On Alline, see Rawlyk, *Canada Fire*; George A. Rawlyk, ed, *Henry Alline: Selected Writings*, Sources of American Spirituality (New York: Paulist Press, 1987); George A. Rawlyk, ed., *New Light Letters and Songs* (Hantsport: Lancelot Press, 1983); J. M. Bumsted, *Henry Alline* (Toronto: University of Toronto Press, 1971).

[11] Brian C. Cutherbertson, ed., *Journal of John Payzant* (Hantsport: Lancelot Press, 1981) 47.

[12] Stephen Jones to Edward Manning, October 31, 1796, Edward Manning Collection, Esther Clarke Wright Archives, Acadia University (Wolfville, Nova Scotia).

religious periodicals; and he was involved with the founding of schools that eventually became Colby College in Maine and Acadia University in Nova Scotia. The self-educated former enthusiast acquired a reputation as "a man of abilities and great reading." The piety he sought to cultivate was, as he once expressed it, "learned, and yet truly evangelical."[13]

"Holy Simpathy": Evangelical Sentiment and Emotional Self-Fashioning

Manning's tears are just the most dramatic instance of the role of affections and sentiment in his pious reading. Manning not only responded emotionally to texts; he also used his sympathetic reading—especially of biographies—as a means of emotional self-fashioning, aspiring to emulate the sentiments of the godly women and men he encountered on the page. His sympathetic reading reflects the importance of and the anxieties about the affections in Baptist culture, and of sentiment in the early nineteenth-century experience of reading.

Manning was "melted to tears" by reading, among many others, the memoirs of David Brainerd, Ann Judson, George Boardman, Heman Lincoln, and William Wilberforce. By far the most tears dropped onto the pages of the biography of his "favorite author," Andrew Fuller, and on Fuller's memoir of Samuel Pearce.[14] The religious biographies that Manning read were among the period's most popular, included in an informal canon of evangelical texts.[15] Biographies generally were ubiquitous in late eighteenth- and early

---

[13] Manning Diary, June 5 and July 10, 1823.

[14] Manning Diary, September 5, 1833 (Judson); April 22, 1834, and March 29, 1837 (Lincoln); March 26, 1835 (Brainerd); April 13, 1835 (Boardman); January 3, 1839 (Wilberforce); November 17 and December 7, 1821 (Fuller); January 22, 1822, and December 23, 1826 (Pearce).

[15] Candy Gunther Brown, *The Word in the World: Evangelical Writing, Publishing, and Reading in America 1789–1880* (Chapel Hill: University of North Carolina Press, 2004) 7–9, 88–95. See also Mary Kupiec Cayton, "Canonizing Harriet Newell: Women, the Evangelical Press, and the Foreign Mission Movement in New England, 1800–1840" in *Competing Kingdoms: Women, Mission, Nation, and the American Protestant Empire, 1812–1960*, ed. Barbara Reeves-Ellington, Kathryn Kish Sklar, and Connie Anne Shemo (Durham: Duke University Press, 2010) 69–93; Joan Jacobs Brumberg, *Mission for Life: The Judson Family and American Evangelical Culture* (New York: New York University Press, 1984) chap. 3. Nineteenth-century evangelical readers also continued to circulate many of the Protestant "steady sellers" of earlier generations; David D. Hall, *Cultures of Print: Essays in the History of the Book* (Amherst: University of Massachusetts Press, 1996) 61–68.

nineteenth-century print, and Scott Casper has demonstrated that most biographies published in the period from 1820 to 1860 were didactic in orientation. Memoirs of the great and the obscure were read to shape character and feeling, whether Republican virtue, female domestic sentiment, or evangelical affections.[16]

Sympathy was central to Manning's reading of these biographies, as he strongly identified with the circumstances—and feelings—of their subjects. Of David Brainerd, Manning wrote, "I feel much simpathy for him…I have experienced much of that gloom, and temptations he has experienced…. The feelings he endured…I have felt in my soul."[17] Of the memoirs of Samuel Pearce, he wrote, "I find so many things that I have experienced that I feel truly an affection for [him]"—an affection, he says, that "would warm me in Greenland, comfort me in New Zealand, and make me happy in the Valley of the Shadow of Death."[18] Manning found connections between his own biography and those he read, observing common trials, moments of pastoral transition, interest in the missionary cause, or even similarities in health complaints. Although Manning was certainly moved by extraordinary events or exceptional characters, he proposed that what made biographies "most useful" was "their plainness and simplicity, or being common to all Christians."[19] While reading an account of the missionaries in Burma, he declared simply, "My heart hath sympathized with them."[20] Manning not only sympathetically identified with the subjects of biographies—he aspired to emulate their affections. Reading the memoir of David Brainerd, Manning exclaimed, "O that I could feel as that dear man of God did!"[21] Identifying with the suffering of Samuel Pearce, Manning sought to regulate his feelings in a similar way: "O that I could feel the composure of Pierce, and feel the happiness he enjoyed."[22]

The teary-eyed Nova Scotian was reading at the trailing edge of what has been described as a culture of sensibility—a period during which affections and sentiments played a significant role in moral philosophy, polite society,

---

[16] Scott E. Casper, *Constructing American Lives: Biography and Culture in Nineteenth-Century America* (Chapel Hill: University of North Carolina Press, 1999).
[17] Manning Diary, March 25, 1835.
[18] Manning Diary, April 20, 1818.
[19] Manning Diary, December 6, 1821.
[20] Manning Diary, December 20, 1826.
[21] Manning Diary, March 25, 1835.
[22] Manning Diary, March 17, 1835.

and literature. Sympathy, in particular, indicated a person's capacity to imaginatively enter into another's circumstances. That the title of the first American novel was *The Power of Sympathy* indicates that Manning's reading with "holy simpathy" had its fictional counterpart. Novels, though conspicuously absent from mention in Manning's diary, joined biography as the period's other narrative genre for shaping sentiment.[23] Elizabeth Barnes summarizes the literary and emotional milieu: "Sympathetic identification emerges in the eighteenth century as the definitive way of reading literature and human relations."[24] It appears that Manning and fellow evangelicals read memoirs in the same way that some of their contemporaries read sentimental novels; they identified personally and sympathetically with the central characters, sought to imitate their virtues, cultivated their capacity for appropriate sentiment, and read these texts with intense emotions. As with the more didactic novels, readers of evangelical biographies sought both sentimental sanctification and readerly satisfaction. Rather than Manning's tears being idiosyncratic, his response of being "melted to tears" was, in the Puritan and sentimental traditions, "the highest form of reading."[25]

Yet Manning did question the religious nature of this sympathetic identification. He recorded one particularly heightened response to reading about Fuller's death: "My feelings have been wrought up to such a degree that I

---

[23] There is a large literature on the culture (or cult) of sensibility in eighteenth- and nineteenth-century Anglo-American society. Among the most helpful introductions are G. J. Barker-Benfield, *The Culture of Sensibility: Sex and Society in Eighteenth-Century Britain* (Chicago: University of Chicago Press, 1992) and Janet Todd, *Sensibility: An Introduction* (London: Methuen, 1986). Stokes, *Altar at Home*, and Van Engen, *Sympathetic Puritans*, assess literary scholarship on sentimental novels in relation to religious history. The canonical text for the sympathetic underpinnings of eighteenth-century moral philosophy is Adam Smith's *The Theory of Moral Sentiments*, ed. Knud Haakonssen (1759; Cambridge: Cambridge University Press, 2002) which begins by describing sympathy: "By the imagination we place ourselves in his situation, we conceive ourselves enduring all the same torments, we enter as it were into his body and become in some measure the same person with him" (12). William Hill Brown published *The Power of Sympathy* in 1789; for discussion, see Cathy N. Davidson, *Revolution and the Word: The Rise of the Novel in America*, 2nd ed. (Oxford: Oxford University Press, 2004) chap. 5.

[24] Elizabeth Barnes, *States of Sympathy: Seduction and Democracy in the American Novel* (New York: Columbia University Press, 1997) 2. The same theme is also present in the period's hymnody, as in this verse from John Fawcett's "Blest Be the Tie that Binds" (1782): "We share our mutual woes, // our mutual burdens bear, // and often for each other flows // the sympathizing tear." I am grateful to Derek Murray for suggesting this connection.

[25] Van Engen, *Sympathetic Puritans*, 172.

suppose 20 times I could scarcely contain myself." He reflected, "Surely this cannot be all religion, but a sort of sympathy. If it was real evangelical Religion, why not when I think of the Dying of the dear Lord Jesus."[26] Were his tears symptomatic of a religious inclination, or of some baser response of the passions? In his pious reading, Manning sought to cultivate what he called, "the holy sympathy the gospel produces in the poor soul," but he did worry about excessive or misplaced sympathy.[27]

Indeed, sentiment in late eighteenth- and early nineteenth-century print was contested terrain. Manning's occasional worries about excessive sympathy reflect wider concerns about readers' becoming too absorbed by sentimental novels. At its most extreme was the European phenomenon described as a "reading mania," or what Robert Darnton called an "epidemic of emotion," as readers were overwhelmed by sentiment in novels by Jean-Jacques Rousseau in France, and earlier by [Samuel] Richardson in England, or [Gotthold] Lessing in Germany. Readers had an "overwhelming desire to make contact with the lives behind the printed page," occasionally taking their sympathy and emulation to the point of obsession. The rise of sentimental fiction generated worries that reading novels encouraged a dangerous surplus of emotion ungoverned by reason. Others believed that the emotional satisfactions of escapist literature discouraged readers from attending to less fictional obligations.[28] And though it is not noticeably marked as such in Manning's diary, controversy over sentiment often had a gendered aspect. Manning more than exemplifies one of the period's ideal types, "The Man of Feeling," though even this

---

[26] Manning Diary, December 7, 1821.

[27] Manning Diary, March 30, 1835. At other times Manning worried that his reading was not feelingly sensible enough: "I think there is nothing in any publications that interests my feelings," Manning Diary, January 15, 1825.

[28] Robert Darnton, "Readers Respond to Rousseau: The Fabrication of Romantic Sensitivity," in *The Great Cat Massacre and Other Episodes in French Cultural History* (New York: Basic Books, 1984) 243–44; Reinhard Wittman, "Was There a Reading Revolution at the End of the Eighteenth Century?" in *A History of Reading in the West*, ed. Guglielmo Cavallo, Roger Chartier, and Lydia G. Cochrane (Amherst: University of Massachusetts Press, 1999) 295–301; James Van Horn Melton, *The Rise of the Public in Enlightenment Europe* (Cambridge: Cambridge University Press, 2001) 110–19. For general worries about sentimental fiction, see Davidson, *Revolution and the Word*, 110–20. For specifically evangelical critiques of novels (even as others employed sentimental forms for religious ends) see Brown, *Word in the World*, 95–105; Richard D. Altick, *The English Common Reader: A Social History of the Mass Reading Public, 1800–1900* (Columbus: Ohio State University Press, 1998) 108–24.

expression of feeling masculinity had to be cautious of supposed feminine excess.[29] Sympathetic and tearful Edward Manning, then, was not the only early nineteenth-century reader to use texts for emotional self-fashioning or to worry about excessive sympathy and tears while reading.

"General Illumination": Expanding Print, Expanding Missions

Missions literature also brought Manning to tears. In January of 1825 he wrote, "I spent the evening reading Baptist magazines and read out loud so that Mrs Manning and Mary might hear, and partake of the feast. O how many times I wept for joy, and I trust holy sympathy, with the many precious souls and in knowing what God is doing in our world."[30] Again, he records, "Received the American Baptist Missionary Magazine, 131st number. The conversion and suffering of the converted Jews at and near Constantinople, the conversion of two Buddhist priests at Celon, the 10th Anniversary of an Association in Connecticut…seems almost to overwhelm me."[31] At still another time, he briefly noted, "Read The Success of the Burman Mission, in the American B[aptis]t M[issionar]y M[agazi]ne, which melted me often to tears."[32] These, and many other instances, capture the intensely emotional experience of evangelicals interpreting the early decades of the missionary movement, and the sensations of readers encountering a flood of information through periodical literature. Manning gives us an individual perspective on the not coincidental overlap between a revolution in reading and the missionary expansion of the Second Great Awakening.

Manning's emotional experience of the dramatic expansion of missions

---

[29] Henry MacKenzie first published *The Man of Feeling* in 1771; for discussion, see Barker-Benfield, *Culture of Sensibility*, 141–48. Eustace, *Passion is the Gale*, 244–47, observes that tears *of sympathy* (rather than self-centered feelings) indicated a mature sensibility in both men and women. The essays in *Sentimental Men: Masculinity and the Politics of Affect in American Culture*, ed. Mary Chapman and Glenn Hendler (Berkeley: University of California Press, 1999) argue for the persistence of the "Man of Feeling" ideal into the nineteenth century and beyond. For general treatments of evangelicalism and masculinity, see Leonore Davidoff and Catherine Hall, *Family Fortunes: Men and Women of the English Middle Class, 1780–1850* (London: Hutchinson, 1987); and John Tosh, *A Man's Place: Masculinity and the Middle-Class Home in Victorian England* (New Haven: Yale University Press, 1999) and *Manliness and Masculinities in Nineteenth-Century Britain: Essays on Gender, Family and Empire* (London: Pearson Longman, 2005).
[30] Manning Diary, January 17, 1825.
[31] Manning Diary, January 3, 1828.
[32] Manning Diary, January 18, 1832.

cannot be separated from the concurrent explosion of print media, and especially the periodical press. It was, simply, an overwhelming time to be a reader. Historians, going back at least to Rolf Engelsing, have described this period as a reading revolution. Innovations in technology and transportation enabled the radical shift in print—from scarcity to abundance. Readers like Manning had access to books and periodicals on a scale unimaginable even a single generation earlier.[33] Missionary magazines and memoirs were central to the expansion of the religious periodical press; while this story has been well told from the perspective of publishers and tract agencies, Manning's record of reading these missionary periodicals captures the novelty and emotional impact of both the missionary message and the periodical medium.[34] "Am much taken," he writes, "with the American Baptist M. Magazines, 105, 106, 107, and 108th No[s.]!"[35] Again: "Employed this day principally in reading the American M[issionary] Magazine, and truly it has been a feast to me."[36] Or simply, "The A[merican] B[aptist] Magazine. Surely the Lord is doing wonders in our world."[37]

Yet abundance introduced new reading anxieties. Manning's entry for January 15, 1825, describes his usual pleasure in reading the latest missionary news: "Read almost all day the magazines lately come to hand. Surely it hath been a feast to my soul to read of...Carey, Ward, Judson.... The account of the success of the gospel among the Aborigines of America.... The experience of the African. All good." But then he admitted, "I fear I have not read my Bible enough, nor prayed enough. I fear I am too much delighted with other

---

[33] For discussion and critique of Engelsing's *Leserevolution* (reading revolution) thesis, see Robert Darnton, *The Kiss of Lamourette: Reflections in Cultural History* (New York: Norton, 1990) 165–67; Hall, *Cultures of Print*, 184–87; Davidson, *Revolution and the Word*, 141–42; Leah Price, "Reading: The State of the Discipline," *Book History* 7 (2004): 303–20; Wittman, "Was There a Reading Revolution," 284–312. Daniel Walker Howe, *What Hath God Wrought: The Transformation of America, 1815–1848*, Oxford History of the United States (New York: Oxford University Press, 2007) chap. 6 discusses a wider "communications revolution" in this period.

[34] On the expanding evangelical print culture of the late eighteenth and early nineteenth centuries, see Brown, *Word in the World*; David Paul Nord, *Faith in Reading: Religious Publishing and the Birth of Mass Media in America* (Oxford: Oxford University Press, 2004); Nathan O. Hatch, *The Democratization of American Christianity* (New Haven: Yale University Press, 1989) chap. 5.

[35] Manning Diary, December 28, 1825.
[36] Manning Diary, September 29/30, 1823.
[37] Manning Diary, April 4, 1829.

publications, and not enough with the Bible."[38] This was a frequent concern, and on another occasion he wrote, "Am much pleased with the magazines. I fear I read them more than I ought, because while reading them and other books, the Bible, the best of Books is neglected."[39] Manning worried that his delight in the steady stream of missionary periodicals was a distraction from more necessary reading. His was a particularly religious version of the problem of abundance. Engelsing's classic formulation of the reading revolution argues that the shift from scarcity to abundance entailed a concomitant change in styles of literacy, from "intensive" to "extensive" reading. Rather than read a small number of (often religious) texts repeatedly, readers consumed more texts, but less attentively. If the worry about novels was too much sentiment, the worry about the expansion of print was that there was simply too much to read—or, as Ann Blair said of an earlier period, there was too much to know.[40] It could be difficult for readers like Manning to regulate both their time and their emotional preoccupations with so much reading on offer.

Manning's experience, however, supports the historiographic reconsideration of the idea of a reading revolution. His reading, after all, was nothing if not intense, and exhibited many characteristics of what David Hall has called "traditional" literacy—rereading, emotional identification, sociability, and devotional ends. Manning appears to have adapted "intensive" strategies of reading to the "extensive" conditions of nineteenth-century print culture, applying that traditional style of reading to new genres, such as memoirs and missionary periodicals.[41] His reading bears witness to continuities in literacy and evangelical devotion, as well as adaptation and change.

Manning's tears also had a theological context. He wept because he perceived the events he read about to have unparalleled theological significance, interpreting them in a frame of optimistic millenarian eschatology. For Manning, news of Burmese missions, widespread Bible distribution, the success of the temperance movement, or nearby revivals was signs of spiritual progress,

---

[38] Manning Diary, January 15, 1825.
[39] Manning Diary, July 26, 1822.
[40] Ann Blair, *Too Much to Know: Managing Scholarly Information before the Modern Age* (New Haven: Yale University Press, 2010).
[41] See Darnton, "Readers Respond," 250–51; Hall, *Cultures of Print*, 184–87.

portending the millennium.[42] Reading of such developments in the *American Baptist Missionary Magazine*, Manning declared, "Those missionary exertions and the Bible Societies and other similar institutions equally benevolent will be owned and blessed of God for the introduction of [the] Millennial State and Glory."[43] Manning described this millennial progress as "general illumination," a term that signals the importance of knowledge, and by extension, print, to Manning's millennial optimism.[44] "Knowledge" was critical; the successes of God's kingdom were not just to happen, but also to *be known*. "Knowledge," Manning optimistically declared, "generally is increasing."[45] It is difficult to overstate how instrumental print was to missions, reform, and revivals. But reading and print per se also had missionary and eschatological significance as the means of general illumination—a significance compounded in experience by the rapid expansion of the religious periodical press. Freighted with such theological meaning, it is not so extraordinary that the arrival of the magazines caused Manning to weep for joy and to be melted to tears.

Imperial Emotions? Feelings and the Experience of Empire

Manning's sentimental reading also raises questions about the emotional and religious experience of empire and colonization. What does his response to missionary news from India tell us about the long-distance encounter with the Other? Did British North Americans feel differently about imperial expansion than those closer to the metropole? How did Manning's location in a white settler colony shape his sympathy for non-white fellow subjects or his sense of connection to metropolitan Britons? Were there "imperial emotions?"[46] How did religious feelings subvert or inadvertently coincide with imperial affections? How did citizens of British North America perceive the place of American missionaries across the globe? Manning's record of reading

---

[42] David W. Bebbington, *Evangelicalism in Modern Britain: A History from the 1730s to the 1980s* (Grand Rapids: Baker, 1989; 1992) 62, 81–86.

[43] Manning Diary, April 29, 1818.

[44] Manning Diary, November 29, 1824.

[45] Manning Diary, July 29, 1825.

[46] The phrase is from Jane Haggis and Margaret Allen, "Imperial Emotions: Affective Communities of Mission in British Protestant Women's Missionary Publications c. 1880–1920," *Journal of Social History* 41, no. 3 (2008): 691–716.

does not definitively settle these questions, but his experience does affirm that they are worth asking.

Reading the outpouring of missionary literature was the primary means of "bringing the Empire home."[47] British subjects—like Manning—who had no access to official imperial communications or who did not directly participate in global trade experienced the expansion of the British Empire as "missionary intelligence." Susan Thorne observes that through its extensive print culture, the missionary movement "encouraged Victorian evangelicals to think about colonized people on a regular basis"; most of what evangelicals knew of the colonies and their inhabitants they learned from the pages of missionary periodicals.[48] It is striking how much Manning, a largely self-educated reader, living in rural, provincial Nova Scotia, came to know and care about events in India and Burma. Benedict Anderson has influentially argued that expanding print made it possible for readers to see themselves as abstracted participants in a common national project—members of an "imagined community."[49] Missionary periodicals—as one religious variety of print—helped readers to imagine, or perhaps feel, their connections in that global community.

Manning recorded in his diary that "Reading the Intelligence from Burmah…tend[ed] to excite various immotions."[50] Indeed, with an imperial context in mind, at least three kinds of tears can be identified: tears of sympathy, tears of pity, and tears of grateful belonging—together suggesting that the experience of empire was complex and deeply felt. First, Manning sympathetically identified with the evangelical work and personal suffering of the missionaries he read about. Their experiences elicited powerful, tearful responses: "I was so overcome that it was with much difficulty that I could keep from crying out loud; from tears I could not."[51] Despite the many differences between Burma and British North America, Manning felt connected: "Have

---

[47] Susan Thorne, "Religion and Empire at Home" in *At Home with the Empire: Metropolitan Culture and the Imperial World*, ed. Catherine Hall and Sonya O. Rose (Cambridge: Cambridge University Press, 2006) 146.

[48] Thorne, "Religion and Empire at Home," 144, 154; Elizabeth Elbourne, *Blood Ground: Colonialism, Missions, and the Contest for Christianity in the Cape Colony and Britain, 1799–1853* (Montreal and Kingston: McGill-Queen's University Press, 2002) 14.

[49] Benedict Anderson, *Imagined Communities: Reflections on the Origin and Spread of Nationalism*, rev. ed. (London: Verso, 1983; 2006).

[50] Manning Diary, January 2, 1821.

[51] Manning Diary, November 6, 1830.

been reading the sufferings of the missionaries in Burmah. My heart hath sympathized with them."[52] Manning often compared his work with that of missionaries, or imagined a younger self engaging in that vaunted overseas task.[53] As with other varieties of eighteenth- and nineteenth-century benevolence and humanitarianism, sympathy underpinned participation in the missionary movement.[54] It was sympathy that drew Manning feelingly close to far-flung places and peoples.

As Laura Stevens has observed, however, missionary texts, written to confirm eschatological expectations and to raise support, tended to place Anglo-American missionaries—rather than indigenous inhabitants—at the center of their narratives, and therefore as the primary objects of sympathy.[55] So while he wept tears of sympathy for the missionaries, Manning also, secondly, cried in pity for the Burmese or Indian people. "Why," he wrote, "do [we] not feel more for the heathen, buried in horrible idolatry[?]"[56] Pity, compared with sympathy, is a feeling borne of a perceived imbalance of power or knowledge—a feeling of difference, rather than identification.[57]

Note, for example the combination of melting affection and superiority in Manning's diary entry for October 3, 1834: "This day rec'd the A[merican] B[aptist] Magazine for September, and am much affected with the acc't of the success of the missionaries in Burmah.... O how shocking, and how horrible

---

[52] Manning Diary, December 20, 1826.

[53] See, for examples, Manning Diary, April 20, 1818; February 1, 1820; December 1, 1824; September 13, 1831; April 13, 1835.

[54] On sympathy and humanitarianism, see Smith, *Theory of Moral Sentiments*; Laura M. Stevens, *The Poor Indians: British Missionaries, Native Americans, and Colonial Sensibility* (Philadelphia: University of Pennsylvania Press, 2006); Norman S. Fiering, "Irresistible Compassion: An Aspect of Eighteenth-Century Sympathy and Humanitarianism," *Journal of the History of Ideas* 37, no. 2 (1976): 195–218; Tony Ballantyne, *Entanglements of Empire: Missionaries, Māori, and the Question of the Body* (Durham: Duke University Press, 2014) chap. 6; Karen Halttunen, "Humanitarianism and the Pornography of Pain in Anglo-American Culture," *American Historical Review* 100, no. 2 (1995): 303–34. On the limits and contradictions of such sentiment in actually enacting humanitarianism, especially abolition, see Christopher L. Brown, *Moral Capital: Foundations of British Abolitionism* (Chapel Hill: University of North Carolina Press, 2006) chap. 1.

[55] Stevens, *Poor Indians*, esp. 7–22. See also Edward Said, *Orientalism* (London: Penguin, 1977); Haggis and Allen, "Imperial Emotions."

[56] Manning Diary, November 10, 1838.

[57] Stevens, *Poor Indians*, 7–8.

is heathen idolatry. It melted me to tears today to think of our superior privileges. O that tears of gratitude might often swell."[58] Sincere feelings did not entirely overcome the implicit assumptions of difference between Anglo-American missionaries and colonial subjects.

That same diary entry also identifies a third category of imperial tears: "tears of gratitude" for "our superior privileges." It may be that reading helped Nova Scotians feel more closely tied to Britain, belonging to something larger. The reading of missionary periodicals gave Manning and other British North Americans (and provincials in places like Edinburgh and Manchester) a common textual and emotional experience that helped them feel themselves to be full participants in the British Empire, aligned sentimentally with the metropole.[59] Manning's sympathy, however, did not neatly coordinate with British nationalism, since American missionaries as often moved him as by their British counterparts. Readers like Manning experienced missionary and imperial expansion as interwoven, but not identical, narratives. From his location in Nova Scotia, Manning participated in a transnational community—an evangelical community with missionary goals and an eschatological (rather than strictly imperial) interpretation of global events. It was a textual community mediated by the reading of missionary periodicals. And it was an emotional community knit together by pity (for the "heathen"), by sympathy (for

---

[58] Manning Diary, October 3, 1834.

[59] See Stevens, *Poor Indians*, 14. For the role of print to mediate a distinctive version of provincial British identity, see Michael Eamon, *Imprinting Britain: Newspapers, Sociability, and the Shaping of British North America* (Montreal and Kingston: McGill-Queen's University Press, 2015); Linda E. Connors and Mary Lu MacDonald, *National Identity in Great Britain and British North America, 1815–1851: The Role of Nineteenth-Century Periodicals* (Farnham: Ashgate, 2011). Catherine Hall, *Civilising Subjects: Metropole and Colony in the English Imagination, 1830–1867* (Chicago: University of Chicago Press, 2002) among others, has urged reconsideration of how colonization *and* missionary activity affected the metropole, but less attention has been given to how those same expansionist activities have affected mostly white settler colonies (like Nova Scotia)—which fell ambiguously between the metropole and other colonies. Also see Hilary M. Carey, *God's Empire: Religion and Colonialism in the British World, c.1801–1908* (Cambridge: Cambridge University Press, 2011). For a helpful overview of the place of British North America in the historiography of Britain and the British Empire, see Nancy Christie, "Introduction: Theorizing a Colonial Past: Canada as a Society of British Settlement," in *Transatlantic Subjects: Ideas, Institutions, and Social Experience in Post-Revolutionary British North America*, ed., Nancy Christie (Montreal and Kingston: McGill-Queen's University Press, 2008) 3–41.

missionaries), and by the shared experience of tears.[60]

Conclusion

Studying Edward Manning's reading through his diary, we might observe, as Robert Darnton did of readers of Rousseau's *Nouvelle Héloïse*, that "one is struck everywhere by the sound of sobbing."[61] It is difficult for modern readers to recover this experience of reading. Yet the strangeness of Manning's intense emotional encounter with texts is far more understandable in the context of the reading revolution and the evangelical and Baptist piety of the nineteenth century. His tearful reading is less idiosyncratic when considered alongside the period's hopes and fears about sentimental fiction and sympathetic biographies. Manning offers a reader's experience of the novelty of missionary expansion and the overwhelming abundance of periodical print. His emotions were rooted in an optimistic, eschatological interpretation of missions and expanding print, and they give us some clues about the role of feelings in the lived experience of empire. It turns out that tears and feelings, as well as ideas, shaped the culture of the Protestant Atlantic in which Manning participated.

---

[60] The idea of a "textual community" is found in Brown, *Word in the World*, esp. 9–14. The concept of "emotional communities" draws on Barbara H. Rosenwein, *Emotional Communities in the Early Middle Ages* (Ithaca: Cornell University Press, 2006). See also Susan Broomhall, introduction to *Spaces for Feeling: Emotions and Sociabilities in Britain, 1650–1850*, ed. Susan Broomhall (New York: Routledge, 2015) 1–2; and Van Engen, *Sympathetic Puritans*, 4. Stevens, *Poor Indians*, 198 (and elsewhere) explores how early missionary texts provided readers with "an affective basis for the building of transatlantic communal ties," as feelings of sympathy, pity, and belonging were transferred from religious to imperial communities. Ballantyne, *Entanglements of Empire*, 27, argues that rather than oppose or conflate imperial and missionary activity the latter should be seen "*within* an imperial framework," but is not the whole picture.

[61] Darnton, "Readers Respond," 242. See also, Vincent-Buffault, *The History of Tears*, 10–14.

Chapter 8

The Mission of Isabel Crawford: Applying the Pattern of Revival

Marilyn Färdig Whiteley

When Isabel Crawford was ten years old, she attended a prayer meeting in the Baptist church in Woodstock, Ontario. During the meeting, all those who wanted to be Christians were invited to stand. The service was a special one, and this was the first time that Crawford had heard such an invitation. Nearly twenty years later she wrote, "To everyone's astonishment I arose & was surprised that every sinner didn't stand up." She continued, "After a while I was converted & applied for baptism but was put off from week to week in order to give the deacons a chance to watch me."[1]

They watched her because she was a lively child and, by her own account, "the terror of the town."[2] She explained,

> I learned enough history to know that my relatives were all well educated and prided themselves on their blue blood; enough geography to be in unknown quarters when there was music or a French lesson on the breeze; enough arithmetic to calculate by distance when I was forbidden to be on the street and caught sight of my mother turning the corner; enough grammar to puzzle strangers who couldn't reconcile such good English with such bad behaviour; enough music to alarm every living

---

[1] Notebook Illinois, clipping "Sketch of Miss Crawford's Life." The writings of Isabel Crawford are found in the Isabel Crawford Collection of the denominational archives of the American Baptist Historical Society (ABHS). The collection includes Crawford's journals and diaries from 1891 through 1948 as well as one unlabelled journal from 1954. In addition, the collection contains notebooks, generally three–ring binders. Any footnote that does not include another specific reference is from the Isabel Crawford Collection of the ABHS. Each note gives the name of the book (e.g., Journal 1902) followed by whatever specific location is provided; sometimes the date of the entry is available, sometimes the page number(s) and sometimes both.

[2] Isabel Crawford, *Joyful Journey* (Philadelphia: Judson, 1951) 54.

creature within sound, and enough physiology to know that I was in perfect health.[3]

Even when her request was being considered, young Isabel showed her independent spirit:

> At last I was sent into the anti-room [sic] to await the decision of the church. I walked in one door & round to another and opened it & sat down & listened & saw everything that was done.
> One good brother said he knew I was pretty lively but he believed the grace of God could do anything for me. Another brother said he had been watching me & he did think at first that there was a change but he didn't know—
> Poor old "Grandma Birtch" then arose & said—
> "Brothers & Sisters I hain't done much watchin' but I've done considerable talkin' & I'm satisfied that Bella is a converted girl & I move she be received."
> The motion was seconded & I saw the deacons & one other man who didn't vote.[4]

Crawford was baptized about two months before her eleventh birthday, but then she had a new concern, that of "falling from grace." She wrote, "I simply couldn't sit up and be good, and say verses in a class any longer. I had to be up and doing."[5] And so, three months after her baptism, she volunteered to teach Sunday school, partly out of newfound Christian zeal and partly from the fear that she would misbehave if she continued to attend her old class. A member of her church had begun a Sunday school mission in a poor section of Woodstock, but he was understandably skeptical about the capabilities of an eleven-year-old. When he told her that the school already had enough teachers, she persisted: "'How about seats?' [she] asked. 'Have you any empty ones? If so, I can fill them.'" And so the next Sunday she arrived with a small class of boys about her own age, "the toughest looking urchins ever to enter a Sunday school."[6] She continued to add students to the class; many of them older than she, and both Crawford and the class thrived. Thus, at age eleven, Isabel Crawford had experienced conversion, a period of surveillance, baptism,

---

[3] Notebook Illinois, clipping "Sketch of Miss Crawford's Life."
[4] Journal 1893–94, 10. This is how Crawford's dialogue appears in her journal.
[5] Isabel Crawford, *A Jolly Journal* (New York: Revell, 1932) 35.
[6] Journal 1942–43, 20.

and Christian activity, a pattern that remained her model for the rest of her life.

Isabel Crawford was born on May 26, 1865, in Cheltenham, Ontario, north of Toronto. Both of her parents were Irish, and they had immigrated to Canada a few years earlier. Isabel's father, John Crawford, was a Baptist preacher, and when Isabel was three, the family moved to Woodstock, Ontario, where her father taught in the theology department of the Canadian Literary Institute. In 1880, he founded his own school, Prairie College, in Rapid City, Manitoba. Hoping to train Baptist ministers for the western prairies, the family moved west. The school closed after three years, and John took a pastorate in St. Thomas, North Dakota, leaving Isabel and her mother to help close the college. During this time, Isabel became seriously ill. She spent six months in bed with pain and fever. Finally, she recovered, but the quinine that she credited with saving her life also took away most of her hearing.

Isabel spent the next seven years with her parents in North Dakota and the eight months after that in Wingham, Ontario, where her father held a pastorate. Then he retired, and her parents went to live with one of their two married daughters. Now Isabel was no longer needed as a companion and help to her parents. As she put it, she had "a life that had to be placed somewhere," and she decided to become a missionary. So, at the age of twenty-eight, she headed to Chicago to the Baptist Missionary Training School.

The courses and fieldwork at the training school occupied most of Crawford's time, but she also took advantage of the opportunities offered by the city. One evening she attended meetings led by Dwight Moody. His appearance surprised her: "Instead of seeing a nice, gentlemanly, neat man with a winning face I beheld a person measuring about 100 inches round where the waist ought to be, medium height, coat open & flapping, full grayish frizzy beard & moustache, very thick red lips, & a penetrating dark eye. This was the great Dwight Lyman Moody." [7] She was also surprised at the "off hand way" in which he conducted the meeting, but afterwards she wrote, "I returned home feeling that I had seen one of the greatest men the world has ever known."[8]

Another day, she visited the Board of Trade, where grains and grain fu-

---

[7] Journal 1891–93, 87.
[8] Journal 1891–93, 91.

tures were bought and sold. From the visitors' gallery, she watched the merchants shout their orders and the telegraph boys rush about. In her journal she wrote, "I never want to hear another word against revival meeting excitement, from a person of the world, for I have been at genuine old time Methodist revivals & Salvation Army camp meetings but never have I witnessed anything that would begin to compare with the excitement at the Board of Trade May 21 1892."[9] This is the only indication in her writing that she was acquainted with more enthusiastic revival practices, and for her, the quieter call to conversion that she had experienced remained the norm.

Following Isabel Crawford's graduation in 1893, the Women's Baptist Home Mission Society assigned her to work among the Kiowas in southwestern Oklahoma. She arrived at Elk Creek in November of 1893. Although she made some progress at Elk Creek, she was frustrated. A Baptist missionary couple also served the small group of Kiowas there, while larger Kiowa camps had no one to bring them the gospel. Thus after two and a half years, and before receiving permission from the women's board, Crawford accepted the invitation of the Kiowa chief at Saddle Mountain to go there—alone—to open a new mission.

In her journal, Crawford described her first meeting at Saddle Mountain. Twenty-five people sat under the shelter of two wagon sheets held up by six poles. Crawford asked: "Are there any Christians here?" No one responded. "Are there any who would like to give up the old roads and let the Holy Spirit teach the new?" At this, two men raised their hands, and the younger spoke: "Some Indians say when they are baptized that they bury all their bad roads and then they pick them up again and go off with them. I don't want to be that kind. I want to be a white-man Christian."[10] The speaker was Lucius Aitsan. He had been educated at the Carlisle Indian Industrial School in Pennsylvania and had worked as an interpreter for several missionaries. But he had not been converted, and he wanted to know more about Christianity.

Aitsan learned and was converted. He and his wife were the first to be baptized at Saddle Mountain, and Crawford had no doubts that their conversion was genuine. But as time went on she probably developed a greater appreciation of the quandary facing the deacons in Woodstock, Ontario.

The Kiowas to whom she brought "the Jesus road" were not children,

---

[9] Journal 1891–93, May 21, 1892, 34.
[10] Isabel Crawford, *Kiowa: The History of a Blanket Indian Mission* (New York: Revell, 1915) 24.

but the Christian message was new to them. They were in a period of transition. Bison no longer roamed the prairies, and the former hunters had been forced to live on a reservation where they were expected to take up farming. Agriculture was not central to their tradition, and the land assigned them was ill suited to the crops for which they were given seeds. The government's solution was to pay them allotments, but when the people gathered to receive their payments, many were tempted to gamble. After one such gathering Crawford wrote, "My heart was sickened by seeing the professing Christians gambling but it is just what we must expect. They come forward at camp meetings & are baptized some of them confessing their sins before they are converted I fear & then they go back to their camps without more instruction & naturally are tempted more than they can stand and fall."[11]

After she had moved to Saddle Mountain, Crawford went back to her former mission to attend a camp meeting. Lone Wolf was a chief at Elk Creek. Crawford wrote, "Lone Wolf at last asked for baptism & when I made the motion to receive him at Bro Hicks request I trembled from head to foot. What if he isn't really converted after all, but scheming for power! We can't be divine however & know the hearts of the people. His testimonies [sic] all along have been that of a Christian but his life in many ways seems schemy [sic]. He's a born schemer anyhow & the Lord only can fathom his heart."[12]

Crawford returned to Saddle Mountain after the meetings, so she could not nurture Lone Wolf in the faith. At her own mission, however, she sought to do more than just lead people to conversion: she continued to teach them what they needed to follow "the Jesus road." And just as she had put herself to work after her conversion and baptism, she formed the new Christians into a mission society. The men as well as women made quilts that they sold when people from many camps gathered to receive their allotments. The money went toward establishing a mission on the Hopi Indian reservation in Arizona and toward building a church at Saddle Mountain. Thus Crawford followed the model with which she was familiar, holding services with a call to conversion, expressing concern about whether those who claimed it were truly converted, and putting the baptized converts to work in addition to teaching them to walk "the Jesus road."

---

[11] Journal 1896–97, 116–17.
[12] Journal 1896–97, July 22, 1896, 120.

Crawford's work was highly successful, but in 1906, a controversy caused her to leave Saddle Mountain.[13] The women's board then assigned Crawford to do deputations work from coast to coast. Early in 1914 she was appointed general missionary in the eastern part of the state of Washington. At Easter she observed, "I came up yesterday to help in evangelistic meetings.... I did a little visiting, talked & prayed with some of the young people *in their homes* but when it came to going round urging people to come forward in the meetings the Holy Spirit did not lead me on. That is not my line of work. Some are called to be evangelist & others to something else, and the master unites the different efforts & brings his own results."[14] In all of Crawford's writing this statement is unique in articulating her understanding of her relationship to traditional revival evangelism.

Around this time, Crawford witnessed the revival preaching of Billy Sunday for the first time. She did not hear him preach: she only saw him, for no "seats anywhere near the front were to be secured for love or money."[15] Three years later saw him again. This time she observed, "The more I hear him the more I glory in his clear grit."[16] From further comments, clippings, and quotations in her journal it is clear that Crawford developed an admiration for Sunday, even though the former baseball player's colloquial style was considerably different from her own.

There was not enough work in eastern Washington to require a full-time missionary, so soon Crawford returned to deputation work, though she found it tiring and less satisfying. Thus late in 1915, Crawford was delighted to be assigned to service on four reservations in western New York State. Crawford recognized that this would be different from Oklahoma. The Kiowas in Oklahoma had been in a difficult period of transition when Crawford arrived there, and some of their leaders recognized the potential of Christianity to help negotiate this transition. In contrast, missionaries had been among the Senecas and Tuscaroras in New York from early years. Crawford wrote that

---

[13] In the absence of a pastor, Crawford explained to the congregation that the Lord's Supper belonged to the church, and they could select one of their number to administer the Supper. Her supervisors took exception to her action. For a full description of the controversy, see Marilyn Färdig Whiteley, *The Life of Isabel Crawford: More Than I Asked For* (Eugene, OR: Wipf & Stock, 2015) chap. 6.

[14] Journal 1914–15, April 12, 1914, 14–15.

[15] Journal 1913–14, 154.

[16] Journal 1916–17, April 15, 1917, 54.

they "had heard so much *more* about *other things* & had seen civilization dominated by these other things that had it not been for the Holy Spirit in their own hearts, they would have supposed that the gospel was a mere fad with some of the white people & not a reality with any but the preachers."[17] The problem now was that there were a number of nominal Christians and a number of churches, but very little preaching, nurture, and pastoral care.

Although these New York circumstances differed from those in Oklahoma, in January Crawford undertook a familiar and comfortable task: she participated in "special meetings" on the Tonawanda reservation. She wrote, "From house to house we went nearly every day for two weeks, singing & praying & exhorting.... I was thrilled through & through to the heart in witnessing such evidences of the working of the Spirit in lives which were all but snowed under."[18] In March, special meetings were held on the Cattaraugus reservation, although, she observed, "It was a season of refreshing rather than of conversions!"[19]

Times of "refreshing rather than conversions" were common on these reservations where the gospel had first been proclaimed many decades earlier, although some participants in these services experienced conversion. In February of 1918 Crawford wrote,

> The meetings are over. Every day from 5 to 8 Indian men have tramped the reservation from door to door, reading the Bible, praying, singing & exhorting in every home. 83 homes were visited. 13 backsliders reclaimed & 10 professed conversion.... Every night there were meetings in the church well attended & full of inspiration.[20]

Crawford continued her report: "Do not think for a moment that I took the lead in this evangelistic effort for I did not. The Indians have their own good way of conducting the affairs of their church & all I did was to let it be known that I would always be ready to help in any way they wanted me to. The Canadian Tuscaroras plan to hold their special services at Easter time & then it will be our Tuscaroras turn to go over & help them as they have helped us."[21]

At Saddle Mountain, Isabel Crawford had worked to teach the Kiowa

---

[17] Journal 1915–16, November 17, 1915, 6.
[18] Journal 1915–16, January 8–21, 1916, 21.
[19] Journal 1915–16, March 26–April 10, 1916, 69.
[20] Journal 1917–18, February 4, 1918, 56.
[21] Journal 1917–18, February 4, 1918, 59.

Christians self-reliance. Here she affirmed the Native Americans' initiative in revival work. There was, however, one native man on the Allegany reservation whose initiative she found dangerous. This was Fillmore Jackson, a Baptist supply pastor with no theological training. Crawford shared Jackson's enthusiasm for revival but not his belief regarding what should happen next. He preached that baptism was necessary for salvation: people could not be saved without it. Crawford was confident in her understanding of the Baptist principles that she had learned from her pastor-father and at the training school; she disagreed with Jackson. For her, belief, not baptism, was crucial. Furthermore, she saw this as no abstract theological point. Jackson was rushing people into baptism before they were truly converted, before they "believed," and then they were left to flounder.

In February 1919, Crawford spoke at an evening service. Jackson expected to perform baptisms, but Crawford cautioned those present. She stated,

> Jesus is our example in all things. He was immersed when he was a grown man & knew what He was doing. He commanded all of his followers to obey Him in this & everything else. He saved the poor converted thief without baptism to teach us that it was not necessary to salvation…. Is it right to hurry people into the Church teaching them what Jesus never taught, that baptism would save them? Many Indians & white people who have come up to the front *for prayers* have been pulled into the churches unconverted & unprepared meet their God. This is not right and I do ask you to be careful tonight in all that you do. The business is not *yours*, but *His*. You are only His agent, so do try to be careful. I was not baptized for six months after I was converted & how thankful I am today that the Church was faithful in being careful.[22]

No baptisms were administered.

Crawford wanted churches to be careful, as her Baptist church in Woodstock, Ontario, had been careful. She wanted lapsed Christians to be refreshed and then nurtured in their faith, and she wanted new Christians to be both trained and observed before they entered the church. Her labour on four reservations and her speaking assignments away from the reservations kept her on the move, but she worked when she could to provide the nurture she felt was needed. At the church near which she had her room and board, she held

---

[22] Journal 1919, February 21, 1919, 18–19. "Six months" does not correspond with Crawford's other statements about her baptism.

a Sunday afternoon Bible school for children, and she turned the Sunday morning service into a Bible class for adults.

The situation with Fillmore Jackson, however, became more difficult. At a week of "special meetings" in March of 1921, Jackson took a leadership role, and things quickly went awry. As the meetings proceeded, Crawford found herself receiving instructions from Jackson, delivered by the sexton, and the newly elected deacon took her secondary place in leadership. She was permitted to speak at the final meeting only when the program committee insisted on it.[23]

After the services had ended, Crawford requested a meeting of the missionary committee. The meeting ended with support for Crawford, but soon she realized that the chairman of the missionary committee had "backed down," and the resolutions passed at the meeting had not gone forward for signing.[24] Greatly discouraged, she resigned from the work on the New York reservations and returned to life on the road, visiting churches and making presentations to inspire her hearers with the importance of the missionary task. She continued to do deputation work for nine years, until her retirement in 1930.

Crawford settled in Florida. So long as she was able, she taught a Sunday school class and retained her interest in evangelism using the pattern of revival that she had known since childhood. In February of 1940, Crawford traveled around Florida with one friend and with her niece, Eva Cline, who had come to Florida to visit Crawford. At Okeechobee they met Willie King, a Baptist missionary. He made them welcome, and with him they went to a Seminole encampment. King began holding a service and then turned it over to Crawford, who gave "a simple gospel message."[25] After an Indian dinner and a hearty invitation to return, the travelers left for home. Early on the morning of Easter Sunday, April 13, the three headed back to the Okeechobee area. Willie King was waiting for them, and the Seminoles were ready. When the congregation was assembled, each of the three visitors spoke. Crawford wrote later, "No Indians responded but the promise of the Holy Spirit's power must follow the Word!" Crawford would not be present to follow up the evangelistic preaching, but she retained the hope that Willie King would witness the

---

[23] Journal 1920–21, March 21, 1921, 126.
[24] Journal 1920–21, April 27, 1921, 161–62.
[25] Journal 1940–41, February 16, 1940, 58.

next stages of revival. Returning home she wrote, "It was a long drive but if one poor Seminole finds the resurrection light we felt it was worthwhile."[26]

In April of 1942, Crawford moved back to Ontario, to spend the rest of her days with two nieces. She died on November 18, 1961, at the age of ninety-six. As a child, Isabel Crawford had waited impatiently to be accepted for baptism after her conversion at a revival. As a missionary, she continued to use the familiar revival pattern of conversion, a period of surveillance, baptism, and Christian activity. As a child, Crawford chaffed at how slow the deacons in Woodstock, Ontario, had been to acknowledge that she had been truly converted, but as a missionary she came to understand their wisdom.

---

[26] Journal 1940–41, April 13, 1940, 68.

Part 2

Europe

9

Andrew Fuller and the Revival of Eighteenth-Century Particular Baptist Life

Peter Morgan

Andrew Fuller (1754–1815) was arguably the foremost English Baptist minister of his generation. Although he spent the whole of his career as a local church pastor, firstly at Soham, Cambridgeshire (1775–1782) and then at Kettering, Northamptonshire (1782–1815), he also exercised a wider and extremely influential ministry as a theologian, apologist, and missionary statesman. He was a central figure in the "profound revitalization" of English Calvinistic (or "Particular") Baptist life, which took place during the final decades of the eighteenth century.[1] This "Revival"[2] was characterized by evangelical theological commitments, lively biblical exposition, close friendships between like-minded ministers, a stress on corporate intercessory prayer, vigorous evangelism, and, finally, remarkable growth both at home and abroad.[3] Fuller's church at Kettering was a prime example of this growth "at home,"

---

[1] Michael A. G. Haykin, "A Habitation of God, through the Spirit: John Sutcliff (1752–1814) and the Revitalization of the Calvinistic Baptists in the Late-Eighteenth Century," *Baptist Quarterly (BQ)* 34, no. 7 (July 1992): 306. "Particular" because of their belief in particular rather than general redemption. For the essential features of eighteenth-century Baptist life in its wider setting, see David W. Bebbington, *Baptists Through the Centuries* (Waco, TX: Baylor University Press: 2010) 65–101.

[2] The term "Revival" has been deployed in a number of ways, as noted by David W. Bebbington, *Victorian Religious Revivals: Culture and Piety in Local and Global Contexts* (Oxford: Oxford University Press, 2012) 3. It is common for historians of eighteenth-century Particular Baptist life to speak of what happened at the end of the century as a Revival, due to the large number of conversions, the global impact, and because the revivication was fed by an evangelicalism which flowed from the transatlantic Evangelical Revival of the 1730s.

[3] For Fuller's ministry in context, see Peter J. Morden, *The Life and Thought of Andrew Fuller (1754–1815)* (Milton Keynes, UK: Paternoster, 2015).

with its meeting house enlarged twice during Fuller's pastorate to accommodate the large numbers of people flocking to services. The growth "abroad" came through the formation, in 1792, of the Particular Baptist Society for Propagating the Gospel among the Heathen (henceforth the BMS). Fuller became the home secretary of the BMS, serving the Society in this capacity from its inception until his death in 1815, combining this demanding role with his continuing duties at Kettering. As BMS secretary he worked tirelessly to support those sent out to serve in cross-cultural mission overseas, such as his young friend William Carey (1761–1834). As Brian Stanley has stated, the BMS's formation marked the opening of a "new chapter," not only in the history of Christianity, "but also in the history of the relations between the Western and the non-Western world." There were precedents for Protestant cross-cultural engagement, but the founding of the new Society was still "a turning point in the history of Christian missionary endeavour,"[4] with others following where the Particular Baptists had led.[5] Through the BMS, the Revival in English Particular Baptist life, and Fuller's own role in this would have far-reaching implications.

Fuller's life and thought, together with his own influence on the wider story of Particular Baptist Revival, has been the subject of recent studies, and his importance to the history of global Christianity is increasingly recognized.[6] Less well known is the way his involvement in the Revival refashioned his own personal spirituality, that is, the way he related to God and lived out his Christian life.[7] This chapter draws from Fuller's unpublished autograph manuscript diary, held at Bristol Baptist College, England, as well as from published primary material, to argue that his immersion in the Revival radically

---

[4] Brian Stanley, *The History of the Baptist Missionary Society, 1792–1992* (Edinburgh: T&T Clark, 1992) 1–2.

[5] For example, the nondenominational London Missionary Society, founded in 1795, and the Anglican Church Missionary Society, established in 1799.

[6] For his thought, see, especially, Chris Chun, *The Legacy of Jonathan Edwards in the Theology of Andrew Fuller* (Leiden: Brill, 2012); in addition, for his life and influence, see Michael A. G. Haykin, *One Heart and One Soul: John Sutcliff of Olney, His Friends and His Times* (Durham: Evangelical Press, 1994) 133–52. For an excellent survey of Fuller scholarship up to 2012, with few stones left unturned, see Nathan A. Finn, "The Renaissance in Andrew Fuller Studies: A Bibliographic Essay," in *Southern Baptist Journal of Theology* 17, no. 2 (Summer 2013): 44–61.

[7] For this understanding of spirituality, see, e.g., Linda Wilson, *Constrained by Zeal: Female Spirituality among Nonconformists 1825–1875* (Carlisle: Paternoster, 2000) 4; Susan M. Schneiders, "Christian Spirituality: Definition, Methods and Types," in *New SCM Dictionary of Christian Spirituality*, ed. Philip Sheldrake (2005) 1.

reshaped his spirituality. This reshaping took place as he came under the influence of evangelical forces and— crucially— came to engage wholeheartedly in evangelical activity.

Fuller's Introspective Spirituality, 1769 to early 1792

Fuller's spirituality from the time of his conversion experience in 1769 to the beginning of 1792 was characterized by a good deal of introspection and unhappiness. His personal diary often paints a bleak picture. During his first pastorate at Soham he had sometimes questioned his own salvation. In a diary entry for 12 September 1780 he declared,

> Very much in doubt respecting my being in a state of grace.... The Lord have mercy on me, for I know not how it is with me. One thing I know, that if I be a Christian at all, real Christianity in me is inexpressibly small in degree. O what a vast distance is there between what I ought to be, and what I am! If I am a saint at all, I know I am one of the least of all saints. I mean, that the workings of real grace in my soul are so feeble, that I hardly think they can be feebler in any true Christian..... I think of late, I cannot in prayer consider myself as a Christian, but as a sinner casting myself at Christ's feet for mercy.[8]

In the first and final sentences of this extract Fuller expresses significant doubt as to his "eternal security." The manuscript diary from his time at Kettering offers ample evidence that doubt and struggle remained keynotes of his inner life during the first decade of his ministry there. He did not explicitly doubt his salvation in his diary entries from 1784 onwards (at least in those which survive), but he did come very close to doing this and he was repeatedly negative about his own spirituality. On November 29, 1784 he wrote,

> Much dispirited, on account of my carnal-mindedness and perpetual propensity to depart from God. My life seems to have been one continued series of departures from God.... The sins of my *life* are *many*; but the sin of my nature seems to be but one—one continual disposition to

---

[8] John Ryland Jr., *The Work of Faith, the Labour of Love, and the Patience of Hope Illustrated in the Life and Death of the Rev. Andrew Fuller*, 2nd ed. (London: Button & Son, 1818) 78. The diary for the period before 1784 is not extant, but Ryland had access to it as he worked on Fuller's biography.

do evil, and aversion to draw near to God.[9]

At the turn of 1784/1785 his comments were briefer but, if anything, the language was stronger. "What good I have done I scarcely know. Great has been my sin against God. I feel myself a vile wretch!"[10] A series of entries made between June 3 and 6, 1785, show him very "low" and "depressed." He felt "guilty" because of his "vain wandering heart": "O I tremble at myself!," he exclaimed.[11] "Darkness and confusion of mind" overwhelmed him[12] and his "sorrow of heart" was so overpowering he felt physically ill.[13] Indeed, it appears that on many occasions his mental stress manifested itself in physical symptoms, including chest pains, fevers, and vomiting. There were many disturbed nights. He had terrible nightmares, dreaming, for instance, that he had "fallen into *some great wickedness*" following which he had been publicly exposed as a terrible sinner, his life and ministry irrevocably ruined.[14] His final surviving diary entry for 1786 was made on Sunday, June 11, at which point the diary abruptly breaks off. The next entry is dated October 3, 1789, over three years later. His "tombstone" biographer, John Ryland Jr. (1753–1825), stated that between sixteen to eighteen leaves had been torn out of the original volume (presumably by Fuller himself),[15] but in his October 3, 1789, entry the Kettering pastor also confessed to have written nothing for "upwards of a year and a half." The reason for this, he said, was that "it seemed to me that my life was not worth writing," characterized as it was by "lukewarmness" and "carnality."[16] Looking back on this period eight years later, in a letter sent to BMS missionary John Thomas (1757–1801) in India, he wrote of "a deep dejection" that had gripped him, which, although he "strove to throw it off in company," soon returned when he was in private.[17]

---

[9] Andrew Fuller, "Diary and Spiritual Thoughts" [1784–1801], bound autograph MS, Bristol Baptist College Library (G 95 b) November 29, 1784. Underlining in original.

[10] "Diary and Spiritual Thoughts," January 1, 1785.

[11] "Diary and Spiritual Thoughts," June 3, 1785.

[12] "Diary and Spiritual Thoughts," June 6, 1785.

[13] "Diary and Spiritual Thoughts," June 5, 1785. Cf. June 6, 1785.

[14] "Diary and Spiritual Thoughts," October 31, 1785. Underlining in original.

[15] Ryland, *Fuller*, 119. This is not apparent from the rebound "Diary and Spiritual Thoughts"; Ryland's father, John Collett Ryland (1723–92) was also a Baptist minister of some repute. All references to "Ryland" in this chapter are to the son, Ryland Jr.

[16] "Diary and Spiritual Thoughts," October 3, 1789.

[17] Fuller letter to John Thomas, May 16, 1796, in Ryland, *Fuller*, 159.

It is important to be aware that Fuller's diary does not necessarily give a totally rounded picture of his spiritual life. Bruce Hindmarsh, in his study of John Newton (1725–1807), comments that because his subject's diary was used as a means of "disciplined self-examination," its confessional and sometimes "self-recriminatory" tone may not have been reflective of his spirituality as a whole.[18] In other words, taken on its own, the diary is likely to be a distortion of Newton's spiritual life, a distortion created by the medium itself. The same is probably true for Fuller, and Hindmarsh's words of caution need to be borne in mind as one evaluates the material in the diary. Most likely, the Kettering pastor's state of mind was sometimes brighter than the extracts just cited, and others like them, might lead one to believe. Nevertheless, his letter to Thomas written years later confirms the basic impression given by the diary. Much introspection and agonized soul searching marked Fuller's spirituality from 1769 to 1790. Furthermore, from the middle of 1786 for three years he experienced a deep spiritual depression, a "dark night of the soul."[19]

Reasons for Fuller's Spiritual Struggle

What were the factors influencing Fuller's depressed spiritual state for much of the period 1769-1792? His family circumstances, which were often difficult, are relevant. Those circumstances included the tragic death of several children. The fatal illness of one daughter, called Sally, caused him particular grief. On Friday, December 17, 1785, he recorded in his diary that his daughter was "ill with the measles [*sic*]." He added, "I think if God should take either of my children from me... I could scarcely sustain it. On this account I have many fears."[20] Sally was six years old. For a while it seemed she might recover. In Fuller's entry for December 19, his relief was palpable: "Bless the Lord, my child is revived tonight!" he exclaimed.[21] But his joy was short lived. Sally became unwell again and in the early months of 1786 her condition

---

[18] D. Bruce Hindmarsh, *John Newton and the English Evangelical Tradition: Between the Conversions of Wesley and Wilberforce* (Oxford: Clarenden Press, 1996) 222.

[19] The phrase, "dark night of the soul," is from John of the Cross. For a classic treatment of spiritual depression from an evangelical perspective, see D. Martyn Lloyd Jones, *Spiritual Depression :Its Causes and Cures* (Glasgow: Pickering & Inglis, 1965).

[20] "Diary and Spiritual Thoughts," December 17, 1785. Sally's brother, Robert, would also predecease his father.

[21] "Diary and Spiritual Thoughts," December 19, 1785.

steadily worsened.[22] Fuller was concerned not only about her physical health but also with her spiritual state and he agonized over whether or not this was secure.[23] Many diary entries could be adduced to show his deep distress at what he correctly guessed was a terminal decline, from the frequent references to the failing health of his "dear little girl"[24] to a simple but poignant, "Lord help me!"[25] At one point he threw himself on the floor and "wept exceedingly," crying desperately to God in prayer.[26] With his daughter close to death he himself became ill with what John Webster Morris, one of his biographers, described as "an agony of grief." In this state he contracted a fever that "confined him to bed for several days."[27] Watching his beloved daughter wasting away had weakened him to the extent he had a further bout of severe physical illness.

Sally finally died on May 30, 1786. In his diary Fuller wrote of the moment he heard the news,

> I heard as I lay very ill in bed in another room I heard [sic] a whispering—I enquired…and all were silent…all were silent! But all is well! I feel reconciled to God! I called my family around my bed—I sat up & prayed as well as I could—I bowed my head and worshipped, and blessed a taking as well as a giving God.[28]

The shaky grammar and the repetition of "I heard" conveys a little of his state of mind. His worship of a "taking as well as a giving God" says something powerful about his Christianity and his determination to "walk by faith" whatever the circumstances. Nevertheless, one almost senses he was trying to convince himself as he wrote, "all is well" in a shaky hand.

Sally's funeral took place on June 1. Seeing her in the open coffin was,

---

[22] See, e.g., "Diary and Spiritual Thoughts," and the entries headed, January 1–8, January 29–February 5, and March 12–April 16, 1786.

[23] "Diary and Spiritual Thoughts," April 28, 1786.

[24] "Diary and Spiritual Thoughts," February 12–19, 1786.

[25] "Diary and Spiritual Thoughts," March 12–April 16, 1786. Cf. his reference to "heart-rending grief," Ryland, *Fuller*, 273.

[26] Ryland, *Fuller*, 274.

[27] John Webster Morris, *Memoirs of the Life and Death of the Rev Andrew Fuller*, 1st ed. (High Wycombe, 1816)], 2nd ed. (London: Wightman and Cramp, 1826) 42; Ryland, *Fuller*, 274.

[28] "Diary and Spiritual Thoughts," May 30, 1786.

Fuller recorded, "almost too much" for him in his "weak and afflicted" condition.[29] He would try to look to God as his source of healing, yet the death of his "beloved" Sally would cast a shadow over his life for many years to come. Events such as these contributed significantly to his low spiritual state. Fuller comes close to recognizing this himself, saying that it was after Sally died that his heart began "wretchedly to degenerate from God."[30] For him, personal tragedy and spiritual depression were linked.[31]

Fuller's own temperament was also an important factor contributing to his spiritual struggles. He was a deep thinker who also felt with a real intensity. Behind a phlegmatic exterior was a man of tender conscience and strong emotions. Sometimes these emotions broke out into the open, but most often they were hidden from all but his closest friends. His feelings in the 1780s sometimes swung from one extreme to another over a few days, with joy and despair both passionately felt. Even his better days were emotionally charged and most likely exhausting. Sunday, June 26, 1785, was, he confided in his diary, one of the best days he had experienced for "years." In the morning service he preached on the grace of God from Acts 4:33, "Great grace was upon them all." His feeling that God was with him was so overwhelming he wept copiously during his message, so much so that it was only with great difficulty that he finished his sermon.[32] Such high emotion came with a price however and, fairly predictably, by the following Wednesday he was "very low and unhappy" again.[33] Mood swings like these were not unusual, although in the period following 1786 it appears his darker feelings almost completely eclipsed any sense of joy.

Nevertheless, important as these circumstantial and temperamental factors were in shaping Fuller's spiritual life, the model of spirituality he had imbibed was also significant. Aspects of sixteenth- and seventeenth-century Puritanism molded the way he related to God. Fuller's habit of keeping a confessional diary was rooted in the Puritan soil from which the English Particular Baptists had sprung. In much Puritan spirituality, the confessional diary

---

[29] Ryland, *Fuller*, 275.
[30] "Diary and Spiritual Thoughts," October 3, 1789.
[31] For more on the tragedies Fuller faced, which included the illness and death of his first wife, Sarah (née Gardiner) (1756–1792) see Morden, *Fuller*, 43–46, 97–106. Fuller married his second wife, Ann Coles (d. 1825) in 1794.
[32] "Diary and Spiritual Thoughts," June 26, 1785.
[33] "Diary and Spiritual Thoughts," June 29, 1785.

was an important tool helping the "godly" to engage in detailed, rigorous self-examination. Those who had made professions of faith were encouraged to examine themselves for evidence they were truly part of the elect, recording their reflections in their journals. Such self-examination would most likely be hard work, with a positive outcome as far as assurance was concerned far from certain. According to the Puritan divine Thomas Brooks (1608–1680), the Christian who wanted to attain assurance of salvation "must work, and sweat and weep..... He must not only dig, but he must dig deep before he can come to the golden mine. Assurance is such precious gold, that a man must win it before he can wear it."[34] Some of the classic expressions of the Puritan struggle for assurance are found in the writings of John Bunyan (1628–1688), for example, in *Grace Abounding to the Chief of Sinners*, which Fuller had read.[35] Even if assurance was at last attained, continued self-examination was still encouraged in order to sustain growth in godliness.[36] As already noted, Fuller's diary provides evidence of a lack of assurance, and many entries reveal his own commitment to self-examination.[37] He looked inside himself for evidence of growth in godliness and believed there was very little; rather, his self-examination seemed to suggest to his sensitive temperament he was a vile sinner, habitually rebelling against God.

However, we especially need to consider the theology known as High Calvinism if we are to understand more completely Fuller's spiritual depression. This is because it is a High Calvinistic mutation of Puritan themes that his diary most often reveals. High Calvinism impacted many Particular Baptist congregations during the early to mid 1700s with Fuller's church in Soham

---

[34] Thomas Brooks, *Heaven on Earth* (1654; London: Banner of Truth, 1961) 139. Cf. the discussion in David W. Bebbington, *Evangelicalism in Modern Britain: A History from the 1730s to the 1980s* (London: Unwin Hyman, 1989) 42–47.

[35] See, e.g., John Bunyan, *Grace Abounding to the Chief of Sinners* (1666; Harmondsworth, Middlesex: Penguin, 1987) paragraphs 59–61, p. 19; paragraph 78, p. 23.

[36] John Coffey has shown that Puritan views on assurance were more diverse than has often been supposed, while accepting the view I am describing in this paragraph as the mainstream one. See Coffey, "Puritanism, Evangelicalism and the Evangelical Protestant Tradition," in *The Emergence of Evangelicalism: Exploring Historical Continuities*, ed. Michael A. G. Haykin and Kenneth J. Stewart (Leicester: InterVarsity Press, 2008) 265–66.

[37] Systematically at the beginning of every New Year, although at many other times too. See "Diary and Spiritual Thoughts," New Year's Day (Jan. 1) 1784, 1785, and 1786. Many entries already cited in this chapter are also relevant.

(he had grown up there before he became its pastor) no exception. This theology exalted the sovereignty of God in salvation in ways that greatly minimized the importance of human response.[38] In particular, according to High Calvinists, it was no person's "duty" to repent and believe the gospel, since total depravity rendered such a response impossible. The logical corollary of this was a lack of invitational evangelistic preaching. As Fuller himself later put it, ministers said nothing to "sinners...inviting them to apply to Christ for salvation."[39] By the early 1780s he had essentially broken with High Calvinism and its accompanying "noninvitation, nonapplication" approach to preaching as far as his published writings and public ministry were concerned. Through the influence of his friends, especially Robert Hall Sr. (1728–1791), John Ryland, and John Sutcliff (1752–1814), and through reading works by the New England philosopher/theologian Jonathan Edwards (1703–1758), he adopted an evangelical Calvinism. He now had no scruple about inviting sinners to trust in Christ. Moreover, his theological treatise, *Gospel Worthy of All Acceptation*, first published in 1785, became the most influential statement of the Edwardsean evangelical approach that was increasingly being adopted by the Particular Baptists towards the end of the eighteenth century. It was this theology that was one of the motors for the Revival in English Calvinistic Baptist life.[40] Yet, as Fuller took his leave of High Calvinism, it was the spirituality associated with it that he found hardest to shake off.

High Calvinistic spirituality had taken some of the Puritan emphases and developed them in particular ways. The Puritan stress on self-examination was emphasized yet further, resulting in a spirituality which was introspective in the extreme. Even if there had been a great desire for evangelistic work, little time would have been left for it. Furthermore, the balance and pastoral concern that characterized the best of Puritan spirituality was lost. Puritans

---

[38] Keith S. Grant, *Andrew Fuller and the Evangelical Renewal of Pastoral Theology* (Milton Keynes, UK: Paternoster, 2013) 28. Grant's brief survey of High Calvinism (26–28) is extremely well done. For an alternative, more detailed treatment, see Peter Toon, *The Emergence of Hyper Calvinism in English Nonconformity 1689–1765* (London: Olive Tree, 1967). High Calvinism was a departure from earlier, Puritan emphases that sought to hold divine sovereignty and human responsibility in more careful balance.

[39] Ryland, *Fuller*, 31–32.

[40] See Peter J. Morden, "Biblical Renewal for Mission: Andrew Fuller and Eighteenth-Century Baptist Life," *Bulletin of the Strict Baptist Historical Society* (Autumn 2011) 1–20; Morden, *Fuller*, esp. 43–68.

contended for "experiential" spirituality and so feelings were important, but feelings were to be grounded on the objective truths of Scripture. In High Calvinism, the subjective tended to overpower the objective. Much importance was placed on feelings as a barometer by which spirituality was measured, and this is one of the most striking features of Fuller's diary when it is viewed in the round. If he felt some "tenderness" in preaching or in administering the Lord's Supper, that was recorded as a positive sign of spiritual life;[41] if he felt "cold," that was noted as a negative and taken as a sure sign of spiritual deadness.[42] The cold feelings engendered further negative reflections about his spiritual life and were the cause of much self-recrimination. They locked Fuller into a downward spiral from which—for a time—he found it impossible to escape. Thus, important as circumstances and temperament were in causing his introspection and spiritual depression, the model of spirituality he had imbibed also contributed considerably to this.

Embracing Evangelical Spirituality, mid 1792 to 1796

Then, during the years 1792–1796 there was a quite definite shift in the tenor of Fuller's spiritual life. References to joy," "peace," and "happiness" became common, in his diary and in other writings. He gained a far greater assurance of salvation, and the self-recriminatory tone faded out almost entirely. Unhappiness and doubt occasionally resurfaced, but rarely, and the extant evidence points to the period of 1792 to 1796 as being watershed years, which brought about a lasting transformation in his spiritual life.

A diary entry dated July 18, 1794, describes the change that had taken place. Reflecting back on the previous two years Fuller recorded that he had "experienced perhaps as much peace and calmness of mind, as at any former period." He continued,

> I have been enabled to walk somewhat more near to God than heretofore; and I find that there is nothing that affords such a preservative against sin. "If we walk in the Spirit, we shall not fulfill the lusts of the flesh." This passage has been of great use to me, ever since I preached from it, which was on June 3, 1792. The idea on which I then principally insisted was that sin is to be overcome, not so much by a direct or mere resistance of it, as by opposing other principles and considerations to it. This sentiment has been abundantly verified in my experience: so far as

---

[41] "Diary and Spiritual Thoughts," September 23, 1784.
[42] "Diary and Spiritual Thoughts," October 12, 1784.

I have walked in the Spirit, so far has my life been holy and happy: and I have experienced a good degree of these blessings, compared with former times; though but a very small degree compared with what I ought to aspire after.[43]

This is worth quoting at length, firstly because it illustrates powerfully the very real change that had taken place: in contrast to his previous experience, now there was "peace," "calmness of mind," and (in Fuller's view) a "closer walk" with God. He dates the beginnings of this change to mid-1792. Also, his evangelicalism is highlighted, especially his experiential, "enlightened" biblicism. Biblical truth was empirically tested and "verified" in his own experience. The affinities between eighteenth-century evangelicalism and aspects of the Enlightenment are seen here in Fuller's life.[44] But most important, in terms of his spirituality, was the way he was now defining the path to spiritual growth positively (walking in the Spirit), rather than negatively (resistance of sin). Sin was still to be resisted, obviously, but this was not to be done through what he now believed was as a morbid preoccupation with it, but rather by focusing elsewhere, on other "principles and considerations." What these "principles and considerations" were is shown in the following extracts.

The year 1792 is the year the BMS was founded, with Fuller taking on the role of secretary. A survey of the ways he gave himself wholeheartedly to this work is presented elsewhere.[45] But the BMS was also crucial to the remodeling of his spirituality. On July 18, 1794, he wrote the following in his diary:

> Within the last year or two, we have formed a Missionary Society; and have been enabled to send out two of our brethren to the East Indies. My heart has been greatly interested in this work. Surely I never felt more genuine love to God and to his cause in my life. I bless God that this

---

[43] Ryland, *Fuller*, 124. Fuller's text was Galatians 5:16. Cf. Fuller's letter to John Ryland, April 2, 1795, in Ryland, *Fuller*, 227: "Sin is to be overcome, not by maintaining a direct opposition to it, as by cultivating opposite principles."

[44] The Enlightenment was a complex and diverse phenomenon. It is important to recognize there were many variations and that it was far from being a monolithic, unified movement. Nevertheless, there were certain core characteristics which crossed national and other boundaries and for this reason I refer to "Enlightenment" with an uppercase E. For more on Fuller's "enlightened" patterns of things, see Morden, *Fuller*, 66–67; 92–96.

[45] Most recently in Morden, *Fuller*, 109–23; 162–81.

work has been a means of reviving my soul. If nothing else comes of it, I and many others have obtained a spiritual advantage.[46]

Six months earlier he had written to Ryland, "I have found the more I do for Christ, the better it is with me. I never enjoyed so much the pleasures of religion, as I have within the last two years, since we have engaged in the Mission business. Mr Whitfield [sic] used to say, 'The more a man does for God, the more he may.'"[47] These quotations tie the sea change that had taken place in Fuller's spirituality to his evangelical activism, specifically his activity on behalf of the BMS. It was this, after many years of struggle that provided the decisive breakthrough in his quest for peace, assurance, and by his own testimony, happiness.

Why did his involvement with the BMS have such a significant and, as Fuller believed, such a positive effect on his spirituality? His temperament should be mentioned again. A number of the quotations in this chapter have suggested he was happier in company than he was on his own, and happier too when he was actively involved in doing something. This is confirmed by other comments, both from Fuller himself and from his friends. Also revealing is that he never had a "study" in which to work, although there were rooms in his house he could have used for this purpose. Throughout his life at Kettering, the desk from which he did all his writing was in the sitting room, and "he worked with his family around him."[48] The suspicion must be that constitutionally he was far more suited to a spirituality which majored on outward-facing activity rather than inward-facing contemplation. As Morris commented bluntly, "if spirituality consists in an aptness for spiritual exercises…, Mr Fuller was not eminent."[49] Yet this on its own is not sufficient explanation for what was happening. Fuller, like so many others of varying temperaments, was now being swept along in the evangelical current. The cause of worldwide Revival, to which the Kettering pastor now gave himself in a blaze of intense activity, was also a means to personal renewal.

---

[46] "Diary and Spiritual Thoughts," July 18, 1794. The "two brethren" were the aforementioned Carey and Thomas.

[47] Andrew Fuller letter to John Ryland, December 3, 1793. Ryland, *Fuller*, 226.

[48] Morris, *Fuller*, 1st ed., 475; Gilbert Laws, *Andrew Fuller: Pastor, Theologian, Ropeholder* (London: Kingsgate, 1942) 70, "Under such circumstances he penned all his letters to the missionaries…and generally conducted all the work of the [BMS] committee."

[49] Morris, *Fuller*, 1st ed., 478. Morris was surveying the whole of Fuller's ministerial career.

"Why Christians in the Present Day Possess Less Joy than the Primitive Disciples"

Fuller drew together the key emphases of his newfound evangelical spirituality in a circular letter written for the Northamptonshire Association of Particular Baptist Churches in 1795, expounding his chosen themes with passion. This letter, which was later published, is well worth a detailed examination. Fuller took as his title, "Why Christians in the Present Day Possess Less Joy than the Primitive Disciples." A vital reason the early believers experienced more joy, he declared, was their strong sense of assurance. Indeed, Fuller insisted that they enjoyed a "settled persuasion of their interest in Christ." He stated, "In all the New Testament we have scarcely an instance of a Christian being at a loss to perceive the evidence of his Christianity. What are called doubts and fears among us, and which make up so large a portion of our religious experiences, seem to have occupied scarcely any place amongst them."[50]

Fuller continued to attack the High Calvinist spirituality that he believed was responsible for his own painful struggles,

> The language that we are in the habit of using, when speaking of our love, or faith, or obedience, betrays a sad defect in the exercise of these heavenly graces.... I *desire* to love, I *would* believe, I *wish* to be obedient, are expressions which frequently occur in our prayers and hymns. Such language is unknown in the Scriptures, unless it be found in the character of the slothful.[51]

Fuller had rarely been so bold, openly attacking the High Calvinist spirituality prevalent in many Particular Baptist churches. Christians could and should be more certain, more definite. But where could this sense of assurance come from? Fuller insisted that his reader's focus should shift from a concentration on themselves (I desire, I would, I wish) to a concentration on the great truths of the gospel. The joy and peace the early Christians experienced came, first of all, through believing the good news. They believed in Christ, in his atoning sacrifice and in the promises of God regarding the future. In "laying

---

[50] Andrew Fuller, "Why Christians in the Present Day Possess Less Joy than the Primitive Disciples," in *The Complete Works of the Rev. Andrew Fuller, With a Memoir of his Life by the Rev. Andrew Gunton Fuller*, vol. 3, ed. Andrew Gunton Fuller, Joseph Belcher (rev. ed.); 3rd ed. (Harrisonburg, VA: Sprinkle Publications, 1845; 1988) 326. For the full text of the letter, see 325–31.

[51] *Works*, 3:326. Italics in original.

down his life" Christ had delivered all that would believe "from the wrath to come." For Fuller, this gospel and these promises had not changed, nor had they lost any of their power, for Christ was the same, "yesterday, today, and forever." Therefore, the same joy and assurance was available, and through the same route. He and his readers could have confidence in God and his promises. They needed to stop looking for subjective indicators within themselves that they were truly part of God's elect, and instead trust in God. To sum up, because Christ and his gospel had not changed, contemporary Christians could have the same assurance and joy as "primitive" ones— if they maintained the same focus and exercised the same faith.[52]

The note Fuller struck in his Association address that present assurance should be the normal experience of believers, was thoroughly evangelical.[53] During the first "Great Awakening," Jonathan Edwards would meet in his study with those who claimed to have undergone a decisive spiritual experience. If he was satisfied this was genuine, he would assure them they were converted.[54] Fuller's view was perhaps less focused on experience than that of Edwards and some other evangelicals in that Fuller tended to stress the objective work of Christ more than feelings, although such feelings (the possession of the "joy" that was spoken of in the Association letter), were nevertheless important to him. This more confident approach to assurance was one of the defining characteristics of eighteenth-century evangelicalism.[55] It was a break from High Calvinism, but also represented a shift away from the Puritan view of assurance discussed earlier in this chapter. For the Puritans, assurance was often the fruit of a long struggle; Fuller (his own earlier struggles notwithstanding), now believed that it should come through trusting the promises of God. And where for the Puritans assurance had been "a crown

---

[52] *Works*, 3: 326–27. Hebrews 13:8.

[53] Bebbington, *Evangelicalism in Modern Britain*, 46.

[54] Bebbington, *Evangelicalism in Modern Britain*, 47–48, convincingly links this view with Enlightenment empiricism.

[55] It is true that some eighteenth-century evangelicals, such as John Newton, exhibited a more typically Puritan approach to assurance. Such people were probably more numerous than previously thought, especially in Calvinistic Dissent. See D. Bruce Hindmarsh, *John Newton and the English Evangelical Tradition* (Oxford: Clarendon Press, 1996) chap. 6, and David W. Bebbington, "Evangelical Conversion, c. 1740–1850," *Scottish Bulletin of Evangelical Theology* 18, no. 2 (2000): 122–24. Nevertheless, they were still in the minority and a more confident doctrine of assurance increasingly became the norm.

that few wear," for Fuller it should be the present possession of all believers.[56]

The way to assurance and joy, therefore, was through believing and being "rooted and grounded" in the gospel. But Fuller then struck a second note, one that he emphasized strongly. Trusting in the gospel was not the only thing the primitive Christians did. Yes, they believed the gospel, but they also went out and spread it. The early Christians were "commissioned to publish glad tidings to every creature, and persuaded that the cause in which they were engaged would sooner or later universally prevail." Consequently, "they laboured with courage and assiduity, and the work of the Lord prospered in their hands."[57] Moreover, Fuller was clear that for them, this approach had led to assurance and great joy. He declared, "The primitive Christians were all intent on disseminating the gospel through the world; and it was in the midst of this kind of employment, and the persecutions which attended it, that they are said to have been 'filled with joy and with the Holy Ghost.'"[58]

Once again, Fuller drew straight lines from the experience of early Christians to those in his own day. The Kettering pastor's fundamental point was quite simple: joy would come for believers in his own day when they stopped focusing on their own comfort and became "swallowed up" in a vigorous concern for the salvation of others.[59] He once again drove this home with a strong challenge to any of his readers whose spirituality had been shaped by their High Calvinist milieu, "If a portion of the time which we spend in ransacking for evidence in the mass of past experiences, were employed in promoting the cause of God in the world, and seeking the welfare of the souls and bodies of men, it would turn to a better account. In seeking the salvation of others we should find our own."[60]

For the sake of balance, it is important to note that Fuller never completely repudiated self-examination. In a sermon entitled "Advice to the Dejected" (not dated, but internal evidence shows it must have been given later than 1792), he says he does not want to discourage "all remembrances of past

---

[56] For a discussion of how this more confident approach links to Enlightenment epistemology, see Peter J. Morden, "John Bunyan: A Seventeenth-Century Evangelical?" in *Grounded in Grace: Essays to Honour Ian M. Randall*, ed. Pieter J. Lalleman, Peter J. Morden, and Anthony R. Cross (London: Spurgeon's College / Baptist Historical Society, 2013) 44–46.
[57] *Works*, 3:326.
[58] *Works*, 3:329; Acts 8:52
[59] *Works*, 3:329.
[60] *Works*, 3:329.

experiences," and criticizes preachers who "cry down...all marks and signs of internal Christianity, taken from the work of sanctification in the soul."[61] He continued to have a high regard for the Puritans, for example recommending in 1796 that John Thomas read the work of the Puritan theologian John Owen's (1618-1683) on the mortification of sin, and promising to send a copy to India for him.[62] Nevertheless, on the occasions when he recommended some form of spiritual self-examination he was careful to qualify the recommendation immediately with the sort of comments he made in his Association letter.[63] There is a real sense in which, at least on this issue, he was not only leaving High Calvinism, but also departing from Puritan emphases.

Fuller referred explicitly in his Association letter to work on behalf of the BMS:

> We appeal to your own hearts, brethren, with respect to your late disinterested exertions for carrying the gospel amongst the heathen, we appeal to those of you especially who have had the undertaking most at heart, whether...you have not felt more of the joyful part of religion than you did before; yea, may we add, more than at any former period in your remembrance.[64]

He effectively challenged his readers to theological reflection on their recent experience of active commitment to the cause of world mission. All of this was of course deeply rooted in his own experience. In fact, the whole letter is shot through with autobiography. Fuller is charting his own journey from an introspective, uncertain, unhappy, and, he believed, an ultimately unholy piety to a God-centered, expansive, confident, joyful, and supremely activist spirituality.

Before considering Fuller's spirituality in the final phase of his ministry, it is worth reflecting briefly on the inter-relationship between activism and assurance in his spiritual development. It is common for historians and commentators on eighteenth-century evangelicalism to speak of how a confident knowledge of eternal security was, for men like the early eighteenth-century evangelicals George Whitefield (1714–1770) and John Wesley (1703–1791),

---

[61] *Fuller's Works*, 1:234. See his argument on 234–35 as a reason for dating this message post-1792.

[62] Fuller letter to John Thomas, May 16, 1796, in Ryland, *Fuller*, 160.

[63] See e.g., *Works*, 1:471.

[64] *Works*, 3:329.

the essential motor for an activism that showed itself especially in the pursuit of conversions.⁶⁵ For Fuller, an evangelical whose life and career straddled the eighteenth and the nineteenth centuries, the relationship between assurance and activism was more complex and, if anything, reversed. Rather than assurance and "joy unspeakable" leading to activism, activism in the service of the gospel was the key that unlocked the door to joy and assurance. In highlighting this, this chapter seeks to contribute to an understanding of the dynamics involved in the development of evangelical spirituality during this period.

Further Developments

How did Fuller's evangelical spirituality work itself out in the rest of his life and career? From the mid-1790s he began to experience some serious health issues and his workload increased to unmanageable proportions. He himself believed, as early as 1800, that he was in danger of neglecting not only "my own family" but also "my own vineyard, my own soul."⁶⁶ There were some signs that this unceasing activity, which had initially brought him such happiness, was becoming so great a weight as to rob him of some of his joy. "I sit down almost in despair," he wrote to John Sutcliff in 1800, "under this...load my heart has often of late groaned for rest."⁶⁷ It is hard to avoid the impression that Fuller was simply doing too much.

His work on behalf of the BMS bulked large and he had many other duties to attend to alongside this. He continued to write and (when he was there) pastor the church at Kettering. One of his letters captures his dilemma,

> [Samuel] Pearce's memoirs are now loudly called for. I sit down almost in despair... My wife looks at me with a tear ready to drop, and says, "My dear, you have hardly time to speak to me." My friends at home are kind, but they also say, "You have no time to see us or know us, and you

---

⁶⁵ David K. Gillett, *Trust and Obey: Explorations in Evangelical Spirituality* (London: Darton, Longman, and Todd, 1993) 60–61, describes assurance as adding "another octane to faith;" David W. Bebbington, "The Enlightenment and Evangelicalism," in *The Gospel in the Modern World: A Tribute to John Stott*, ed. Martyn Eden and David F. Wells (Leicester: IVP, 1991) 72.

⁶⁶ Andrew Gunton Fuller, *Men Worth Remembering: Andrew Fuller* (London: Hodder and Stoughton, 1882) 91.

⁶⁷ Gunton Fuller, *Men Worth Remembering*, 91–92.

will soon be worn out." Amidst all this there is "Come again to Scotland—come to Portsmouth—come to Plymouth—come to Bristol."[68]

In 1801, Robert Hall Jr. (1764–1831), having heard that Fuller had indeed recently visited Plymouth and Bristol, expressed his fears for Fuller's health in a letter to Ryland, "If he is not more careful he will be in danger of wearing himself out before his time. His journeys, his studies, his correspondencies [sic] must be too much for any man."[69] Yet Fuller was still pursuing his usual exhausting schedule. At one stage, in 1807, he was feeling so overwhelmed that he wrote to Ryland saying "I could almost wish I could shut myself up in a monastery."[70]

Comments such as these are not typical, and Fuller's tone in most of his correspondence remained positive till the end of his life. The success of the BMS was a particular source of joy, even whilst his work on the Society's behalf caused strain. When reports of the Mission's first Indian converts reached England, Fuller was elated. He wrote to the new Christians on behalf of the home committee, stating,

> In you we see the first fruits of Hindustan, the travail of our Redeemer's soul, and a rich reward for our imperfect labours. You know, beloved, that the love of Christ is of a constraining nature. It was this, and only this, that constrained us to mediate the means of your conversion. It was this that constrained our brethren that are with you to leave their country and all their worldly prospects, and to encounter perils, hardships and reproaches. If you stand fast in the Lord and are saved this is their and our reward.[71]

The spiritual dynamic Fuller had discovered—that activity in God's service led to increased joy— was sometimes stretched to breaking point. Nevertheless, he never slackened his commitment to spread the gospel and when there was "fruit" from these labours then this was also rich reward.

---

[68] Fuller letter to unnamed correspondent, March 1800, in Gunton Fuller, *Men Worth Remembering*, 91–92. Samuel Pearce (1766–99) had been the pastor of Cannon Street Baptist Church, Birmingham.

[69] Robert Hall Jr. letter to John Ryland, May 25, 1801, in Geoffrey F. Nuttall, "Letters from Robert Hall to John Ryland, 1791–1824," *BQ* 34, no. 3 (July 1991): 127.

[70] Fuller letter to John Ryland, January 13, 1807, in Ryland, *Fuller*, 249.

[71] Fuller letter to Brother Krishna, Sister Joymonee…August 19, 1801, Letters to Carey, Marshman and Ward. Fuller alluded to 2 Cor. 5:14, "For the love of Christ constraineth us…."

Conclusion

Andrew Fuller's spirituality was radically reshaped as he embraced evangelicalism and participated in the Revival of eighteenth-century Particular Baptist life. This reshaping did not happen without a struggle. Fuller was practicing evangelical ministry by the early 1780s and had a thoroughly worked through evangelical theology from at least 1782, yet the 1780s saw his personal spirituality resistant to evangelicalism. At times he lacked assurance of salvation, and his patterns of piety owed more to Puritanism and, especially, High Calvinism than to evangelical forces. But from 1792 his spirituality was transformed. It became more outward facing, confident and—by Fuller's own account—joyful. A range of factors can be adduced to account for this change, including the impact of evangelical theology. Nevertheless, involvement in evangelical activity, especially promoting the cause of overseas mission, was extremely significant. The foundation and early progress of the BMS is an event of great importance in the history of world mission; it was also transformative for the Society's first secretary.

10

"Uſeful Learning": Theological Training and the Particular Baptist Revival in the Long Eighteenth Century

Anthony R. Cross

An Overlooked "Means" for the "Happy Revival"

In 1702, Hercules Collins noted, "there is ſo little Proviſion made in the Churches of Chriſt for a future Miniſtry."[1] This led him to three principal matters in which he believed the contemporary church was "careleſs," the first recognized that as "the Schools of Chriſt" the churches needed to

> "be ſtir'd up to ſee what Spiritual Gifts God hath given them, *and put them into their proper Exerciſe*." Secondly, all pastors and teachers would "look upon it as their Duty to inſtruct thoſe Members who are moſt capable into the knowledg of Goſpel Myſteries." Thirdly, that "the Members of Churches, eſpecially thoſe to whom God hath given a good degree of ſpiritual Knowledg, would not always content themſelves to be only Hearers, but to ſtir up thoſe Gifts in an humble manner, *and put them in uſe for the Churches Edification*."[2]

At his funeral twelve years later, John Piggott exhorted Collins's congregation to "look up to heaven, and pray to the Lord of the Harveſt that he

---

[1] The long, medial, or descending *s* (ſ) is used in quotations where that letterform is found. It is a form of the minuscule (lowercase) letter *s*, which was formerly used where *s* occurred in the middle or at the beginning of a word (e.g. "ſinfulneſs" for "sinfulness" and "ſucceſsful" for "successful"). The modern letterform was called the terminal, round, or short *s*.

[2] Hercules Collins, *The Temple Repair'd: or, An Essay to revive the long-neglected Ordinances, of exerciſing the ſpiritual Gift of Prophecy for the Edification of the Churches; and of ordaining Miniſters duly qualified. With proper Directions as to Study and Preaching, for ſuch as are inclin'd to the Miniſtry* (London, 1702) 3 (original italics removed; italics added).

would fend forth Labourers into his Harveſt," reminding them that God gives his Spirit

> "in what meaſures he pleaſes, and qualify whom he will *for the Miniſtration of the Goſpel.*"³ Piggott immediately warned the congregation, "let not that make you defective on your part: You muſt not expect that Preachers will drop down from heaven, or ſpring out of Earth; but due care muſt be taken for the incouragement of humble men that have *real Gifts*, and let ſuch be train'd up in *uſeful Learning*, that they may be able to defend the Truths they preach."⁴

The High Calvinist John Brine recognized that the church was "in a declining State" and that it needed to make "Application unto God for a Revival." On the basis of Zechariah 4:6, he identified the Holy Spirit as "the ſole Cauſe of a happy Revival."⁵ According to Brine, the means for revival were the recovery and practice of those duties the neglect of which had resulted in "Loſs to ourſelves." The "proper Attendance" to Bible reading and meditation, prayer, hearing the gospel, and celebration of the ordinances, Brine believed, were "uſually bleſſed of God; to the Increaſe of heavenly Knowledge, the Eſtabliſhment of Faith, and indeed unto the Improvement of every Grace of the Spirit. This is that precious Reward, which God has given us Ground to hope for, in keeping His Commandments."⁶ Brine, Gill, and other High Calvinists were "pro-revival in the sense that they favored a genuine renewal of the church," but they were so "in Old Dissenting terms," to which Philip Roberts importantly reminds us that while they were not anti-evangelistic, they were non-missionary.⁷

---

³ John Piggott, "To the Church of Chriſt, Lately under the Paſtoral Care of the Deceas'd Mr. Hercules Collins," in *Eleven Sermons Preach'd upon Special Occaſions, By the Late Reverend Mr. John Piggott, Miniſter of the Goſpel. Being all that were Printed in his Life-time* (London: John Darby, 1714) 201–40 (239, original italics removed; italics added).

⁴ Piggott, "To the Church of Chriſt," 239 (italics original).

⁵ John Brine, *A Treatise on Various Subjects*, 2nd ed. (London, 1766) 302. The whole of chap. 11 is "Of the Ways and Means of a Happy Revival, under Decays of Grace," 302–16.

⁶ Brine, *Treatise*, 259. He immediately continues negatively, "On the contrary, we muſt expect Him to hide His Face from us, if we ſeek Him not, in thoſe Ways, wherein, He has promiſed to meet and bleſs us. For ſuch Neglect is, both a Violation of His Command, and a Regardleſsneſs of our own Good."

⁷ R. Philip Roberts, *Continuity and Change: London Calvinistic Baptists and the Evangelical Revival 1760–1820* (Wheaton, Ill.: Richard Owen Roberts, 1989) 79.

Moderate Calvinists also recognized the parlous state of the churches, but took a different path to that advocated by the High Calvinists, whose theological convictions continued to advocate election, the gospel, and sound doctrine, but minimized "the church's evangelistic imperative."[8] Writing mid-century, Benjamin Wallin resisted despair when he called on those who feared the Lord not to "give up their Hopes of Recovery," and to focus on God and see what he would do:

> The Eye of God is upon all things; and with him all things are poſſible. He is able, and will in his Time revive our dry Bones; as with him is the Residue of the Spirit; and as in all Ages he hath been the hope of Iſrael, and the Saviour therof in the Day of Trouble. In the mean Time, it becomes them to exert themſelves *in the Uſe of all appointed Means*, waiting in Hope to ſee what God will do.[9]

The best known occurrence of the language of "means" comes in both the title and pages of Carey's manifesto for world mission, part of the title of which is "*to use Means for the Conversion of the Heathens*," while in his discussion of these means he asserted, "We muſt not be contented however with praying, *without exerting ourſelves in the uſe of means* for the obtaining of thoſe things we pray for."[10] This call for exertion and use of the divine means was key in the development and spread of Baptist evangelical Calvinism in the eighteenth-century.

Of Education Funds and Societies: First Attempts among the Particular Baptists

The importance of providing a learned ministry can be traced at least as far back as 1675, when prominent London ministers sent a letter inviting

---

[8] Raymond Brown, *The English Baptists of the Eighteenth Century: A History of the English Baptists* (London: Baptist Historical Society, 1986) 2:5.

[9] Benjamin Wallin, *A Humble Address to the Churches of Chriſt* (London, 1750) 1 (original italics removed, italics added).

[10] William Carey, *An Enquiry into the Obligations of Christians, to use Means for the Conversion of the Heathens. In which the Religious State of the Different Nations of the World, the Success of Former Undertakings, and the Practicality of Further Undertakings, are Considered* (Leicester, 1792) 81 (italics original). This section of the book, 77–87, is headed, "An Enquiry into the Duty of Chriſtians in general, and what Means ought to be uſed, in order to promote this Work."

English and Welsh churches to meet the following May in London, in Rippon's words, "to form a plan for the providing an orderly standing ministry in the church, who might give themselves to reading and study, *and so become able ministers of the new testament.*"[11] Whether the proposed meeting ever took place Ivimey did not know, but he did remark, "It…proves that the learned men who were amongst the Baptists, and pastors in their churches were very desirous of providing a learned ministry, which could not now be expected without establishing seminaries of their own, as the universities and public schools were shut against them."[12]

The matter reappeared in 1689 when more than one hundred churches gathered at the first national Assembly of the Particular Baptists to consider "the present state of the baptized congregations…in the country."[13] The invitation lamented "the present condition of our churches… fearing that much of that former strength, life, and vigour, which attended us is much gone;…the interest of our Lord Jesus Christ seems to be much neglected, and the congregations…languish …. " The causes of this led them to conclude "That the great neglect of the present ministry is one thing, together with that general unconcernedness there generally seems to be, of giving fit and proper encouragement for the raising up an able and honourable ministry for the time to come…."[14] The assembly observed that the neglect of making "Goſpel-Proviſion" for the financial support of such ministers resulted in them being "ſo incumbred with Worldly Affairs, that they are not able to perform the Duties of their holy Calling" to the detriment of the preaching of the gospel.[15]

---

[11] John Rippon, A brief essay towards an history of the Baptist Academy at Bristol; read before the Bristol Education Society, at their anniversary meeting, in Broadmead, August 26th, 1795 (London, 1796) 9–10; and Joseph Ivimey, *A History of the English Baptists: including an Investigation of the History of Baptism in England from the Earliest Period to which it can be traced to the close of the Seventeenth Century*, 4 vols. (London, 1811–30) 1:416.

[12] For Ivimey's discussion of this, see, *History*, 1:415–16. For detailed discussion of Baptist schools, academies, and, eventually, what we now call colleges, see Anthony R. Cross, *"To communicate simply you must understand profoundly": Preparation for Ministry Among British Baptists* (Didcot: Baptist Historical Society, 2016) chaps. 1–4.

[13] Ivimey, *History*, 1:478. For the letter of invitation, signed "London, July 22, 1689" by, among others, William Kiffen, Hanserd Knollys, and Benjamin Keach, see 1:478–81.

[14] Ivimey, *History*, 1:479.

[15] *A General Epiſtle to the Churches," A Narrative of the Proceedings of the General Aſſembly of divers Paſtors, Meſſengers and Miniſtring Brethren of the Baptized Churches, met together in London*,

The assembly's concern was wholly kerygmatic and evangelistic, and was set out in three points. First, to support those churches that were financially unable to maintain their own ministry, so "that their Minifters may be encouraged wholly to devote themfelves to the great Work of Preaching the Gofpel." Secondly, "To fend Minifters that are ordained (or at leaft folemnly called) to preach, both in City and Country, where the Gofpel hath, or hath not yet been preached." Finally, "To affift thofe Members that fhall be found in any of the aforefaid Churches, that are difposed for Study…in attaining to the knowledg and underftanding of the Languages, Latin, Greek, and Hebrew."[16] This first national assembly was not concerned simply for the internal welfare of the churches. While the gift of the Spirit was essential, this in no way obviated the need for education, because the assembly later resolved that "the Graces and Gifts of the Holy Spirit" are "sufficient to the making and continuing of an Honourable Miniftry in the Churches," and that those "now in the Miniftry, or that may be in the Miniftry, [are] to attain to a competent knowledge of the Hebrew, Greek, and Latin Tongues, that they may be the better capable to defend the Truth againft Oppofers."[17]

By 1693 the assembly's tone had significantly changed and become more cautious of the benefits of such an education, resulting in no action being taken. Following 1693, the national assembly met twice yearly, in Bristol and London.[18] However, the London-based discussions for an educated ministry faltered due to lack of financial support. It was left, then, to the Bristol meeting of 1693 to take up the cause of ministerial calling and training,[19] and what Bristol had that London did not was a visionary benefactor in the person of the Broadmead elder and businessman Edward Terrill.

---

from Septemb. 3. to 12. 1689, from divers parts of England and Wales: Owning the Doctrine of Perfonal Election, and final Perfeverance (London, 1689) 5. Narrative of the Proceedings is also printed in Ivimey, *History*, 1:480–511.

[16] *Narrative of the Proceedings* (1689) 12.

[17] *Narrative of the Proceedings* (1689) 18 (italics removed); also in Ivimey, *History*, 1:500.

[18] On the importance of Bristol and London for the development of ministerial education, see Harry Foreman, "Baptist Provision for Ministerial Education in the 18th Century," *Baptist Quarterly* 27, no. 8 (October 1978): 358–69 (esp. 358–63).

[19] Ivimey, *History*, 1:528.

The Bristol Tradition

In 1679 Terrill made provision for the support of a minister at Broadmead who was "well skilled" in Hebrew and Greek, and whose primary work was to prepare young men for ministry throughout the country.[20] The Bristol Academy began in 1720[21] when two Welsh students came to Broadmead to study under its minister, Bernard Foskett.[22] In 1770, the third principal of the Bristol Academy, Caleb Evans, separated the academy from the Broadmead church through the Bristol Education Society,[23] the twofold purpose of which was "The education of pious candidates for the miniſtry" and "the encouragement of miſſionaries to preach the goſpel wherever providence opens the door for it."[24]

The Theological Emphases of the Bristol Tradition

While the influences of the Evangelical Revival were also in evidence in the Northwest and London,[25] the Bristol Tradition was the powerhouse of

---

[20] "Edward Terrell's Charity," in *The Bristol Charities*, ed. Thomas John Manchee (Bristol, 1831) 1:280–84 (esp. 281). See Anthony R. Cross, "The Early Bristol Tradition as a Seedbed for Evangelical Reception among British Baptists, c.1720–c.1770," in *Pathways and Patterns in History: Essays on Baptists, Evangelicals, and the Modern World in Honour of David Bebbington*, ed. Anthony R. Cross, Peter J. Morden, and Ian M. Randall (London: Spurgeon's College/Didcot: Baptist Historical Society, 2015) 50–77 (esp. 53–54); and Roger Hayden, *Continuity and Change: Evangelical Calvinism among Eighteenth-Century Baptist Ministers Trained at Bristol Academy, 1690–1791* (Chipping Norton: Roger Hayden and Baptist Historical Society, 2006) 21.

[21] The case that Bristol Baptist College should, therefore, be dated from 1720, and not 1679, is set out in Cross, "Early Bristol Tradition," 54n21.

[22] Namely, Thomas Rogers and John Phillips. See G. F. Nuttall, "Welsh Students at Bristol Baptist College, 1720–1797," *Transactions of the Honourable Society of Cymmrodorion* (1978): 171–99 (see 197 and 196 respectively).

[23] See "An Account of the Constitution of the Bristol Education Society" (dated June 7, 1770) in *An Account of the Bristol Education Society*, 1–7.

[24] Caleb Evans, *The Kingdom of God: A Sermon Preached in Broad-mead, Bristol, before the Briſtol-Education-Society*. August 16, 1775 (Bristol: W. Pine, T. Cadell, M. Ward &c., [1775]) 24.

[25] See Ian Sellers, ed., *Our Heritage: The Baptists of Yorkshire, Lancashire and Cheshire 1647–1987* (Leeds: Yorkshire Baptist Association, 1987) 14–20. Sellers examines the revival's impact in the north from 1750 to 1787, and at 21–29 up to 1837; Roberts, *Continuity and Change*, focuses on the capital.

proto-Evangelicalism through its academy.[26]

The first four principals of the Bristol Academy were ardent advocates of Evangelical faith: conversionism, activism, biblicism, and crucicentrism.[27] Elsewhere I have discussed in some detail the Evangelical Calvinism of Foskett, and Hugh and Caleb Evans,[28] so it is necessary only to illustrate how the fourth principal, John Ryland, upheld these characteristics. In his ordination confession of faith, Ryland began with "the firm Belief of the Scriptures of Truth being truly & certainly a Revelation from God," inspired and authoritative, and instrumental "in the Conversion of Men's hearts and the Reformation of their lives."[29] Accepting both original sin and guilt, he believed that no one could ever "have been sav'd without an Atonement and Satisfaction of infinite Value."[30] God's Son made "an Offering for Sin" when he was "deliver'd unto the accursed Death of the Crofs, for our offences." Ryland's moderate Calvinism is clear when he declared, "God discovers his *infinite Love to Righteousnefs* by bestowing Pardon, salvation & Glory" on his elect.[31] On the Modern Question, however, he concurred with the emerging Evangelical Calvinists, and this vision extended globally.

> I believe that the risen Savior has commanded Repentance and Remission of Sins to be preach'd in his Name *among all Nations* & his Gospel to be publifed *to every Creature*—That his Ministers are commissioned to assure their hearers in general that all Things are ready, the Gospel Feast is provided *for all comers*; Jesus who saves to the uttermost will in no wise cast out or reject *any that apply to him*....[32]

---

[26] Hayden's *Continuity and Change* focuses on Baptists in the southwest. See also Cross, "Early Bristol Tradition."

[27] David W. Bebbington, *Evangelicalism in Modern Britain: A History from the 1730s to the 1980s* (London: Unwin Hyman, 1989) 2–17.

[28] See Cross, "Early Bristol Tradition," 57–59, on Foskett, and 64–65 on Hugh and Caleb Evans.

[29] John Ryland Jr., "A Confession of Faith delivered by John Ryland, junr of Northampton at his Ordination to the Pastoral Care of the Church in College Lane, June.8.1781" (a twenty-three page, handwritten MS, in Bristol Baptist College Library, G97a/Ryl/02) 3.

[30] Ryland, "Confession of Faith," see 9–10, and quotation from 11.

[31] Ryland, "Confession of Faith," 12 (underlining original). On God's sovereignty and grace, see 14–15.

[32] Ryland, "Confession of Faith," 13 (italics added).

In 1812, Ryland brought together the importance of theologically educated ministers and mission, when he declared that students "must be influenced by an ardent desire to know, enjoy, resemble, serve, and glorify God himself; *and to bring others to unite with him in the same exalted purpose.*"[33] During his thirty-two years as principal, twenty-six students went to serve with the Baptist Missionary Society (BMS).[34] He is, perhaps, best known for his encouragement of William Knibb, a member of the Broadmead church where he was also pastor.[35]

In the early years, however, the academy's mission emphasis was directed to home mission. During vacations students regularly itinerated.[36] In 1773, the Bristol Education Society supported a gospel mission to Cornwall with Benjamin Francis as the itinerant preacher. A mission followed this in 1776 to North Wales, a leading figure in which was another former student, Thomas Llewelyn.[37] Later John Saffery of Salisbury[38] and William Steadman

---

[33] John Ryland, *Advice to Young Ministers, respecting their preparatory Studies. A Sermon, Preached Jun 25, 1812, in the Meeting-House in Devonshire-Square, London; before the Subscribers to the Academical Institution at Stepney, for the Education of Candidates for the Ministry, of the Baptist Denomination* (Bristol: E. Bryan, 1812) 6–7 (italics added).

[34] See Norman S. Moon, *Education for Ministry: Bristol Baptist College 1679–1979* (Bristol: Bristol Baptist College, 1979) 35.

[35] See, e.g., John Howard Hinton, *Memoir of William Knibb, Missionary in Jamaica* (London: Houlston and Stoneman, 1847; 1849) 5–31. The Baptist Mission in Jamaica was founded in 1813 by the work of another of Ryland's students, John Rowe. See Stephen Albert Swaine, *Faithful Men; or, Memorials of Bristol Baptist College, and some of its most Distinguished Alumni* (London: Alexander & Shepheard, 1884) 274–75. On the connection between the academy and Jamaica, see 274–81.

[36] Moon, *Education for Ministry*, 20.

[37] On the Cornwall and other such missions, see, e.g., Hayden, *Continuity and Change*, 129–31; and on the North Wales mission, see T. M. Bassett, *The Welsh Baptists* (Swansea: Ilston House, 1977) 100–107. Llewelyn studied at the academy c.1740–c.1742.

[38] On whom, see "Extract from the Funeral Sermon for the late Rev. John Saffery, delivered in the Baptist Meeting-house, Brown Street, Salisbury, Monday Evening, March 14, 1825," *Baptist Magazine* 17 (May 1825): 189–91, which recounts his call to ministry, 189, that "It was soon discovered that Mr. S. possessed talents for public *usefulness*, and, according to the usage of our churches, he was invited to exercise them" (italics added). It was also noted that his "impressive" preaching and "labour" were not in vain, as the Salisbury church was "composed, for the most part, of those who were turned to God by his *instrumentality*" (italics added). "He was remarkably distinguished by his uniform and glowing zeal for the spread of the gospel, and the enlargement of the Redeemer's kingdom at home and abroad," as evidenced through his practise and advocacy of itinerant ministry, as well as promotion of the Baptist Missionary Society. See

of Broughton shared in 1796 in an evangelistic tour of Cornwall, sponsored by the BMS.³⁹

Able, Evangelical, Zealous, and Lively

The Bristol Education Society's vision extended beyond the domestic ministry to one throughout the British Empire, "To the end that diffenting congregations, efpecially of the Baptift denomination, in any part of the Britifh dominions, may, if it pleafe God to fucceed our endeavours, be more effectively fupplied with a fuccession of able and evangelical minifters...."⁴⁰

Three years later, Hugh Evans set out its aims:

[T]o improve the minds of thofe pious perfons who are recommended by the churches to its patronage, by proper cultivation, reading, ftudy and converfation. To inftruct them into the knowledge of the languages in which the fcriptures were written, to give them a juft view of language in general, and...to teach them to exprefs themfelves with propriety.... [T]he defign of this inftitution is to contribute what we can, towards the church and world's having *able minifters* of the new teftament. Such as may be qualified to explain, illuftrate, defend, improve, and enforce divine truths and duties.... Such as, being in a meafure judges of words or language, fhall be able to feek and find out acceptable words, and thus more fully and agreeably convey to their hearers the knowledge of divine things ...⁴¹

Caleb Evans employed the language of instrumentality when summing

---

also John Saffery, *The Importance of Strenuous Exertions in the Cause of Christ* (1805) *Circular Letter From The Elders, Ministers, and Messengers, of the Several Baptist Churches of the Western Association Assembled at Kingsbridge, Devon, On Wednesday and Thursday, 5th and 6th June, 1805*, transcribed from the Western Baptist Association Minutes (1805) 1–11, at John Saffery, "The Importance of Strenuous Exertions in the Cause of Christ (1805)" last accessed 30 June 2015, http://www.oocities.org/baptist_documents/1805.cl.british.exertion.html.

³⁹ See Brian Stanley, *History of the Baptist Missionary Society 1792–1992* (Edinburgh: T&T Clark, 1992) 18.

⁴⁰ "An Account of the Constitution of the Bristol Education Society," in *An Account of the Bristol Education Society: Began Anno 1770* (Bristol: W. Pine, [1770]) 1. Cf. Ryland, *Advice to Young Ministers*, 23–24, who, addressing students of the London Education Society/Stepney College in 1812, spoke of those who would support them in their studies "in hope that our churches may be furnished with a succession of able and faithful ministers."

⁴¹ Hugh Evans, *The Able Minifter. A Sermon, Preached in Broad-mead, before the Briftol Education Society, August 18, 1773* (Bristol, 1773) 43 (italics original).

up his father's aim, and bequeathed to the Bristol tradition the famous words that it was "not merely to form fubftantial fcholars but as far as in him lay he was defirous of being made an inftrument in God's hands of forming them, *able, evangelical, lively, zealous Minifters of the gofpel.*"⁴² Caleb further stated that "it is the higheft ambition of your Friends and Tutors indulge refpecting you, to fee you *able, faithful, and fuccefsful, Minifters of the New Teftament*...."⁴³ Writing three years after the formation of the BMS, Rippon's shortened version of the society's goals immediately continued, "and that Missionaries may be sent to those places where there is an opening for the gospel."⁴⁴

The able minister is also to be "zealous," a word which appears to be practically synonymous with "lively." For Hugh Evans, only God "can make able minifters of the new teftament. But as he is pleafed to make ufe of inftruments to effect his own purpofes, the honor *you* are ambitious of, is that of being employed by him, in the accomplifment of the great and defirable work of raifing up *able minifters* of the gofpel," because "The harveft truly is plenteous, but able laborers very few," hence the "great need…of able and zealous minifters to vindicate and eftablish the truth as it is in Jefus."⁴⁵ To whatever services ministers are called, then, they should be attended to "with diligence and zeal."⁴⁶

---

⁴² Caleb Evans, *Elisha's Exclamation! A Sermon, Occafioned by the Death of The Rev. Hugh Evans, M.A. Who departed this Life, March 28, 1781, In the 69th Year of his Age. Preached at Broadmead, Bristol, April 8, 1781. Publifhed at the Requeft of the Congregation* (Bristol, 1781) 31. This quotation is often wrongly attributed to Caleb Evans's Address to the Students in the Academy at Bristol. April 12, 1770, in John Rippon, *Baptist Annual Register, Including Sketches of the State of Religion among Different Denominations of Good Men at Home and Abroad*, 4 vols (1790–1802) 1:345–51. So Moon, Education for Ministry, 11 and 115n 23; who is followed, e.g., by W. M. S. West, Bristol Tradition: Then and Now (n.p. [Bristol]; n.p. [Bristol Baptist College], n.d. [1987]) n.p. [9].
⁴³ Caleb Evans, *Address to the Students in the Academy at Bristol, 351* (italics original).
⁴⁴ Rippon, *A brief essay*, 34. In this he is followed by Ivimey, *History*, 3:26.
⁴⁵ Hugh Evans, *The Able Minifter*, 4 (italics original).
⁴⁶ Hugh Evans, *Ministers defcribed, under the Characters of Fathers and Prophets, and their Death improved* (Bristol, 1773) 4. Cf. Hugh and Caleb Evans's assistant tutor, and minister of the Pithay, Bristol, James Newton, *The Good Steward: A Sermon, Preached at Broad-Mead, Bristol, before the Education Society, August 14, 1776* (Bristol, [1776]) 29, "May we be excited to greater activity in our ftations." He looks forward to the pleasure that will come when the Lord approves faithful stewardship with "Well done good and faithful fervants! Let this fire our fouls with an holy zeal." In Caleb Evans and Hugh Evans, *A Charge and Sermon, delivered at the Ordination of the Rev. Thomas Dunscombe* (Bristol, 1773) 19, Caleb Evans also holds out God's "Well done

Theological training and study helped ministers not only to a greater understanding of the Scriptures but also to be better communicators of the gospel message. When combined with the presence of God, the result of their preparations in the study, was well-expressed by Samuel Wilson, who was an early Baptist to emphasize heart religion which was so characteristic of the Evangelical Revival:

> if you are favoured with the greateſt Liberty of Mind in your private Preparations, you will equally need the Preſence of God in your public Miniſtrations; not only to bring your former Thoughts to remembrance, but eſpecially to warm your Heart with Divine Truths, that you may ſpeak feelingly, and *with proper Zeal and Earneſtneſs*, as one who is thoroughly concerned, in the Hand of God, *to be uſeful to the Souls of Men*. A Preacher who is viſibly unaffected with what he delivers to others, is not likely to ingage the Attention, or be of any conſiderable Service to thoſe who hear him. Pray then…that when you are preaching the Goſpel, you may have all proper Utterance; *That your Tongue may be as the Pen of a ready Writer.*[47]

The origins of the BMS owe much to the Northamptonshire Association,[48] and many of the prime movers of the society also had theological connections with the Bristol Academy. Though Robert Hall Sr., minister at Arnesby, did not receive a formal theological education, he was far from theologically illiterate. His *Help to Zion's Travellers*[49] inspired much that was to

---

good and faithful ſervant" as the minister's reward, adding, "Surely the thought *will revive* and *rouſe* you!" (italics original). On the meaning of "zealous," see Cross, "Early Bristol Tradition," 74–75.

[47] Samuel Wilson, *The Duties of a Pastor and Deacons: Recommended in a Sermon Preach'd at the Ordination of the Rev. Mr. Thomas Flower, jun. As Pastor; and Mr. T. Kenward and Mr. S. Stinton, As Deacons: April the xxixth, MDCCXXXVI. At the Meeting-Place in Unicorn Yard, Toolyſtreet* (London: John Wilson, 1736) 19–20 (first two italics added, third original).

[48] See Stanley, *History*, 14, "Although there was no reference in the title to the Northamptonshire Association, the Society was in every respect a child of the Association." See also 4–6, 9–11 and 13–15; and R. L. Greenall, ed., *The Kettering Connection——Northamptonshire Baptists and Overseas Missions* (Leicester: University of Leicester, n.d. [1993]).

[49] Robert Hall, *Help to Zion's Travellers: being An Attempt to remove various Stumbling Blocks out of the Way, relating to Doctrinal, Experimental, and Practical Religion* (Bristol, 1781). This book, being a revised and expanded version of his sermon on Isaiah 57:14 ("Caſt ye up, caſt ye up, prepare the way, take up the ſtumbling-block out of the way of my people") delivered to the Northamptonshire Association annual meeting in 1779. On Robert Hall Sr., see Rippon, *Baptist Annual Register*, 1:226–41.

come, influencing, among others, both Carey and Fuller.⁵⁰ Of Hall Sr., a close friend recorded how he "laid in a large ſtock of uſeful knowledge." The result was that "in the hands of God" his ministry "was effectual to the converſion of great numbers; and in this particular he was diſtinguiſhed in a manner not very common, for the laſt years of his life were the moſt ſucceſsful."⁵¹

The "grand object" of John Sutcliff's 1784 Prayer Call for the "revival of our churches" was "that the Holy Spirit may be poured down on our miniſters and churches, that ſinners may be converted, the ſaints edified, and intereſt of religion revived, and the name of God glorified…let…the ſpread of the goſpel to the moſt diſtant parts of the habitable globe be the object of your moſt fervent requeſts."⁵²

Of the thirteen[53] founders of the BMS, three were former students at Bristol (John Sutcliff, Samuel Pearce, and Thomas Blundell), one was a present student (William Staughton), and a good case can be made that John Ryland had learnt from his Bristol-trained father, both as his assistant at John Collett Ryland's school[54] and also in the ministry at College Street, Northampton. Though others were not college-trained, this does not mean they were not theologically driven. In many ways both Carey and Fuller were theologically self-taught, yet Sutcliff gave him Carey's first Latin lesson;[55] he then

---

[50] Equally as important to Carey and Fuller was Hall Sr.'s preaching and counsel. See Eustace Carey, *Memoir of William Carey, D.D.* (Boston: Gould, Kendall and Lincoln, 1836) 11; and John Ryland, *The Work of Faith, the Labour of Love, and the Patience of Hope illustrated; in the Life and Death of the Reverend Andrew Fuller, late Pastor of the Baptist Church at Kettering* (London: Button & Son, 1816) 56, 58, 68.

[51] Rippon, *Baptist Annual Register*, 1:238–39.

[52] [John Sutcliff], "P.S." in Richard Hopper, *The Nature, Evidences, and Advantages, of Humility, Represented in a Circular Letter from the Ministers and Messengers of the Baptist Association, Aſſembled at Nottingham*, June 2, 3, 1784 ([1784]) 12.

[53] For the attenders, see Stanley, *History*, 14n45.

[54] John Collett Ryland ran a boarding school that began in Warwick in 1748 and then moved to Northampton in 1760, and to Enfield in 1785; he was assisted by his son John Ryland (who had also studied at his father's school) and the later principal of Stepney College, William Newman. One of his most famous pupils was Robert Hall Jr. See W. T. Whitley, "J. C. Ryland as Schoolmaster," *Baptist Quarterly* 5, no. 3 (July 1930): 141–44 (esp. 143–44); and Seymour J. Price, "Dissenting Academies, 1662–1820," *Baptist Quarterly* 6, no. 3 (July 1932): 125–38 (esp. 135–37).

[55] Ivimey, *History*, 4:438n*; [Maurice F. Hewett], "Sutcliff's Academy at Olney," *Baptist Quarterly* 4, no. 6 (April 1929): 276–79 (276). at 279, Hewett comments, "The B.M.S., in its earliest stages, owed as much to Sutcliff as to any man."

taught himself the biblical languages, as well as Dutch and French.[56] As for Fuller, John Ryland, for example, helped teach him Hebrew.[57]

Academies in the North and Wales

Founded in 1804, the Northern Education Society led to the founding of the college at Horton,[58] and was in large part the work of John Fawcett, who, though never academy-trained, ran a day school and trained young men for the Baptist ministry.[59] His students included John Sutcliff, John Foster the minister and essayist, and William Ward, a Serampore colleague of Carey and Marshman.[60] Fawcett echoed the sentiments of the Bristol Tradition when he announced: "The grand design we have in view is to furnish the churches of Christ with *lively, zealous, judicious, disinterested ministers of the Word.* We need not say how much they are at present wanted." He continued,

> We purpose (through Divine assistance) to use all proper endeavours for impressing the minds of those who may come under our care, with a *deep and lively* sense of the awful and important nature of the work;…and assist their progress *in all the branches of useful knowledge.* And in order to preserve *a lively sense of Divine things* on their minds…ever remembering that those ministers who live nearest to God are the most likely, by their labours, to bring others to him, and consequently answer the important

---

[56] See Timothy George, *Faithful Witness: The Life and Mission of William Carey* (Leicester: InterVarsity Press, 1991, 1992) 23–24.

[57] See Ryland's notes for Fuller in a notebook entitled "Dr J. Ryland's Hebrew Notes on Psalms 1 and 23," in Bristol Baptist College Library (OS G 95A 16031). I am grateful to the Rev. Dr. Peter J. Morden for drawing my attention to this.

[58] See William Medley, *Rawdon Baptist College. (Horton 1804. Rawdon 1859.) Centenary Memorial* (London: Kingsgate, 1904); A. C. Underwood, "The Early Relations of Horton Academy and Rawdon College with Lancashire," *Baptist Quarterly* 5, no. 3 (July 1930): 130–36; and Peter Shepherd, *The Making of a Northern Baptist College* (Manchester: Northern Baptist College, 2004) 8–10, 17–19, 25–31.

[59] See Ian Sellers, "Other Times, Other Ministries: John Fawcett and Alexander McLaren," *Baptist Quarterly* 32, no. 4 (October 1987): 181–99 (184).

[60] See J. E. Ryland, ed., *The Life and Correspondence of John Foster: With Notices of Mr. Foster as a Preacher and Companion by John Sheppard*, 2nd ed., 2 vols. (London: Jackson and Walford, 1848) 1:8–13; and Samuel Stennett, *Memoirs of the Life of the Rev. William Ward, Late Baptist Missionary in India; containing a Few of His Early Poetical Productions. And a Monody to his Memory* (London: J. Haddon, 1825) 34–49.

ends of a gospel ministry.[61]

During his lifetime, Fawcett paved the way for the Northern Education Society and the academy's first President, Dr. William Steadman.[62] In 1815, Steadman, one of Caleb Evans's students, set out the society's "plan of education" as "to form as correct an idea as possible of the state of those churches with which the young men were likely to be connected after their studies closed, with a view to cultivate that in them which would be likely to make them *acceptable and useful*."[63]

As a society "founded on such principles as secured an attachment to evangelical truth," its aim was also to "cultivate those branches of literature, which form the man and the scholar, in connection with those virtues and graces, that stedfast adherence to the truth as it is in Jesus, and that zeal for the advancement of his kingdom, and that love to the souls of men, which constitute and adorn the character of a gospel minister."[64]

Of these educated ministers, Steadman spoke of their "usefulness," and that they "have met with the divine approbation."[65] The able minister is to evince zeal "in the sacred cause,"[66] be zealous in preaching,[67] and "must possess the facility of acquiring as well as of imparting, knowledge."[68] In short,

---

[61] John Fawcett Jr., *An Account of The Life, Ministry and Writings of the late Rev. John Fawcett, D.D., who was the Minister of the Gospel Fifty-Four Years, First at Wainsgate, and Afterwards at Hebdenbridge, in the Parish of Halifax; Comprehending Many Particulars Relative to The Revival and Progress of Religion in Yorkshire and Lancashire; and Illustrated by Copius Extracts from the Diary of the Deceased, from his Extensive Correspondence, and other Documents* (London: Baldwin, Craddock, and Joy, 1818) 176–77 (italics added) letter dated June 18, 1773.

[62] See Thomas Steadman, *Memoir of the Rev. William Steadman*; and Sharon James, "Revival and Renewal in Baptist Life: The Contribution of William Steadman (1764–1837)" *Baptist Quarterly* 37, no. 6 (April 1998): 263–82. The importance of academy tutors' influence on students did not evade William Steadman, *The Able Minister: A Sermon, The substance of which was delivered at Bradford, Yorkshire, August 3, 1825* (London, 1825) 28: "By the wise admonitions, the pious examples, the biblical and theological instructions of well-qualified tutors, who set patterns of diligence and zeal as ministers, and act the part of pastors to them while under their care, they may be expected to acquire a greater degree of fitness for the office of ministers and pastors themselves."

[63] Thomas Steadman, *Memoir of the Rev. William Steadman*, 318 (italics added).

[64] William Steadman, *Able Minister*, iv–v.

[65] William Steadman, *Able Minister*, 2–3.

[66] William Steadman, *Able Minister*, 16.

[67] William Steadman, *Able Minister*, 17.

[68] William Steadman, *Able Minister*, 20.

according to Steadman, "the character of an able minister" is constituted by four things: grace, gifts, a "portion of acquired knowledge," and "the constant supply of the Holy Spirit."[69] The Spirit must "keep alive those graces—he must animate that zeal—he must keep up that holy courage which forms the radical qualifications for his great work," improving the gifts he has already bestowed, and sanctifying "those improvements which human effort supplies." The able minister must experience the Spirit's aid, for not only is the "influence" of the Spirit "necessary to be shed on others" to bring success from the minister's labours, but the Spirit's influence must continually be shed on the minister, for without this "his engagements" will fail, his testimony to others will be "destitute," and he will suffer his great master's disapproval.[70]

The studies to which students should give themselves must be those that "influence their minds...*with love to Christ and to the souls of men*."[71] Steadman exhorted his students to "resolve in the strength of divine grace to become *able ministers of the New Testament* — repair, if they can be repaired, the breaches death has made among us — fill our vacant pulpits — augment the number of our churches, and contribute your quota, and that a large one, towards extending the empire of the Redeemer from Pole to Pole."[72]

In 1807, a third college was established in Abergavenny, its origins being attributed by Mervyn Himbury to "the evangelical zeal of the Rev. Micah Thomas and his friends."[73] Thomas, like many other Welsh ministers, was a former student at the Bristol Academy. In his ordination sermon to Thomas, Ryland exhorted him to, "Strive...to win fouls to Chrift. Let it be your concern to act in unifon with him.... Go and feek for the loft fheep which the Son of God hath purchafed with his own blood. Labour for your divine Lord, that you may gather in his harveft...Endeavour to advance his kingdom

---

[69] William Steadman, *Able Minister*, 19–31.
[70] William Steadman, *Able Minister*, 30. On 31, Steadman is probably referring to Robert Hall's *Help to Zion's Travellers*.
[71] William Steadman, *Able Minister*, 32 (italics added).
[72] William Steadman, *Able Minister*, 35 (italics original).
[73] D. Mervyn Himbury, *The South Wales Baptist College (1807–1957): Published on the Occasion of the Ter-Jubilee of the College 1957* (1957) 15. E.W. Price Evans, "Rev. Micah Thomas, Abergavenny, 1778–1853," *Baptist Quarterly* 14, no. 3 (July 1951): 109–13 (at 112) states that Thomas was "a qualified Calvinist, more or less of the school of Andrew Fuller," and as a preacher, "scriptural and expository."

among men."⁷⁴ Ultimately, Christ is the sower and reaper, and the harvest will be "ample," the prospect of which led Ryland to exclaim, "Oh! ſhall not this be enough to make us diligent, all zeal and activity in the cauſe of Chriſt, and faithful unto death?"⁷⁵

Following his retirement as tutor, Micah Thomas praised the developments under its new tutor, Thomas Thomas,⁷⁶ with the benediction, "May the great Source of every good gift, and of every perfect gift, prosper his [Thomas Thomas'] endeavours: and may the extraordinary zeal now so laudably put forth by the friends of the Institution, continue, like an ardent flame, unquenchably to burn!"⁷⁷

An Institution for London

The founding of the colleges at Horton and Abergavenny stirred up interest in London for their own college.⁷⁸ The Baptist Education Society was formed in 1804.⁷⁹ Six years later the Stepney Academy was opened, largely as a result of "the wisdom and influence of the venerable Abraham Booth."⁸⁰ Though he, too, lacked a formal education, nevertheless he made up for this in later life,⁸¹ being taught some Hebrew, and Latin and Greek by a Roman

---

⁷⁴ John Ryland, "Sketch of a Charge given to the Rev. Mr. Toms, of Chard, and to the Rev. Micah Thomas, of Ryford, in 1802, by Dr. Ryland," in Rippon, *Baptist Annual Register*, 4:1079–88 (1082). The sermon is based on John 12:26.

⁷⁵ Ryland, "Sketch of a Charge," 1087.

⁷⁶ See Arthur J. Edwards, *Thomas Thomas of Pontypool: Radical Puritan* (Caerleon: APECS, 2009); J. Jenkyn Brown, "Memoir to Micah Thomas of Abergavenny, 1778–1853," *Baptist Magazine* 46 (October 1854): 593–98; and E. W. Price Evans, "Dr. Thomas Thomas, of Pontypool," *Baptist Quarterly* 3, no. 3 (1926): 130–36.

⁷⁷ Micah Thomas, "A Brief Memorial of the Baptist Academy, Late of Abergavenny, Monmouthshire," *Baptist Magazine* 29 (1837): 359–61 (360).

⁷⁸ Arnold H. J. Baines, "The Pre-History of Regent's Park College," *Baptist Quarterly* 36, no. 4 (October 1995): 191–201 (198).

⁷⁹ This is not to be confused with the earlier, short-lived society of the same name founded in 1752, on which see Baines, "Pre-History."

⁸⁰ George Pritchard, *Memoir of the Rev. William Newman, D.D.: More than Forty Years Pastor of the Baptist Church at Old Ford; President & Theological Tutor of the Academical Institution at Stepney from its Commencement (1811) to 1826* (London: Thomas Ward, 1837) 179. See R. E. Cooper, *From Stepney to St. Giles': The Story of Regent's Park College 1810–1960* (London: Carey Kingsgate, 1960) 26–30.

⁸¹ *The Works of Abraham Booth, Late Pastor of the Baptist Church assembling in Little Prescot Street, Goodman's Fields, London. With some account of his Life and Writings*, 3 vols. (London: J.

Catholic.

For Booth, the establishment of the college was in no way divorced from the centrality of preaching, serving the churches, and furthering mission. Booth echoed Carey's beliefs and set out the Society's aims:

> Preach the gospel, or proclaim the glad tidings, "to every creature,"...[T]hough it be from Jesus only that ministerial gifts, with all the genuine success that attends the exercise of them, proceed; and though we are by no means warranted to consider a learned education as *essential* to the discharge of the duties of a Christian Ministry; yet we cannot but reflect, with much concern, on that degree of illiteracy which is sometimes observable in those who preach the Gospel of Christ. To remedy so obvious a defect in our immediate connexion, a Society has been formed; the principal design of which is, to assist persons of good character and of promising talents for the ministry, in the acquirement of important knowledge...to assist them in forming scriptural views of divine truth, and of duties enjoined by it: and to communicate their ideas to others in a perspicuous manner.[82]

Evangelical Baptists and the Spread of Education

Once the Universities of Oxford and Cambridge were again closed to Dissenters with the restoration of the monarchy, many Baptist ministers established day and boarding schools,[83] often also called academies. Among

---

Haddon, 1813) 1:xviii–xix and xxxvii–xxxix. See also 1:lxxviii–lxxix. His 1769 ordination confession of faith is reproduced on 1:xxviii–xxxvii. For his biblicism, see 1:xxviii–xxxi; crucicentrism, see 1:xxxii–xxxiii; conversionism, see 1:xxxiii–xxxiv; and activism, see 1:xxxvi, where he speaks of his needing to be "faithful in that ministry" in which he must preach to others, and also his Glad Tidings to Perishing Sinners: or, The Genuine Gospel a Complete Warrant for the Ungodly to Believe in Jesus (London, 1796) a second edition of which appeared in 1800.

[82] George P. Gould, *The Baptist College at Regent's Park: A Centenary Record* (London: Kingsgate, 1910) 17 (italics original). On Booth's involvement, see 16–18, 22–23 and 30–31. See also Baines, "Pre-History," 198, where he quotes from the *Rules of the Baptist Education Society, established in London 1804, reprinted with a list of subscribers* (1807).

[83] "Dissenters' Schools, 1660–1820," *Transactions of the Baptist Historical Society* 4, no. 4 (1914): 220–27, provides an extensive list with brief details of Dissenters' contributions to general education, many Baptist schools among them.

their number were Joseph Stennett,[84] Thomas Crosby,[85] Daniel Turner,[86] John Ash,[87] Rees Evans,[88] and John Ward.[89] The importance placed on theological education also led to the education of the young in the form of catechisms published by, among others, William Collins (d.1702),[90] Benjamin

---

[84] "Some Account of the Life of the Reverend and Learned Mr. Joſeph Stennett," in *The Works Of the late Reverend and Learned Mr. Joſeph Stennett: In Five Volumes. To which is prefix'd Some Account of his Life*, 4 vols. [not the 5 referred to in the title] (London: J. Darby et al., 1732) 9, notes that Stennett taught for five years before entering the ministry; and Price, "Dissenting Academies," 131.

[85] See Thomas Crosby, *The History of the English Baptists, from The Reformation to the Beginning of the Reign of King George I*, 4 vols. (London, 1738–40) a three-page advertisement for his boarding school at Horselydown, Southwark, for "Young Gentlemen" follows the appendix; and Price, "Dissenting Academies," 1:134.

[86] The hymn writer Daniel Turner ran a short-lived academy in Hemel Hempstead (c.1738) see Price, "Dissenting Academies," 131, for which Turner wrote *An Abstract of English Grammar and Rhetoric: containing the Chief Principles and Rules of both Arts, neceſſary to the Writing the Language Correctly and Handſomely. In a New, Eaſy and Diſtinct Method. Designed to Introduce the Engliſh Scholar to a juſt Notion of the Propriety, and Beauty, of his Mother Tongue* (London: R. Hett, 1739).

[87] Dr. John Ash, the lexicographer, ran an academy at Pershore. See Price, "Dissenting Academies," 132; Ash wrote a number of books on education; see Ivimey, *History*, 4: 561–62, and Swaine, *Faithful Men*, 61–64.

[88] Before being called to Trosnant Academy, Rees Evans opened a private school in Bedwelty in 1740, so S. Gummer, "Trosnant Academy," *Baptist Quarterly* 9, no. 7 (July 1939): 417–23 (at 420).

[89] Ward, a member of the Little Wild Street Baptist Church, opened a school in Tenter Alley, Moorfields, in 1710, and some of his pupils later became Baptist preachers having improved their "'Latin, Greek, and Hebrew, and other studies suited to the Profession of Divinity,'" among them John Gale, Isaac Kimber, and Samuel Wilson. See [William Brock], "John Ward, LL.D., F.R.S., F.S.A.," *Transactions of the Baptist Historical Society* 4, no. 1 (April 1914): 1–32 (esp. 2–3 and 26). See also [W. T. Whitley], "Pupils of John Ward," *Transactions of the Baptist Historical Society* 4, no. 4 (1914): 219.

[90] [William Collins], *A Brief Inſtruction in the Principles of the Chriſtian Religion: Agreeable to the Confeſſion of Faith, put forth by the Elders and Brethren of many Congregations of Chriſtians (baptized upon Profeſſion of their Faith) in London and the Country; owning the Doctrine of Perſonal Election, and Final Perseverance* 5th ed. (London, 1695). For William Collins as the author, see the account of the General Assembly of Particular Baptists in London in 1693 in Ivimey, *History*, 1:533. It was reprinted numerous times in the next hundred years, e.g., *The Baptiſt-Catechiſm: or a Brief Instruction in the Principles of the Christian Religion ...*, 15th ed. (London:, 1747) and 16th ed. (London, 1764) and *The Baptist Catechism, commonly called Keach's Catechism. Compared with the Early Editions, and reviſed by John Rippon, D.D.* (London, 1794). On the question of the

Stinton,[91] Benjamin Beddome,[92] and Robert Robinson,[93] but the most long-lasting impact was through the spread of Baptist colleges and seminaries worldwide. For example, another student from the Bristol Academy, William Staughton, took Caleb Evans's pattern with him to America and founded the Philadelphia Education Society in 1812, the Philadelphia Theological Institute, and Columbian College, the first Baptist university in America, later renamed George Washington University.[94] Of the Serampore Trio of Carey, Marshman, and Ward, Timothy George observes, "next to preaching and Bible translation, education was the most important means employed…in their efforts to evangelize India."[95] Together they established Serampore College

---

origins and authorship of the catechism, see Jonathan W. Arnold, *The Reformed Theology of Benjamin Keach* (1640–1704) Centre for Baptist History and Heritage Studies 11 (Oxford: Regent's Park College, 2013) 57–59 and 68.

[91] Benjamin Stinton, *A Short Catechism, Wherein the Principles of the Chriſtian Religion Are Taught in the Words of the Sacred Scriptures themſelves*, 2nd ed. (London, 1730).

[92] Benjamin Beddome, *A Scriptural Exposition of the Baptist Catechism by way of Question and Answer*, 2nd ed. (1752; Bristol, 1776).

[93] Robert Robinson, *A Plan of Lectures on the Principles of Nonconformity for the Instruction of Catechumens*, 6th ed. (1797) in Robert Robinson, *Miscellaneous Works of Robert Robinson, Late Pastor of the Baptist Church and Congregation of Protestant Dissenters, at Cambridge; in Four Volumes: to which are prefixed Brief Memoirs of His Life and Writings*, 4 vols. (Harlow: B. Flower, 1807) 2:187–256.

[94] See S. W. Lynd, *Memoir of the Rev. William Staughton, D.D.* (Boston: Lincoln, Edmands, 1834); and Roger Hayden, "William Staughton: Baptist Educator and Missionary Advocate," *Foundations* 10, no. 1 (January–March 1967): 19–35, and "Bristol Baptist College and America," *Baptist History and Heritage* 14, no. 4 (October 1979): 26–33.

[95] George, *Faithful Witness*, 143. See also G. E. Smith, "Patterns of Missionary Education: India 1794–1824," *Baptist Quarterly* 20, no. 7 (July 1964): 293–312; and M. A. Laird, "The Serampore Missionaries as Educationists 1794–1824," *Baptist Quarterly* 22 no. 6 (April 1968): 312, 320–25.

(fl. 1818),⁹⁶ and a major part of their efforts were channelled towards education,⁹⁷ a key aim of which was to train an indigenous ministry.⁹⁸ This pattern of founding schools and colleges and training local men for ministry was followed in different countries where the Baptist missionaries served, among them Calabar College in Jamaica, which was founded in 1843.⁹⁹

Conclusions

The importance of theology for the Evangelical Revival in general and revival among the Baptists in particular is widely recognized, but what is less noted is that theology requires the provision of theological education. The rise of Fullerism/evangelical Calvinism, whether seen as a development of moderate Calvinism prevalent in the seventeenth century or as a new expression of Baptist theology, or a combination of both, could not have occurred without the convictions of a growing number of Baptists, individually (Terrill, Fawcett, Thomas, and Booth) and corporately (the early General Assemblies, the three academies, and two education societies), to provide a theologically literate ministry. In their advocacy of theological education, many Baptists adopted a group of theologically rich and practical terms—"useful," "able," "evangelical," "zealous," "lively," "duty," "means" and "instrument"—to

---

⁹⁶ See E. Daniel Potts, *British Baptist Missionaries in India, 1793–1837: The History of Serampore and its Missions* (Cambridge: Cambridge University Press, 1967); George Howells and A. C. Underwood, *The Story of Serampore and its College* (Serampore and Calcutta: Faculty of Serampore College, 1918); and George Howells and Members of the College Faculty, *The Story of Serampore and its College* (Serampore: n.p., 1927).

⁹⁷ See, e.g., Stanley, *History*, 156–62. Laird, "Serampore Missionaries as Educationists," highlights the influence of Sunday schools, dissenting boarding schools, and dissenting academies on Serampore College.

⁹⁸ Brian Stanley, "Planting Self-Governing Churches: British Baptist Ecclesiology in the Missionary Context," *Baptist Quarterly* 34, no. 8 (October 1992): 378–89 (esp. 379–81); and J.T.K. Daniel, "Ecumenical Pragmatism of the Serampore Mission," *Indian Journal of Theology* 42, no. 2 (2000): 171–77 (esp. 173).

⁹⁹ Following their independence from the BMS in 1842, the Jamaican Baptists founded their own Jamaica Baptist Missionary Society and, in 1843, established their own theological college, Calabar Institution, something that had been aired a decade earlier. See H. O. Russell, "A Question of Indigenous Mission: The Jamaican Baptist Missionary Society," *Baptist Quarterly* 25, no. 2 (April 1973): 86–93; Stanley, *History*, 84–85, 87, 89; and E. B. Underhill, *Life of James Mursell Phillippo, Missionary in Jamaica* (London: Yates & Alexander, 1881) 199, 204–6, and *The West Indies: Their Social and Religious Condition* (London: Jackson, Walford, and Hodder, 1862) 292–97. See also Gordon A. Catherall, "Bristol College and the Jamaican Mission: A Caribbean Contribution," *Baptist Quarterly* 35, no. 6 (April 1994): 294–302 (at 300).

achieve the goals of this theological education, which included not only the better understanding of God's word, but the greater ability to communicate the gospel, which, through the divine attendance and operation of the Spirit resulted in the building up of the church and the spread of the gospel through the conversion of sinners.

What we have also seen is, first, that for a growing number of Baptists there was a natural and inseparable connection between the provision of a quality ministry and the churches' effectiveness in God's mission. Secondly, that there was an intimate connection between knowing the Bible (not least through the biblical languages) and divine truths, and the emphasis on the warmed heart. It wasn't enough just to understand the truth; the minister had to be passionate/zealous about it. Usefulness was the result of zeal, and together made the man of God

11

John Ryland Jr. (1753–1825), Evangelical Calvinism, and the Evangelical Revival

Chris W. Crocker

The year was 1774. The guest preacher, a man of growing local repute, ascended into the pulpit of the Sheepshead Baptist Church.¹ His name was John Ryland Jr., son of John Ryland Sr. (1723–1792), pastor of College Lane Baptist Church, Northampton.² Ryland had been invited to preach by his friend William Guy (1739-83), who was the new pastor at Sheepshead.³ Ryland recorded, "My dear friend Mr. Guy went to Sheepshead this spring, where a remarkable revival took place. I went to see him May 1st where the meeting-house would not contain half the people, and I was obliged to come out of the pulpit, and go with a thousand people into Mr. Oram's yard, where I preached in a waggon."⁴ A few months later Ryland informed his friend John Sutcliff (1752–1814): "You ask if I have heard of the revival at Sheepshead—I have *seen* it. The instrument is Mr. Guy...the plainest rough-hewed preacher you

---

¹ The area is now called Shepshed and the church is known as Charnwood Road Baptist Church. This congregation represents the group known as Particular Baptists, hereafter referred to as Baptists. John Collett Ryland pastored there from 1759 to 1786. See Peter Naylor, "John Collett Ryland," in *The British Particular Baptists, 1638–1910*, vol. 1, ed. Michael Haykin (Springfield, MO: Particular Baptist Press, 1998) 184–201.

² For preliminary reading on John Ryland Jr., see James Culross, *The Three Rylands: A Hundred Years of Various Christian Service* (London: Elliot Stock, 1897) and Grant Gordon, "John Ryland Jr. (1752–1825)" in *The British Particular Baptists, 1638–1910*, vol. 2, ed. Michael Haykin (Springfield, MO: Particular Baptist Press, 2000).

³ See John Ryland, *Seasonable hints to a bereaved church; and the blessedness of the dead, who die in the Lord. A sermon preached at Sheepshead occasioned by the death of Rev. W. Guy* (Northampton: T. Dicey and Co, 1783) Bristol Baptist College Archives (hereafter BBCA) 13536. Ryland first met Mr. Guy when he had studied at his father's school; John Ryland, *Autograph Reminiscences* (1807) BBCA 14883, 47, and through this they became "very intimate" friends; see Ryland, *Reminiscences*, 45.

⁴ Ryland, *Reminiscences*, 49.

ever saw or heard...three Sabbaths back twenty-four gave in their experience there, the Church lasted from 4 in the afternoon till 12 at night."[5] The day after Guy's ordination in October this "remarkable revival" was marked when he baptized forty-three people.[6] Such an awakening appears all the more remarkable when set against the backdrop of "the godless eighteenth-century."[7]

From this occurrence several deductions can be made: a revival had taken place in which Ryland had been a direct participant; a new and exciting work seemed to be dawning amongst these Baptists; Ryland, though important, was not singularly involved or responsible for the revival; and there was a new generation of pastors who were longing for, reflecting upon, and promoting revival, as well as assuming new roles of leadership. From this episode and subsequent discussions, revival or awakening may be defined as the act by which an individual or group, in a locality or region, is quickened in their interest, affection, and devotion to Jesus Christ.[8] Such a phenomenon was perceived by those present to be a sovereign work of the Holy Spirit.[9] By itself this episode would tell us little about Ryland's significance for revival, but this precocious son of an influential Baptist pastor is not to be underestimated.

In a letter from young Ryland to John Newton in 1773, no longer extant, Josiah Bull records the contents of Ryland's "sorrowful epistle:"[10]

---

[5] John Ryland, "Letter to John Sutcliff," August 26, 1774. American Baptist Historical Society Records (hereafter ABHSR); See Michael Haykin, *One Heart and One Soul: John Sutcliff of Olney, His Friends, and His Times* (Darlington Co. Durham: Evangelical Press, 1994).

[6] Ryland, *Reminiscences*, 49.

[7] Culross, *The Three Rylands*, 18. This was a description of the religious condition of England as described by philosopher Thomas Carlyle (1775–1881) and likely an allusion to a phrase repeated throughout a chapter in Carlyle's *Past and Present*, book 4, chapter 1: "Horoscope" (New York: William H. Colyer, 1844) 165-205

[8] This can apply to both the church and new converts as noted in a nineteenth-century definition of revivals as "those outpourings of the Spirit, which result in the quickening of the church and the conversion of sinners." Quoted by Wesley Banner, *Christian Advocate* [American Methodist periodical] (February 1849) n.p.

[9] This, Ryland affirmed: "sinners always resist the Holy Spirit, as far as they can; if he were not almighty, none would be converted"; Ryland letter to Sutcliff, ABHSR. See also Michael Haykin, "'The Sum of All Good': John Ryland Jr. and the Doctrine of the Holy Spirit," *Churchman* (1989) 103-4.

[10] This is how Newton refers to Ryland's letter when he responds to it on July 31, 1773. See Grant Gordon, ed., *Wise Counsel: John Newton's Letters to John Ryland Jr* (Edinburgh: Banner of Truth Trust, 2009) letter 7, 43.

JOHN RYLAND JR., EVANGELICAL CALVINISM, AND THE EVANGELICAL REVIVAL

[Ryland] had written to Olney in a very desponding tone as to the state of things in the religious world. He speaks of error abounding on the one hand and lukewarmness on the other. He is staggered sometimes, and knows not what to think of things—either Satan or unbelief, or both, say, Christ is asleep, and cares not that the ship is going to the bottom.[11]

So moved, Ryland set forth his three great objects in life, which he recalled in 1788 when reflecting upon the Prayer Call of 1784: "our chief design was to implore a revival of godliness in our own souls, in our churches, and in the church at large."[12] As Ryland exerted himself to achieve these ends he became a man of "considerable usefulness."[13] This chapter will trace the experiential and relational origins of Ryland's evangelical Calvinism, examine and define his theological development, and demonstrate how this evangelical Calvinism in action impacted Ryland's usefulness in revival.

Early Revival Experience

Ryland's life was not without an experiential impression of revival that shaped both his theology and desire to see continued awakening.[14] Benjamin Beddome (1717–1795)—a Baptist pastor who had experienced revival in his own congregation, knew leading figures in revival, and had read widely on the subject—left a lasting impression upon Ryland.[15] He had experienced Beddome's preaching on a number of occasions, recollecting listening to him

---

[11] Josiah Bull, *"But now I see": The Life of John Newton* (Edinburgh: Banner of Truth Trust, 1868) 166.

[12] J. E. Ryland, ed., *Pastoral Memorials Selected from the Manuscripts of the Late Rev'd. John Ryland, D.D. of Bristol a Memoir of the Author in Two Volumes* (London; Holdsworth, 1827) 1:17. Ryland also states in his 1775–1776 diary that he had "anxious concern for more powerful godliness in my own soul, and for the welfare of the church, the honor of religion, and the salvation of souls"; Ryland, *Reminiscences*, 57.

[13] This is a term borrowed from John Newton adopted as a life phrase to describe Ryland. Newton recognized that Ryland's gifts would "qualify him for considerable usefulness"; Gordon, *Wise Counsel*, letter one, 12).

[14] This chapter will not focus on his father's influence or their complex relationship, but it can be stated that John Collett Ryland was a moderate High Calvinist of evangelical catholicity.

[15] Roger Hayden, *Continuity and Change: Evangelical Calvinism among Eighteenth-Century Baptist Ministers Trained at Bristol Academy, 1690–1791* (London: Baptist Historical Society, 2006) 152. For more on Beddome, see Michael Haykin, "Benjamin Beddome," in *The British Particular Baptists, 1638–1910*, vol. 1, ed. Michael Haykin (Springfield, MO: Particular Baptist, 1998) 166–82. Beddome's lasting impression on the Rylands can be seen in that Ryland's granddaughter was named Jane Beddome Ryland.

"with much pleasure."[16] Beddome had a profound ministry in the Cotswolds and was the pastor who baptized Ryland's father. John Collett Ryland had been converted in 1741 at the "remarkable awakening in Bourton" where more than forty people were brought to repentance and faith,[17] himself a graduate of Bristol Baptist Academy, ministered in Bourton-on-the-Water from 1740 to 1795 and his church saw great numerical growth with one hundred being added to membership in his first decade.[18]

Revival was not simply a historic family reality but rather something that Ryland experienced personally. Over the course of 1766–1767, Ryland himself began to wrestle with his sin and need for salvation.[19] Though raised hearing the gospel in church, in the fall of 1766 the conviction of sin had not been "of an abiding nature...till near the close of my thirteenth year."[20] Writing on December 17, 1766, he recalled that a year prior there had been an "awakening" among some of his friends, who formed a religious society on the playground.[21] Ryland was half put out when his company was passed over because they were discussing "something better."[22] Ryland set about, under great introspective turmoil, to wrestle with what this something better was and read a number of Puritan works to aid him in his quest.[23] Finally, after wrestling for many months, in late January 1767 he records his first affirmative profession of faith: "Yes, Lord, I am thine!"[24] Through the many connections with

---

[16] Ryland, *Reminiscences*, 36.

[17] Culross, *The Three Rylands*, 13. See also William Newman, *Rylandiana: Reminiscences Relating to the Rev. John Ryland, A.M. of Northampton, father of the late Rev. Dr. Ryland of Bristol* (London: George Wightman, 1835) 24–25.

[18] Haykin, "Benjamin Beddome," 173.

[19] See Ryland, *Reminiscences*, 155–29. See also Bruce D. Hindmarsh, *The Evangelical Conversion Narrative: Spiritual Autobiography in Early Modern England* (Oxford: Oxford University Press, 2005); and H. Wheeler Robinson, "The Experience of John Ryland." *Baptist Quarterly*, 4, no. 1 (1928): 17-26.

[20] Ryland, *Reminiscences*, 15.

[21] Ryland, *Reminiscences*, 15–16. See also Timothy Wheelan, "John Ryland at School: Two Societies in Northampton Boarding School," *Baptist Quarterly* 40 (April 2003): 110.

[22] Ryland, *Reminiscences*, 17. "Something better" refers to "Jesus Christ and the salvation of souls."

[23] Ryland, *Reminiscences*, 18. That is, Joseph Alliene, Richard Baxter, and John Bunyan.

[24] Ryland, *Reminiscences*, 25. He went on to write: "Thou wilt save me. O Joy! O sweet night, or rather O sweet Jesus. O the love of Christ my God! Thou art my All, and I am thine!...Bless the Lord O my soul. Bless the Lord. O God give me grace and strength to serve thee. Take my heart and fashion it after thy will."

traveling preachers of both his father, and later John Newton, young Ryland "was privileged to hear many major evangelical leaders."[25] Perhaps one of the most notable of his day, George Whitefield (1714–1770), came to visit Ryland Sr. and was invited to preach.[26] At 8 a.m. on September 8, 1767 Ryland listened to a sermon from Isaiah 61:10, which Ryland described as "a most affectionate discourse, to a crowded congregation. I wished he could have held on till midnight."[27] Whitefield's message seems to represent the culmination of numerous factors that had shaped Ryland's relationship with Christ, for just four days later Ryland was baptized. Ryland's personal experience of "awakening" gave him the foretaste that enlivened him to invite others to share what he had experienced.

Ryland experienced two revivals in Northampton, which included the flourishing ministry at his father's boy's boarding school and in ministry with his congregation.[28] In April 1772, after having had "anxious concern" for their souls, Ryland tasted firsthand an awakening amongst the students:[29] "We had a very extraordinary awakening among the boys, many being deeply impressed; I used to go from room to room, after they were in bed, talking to them, while many were weeping and praying, 'Lord give me an interest in Christ!'"[30]

---

[25] Gordon, *Wise Counsel*, 22. Ryland was also able to hear notable preachers such as Rowland Hill (1744–1833) John Gill (1697–1771) and Augustus Toplady (1740–1778) among others.

[26] Milton J. Coalter Jr., "George Whitefield," *Dictionary of Evangelical Biography*, vol. II (Oxford: Blackwell Publishers Ltd.) 1180–81; He was invited to preach at Castle Hill. This is a hill in Northampton very suitable to open air preaching but here likely refers to Castle Hill Congregational Church, built in 1692 and home to the preacher, Phillip Doddridge (1702-51).

[27] Ryland, *Reminiscences*, 29.

[28] In both settings Ryland came to have an ever-increasing role alongside his father. In June of 1771 Ryland writes that he "constantly assisted my Father in the school and in preaching"; Ryland, *Reminiscences*, 44.

[29] Ryland, *Reminiscences*, 38, 39, 45. In July of 1769 he lamented that while several boys had joined their "praying society" the boys "in general seemed rather hardened than softened [spiritually]." The prayer society is an example of how Ryland was beginning to value prayer. An experience of the power and importance of prayer, long before he had read Edwards, came from a story his "dear mother" recalled from when his father was at death's door because of smallpox, "I have often heard my mother speak of the extraordinary spirit of prayer, which then prevailed among the people of his charge, & the great concern expressed for his life." Ryland, *Reminiscences*, 10.

[30] Ryland, *Reminiscences*, 46.

Ryland not only witnessed awakening at the school but also in his home congregation. He noted that, "his [father's] ministry there was very successful, the congregation increased exceedingly, and the meeting-house was twice enlarged," and in 1774 that "many were awakened at Northampton this spring."[31] These early examples of revival demonstrate that Ryland was aware of and deeply impressed by the revivals he experienced.[32]

Influential Mentors

Ryland was not alone in developing his theology of revival. Aside from early experiences, three eminent divines also profoundly influenced Ryland's theology and pastoral character. Those included John Newton, Robert Hall Sr., and, through his writings, Jonathan Edwards. Ryland described the former two pastoral divines as "the counsellors of my youth," and the latter theologian as "the greatest, wisest, humblest and holyest of uninspired Men!"[33]

John Newton (1725–1807), whom Ryland affectionately referred to as "father Newton," served as the evangelical vicar in nearby Olney (1764–1779),

---

[31] Ryland, *Reminiscences*, 12 and 48. Included among these was his wife to be! Michael Haykin, *One Heart, One Soul*, 72, notes that such was the success of his ministry that leading evangelical figures such as George Whitefield, Howell Harris, John Newton, Augustus Toplady, and Rowland Hill took notice of this "great work" in Northampton. Of those who were added into membership, Ryland Sr. notes in the church minute book that between 1760 and 1767, 109 new members were added. "New members added since 16 February 1760," *Northampton Church Book*, Northampton Record Office.

[32] Ryland was impressed by events such as these, which is highlighted in Ryland's correspondence with the Welsh Baptist pastor John Williams (1767–1825) who had moved to the United States, about revivals sweeping whole communities (as was common in America). He stated he had ever only seen this once in England in the case of Sheepshead, a fact he recollected in 1807, over thirty years after the event. John Ryland, "Letter to John Williams," August 28, 1807, ABHSR.

[33] John Ryland, *The indwelling and righteousness of Christ no security against corporeal death, but the source of spiritual and eternal life....* (London: W. Button, 1815) 37. Ryland's comment in 1773 on the inside cover of his copy of *The Life and Character of Jonathan Edwards* (Boston, 1765) BBCA 13898. This chapter will focus on Newton. For more on Hall see Michael Haykin, "Robert Hall," in *The British Particular Baptists, 1638–1910*, vol. 1, ed. Michael Haykin (Springfield, MO: Particular Baptist Press, 1998) 203–11. He was a founding member of the association, an influential pastor, a ministerial member, and a mentor, and he held the position of moderator on seven occasions.

and then as rector at St. Mary Woolnoth in London (1779–1807).[34] Ryland and Newton's "unique and enduring friendship" began on January 17, 1768, when Ryland first heard him preach in Olney.[35] Not long after Ryland went to visit Newton for several days and remembered that he "had much pleasure in his conversation, and that of several of his poor people whom he took me to see. Heard him preach 3 times...."[36] The two would connect regularly; after Newton moved to London, and Ryland to Bristol, they maintained regular correspondence.[37]

Newton provided Ryland with much pastoral wisdom.[38] Specific to his High Calvinistic theology and disposition he influenced Ryland in two significant ways, as seen in his 1771 and 1772 letters. In 1771, the same year Ryland had begun to engage in public ministry, he published a collection of his adolescent verses, *Serious Essays*, which was prefaced by a twenty-two-page barrage defending High Calvinism.[39] Newton, unable to personally meet Ryland quickly, wrote to "act the part of a friend by letter."[40] Sensing Ryland's teachable disposition, Newton rebuked Ryland for his "vanity" (for disclaiming friendly assistance in the composition of his verse) and also his "great impropriety" (his arrogance in presuming that at such a young age he could speak, *ex cathedra* as it were, on subtle theological distinctions on which there was considerable disagreement among the greatest divines). On the point of

---

[34] Gordon, *Wise Counsel*, 403. Newton represented a growing evangelical minority within the Church of England. For more on Newton see Jonathan Aitken, *John Newton: From Disgrace to Amazing Grace* (London: Continuum, 2007).

[35] Gordon, *Wise Counsel*, 404; Ryland, *Reminiscences*, 31.

[36] He stayed with Newton in Olney from August 28 to September 3; Ryland, *Reminiscences*, 36.

[37] There are eighty-three known letters (1771–1803) from Newton to Ryland. For a superb record of the letters between these two friends see Gordon, *Wise Counsel*. On July 28, 1795, Newton reflected on the significance of their friendship, writing, "the remembrance of past times revived and gave me pleasure. We began when you were a lad and I a curate and we have gone on till you are grown into a doctor and I am dignified with the title of rector. Our friendship, now grown old, will I hope continue to the end, whatever changes may yet await us; yea, and subsist and flourish in a better world." Gordon, *Wise Counsel*, letter 67, 317.

[38] For more on Newton's theological influence on Ryland see Bruce D. Hindmarsh, *John Newton and the English Evangelical Tradition between the Conversions of Wesley and Wilberforce* (Oxford: Clarendon Press, 1996) 142–59.

[39] John Ryland, *Serious Essays on the Truths of the Glorious Gospel, and the Various Branches of Vital Experience. For the Use of True Christians* (London: J. W. Pasham, 1771). BBCA 13535.

[40] Gordon, *Wise Counsel*, letter one, 11.

Ryland's vanity Newton had much to say: "The doctrines of grace are humbling, that is in their power and experience, but a man may hold them all in the notion, and be very proud. He certainly is so, if he thinks his assenting to them is a proof of his humility, and despises others as proud and ignorant in comparison of himself."[41] Likewise, the theological issue of eternal justification was dealt with in the letters when Newton offered practical advice regarding the condescending tendency of High Calvinism, where many, he said, "have appeared to be rather wise than warm, rather positive than humble, rather captious than lively, and more disposed to talk of speculations than experience."[42]

Newton was constrained by the unpopularity of his theological stance within the Establishment, but nonetheless remained Calvinistic and used such principles as part of a wider theology and not simply as a hobbyhorse.[43] As such, he helped steer Ryland towards a more biblical theology and spirituality than one predominated by one single prejudice. William Jay (1769-1853), leading evangelical congregational preacher in Bath, recounted a conversation with Newton in which Jay said, "'I am more of a Calvinist than anything else; but I use my Calvinism in my writings and my preaching as I use this sugar'"— taking a lump, and putting it into his tea-cup, and stirring it, adding, "'I do not give it alone, and whole; but mixed and diluted.'"[44]

Newton wisely noticed both the theological and practical dangers of the High Calvinism with which Ryland was dallying. Newton's wise counsel and personal example did much to influence Ryland's reflection on High Calvinism, as did his lending of theological works. He and Ryland are known to have exchanged many books; however, the work of the greatest significance was

---

[41] Gordon, *Wise Counsel*, letter one, 15.

[42] Gordon, *Wise Counsel*, letter two, 21.

[43] Bruce D. Hindmarsh, "'I am a sort of a middle-man': The Politically Correct Evangelicalism of John Newton," in *Amazing Grace: Evangelicals in Australia, Britain, Canada and the United States*, ed. G. Rawlyk et al. (Montreal: McGill-Queens, 1994) 21. Whereas Ryland, being a Particular Baptist, had much more liberty to purport his views and could therefore be more vocally Calvinistic, Newton saw great dangers in "separating those things which God hath joined together, and insisting on some parts of the word of God almost to the exclusion of the rest." Gordon, *Wise Counsel*, letter two, 21.

[44] G. Redford, and J. A. James, eds. *The Autobiography of William Jay* (1854; reprint, Edinburgh: Banner of Truth Trust, 1974) 272; For more on Jay see Tudor Jones, "William Jay," *Dictionary of Evangelical Biography*, vol. 1 (Oxford: Blackwell Publishers Ltd., 1995) 606.

Smalley's sermons on moral and natural ability that Ryland received in 1776.[45] Though the American theologian of revival, Jonathan Edwards (1703–1758), died when Ryland was only five years old, his legacy through his written works and relations had the most profound impact upon Ryland.[46] This is best illustrated in Ryland's naming his son Jonathan Edwards Ryland (b. 1797).[47] In light of his belief that Edwards reflected life-giving orthodoxy, he could state years later that, "if I knew that I should be with Sutcliff and Fuller tomorrow, instead of regretting that I had endeavoured to promote that religion delineated by Jonathan Edwards in his *Treatise of Religious Affections* and in his life of David Brainerd I would recommend his writings …with the last effort I could make to guide a pen."[48] Edwards would play a leading role in Ryland's theological reformation.

Ryland's Evangelical Calvinism Developed and Defined

In Newton's response to Ryland's 1773 sorrowful epistle, he quotes a friend from Cambridge who stated, "There were many high, dry, notional Calvinists in that part of the country."[49] Indeed such High-Calvinistic coolness had swept across much of nonconformity, and has been duly noted as a

---

[45] John Smalley, *Natural and Moral Inability: Two Sermons; or The Inability of the Sinner to Comply with the Gospel, his inexcusable guilt in not complying with it, and the consistency of these with each other, illustrated, Two Discourses* (London, 1769). The New England theologian John Smalley (1734–1820) was an associate of Jonathan Edwards.

[46] See George Marsden, *Jonathan Edwards: A Life* (New Haven: Yale University Press, 2004). Ryland was introduced to Jonathan Edwards Jr. by John Erskine and they maintained an active correspondence; Jonathan Yeager, "The Letters of John Erskine to the Rylands," *Eusebeia: The Journal of the Andrew Fuller Center for Baptist Studies* 9 (2008): 183.

[47] Diary entry of December 27, 1795. His first son was named Jonathan Tyler Ryland; had his second son survived infancy, Frances Ryland wrote, he was "to have taken the name of Jonathan Edwards." See Timothy Wheelan. *Nonconformist Women Writers, 1720–1840* (London: Pickering and Chatto, 2011) 361. Despite the sad reality of eighteenth-century infant mortality, Ryland persevered to name yet another son after his favorite theologian.

[48] J. E. Ryland, *Pastoral Memorials*, 1:15. For more on Andrew Fuller (1754–1815) see Peter Morden, *Offering Christ to the World: Andrew Fuller (1754–1815) and the Revival of Eighteenth Century Particular Baptist Life* (Milton Keynes, UK: Paternoster, 2003); and Peter Morden, *The Life and Thought of Andrew Fuller, 1754–1815* (Milton Keynes, UK: Paternoster, 2015).

[49] Gordon, *Wise Counsel*, 43.

leading cause in Baptist decline.[50] For instance, by 1689 Baptist congregations had rapidly increased to three hundred, and yet the ensuing settledness saw that decline to 220 in 1715 and 150 in 1750.[51] Amongst Baptists this issue actually had its birthplace and demise in Northamptonshire.

The controversy in question was the "Modern Question" and was defined by Ryland as "whether it be the duty of all men to whom the gospel is published, to repent and believe in Christ."[52] This was a consuming theological controversy within Calvinistic circles throughout Ryland's lifetime.[53] The question produced those who responded in the affirmative (Evangelical Calvinists) or the negative (High Calvinists). Ryland acknowledged that the zeal of many "good men" to guard the five points of Calvinism, and any antinomian tendencies "were driven into an extreme."[54] As a result, men such as John Gill and John Brine, who took the negative side, believed "it is not the duty of the unregenerate to believe in Christ."[55] They believed that as only the elect

---

[50] Nonconformity was troubled by nominalism, primary theological disputes stemming from intellectualism, and the spiritual dangers of political stability and wealth; Hayden, *Continuity and Change*, 37. Though traditional Baptist historiography tended to label High Calvinism as the sole cause of decline amongst Baptists, recent studies have expanded that list to include a number of factors such as burnout from persecution; church building instead of evangelism; internal vs. external focus; traditionalism; failing to acknowledge awakenings outside of Baptist circles as legitimate; and internal secondary theological disputes; Michael Haykin, *Ardent Love for Jesus: Learning from the Eighteenth-Century Baptist Revival* (Bridgend, Wales: Bryntirion Press, 2013) 17, 19–20).

[51] Michael Haykin, "'The Lord is Doing Great Things and Answering Prayer Everywhere': The Revival of the Calvinistic Baptist in the Long Eighteenth Century" (unpublished paper) 1; W. T. Whitley, "The Baptist Interest under George I," *Transactions of the Baptist Historical Society*, 2 (1910–1911): 95–109; and John Collett Ryland list, Warwick Church Book, 1714–1779 (Warwick Record Office) 19–21.

[52] Ryland, *Andrew Fuller*, 6. For more on the Modern Question see Ryland, *Andrew Fuller*, 6–11; Hindmarsh, *John Newton and the English Evangelical Tradition*, 144–46; Geoffrey F. Nuttall, "Northamptonshire and the Modern Question: A Turning-Point in Eighteenth-Century Dissent," *Journal of Theological Studies* 16 (1965): 101; Hindmarsh, *John Newton and the English Evangelical Tradition*, 142–59; and Gerald Priest, "Andrew Fuller's Response to the 'Modern Question'—A Reappraisal of the Gospel Worthy of All Acceptation," *Detroit Baptist Seminary Journal* 6 (Fall 2001): 45–73.

[53] See Alan P.F. Sell, *The Great Debate: Calvinism, Arminianism and Salvation* (Eugene, OR: Wipf & Stock, 1998) 52–53.

[54] John Ryland, *The Work of Faith, the Labour of Love, and the Patience of Hope Illustrated in the Life of Andrew Fuller* (London: Button & Son, 1816) 5–6; BBCA 13532..

[55] J. E. Ryland,, *Pastoral Memorials*, 1:14.

can be saved, Christ should not be offered to sinners, essentially annihilating the apostolic commission.⁵⁶ Ryland, affected by this when he entered the ministry, recalled that though he "endeavoured to say as much to sinners as my views of this subject would allow," he was "shackled" and "carefully avoided exhorting sinners to come to Christ for salvation."⁵⁷ What worried those who took the affirmative side was that in "calling on sinners to repent and believe the Gospel" their act would be accused as "a piece of robbery against the Holy Spirit" as it would imply an innate ability to believe on the part of the hearer.⁵⁸ As a result, Baptist preachers "were too much restrained from imitating our Lord and his apostles, in calling on sinners to 'repent and believe the gospel.'"⁵⁹ Christian obedience and evangelism, along with the ensuing personal spiritual benefits, were thus greatly stifled by the negative side. The theological reformation that followed amongst Ryland and his friends was a quest to discern how evangelism and particular redemption could be reconciled within a Calvinistic system.

For Ryland the blame was clear: "Through the influence of Mr. Brine and Dr. Gill, who both took the negative of the question...this opinion spread pretty much among ministers of the Baptist denomination."⁶⁰ In his published work entitled *Serious Remarks II*, Ryland argues that High Calvinism was false Calvinism and suggests that he rediscovered earlier "Calvinistic divines" who had indeed answered the Modern Question in the affirmative.⁶¹ Thus, the

---

⁵⁶ J. E. Ryland, *Pastoral Memorials*, 1:14.

⁵⁷ John Ryland, *Serious Remarks on the Different Representations of Evangelical Doctrine by the Professed Friends of the Gospel*, in 2 parts (Bristol: Button & Son, 1817 and 1818) pt. 2, p. 8.

⁵⁸ Ryland, *Andrew Fuller*, 9. This was a term used by Joseph Hussey (1659–1726) in *God's Operation of Grace but No Offers of Grace*) (1707) and W.T. Whitley, *Calvinism and Evangelism, Especially in Baptist Circles* (London: Kingsgate, 1933) 27.

⁵⁹ Ryland, *Andrew Fuller*, 5–8.

⁶⁰ In *Continuity and Change*, Hayden views the Western Association, and other provincial regions, as preserving Evangelical Calvinism from the influence of the High Calvinism of many notable London pulpits. This view is also supported by Ryland himself: "The Baptists in the West of England, indeed, knew but little of the controversy, carried on in Northamptonshire and Yorkshire, respecting what was called "The Modern Question": therefore, some of their ablest ministers were stigmatized with the name of West-Country Calvinists, by those who thought themselves sounder in the faith, than the great reformer at Geneva"; Ryland, *Serious Remarks*, pt. 2, pp. 3–4; Ryland, *Andrew Fuller*, 8; and Ryland, *Reminiscences*, 36–37.

⁶¹ Ryland writes: "As far as I can learn, all the Calvinistic divines in Britain, both Conformists and Non-conformists, were agreed, till some considerable time after the beginning of the last century, on this subject"; Ryland, *Serious Remarks*, pt. 2, pp. 3–4. Ryland's historic view

Northamptonshire Baptist Association became the catalytic center for reform that challenged "false Calvinism's" hold over the Baptists. Ryland and his friends became agents advocating this evangelical Calvinism that swept most of the denomination with new life.

As early as February 1774, Ryland was introduced to Edwards by reading an abridgement of *On the Affections*.[62] In late May 1775, Ryland read Edwards's *Life of David Brainerd*, a book that he prized "above almost all others."[63] This Ryland read "with great interest, and I trust with humiliation and profit."[64] On the cover of his personal copy of this book he remarked, "O for the like Spirit that rested on this blessed Man whose life is here in related. Where is the Lord God of Elijah!!!"[65] The testimony of Brainerd's life had a profound spiritual effect on Ryland, especially "that power of godliness" in him, which spurred Ryland toward revival both personal and corporate.[66] In October 1775, Ryland declared, "This [*On the Affections*] and the *Life of David Brainerd* I trust renewed me more of the Nature of True Religion than I ever saw before."[67] His theological reflection surrounding these works all coincided with his resolve "to get a more decided conviction of the Truth of the affirmative side of the Modern Question, and a clearer view of the nature of Faith in Christ" in the fall of 1775.[68] Then in 1776 he borrowed a volume of Amer-

---

is in line with contemporary arguments that stress evangelicalism's continuity with the Puritans. See Michael Haykin and Kenneth J. Stewart, eds. *The Advent of Evangelicalism: Exploring Historical Continuities* (Nottingham, UK: Intervarsity Press, 2008). This work includes David Bebbington's own reassessment, and stresses Evangelicalism's continuity rather than its discontinuity as originally argued in *Evangelicalism in Modern Britain: A History from the 1730s to the 1980s* (New York: Routledge, 1989) chap. 2.

[62] Jonathan Edwards, *A Treatise Concerning Religious Affections* (1746). He read the full work in the fall of 1775; Ryland, *Reminiscences*, 56.

[63] Jonathan Edwards, *An Account of the Life of the Late Reverend Mr David Brainerd* (Edinburgh: William Gray, 1765 [1749]) Ryland's copy, BBCA 13881, cover.

[64] Ryland, *Reminiscences*, 50.

[65] Ryland's personal copy of Edwards, *David Brainerd*, front cover.

[66] Ryland, *Reminiscences*, 51. In John Ryland, *Salvation Finished: A Funeral Sermon on Robert Hall Senior; with Appendix on the Church at Arnesby and Its Pastor* (1791) (BBCA 13536) 34, Ryland similarly wrote, "never met with any human composure, more suited to illustrate and promote pure and undefiled religion."

[67] Ryland, *Reminiscences*, 56.

[68] Ryland, *Reminiscences*, 55. To accomplish this he not only read Edwards but Samuel Rutherford and Jonathan Dickinson's *Letters*.

ican sermons from Newton. Among these were Smalley's two sermons on natural and moral ability. Smalley's sermons were significant for Ryland and friends to whom he lent them, "in settling our minds respecting some theological difficulties."[69] Thus Newton, Edwards, and finally Smalley helped to academically unhinge the High Calvinism of Ryland and his circle regarding the Modern Question.[70] The period from 1774 to 1776 had seen a seismic period of theological reformation for Ryland. By the time of his ordination council on June 8, 1781, his theology had been orientated in a renewed direction.[71]

The years from 1768 through to the late 1770s represent a period in which Ryland's theology was reformed, but there was one additional element yet to be built upon it: prayer and revival. On March 15, 1784, Dr. John Erskine (1721–1803) sent a letter from Scotland to Ryland in which Erskine wrote, "I beg your acceptance of President Edwards on prayer for the revival of religion. I know not if there is another copy in Scotland."[72] Enclosed in the package was a copy of *An Humble Attempt* that would be the spark that fanned the flames of the Prayer Call of that same year.[73]

---

[69] Ryland, *Reminiscences*, 57.

[70] Hindmarsh, *John Newton and the English Evangelical Tradition*, 154.

[71] In all likelihood it had emerged some years prior as his preface statement remarks that his people "are already acquainted with my sentiments" amongst whom he did not use "any disguise." John Ryland, *A Confession of Faith delivered by John Ryland jur of Northampton at his Ordination to the Pastoral Care of the Church in College Lane, June 8, 1781*; BBCA 14884.

[72] "The Correspondence of John Erskine to the Rylands," University of Edinburgh Collection. See also: Jonathan Yeager, "The Letters of John Erskine to the Rylands," *Eusebeia: The Journal of the Andrew Fuller Center for Baptist Studies* 9 (2008): 183–95. For more on Erskine see Jonathan Yeager, *Enlightened Evangelicalism: The Life and Thought of John Erskine* (Oxford: Oxford University, 2011) 12. Erskine was an evangelical transmitter of ideas. There are eighty-six known letters to Ryland in which he was forwarded four hundred items. Of the known correspondents of Erskine, Ryland was the most prolific. Erskine also propagated Ryland's works, ensuring they had a wider audience.

[73] Jonathan Edwards, *An Humble Attempt to Promote Explicit Agreement and Visible Union of God's People in Extraordinary Prayer* (Boston, 1747); The Prayer Call built upon an already developing prayer culture within the association. Ernest Payne, *Prayer Call of 1784* (London: Baptist Laymen's Missionary Movement, 1941). The Prayer Call was written by John Sutcliff and issued in 1784 by the Northamptonshire Baptist Association after its annual meeting calling on member churches to pray and bewail "the low estate of religion, and earnestly implore a revival of our churches, and of the general cause of our Redeemer, and for that end to wrestle with God for the effusion of his Holy Spirit, which alone can produce the blessed effect" (cf. Ezekiel 36:37).

After rapidly absorbing *An Humble Attempt* Ryland quickly passed it on to others in time for the June association meeting where Fuller would speak on the subject and Sutcliff would issue the Prayer Call.[74] But was Ryland simply a conduit of evangelical material for this band of brothers in Northamptonshire that led to the rediscovery of evangelical Calvinism and provided the impetus for revival among the Baptists (and beyond), or was he something more?[75] Gordon and Hindmarsh have Ryland following Fuller theologically, whereas Noll and Champion have Sutcliff and Fuller following Ryland, and Fuller biographer Peter Morden states Ryland's influence was indirect but important; but which was it?[76] High-Calvinism and the "godless eighteenth-century" had produced ripe ground for such reflection, and evangelical Calvinism's entry into Northamptonshire cannot necessarily be pinned to any one individual, as together—simultaneously—they were reflecting on the nature of revival and seeking it for themselves. For example, Ryland's son J. E. Ryland noted that, "several other ministers were led to adopt a similar view."[77] However, it is interesting that the insinuated distinction made by Ryland's son, is that these brothers "were led," not just through reflection or by the Spirit, but by his father. While this could be attributed to family pride, there is strong reason to believe that in this fellowship, whereas Fuller may have gone on to theologize and popularize evangelical Calvinism and William Carey (1761–1834) drew practical, missional conclusions from it, it was Ryland amongst

---

It was suggested that churches set apart the first Monday of each month for this effort. The practice quickly spread to other Baptist associations and other denominations across England.

[74] June 2 and 3, 1784, were the dates for the association gathering in Nottingham from which the Prayer Call was issued.

[75] Ryland "always considered him [Fuller], Brother Sutcliff and myself as more closely united to each other than either of us was to anyone else"; Ryland, *Andrew Fuller*, 9.

[76] Hindmarsh, *John Newton and the English Evangelical Tradition*, 149 (here he even suggests Fuller developed his Fullerism independently because of his geographic isolation within the Northamptonshire Association); Gordon, *Wise Counsel*, 173; Mark Noll, *The Rise of Evangelicalism: The Age of Edwards, Whitefield and the Wesley's* (Downer's Grove: InterVarsity, 2003) 196; Leonard Champion, "The Theology of John Ryland, Its Sources and Its Influences," *Baptist Quarterly* 28 (January 1979): 22; and Peter Morden notes Ryland's influence on Fuller was indirect but still important; Morden, *Offering Christ to the World*, 39–40.

[77] J. E. Ryland, *Pastoral Memorials*, 1:15–16. The other ministers include Fuller, Carey, Hall Sr., and Sutcliff.

this brotherhood who acted the part of the Baptist bishop.[78] Ryland first met Sutcliff on July 22, 1773, and Fuller in 1776.[79] That Ryland was Sutcliff's conduit for many theological works has already been noted; the same was true of Fuller.[80] Ryland's academic learnedness coupled with his piety and evangelical connections meant that, in Northamptonshire, he was the likely fixture to become aware of, receive, and promote information he deemed important. Add to this the ministerial position he inherited from his father at College Lane, the leading church with the most prominent pastor in the association, and the esteem in which he was held, one can see how Ryland Jr. was more than just a conduit for Edwards. He was captivated by Edwards, and became Edwards's apostle using his position to advocate for evangelical Calvinism and labor for revival. While a strong level of mutuality must be admitted in this circle, that Ryland took a lead role cannot be rightly denied.

The significance of Edwards's ultimate influence over Ryland and his friends is captured in correspondence between Fuller and Ryland in 1815 in which Fuller wrote, "We have some who have been giving out of late that if Sutcliff and some others had preached more of Christ and less of Jonathan Edwards, they would have been more useful." To this criticism Fuller immediately made the reply: "If those who talk thus preached Christ half as much as Jonathan Edwards did, and were half as useful as he was, their usefulness would be double what it is."[81] Ryland defines "evangelical [or Gospel] truth" as a "system of truth which is taught us in the gospel of Jesus Christ.... It is good news of salvation by grace, from sin and its just but awful consequences, through the mediation and atonement of the blessed Redeemer, and the renewing influences of the Holy Spirit."[82] He goes on to add the necessity of sovereign grace and the five points of Calvinism as intrinsic to this religion.[83]

---

[78] Andrew Fuller, *The Gospel Worthy of All Acceptation*, 1st ed. (Northampton: T. Dicey, 1785); and William Carey, *An Enquiry into the Obligations for Christians to use Means for the Conversion of the Heathens* (1792; London: Kingsgate, 1961). For more on Carey see S. Pearce, *William Carey: The Father of Modern Missions* (London: Wakeman Trust, 1993).

[79] Ryland, *Reminiscences*, 47.

[80] Champion, "The Theology of John Ryland," 22. Ryland lent Fuller a number of Edwards's works and other American publications; Morden, *Offering Christ to the World*, 39–40.

[81] Ryland, *Andrew Fuller*, 545.

[82] John Ryland, *The Practical Influence of Evangelical Religion* (London: B. J. Holdsworth, 1819) 6.

[83] Ryland, *Practical Influence*, 6; See also Ryland, *Andrew Fuller*, 5.

Theologically, Ryland had been a High Calvinist. Through his own experience, study of Scripture and theology, group reflection, and the witnessing of revival around him, he was led to abandon this system that had shackled his ministry.[84] Contrary to most Baptist historiography about Ryland's theology that describes it as developing, moderate, and progressing, for Ryland at least, his formation was viewed as simply *ad fontes*, rediscovery or reformation. While it can often anachronistically be labeled Fullerism, evangelical, or moderate Calvinism, Ryland employed other terms to describe his stance.[85] He used words such as "pseudo Calvinist," and "false Calvinist," to describe High Calvinism, and "first Calvinists" and "strict Calvinism," to describe what he saw as authentic Calvinism.[86] For Ryland, the difference was between false Calvinism and true Calvinism, and true Calvinism was synonymous with "evangelical truth," evangelicalism, and authentic orthodox Christianity.[87] For Ryland, nothing novel was discovered; rather he and his friends acted as reformers recalling their denomination back to something that once was. In so doing, they recaptured a spirituality and urgent sense of mission that radiated throughout Baptist and evangelical ranks.

---

[84] Ryland., *Pastoral Memorials*, 1:15.

[85] Ryland does employ this term at least once (Ryland, *Andrew Fuller*, 4); however, it is not used in a sense of progressively moderating but rather something that was in the extreme being made moderate towards a center.

[86] Ryland, *Serious Remarks*, pt 1, p. 22; The charge by Bruce Hindmarsh ("I am a sort of middle-man," 13) that Hyper-Calvinism did not come into vogue until the nineteenth century and is thus anachronistic would be false because Fuller was using this term in the eighteenth century in a derogatory manner. Fuller stated, "with respect to the system of doctrine which I had used to hear from youth, it was in the hyper-Calvinistic strain...." See Andrew Fuller, *The Reformed Reader*, accessed March 2015, http://www.reformedreader.org/rbs/afuller.htm; Ryland, *Serious Remarks*, pt. 2, p. 6; see also Ryland, *Andrew Fuller*, 9–10 (literally "the strictest Calvinism"). This was also a term used by Andrew Fuller, and he did not utilize strict to mean prohibitive but rather a system strictly following true Calvinism.

[87] Ryland, *Reminiscences*, 35; As Robert Hall Jr. (1764–1831) put it in Ryland's funeral sermon: "The two extremes [against] which you are well aware he was most solicitous to guard the religious public were, Pelagian pride and Antinomian licentiousness; the first of which he detested as an insult on the grace of the gospel; and the last, on the majesty and authority of the law." Robert Hall Jr., "A sermon occasioned by the death of the Rev. John Ryland, D.D. preached at the Baptist meeting, Broadmead, Bristol, June 5, 1825," in *The Works of the Rev. Robert Hall*, ed. A. M. Olinthus, Gregory and Joseph Belcher (New York: Harper & Bros., 1854) 221.

JOHN RYLAND JR., EVANGELICAL CALVINISM, AND THE EVANGELICAL REVIVAL

Evangelical Calvinism in Action

The outworking of Ryland's theology had many practical implications for religion. He was one of the defining figures amongst Baptists during his lifetime and was recognized as a leading evangelical character, which contributed greatly to revival through the spread of evangelical Calvinism. While the Baptists were at a congregational low of 150 in 1750, Ryland played a significant role in the rapid growth of the denomination to 382 congregations in 1794, 445 in 1798, 926 in 1832, and 1,947 in 1839; a 1,300 percent growth![88] John Briggs offers four essential ingredients behind this Baptist revival: (1) the influence of Edwardsianism (2) renewed leadership and association life (3) a new sense of spiritual vision and cooperation towards local and international mission, and (4) corporate prayer.[89] Ryland was at the heart of each of these, exercising his threefold purpose. Historians Cox, Orr, Cook, Payne, Haykin, Briggs, and Noll have all noted that the human origins of not only the Baptist revival but the Evangelical Revival (1790s–1830s) in England as a whole, find their direct roots in Ryland, his close friends, and the Prayer Call of 1784.[90] Ryland's usefulness was such that he not only contributed to an expansive, confident, and influential denomination, but also to the wider advance of religion and its transformative impact on English society into the Victorian era.[91] In addition to his theology, Ryland's usefulness was demonstrated as a

---

[88] See John Rippon, *Baptist Annual Register* (London, 1797) 2:16, 23; Rippon, *Baptist Annual Register* (London, 1801) 3:40, 42; and *Census of Great Britain, 1851*, "Religious Worship, England and Wales, Reports and Tables" (London: George E. Eyre and William Spottiswoode, 1853) 61.

[89] John Briggs, ed., *Pulpit and People: Studies in Eighteenth Century Baptist Life and Thought* (Milton Keynes, UK: Paternoster, 2009) 7.

[90] F. A. Cox, *History of the Baptist Missionary Society, from 1792 to 1842* (London, 1842) 1:10–11; J. Edwin Orr, *The Eager Feet: Evangelical Awakenings 1790–1830* (Chicago: Moody, 1975) 95, 191–92, 199; Paul E. G. Cook, "The Forgotten Revival," in *Preaching and Revival* (London: Westminster Conference, 1984) 92; Payne, "Prayer Call of 1784," 1; Haykin, "The Lord is doing Great Things," 33–34; and Noll, *Rise of Evangelicalism*, 145.

[91] Hindmarsh, *John Newton and the English Evangelical Tradition*, 145; and John Wolfe, *The Expansion of Evangelicalism: The Age of Wilberforce, More, Chalmers and Finney* (Downer's Grove: Intervarsity, 2007) 90.

pastor and educator,[92] through his evangelical catholicity,[93] as a Baptist Missionary Society founder,[94] and through his pen.[95]

Summary

Ryland experienced first-hand what historians have subsequently termed "the Great Evangelical Revival." Ryland's acquaintance with awakenings such as those of Beddome and other leading preachers, his own conversion experience, and revivals in the church and school in Northampton, along with influential mentors such as Hall, Newton, and Edwards all served to influence his theology. Throughout the 1770s, he recast his doctrinal stance, rediscovered his authentic Calvinistic heritage, and contextualized it for a new era to purport what it meant to truly be a Particular Baptist. Stemming from these

---

[92] Ryland pastored the nationally significant congregations of College Lane, Northampton (1771–1793) and Broadmead, Bristol (1793–1825); he served as president of the Bristol Baptist Academy (1793–1825). His arrival in 1793 to the joint office, in the words of Newton, was in the "general interest of the Baptists"; Gordon, *Wise Counsel*, letter 55, 263. Andrew Fuller said, "Perhaps, there could not have been a station in which you would have had so fair an opportunity of propagating gospel truths"; Andrew Fuller, "Letter to John Ryland," December, 3, 1793 (AB-HSR). Some two hundred students were trained for ministry of which twenty-six became BMS (Baptist Missionary Society) missionaries; Gordon, *Wise Counsel*, 297) many of them going on to have influential roles themselves at home and abroad as "Ryland's boys." (Haykin, "Sum of all Good," 336–37).

[93] A survey of Ryland's connections reveals a who's who of Baptists, and to a lesser but still valid extent, wider Evangelicalism, as he engaged in and helped found numerous Baptist and pan-evangelical causes and societies.

[94] While Fuller and Ryland both recognized Carey's genius behind the idea of missions found in *An Enquiry* (Ryland, *Andrew Fuller*, 146–47) it was the theology of Ryland and his friends that was the incubator for Carey's work and the formation of the BMS. Indeed, Ryland had baptized Carey in 1783 and he would remain a close personal friend and mentor of many of the BMS missionaries. Carey also noted that it was Ryland, Fuller, and Sutcliff who "held the ropes" of the mission; J. W. Morris, *Memoirs of the Life and Death of the Rev. Andrew Fuller* (London: Button & Son, 1816) 101. As a founding member, Ryland tirelessly strove to promote the ends of the mission, especially in the West Indies. After Fuller died in 1815, Ryland took up the reins of the BMS as secretary.

[95] Ryland exerted an influence beyond himself via his prolific pen. Not counting his travels prior to 1792, he traveled 36,000 miles by horse, and preached a total of 8,691 sermons at some three hundred locations during his lifetime; John Ryland, "Account of Journeys since 1792," BBCA 14884). He published numerous sermons, theological works, the first biography of Andrew Fuller, and over ninety-nine hymns. Though not necessarily original, Ryland's academic and spiritual prowess was a practical means by which he zealously defended and promoted the principles and causes he believed in.

convictions and their promotion, Ryland significantly contributed to the subsequent revivals that swept across Britain and beyond its shores through his foundational work with the BMS, his evangelical catholicity, and the instrumental denominational positions he held, as well as through his written works. Thus, Ryland fulfilled his threefold calling to utility.

12

The Hymns of Anne Steele in John Rippon's *Selection of Hymns*: The Sung Theology of the English Particular Baptist Revival

Joseph V. Carmichael

Anne Steele the Hymn Writer

Anne Steele (1717–1778), the poetically gifted daughter of a Particular Baptist pastor, composed hymns for personal devotional purposes and also to supplement the collection of the hymns of Isaac Watts (1674–1748) that were sung in her father's congregation. Once celebrated as "the female Poet of the Sanctuary,"[1] Steele's pen placed her at the head of a group of Particular Baptist pastor hymn writers whose evangelical and theologically compelling hymns—once warmly received—have been practically forgotten.[2] Writing in the midst of the evangelical revival in England along with such famous hymn writers as Charles Wesley (1707–1788), William Cowper (1731–1800), and John Newton (1725–1807), she and this group followed Isaac Watts into the "Golden

---

[1] Edwin F. Hatfield, *Poets of the Church* (Wentworth Press, 2016) 570, cited in Henry S. Burrage, *Baptist Hymn Writers and Their Hymns* (Portland, Maine: Brown Thurston and Co., 1888) 46.

[2] Baptist authors collectively wrote 263 of the 588 hymns in John Rippon's *A Selection of Hymns, from the Best Authors, including a Great Number of Originals, Intended to be an appendix to Dr. Watts's Psalms and Hymns* of 1787 and have a substantial number of hymns in The Baptist Hymnal of 1883, but have notably fewer hymns in *The Baptist Hymnal* published in 1991. Anne Steele has none in this last named hymnal. Other notable Particular Baptist hymn writers of the era include Joseph Stennett I (1663–1713) Benjamin Wallin (1711–1782) Benjamin Beddome (1717–1795) Samuel Stennett (1727–1795) Benjamin Francis (1734–1799) John Fawcett (1739–1817) and John Ryland Jr. (1753–1825). W. R. Stevenson regards Steele as "by far the most gifted Baptist hymn writer of this period." Stevenson, "Baptist Hymnody, English," in *A Dictionary of Hymnology: Setting Forth the Origin and History of Christian Hymns of All Ages and Nations*, rev. ed., ed. John Julian (London: John Murray, Albemarle Street, 1907) 1:111–12.

Age of Hymnody."³ In fact, hymnologist Louis F. Benson says that the publication of Steele's volumes in 1760 under the pseudonym Theodosia launched Baptist hymnody into its own golden age.⁴ History has shown that Steele, who has been called the "all-time champion Baptist hymn writer of either sex,"⁵ is "the only woman of that period whose hymns have stood the test of time."⁶

Steele's father, Particular Baptist pastor William Steele (1689–1769), a successful timber merchant, had taken over the pastorate of the Baptist chapel at Broughton from his uncle, Henry Steele (1655–1739), who died in 1739 after serving that church for forty years. From an early age Anne was involved in the life of this Baptist congregation. J. R. Broome says of William, to whom Anne was very close all his life, "Doctrinally, in his preaching he followed the 1689 Confession of Faith,"⁷ which has been called "the classic expression of Calvinistic Baptist doctrine."⁸ Interestingly, the framers of the Second London Confession made a subtle but significant change to the Westminster Confession of Faith. Regarding the religious worship of God, the Second London Confession adds that not only the Psalms, "but also "Hymns and Spiritual Songs" are appropriate in the religious worship of God.⁹ The composition of theologically robust and experientially rich hymns, endorsed by this reissued confession of faith, became a treasured resource for expressions of "the doctrines of our faith and practice," just as the framers declared of the

---

³ See *Christian History* 10, no. 3 (1991) which is dedicated to the topic of the hymns of the eighteenth century. The title of the issue is "The Golden Age of Hymns."

⁴ Louis F. Benson, *The English Hymn: Its Development and Use in Worship* (Philadelphia: Presbyterian Board of Publication, 1915) 213.

⁵ Hoxie Neale Fairchild, *Religious Trends in English Poetry* (New York, 1942) 2:111, in Richard Arnold, ed., *English Hymns of the Eighteenth Century: An Anthology*, with introductions by Richard Arnold, American University Studies, ser. 4, vol. 137 (New York: Peter Lang, 1991) 318.

⁶ J. R. Broome, *A Bruised Reed: The Life and Times of Anne Steele, Together with Anne Steele's Hymns, Psalms, and a Selection of Her Prose Works* (Harpenden, UK: Gospel Standard Trust, 2007) 151.

⁷ Broome, *Bruised Reed*, 194. Broome lists excerpts from one of his sermons, showing it to be Evangelical, Calvinistic, and Gospel-driven. See 194–98.

⁸ Michael A. G. Haykin, *Kiffin, Knollys and Keach—Rediscovering Our English Baptist Heritage* (Leeds, UK.: Reformation Trust Today, 1996) 62.

⁹ Second London Confession (1677, 1688/89) 22:5, in William L. Lumpkin, *Baptist Confessions of Faith*, rev. ed. (Valley Forge, Penna.: Judson Press, 1969) 281.

confession.[10] Baptist hymn writing and congregational hymn singing also became more prominent and permanent elements of typical Particular Baptist piety and worship.

Writing her hymns self-consciously as a Particular Baptist, Steele also sought to pattern her compositions after Isaac Watts.[11] However, in considering the lyrical content, theology, and experiential elements in Anne Steele's hymns, it is also true that Steele's physical and emotional suffering was the crucible from within which she composed many of her hymns. While the popularizing of "hymn stories" over time has caused a sentimentalizing and inaccurate reporting of the range of Steele's sufferings,[12] there is no doubt that she lived through much physical and emotional pain in her life. From her childhood she endured high fever and seizures caused by malaria (eventually leading to a nervous disorder) as well as severe toothaches, stomach aches, and other bodily afflictions.[13] Writing from the experience of faith in God as it was tested through life's dark providences allowed Steele's hymns to be suffused with a sense of the reality of life in a fallen world. This added credibility to her role as a hymn writer. Broome posits, "Her ill-health over many years had been sanctified to her and out of it she had learnt that faith in the Son of God was the only source of help, happiness, and hope."[14] Cynthia Aalders finds in Steele's writings a "persisting sensitivity to God's response to the suffering she witnessed and experienced in the world."[15] Additionally, Steele lived through decades of British involvement in war and its harsh conditions within a family who sold timber to the Navy for the making of warships. Such "a lived experience" also led Steele to write about historic events.

While Steele highlights the experiential nature of eighteenth-century

---

[10] Lumpkin, *Baptist Confessions of Faith*, rev. ed., 239.

[11] Broome, *Bruised Reed*, 163.

[12] For example, surviving letters regarding the story of the drowning incident of her fiancé before their wedding show this story to be of questionable veracity. In fact, not only did her potential suitor not drown the day of or before a scheduled wedding, it does not appear the couple was even engaged. See especially J. R. Watson and Nancy Cho, "Anne Steele's Drowned Fiancé," *British Journal of Eighteenth-Century Studies* 32 (2005): 117–21.

[13] Sharon James, *In Trouble and in Joy: Four Women Who Lived for God* (Darlington, UK: Evangelical Press, 2003) 140.

[14] Broome, *Bruised Reed*, 165.

[15] Cynthia Y. Aalders, *To Express the Ineffable: The Hymns and Spirituality of Anne Steele*, Studies in Baptist History and Thought 40 (Milton Keynes, UK: Paternoster, 2008) 112.

hymnody, she wrote from the standpoint of deep theological convictions. Two points about the doctrinal nature of her hymns should be noted. First, the Scriptures were the foundation from which Steele composed her hymns. Steele gave her hymns individual titles and often included a Scripture reference to go with each one.[16] Commenting on the depth of this characteristic in Steele's hymnody, Aalders says, "This scriptural element becomes part of the formal nature of her hymnody, so that a great deal of her meaning is directed by her consistently biblical approach."[17] Bringing to mind David Bebbington's work on Evangelicalism, Nancy Cho adds, "Steele's hymns are resolutely Evangelical: word-centred, crucicentric, and encouraging a personal relationship with Christ."[18] Steele's hymns were not only biblical, however. There was also a confessional nature to them. Particular Baptist congregations of the day often supported and taught a confessional theology based on their theological beliefs as expounded in the Second London Confession. An examination of her hymns in Rippon's *Selection of Hymns* demonstrates that confessional Baptist theology was part and parcel of Steele's poetic output. This also illustrates L. G. Champion's contention that a renewed theology contributed to a rediscovery by the English Particular Baptist community of their evangelical mission as Calvinistic Baptists.[19]

Particular Baptist Hymn Writers, Steele's Hymns, and Rippon's Hymnal

Benjamin Keach has been credited with permanently laying the foundation for hymn singing among the Particular Baptist churches.[20] Samuel J. Rogal credits the ingenuity of Keach: "He managed to form a primitive model for what would come early in the eighteenth century—the hymn and the

---

[16] Rippon includes Steele's biblical references, but sometimes modifies the titles of Steele's hymns in his hymnal.

[17] Aalders, *To Express the Ineffable*, 92.

[18] Nancy Jiwon Cho, "'The Ministry of Song': Unmarried British Women's Hymn Writing, 1760–1936" (PhD diss., Durham University, 2007) 71.

[19] L. G. Champion, "Evangelical Calvinism and the Structures of Baptist Church Life," *Baptist Quarterly* 28 (1980): 197.

[20] See Benson, *English Hymn*, 99–100.

hymnbook as instruments to complement publicly moral and religious expression."[21] Though Keach wrote doctrinally sound hymns, it is often observed that they simply lacked the poetic quality necessary to press his hymn singing movement forward.[22] Joseph Stennett I followed Keach by just a few years, publishing two collections of evangelical hymns.[23] Stennett, however, was not only said to be a "good poet" by poet laureate Nahum Tate (1652–1715), but was praised by Isaac Watts for his "beautiful language" as Watts "was not ashamed to confess that he borrowed some of his lines from Stennett's hymns."[24] B. A. Ramsbottom points out the importance of Stennett in the fledgling Particular Baptist hymn movement: "Humanly speaking, Joseph Stennett's hymns are the reason why hymn singing did not "sink into oblivion" among the Baptists.[25]

Following the beginnings by these two men and prior to the explosion of hymn writing during the generation of Steele and other Baptist hymn writers, the Independent Isaac Watts burst upon the scene with the publication of his *Hymns and Spiritual Songs* in 1707 and *Psalms of David* in 1719. Eventually published together, these hymns, as they gradually made their way into Particular Baptist congregations, filled the gap in the worship of Particular Baptists until 1769 when John Ash (1724–1779) and Caleb Evans (1737–1791) published *A Collection of Hymns Adapted to Public Worship*. This hymnal, known as the Bristol Collection, due to its editors' association with the Bristol Baptist Academy, included some of Watts's most popular hymns. This hymnbook is not only widely known as the first Baptist hymnal, but also as one of the early successful attempts at collecting hymns in the same volume from a variety of authors and denominational backgrounds. According to Benson, however, it was the desire of the editors to supersede Watts as the Particular Baptist hymnal of choice that eventually led to their hymnal being superseded by another: John Rippon's (1751–1836) *A Selection of Hymns, from*

---

[21]Samuel J. Rogal, *A General Introduction to Hymnody and Congregational Song*, ATLA Monograph Series 26 (Metuchen, NJ: American Theological Library Association and Scarecrow Press, 1991) 81.

[22]For example, see Benson, *English Hymn*, 110–14.

[23]Benson, *English Hymn*, 100.

[24]B. A. Ramsbottom, "The Stennetts," in *The British Particular Baptists: 1638–1910*, ed. Michael A. G. Haykin (Springfield, MO: Particular Baptist Press, 1998) 1:137.

[25]Ramsbottom, "Stennetts," 137.

the *Best Authors, including a Great Number of Originals; Intended to be an Appendix to Dr. Watts's Psalms and Hymns*, first published in 1787. Ken R. Manley explains the Particular Baptist community's affinity for Watts: "Baptists found the hymns of Watts eminently suitable: they were doctrinally orthodox, objective in tone, rich in emotion but free from frivolities. The grace of God, the person of Christ, and his redemptive action were central themes of his hymns."[26]

Rippon wisely chose to supplement Watts rather than try to replace him, as it was Watts's own "homiletical hymnody" that endeared him to the Baptists, inspired some of their own hymn writing endeavors, and spurred Rippon's idea toward publishing a new hymnal.[27] Rippon included fifty-two of Steele's hymns in his wildly successful hymnal,[28] which sold approximately 200,000 copies in Britain and over 100,000 in America.[29] Rippon chose hymns based on evangelical convictions expressed in the lyrics through vibrant poetry that would speak to the affections. He specifically sought to "encourage appeals to the conscience of sinners" while emphasizing the work of the Holy Spirit.[30] Steele's chosen hymns contribute to these ends. Thus Manley posits that Rippon's *Selection of Hymns* was one among the many ways he encouraged the revival among Particular Baptists during the last quarter of the eighteenth century and the first quarter of the next as it "introduced to the Baptist community many of the songs of the Revival, endorsing their Evangelical piety."[31]

Through his *Selection of Hymns* John Rippon disseminated the sung theology and piety of the golden age of Baptist and evangelical hymnody.[32] Manley says, "Rippon understood that hymns are a force for unity as well as for

---

[26]Ken R. Manley, *"Redeeming Love Proclaim": John Rippon and the Baptists*, Studies in Baptist History and Thought 12 (Carlisle, Cumbria, UK: Paternoster, 2004) 86.

[27]See Manley, *Redeeming Love Proclaim*, 86–87.

[28]See Manley, *Redeeming Love Proclaim*, 287–89. Manley's table lists fifty-three hymns for Steele in Rippon's hymnal, but for this research only fifty-two were identified. See Manley "*Redeeming Love Proclaim*," 289, for his numbers.

[29]Rippon, preface to *Selection of Hymns*, iii–iv.

[30]Ken R. Manley, "John Rippon and Baptist Hymnody," in *Dissenting Praise: Religious Dissent and the Hymn in England and Wales*, ed. Isabel Rivers and David L. Wykes (Oxford: Oxford University Press, 2011) 103.

[31]Manley, *Redeeming Love Proclaim*, 6.

[32]For the present thesis, Steele's hymns were evaluated as printed in John Rippon, ed., *A Selection of Hymns, from the Best Authors, including a Great Number of Originals; Intended to be an*

shaping and strengthening faith."[33] The widespread use of Rippon's *Selection of Hymns* "among Baptists was a theologically unifying force of almost incalculable significance."[34] Rippon's hymnal met specific theological, pastoral, and devotional needs among the Baptist community. Through the vehicle of Rippon's hymnbook and the hymns therein, such as those by Steele, Baptists together affirmed their religious convictions and emotions "in the unifying experience of worship,"[35] reviving their spiritual vitality. Among Baptists and other Dissenters, this hymnal functioned practically as a prayer book. Rippon's collection of hymns, according to Manley, is illustrative of "the devotional content of Baptist worship during his lifetime and [is] a valuable pointer to Baptist spirituality for the period."[36]

Steele's hymnody as mediated through Rippon's *Selection of Hymns* contributed to the hymnal's devotional influence on the person in the pew. One aspect of the usefulness of Rippon's hymnal for research is that it is a collection of hymns from a variety of authors carefully arranged and organized systematically according to theological, ecclesiological, devotional, and practical concerns. Rippon organized it into seventeen distinct subjects with various subheadings that reveal what he wanted to communicate through the hymns he chose.[37] These headings emphasize the doctrines that needed to be emphasized in the face of errors and the overall outline of the major theological convictions of the Particular Baptists. Rippon begins with the foundational doctrinal themes of God, Creation and Providence, the Fall of Man, Scripture,

---

Appendix to Dr. Watts's Psalms and Hymns, 32nd ed. (London, 1830). The reason: "Rippon's Selection became, in connection with Watts, a standard of Baptist Hymnody, which it did so much to enlarge." Louis Benson notes the enormous impact of Rippon's Selection of Hymns: Not only was it a "standard of Baptist hymnody,...it also served as a source book for makers of many hymnbooks in the church outside,...carried forward Particular Baptist hymnody to our own time [1915], being used in Spurgeon's Tabernacle till 1866 in connection with Watts. It also was a link of connection between Baptist Hymnody in England and America, and was reprinted in New York as early as 1792." Therefore, "Rippon's Selection put American Baptists in early possession of much of the Evangelical Hymnody." See Benson, *English Hymn*, 145 and 362.

[33]Manley, *Redeeming Love Proclaim*, 82.
[34]Manley, *Redeeming Love Proclaim*, 85.
[35]Manley, "John Rippon and Baptist Hymnody," 103.
[36]Manley, *Redeeming Love Proclaim*, 84.
[37]J. R. Watson laments the lack of organization among other Dissenters' hymnbooks. See Watson, *English Hymn*, 91. Rippon was innovative in his careful arrangement, marking, and indexing of hymns in the *Selection of Hymns*.

Christ, and the Spirit. Having laid a theological base, he moves to the realm of Christian experience, both individually and corporately, with the Christian Life, Worship, the World (its vanity), the Church, Baptism, and the Lord's Supper. The final group provides hymns for Times and Seasons, Time and Eternity, Death and Resurrection, Judgment, and heaven and Hell. Steele's fifty-two hymns are proportionally distributed throughout the major sections.[38] An analysis of Steele's hymns in the *Selection of Hymns* provides a comprehensive illustration of the sensibilities of Baptist thought, theology, and piety, as well as the worship practices valued by the English Baptist community during their period of revival.

Steele's Hymn's in Rippon's Hymnal: A Case Study

Any discussion of Steele that considers her approach to her craft and the influences her poetry had on others must mention the one about whom she said, "O could I write like Watts."[39] Isaac Watts's influence upon Steele is crucial to consider in any discussion of her growth, development, and impact as a hymn writer. Steele followed Watts in many ways: in the interplay of observation and internal conviction, of theology and experience, and of orthodoxy and practice in her hymns. For example, both hymn writers saw the handiwork of a Creator in the natural order. These observations of general revelation led them each to consider their own and humankind's standing before God as found in the special revelation of Holy Scripture. Watson says of Watts, "His joy in the created world, which is found so impressively in his hymns,…becomes an important part of his theology."[40] Inhabited with a sense of the awe and power of the Creator of such a world, Watts "reaches great heights of grandeur, such as 'God of the seas! Thy thundering voice / Makes all the roaring waves rejoice, / And one soft word of thy command, / Can sink them silent in the sand.'"[41] Steele, likewise, ascends such heights in "Praise for

---

[38] It should be noted that she does not have hymns in the following small sections: the Fall of Man, the World, and Judgment, with each of these sections containing only five, five, and ten hymns, respectively. She also does not have a hymn on baptism. She has notable and balanced representation, however, in the other thirteen sections. See Manley, *"Redeeming Love Proclaim,"* 286.

[39] Anne Steele, in Broome, *Bruised Reed*, 163.

[40] Watson, *English Hymn*, 134.

[41] Broome, *Bruised Reed*, 162.

National Peace, Psalm xlvi:9,"[42] "Great Ruler of the earth and skies, / A word of thy Almighty breath / Can sink the world, or bid it rise; / Thy smile is life, thy frown is death." While Broome still finds in Watts a "greater realization of the majesty and glory of God" than in Steele, he does propose, "when however it came to matters of the soul, then Anne equaled him."[43] Further, echoing Watson, he suggests that "her best hymns…are those which testify of her love for Christ,"[44] a characteristic that Steele valued in Watts's compositions.

Steele shared Watts's profound sense of awe with regard to Christ's person and work and a sincere desire to be with him.[45] A consideration of each poet's reflection on Christ's role as Redeemer set against the backdrop of a desire to be with him in heaven illustrates. In a piece of prose, as he dreams of Christ's return, Watts offers a glimpse into the inspiration behind his Christ-focused hymns, "O happy day and happy hour indeed, that shall finish the long absence of my beloved, and place me within sight of my adored Jesus! When shall I see that lovely, that illustrious Friend, who laid down his own life to rescue mine, his own valuable life to rescue a worm, a rebel that deserved to die?"[46] Watson suggests, "There is only one thing which Watts insists upon as greater [than the idea of God as Creator], and that is God as Redeemer."[47] Steele followed suit, writing of heaven, "Dear Saviour! Let thy Spirit seal / Our int'rest in that blissful place; / Till death remove this mortal veil, / And we behold thy lovely face."[48] And in "The Wonders of Redemption," one of her many hymns detailing the work of Christ on behalf of sinners, Steele declares, "Yes! the Redeemer left his throne, / His radiant throne on high, / (Surprising mercy! love unknown) / To suffer, bleed, and die."[49] Like Watts

---

[42]Steele, "Praise for National Peace, Psalm xlvi: 9," hymn no. 531 in Rippon, *Selection of Hymns*, 684, 686.

[43]Broome, *Bruised Reed*, 165.

[44]Broome, *Bruised Reed*, 169.

[45]These two somewhat inseparable themes contributed to Watts's desire to paraphrase the psalms from the vantage point of their fulfilment in Christ and also formed the theological and experiential foundation of the hymns of his follower, Steele.

[46]George Burder, ed., *The Works of the Reverend and Learned Isaac Watts, D.D.* (London, 1810) i. 394 in Watson, *English Hymn*, 136.

[47]Watson, *English Hymn*, 146.

[48]Steele, "The Worship of Heaven, John 17: 24," hymn no. 587 in Rippon, *Selection of Hymns*, 762–63.

[49]Steele, "The Wonders of Redemption," hymn no. 485 in Rippon, *Selection of Hymns*, 631–32.

before her, Steele constantly explored Christ's works accomplished in the place of and for his own sinful, but redeemed, people.

Further consideration of "The Wonders of Redemption"[50] offers an opportunity to conclude the discussion of Watts's influence on Steele while also offering an example of some of her own personal elements of the craft of hymn writing which contributed to her influence on Particular Baptists who sang from Rippon's hymnal. Listed in Rippon as a hymn to be sung alongside the Lord's Supper, "The Wonders of Redemption" displays vintage Anne Steele. Here she poetically, in a vibrant 8.6.8.6 meter, reflects upon Christ's complete body of work accomplished for the sake of sinners as well their proper response to it. With the first half of this hymn of six verses she begins with questions before moving to exclamations and parenthetical remarks. She uses a variety of names for God as well as graphic terms for sinful humans throughout the piece. The second half of the hymn is a prayer addressing the second person of the Trinity, acknowledging his sacrifice and its benefits for believers, and requesting his power to be at work in her life. So the Baptist pastor Rippon uses Steele's prayerful, Christ-centered hymn, like the Puritans before him, to relate the ordinance of "the Lord's Supper to redemption," emphasizing "God's gracious act of love and the forgiveness of sins rather than self-offering."[51] The hymn is listed in full so that its impact may be felt and these poetic devices recognized as she expresses substitutionary atonement theology:

1 And did the holy and the just,
    The Sovereign of the skies,
Stoop down to wretchedness and dust,
    That guilty worms might rise?

2 Yes! the Redeemer left his throne,
    His radiant throne on high,
(Surprising mercy! love unknown)

---

[50]Rippon, *Selection of Hymns*, 631–32. Steele added a Scripture reference, 1 Peter 3:18, "For Christ also hath once suffered for sins, the just for the unjust, that he might bring us to God, being put to death in the flesh, but quickened by the Spirit." See *Works*, 1:168.

[51]Karen Smith, "The Covenant Life of Some Eighteenth-Century Calvinistic Baptists in Hampshire and Wiltshire," in *Pilgrim Pathways: Essays in Baptist History in Honour of B. R. White*, ed. William H. Brackney and Paul S. Fiddes with John H. Y. Briggs (Macon, Ga.: Mercer University Press, 1999) 179.

> To suffer, bleed, and die.
>
> 3 He took the dying traitor's place,
>   And suffer'd in his stead;
> For man (O miracle of grace!)
>   For man the Saviour bled!
>
> 4 Dear LORD! what heav'nly wonders dwell
>   In thy atoning blood!
> By this are sinners snatch'd from hell,
>   And rebels brought to GOD.
>
> 5 JESUS! my soul adoring bends
>   To love so full, so free;
> And may I hope *that* love extends
>   Its sacred powers to me!
>
> 6 What glad return can I impart
>   For favours so divine?
> O take my all—this worthless heart,
>   And make it only thine.

These lines reveal an intersection of the poet, the theologian, and the worshiper in the pew. Such a meeting within a hymn is one of the characteristics Steele found worth emulating in Watts. A few points should be briefly highlighted. First, Steele, like Watts, found at the center of her assurance and praise "the grace of God and the person of Christ, and his redemptive action."[52] They both shared an evangelical vision of sinners saved by grace through faith in Christ alone. This hymn is one of many of Steele's testimonies to such a vision.

Second, specific words that sometimes sound strange to modern ears were used by Steele, following Watts, to establish a proper theological understanding of man's fallen nature before God—"wretchedness," "guilty worms," "dying traitor," "sinners," and "rebels." Cynthia Aalders states matter-of-factly

---

[52]Watson, *English Hymn*, 152.

that these words are simply Steele's way of expressing that "as with other eighteenth-century Calvinistic Baptists, Steele had a large view of her own sinfulness."[53] These words are not meant to leave singers (and sinners) in the depths but to elicit joy at the consideration of the Redeemer's self-giving love.

Finally, these previous points position Steele in the line of the Augustan tradition of Watts with its clear expression of the truth it intends to convey while also offering a didactic purpose, in this case, teaching the doctrines of redemption and substitutionary atonement. Watson says that for Isaac Watts, "Hymns show the mind of a poet applied with skill and dedication to the expression of his belief."[54] Steele exemplifies this characteristic. Aalders elaborates, "The ability to convey clear meaning is of especial importance to the hymn writer, as congregations are meant to sing and understand what they are singing without the benefit of time to reflect at length on the hymn writer's words."[55] Simplicity and clarity were marks of both Watts and Steele.

This hymn also reflects some aspects of Steele's style that take her beyond Watts. For example, it illustrates her use of the question, the exclamation, and the parenthetical remark. These aspects of Steele's writing style reveal something of her personality, her approach to God, and her artful process of writing about him. Watson finds Steele at her best when not only making statements, but also asking questions and making exclamations: "She employs them to probe further than the statements themselves can do, because they gesture towards the unanswered, the mysterious, and the unknown."[56] The final two stanzas of the hymn allow for further reflection on this characteristic of Steele's writing: In the first of these last two stanzas Steele uses two exclamations. The first contrasts her sturdy approach to her Savior, "Jesus!" with the second, which she uses to turn her slight doubt as to whether he will extend his love to her into Christian assurance by placing an exclamation point where a question mark might have been expected. The question in the final stanza offers an application of her faith in response to the love of Jesus toward her. And as in the earlier verses, the parenthetical remark here demonstrates the wonder and mystery of a holy God giving himself, in Christ, to the undeserv-

---

[53]Aalders, *To Express the Ineffable*, 84.
[54]J. R. Watson, ed., *An Annotated Anthology of Hymns* (Oxford: Oxford University Press, 2002) 121.
[55]Aalders, *To* Express the Ineffable, 90.
[56]Watson, *English Hymn*, 198.

ing. So Steele uses grammar and punctuation to generate questions and exclamations for evangelical purposes, as "through them her hymnody celebrates not just the doctrine of grace, but the application of that grace to human experience." It is her ability to share with readers and singers personal reflections of faith in the midst of difficulties that is another exemplary characteristic of Steele as a hymn writer.

To summarize, the first two verses, one a question and the next an answer, work in parallel in proclaiming that it was indeed the "Sovereign" who was also the "Redeemer." The punctuation and grammar highlight the mystery and astonishment of such news. Taken with the third and fourth verses, these lines of the hymn display when Steele is most bold in her lyrical development. Aalders explains, "These moments most often occur in the context of her devotion to Christ—that is, her joy as she hopes for redemption and her anticipation of spiritual fulfilment made possible by Christ's sacrifice."[57] The last two verses illustrate that for Steele a consideration of the atonement contributed to her desire to commit her life in all its parts to Christ as "a living sacrifice"[58] in gratitude for his saving work. She also expresses an affinity with the Apostle Paul's desire: "That I may know him,…and the fellowship of his sufferings, being made conformable unto his death."[59] And so in a crucicentric hymn revealing Steele at her best she expresses both her evangelical emphasis on the cross of Christ and complements through poetry what Manley considers "the Christocentric emphasis of Baptist preaching."[60]

Conclusion

J. R. Watson explains that congregations that sing hymns "interpret the hymns…in the way they have come to understand them, almost unconsciously, in the light of doctrine, belief, and history. Those people who share certain things sing hymns: Bible reading, doctrine, common prayer, and moral precept.…Congregations sing because of what they believe, and believe because of what they sing."[61] Manley suggests, "Like any good hymnbook Rip-

---

[57]Aalders, *To Express the Ineffable*, 163.
[58]From Romans 12:1.
[59]Philippians 3:10.
[60]Manley, "John Rippon and Baptist Hymnody," 105.
[61]Watson, *English Hymn*, 18–19.

pon's helped to define and interpret the Christian faith for its own generation."[62] Steele's fifty-two hymns in the *Selection of Hymns* collectively offer a glimpse into the theological, spiritual, experiential, and evangelical tenor of Baptist life as it was spiritually renewed and revived from the 1780s to the 1830s.

Steele covers a wide breadth of doctrine and reveals a robust piety in her gospel-driven, biblically sound, articulately expressed, and emotionally compelling compositions showcased by Rippon in his popular hymnal. One writer said of Steele that no woman "has so largely contributed to the familiar hymnology of the church as the modest and retiring, but gifted and godly, Anne Steele."[63] Writing during the golden age of the English hymn and ushering in the golden age of Baptist hymnody, she wrote evangelical hymns that directed the congregation to sing praises to God in worship, taught of the depth and richness of the theology of the Scriptures as taught in the Second London Confession, and gave believers a prayerful avenue through which to express their affections for God and the emotions that come from living in a sin-stained world. Further, they collectively illustrate the themes of those preachers of the Baptist revival: "personal renewal, the revival of the church, and Spirit-empowered witness."[64] It was the people in the pew who sang the hymns of Rippon's *Selection of Hymns*. As they sang they were influenced by such hymn writers as Anne Steele in the shaping and strengthening of their faith. Through her legacy of songs proclaiming the scope of vibrant evangelical Calvinism to believers and any who would simply respond to Christ in faith, Steele nurtured the spiritual revival in Particular Baptist worship and congregational life in the decades immediately following her death in 1778.

---

[62] Manley, *Redeeming Love Proclaim*, 135.

[63] Hatfield, *Poets of the Church*, 570, cited in Henry S. Burrage, *Baptist Hymn Writers and Their Hymns* (Portland, Maine: Brown Thurston and Co., 1888) 46.

[64] Michael A. G. Haykin, "'A Habitation of God, Through the Spirit': John Sutcliff (1752–1814) and the Revitalization of the Calvinistic Baptists in the Late Eighteenth Century," *Baptist Quarterly* 34 (1992): 316.

13

Baptists and the Second Evangelical Awakening in England, 1859–1865

Terry G. Carter

J. Edwin Orr, undoubtedly the most renowned revival historian of the twentieth century, wrote two books on what was termed "The Second Evangelical Awakening." In 1949 he published a history detailing the awakening in Britain followed by a 1952 volume focusing on America. The awakening between 1859 and 1865 impacted Ireland, Wales, Scotland, and America. Some question its impact on England. Orr proposed that the "pattern of the Awakening in England was noteworthy, for it included full-scale Revival of the spontaneous and immediate type...[and] other movements following the metropolitan London pattern" which took place over several years as the right atmosphere and leadership developed.[1]

In making his argument for the English awakening, Orr relied heavily on a weekly periodical entitled *The Revival*. This magazine was established with the primary purpose of chronicling and promoting the revival effort. David Bebbington in *Evangelicalism in Modern Britain* questions the reliability of *The Revival*. "Morgan (the editor) deliberately created the impression that a single phenomenon, revival, was already aflame throughout Britain." Bebbington argues that the range of the revivals in Britain was quite limited. Mass conversions and physical prostrations that often characterize revival appeared in America, Ulster, Wales, and Scotland but "were rare in England." Cornwall and North Devon experienced some revival events but those were primarily community affairs "confined to the periphery" and most often "single occupational groups."[2] Clearly Orr and Bebbington disagree on the extent

---

[1] J. Edwin Orr, *The Second Evangelical Awakening in America*, (London: Marshall, Morgan & Scott, 1952) 88.

[2] David W. Bebbington, *Evangelicalism in Modern Britain: A History from the 1730s to the 1980s* (Abingdon: Taylor and Francis Group, 2005) 116–17.

BAPTISTS AND THE SECOND EVANGELICAL AWAKENING IN ENGLAND, 1859–1865

and impact of the Second Evangelical Awakening in England. This chapter seeks to carry the discussion to a more specific arena focusing on how English Baptists were involved and affected by the movement. Once again, Orr argued for strong English Baptist involvement and huge gains to Baptist churches in the wake of the revival. Orr correctly stated that English Baptists supported the revival and often discussed awakening events in Ireland, Scotland, America, and Wales. Even the Baptist Union approved of the revival idea. Orr boasted that the most famous English Baptist preacher, Charles Haddon Spurgeon, was an "unqualified friend" of the Awakening and lamented that more churches had not experienced it. Spurgeon believed many "ministers and churches had slighted its golden opportunities."[3]

Orr concluded that Baptists in England gained great numbers due to the revival. He cited W. T. Whitley's claim that between 1860 and 1870 more Baptist churches were founded than in any period before or since. Orr argued that the number of new churches "must be taken as an index of the ingathering into Baptist churches." He noted that Baptists in England and Wales numbered 250,000 in 1865 and that 100,000 of those resulted from the revival. In Appendix B of *The Second Evangelical Awakening in Britain*, Orr offered more detail. The Baptist Union reported 43,586 additions in the seven years of the revival era, but Orr believed nonreporting churches averaged a thousand each during that period, increasing the number to 75,586. He followed with some mathematical logic. "Adding 25,000 as the number of accessions needed to equal the loss of membership due to a death-rate of 2 percent per annum, a total of 100,000 accessions of converts is found, a very high proportion in a total membership of 250,000."[4]

One might ask if there is sufficient information to support Orr's conclusions. Using research data from periodicals such as *The Baptist Magazine* and *The Baptist Reporter*, church histories covering this period, and annual reports of associations and churches, this chapter will offer reasonable doubt to some of Orr's assertions. If the revival heavily impacted English Baptists, surely denominationally related publications would reflect that. In the process of the discussion, concessions will be made to Orr regarding the participation of some key Baptist leaders in revival activities and that English Baptists supported and appreciated the revivals in Ulster, Wales, America, and Scotland.

---

[3] J. Edwin Orr, *The Second Evangelical Awakening in Britain* (London: Marshall, Morgan & Scott, 1949) 190–91.

[4] Orr, *Britain*, 271.

They subsequently called for similar activity in England. In spite of these concessions, evidence that the revival came to Baptists in England is lacking. As if in a court of law, I contend that reasonable doubt concerning Orr's claims exists. First, let's consider the concessions to Orr's arguments.

Baptist Support and Involvement in the Evangelical Awakening

Although *The Revival* magazine mentioned Baptists occasionally, little specific attention was given them compared to other denominations like Methodists. The magazine did offer sufficient examples showing Baptist support for the revival. Early on leaders called for prayer meetings for an awakening they all hoped would come. The Queen St. Baptist Chapel in Woolwich hosted some of those. In Deptford, also in the London area, Christian churches united for prayer in the Lecture Hall. A General Alexander conducted the meeting, surrounded by ministers from Anglican, Wesleyan, Independent, and Baptist churches. In Clippenham a public prayer meeting convened in the New Baptist Chapel.[5] *The Revival* recorded that God had visited Whittlesea in Cambridgeshire with a mighty work in the "name of the Holy Child." Daily prayer meetings convened in the General Baptist church and thirteen were converted.[6] Baptists surely earnestly desired and prayed for revival.

Some Baptist preachers took active roles in revival efforts. In Cheddar, Charles Haddon Spurgeon preached to a crowd of eight to ten thousand.[7] Baptist Noel, twice president of the Baptist Union, preached to revival crowds, led in prayer meetings, and promoted the Evangelical Alliance, a key organization in the promotion of revival effort.[8] Other, less prominent Baptists played revival roles as well. In Torrington, a Baptist minister's wife held Bible classes with fifty to sixty women attending.[9] Clearly, Baptists favored the revival and some participated. However, this fact does not mean revival growth

---

[5] "Woolwich," *The Revival* 15 (November 5, 1859): 116; "Deptford," *The Revival* 17 (November 19, 1859): 135; "Clippenham," *The Revival* 17 (November 19, 1859): 135.

[6] "Whittlesea, Cambridgeshire," *The Revival* 24 (January 7, 1860): 3.

[7] "Cheddar," *The Revival* 166 (September 25, 1862): 146.

[8] "The Week of Prayer," *The Revival* 181 (January 8, 1863): 19; "The Week of Prayer," *The Revival* (January 15, 1863): 31–32; William Brackney, "Baptist Contributions to Protestantism," *Baptist Heritage and the 21st Century* (pamphlet series) www.baptisthistory.org/bhhs/21stcentury/contributionprotestantism.html. For Baptist Noel see also David Bebbington, "Life of Baptist Noel," *Baptist Quarterly* 24 (October 8, 1972): 389–411.

[9] "Torrington," *The Revival* 198 (May 7, 1863): 226–27.

for the denomination. What evidence exists to show a significant positive revival impact on the Baptists in England? Let's shift gears and investigate that aspect.

Selected Baptist Periodicals and the Revival

Logically, if a great revival occurred among Baptist churches, Baptist magazines would cover it. Indeed, periodicals like the *Baptist Magazine* and *The Baptist Reporter* included multiple articles and references chronicling revival activities around the world. Some articles even analyzed these events, outlining causes and effects. However, what seem to be missing are regular discussions of revivals going on in English Baptist churches.

Reports of Revivals: As early as 1858 *The Baptist Magazine* reported on the awakening occurring in America. In the May edition the editor desired to print a "full discussion of the great religious awakening going on in America." However, need for more information caused the editors to adjust that intention in order to avoid speculation. They opted "to give copious cuttings from transatlantic newspapers, both secular and religious." The editors borrowed excerpts from *The New York Examiner, The New York Tribune, The Boston Traveler, The New York Independent* (all secular papers), and *The New York Protestant Churchman*. These articles described events that some thought surpassed the Great Awakening of Edwards's time.[10] More followed in the August and September editions of the *Magazine*.[11]

The American revival continued as a focus for the next few years. An article entitled "The American Revival" appeared in the April 1859 edition of the *Baptist Magazine* recounting details about the awakening. The writer shared, "The secret of the American revival is this: Christians have begun to act upon the principle that 'whoever apprehends the gospel for himself should preach it to his fellow.' Their motto is, 'Every man a missionary.'"[12]

Coverage of revivals in other countries also appeared. The *Irish Chronicle* (found bound with the *Baptist Magazine*) regularly updated British Baptists on the awakening in Ireland. In September of 1859 the *Chronicle* reported a

---

[10] "The Religious Revival in America," *Baptist Magazine* 50 (May 1858): 297–300.
[11] "The Revival in America," *Baptist Magazine* 50 (August 1858): 469; "A Sunday in New York," *Baptist Magazine* 50 (August 1858): 485; "Thoughts on Revival," *Baptist Magazine* 50 (September 1858): 555.
[12] "The American Revival," *The Baptist Magazine* 51 (April 1859): 219.

revival in Banbridge, Ireland. A letter by Mr. Eccles dated August 13, 1859, states, "Banbridge and neighborhood are now visited by that wave of salvation which had previously blessed some other districts in the north."[13] The following month the *Chronicle* printed a letter from C. J. Middleditch to the editor of the *Freeman* concerning the revival in Northern Ireland. Based on observations of spiritual conviction and the physical manifestations in the new converts, Middleditch referred to it as a "remarkable movement." He mentioned specifically Coleraine and following articles in the *Chronicle* detailed similar revival activity in Londonderry and Letter-Kenny. Apparently Northern Ireland felt the strong wave of revival in several towns.[14] These reports on Ireland continued in the magazine for the next few years. Likewise, the *Baptist Reporter* covered the Irish revivals in 1858 until the awakening began to cool in 1862.[15]

As the revivals spread, English Baptists maintained a keen interest in the subject. The *Baptist Reporter* published reports on Wales (May 1859, January, February 1861), France (September 1861), Scotland (November 1859, May, April, June, and December 1861), and Sweden (January, February 1859).[16] Baptist periodicals informed, encouraged, and promoted the idea of revival worldwide and the examples given above represent only a few.

Educational Articles Concerning Revivals: As a method of promoting the awakening, the *Baptist Magazine* and the *Baptist Reporter* provided space for analyzing revivals. Even as early as September 1858 the *Baptist Magazine* printed an article responding to the American revival. The article delineated lessons to be learned from the awakening in America. The first lesson expressed shock at the low state of religion in England since the revival reports caused "astonishment and incredulity." The writer argued that since the

---

[13] "The Religious Awakening in Ireland," *Irish Chronicle* (September 1859): 593–96.

[14] "The Religious Revival in Ireland," *Irish Chronicle* (October 1859): 657–59; "Coleraine," *Irish Chronicle* (October 1859): 659.

[15] "A Visit to Londonderry," *Baptist Reporter* (April 1861): 118–19.

[16] "Religious Revivals in Wales," *Baptist Reporter* (May 1859): 134–35; "Welsh Statistics," *Baptist Reporter* (January 1861): 29; "The Quarry-Men in Wales," *Baptist Reporter* (February 1861): 55; "France," *Baptist Reporter* (September 1861): 278; "Revival in Scotland," *Baptist Reporter* (November 1859): 326–27; "Scotland," *Baptist Reporter* (May 1861): 149–151; "Scotland," *Baptist Reporter* (June 1861): 184; "Results of the Revival in Scotland," *Baptist Reporter* (December 1861): 371–72; "Religious Awakening in Sweden," *Baptist Reporter* (January 1859): 37; "Religious Revivals in Sweden," *Baptist Reporter* (February 1859): 87–89.

church is the body of Christ animated by Christ's Spirit, any lack of revival derives not from the slackness of God, but of the members. The article called the churches in England to repentance. A second lesson called for increased fidelity.[17] A year later another article entitled "Lessons of the Recent Revivals of Religion" drew from a circular letter written by Rev. C. M. Birrell to the Lancashire Association. Birrell, focusing on America and Ireland, suggested an investigation of "person religion" should be conducted among English Baptists to see if there is "neglect in the souls" of its members. He called the church to "diligence in communicating sound instruction" and followed it with a quote from a transatlantic minister. "I have almost uniformly remarked that, when the subjects have been early and competently instructed, the impressions have been permanent." Rev. Birrell did warn against manipulation to stir up revival which always resulted in "disastrous effects." He ended the lessons calling for a kind of character and faith that would "secure the confidence of the ungodly" and the need for "contrition and confession to the throne." These might result in ending the "wintry scene."[18]

Likewise, the *Baptist Reporter* promoted the revival spirit with similar articles on revivalism. In October of 1859 an article entitled "The Religious Revivals" highlighted events occurring in the British Isles but not yet in England. However, hope prevailed for England since men like Mr. Thomas Cooper had witnessed an uplifting service in a Wesleyan church at Malton and was convinced revival fires were soon arriving in England. "The great outpouring of God's spirit all over England is at hand."[19] The *Reporter* sported a regular section called "Revivals and Awakenings" designed to highlight and encourage revivalism. In 1861 that section included an article entitled "The Machinery of Revival." The author argued that awakening comes about by God and contains less excitement and extravagance than people often imagine. The hymns sung at revivals focus on "the fundamental doctrines of salvation" and the prayers are "short and to the point." Revival preaching seeks to awaken the awareness of sin and guide the sinner to peace. "Earnest, pointed, faithful gospel preaching is the preaching God is blessing. Crowds run to hear such men as Weaver and Carter, for they preach them a full, free and present

---

[17] "Thoughts on the Revival," *Baptist Magazine* 50 (September 1858): 555–59.
[18] "The Lessons of Recent Revivals of Religion," *Baptist Magazine* 51 (September 1859): 558–64. See also "Religious Revival," *Baptist Magazine* 51 (May 1859): 161–66.
[19] "The Religious Revivals," *Baptist Reporter* (October 1859): 297–301.

salvation." The writer encouraged more of the same.[20]

Reports on Revival in England

In addition to worldwide reports, Baptist periodicals sought to keep the people informed of revival activity in England and build a hunger for spiritual awakening. Often these reports carried little or no detail concerning numbers or denominations. A few examples follow.

In June of 1861 a notice of a special work going on in Norfolk made the *Baptist Reporter*. The write-up was short and void of details. "In the city of Norwich and in Lowestoft there has been a very gratifying and encouraging awakening. Great numbers, we are told, are under serious convictions." The article added that similar activity was under way in other places in the country. These events resulted from the blessing of God, which accompanied preaching, and prayer.[21] Denominational involvement and numbers are absent in the account. The next year the *Reporter* covered a movement in Frome. The story, borrowed from *Revival* magazine, simply stated the source as "a writer." The writer promised an account of the "Lord's power" being manifested in connection with activities in Frome, but the write-up was brief and without denominational specifics. It did mention the revival spreading to a Sabbath school.[22]

Again in 1862 the *Reporter* borrowed from *Revival* magazine concerning a movement in Westmoreland. The details derive from a letter by Mr. William Carter "who, we presume, is an itinerating Evangelist." The *Reporter* apparently knew little of William Carter, who was a key evangelist of the time. Carter recounted his time in Windermere and Kendal in the Lake District. He reported good meetings in which some of the "vilest sinners" and nominally religious were saved. Carter preached to a packed Kendal Town Hall and reported conversions too numerous to really call. "It would be impossible for me to enumerate the many cases of conversion which came under our notice."[23] Carter mentioned no denominational affiliations. Perhaps Baptists were involved but again the report is silent. Just south of the Lake District in Lancashire an 1863 revival accompanied one of the worst economic disasters in that area. The time known as the Cotton Famine occurred in the years

---

[20] "The Machinery of Revivals," *Baptist Reporter* (October 1861): 310–11.
[21] "Norfolk," *Baptist Reporter* (June 1861): 184.
[22] "Revival Incidents," *Baptist Reporter* (April 1862): 121–22.
[23] "Westmorland," *Baptist Reporter* (June 1862): 186–87.

following a cotton boom. Many left for places like Canada, Australia, and South Africa. During this depression a "glorious work" happened in the area around Manchester. Meetings in the Circus in Manchester boasted two thousand in attendance. Spiritually they termed it as "wildfire." The tragedy of unemployment and mass emigration turned into a good thing according to the writer. "The cotton famine has been the means of blessing hundreds." Once again the article made little comment about denominational affiliations with the exception of a vicar being involved.[24]

How about Baptist revivals? The *Baptist Messenger* in 1859 included a word from Fenny Stratford Baptist church. For twelve years a moral blight existed and religion languished in the area. Then the Lord sent a "spiritual shower." Weekly prayer meetings grew from six to sometimes sixty. Having been without a pastor, God finally sent to the Fenny Stratford church the Rev. C. H. Hosken and the increase began weekly. On December 5, Hosken baptized five women with six people waiting to be baptized. The church expected a Pentecostal blessing. Although this sounds revival-like, the magazine section on baptisms indicated other churches reporting even more baptisms than Fenny Stratford (Llanelly church, twenty baptisms). Perhaps Fenny Stratford just had a good year compared to years before. Surely if strong revival events took place among Baptists in England during this time, the magazines would have published more articles about that.

Although this chapter has relied heavily on the information from two periodicals that represented Particular Baptists (*Baptist Magazine*) and General Baptists (*Baptist Reporter*), other periodicals were investigated and revealed no widespread revival activity among Baptists in England. Obviously, exceptions existed but proved to be seemingly rare. The following magazines, *The Primitive Church (or Baptist) Magazine* (1859, 1861–1865), *The British Baptist Reporter* (1863), *The Gospel Herald or Poor Christian's Magazine* (1864) and the *Voice of Truth or Baptist Record* (1865) offered revival reports but little on Baptists. It appears there was little to report.

Baptist Union, Association, and Church Reports and Histories

Undoubtedly between 1859 and 1865 active revivals occurred in some places in the British Isles but our research to this point shows sparse evidence of English Baptist revivals. Minutes and reports from churches and histories

---

[24] "Lancashire," *Baptist Reporter* (May 1863): 148–52.

of churches should provide that evidence if it exists. Let's look at the minutes of the annual meetings of New Connexion General Baptists and numerous church histories. Admittedly these represent a limited periodical selection but certainly offer us clues into revival activity and Baptist acknowledgments of such activity.

Minutes of the Annual Association of the New Connexion of General Baptists

New Connexion General Baptists, being most closely associated theologically with revival active Wesleyans, would seem to be most likely affected by the awakening. However, the minutes of the associational meetings from 1859 to 1865 show little evidence of a revival activity. Some glowing reports from individual churches surfaced but not in sufficient numbers to support a widespread revival scenario. For instance, the church at Hinkle reported in 1860 that they had experienced "manifestations of the Spirit's presence." The pastor's ministry proved effective, the offering was sufficient, the Sabbath school totalled 350 scholars and the seats were filled at meetings. Praed Street church reported in 1861 that the congregation occasionally ran out of room "and our present prosperity is greater than at any former period in the history of our church." In their 1862 minutes Ilkeston reported the faithful preaching of the Gospel that "was accompanied by the power of the Holy Spirit. Many have been converted unto God, the great part of who were from the Sabbath school, which is in a flourishing condition." In spite of this report, they complained of budget problems and the fact that only 120 of the 229 members were attending: clearly not a great revival story. The good work at Ilkeston continued in 1863 with reports of good attendance and a "goodly number" added to the Sabbath school. In 1862 Call Lane church recorded a similar growth in the Sabbath schools. Halifax also testified of a noteworthy year stating "the goodness of God to us during the year calls for devout thanksgiving." They stated that the word was faithfully preached and resulted in the "conversion of many sinners." The following year's minutes revealed a similar trend.[25]

---

[25] The following minutes were all printed in Leicester by Winks & Son: Minutes of the Ninetieth Annual Association of the New Connexion of General Baptists 1859 (1859); Minutes of the Ninety-First Annual Association of the New Connexion of General Baptists 1860 (1860)

BAPTISTS AND THE SECOND EVANGELICAL AWAKENING IN
ENGLAND, 1859–1865

Although the above examples are remarkable, the majority of Baptist churches reporting provided less stellar notes such as "so little prosperity," "suffered additional losses," "year mingled with joy and sorrow," "year of heavy trial," and "mourn the want of more vital godliness." One might conclude that the associational reports reveal what would be considered normal for associational records in any given year—reports of some very fruitful churches while other churches reveal a struggle. Nevertheless, the New General Connexion minutes do not point to a broad awakening scenario.[26]

Individual Church Histories and Regional or City Church Histories

An important record concerning revival activity within churches and associations would be the histories of those bodies. A study of these should give us a sense of revival trends during a particular time period. An investigation of one hundred two histories of churches and associations reveals no more revival activity than was described in the Baptist periodicals.

Frederick Overend, who wrote the history of Ebenezer Baptist Church in Bacup made a clear statement. "There seems little evidence that the Revival Movement of 1859, which affected many parts of the country, brought any great quickening to the Berkshire Baptist churches." He does concede that the Isley church under the pastoral leadership of Henry Fuller experienced "much aggressive work." Maybe leadership accounted for Isley's positive results.[27] In the history of the Baptist Church at Farsley the unknown author included a section called "Notable Events." He listed in 1859 a burial ground purchased and a Baptist School built. On the 1863 entry he mentioned a Sunday evening sermon being instituted. He specified no exceptional growth.[28]

23; Minutes of the Ninety-Second Annual Association of the New Connexion of General Baptists 1861 (1861) 19–20; Minutes of the Ninety-Third Annual Association of the New Connexion of General Baptists 1862 (1862) 24, 31; Minutes of the Ninety-Fourth Annual Association of the New Connexion of General Baptists 1863 (1863) 26–27, 31, 40; Minutes of the Ninety-Fifth Annual Association of the New Connexion of General Baptists 1864 (1864) 18, 25–28, 30–31.

[26] Minutes (1862) 26–27.

[27] Frederick Overend, *History of the Ebenezer Baptist Church Bacup* (London: Kingsgate, 1912) 110.

[28] Baptist Church, Farsley; *Record of 150 Years, 1777–1927* (cover page missing and no page number available)

A few of the histories did record stories of exceptional spiritual movements. In Radnorshire the churches at Evenjobb and Gladestry experienced revival. Before the new pastor, Mr. Phillips, arrived in 1860, the revival had begun. By the end of June 1861, eighty people were baptized and in the next two years many more. The ministry seemed to advance until the departure of Mr. Phillips in 1868.[29] The Baptist church in Farsley felt the revival spirit under the preaching of a Mr. Parker. He commenced a series of discourses in November of 1863. The discourses were described as "super-excellent." They generated a revival feeling and a "tone of piety." "By the beginning of February, there were decisive indications of a coming shower of blessings." Church meetings increased in frequency even while Mr. Parker was away in Scotland. During this time a supply preacher from Liverpool, Mr. Dawson, filled the pulpit. By the time Parker returned attendance had increased greatly. These "soul refreshing meetings were continued nightly for seven weeks." The revival movement lasted through 1864 being described as "the most prosperous the church has enjoyed except for 1843." During 1864 baptisms were regular and multiple. "In March four were baptized; in April five; in May eight; in July eleven; in August eleven; in September four…" Forty-six were added to the church by baptism that year. These years were spiritually alive for the Farsley church.[30]

Particularly interesting are revival stories associated with churches without pastors. For instance, Providence Chapel in Lumb called Mr. Brotherton in August of 1860 as pastor. He experienced a fruitful ministry, baptizing at least twenty that year. Unfortunately, he moved to South Africa and for nearly four years the church used supply preachers. Between the years of 1862 and 1865 the church reported "great blessing." The meetings were well attended resulting in a great harvest of forty-two baptisms.[31] Earlier we discussed a magazine article about a Norfolk revival, which lacked any detail. The history of Baptist churches in Norfolk states: "Aylsham baptized forty-six in 1863, Ingham, in the remote countryside, in 1868 reported twenty-two baptisms,

---

[29] John Jones, *The History of the Baptists in Radnorshire* (London: Elliot Stock, 1895) 42–43.

[30] *The Centenary Volume of the Baptist Church*, Farsley (Leeds: H. W. Walker, 1877) 26–27.

[31] Edward Nuttall, *History of the Baptist Church and Congregation Meeting in Providence Chapel, Lumb* (London: Yates and Alexander, 1879) 68–69.

while Swaffham went from strength to strength, baptizing twenty-six in 1867 and a similar number in 1868; thirty-two in 1873, thirty-four in 1877, and twenty-four in 1878."[32] Obviously, some of the Norfolk churches experienced revival even beyond awakening dates.

Although the church and associational histories indicate a few English Baptist churches experienced revival events during the period of the Evangelical Awakening, the majority of the histories made no mention of a revival. Seventy-five of the church histories record nothing at all concerning revival, and nineteen of the associational or regional histories fail to mention it. [33] Surely, if as Orr claimed, an awakening took place adding 100,000 members to Baptist churches, more than a few Baptist histories would report the event. Most are silent.

Conclusion

J. Edwin Orr wrote a great deal chronicling the "Second Evangelical

---

[32] *The Baptists in Norfolk* (London: Camelot, 1957) 93.

[33] See also church histories of the following churches and associations. North Devon; Millington and Lymm; Mt. Zion, Edgeside; Pembroke; Bethel, Latchford; Blenheim, Leeds; Park Street, Luton; Odgen Baptist Chapel, Newhey; Nantwich, Aenon, Milnsbridge, Little Wild Street, Lincoln's Inn Fields; College Street Chapel, Northhampton; Friar Lane, Nottingham; New Road, Oxford; George Street and Mutley Chapels, Plymouth; Lymington, Hants; South Parade Chapel, Leeds; Meltham; Ebenezer, Scarborough; Steep Lane, Sowerby; Tottlebank, Greenodd; Tiverton, Devon; Upton Chapel; Bethel, Briggate; Townhead Street, Sheffield; Greek Street, Stockport; Stafford; Sutton-in-Craven; Roomfield, Todmorden; King Street, Oldham; Rishworth; Vale; Wakefield; Weston-by-Weedon; Castle Hill, now Doddridge; Angmering; Westgate Road, Newcastle-upon-Tyne; Kingsbridge, Devon; Broughton Chapel; Bridlington; Bluntisham; West Street, Rochdale; Country Baptist, East Yorkshire; Battersea Chapel; Wem; Wantage; Salendine Nook Chapel, Huddersfield; Walgrave; Heptonstall Slack; Hinckley; Gildersome, York; George Street, Hull; Northgate-End Chapel, Halifax; Queensbury; Bethesda, Barnoldswick; Ebenezer, Bacup; Atch Lench; Hill Cliffe, Warrington; First Baptist, Bradford; Blackpool; Broadstone, Hedden Bridge; Friar Lane, Leicester; Baptist Churches of Lancashire; Keighley; First General, Derby; Earby; Hunslet Tabernacle, Leeds; First Baptist, Halifax; Trinity Road, Halifax; Trinity, Haslingden; Stevington; Nottinghamshire Baptists; Canon Street Memorial, Birmingham; Fuller Church, Kettering; Cloughfold; Hebden Bridge, Yorkshire; Yorkshire Baptists; Lancashire and Yorkshire Associations; Falmouth Baptists; Berks Baptist Association; Baptists in Bridgewater; Accrington Baptists; Saffron Waldron; Melbourne Baptists, Derbyshire; Baptists in Bolton; Baptists of Surrey; Baptists of Weston-by-Weedon and Sulgrave; Liverpool Baptists; Bristol Baptists; Pudsey; Worcestershire Association (2 separate histories); Baptists of Yorkshire; Suffolk Baptists; Baptists of North-West England; Birmingham Baptists; Radnorshire Baptists; Kent and Sussex Associations. These histories have little to say of the awakening among Baptists.

Awakening." He no doubt proved that revival fires burned in many countries between 1859 and 1865. However, his argument relating to English Baptists appears to be a bit of an overreach. What can we conclude from the data considered? First, English Baptists knew of the revivals in America, Wales, Ireland and Scotland. They discussed them often in print, prayed earnestly and desired similar fires to invade their churches. Indeed, a few Baptist churches realized exceptional growth between 1859 and 1865. Secondly, the evidence reveals these revival fires were certainly sparsely scattered across English Baptist life. The selected Baptist periodicals, minutes, reports from numerous churches and histories covering the time period offer little support of Orr's argument for an English Baptist awakening. Certainly an awakening of such major proportions would have demanded significant time and space coverage in church and denominational correspondence and reports. I struggled to find such evidence. While silence is most often not the best argument for a challenge, in this case it may be.

Chapter 14

"A larger outpouring of the Spirit of God": British Baptists and the 1859 Revival with a Focus on Scotland

Brian Talbot

The extraordinary spiritual awakening—"a larger outpouring of the Spirit of God"[1]— that began in the United States in the autumn of 1857 and over the next few years spread to Ulster, England, Wales, Scotland, the West Indies, continental Europe, and Scandinavia, even as far away as India, Australia, and New Zealand[2] has until recent years received comparatively little coverage in scholarly literature. A variety of explanations have been put forward to explain this anomaly including scholarly fascination with earlier awakenings, a focus on the division of major Protestant denominations in that country over the issue of slavery, and the Civil War in the years that followed,[3] together with the apparent anomaly of a "businessmen's awakening" in the midst of what has been described as the "feminization" of American Protestantism.[4] There was also perceived to be a growing focus on more secular concerns in society

---

[1] *The Freeman* 5 (November 2, 1859): 665.
[2] Charles Seaver, 'The Ulster Revival', in *The Ulster Revival and Its Religious Features and Physiological Accidents by the Right Rev. Lord Bishop of Down, Connor, and Dromore; the Right Rev. Charles Seaver, incumbent of St John, Belfast; The Rev. J. A. Canning, Presbyterian minister Coleraine, and the Rev. James McCosh LLD, being papers read to the Evangelical Alliance in Belfast, 22 September 1859* (London: James Nisbet and Co., 1959) 7; C. M. Birrell, "The Lessons of Recent Revivals of Religion," Circular Letter of the Lancashire Association, Baptist Magazine 52 (September 1860): 559, 564; Oscar Bussey, "The Religious Awakening of 1858–60 in Great Britain and Ireland" (PhD diss., University of Edinburgh, 1947) i.
[3] Kathryn Teresa Long, *The Revival of 1857–58 Interpreting an American Religious Awakening* (New York: Oxford University Press, 1998) 3–4.
[4] Ann Douglas, *The Feminization of American Culture* (New York: Knopf, 1977) cited in Long, *Revival of 1857–58*, 4.

at that time,[5] together with scholarly skepticism that anything particularly significant had taken place in the Anglo-Saxon world.[6] This study will first present brief comments on the revival in the USA, then on the events in Ulster, England, and Wales, prior to its focus on this movement's impact on the Christian church in Scotland with particular reference to Baptist churches in that country.

British Christians, like their Evangelical colleagues in the USA, were inspired by the decision of Jeremiah Lanphier, a former businessman now city missionary, to launch a prayer meeting for working men during their lunch hour in Fulton Street Dutch Reformed Church in lower Manhattan, in the heart of New York's business district.[7] It had begun slowly on September 23 1857, but soon saw a steady increase in attendance and consequently the formation of other prayer meetings in other cities in America. These united prayer meetings were nondenominational and often led by lay people. This was a departure from previous awakenings in which a prominent clerical presence had been the norm. In other respects, however, it was a much broader Great Awakening fitting the traditional Reformed pattern of such events. It has been called the closest thing to a national revival of the Christian faith in American history, an event that touched the lives of millions of Americans associated with the range of Protestant churches.[8] *The Presbyterian Magazine*, published in Philadelphia, recorded in June 1858: "It is not confined to a single section of the country, not to a single Christian denomination, but with some exceptions, it extends to all."[9] On both sides of the Atlantic there was a clear move by clergymen of traditional Reformed theological opinions, in

---

[5] The analysis of Fletcher Harper, editor of *Harper's Weekly*, in an 1854 editorial article, cited by Timothy L. Smith, *Revivalism & Social Reform: American Protestantism on the Eve of the Civil War* (New York: Harper Torchbooks, 1957) 15.

[6] John Kent, *Holding the Fort: Studies in Religious Revivalism* (London: Epworth Press, 1978) 31. With reference to Scotland, this perspective is articulated by C. J. Marrs, "The 1859 Religious Revival in Scotland: A Review and Critique of the Movement with particular reference to the City of Glasgow" (PhD diss., University of Glasgow 1995) 204–6, 340–43.

[7] For example, *The Wynd Journal* 55 (October 13, 1860): 435. William Arthur, *Beginnings of A Great Revival: The Awakening in Ulster, Connor* (London: Hamilton, Adams & Co., and John Mason, 1859) 3–9; Samuel Coley, *The Life of Rev. Thos. Collins* (London: Elliott Stock, 1869) 441.

[8] Long, *Revival of 1857*, 7.

[9] *Presbyterian Magazine* 8 (June 1858) (Philadelphia: Joseph M. Wilson) 248.

1858,[10] to emphasize that what was happening was quite distinct from the new measures and techniques of Charles Finney and other revivalist campaigners.[11] In the United Kingdom words attributed to Baptist leader Charles Haddon Spurgeon represented the message that many Christians across the Protestant churches would have affirmed: "Providence had sent [James] Caughey, and [Charles] Finney, and such wide famed revivalists, packing, that honour might be given to the Lord alone."[12] It is this interpretation of the Revival that has been broadly accepted within the Christian churches.[13] Although definitive data of the number of converts is impossible to obtain, Edwin Orr, the well-known historian of revival, gives very plausible figures, with approximately one million new believers added to the main Protestant denominations in America in 1858 and 1859.[14] This figure is only slightly higher than those given by Roy Fish.[15] It was clear that a remarkable religious revival had taken place in America between 1857 and 1859. However, it was not confined to that country. Ulster, which had close connections to America, also experienced a sizable awakening influenced by the events taking place in America.

Ulster, in the three decades prior to the Revival, had seen significant growth both in the numbers of Evangelical Presbyterian clergymen and a

---

[10] For example, Samuel I. Prime, *The Power of Prayer;* Talbot W. Chambers, *The Noon Prayer Meeting of the North Dutch Church*; William C. Conant, *Narratives of Remarkable Conversions and Revival Incidents*; James W. Alexander, *The Revival and Its Lessons* (New York: The American Tract Society, 1858) and Samuel I. Prime, ed., *The New York Pulpit in the Revival of 1858* (New York: Sheldon, Blakeman and Co.,1858).

[11] For more detailed information on the contrast between the more traditional approach to revival and evangelism and the newer approaches, see R. Carwardine, *Trans-Atlantic Revivalism: Popular Evangelicalism in Britain and America, 1790-1865* (Westport, CT: Greenwood, 1978) 3-56; and Iain H. Murray, *Revival and Revivalism: The Making and Marring of American Evangelicalism 1750-1858* (Edinburgh: Banner of Truth Trust, 1994) 225-98.

[12] Quoted by Coley, *Life of Rev. Thos. Collins*, 441.

[13] Long, *Revival of 1857*, 11-25.

[14] J. Edwin Orr, *The Event of the Century: The 1857-1858 Awakening* (Wheaton, IL: International Awakening Press, 1989) 319-27. See also J. Edwin Orr, *The Second Evangelical Awakening in Britain* (Marshall, Morgan & Scott, 1949) 34-37.

[15] Roy J. Fish, *When Heaven Touched Earth: The Awakening of 1858 and Its Effects on Baptists* (Azle, Texas: Need of the Times Publishers, 1996) 271. See also the comments and analysis of the figures given in Carwardine, *Trans-Atlantic Revivalism*, 159-62

growing consciousness of previous revivals, which had led by 1857 to an increased number of prayer meetings for a fresh awakening.[16] News from America was shared across the province by Presbyterian ministers William McClure and Professor William Gibson, which significantly raised expectations of imminent revival. A few Presbyterian clergymen such as Isaac Nelson, minister of Donegall Street Presbyterian Church, Belfast, were noted critics of the campaign.[17] Although Presbyterians and their ministers dominated Evangelical church life in Ulster at that time, when the Revival began it was largely led by the laity and involved all the Protestant denominations.[18] Thomas Pewtress and C. J. Middleditch, the secretary and treasurer respectively of the Baptist Irish Society, in a short report from their mission agency to British Baptists commending "the present religious awakening," observed that "In its earlier stages, the Revival was almost, if not entirely, independent of ministerial services."[19] In August 1859 Scottish Baptist minister John Williams wrote an article in which he expressed his concern that new converts of the Revival were encouraged to speak about their experiences too soon at public meetings in Ulster.[20] Baptists had been invited to take part in united prayer meetings in Northern Ireland, for example, in Armagh in September 1859.[21] However, it was a more cautious welcome in some other parts of the province. A balanced

---

[16] For example, Seaver, "Ulster Revival," 6–7. Arthur, *Beginnings of a Great Revival*, 6. Details of the young men involved the earliest recorded prayer gathering associated with the revival at Kells in the parish of Connor, as early as September 1857, are given in Orr, *Second Evangelical Awakening*, 38–39. There are records of talks and sermons related to past revivals being delivered in the places where revival occurred in 1859. See Nicholas M. Railton, *Revival on the Causeway Coast: The 1859 Revival in and around Coleraine* (Fearn, Ross-shire: Christian Focus, 2009) 59–60. See also David Hempton and Myrtle Hill, *Evangelical Protestantism in Ulster Society 1740–1890* (London: Routledge, 2014) 145–51.

[17] I. Nelson, *The Year of Delusion: "A Review of a Year of Grace"* (Belfast: Mayne, 1860) 77, cited by Orr, *Second Evangelical Awakening*, 39. See also Ian Randall, *Rhythms of Revival: The Spiritual Awakening of 1857–1863* (Milton Keynes, UK: Paternoster, 2010) 33–35, and Hempton and Hill, *Evangelical Protestantism*, 151–55; For details on the nature of the controversy in Irish Presbyterian ranks concerning the revival see Daniel Ritchie, "Confessional Calvinism and Evangelical Assurance: Isaac Nelson, Ulster Revivalism and the Assurance Controversy in the Presbyterian Church in Ireland, c.1859–1867," *History* 100 (339) (January 2015) 85–106.

[18] *The Freeman* (June 22, 1859): 367; (August 10, 1859): 471.

[19] *The Freeman* 5 (October 12, 1859) 618; this is supported from other sources by Hempton and Hill, *Evangelical Protestantism*, 150–51.

[20] *The Freeman* (August 17, 1859): 489.

[21] *The Freeman* (September 28, 1859): 584.

appraisal of the overall picture came from the pen of Charles Kirtland, a Baptist minister from Canterbury, who had spent considerable time in Ulster preaching and evaluating the progress of the Revival. Kirtland wrote:

> And one of the most delightful features connected with the Revival, is the distribution of its blessings among all Evangelical Churches. Sectarian jealousies have in some places rather disturbed the harmonious feeling and action of the various bodies of Christendom, and put a weapon into the hands of those who hate and revile the good work; but they cannot interfere with its onward progress.[22]

Baptists in Ulster certainly had experienced some persecution during the Revival, especially when numbers in their ranks grew or new congregations were planted.[23] Overall, attendances in their approximately thirty congregations increased, and two or three new churches were planted as a result of the Revival.[24] It also led to the formation of an association of Baptist churches in Ireland.[25] The Hon. Baptist Noel, an English Baptist minister, who was an enthusiastic supporter of and participant in the Revival in Ireland, reported to an Evangelical Alliance meeting that "100,000 converts was probably under the mark."[26] However, the vast majority of these converts either were already associated with Presbyterian causes or chose to join them following this religious awakening in Ulster.

In mainland Britain there was a broad welcome for the Revival amongst Evangelical Christians, even if some accounts of the cooperation painted too rosy a picture at times.[27] There was, though, predictable opposition from less sympathetic theological traditions, like the High Church Anglicans.[28] Baptists

---

[22] *The Freeman* (January 25, 1860): 53.

[23] For example, *Irish Chronicle* [bound with the monthly issues of *Baptist Magazine*] (November 1860): 737; (February 1861): 125; (September 1861): 600; (November 1861): 734.

[24] *Irish Chronicle* (February 1860): 130–31. *The Freeman* (September 19, 1860): 601.

[25] "The Association of Baptist Churches in Ireland," *Irish Chronicle* (August 1862): 541-42.

[26] Cited by *Wynd Journal* (April 7, 1860): 223, and by G. C. Morgan, *R.C. Morgan, His Life and Times* (London: Pickering and Inglis, 1909) 96.

[27] *The Revival* 6, no. 171 (October 30, 1862): 201–3.

[28] For details see Orr, *Second Evangelical Awakening*, 184–207.

warmly welcomed it, with the denominational periodical *The Freeman*[29] providing favourable and fair coverage of its progress. Baptist Noel and Charles Haddon Spurgeon were two of the most prominent English Baptists promoting it.[30] The Metropolitan Tabernacle was one of many churches built or extended in the decade following the growth of the Revival years. London Baptist numbers had increased by 33,325 in the 1860s, a growth of 60 percent in that decade. Overall, English Baptists may have gained as many as 80,000 new members through this Revival by 1865, and Welsh Baptists 20,000.[31] The Revival in Wales like Ulster was significantly influenced by a minister who had been involved in the awakening in America, although the movement spread without obvious leadership through the strong chapel networks that warmly welcomed the Revival.[32] *The Freeman*, in a summary of the progress of the Revival, noted as early as October 1859:

> Throughout the whole principality the movement is progressing, and is sustained by the united efforts and prayers of Episcopalians, Methodists, Independents and Baptists in every county and town the awakening is felt.... Meetings for prayer are numerous and at each the special object of petition is for a more abundant outpouring of the Holy Spirit.[33]

---

[29] [News of Revival] "We have read, we may say with joy ..." in connection with a report on an Evangelical Alliance conference on the Revival, *The Freeman* (October 5, 1859): 599. The lengthy article was very supportive of the Revival.

[30] Orr, *Second Evangelical Awakening*, 190–91; see also C. H. Spurgeon, *New Park Street Pulpit*, vol.5 (1860) 82. See also Spurgeon's commendation of the Revival in *The Revival* (December 17, 1863) [in Orr, *Second Evangelical Awakening* 191n].

[31] Orr, *Second Evangelical Awakening*, 191 and Appendix B, 270–71. Overall, the numerical gains from this Revival outside of London for English Baptists were quite small. For more details on English Baptists and the 1859 Revival see Terry Carter, "Baptists and the 'Second Great Awakening' in England, 1859–65," paper presented at the International Conference on Baptist Studies, University of Manchester, United Kingdom (July 15–18, 2015) and published as chapter 13 of this book.

[32] Enthusiastic responses followed Humphrey Jones's preaching, together with that of a newly converted Calvinistic Methodist minister, David Morgan. Holmes, *Religious Revivals in Britain and Ireland 1859–1905*, 35–36.

[33] *The Freeman* (October 26, 1859): 650. "In other Revivals preaching was the great instrument; in this, prayer has been the prominent instrument," *The Freeman* (October 5, 1859): 599. A contrary view claiming that too much emphasis was placed on prayer meetings and not enough on the input of laypeople was given in *Baptist Magazine* 6 (April 1859): 219–21. Overlooked in that article was that many of the prayer meetings had been started and led by lay people. Good examples of united prayer gatherings in which a Baptist played a prominent role took place in

Particularly significant was the desire for unity in Baptist ranks, something of little concern to many of these churches at the beginning of the 1860s. By 1865, two thousand of the twenty-four-hundred Particular Baptist congregations in England had joined the Baptist Union of Great Britain.[34] The letters pages of *The Freeman* and *The General Baptist Magazine* had regular correspondence on the subject of union between Particular and General Baptists,[35] the majority of it in favour of this proposal. A few voices had advocated it prior to this Revival; indisputably many more were favourable following it.

Scottish Evangelicals had eagerly sought news on the progress of the Revival in America and then in Ulster. It was claimed that visitors to and from Ireland had gone all over Scotland giving addresses on Revival in the summer of 1859.[36] However, conferences to discuss the American awakening and numerous prayer meetings to plead for Scotland to experience this blessing had already been established during the previous year.[37] *The Scottish Guardian* was a prominent source of information for the Christian community on this subject. The primary focus of the July 26, 1859, issue was the Ulster Revival.[38] Rev. Adam Smith of Girvan noted that prayer had been offered in New York for the spiritual needs of Coleraine in Ulster, which subsequently was greatly affected by the awakening. The Christians of Coleraine in turn had focused in prayer for the people of Port Glasgow,[39] one of the first communities in Scotland to see signs of revival in July 1859.[40] From August that year nightly meetings at the Seamen's Chapel in Greenock resulted in over one thousand professions of faith in Christ in only six months.[41] By early September 1859

London in January 1860; *The Freeman* (December 7, 1859): 745–46; and in Scarborough in January and February 1860; *The Freeman* (February 16, 1859): 68.

[34] Orr, Second Evangelical Awakening, 190–91.

[35] For example, *The Freeman* (June 3, 1857): 314; (June 20, 1860): 395; (July 11, 1860): 441; (July 18, 1860): 457; (July 25, 1860): 473–74. *General Baptist Magazine* (April 1861): 146–48; (May 1861): 181–85; (June 1861): 220–21; (August 1861): 298–300.

[36] *The Witness* (September 7, 1859) cited by Bussey, "Religious Awakening of 1858–60," 93.

[37] Bussey, "Religious Awakening of 1858–60," 93.

[38] *Scottish Guardian* 28 (July 26, 1859).

[39] *The Revival* (August 27, 1859) cited by Orr, *Second Evangelical Awakening*, 59–60.

[40] *Scottish Guardian* 28 (August 9, 1859). For more details see Harry Sprange, *Children in Revival* (Fearn: Christian Focus, 2002) 128–30.

[41] *The Revival* (January 28, 1860): 30. *Wynd Journal* (April 28, 1860): 242, had a lower figure of "nearly 900" with reference to these meetings in Greenock.

"refreshing showers of God's reviving grace" had been witnessed in Aberdeen and Dundee, together with earlier reports of the outpouring of God's most blessed Spirit" in the West of Scotland from Port Glasgow and Greenock, Rothesay, Ardrossan, Glasgow, and Airdrie.[42] It would be accurate to refer to waves of revival fervour punctuated by periods of regular services and activities in the churches between 1859 and 1863. It is very difficult to determine the number who professed faith in Scotland during those years.[43] What is abundantly clear from eyewitness accounts are the large numbers of attendees at Revival meetings and numerous professions of faith reported in local communities across Scotland. It is also acknowledged that a large proportion of those attending already had a connection with one of the three main Presbyterian churches in Scotland and that many of those professing faith were already members of one of those bodies. Analysis of membership increases would not find reference to these people. There were, though, significant membership increases, for example, in the United Presbyterian Church (UPC).[44] The Free Church of Scotland was also openly supportive of the Revival while the Church of Scotland was divided on the issue. It is no surprise that the Revival had more impact on the former than the latter body. Very few Baptist churches were founded in the aftermath of the Revival,[45] though significant renewal in some existing causes undoubtedly occurred. The network of churches that gained the most proportionately from the Revival was the Scottish Brethren. From only four known assemblies prior to 1860,[46] the foundations of many more congregations were laid in the next decade; so that by

---

[42] John Williams, "The Revival in Glasgow," *The Freeman* (September 14, 1859): 552.

[43] For discussion of the issues involved, see Marrs, "1859 Religious Revival in Scotland," 96–100, and Orr, *Second Evangelical Awakening*, 76–77.

[44] In 1859, 477 of its congregations added 15,314 new members, an average of thirty-three people; Orr, *Second Evangelical Awakening*, 76–77. The number of prayer meetings in its congregations doubled and the ongoing Sunday attendance figures across the country remained at approximately 50 percent higher than before the Revival. See *The Church in Victorian Scotland* (Edinburgh: St Andrews Press, 1975) 185–86.

[45] James Gordon, "The Latter Nineteenth Century," in *The Baptists in Scotland: A History*, ed. D. W. Bebbington (Glasgow: Baptist Union of Scotland, 1988) 55.

[46] N. Dickson, "Scottish Brethren: Division and Wholeness 1838–1916," *Christian Brethren Review Journal* 41 (1990): 5–41; cited by D. E. Meek, "Revivals," in *Dictionary of Scottish Church History and Theology*, ed. N. M. de S. Cameron et al. (Edinburgh: T&T. Clark, 1993) 711–18.

1870 the Brethren were firmly established in many locations within Scotland.[47]

What were the distinctive features of this awakening in Scotland and how did Baptists respond to these developments? The first significant factor to characterize this spiritual renewal movement was its basis in united interdenominational prayer meetings, as highlighted in the previous chapter. Excitement increased as reports of events in Ulster were shared around the country; additional prayer meetings were springing up or growing in attendance in an increasing number of communities, for example, in Port Glasgow, which saw the first signs of an awakening in July 1859:[48] "We are greatly encouraged...that the movement is assuming the same form here as in America and Ireland. The revivals in those lands have, in an important sense, been 'prayer-meeting revivals.'"[49] John Williams, Revival correspondent from Scotland for *The Freeman* and minister of North Frederick Street Baptist Church, Glasgow, wrote: "I believe God is about to do a great work among us. Our daily united prayer meeting is crowded, and it is very refreshing to see Christians of every denomination in such goodly numbers uniting to pray for the outpouring of the Holy Spirit."[50] Eyemouth in Berwickshire had seen "a remarkable outpouring of the Holy Spirit." The local population had been only two thousand people, but almost every home had been affected by the Revival. Every weeknight the four churches—Baptist, Methodist, Free Church, and United Presbyterian—had been open for prayer meetings with seats quickly taken. "The most cordial union exists among the ministers of the town, as well as among all Christians. Denominationalism is out of sight, and all are cooperating most heartily on behalf of Christ alone."[51] Christians committed to

---

[47] Neil T. R. Dickson, *Brethren in Scotland 1838–2000* (Carlisle: Paternoster, 2002) 855–89.

[48] *The Freeman* (August 17, 1859): 489, reported "as many as sixty" conversions at Port Glasgow "within the last fortnight." See also *Scottish Guardian* 28 (August 9, 1859). For more details, see Sprange, *Children in Revival*, 128–30.

[49] John Williams, "The Revival in Scotland," *The Freeman* (October 26, 1859): 649.

[50] *The Freeman* 5 (August 17, 1859): 489. See also *Scottish Guardian* 28 (August 26, 1859). Other examples include Helensburgh, where "the [united] prayer meetings are crowded....Here Presbyterians, Baptists and Independents are unitedly and heartily promoting the work of the Lord"; *The Freeman* 5 (October 26, 1859): 649. United prayer meetings were launched in the west end of Edinburgh where "the Rev. Jonathan Watson [Minister of Dublin Street Baptist Church] and others conducted the exercises." *Wynd Journal* (February 4, 1860): 145.

[51] *The Freeman* 5 (December 21, 1859): 778.

praying together, whether for one another or for people currently outside their faith, would have found it only a small step to engage in evangelistic endeavours together.

There was no doubt that Scottish Evangelical Christians worked more closely together in evangelistic work during this time of Revival.[52] Several examples of cooperative work illustrate this activity followed by some that highlight the limitations of joint ventures in mission. The former included the Carrubbers' Close Mission, an interdenominational outreach agency set up in Edinburgh to evangelise working men and women unfamiliar with church attendance in the city.[53] In April 1860, its leaders with the backing of key representatives of Established, Free, United Presbyterian, and Baptist [Jonathan Watson] churches sought successfully to obtain the empty Theatre-Royal building in the city for evangelistic events.[54] In Perth the large city hall was obtained for a series of evangelistic events that drew large crowds with encouraging numbers of professions of faith. Evangelist Duncan Matheson commented on that mission:

> A very pleasing feature was the cordial co-operation of the different ministers of the town—the Revs Milne, Davidson, Dymock, Tulloch (Free Church), Knowles and Neaves (Independent), Brown (Baptist), Frame (United Presbyterian)—taking part in the services. All felt how good it was for brethren to dwell in unity, seeking to make known from one platform the same blessed Jesus.[55]

Many examples could be cited of united efforts, but it must be admitted there were some tensions and differences of opinion between churches over

---

[52] Bussey, "Religious Awakening of 1858–1860," concludes,: "At no former revival had there been such a measure of unity among the various denominations." 333.

[53] Anon, *These Fifty Years: The Story of Carrubber's Close Mission Edinburgh 1858–1909* (Edinburgh: Tract and Colportage Society of Scotland, 1909) 14, cited by Christina Lumsden, "Class, Gender and Christianity in Edinburgh 1850–1905: A Study in Denominationalism," (PhD diss., University of Edinburgh, 2012) 152–53.

[54] *Wynd Journal* (April 28, 1860): 242; (May 5, 1860): 254–55. Another example of joint mission initiatives was those led by American evangelist Edward Payson Hammond. His particular focus was on evangelism amongst children. In little more than a month in Glasgow, in March 1860, he had preached in Free Church, United Presbyterian, Baptist and Independent pulpits with acceptance. *The Freeman* (April 3, 1861): 213. See also Carwardine, *Transatlantic Revivalism*, 185–86, for more details on Hammond.

[55] *The Revival* (February 26, 1863): 100.

which approaches to evangelistic endeavours were or were not acceptable.[56] Baptist minister John Williams in Glasgow recorded his distress at the bad theology and new religious measures being promoted by Dr. Walter and Mrs. Phoebe Palmer in the John Street Methodist Church in that city. He cited the words of an article on the Palmers in *The Scottish Guardian*: "'We should be sorry to see the same machinery set in motion in our Presbyterian Churches.' I have this confidence that such machinery never will, never can, be set in motion in our Baptist Churches."[57] In Edinburgh, the "Morrisonians," that is, those favouring the new measures of Charles Finney, associated with Brighton Street Evangelical Union Church, where John Kirk was the minister, but were unwelcome to participate in joint evangelistic events organised by the Carrubbers' Close Mission. However, the Brighton Street congregation hardly helped their cause by infiltrating enquirers' meetings at these events and seeking to direct those professing faith to their own place of worship or by handing out their tracts to people attending events at other churches![58] Some Presbyterians would have no dealings with "Plymouthists," a name used negatively to refer to people associated with the Scottish Brethren.[59] These recorded negative examples were few in Scotland, compared to the more sustained opposition some Baptists experienced in Ireland,[60] but the difference lay in where acceptable boundaries of evangelical unity should be placed. In Ireland, some Presbyterians clearly saw acceptance of infant baptism as a non-negotiable basis for working together in mission. Whereas in Scotland, the unity was centred on a common Reformed faith which most Scottish Baptists shared with Presbyterian and Independent colleagues, and through the Evangelical Alliance.

A third feature of this awakening was that the most effective speakers were laymen and occasionally lay women. Scottish Christians who were willing to engage in united prayer meetings and cooperative evangelistic events were generally willing to receive laymen and in most cases lay women to preach at these events. *The Freeman* in August 1859 cited with favour a lecture

---

[56] This is highlighted in Meek, "Revivals," 717.

[57] *The Freeman* (January 25, 1860): 53. Williams opposed both holiness theology and women serving in churches as preachers; for more details of the Palmers see Carwardine, *Transatlantic Revivalism*, 182–84.

[58] *Wynd Journal* (December 17, 1859): 94.

[59] *The Revival* (January 21, 1864): 34.

[60] See note 24.

of Professor William Martin, principal of Marischal College, Aberdeen, which highlighted the prominence of laymen in the Revival in Aberdeen. "Laymen had been stirred up to extraordinary effort, and God had given them the word for both perishing sinners and slumbering saints." He went on to note that after news of the extraordinary events taking place in America was shared: "Two laymen in simple faith next began a daily united prayer meeting in Aberdeen." The preacher, invited by Martin, whom God used to bring people to faith "was an Englishman...a layman and a lawyer" called Reginald Radcliffe.[61] There were those who were delighted at this development. *The Freeman* in October 1859 carried an article with these words: "No popular minister— no exciting 'Revivalist'—inaugurated or sustained the movement. Mr Finney is in Edinburgh, holding special meetings. But he has done nothing towards the originating and very likely will do but little towards extending, the Revival in Scotland."[62] The effectiveness of the ministry of these laymen undoubtedly convinced the majority of Protestant Evangelicals of God's favour on their labours. The social background of the preachers was carefully considered when they were invited to preach in specific locations. James Gall, of the Carrubbers' Close Mission, admitted in a report in *The Wynd Journal* that Donald Ross, a former West Port Free Church missionary in Edinburgh, and later Brethren member[63] had been invited to speak to a congregation in "John Knox's Church...almost exclusively...the poor," while Reginald Radcliffe would address the crowds in the New Assembly Hall in Edinburgh "to a large extent of the better classes."[64] *The Revival* newspaper celebrated that all social classes could hear the gospel being preached through these laymen. "Thus, Mr. North to the upper classes, Mr Radcliffe to the middle classes, and Richard Weaver to the masses, were the men chosen of God to begin the work."[65] Brownlow North, grandson of an Anglican bishop and nephew of Lord North, prime minister under George III,[66] alongside Hay Macdowall

---

[61] *The Freeman* (August 24, 1859): 505. For more details of this visit see *Recollections of Reginald Radcliffe by His Wife* (London: Morgan and Scott, [1896]) 36–58.

[62] *The Freeman* (October 26, 1859): 649.

[63] Dickson, *Brethren in Scotland*, 42. See also C. W. R[oss], ed., *Donald Ross: Pioneer Evangelist of the North of Scotland and the United States of America* (Kilmarnock, 1903) 30–32.

[64] *Wynd Journal* (October 20, 1860): 411.

[65] *The Revival* (September 14, 1861): 81–83.

[66] K. Moody Stuart, *Brownlow North: His life and Work* (1878; London: Banner of Truth, 1961) 5.

Grant, a member of a Scottish gentry family,[67] were the two evangelists of this awakening that came from the upper classes. Richard Weaver, a former miner,[68] was the most effective evangelist of that era in communicating the Christian faith to the working classes. There were, though, others such as Duncan Matheson, a former stonemason,[69] and a cooper named James Turner[70] who had great success in proclaiming the Christian faith to working class men and women in the northeast of Scotland. There were other laymen and laywomen preachers[71] who also had significant acceptance of their preaching gifts during the Revival. Most Scottish Baptists in common with those in other Scottish Evangelical Churches accepted this innovative use of lay evangelists in promoting this cause. In light of this development it is not surprising that their experiences during these years led Scottish Baptists to see the benefits of closer ties with one another.

The fourth and last feature of the Revival influence was its impact in encouraging Scottish Baptists to come together to form the Baptist Union of Scotland. In 1859, there had been very limited interest in Baptist union.[72] The connection between Baptists in Scotland and the Revival was made plain in the 1859 annual report of the Scottish Baptist Association (SBA).

The report, which was read at a business meeting, referred to the origin of the Association as having arisen out of an earnest desire on the part of members of the churches for a larger outpouring of the Spirit of God, and to the coincidence that at the very time the same desire had taken possession of the hearts of Christians in America, Sweden, and elsewhere, which had been followed by actual Revival in these countries, and now in this. The report

---

[67] Mrs. Gordon, *Hay Macdowall Grant of Arndilly* (London: Seeley, Jackson & Halliday, 1876) 3.

[68] R. C. Morgan, *The Life of Richard Weaver the Converted Collier* (Morgan and Scot, 1861).

[69] John Macpherson, *Life and Labours of Duncan Matheson, the Scottish Evangelist* (London: Morgan and Scott, 1871) 16–17.

[70] E. McHardie, *James Turner, or How to reach the masses* (London: T. Woolmer, 1889) 1.

[71] For details of these women preachers, see Dickson, *Brethren in Scotland*, 74–77; ibid, "Modern Prophetesses: Women Preachers in the Nineteenth-Century Scottish Brethren," *Records of the Scottish Church History Society*, 25, no. 1 (1993): 89–117; On a wider canvas see Olive Anderson, "Women Preachers in Mid-Victorian Britain," *Historical Journal* 12, no. 3 (1969): 467–84, together with Donald M. Lewis, "'Lights in Dark Places': Women Evangelists in Early Victorian Britain, 1838–1857," in *Women in the Church*, ed. W. J. Shiels and Diane Wood (Oxford: Basil Blackwell, 1990) 415–27.

[72] *The Freeman* 5 (June 1, 1859): 311.

gratefully acknowledged that many of the churches connected with the Baptist denomination had participated in these tokens of God's mercy and grace.[73]

Arminian and Calvinistic Baptists in Scotland were united in favour of the 1859 Revival. The growth in the churches would act as an incentive to further collective efforts in prayer and evangelistic activity. The 1861 annual report that the SBA declared that it "was designed to promote the cause of revivals."[74] When the focus was on shared activities such as prayer and evangelism, as mentioned in this context, the ties between Scottish Baptists were becoming more firmly established. The 1856 assembly of the SBA linked these two activities:

> The objects of the association were— first, to promote the revival of spiritual religion in the denomination.... The chairman made several remarks on each of these objects, but dwelt particularly on the first, showing the necessity there was for increased earnestness and activity on the part of the ministers, deacons, and members. Addresses of a practical character...were afterwards delivered.[75]

Scottish Baptists like counterparts in Ireland and England formed a union of congregations to facilitate closer cooperation between them. In the context of Revival blessings from God the theological differences between Baptists, and those between Baptists and other evangelical Christians, appeared to be much smaller than previously thought. In his presidential address, William Tulloch, the president of the Baptist Union of Scotland in 1881, highlighted what he believed was a main source of encouragement that strengthened ties between Baptists in Scotland.

> The Union was in fact born of a revival.... Quickened souls in all the churches...having been providentially led to cooperate in special efforts on behalf of the perishing, both ministers and people felt how good it was to work together for their common Lord. This excited in the minds of some of us a strong desire to see the body to which we belonged...take its part in so noble a work. The breath of heaven, which was then imparting new spiritual life to multitudes, could breathe on the Baptist churches too, and drawing together the scattered members of the body

---

[73] *The Freeman* 5 (November 2, 1859): 665. The SBA was formed in 1856 by a small group of individuals committed to promoting closer working ties between Scottish Baptists.

[74] *The Freeman* 7 (October 30, 1861): 697.

[75] *The Freeman* 2 (October 29, 1856): 649.

make them instinct with the life of God.[76]

Promoting the cause of Revival clearly brought many Scottish Baptists closer together and as a result it strengthened the support for the work of the new Scottish Baptist Association.

Scottish Baptists considered that they had experienced a larger outpouring of the Spirit of God between 1859 and 1863 through the Revival movement that had a lasting impact on the churches not just in Scotland, but also in the USA, other parts of the United Kingdom, and to a smaller degree in some other countries affected by it. The pattern of this awakening followed in the footsteps of earlier Revivals, but it also had some new features with its significant origins in the prayer groups seeking revival; closer cooperation in mission across denominational barriers, together with the particularly prominent role laymen, and to lesser extent lay women, played in its promulgation, together with a recognition of the benefits of closer union in their own ranks. Over the course of the 1860s this would lead to more effective working relationships and then to the formation of the current Baptist Union of Scotland in 1869.[77]

---

[76] W. Tulloch, "Presidential Address," *Fourteenth Annual Report of the Baptist Union of Scotland* (Glasgow: Baptist Union of Scotland, 1882) 42.

[77] Brian R. Talbot, *Search for a Common Identity: The Origins of the Baptist Union of Scotland, 1800–1870* (Carlisle: Paternoster, 2003) 277–317.

15

Baptists and Revival in Nineteenth-Century Scotland

Harry Sprange

At the beginning of the nineteenth century, Baptists in Scotland were small, weak, and isolated. Religious liberty had come late to the country with no tradition of so-called independency before 1730. By 1800, when the population of Scotland was only 1.6 million, it is estimated that there were only a thousand full members of independent churches—maybe a total community of four thousand if families and "hearers" are added. Included in this estimate would be the eleven "Scotch Baptist" churches we know of, plus the totally isolated and independent church in Keiss (Caithness) that has the extraordinary claim of being the oldest continuing Baptist witness in Scotland, dating from 1750.[1]

The Scotch Baptists were insular, struggled for their own survival, and had a tendency for division. However, south of the Border, from 1785 Andrew Fuller and William Carey had opened the discussion of the use "means" for the conversion of the "heathen" within the Baptist churches. Among the Scottish leaders, Archibald McLean from Edinburgh and James Watt in Glasgow certainly carried a burden for evangelism. The only link with revival that we can trace with any certainty is that McLean had heard Whitefield preach in his youth in the west of Scotland.

The other tenuous link from the eighteenth century comes from another unlikely source. In 1796, Rev. Charles Simeon from Cambridge was passing through central Perthshire and seems to have led Rev. Alexander Stewart, the parish minister of Moulin by Pitlochry, into assurance of salvation. Stewart's preaching changed, and towards the end of 1798 his congregation became concerned about their own salvation when he began to teach fundamental

---

[1] Derek Murray, "The Seventeenth and Eighteenth Centuries," in *The Baptists in Scotland: A History*, ed. David W. Bebbington (Glasgow: Baptist Union of Scotland, 1988) 17, 21.

doctrines; by the beginning of 1799, weekly conversions were reported. By March, there was a general awakening in the two villages, with seventy people "truly enlightened" out of sixty-seven families.[2] This was an amazing proportion of the local populace and was the first clear evidence of revival in Scotland since the Whitefield era of the 1740's.[3] When Stewart left the parish in 1805, his successor was unsympathetic. W. J. Couper claimed that most of his converts became Baptists![4] One of the converts from Logierait, another Alexander Stewart, became a Haldane missionary, operating farther north in Scotland. He accepted believer's baptism and later emigrated to Upper Canada, establishing the first Baptist cause in Toronto.[5]

The Haldane brothers' Society for Propagating the Gospel at Home (SPGH) sent John Farquharson into Breadalbane as an itinerant preacher. Revival commenced in Ardeonaig and spread from there around Loch Tay. At a prayer meeting in April 1802, fourteen fell to the ground crying for mercy, and whole nights were spent in prayer. Congregations of three hundred gathered, meeting in the open air or in tents. One of the converts, twenty-year-old John Campbell, spent eight months of 1804 preaching throughout the district. As a result, Independent congregations sprang up in the area. When the Haldanes accepted believer's baptism, the SPGH movement split. Yet four Baptist churches were established in the area: Killin, Lawers, Glenlyon, and Aberfeldy. By 1844, the largest Baptist church in Perthshire was at Tullymet with 131 members.[6] Incidentally, it was at Tullymet in 1835, that the first attempt to link the Baptist churches into a union was made, calling itself the Scottish Baptist Association.[7] Revival again occurred under the parish minister of Ardeonaig, Robert Findlater, from 1816 to 1819 and

---

[2] Glasgow Revival Tract no. VI 1839, reprinted in *Restoration in the Church* (Tain: Christian Focus Publications, 1989) 74.

[3] A few notable exceptions of revival existed between 1763 and 1766 in the form of local revivals in the far north of Scotland under James Croy of Calder. Croy influenced William Mackenzie of Tongue, who from 1773 saw signs of weekly conviction of sin in his congregation. See Tom Lennie, *Land of Many Revivals* (Tain: Christian Focus Publications, 2015) 154–57.

[4] W. J. Couper, *Scottish Revivals* (Dundee: Mathew & Co., 1918) 86.

[5] Lennie, *Land of Many Revivals*, 190n83.

[6] J. Quinn, "Tayside," in *The Baptists in Scotland: A History*, ed. David W. Bebbington (Glasgow: Baptist Union of Scotland, 1988) 241.

[7] For details of formation of Baptist Union of Scotland see D. B. Murray, *The First Hundred Years* (Glasgow: Baptist Union of Scotland, 1969).

spread up Glen Lyon. It was claimed that only four or five families were left untouched, and some of these joined the Baptist congregation.[8] The Presbyterians blamed the arrival of sectarianism for the decline of this move of the Spirit.

Despite what he called "inherent weaknesses" in the Scotch Baptist movement, Derek Murray made the extraordinary claim that, "By giving laymen the chance to exercise gifts of preaching and leadership, by introducing congregational hymn singing, by efforts of evangelism largely unrecorded, by fidelity to Scripture and by disseminating their principles in print, a few men and women played a great part in preparing for the revivals of the nineteenth century."[9]

Also helpful is Alexander MacRae's statement: "The awakenings that took place throughout the north, almost simultaneously, in districts far removed from one another, during the first two decades of the century, did more for the moral and intellectual development of the people than it is possible now to compute."[10] While he is generous enough to concede, "in Kintyre, Breadalbane, Skye, and Caithness, the first revivals on record took place under the preaching of the Haldanes and their evangelists; while in Tiree and elsewhere a work of grace, that spread to all denominations, began among the Baptists,"[11] he hardly mentions the Baptist contribution in the rest of his book!

It is important to understand that this was a time of tremendous social upheaval. The Agricultural Revolution was well under way and the Highland clearances had begun. Meanwhile, increasing mechanization of the Industrial Revolution was just beginning in the cities, with the introduction of steam and waterpower into weaving. The French Revolution had fostered a radical political consciousness. Donald Meek and Derek Murray deduced, "it is at least significant that Baptist principles took root in those parts of the Lowlands and Highlands in which social change was most noticeable."[12]

The Baptist cause really came to life in Scotland in the first decade of the

---

[8] Lennie, *Land of Many Revivals*, 211.
[9] Murray, "Seventeenth and Eighteenth Centuries," 24.
[10] Alexander MacRae, *Revivals in the Highlands and Islands* (Stoke: Tentmaker Publications, 1998) 10.
[11] MacRae, *Revivals in the Highlands and Islands*, 10.
[12] Derek Murray and Donald E. Meek, "The Early Nineteenth Century," in Bebbington, *Baptists in Scotland*, 28.

nineteenth century. Christopher Anderson had gathered a church, later to be known as Charlotte Chapel, at Richmond Court in Edinburgh in 1808 and founded in the pattern of the "English" Baptist churches. Influenced by the formation of the Baptist Missionary Society, they began sending evangelists not only to India but also into the Highlands as the Scotch Itinerant Society. In 1816, some of the former SPGH missionaries who had become Baptists linked with the "Scotch" Baptists of Perth and Glasgow and formed the Baptist Highland Mission. By 1827, these various strands had merged into the Baptist Home Missionary Society for Scotland, supporting twenty-one preachers by 1829, the first being Lachlan Mackintosh of Grantown on Spey. Anderson was also influential in the forming of the first Gaelic School Society in 1811, which is discussed below.[13]

One of the first men to be sent out by Anderson was Dugald Sinclair from Bellanoch. He had become a Baptist in 1801, trained in Bradford, and was appointed to be a missionary in Argyll and the Western Isles. There was a huge response to his preaching on Islay and Jura in 1812. Donald Meek claims that, "when harvesters left their labor to attend a religious service, it was usually indicative of deep spiritual interest in the kind associated with revivals or awakenings."[14] When speaking about work in these scattered rural communities it is important not to judge the results by numbers but by the depth of the preaching and the impact it had on the hearers. None of these pioneer Baptist evangelists would have thought of themselves as revivalists; nevertheless the conviction of sin that they saw can justifiably be seen as revival, as much as the later mass movements in more urban settings. On Colonsay in 1814 his congregation grew to four hundred, half the population of the island, and following his preaching on baptism by immersion in 1815 the Baptist church was founded. Later in life he immigrated to Lobo in Canada in 1831.[15]

There were other itinerants who operated independently with no official backing, for example, Donald MacArthur of Strachur, who began preaching following his conversion. He was baptized in 1801 and later pastored the Bap-

---

[13] H. A. Sprange details all references to revival in GSS schools in *Children in Revival* (Tain: Christian Focus Publications, 2002) chap. 2(e).

[14] Donald E. Meek, "Dugald Sinclair," *Scottish Studies* 30 (1991): 74.

[15] Lennie, *Land of Many Revivals*, 234n96.

tist church in Bute while continuing to travel. According to a description written in 1827, "Many were so affected under his preaching as to fall down and cry out."[16] After much opposition he decided to immigrate to America where he joined the Seventh Day Baptists in 1810.

Another self-supporting preacher was the colorful Sinclair Thomson, the first Baptist in Shetland. He was baptized in August 1815, but as early as 1810 his preaching had attracted hundreds from his base at Dunrossness; hundreds were awakened under his ministry. He founded six other churches in the islands, appointing ministers from among his own converts.[17]

In a short chapter it is not possible to cover in detail every local revival in the century, but it does seem possible to suggest that almost all the Baptist churches in the Highlands and Islands were either started or established out of a small scale revival move of the Holy Spirit. Donald Meek has suggested[18] that the cholera outbreak of 1832 precipitated a spiritual concern in many communities across Scotland, and marked growth can be traced in the Baptist churches in Lochgilphead, Tobermory, and Grantown on Spey that year.[19] At the last of these, the meeting-house was enlarged to seat 100 more people, and was immediately filled with attendees regularly coming under conviction of sin.[20] Towards the end of 1834, a powerful revival was triggered by a visit from Duncan Dunbar who had been known as a local lad but had become a minister in New York. The pastor, Peter Grant, reported baptisms almost every month for a period of four years. Fourteen young men, all new converts, started a Sunday morning prayer meeting; nine Sabbath schools were commenced in outlying preaching stations and sixty members were added at Grantown.[21] Grant also assisted his colleague, William Hutchison, at Kingussie

---

[16] From *An Account of the Present State of Religion throughout the Highlands of Scotland* (Edinburgh, 1827) quoted in both Lennie, *Land of Many Revivals*, 185, and Donald E. Meeks, "The Highlands," in Bebbington, *Baptists in Scotland*, 281.

[17] See J. A. Smith, *Sinclair Thomson, The Shetland Apostle* (Lerwick: Shetland Times, 1969) for full biography, summarized in Lennie, *Land of Many Revivals*, 235.

[18] Donald E. Meek in "Gaelic Bible, Revival and Mission: The Spiritual Rebirth of the Nineteenth-Century Highlands," in *The Church in the Highlands*, ed. James Kirk (Edinburgh, 1998) quoted by Lennie, *Land of Many Revivals*, 263.

[19] Lennie, *Land of Many Revivals*, 272–73.

[20] Baptist Home Missionary Society for Scotland (BHMS) report for 1833.

[21] BHMS 1836; see also Sprange, *Children in Revival*, 115–22.

where there was a minor awakening that added eighteen to the church.[22]

Duncan Cameron was appointed to Lawers and in 1839 addressed three hundred on a hillside on a Sunday evening. He complained that he could not visit all the places requesting a preaching visit around Loch Tummel and Loch Rannoch. Over two hundred people, some of whom may have walked up to fourteen miles, were present at a baptism in the remote and sparsely populated district of Rannoch. Cameron was engaged in praying with enquiries until 2:00 in the morning.[23] A renewed work was reported in Tullymet in 1840. Work progressed under Donald Grant from Grantown with many in great distress but "no groanings or swoonings." "simply speaking the truth in love on the Lord's Day, and from house to house" advanced the work.[24]

Grantown was visited again by revival in 1857 and membership increased to 203. In all Grant had seen 375 members added since the commencement of his ministry in 1828; fifty had died, thirty-six had been excommunicated, and others had moved away.[25]

Perhaps it was in the Hebridean islands that the Baptist evangelists made their greatest impact. John Farquharson had moved to Skye from Lochtayside in 1805 and itinerated around the north and west of the island before immigrating to Nova Scotia later that year. He may have been the first evangelical preacher to visit the island. Steve Taylor claims that both Donald Martin, minister of Kilmuir, and Donald Munro, the blind catechist, were converted through his open air preaching in Uig.[26] Munro started a prayer meeting. A number of those attending received believer's baptism from an unknown visitor and formed the nucleus of a Baptist Church in Uig in 1808; Taylor deduces the visitor was Walter Munro, later of Fortrose and Inverness.[27]

In 1826, William Fraser was appointed to Uig. Under his evangelistic ministry the church grew to about sixty, with up to three hundred attending his services. In 1831, he immigrated to Breadalbane, Ontario, where he saw one hundred members added to his church in fourteen months.[28] Other Uig

---

[22] BHMS 1836 and 1837.
[23] BHMS 1843, and Lennie, *Land of Many Revivals*, 355–56.
[24] BHMS 1840.
[25] BHMS 1857.
[26] Steve Taylor, *The Skye Revivals* (Chichester: New Wine Press, 2003) 23, 25.
[27] Taylor, *Skye Revivals*, 73.
[28] Taylor, *Skye Revivals*, 74–75.

Baptists went on to significant ministries in the New World, notably Samuel MacLeod, who left in 1829 for Prince Edward Island (Lyndale), and Murdoch Ross, who went to Cape Breton (Margaree Baptist Church).

Angus Ferguson, a native of Mull, which had experienced revival in 1832,[29] moved from Mull to Uig on Skye in 1836. Within a year, their three hundred-seat chapels were packed to capacity. A severe outbreak of smallpox occurred in 1838 and stimulated prayer. Ferguson reported "a great revival in Uig; the appearance is more promising than any I have ever yet seen." He then records preaching to a congregation of four hundred before proceeding to a baptism in the local river. He concluded his report: "There is a great reformation in this place."[30] By June 1839, he had a regular congregation of four hundred. The following March, he claimed that in the Kilmuir/Staffin district "large houses, containing two or three hundred, were crowded to excess."[31] Interestingly, he does not claim it to be revival, for in December he wrote, "our meetings were well attended and apparently deep impressions made…although there is no appearance of revival at present, yet we hope for better days." However, shortly afterwards the church began to be seriously depleted by emigration to America.

Farther south on Skye, James MacQueen, a member of the Grantown-on-Spey church, had been sent to Broadford in 1825; crowds soon gathered to hear his preaching. He was transferred to Lochcarron in 1833, where he preached to congregations of up to four hundred in the open air since there was no building large enough to meet in. By 1834, his regular congregation was two to three hundred on the Lord's Day and between sixty and two hundred on weekdays. He returned to Broadford in June 1836 to be ordained as an elder in that church. By December 1838, MacQueen was complaining that only half of his congregation could get into the building and he had to preach in a field to between four and five hundred.[32] He continued to visit Wester Ross, traveling as far north as Gairloch. In June 1839, there was a similar thirst for preaching with six to eight hundred attending on the Lord's Day in Lochcarron,[33] while in Applecross "there was such a desire to hear that a house

---

[29] Donald E.Meek, *Sunshine and Shadow* (Edinburgh: Tiree Books, 1991) 7.
[30] BHMS 1838.
[31] BHMS 1840.
[32] BHMS 1839.
[33] BHMS 1839.

could not contain the people; they stood outside under wind and rain, and in the dark."[34]

Skye was visited by a much more general revival in 1842, starting in the northwest under the preaching of the parish minister of Snizort, Rev. Roderick Macleod. He preached weekly for two months to thousands at a remote road junction known as Fairy Bridge. Initially MacQueen was hesitant, writing in September, "They had the sacrament last week, and, I hear, that between twelve thousand and fifteen thousand attended, and that hundreds fell down as if dead. This usually commences with violent shaking and crying out, and clapping of hands. Those affected were mostly women and children…if it be of man it will come to naught." By December he appeared reassured: "I never saw the church so lively and zealous as at present…I never saw such a general desire to hear in every part of the station, and, indeed throughout the whole island. This awakening…has extended to all the parishes of the island. There is a wonderful change in the conduct of the people, and much attention is paid to the word of God."[35] In March 1843, MacQueen continued, "As to the revival things are more moderate. The crying and fainting are dying away in most places, but the desire to hear is the same. The revival has extended to the mainland; in some parishes it is at its height, and the people are carried home in carts." The Gaelic Schools Society reported in 1842 that, "With scarcely an exception, the fourteen schools in Skye all shared in the outpouring of the Holy Ghost." The following year the society added, "There are few families in the whole island of Skye where there has not been one or more individuals seriously impressed."[36] The 1843 "Disruption" left many churches without settled ministry; lay revival converts conducted services, while the Baptists continued to draw open-air crowds of a thousand persons.

In the more southern islands, revival in Tiree spread from the Congregationalists to the Baptists, and at the end of 1840 their pastor, Duncan MacDougal, wrote in poetic language: "Our winter is past, the rain is over and gone, the time of the singing of birds is come, and the voice of the turtle is heard in our land."[37] The following year he could write, "The whole church is revived and animated with more zeal and love than ever before." MacDougal recorded that a desire to hear existed all over the island. He knew of over forty

---

[34] BHMS 1842.
[35] BHMS 1843.
[36] Gaelic Schools Society report for 1843.
[37] BHMS 1840.

under conviction of sin at the same time "mostly among grown up and old people," and there were frequent baptisms. On one occasion, in April 1840, a baptism attracted a crowd of three to four hundred. Another thirty-two were baptized in September 1845, eight more in nearby Colonsay. Church membership peaked at one hundred, but dropped to thirty-two in 1851 due to mass emigration, partly due to potato blight.[38]

After MacDougal's death, the next pastor was John MacFarlane. His family had been touched by the revival of 1839–1846, after which three of his brothers also became ministers: Duncan in Tobermory, James in Elgin, and Robert into the Established Church in Glenorchy. A second wave of blessing came to Tiree with the 1874 Moody and Sankey mission to Scotland. According to Meek, Duncan had heard Moody preach in Glasgow and invited him to the islands; Moody declined but suggested that Duncan preach God's love for sinners in a similar manner. Duncan came to Tiree in August 1874 to assist his brother with a baptism and was asked to share news of the mainland meetings. Nightly meetings shared with the Independents and the Parish Church began all over the island with five to six hundred attending every night, and sixty to eighty remaining behind for the subsequent enquirers' meeting. It was estimated that three hundred were converted by the end of the year, with 116 of these joining the Baptist church after baptism.[39] Meek goes on to claim, "the current of revival flowed so strongly after 1874 that it is difficult to talk about revivals as isolated events in the life of the church. The record shows peaks in a wave of spiritual interest, as in 1885, 1895, 1898, and 1901–1902."[40]

Independency had been established in Orkney through the work of Haldane's preachers, and a Baptist church established in Westray. The pastor, William Tulloch, in 1843 reported "a great shaking" and a "deep work of grace," and in February a hole was cut in the frozen loch to baptize eleven converts. That year the church added thirty-six members and claimed another twelve were seeking admission.[41] Another William Tulloch was pastor in Elgin when, in the spring of 1855, there was "a most precious and refreshing shower" of the Holy Spirit, resulting in six baptisms in a month; by November

---

[38] Donald E. Meek, *Island Harvest* (Edinburgh: Tiree Books, 1988) 10.
[39] Meek, *Island Harvest*, 17–19.
[40] Meek, *Island Harvest*, 30.
[41] BHMS 1844.

he was describing "a more copious shower."[42] Lennie claims that "stirrings among Baptist congregations were especially prominent in these years [1851–1857],"[43] and it would not be possible to record every example of these local moves of the Holy Spirit. For example, John Fisher makes a passing reference to revival on the island of Stroma (population only 330) just before 1870, which resulted in the construction of a Baptist chapel seating 180, but Fisher gives no details.[44]

The national awakening of 1859–1861 that occurred across Scotland and elsewhere has been studied in several accounts.[45] One of the first churches in Glasgow where revival was reported was in the North Frederick Street Baptist Chapel. On Thursday, August 18, "young and old were crying and weeping for mercy."[46] This church had been open less than a year, and in 1860 invited Rev. T. W. Medhurst from Coleraine to the pastorate. It would be interesting to discover if it had an earlier direct connection with the revival in Ulster that had preceded the work of the Spirit in Scotland by some months.

It is not possible to cover the second half of the century in the same detail for two reasons. One result of the mid-century revival was the extensive cooperation of the churches across the denominations; it is much harder to extract any specific Baptist contribution. The second is to question the use of the word "revival" as appropriate in an era of organized missions with planned campaigns and follow-up meetings, often led by professional evangelists. That is not to suggest that there was no planning in the activities of the early Baptist pioneers, but there was a spontaneity about their activities. There were often totally unexpected results that might indicate a supernatural dimension behind their gospel preaching. Often evangelists were compelled to remain in a village because of the large response to their preaching. That did not happen in the more organized outreaches of the latter nineteenth century. That reopens the debate on what is true "revival," which again is beyond the scope of this chapter.

---

[42] BHMS 1855.

[43] Lennie, *Land of Many Revivals*, 476.

[44] John S. Fisher, *Impelled by Faith* (Stirling: Scottish Baptist History Project, 1996) 33.

[45] See the preceding chapter in this book by Brian Talbot, "A Larger Outpouring of the Spirit of God".

[46] Sprange, *Children in Revival*, 143. Sprange also details the all-night prayer meeting run by children in Elgin Baptist Church in March 1860 and the controversy it provoked in the local press, 269–70, 404–7.

16

Revival Among Scottish Baptists in the Early Twentieth Century

Kenneth B. E. Roxburgh

The revival tradition in Scotland was one that was intimately woven into the experience and expectation of many people within Scottish Christianity. During the eighteenth and nineteenth centuries, recurring periods of spiritual awakening affected the religious life of the Scottish church, often bringing surges of emotional intensity, popular interest, and renewal to the life of the nation.[1] The phenomena of revival, as it affected Scotland, was not uniform in its appearance. During the seventeenth and eighteenth centuries, revival affected parishes within the Church of Scotland, often during communion seasons when the preaching of the crucified Christ, linked to the visible signs of the sacrament, often led to these occasions becoming converting ordinances. Many people who flocked to these corporate expressions of their faith experienced personal renewal and encountered immediacy in their experience of the presence of God.[2] It was not, however, until 1859 that the national movement impacted various denominations and, indeed, the whole country, as Scotland shared in an awakening with truly international proportions, affecting different parts of Great Britain as well as the United States.

In the latter part of the nineteenth century, awakenings began to be associated with significant preachers such as D. L. Moody, whose appearance

---

[1] These included an awakening in Moulin, near Pitlochry (1798) Arran (1804) Skye (1812) and the Isle of Lewis (1824–1835).

[2] M. J. Crawford comments, "the celebration of the Lord's Supper...was a revivalist ritual that served as a conduit for the outpouring of grace." *Seasons of Grace: Colonial New England's Revival Tradition in its British Context* (Oxford: Oxford University Press, 1991) 219. Alexander Whyte spoke of how the Lord's Supper "has been made a converting ordinance to many in all ages of the Church." Cited in W. J. Couper, *Scotland Saw His Glory* (Wheaton, IL: International Awakening Press, 1995) 326.

in the cities of Edinburgh and Glasgow in the 1870s brought many people to faith in Christ.[3] His use of simple language[4] and his anti-intellectual theology characterized as "ruin by sin, redemption by Christ, and regeneration by the Holy Ghost"[5] appealed to ordinary people and drew them into his meetings by the thousands.[6] Moody's message stressed a theology of the love of God demonstrated at Calvary and was warm and moving in its appeal. Unlike many evangelists who preached on hell and judgment, Moody focused on the love of God and the joys of heaven. His mission in Scotland was particularly effective. Several eminent ministers from various denominations endorsed it. Moody had not only demonstrated a "successful model for evangelizing the masses," but his "theological inclusive gospel" converted many ministers to "a more pragmatic theology of mission" and had an impact on the theological issues of the day.[7] There is evidence that, along with other changes, there was

---

[3] Ian Hamilton suggests that "Moody's visits to Scotland (1873, 1881–1882, 1891–1892) helped to transform the face of the church in Scotland." See Hamilton, "D. L. Moody" in *Dictionary of Scottish Church History and Theology* (Edinburgh: T&T Clark, 1993) 605–6. John Coffey has demonstrated that Moody went out of his way to reach men and women who had little contact with the church, holding his meetings in agricultural and city halls rather than churches and chapels, thereby distancing himself from traditional, institutional religion. John Coffey, "Democracy and popular religion: Moody and Sankey's Mission to Britain, 1873–1875" in *Citizenship and Community*, ed. Eugenio F. Biagini (Cambridge: Cambridge University Press, 1996) 93–119.

[4] W. G. Blaikie said, "Moody's sermons were certainly not intellectual, and those who went to his meetings in hopes of hearing something original and brilliant were doomed to disappointment. They were plain, honest, somewhat blunt appeals, but wonderfully brightened and made telling by a copious supply of illustrations, anecdotes and personal reminiscences." Cited in Couper, *Scotland*, 319.

[5] W. S. Hudson, *Religion in America* (New York: Scribner, 1965) 223.

[6] Ken Jeffrey speaks of how Moody "succeeded in reaching the urban masses." *When the Lord Walked the Land: The 1858–62 Revival in the North-East of Scotland* (Carlisle: Paternoster, 2002) 18. However, Couper states that "at the concluding meeting for converts in Edinburgh not fewer than 1,700 were present, young men and women of all social grades, but mainly belonging, it has been ascertained, to the families of Christian professors." *Scotland*, 322.

[7] James Gordon, *James Denney (1856–1917): An Intellectual and Contextual Biography* (Eugene, OR: Wipf & Stock, 2006) 102. Gordon suggests that Denney "looked on Moody-style evangelism with a mixture of intellectual disdain and grudging admiration." See Gordon, *Denney*, 96.

a "growing shift in Scottish Presbyterianism towards a more Arminian perception of salvation."[8] However, following Moody's visit there was sense in the country that revival, as a phenomenon, had virtually disappeared from the religious life of Scotland by the turn of the twentieth century.

Welsh Revival

Thus, when the Welsh Revival occurred in 1904, it was "totally unexpected."[9] By January 1905, some three thousand new members had been added to Baptist churches in the Rhondda Valley with similar numbers being seen in other Baptist associations.[10] R. Tudur Jones describes it as "one of the most remarkable events in twentieth-century Welsh history."[11] It was a movement characterized by the involvement of laity, especially young men, women,[12] and even children, by the absence of preaching, and by prolonged meetings that were taken up with singing, prayer, testimony, exhortations,

---

[8] Janice Holmes, *Religious Revivals in Britain and Ireland, 1859–1905* (Portland, OR: Irish Academic Press, 2000) 72.

[9] T. M. Bassett, *The Welsh Baptists* (Swansea: Iston House, 1977) 377. W. T. Stead, editor of the British *Review of Reviews*, commented, "never in the history of Revival has there been any Revival more spontaneous than this." "Mr. Evan Roberts" in *The Story of the Welsh Revival* (New York: F. H. Revell, 1905) 54. Stead was a friend of William Booth and an active spiritualist who supported the Welsh Revival because of its impact on social reform; he wrote three articles on the movement. Like another person involved in the revival, John Harper, he died on the Titanic's maiden voyage across the Atlantic. See Brynmor P. Jones, *Voices from the Welsh Revival* (Bridgend: Evangelical Press of Wales, 1995) 155. Basil Hall says that "its unordered spontaneity, so frequently commented on by observers, makes it unique in the history of revivals." "The Welsh Revival: 1904–5: A Critique" in *Popular Belief and Practice* (Cambridge: Cambridge University Press, 1972) 295.

[10] See Bassett, *The Welsh Baptists*, 378.

[11] R. Tudur Jones, *Faith and the Crisis of a Nation: Wales, 1890–1914* (Cardiff: University of Wales Press, 2004) 283.

[12] The *Western Mail* reported that "Miss A. M. Rees was, as usual, particularly energetic in all her evangelistic work, and her quiet conversations with dozens of young men were remarkable in every aspect." *Western Mail* for December 8, 1904. Roberts surrounded himself with several young women who took a lead in the singing of hymns and spiritual songs during the revival meetings. Phillips says that there were five "singing sisters," although one, "Madam Morgan Llewelyn, who was a professional singer—are as conspicuous in the movement as Evan Roberts himself." D. M. Phillips, *Evan Roberts, the Great Welsh Revivalist and His Work* (London: Marshall Bros., 1906) 304.

and the free expression of human emotions. It was an example of popular religion unregulated by ordained clergy.[13] The chief characteristic of the message of the revival was the person and work of Christ[14] and "the joys of heaven here on earth rather than the terrors of hell hereafter."[15] When Evan Roberts preached, reporters spoke of how "he frequently dwells on the Passion of our Lord, often breaks into tears as he describes the divine suffering...and instead of directly attacking secular amusements...seeks to draw man from bondage to the world by the superior love of Christ."[16]

Scottish Baptists

The Welsh Revival received many visitors from different parts of the world, including numerous Scottish Baptist ministers who traveled south to experience the movement themselves and returned to encourage an expectation that the awakening could also affect Scotland. The first notice of the Welsh Revival took place in an editorial within the *Scottish Baptist Magazine* for January 1905.

> An extraordinary revival of religion has visited Wales...the meetings [are] emphatically prayer meetings...earnest, brief, personal and urgent...the people do not engage in prayer, but pray with all their hearts, as those who desire a blessing, and will not rest until they obtain it. Men, women, and children have been taking part in the Welsh Revival meetings, many of which are prolonged for hours, without weariness and with comparatively little excitement. In many cases the meetings have no leader, but they have nevertheless proceeded with perfect order...short exhortations, professions of faith, hymns and prayers alternating without

---

[13] G. Campbell Morgan, minister of Westminster Chapel in London, visited the scene of the revival and commented, "There is no preaching, no order, no hymnbooks, no choirs, no organs, no collections, and finally no advertising.... everybody is preaching.... they abandon themselves to their singing...a praying remnant have been agonizing before God...and it is through that the answer of fire has come." See G. Campbell Morgan, "The Lesson of the Revival" in *Story of the Welsh Revival*, 42–44.

[14] E. Cynolwyn Pugh, "The Welsh Revival of 1904–1905," in *Theology Today*, vol. 12, no. 2 (July 1955): 232.

[15] Phillips, *Evan Roberts*, 333. Roberts stated that he was "merely trying to show people the love of Christ as I have experienced it." Arthur Goldrich, "The Story of the Welsh Revival" in *Welsh Revival*, 15.

[16] A. T. Fryer, "The Revival in Wales," *East and West: A Quarterly Review for the Study of Missions*, (April 1905): 181.

restraint, but with an absence of confusion. There are hundreds; we might without exaggeration say thousands of professed conversions. Ministers testify that their membership is increasing at a rate that has scarcely ever been known before...and the people of Wales are manifesting the keenest interest in the present and eternal welfare of their friends and neighbors...this movement is seizing and reforming the indifferent multitudes where regular and evangelical efforts have failed.... Will it visit us? Yes; if we are prepared to use the means—to pray, not in a perfunctory and matter of custom way; but with earnestness and sincerity, that God would send us the blessing.[17]

In March 1905, the editor of the magazine returned to the subject of revival and stated,

The desire for a deep and widespread revival of religion has been growing in connection with our churches and throughout Scotland generally. Everywhere an impression prevails that a revival of no ordinary kind is coming; and this feeling has of late been much accentuated by the remarkable success that has attended the movement in Wales.... We have now arrived at a stage when even worldly people look upon a revival as a thing to be expected.

Responding to the criticism that the revival in Wales was characterized by emotionalism due to the character of the Welsh people and that the "Scotch, on the other hand, and especially the educated among us, set much value on a certain cold stolidity," he argued that

the thing to be aimed at is a legitimate and wise self-control; but self-management does not necessitate the locking-up of the fountains of our emotions...we conduct ourselves best when we allow just that amount of play to our emotions that is justified by the circumstances in which we are placed. To repress emotion when it ought to be expressed is to do violence to our nature.

He concluded his editorial by assuring his readers throughout Scotland that

---

[17] "Revival Times for the Christian Million," *Scottish Baptist Magazine*, January 1905. The magazine also gave a description of the Welsh Revival in a separate article on page 9 describing the ministry of Evan Roberts and his success in different parts of South Wales. The *Revival Times* noted "much blessing in connection with evangelistic services in different parts of Scotland— a new interest...a greater readiness...to respond" and particularly mentioned meetings in Glasgow, Motherwell, and Forfar. May 15, 1905.

The revival has begun in many of our Churches... our own Baptist ministers are in fullest accord with the movement, and prepared to do their utmost to speed its progress...[during] our Union quarterly meetings...on two occasions...our ministers engaged in special prayer for personal quickening and revival in the churches. The prayers were brief, pointed, and earnest to a degree—expressive of the burden of their hearts— showing with what intense anxiety they are seeking the effectual operation of the Holy Spirit.[18]

Scottish Baptist statistics for 1902–1906 indicate a significant rise in both baptisms and membership figures for 1905, when membership rose from 17,334 in 1904 to 18,566, with baptismal figures also rising from 1,319 to 1,970.[19] Among the churches impacted by the revival, four deserve attention: Charlotte Chapel, Edinburgh; Glasgow and Govan; Galashiels, and Stirling.

Charlotte Chapel, Edinburgh

In many of the Scottish communities where congregations were enjoying, eagerly expecting, and praying for a copious outpouring of the Spirit, none was more dramatic than Charlotte Baptist Chapel in the West End of Edinburgh. The revival, as the church experienced it, was a close reflection of what had been known in Wales.

In February 1902, Joseph Kemp accepted the invitation to become the new pastor of Charlotte Chapel. The membership of the congregation numbered one hundred, but only thirty-five were active in attendance. Three years

---

[18] *Scottish Baptist Magazine*, March 1905, 41–42. In 1905, the Baptist Union of Scotland sent postcards to fifty of its ministers asking them if they had "anything special to communicate." Replies came immediately from all over Scotland—from Arbroath, Bellshill, Bowhill (Fife) Bridgeton (Glasgow) Bristo Place (Edinburgh) Clydebank, Cowdenbeath, Denny, Elgin, Forfar, Galashields, George Street (Paisley) Gilcomston Park (Aberdeen) Hawick, Inverkeithing, Kelvinside (Glasgow) Maxweltown (Dundee) Maybole, Motherwell, Orangefield (Greenock) Paisley Road (Glasgow) Partick (Glasgow) Port Ellen (Islay) South Leith, Victoria Place (Glasgow) Stirling and Wishaw. See Alasdair Black, "Pour out Your Spirit: Experiences of the Holy Spirit amongst Baptists in Scotland in the Twentieth Century" in *A Distinctive People*, ed. Brian R. Talbot (Milton Keynes, UK: Paternoster, 2014) 159.

[19]

Year	Churches	Membership	Baptisms
1902	120	16,250	1105
1903	119	16,607	1319
1904	119	17,334	1269
1905	125	18,566	1970
1906	125	19,179	1195

later, 347 new members had been added to the church and the congregation continued to grow in succeeding years, becoming the largest Baptist church in Scotland.

In January 1905, Kemp heard of the Revival in Wales and spent two weeks "watching, experiencing, drinking in, having my own heart searched...then I returned to my people in Edinburgh to tell them what I had seen."[20] J. J. Thomas returned from Wales with Kemp, and on Saturday, January 22, they held a conference on revival that lasted from 3:30 p.m. until midnight. It was to be the first of innumerable prolonged meetings over the coming weeks and months. One of the chief characteristics of these meetings, following the experience of Wales, was that of prayer, testimony, and singing. Even in Sunday services there were occasions when Kemp found it difficult to preach because of the audible prayers of the congregation. The chapel held 750 people, but it was often crowded with every nook and cranny being utilized by young and old, including many children. In 1905, around one thousand people were converted and 203 new members were added to the church, bringing the membership at the end of 1905 to 520. Following a period of relative quietness, a Sunday evening service at the end of 1906 brought a fresh sense of God's presence and "the fire fell...quite suddenly, upon one and another, came an overwhelming sense of the reality and awfulness of His presence and of eternal things.... prayer and weeping began and gained in intensity every moment...prayer broke out, waves and waves of prayer" and when meetings were held on January 1, 1907, at 11:00 a.m., 3:00 p.m., and 6:30 p.m., the pattern of "prayer, confession, testimony and praise" once again characterized the spiritual awakening.[21]

Although the movement in 1906 was a "year of advance," Kemp commented that it was not to the same extent as 1905.[22] By February 1907 the church realized that the dramatic events of the previous two years had finally come to an end. They began to "reorganize the work in the Chapel on generally accepted Church lines," although conversions were experienced throughout the rest of the year.

Kemp believed that the characteristics of the revival that they experienced in Edinburgh was marked by three features: first of a "deep conviction

---

[20] Winnie Kemp, *Joseph Kemp: The Record of a Spirit-Filled Life* (Edinburgh: M. Morgan & Scott, [1936]) 29.

[21] *Charlotte Chapel Record*, December 1908, 20–21.

[22] The Chapel had 130 baptisms in 1905 and 102 in 1906.

of sin" when even "many things thought to be right have been seen to be wrong and sinful.... a thing which may have been in itself perfectly lawful, has been abandoned because it stood in the way of full surrender"; secondly, he identified "prolonged intercession, sometimes for hours...here we have learned something of what Wales experienced;" thirdly, a "new spontaneity and power of the prayer meetings...the stream of prayer flows on unhindered."[23]

In Scotland, Kemp was a frequent speaker at various churches, giving his "lamp light lecture on 'The Welsh Revival'" in a variety of Baptist churches. On some occasions, such as a visit to Aberdeen, the congregation of six hundred continued "in prayer and waited on the Lord till nearly midnight."[24] Yet, when the chapel celebrated its centenary in October 1908, Kemp lamented the "annual statistics sent forth by our different denominations" that indicated, "that the numbers attending our churches are growing less and less."[25]

Glasgow and Govan

By 1870, more than half of the British shipbuilding workforce was based on the Clyde. The area of Govan grew because of this boom in industry and the population increased from nine thousand in 1864 to more than ninety thousand by 1914. Despite its exceptional economic growth, everyday life for most of its population was one of poverty, overcrowded housing, and sickness.[26] Govan became a city of contrasts, filled with challenges for the church at the turn of the twentieth century.

In 1895, the Baptist Union of Scotland supported the work of a young evangelist called John Harper to establish a work in Paisley Road, Govan. A church was constituted with twenty-five members in September 1897. In 1901, when the church had grown to 230 members, a hall with seating for six hundred was built, and over the following four years its membership grew to

---

[23] *Charlotte Chapel Record*, March 1907, 1.
[24] *Charlotte Chapel Record*, June 1907. Kemp also was a speaker in Ayr, Maybole, Stirling and Abbeyhill, Edinburgh, and at a conference on revival in Glasgow.
[25] *Charlotte Chapel Record*, November 1908.
[26] A school board survey of 1906 indicated that a fourteen-year-old living in a poor area of Glasgow was, on average, some four inches shorter than another child from the prosperous West End. A national survey of 1902 revealed that Glasgow as the most overcrowded city in Britain.

445. Its most vibrant period spanned September 1904 to October 1905 when 232 converts were baptized on profession of faith.[27]

John Harper, assisted by Mr. Dunn, held meetings every night for several weeks. The crowds were so large that, in addition to nightly meetings in the Baptist church, the congregation took over the White Memorial Free Church, and both buildings were full for several weeks of nightly meetings.[28] In April 1905, the *Scottish Baptist Magazine* reported that since December 1904 over seven hundred people had professed conversion with one hundred being added to the church membership. In October 1905, the membership stood at 507. By August 1906, there were indications that the revival was ebbing, and the church minutes complained that "had it not been for the spiritual declension which has been quite manifest in our midst the number of conversions would have been very much larger" although most "members are praying for a great revival which will surely be given."[29] In the summer of 1905, Harper's health broke, and in January 1906 his wife died leaving him a baby girl. In 1910, he left to go to London to become pastor of Walworth Road Baptist Church. He traveled to the United States to spend three months in the Moody Church in Chicago when a further movement of revival was experienced. Following a visit to Britain, he sailed back to America to spend three more months in Chicago but died on the Titanic on April 10, 1912. The church in Glasgow renamed its building Harper Memorial Baptist Church.[30]

Galashiels

During a Baptist church business meeting in Stirling Street, Galashiels, the pastor, John Shearer, "earnestly pleaded for a more prayerful spirit being evidenced in order that we might share in the great work of revival Wales was presently experiencing."[31] Shearer spent a week in Wales[32] attending meetings which he described as "strangely solemn, yet ineffably joyous." He spoke of the "great waves of unseen power" which evoked "prayer like a torrent…. God is felt to be very near, and hot tears tell of deep repentance and reawakened

---

[27] *John Harper (1872–1912)* (Harper Memorial Baptist Church, May 1972).
[28] *Scottish Baptist Magazine*, February 1905, 42–3.
[29] Minutes of Church meeting in August 1906.
[30] The new building was opened in 1922 by his daughter.
[31] *Scottish Baptist Magazine*, March 1905, 58.
[32] See "The Revival in Wales" reported in, *Scottish Baptist Magazine*, April 1905, 67–69.

love… strong men [are] broken down in an agony of remorse." He returned to the Scottish Borders "with a new heart and a new Bible,"[33] and "much blessing followed" as the church held nightly meetings from April 3 to July 8, 1905, that resulted in over 120 conversions recorded.[34] The longing for revival continued into 1906 when Shearer "expressed a desire for the spread of prayer" during a deacon's meeting, "and at the end of the meeting all the brethren present engaged in prayer, especially for revival."[35] The number added to the church in Galashiels was not significant, the membership rising from 244 in 1904 to 269 in 1906. This occurred during a period when trade depression hit the Borders area and affected all the churches there.[36]

The influence of the Welsh Revival, with its "conservative evangelical ethos"[37] influenced Shearer's theological concerns. He reflected on his visit to Penuel Chapel, Cwmavon, where ninety men and women were baptized. The pastor, who had previously met resistance to the plan to abandon the use of fermented wine during communion, called for a vote during a spontaneous church meeting, and "to the pastor's joy there was not one dissenting voice." Shearer met Evan Roberts whom he described as combining "manly courage with womanly gentleness…modest and brotherly…a man of God, possessed by the Holy Spirit."[38] Furthermore, Shearer felt that the simple gospel that moved men and women during the revival was in danger of being rejected because of higher criticism. In his presidential address to the Scottish Baptist Assembly in 1936, Shearer spoke of the "danger [that] threatens us at the present moment. The new Rationalism that has invaded the Church has taken our feet from the firm ground of our faith and made us to flounder miserably in a quagmire of doubt." He maintained the need to hold on to the fundamentals of Baptist faith such as belief in the Bible as "the Word of the Living

---

[33] Comment in memorandum notebook in the possession of John Shearer's daughter.

[34] Shearer reported in the *Scottish Baptist Magazine*, June 1905, that 120 had been converted. Stirling Street had thirty-seven Baptisms in 1905.

[35] Minutes of Deacon's Meeting, Stirling Street Baptist Church, January 26, 1906.

[36] See *The Baptists in Scotland: A History*, ed. David W. Bebbington (Glasgow: Baptist Union of Scotland, 1988) 124.

[37] Ian S. Rennie, "Fundamentalism and the Varieties of North Atlantic Evangelicalism" in *Evangelicalism: Comparative Studies of Popular Protestantism in North America, the British Isles, and Beyond, 1700–1990*, ed. Mark A. Noll, David W. Bebbington, and George A. Rawlyk (Oxford, Oxford University Press, 1994) 342.

[38] *Scottish Baptist Magazine*, April 1905, 68.

God" and "our Lord's Deity" which will oppose the "insidious Unitarianism that...is deep seated in the churches of our land." Thirdly, he spoke of the "atoning death" of Christ as a "perfect substitution." This he contended was "the central truth of Christianity." He concluded by mentioning the Lord's Resurrection, the fact of the New Birth that opposed the "New Rationalism" with its "system of psychology," and the Blessed Hope of the Church, which he identified as the imminent return of Christ.[39] For Shearer, the only hope of the church was to be found in a fresh outpouring of the Holy Spirit and a concentration on issues relating to evangelism.[40]

Stirling

At a meeting of deacons on January 11, 1905, Mr. Yuille, the minister, expressed the hope that the great revival in Wales would extend to Scotland and Stirling and that prayer to this end be offered."[41] The church was committed to evangelism and appointed a full-time evangelist who engaged in house-to-house visitation. During a mission led by A. Y. McGregor from Edinburgh, there were 397 converts. The converts resulting from the mission were described as "far in excess of any movement in Stirling within our recollection [and] there were no cases dealt with at the police court this week, but this we are told is merely 'a coincidence.'"[42] The church increased in membership from 150 in 1903 to 222 in 1906.

Role of Women in the Revival

As in Wales, the involvement of women in the revival movement in Scottish Baptist congregations was significant. In May 1905, the church in Victoria Place in Glasgow reported that it was in the fourth week of a special mission. Miss Maggie Condie, whom John McLean, pastor of the church had met on a visit to Wales, was acting as an evangelist, and her "sweet, simple, spiritual singing and testimony" was effective in winning many people to

---

[39] John Shearer, "Forward: The Call to a Great Advance" in *Scottish Baptist Year Book* (1937): 153–157.

[40] See John Shearer, Old Time Revivals: How the Fire of God Spread in Days Now Past and Gone (London, private publication, n.d.).

[41] Records of Stirling Baptist Church, in Stirling County Council Archives, PD 154/2, Deacons' Meeting Book 1890–1911, 210–211.

[42] *Scottish Baptist Magazine*, April 1905, 64.

Christ. Mclean commented that she was booked to conduct meetings in several Baptist churches in Scotland, "and a blessing is sure to attend her consecrated services wherever she goes."[43] Condie then moved on to Shettleston, Glasgow, to hold a special mission when somewhere between 150 and 160 people were converted, with about one hundred of the young converts forming Christian Endeavour societies. The church reported that they had added fifteen new members through baptism and "at present we are having a special season of prayer in view of Miss Condie's return on October fifteenth. Our sister will be with us for a fortnight, and we are expecting great things from God and that many souls will be saved."[44] The following month, the Baptist church in Alexandria held a two-week mission with Miss Condie from Wales, and thirty people professed conversion, some of whom joined the church.[45] The *Charlotte Chapel Record* mentioned the presence of Miss Davies, a Welsh evangelist who was involved in a five-week mission in Coldstream in 1907. In April 1908, the *Record* mentioned that Miss Annie McLaren "recently returned from America is evangelizing with Mr. Frank Weaver."[46]

Welsh Revival, Early Pentecostalism, and Baptists in Scotland

Allen Anderson comments that the "Welsh Revival emphasised the Pentecostal presence and power of the Spirit...the end time Pentecost...that would result in a worldwide revival."[47] The Welsh Revival affected many of the early leaders of Pentecostalism in Scotland.[48] It seems clear that the three

---

[43] *Scottish Baptist Magazine*, May 1905, 87.
[44] *Scottish Baptist Year Book* (1906): 64.
[45] *Scottish Baptist Year Book* (1906): 70.
[46] *Charlotte Chapel Record*, April 1908, 43.
[47] Allan Anderson, "The Pentecostal and Charismatic Movements," *The Cambridge History of Christianity: World Christianities c. 1914– c. 2000*, vol. 9, ed. Hugh McLeod (Cambridge: Cambridge University Press, 2006) 89. Anderson also suggests that "Pentecostalism began in Europe very soon after the Azuza Street revival, but differed from the North American movement" in that it was influenced not only by the holiness tradition but also by the Keswick movement and the Welsh Revival. See Allan Anderson, *An Introduction to Pentecostalism* (Cambridge: Cambridge University Press, 2004) 83.
[48] The influence of the Welsh Revival and the emergence of Pentecostalism have been evaluated differently by historians of the movement. See James Robinson, *Pentecostal Origins: Early Pentecostalism in Ireland in the Context of the British Isles* (Milton Keynes, UK: Paternoster, 2005) 13–15; Neil Hudson, "'You'll never know your future until you know where your past is': British Pentecostalism's Development and Future Challenges," *Evangel*, 21.2 (Summer 2003):

classic Pentecostal denominations in the British Isles were influenced, in one way or another, by news of and direct, or indirect, participation in the Welsh Revival, although the Welsh Revival itself did not include any distinctive Pentecostal signs of speaking in tongues. Donald Gee, one of the early leaders of the Assemblies of God, was converted through the preaching of Seth Joshua, a preacher of the revival. George and Stephen Jeffreys, co-founders of the Elim Pentecostal movement, were converted during the revival in Wales.[49] A. B. Boddy (1854–1930), an Anglican vicar in Sunderland and perhaps the most significant leader of Pentecostalism in Great Britain, had previously visited the Welsh Revival and spent time speaking with Evan Roberts. He returned to his parish to start a prayer meeting for revival to break out in their locality.

Two of the earliest leaders of the movement in Scotland were Eilif and Christina Beruldsen. Eilif Beruldsen was a wealthy ship chandler in Edinburgh; he and his wife were members of Charlotte Baptist Chapel in Edinburgh.[50] Eilif had been elected as a deacon in 1904 and had participated in the revival. In January 1908, Eilif and Christina attended the Faith Mission Conference in Edinburgh where Boddy spoke. Two days later they went to Sunderland where it is reported that they both were baptized in the Spirit and spoke in tongues. Christina spoke of how "my tongue loosened and I spoke in New Tongues for about two hours. All through the night I was singing heavenly music."[51] Although they hoped that their experience of the Spirit would be welcomed within the Chapel, they didn't find any encouragement so they began to hold meetings in their home in Murrayfield, eventually establishing their own Pentecostal mission in the working-class district of Leith, where Donald Gee began his pastoral ministry in 1920.[52]

In May 1908 a series of meetings were held in the church hall of Stirling

---

37–40. See also Neil Hudson, "The Earliest Days of British Pentecostalism," *The Journal of the European Pentecostal Theological Association*, 21 (2001): 49–67.

[49] Robinson, *Pentecostal Origins*, 15.

[50] Colin Whittaker suggests he was an elder of the chapel. See Colin Whittaker, *Seven Pentecostal Pioneers* (Springfield, MO: Gospel Publishing House, 1983) 85. In email correspondence on March 3, 2009, Ian Balfour wrote "Chapel records show that Eilif Beruldsen became a deacon at the December 1904 election."

[51] *Confidence*, April 1908, 11.

[52] See Donald Gee, *Wind and Flame* (Croyden, UK: Assemblies of God, 1967) 32. The initial mission hall was in Bridge Street, Leith. In January 1922, the congregation moved to the Bonnington Toll district of Edinburgh, close to Leith. Whittaker, *Pentecostal leaders*, 86–87.

Baptist church and attracted the attention of the deacons. The minutes of the deacon's meeting recorded that:

> Some discussion arose about certain manifestations in meetings [margin note "gift of tongues"] in the church hall by a company of Christians who were waiting on God for the Baptism of the Holy Ghost and Fire, the suggestion being that they were a hindrance to the work of the church.... On the motion of Mr Taylor it was agreed that none of these meetings be held under the auspices of the church.[53]

The Great War

In the early days of the First World War, church leaders eagerly anticipated a revival of religion, not only in the armed forces but also in the churches.[54] The United Free Church spoke of "larger attendances at church than has been seen for a long time...many began to think that the revival they looked for had come in this most unexpected way."[55] D. S. Cairns, who edited the *Army and Religion Report* published after the war, believed that "the presence of death, sorrow, pain...is awakening the primitive religious sense...making him call out for God."[56] Churches throughout the country were crowded on Sunday, August 9, after Great Britain declared war on Germany. Shortly thereafter, smaller denominations, such as the Baptists, reported 1,293 baptisms in 1914, an unusually high figure.[57] This intensified interest in religion was maintained through January 1915, when the king

---

[53] Cited in Brian R. Talbot, *Standing on the Rock* (Stirling: Stirling Baptist Church, 2005) 60–61. In October 1908, the *Confidence* magazine reported "that about 30 or 60 [rather vague] now have Pentecost with new Tongues" but did not indicate where they were meeting. Report by John Miller from Glasgow in *Confidence,* October 1908, 16–17.

[54] For an examination of this issue see Stewart J. Brown, "A Solemn Purification by Fire: Responses to the Great War in the Scottish Presbyterian Churches, 1914–1919," *Journal of Ecclesiastical History* 45, No. 1 (January 1994): 90.

[55] "From the Synods" in "Report of the Committee on Church Life," *Reports to the General Assembly of the United Free Church* (Edinburgh: United Free Church of Scotland, 1915) 12.

[56] D. S. Cairns, "The Task Before the Church," *Christ and the World at War: Sermons Preached in War-Time,* ed. Basil Matthews (London: J. Clark, 1917) 41–42.

[57] See David Hunt, *Reflecting on Our Past: A Statistical Look at Baptists in Scotland 1892–1997* (Glasgow, November 1997) appendix 2. The next year only 727 baptisms were recorded and this figure went down even further to 619 in 1916. There were slight increases to 781 in 1917 and 868 in 1918.

called for a "Day of Prayer" and "everywhere the churches were filled."⁵⁸ However, the United Free Church was realistic enough to report in May 1915 that through the winter the attendance had lessened and intercessory services had either ceased or were more "sparsely attended than at the beginning of the war."⁵⁹ They concluded that although "large numbers...have made profession of their faith in Christ...we have not seen a great return of the nation to God, nor the great revival which ought to be the outcome of the present terrible experience."⁶⁰ The United Free Church suggested that one reason for the decline in church attendance was that a large number of men had joined the army and also by the introduction of Sunday working.⁶¹ C. M. Black, the Episcopal rector of Christ Church in Edinburgh thought that only "a very few have been religiously affected by the war...the call of religious revival which was sounded at the beginning of the war, has not been answered to any great extent."⁶² Michael Snape comments "the religious revival of 1914–15, like many other smaller revivals in the British army since the 1740s, could not survive the inevitable attrition and disruptions of hard and sustained campaigning."⁶³ Richard Schweitzer suggests that rather than see the war as either a "revivalist or secularizing event," we should recognize that elements of both attitudes can be seen during this time.⁶⁴

---

⁵⁸ The king specifically asked for a Day of Intercession, refusing the use the older term "Day of Humiliation and Prayer," which would have implied that Great Britain shared in the guilt of the war. See "Reflections in Time of War," *Life and Work* (February 1915): 52. Later that year, the Free Church claimed that the war had come as a means of judgment upon Britain because of their national sins, such as "Intemperance...inordinate cravings for amusements...Fostering of Romanism...by sending an envoy to the Vatican...Sabbath Desecration...Neglect of God's Word." See *Free Church Monthly Record* (June 1915): 102–103.

⁵⁹ "From The Synods," 12.

⁶⁰ "From The Synods," 14. Richard Schweitzer comments that when "civilian church attendance returned to pre-war levels, revivalists focused their hopes upon soldiers." See Schweitzer, *The Cross and the Trenches*, xviii.

⁶¹ "Report of Committee on the Present Situation as affected by the War," *Reports to the UF Assembly* (1917) 4.

⁶² See *Life and Work* (December 1916): 245.

⁶³ Michael Snape, *God and the British Soldier* (Abingdon: Routledge, 2005) 167–167. See also Neil E. Allison, *The Official History of the United Board: The Clash of Empires 1914–1939* (United Navy, Army and Air Force Board, 2008) 75.

⁶⁴ Richard Schweitzer, *The Cross and the Trenches: Religious Faith and Doubt among British and American Great War Soldiers* (West Port, CT: Praeger, 2003) xxi.

Fisherman's Revival in North-East Scotland[65]

When the war ended in 1918, a great number of men had perished and attendance at churches appeared to be falling. Baptist Sunday school numbers dropped from 19,838 in 1914 to 18,065 in 1919; Bible class numbers dropped from 3,888 to 2,632. Although the Scottish churches emerged from the war with relatively healthy statistics, which remained on a statistical plateau during the 1920s, it was evident that the religious life of Scotland was changing. Influences, both social as well as religious, would affect the life of the church in the decades to come. By 1921, disillusionment had set in among many of the young men from the fishing communities. They returned home to find that "the church seemed to have lost its hold on many who were brought up in religious homes."[66] The fishing industry had enjoyed a buoyant prewar market and a boom in earnings during the war itself; no less than 80 percent of the herring industry was exported to Germany and Russia. The postwar period saw these markets disappear. In the summer of 1921, the herring fishing industry had a disastrous year, and the British government refused to extend a subsidy for the fishing market. As the boats moved through the season from the west coast of Scotland, to the Shetland Isles, to the northeast of Scotland, and finally to Lowestoft and Yarmouth in England, fishing communities were despairing. It is estimated that in Fraserburgh, "some 600–700 children were undernourished and two hundred were on the verge of starvation."[67] When the fleet moved to East Anglia, there appeared to have been eagerness, as well as an opportunity, to listen to the message of the gospel.[68]

---

[65] The most recent general account is Stanley C. Griffin, *A Forgotten Revival: East Anglia and NE Scotland, 1921* (Bromley, Kent: One Day Publications, 1992). See also Jackie Ritchie, *Floods upon the Dry Ground: God Working among Fisherfolk* (Peterhead: Peterhead Offset, 1983); Donald Meek, "Fishers of Men," *Scottish Bulletin of Evangelical Theology* 17.1 (Spring, 1999); John Lowe Duthie, "The Fishermen's Religious Revival," *History Today* 33 (1983).

[66] Comments by C. N. Johnson (Lord Sands) at meeting in Edinburgh reported in *Scotsman Newspaper*, January 9, 1922, 10. Joseph Johnson, Palmerston Place United Free Church, spoke of "the serious setback to the religious life of the nation by war conditions, and hailed with profound gratitude the present evidences of religious awakening." *Scotsman Newspaper*, January 24, 1922, 8.

[67] Duthie, "Fisherman's Revival," 23.

[68] The *Life and Work* magazine spoke of how "at the close of the summer fishing in Shetland there were signs of its [the revival] coming." "The East Coast Awakening," *Life and Work*, February, 1922, 40.

The revival had its origins in East Anglia when the fishing community from Scotland—men who worked in the boats as well as women who gutted the fish for market—listened to John Troup, a cooper from Wick. Within a few weeks several hundred professed faith in Christ. Families with special connection to the Christian Brethren, Baptist, and Congregational churches along with the Salvation Army appeared to have been particularly affected during the initial stages of the movement. In November 1921, Troup left Yarmouth for Fraserburgh, on the northeast coast of Scotland. After preaching in the open air, he was invited to conduct a series of services in the Baptist church.[69] The Baptist minister, William Gilmour, and the Congregational minister, Thomas Johnstone, were strong supporters of the revival movement and opened their churches to the evangelists, John Troup, William Bruce, another cooper, and David Cordiner, a fisherman from Peterhead. In December, the meetings had outgrown both buildings, and the Church of Scotland gave permission for meetings to be held in the Parish church.

The revival made its greatest impact upon members of the fishing community. In Fraserburgh this made up two thousand people out of a total population of twelve thousand. This was characteristic of the movement right along the Moray coast, "from Peterhead to Wick"[70] when fishing villages were most affected and "the agricultural population" was not "within its scope."[71] The largest proportion of converts was between twenty-five and thirty years of age, many of whom had served in the Navy during the Great War.[72] The Church of Scotland reported that "prominent among the converts are level-headed young men of initiative who earned distinction in the war."[73] The movement was characterized by protracted meetings made up of singing,[74] testimonies, prayer, and fervent preaching from "honest, earnest, enthusiastic young men of sound common sense, with a humble idea of their own ability,

---

[69] The author was minister of the Baptist church in Fraserburgh from 1984–1988 and spoke to several people who were converted during this period of time.

[70] *Scotsman Newspaper*, December 23, 1921, 5.

[71] *Scotsman Newspaper*, December 21, 1921, 9.

[72] *Scotsman Newspaper*, December 22, 1921, 7. In January 1922, R. J. Drummond, former Moderator of the UF Church and minister of Lothian Road, Edinburgh spoke of the "arresting thing is the preponderance of young men upon whom the revival has taken hold." *Scotsman Newspaper*, January 5, 1922, 9.

[73] *Life and Work*, February 1922, 40.

[74] Hymns from the Moody and Sankey revival meetings were commonly used.

with a passionately expressed love for Jesus Christ, and a yearning to bring men to a definite decision for Him."[75] W. P. Paterson, professor of theology at Edinburgh University, spent several days in the area and reported that the "revival was not accompanied by the powerful presentation of the Gospel" but that the "movement was beautiful and profoundly impressive."[76] R. J. Drummond and other colleagues from the United Free Church scorched rumors of excessive emotionalism within the meetings, commenting that any "features of extravagance have been confined to two villages (Cairnbulg and Inverallochy)...and even there have been few and slight."[77] John Hall, minister of Warrender Park United Free Church in Edinburgh, spoke of the "sanity and self-restraint" of the movement "that made one feel that there was a reality under it that gave it the stamp of God."[78] One critic of the movement was W. Major Scott, minister of the Ward Road Congregational Church in Dundee, who complained that the evangelists were "ignorant of nearly everything except the art of working upon the emotions of a crowd of people...and raising their emotion to fever pitch." Scott argued, "Such unhealthy emotionalism had no genuine connection with religion at all." It is doubtful, however, if his criticisms were accurately portraying the revival movement itself,[79] as the parish minister in Fraserburgh reported that the "emotionalism manifested was not excessive."[80] There was some evidence, in the Cairnbulg and Inverallochy villages, of an apocalyptic, millennial emphasis in the preaching of Fred Clark that led some fishermen to give up fishing altogether as they waited for the imminent return of Christ. They also abandoned insuring their boats on the basis that any loss of their material resources would enable them to put their

---

[75] From a report submitted by the Home Mission Committee of the United Free Church, *Scotsman Newspaper*, December 29, 1921, 6.

[76] Paterson was professor of theology at Edinburgh University. See *Scotsman Newspaper*, January 5, 1922, 4.

[77] *Scotsman Newspaper*, December 29, 1921, 6.

[78] *Scotsman Newspaper*, January 5, 1922, 5.

[79] *Scotsman Newspaper*, December 27, 1921, 39. Scott, a graduate of St. Andrews University and Yorkshire United College, was minister of Ward Road Chapel from 1919–1922. W. McNaughton, *The Scottish Congregational Ministry: 1794–1993* (Glasgow: Congregational Union of Scotland, 1993) 258.

[80] See "The Revival in the North-East of Scotland," *British Weekly*, No. 1836, December 29, 1921, 302.

complete trust in God to provide for their needs.[81]

The revival drew considerable interest from church leaders throughout Scotland across the denomination.[82] The United Free Church sent members of their Home Mission Board to Fraserburgh, and W. P. Paterson also traveled to meet with leaders of the movement, spending four days in the Fraserburgh district, interviewing converts and local parish ministers. D. P. Thomson, who would later be the evangelist of the Church of Scotland, then a student for the ministry of the United Free Church, led meetings in the parish church in Fraserburgh, supported by the four Presbyterian churches within the town.[83] Thomson moved to the Congregational Church to lead services during the latter part of December. By then, the newspapers were reporting that "all the excitement of the earlier days has disappeared" and that even the "tide of excitement in the adjoining villages of Cairnbulg, Inverallochy, and St Combs is steadily ebbing."[84] Like many experiences of revival in Scottish history, the movement lasted only a few, but effective weeks.

The impact of the revival movement on the Baptist congregation in Fraserburgh was significant. At a church meeting of April 12, 1922, a letter was read from the Baptist Union of Scotland giving thanks for the "great things God had done." The pastor proposed the following motion, which was "enthusiastically approved" and "that we place on record...our praise and thanksgiving to God for the recent great spiritual awakening and revival experienced in this town...conspicuously owned and blessed of God...resulting in a multitude of redeemed and transformed lives from among young and old with its

---

[81] See "Insurance Policies on Boats Withdrawn," *Scotsman Newspaper*, December 22, 1921, 7.

[82] A meeting in Edinburgh drew W. Graham Scroggie, minister of Charlotte Baptist Chapel, along with other leaders of various denominations.

[83] The *Scotsman Newspaper* commented that he had "done a good deal of evangelical work" and was respected within the denomination and the local community. During his student years Thompson led various evangelistic campaigns throughout Scotland. To encourage team support in this work he founded the Glasgow Students Evangelistic Union. In 1923 Thomson recruited Eric Liddell, famous for his athletic powers, as a member of his team. In 1934, he was appointed an evangelist for the Church of Scotland. See *Scotsman Newspaper*, December 21, 1921, 9. See Frank Bardgett, *Scotland's Evangelist: D. P. Thomson* (Drummond Trust, Stirling, 2010). For his comments on Thomson's connection with Fraserburgh see 68–70.

[84] *Scotsman Newspaper*, December 30, 1921, 5.

corresponding influence on the moral and social life of the whole community."[85] Two deacons added their own proposal and referred in particular to the "soul winning zeal, earnestness and self-sacrificial work of our pastor, Mr. Gilmour."[86] One piece of evidence of the impact of the revival upon the church is the number of baptisms that occurred in 1922. From 1917 to 1922 only twelve people had been baptized in the church.[87] However, in 1922, fifty-six people were baptized.[88] In the following three years only ten people were baptized.[89]

The impact of the movement on social issues was often limited to temperance and the "No License" debate that was under discussion in Scotland.[90] The *Scotsman* newspaper predicted that when another temperance vote was taken, Fraserburgh would "go dry."[91] The Parish minister of Fraserburgh spoke of how "Gambling, drinking, card-playing, betting, swearing— all given up for the better joys and higher aims."[92] This pietistic fervor was sometimes dramatically displayed, as in the fishing village of Cairnbulg when people assembled near the shore and brought what were termed their offerings. These consisted of tobacco, pipes, and pouches, ludo boards and the apparatus of other simple games, as well as earrings and jewelry. When the articles were accumulated, a light was set to the pile, and while it burned the inhabitants stood around and sang and prayed. This was their renunciation of things that, under the influence of religious emotion, they had come to regard as sinful.[93]

The revival, however, did not appear to change the thinking of its participants, either lay or clerical, on the wider systemic social issues of poverty

---

[85] Minutes of Fraserburgh Baptist Church, April 12, 1922.

[86] Ibid. Eight months later Gilmour resigned as pastor and moved to become pastor of New Cumnock Baptist Church in Ayrshire Minutes of Fraserburgh Baptist Church, November 19, 1922.

[87] Two in 1917; three in 1918; none in 1919; five in 1920, and two in 1922.

[88] Eighteen in January; eleven in February; nine in March; six in April; two in May; four in June; three in August, and one in December.

[89] One in 1923; four in 1924, and five in 1925.

[90] The *Scotsman Newspaper* indicated that the "great majority of the fishing population in this part of the county" (Fraserburgh) noted, "No License" at the Temperance Act Polls [in 1913]. *Scotsman Newspaper,* December 23, 1913, 5.

[91] *Scotsman Newspaper*, January 4, 1922, 10.

[92] *British Weekly*, No. 1836, December 29, 1921, 301.

[93] *Scotsman Newspaper*, December 21, 1921, 9.

or unemployment which had affected the fishing communities in the northeast of Scotland.

Although the epicenter of the movement was Fraserburgh and the surrounding areas, the revival movement affected other villages and towns along the Moray Coast as well as cities such as Dundee, Glasgow, and Edinburgh.[94] In January 1922, meetings were held in Ibrox United Free Church where the minister of Harper Memorial Baptist Church, W. A. Ashley, reported on a visit he made under the auspices of the Baptist Union of Scotland to Fraserburgh. He described the movement as "a quiet, intelligent, and undemonstrative movement," and noted, "The churches were enrolling the converts of the moment."[95]

Numerous conversions in various Baptist churches took place throughout Scotland. The Baptist Union of Scotland also saw a rise in the number of baptisms during this period: from 888 in 1921 to 1,104 in 1922. The following year the number of baptisms reached fifteen hundred, although the secretary of the Union indicated "the returns hardly fulfill the high hopes raised in the early months of the year by the tidings of revival in the fishing and other centers. That movement" he concluded "did not become in any sense general, and only a few of our churches report any phenomenal increase."[96] The long-term effects of unemployment and immigration to North America were beginning to affect many of these churches in this period with the Baptists reporting that "one small church noted the loss of sixteen members to emigration within two or three months."[97] In Fraserburgh some twenty-four members left the area to immigrate to the United States in the early 1920s.

The revival among the fishing communities in 1921 and 1922 cannot be accounted for on the basis of any one sociological, economic, or religious reason but as a combination of factors that led to a fervent search for religious security in the simplicity of the message that the evangelists proclaimed. Its long-term impact can be seen in various outcomes. In 1945, D. P. Thomson spoke of how he knew of two hundred people who had entered into pastoral

---

[94] Near the end of December, the *British Weekly* reported that Dundee and Glasgow had witnessed "crowded meetings," the Dundee event being attended by "fifteen hundred" and "over 1,100…in Bethany Hall, Glasgow." December 29, 1921, no, 1836, 305.

[95] *Scotsman Newspaper*, January 11, 1922, 11.

[96] *Scottish Baptist Year Book* (1922) 115; *Scottish Baptist Year Book* (1923) 111.

[97] *Scottish Baptist Year Book* (1923) 111.

ministry or gone overseas as missionaries as a direct result of the revival in Fraserbugh.[98]

Each of the three revivals examined in early twentieth century Scotland were relatively short lived and impacted particular churches in the country. There were similarities between the Welsh Revival and the fisherman's revival in their use of simple gospel preaching of the love of God revealed in the cross of Calvary. It was the passionate praying and the existential experiences of converts that led other people to an awareness of the reality of God's presence and to an encounter with God. The church in Scotland did not experience a resurgence of extraordinary growth in its overall membership, and it would continue to bemoan the "churchless millions" in the country. Membership of all the main churches in the country would remain steady over the following four decades before inexorable decline would set in from the 1960s onward. Baptists would decline from 21,173 in 1920 to just over 14,000 in 2000. Revivals would be a distant memory, and many would realize that even revivals were not the answer to the pressing issues of the twentieth century.

---

[98] Cited in Tom Lennie, *Glory in the Glen: A History of Evangelical Revivals in Scotland 1880–1940* (Fearn: Christian Focus, 2009) 232.

17

British Baptist Revival at the Front in the First World War

Neil E. Allison

The outbreak of the war on August 4, 1914, was generally met with, sometimes enthusiastic, but often muted, support by the Baptist churches of the British Empire.[1] Thousands of young men, encouraged by their community churches to do their duty, volunteered to serve in the British Empire army in defense of Belgium and to defeat the German Zeitgeist that had invaded this little country.[2] K. W. Clements explains "war was morally abhorrent to the Nonconformist Conscience; but that same conscience was aroused by the plight of Belgium, and could not allow Britain to stand by at such a flagrant violation of liberties."[3] There was little doubt amongst Baptist combatants[4] that this war was just and military force could be legitimately sanctified; indeed many Baptists who participated in this conflict considered it a Christian

---

[1] See Stephen Willis, "English Baptist Attitudes to the First World War;" Gethin Mathews, "The Responses of Welsh Baptist Churches to the First World War;" and Brian Talbot, "Scottish Baptist Churches and the First World War," in *Step into Your Place: The First World War and Baptist Life & Thought,* ed. Larry J. Kreitzer (Oxford: Regents Park College, 2014); see also Neil E. Allison, "Fighting the Good Fight: Changing Attitudes to War in the Twentieth Century," in *A Distinctive People: A Thematic Study of Aspects of the Witness of Baptists in Scotland in the Twentieth Century,* ed. Brian R. Talbot (Milton Keynes, UK, Paternoster, 2014).

[2] J. H. Thompson, "The Nonconformist Chaplain in the First World War," in *The Clergy in Khaki: New Perspectives on the British Army Chaplaincy in the First World War,* ed. Michael Snape and Edward Madigan (Ashgate: Surrey, 2013) 21.

[3] K. W. Clements, "Baptists and the Outbreak of the First World War," *Baptist Quarterly* 26, no. 2 (April 1975): 87.

[4] See Neil E. Allison, "A Baptist View from the Trenches: Lockhart Landels Ireland (1887–1916)" *Baptist Quarterly*, vol. 47, no. 2 (June 2016): 76–85.

duty.[5] The formation of the Kitchener's Army[6] of thirty new divisions and its Pals Battalions encouraged men who lived and worked together to volunteer and serve together. These battalions also enabled Sunday schools and church organizations like the Church Lads' Brigade[7] to do the same, which allowed Christian nonconformity to have a spiritually significant impact on this new army.

As Baptists poured into the army, John Howard Shakespeare (1857–1928),[8] the secretary of the Baptist Union of Great Britain and Ireland (BUGBI), saw and took the opportunity to gain formal recognition for Baptists in order to keep denominational integrity for these new recruits. Until that point, it was usual for Baptists in the military to be forced to attend Anglican services with no regard for their own traditions. Shakespeare passionately believed that the Baptist denomination was "the greatest Protestant evangelical community on earth"[9] and used his denominational position and his personal influence and friendship with David Lloyd George to forward his aims of placing the Baptist denomination at the center of national life. Shakespeare gained formal recognition through the provision of commissioned Baptist chaplains to serve the spiritual needs of Baptist soldiers and sailors.[10] This led to the formation of the United Navy and Army Board (U.B.) on January 14, 1915, which would oversee Baptist and Congregational, Primitive and United Methodist military chaplaincy and represent their denominational interests.[11] This new denominational integrity and influence included a freedom

---

[5] Religious rhetoric pervaded the language of war. See Philip Jenkins, *The Great and Holy War: How World War I Became a Religious Crusade* (Oxford: Lion, 2014): 66–82.

[6] He was the First Earl Herbert Kitchener (1850–1916) who as the Secretary for State for War created a vast new army of volunteers at the beginning of the war. On June 5, 1916, he was lost at sea after the ship he was traveling on, *HMS Hampshire*, was sunk by enemy action.

[7] James Duncan, *With the C.L.B. Battalion in France* (London: Skeffington & Son, 1917).

[8] John Howard Shakespeare was born in 1857 in West Riding, Yorkshire, and died March 12, 1928.

[9] Ian M. Randall, *The English Baptists of the 20th Century* (Didcot: Baptist Historical Society, 2005) 50.

[10] D. Lloyd George, *War Memoirs of David Lloyd George*, 2 vols. (London: Odhams Press Limited, 1933).

[11] In 1918 it would change its name to become the United Navy, Army, and Air Force Board after the establishment of the Royal Air Force Service on April 1,1918. For a full introduction to the beginnings and development of the U.B. see Neil E. Allison, *The Official History of the United Board Revised*, vol. 1, *The Clash of Empires 1914–1939* (Norfolk: United Navy, Army

to engage in mission opportunities as was confirmed by J. R. Gould, who recorded in the Deacons' Minute Book of Ayr Baptist Church that "the Pastor (W. C. Charteris) gave a report of the work he was doing at the Front. He stated that he would like to be back amongst us but he felt that the work he was doing at the Front was Pioneer Work for the Denomination at large and it would be a pity to loose [sic] the opportunity which would likely never occur again."[12] Additional credence was given to the chaplains and their work when Shakespeare officially visited the "Front." A. T. Guttery, a Baptist chaplain serving at the Front at the time of Shakespeare's official visit, saw this as evidence that the U.B. had come in out of the cold and that Shakespeare had gained the recognition that normally was reserved only for Anglican, Roman Catholic, and Church of Scotland dignitaries. He wrote, "Bishops had been out to visit the Anglicans, and distinguished people of all sorts to visit the other denominations, but we had not been so highly favoured. *Now* we can hold up our heads with pride as we think of the effect he created."[13]

Opportunities for Baptist pastors to serve and reach out to the soldiers were not limited to signing up to a temporary commission as a military chaplain. Denominational Huts were erected in Britain by Baptists that functioned along similar lines to those of the Young Men's Christian Association (YMCA).[14] While members of the churches served hot drinks and snacks, many pastors became chaplains, providing pastoral care and leading services, often of a revival nature. The YMCA ran huts both abroad and in Britain. At least ninety Baptist pastors served with the YMCA abroad and forty-seven Baptists at a home posting.[15] Oswald Chambers (1874–1917) was probably

---

and Air Force Board, 2014) and Neil E. Allison, *The Official History of the United Board Revised*, vol. 2, *The Clash of Ideologies 1939–1950* (Norfolk: United Navy, Army and Air Force Board, 2015).

[12] Ayr Baptist Deacon Court Minute Book (October 6, 1916).

[13] J. Wallet, "The Rev, A. T. Guttery at the Front," *Baptist Times and Freeman* (October 15, 1915): 664.

[14] See *The Back Parts of War: The YMCA Memoirs and Letters of Barclay Baron, 1915–1919*, ed. Michael Snape (Suffolk: Boydell, 2009).

[15] J. H. Thompson, "The Nonconformist Chaplain in the First World War: The Importance of a New Phenomenon," in *The Clergy in Khaki: New Perspectives on British Army Chaplaincy in the First World War*, ed. Michael Snape and Edward Madigan (Surrey: Ashgate, 2013) 24.

the most notable Baptist to serve in the YMCA in Egypt.[16] Walter E. Young, a soldier serving with the London Regiment, recorded in his memoirs that such outreach organizations were "always crowded to overflowing."[17] Serving as a YMCA chaplain abroad was on occasions no less dangerous than serving in the military. Reverend W. H. Spinks,[18] a Baptist minister serving with the YMCA, was killed in action while, with his own body, trying to shelter a Chinese youth from a heavy bombardment.

Some Baptists served in a variety of chaplaincies during the war. Arthur Cecil Dixon, pastor of Helensburgh Baptist Church, first started as a YMCA chaplain in 1916, serving in this capacity for two years before signing up as a commissioned temporary chaplain. Others such as Frederick George Benskin (1872–1965), the pastor of Broadmead Baptist Church in Bristol, served as a military chaplain, but probably because of his age, he took on senior responsibility for soldiers based in camps or sick in hospital for the Gloucestershire, Somerset, and Wiltshire areas.[19]

Early in the war enthusiasm was high within the Baptist denomination. The BUGBI even had a discussion concerned with the raising of a Baptist corps[20] and the establishment of a Baptist Navy and Army Church although neither came into being.[21] In a sermon Campbell Morgan, minister of Westminster Chapel, London, expressed his hope, held by many Baptists, that the war would indeed be the catalyst for the long awaited revival or at the very least a moral reformation. He openly declared, "War, though caused by man's wickedness could produce the renewal of moral consciousness and the re-birth of the soul."[22] In light of these two significant factors it is unsurprising that Richard Schweitzer argued, "Small military units, functioning akin to civilian

---

[16] David McCasland, *Oswald Chambers: Abandoned to God: The Life Story of the Author of "My Utmost for His Highest"* (Michigan: Christian Art Publishers, 2006).

[17] Walter E. Young, *Walter's War: A Rediscovered Memoir of the Great War 1914–1918* (Oxford: Lion, 2015) 120.

[18] Matthew McLachlan, *Whyte's Causeway Baptist Church: The First Hundred Years, 1852–1952* (Kirkaldy: Whyte's Causeway Baptist Church, 1952) 22.

[19] Brian Bowers, "The Rev. Frederick George Benskin," *Baptist Quarterly* 43, no. 3 (July 2009): 177.

[20] Clements, "Baptists and the Outbreak," 76.

[21] Peter Shepherd, *The Making of a Modern Denomination* (Carlisle: Paternoster, 2001) 102.

[22] Ian M. Randall, "The Role of Conscientious Objectors. British Evangelicals and the First World War," *Anabaptism Today* (February 1996): 11.

communities, experienced local revivals."[23]

It would not be an overstatement to say that culturally the British population largely defined itself as Christian. Most of the British population at the time accepted the "culture of Protestant Christianity, including acceptance of the Bible as the highest religious authority, and of moral principles derived from Protestant Christianity, practice of the Christian rites of passage, and observance of Sunday."[24] Thomas Newell Tattersall (1879–1943),[25] pastor of Fuller Baptist Church, Kettering, and a temporary army chaplain,[26] observed in his diary that some of the soldiers insisted on having a public service on the grounds that "we are Englishmen and mean to keep Sunday."[27] The average British male tended to believe in God, prayed from time to time, and enjoyed singing hymns[28] known from their childhood.[29] The British national cultural identity was Christian[30] and denominational expression of that faith was important for the more committed.

---

[23] Richard Schweitzer, *The Cross and the Trenches. Religious Faith and Doubt among British and American Great War Soldiers* (Westport CT: Praeger, 2003) 191.

[24] Hugh McLeod, *Religion and Society in England, 1850–1914* (London: Macmillan, 1996) 1.

[25] See Neil E. Allison, "T. N. Tattersall D.S.O: His War Experience and Medals," *RAChD Journal* 45 (2006): 31-33.

[26] Robert F. Wearmouth, a Primitive Methodist chaplain serving with the U.B., described the army chaplains' diverse responsibilities by contrasting the extremes the chaplain of any denomination often faced: "For the most part the Padre's job was diverse, difficult and dangerous. On occasion he had to run the Officers' Mess, superintend the men's canteen, sell the cakes, the tea, the Woodbines at five a penny, accompany the troops on their long marches, footslog it on the cobbled roads, be exposed to the sweltering sun or the pouring rain, grope his way through the intense darkness, live with the lads in the narrow trenches, the flimsy shelters, the battered houses, the destroyed villages, the shelter of the ridges. Although unarmed he went sometimes with them over the top, into the fury of the battle, not to fight, but to rescue the fallen, attend the wounded, minister to the dying, reverently bury the dead, write to their loved ones, break the sad news about wounds or death, and to comfort all who suffered or were in distress." Robert F. Wearmouth, *Pages from a Padre's Diary: A Story of Struggle and Triumph, of Sorrow and Sympathy* (Northumberland: Robert F. Wearmouth, 1946) 34.

[27] T. N. Tattersall, *Fuller Magazine* (February 1915).

[28] See A. M. Perkins, *Between Battle* (London: T. Fisher Unwin, 1918) 50.

[29] Michael Snape, *God and the British Soldier: Religion and the British Army in the First and Second World Wars* (London: Routledge, 2005) 245.

[30] There was also a strong Jewish community in Britain and many would choose to serve in the military. They had their own chaplains, who wore the Star of David on their caps and lapels. Other religions were not officially represented in chaplaincy.

Nonconformists in general were passionately dedicated to the committed practice of their Christian faith with their particular church polity being a significant feature of their practice. Baptists were deeply proud of their nonconformity and often defined themselves over and against the Church of England, whose privileged status as the state church was understandably resented. Anglo-Catholic Anglican services were seen as an unacceptable imposition, and this no doubt influenced the thinking of T. N. Tattersall, who believed and expressed the notion that "nothing can make a good Baptist into an Anglican."[31] He explained further his conviction that "Of heaven and hell, of sin and death and judgment one rarely hears him [the British soldier] speak. If he does speak of these things, or of conversion, or of the spiritual life, I know him at once. He is a Nonconformist. Perhaps his identification disc says, C of E, but his speech betrayed him."[32] An anonymous soldier reflected on the importance of his nonconformity: "Months ago our Nonconformist Padre was taken from us, and we have only had the C of E man, although, the Unit is eighty percent Nonconformist."[33] Baptists in particular emphasized and maintained their commitment to evangelism and mission, which was "a particular feature of Baptist life and worship, present from its early stages, though later to be influenced by the Evangelical Revival and other movements"[34] like the crusading Temperance Mission. Baptist ecclesiastical culture emphasized the need for a person to have a converting experience of the love of God through faith in Christ alone and emphasized his death on the cross, his resurrection and ascension, and a lost eternity without him. Receiving Christ would lead to salvation and this inward reality was to be publically demonstrated by believer's baptism, and the desire for a transformed life with a particular emphasis on temperance. Naturally Baptists, along with other nonconformists, would be particularly open and responsive to the gospel ministry of their chaplains and the many evangelists serving alongside them in the ranks. This was partly because it was a familiar experience of their home church life in a context where anything familiar was clung to.

---

[31] T. N. Tattersall, "At the Base," *Baptist Times and Freeman* (December 4, 1914): 880.

[32] T. N. Tattersall, "The British Soldier in Hospital," *Baptist Times and Freeman* (April 9, 1915): 235.

[33] "U.B. Minutes" (September 14, 1916): 148.

[34] Christopher J. Ellis, *Gathering: A Theology and Spirituality of Worship in Free Church Tradition* (London: S.C.M., 2004) 95.

Wartime temporary army chaplains like William Cramb Charteris (1869–1950),[35] pastor of Westray Baptist Church, were passionate about "saving souls." Charteris wrote about the emphasis he placed on his work in 1915: "The men here are just splendid, but the work is great and the task difficult, so we covet your prayers. Many have the veil taken from their eyes and they see beauty in Christ. Many have discovered and rediscovered the great cardinal truths of our religion, and find great comfort in the glorious Gospel of the Grace of God."[36] Frederick James Harry Humphrey (1874–1947),[37] pastor of Fairlop Road Baptist Church and army hospital chaplain, also emphasized the same point and that there was no hesitation in speaking of "sin and atonement and salvation"[38] for "very little there is to say unless one has a Gospel to preach."[39] Preaching remained a key aspect of Baptist ministry even within the army. David John Hiley (1860–1948), a Welshman and pastor at Chatsworth Road serving with a Canadian unit,[40] believed the message was all-important. He had even strained his voice while taking every opportunity to preach in the open air to large numbers of soldiers. Hiley wrote about his passionate commitment to preaching: "I can talk quietly enough by the bedside of the boys, but when I stand on the platform, and look into the faces of a thousand men, they stir my Welsh blood, and warm my Celtic heart. I forget all good advice about talking quietly."[41]

Evangelical[42] Nonconformity was so strong that some units were even

---

[35] See Neil E. Allison, "Shakespeare's Man at the Front. The Ministry of the Rev. William Cramb Charteris OBE MC During the Great War (1914–1918)" *Baptist Quarterly* 14, no. 4 (October 2005): 224–35.

[36] *Scottish Baptist Magazine* (April 1916): 58.

[37] See Neil E. Allison, "The Spirit of Cromwell: Nonconformist Chaplains' War Ministry and Experience (1914–1918)" (London: Congregational Memorial Hall Trust (1978) 2013) 27–30; republished with minor changes as "The Household of Faith" in *International Congregational Journal*, 13, no.1 (Summer 2014).

[38] *Baptist Times and Freeman* (November 9, 1917): 676.

[39] *Baptist Times and Freeman* (August 27, 1915): 559.

[40] Cited in Rod Badams, unpublished MS regarding Spurgeon's students 1856–1891 (2014) 53.

[41] Badams, Spurgeon's students 1856–1891 (2014) 55.

[42] Bebbington defines "evangelical" Christianity as having four key emphases: Biblical inspiration and authority; the human need to experience the grace of God in Christ and the Cross of Christ being central to the gospel message, to be worked out in practical service, and mission work. See David W. Bebbington, *The Nonconformist Conscience: Chapel and Politics 1870–1914* (London: Allen & Unwin, 1982) 1-19.

considered to be predominantly and even officially nonconformist, most notably the Welsh. The Welsh (38th Division), commanded by a Welsh-speaking Congregationalist,[43] was one significant division generally considered to be nonconformist.[44] This Welsh nonconformist influence was verified by T.N. Tattersall, who reflected, "I find most of our Baptists amongst the Welsh. One boy told me of eighty-seven of their company who were Baptists."[45] This is a significant observation as there had been a recent revival in Wales which had "accounted for about half the total increase in membership in England and Wales between 1900 and 1910"[46] for nonconformist congregations. R. Tudur Jones believed that the "The 1904–1905 Revival was one of the most remarkable events in twentieth-century Welsh history."[47] The Welsh Revival continued to be a significant influence on lay and ordained men,[48] who, although now serving in the ranks, continued preaching and working as unofficial chaplains when circumstances and duties allowed. Michael Snape noted that "Many English units also contained a significant smattering of Nonconformist soldiers who, true to their independent traditions, proved remarkably adept at organizing prayer meetings of their own."[49] William E. Sellers concluded, "Always converting work is going on behind the firing line."[50] This was observed by Humphrey, pastor and army hospital chaplain, who reported that "A great work is going forward among the men of the Army and Navy; everywhere it seems that there is a ready hearing and acceptance of the Gospel."[51] Thomas Jones (1867–1940), pastor of George Street Baptist Church in Paisley, described the effect the gospel message was having on the soldiers in the trenches on the front line: "Services are not easily arranged on the peninsula, as being constantly within range of shell fire, the

---

[43] Keith Robbins, *Oxford History of the Christian Church: England, Ireland, Scotland, Wales: The Christian Church 1900–2000* (Oxford: Oxford University Press, 2010) 105.

[44] "Inter-denominational Army Committee Minutes," (I.A.C.) August 18, 1916.

[45] T. N. Tattersall, "Pastor's Letter," *Fuller Magazine* (February 1915).

[46] Peter Shepherd, "Denominational Renewal," *Baptist Quarterly* 37, no 7 (July 1998): 336.

[47] R. Tudur Jones, *Faith and the Crises of a Nation: Wales 1890–1914* (Cardiff: University of Wales Press, 2004) 283.

[48] David Coulter, "The Church of Scotland Chaplains of World War Two" (PhD thesis, University of Edinburgh, 1993) 3.

[49] Snape, *God and the British Soldier*, 163.

[50] William E Sellers, *With Our Heroes in Khaki* (London: R.T.S., 1917): 95.

[51] *Baptist Times and Freeman* (August 27, 1915): 559.

congregating of large companies of men is too risky. Still, we manage to hold services and at times if well sheltered, large numbers attend and all show interest in singing and in the Gospel message."[52] W. C. Charteris likened one of his services where "the sprinkling of Welshmen gave fine zest to the singing" to an Evan Roberts revival meeting.[53]

Most of these new temporary chaplains recognized by the U.B, "focused the individual on personal salvation and ideals of moral behaviour and manifestations of outward piety."[54] A temporary chaplain who would represent the typical Baptist chaplain of the period was Abraham Rees Morgan (1886–1946).[55] He was the pastor of New Park Street Chapel, Holy Head in Anglesey and "was a very enthusiastic and overtly evangelical chaplain and was thus in keeping with the generation of young Welsh Nonconformist ministers influenced by the 1904–1905 Welsh Revival."[56] W. C. Charteris, also influenced by the Welsh Revival which he had personally experienced, sought to "minister to the spiritual needs of officers and men, therefore the record of [his] work was the record of a Gospel ministry, the story of conversions"[57] as "his one business is to preach the Gospel…. Where else can the soldier find strength for his hazardous calling or comfort in suffering and death."[58] Guy Thornton was a New Zealand chaplain responsible for Australian, New Zealand (ANSAC), and British troops. He published his reminiscences, *With the Anzacs in Cairo*,[59] in 1916, which confirms this point. In his memoir he tells "of the gracious revival that visited thousands of our soldiers, in order that the hearts of many parents, whose boys lie buried on the steep slopes of Gallipoli, may be comforted."[60] One such death was that of Private J. Downs, a Welsh Baptist, who shortly before his own death asked his chaplain to "tell my wife

---

[52] *Scottish Baptist Magazine* (December 1915): 191.

[53] *Scottish Baptist Magazine* (April 1917): 58.

[54] Callum G. Brown, *The Death of Christian Britai:. Understanding Secularization 1800–2000* (London: Routledge, 2001) 39.

[55] See Ieuan Elfryn Jones, "A Welsh Perspective on Army Chaplaincy during the First World War: The Letters of Abraham Rees Morgan," in *The Clergy in Khaki: New Perspectives on British Army Chaplaincy in the First World War*, ed. Michael Snape and Edward Madigan (Surrey: Ashgate, 2013) 57–73.

[56] Jones, "Letters of Abraham Rees Morgan," 60.

[57] *Scottish Baptist Magazine* (October 1914): 158.

[58] *Scottish Baptist Magazine* (April 1917): 58.

[59] J. Bryant Haigh, *Men of Faith and Courage* (Auckland NZ: Word Publishers, 1983) 87.

[60] Guy Thornton, *With the ANZACS in Cairo* (London: Allenson, 1916) 12.

I am ready, that to God I have given my trust."[61]

Arguably, at the time, the most famous Baptist army chaplain and revivalist was Ernest Lodge Watson, an Australian who was the pastor of West End Baptist Church Hammersmith, London. He joined the British Expeditionary Force (BEF) as a temporary chaplain on the October 9, 1914, and would be the first Baptist pastor sent to the Front. He was the first of many committed revivalists who set the standards of effective ministry. Watson understood that "Life is very real to every man on the field and the essentials only count."[62] That which was considered essential was the gospel, and his style of presenting this message of salvation was popular with the soldiers. George Kendall, a Primitive Methodist colleague, confirmed Watson's popularity even when conducting public services. In an article entitled "The Revival at the Front" published in the *Baptist Times* in 1915, Kendall reported that one "can always be sure of a crowded parade when Captain Watson is announced to conduct it."[63] Watson's preaching concentrated on Jesus as a loving Redeemer and concluded with a call for the men to get right with God.[64] As Watson told Kendall, the men "only want the truth that grips and heals."[65] He, therefore, illustrated his sermons with "stories that grip. He chose stories from the battlefield, from personal experiences, from the lives of great men."[66] He remembers Watson as a "khaki figure weighing sixteen stone and standing six feet high waving his arms and stamping his feet until the platform threatened to give way, leading the singing of, 'When the roll is called up yonder.'"[67] After such services, he would ask the men to give him their names, addresses, ranks, and regiments if they wanted to follow Christ so he could follow up with them and pray over their names. F. C. Spurr, himself a denominational evangelist, spoke of Watson's immense popularity with the troops and presented a detailed description of Watson's approach to public ministry along with its effect.[68]

---

[61] *Baptist Times and Freeman* (December 4, 1914): 880.
[62] *Baptist Times and Freeman* (December 18, 1914): 912.
[63] *Baptist Times and Freeman* (July 9, 1915): 453.
[64] F. C. Spurr, *Some Chaplains in Khaki: An Account of the Work of Chaplains of the United Navy and Army Board* (London: Kingsgate, 1916) 71.
[65] *Baptist Times and Freeman* (February 19, 1915): 115.
[66] *Baptist Times and Freeman* (July 9, 1915): 453.
[67] *Baptist Times and Freeman* (August 6, 1915): 525.
[68] Spurr, *Some Chaplains in Khaki*, 68–75.

Not everyone was enthusiastic about the new influx of evangelical nonconformist chaplains and the way they ministered to their troops. Morris Murray, a High Anglican regular chaplain, described a Nonconformist service that he had experienced at the Front. "It is a nice little dugout and at the time of my visit, full of nonconformist soldiers with whom a Welsh Padre was praying in English. He was thin and tall and wore no robes. He had that earnest Revivalist look and his voice was at once melodious and odious."[69] This event reveals something of the shock felt by established chaplains who felt the intrusion of this new kind of chaplain. E. W. Hornung, who served as a YMCA hut worker in France during the last year of the war, described his experience of soldiers' revivalist meetings in equally vivid and unappreciative terms:

"The man had an astounding flow of spiritual invective, at due distance the very drum-fire of withering anathema, but sorry stuff of a familiar order at close range. It was impossible not to respect this red-hot gospeller, who knew neither fear nor doubt, nor the base art of mincing words; and he had a strong following among the men, who seemed to enjoy his onslaughts, whether they took them to heart or not."[70] Hornung further refers to preachers like him as "tight-sleeves conjurors; and they spoke from their hearts to many that beat the faster for their words. In that congregation there were no loath members."[71]

There is no greater study than *The Army and Religion* 1919 committee report authored by Dr. David Cairns, which concludes that "there is not so much a revival of religious faith"[72] and cited with approval a hut worker's view that the "crude evangelical way...soon puts more thoughtful men out of rapport."[73] This conclusion was obviously prejudiced against revivalism, discounting the evidence in the report itself as well as being "confined to English

---

[69] Michael Moynihan, *God on Our Side: The British Padre in World War I* (London: Leo Cooper, 1983) 118.

[70] E. W. Homung, *Notes of a Camp-Follower on the Western Front* (London: Constable, 1919) 31–32.

[71] Homung, *Notes of a Camp-Follower on the Western Front*, 31–2.

[72] Dr. David Cairns, *The Army and Religion* (London: Macmillan & Co, 1919) 17.

[73] Cairns, *The Army and Religion*, 43.

and Scottish evidence and does not include Ireland, Wales, or the Dominions"[74] thereby excluding significant Welsh evidence where Baptists were significantly represented. The postwar period continued to discount any evidence for a revival because, as Gethin Matthews explains, "It is the received wisdom that the experience of a total, and utterly brutal, war was a body-blow to many of the old, comfortable, ideas about progress and providence."[75] A German army doctor reflected this view at the time:

> As I look back I see no occasion for the ordinary man to have had religious experiences whilst on service. War is something so opposed to God. It is so full of the Satanic— that is, of the consciously evil—that a pure experience of God can be possible only in the most exceptional cases…. I believe that most of the so-called experiences of God whilst on service are sprung partly from what has been planted in the soul already in the times of peace, partly from the subsequent operations of memory. Most men have seen in war-experience nothing but evil in its nakedness, and so far as they have thought about it at all, have been led to the conclusion that there is no God of truth, good, beauty.[76]

It is therefore unsurprising that "the discourse on the war came to be dominated by anti-revivalist interpretation"[77] dismissing evidence to the contrary as "spasmodic pieties of the danger zone."[78] Until recently "no major published study has ever appeared of the hundreds of Presbyterian or Free Church chaplains who served in the British army during the First World War,"[79] even though Free Church chaplains made up "a quarter of the Army Chaplain's Department" by the end of the war.[80] Historical researchers have recently reevaluated the material still available. Michael Snape, in his study of

---

[74] Cairns, *The Army and Religion*, ix.

[75] Gethin Matthews, "Fighting Baptists: The Response of Baptist Churches to the Great War," *Baptist Quarterly* 45, no. 3 (July 2013): 181.

[76] Herbert Patrick, "A Baptist Doctor with the Prussian Army," *Baptist Quarterly* 1, no. 7 (July 1923) 300.

[77] Schweitzer, *The Cross and the Trenches*, 192.

[78] Cited in Coulter, "The Church of Scotland Chaplains of World War Two," 9.

[79] Snape, *God and the British Soldier*, 84–85.

[80] Michael Snape, "Church of England Army Chaplains in the First World War: Goodbye to 'Goodbye to All That!'" *Journal of Ecclesiastical History*, 62, no. 2 (April 2011): 319. See also Michael Snape's official history, *The Royal Army Chaplains' Department: Clergy Under Fire* (Suffolk: Boydell, 2008) and Peter Howson, *Muddling Through: The Organisation of British Army Chaplaincy in World War 1* (West Midlands: Helion, 2013).

God and the British Soldier, confirms that a revival was "evident throughout the army, notably during the heady if bloody months of 1914–1916."[81] Certainly mainstream Baptists like F. C. Spurr and well-known ministers who served as chaplains like T. N. Tattersall, E. L. Watson, Fredrick Humphrey, Guy Thornton, Thomas Jones, and W. C. Charteris amongst many others confirmed their involvement in revival type services and experiences. There is little doubt that localized revivals did take place between 1914 and 1916, but they lacked discernable evidence of church growth immediately after the war.[82] The answer to this observable fact is simply the attrition of war. John Wolffe estimates that the war "seriously depleted the ranks of the churches. Of the 772,785 men killed a disproportionate number were officers and of these many were Church or Chapel members."[83] Of the Scottish Baptists that served, it is estimated that about one-fifth never returned."[84] It has also been estimated that approximately 35,000 Welshman died of the 272,924 that served.[85] The significance of losses suffered can also be seen at a microscopic level. The Bunyan Meeting Roll of Honour lists 266 men of the church who fought for their country. By the end of the war sixty-five members had been killed, and are remembered on the church's war memorial.[86] That is 24.4 percent of the number who served in the forces. Helensburgh Baptist Church, a small seaside church on the west coast of Scotland, had seventeen members serving in the forces; of these five were killed and that is 29.4 percent.[87] The losses during the First World War were significant for the Baptist denominations.

The attrition of disease also took its toll as troops moved around the

---

[81] Snape, *God and the British Soldier*, 245.

[82] Kenneth D. Brown, *A Social History of Nonconformist Ministry in England and Wales, 1800–1930* (Oxford: Clarendon Press, 1988) 233–234.

[83] John Wolffe, *God and Greater Britain: Religion and National Life in Britain and Ireland, 1843–1945* (London: Routledge, 1994) 194.

[84] John S. Fisher, *Impelled by Faith: A Short History of Baptists in Scotland* (Stirling: Scottish Baptist History Project, 1996) 40.

[85] Chris Williams, "Taffs in the Trenches: Welsh National Identity and Military Service 1914–1918," in *Wales and War: Society, Politics and Religion in the Nineteenth and Twentieth Centuries*, ed. Matthew Cragoe and Chris Williams (Cardiff: University of Wales Press, 2007) 126.

[86] Nicola Sherhod and Neil E. Allison, eds., *Bunyan Meeting History: Padre W. J. Coates Letters from the Front* (Norfolk: Bunyan Meeting & United Board History Project, 2015).

[87] See Neil E. Allison, *Pastor A. C. Dixon, Helensburgh Baptist Church and the Great War (1914–1919)* (Helensburgh: Helensburgh Baptist Church, 2014).

country. Many of them had never ventured farther than the largest town in their own district. The risks from disease involved in simply traveling around the British Isles could be fatal as the troops had little or no immunity to certain diseases. Bunyan Meeting in Bedford recorded, "Many of the soldiers came from isolated parts of Scotland, with little or no immunity to common diseases of the time; thirty-three of the 17,000 men are buried at Foster Hill Road Cemetery, Bedford after an outbreak of measles, scarlet fever, and diphtheria within the camp which affected over 1,000 troops."[88] Later in 1918 an influenza pandemic killed ten times the number of the population than soldiers and sailors killed in action; this included many soldiers. At least one Baptist chaplain died during training soon after joining up. William Heading reported for duty to Number 3 Officers Training School at Tidworth and died only two weeks later.[89]

The "frequent verdict was that the war had brought neither a general revival of religion nor a mass alienation from it."[90] There is ample evidence even from the detractors that at least some localized revivals did take place, and Baptists, along with Salvationists, Congregationalists, and evangelical Anglicans, were at the forefront of these revivals in the army.[91] There may have been a more generalized revival, but the attrition of combat and disease prevented its development into something more significant. Snape explains that the "casualty levels at Ypres, Gallipoli, Loos, and the Somme were such that many of the men who experienced either a religious conversion or a deepening of their faith in 1914–1915 simply did not survive or remain in the army long enough to become hardened or disillusioned. Death, wounding, transfer and reorganization destroyed the original character of many units which had once harboured strong religious cultures."[92] There was an evangelical revival in the truest sense involving most protestant denominations with an evangelical approach, but this story is yet to be fully understood and told.

---

[88] *Bunyan Meeting History*, 15.
[89] See Allison, *Clash of Empires*, 111.
[90] Keith Robbins, *Oxford History of the Christian Church: England, Ireland, Scotland, Wales: The Christian Church, 1900—2000* (Oxford: Oxford University Press, 2008) 157.
[91] See Neil E. Allison, "Free Church Revivalism in the British Army during the First World War," in *The Clergy in Khaki*.
[92] Snape, *God and the British Soldier*, 167–68.

18

"Dumb Dogs that Cannot Bark": The Puritan Origins of Preaching Revival

Jan Martijn Abrahamse

I have felt its power in my own heart; I have the witness of the Spirit within my spirit, and I know it is a thing of might, because it has conquered me, and bowed me down…but my gratitude most of all is due to God, not for books, but for the preached Word—and that too addressed to me by a poor uneducated man, a man who had never received any training for the ministry, and probably will never be heard in this life, a man engaged in business, no doubt of a humble kind, during the week, but who had just enough grace to say on the Sabbath, "Look unto Me, and be ye saved, all the ends of the earth." The books were good, but the man was better. The revealed Word awakened me, but it was the preached Word that saved me.[1]

With these words, Charles Spurgeon described how he himself was "revived" at young age by, in his own words, "a shoemaker, or tailor, or something of that sort."[2] Though the real identity of this preacher remains obscure,[3] Spurgeon often contrasted this lay preacher with the preachers of his youth, who "had not told half the beauty of my Lord and Master."[4]

---

[1] Charles Haddon Spurgeon, *Autobiography*, vol. 1, *1834–1854* (Chicago: Fleming H. Revell Company, 1898) 102–4.

[2] Spurgeon, *Autobiography*, 1:105.

[3] See notably Peter J. Morden, *"Communion with Christ and His People": The Spirituality of C. H. Spurgeon*, Centre for Baptist and Heritage Studies, vol. 5 (Oxford: Regent's Park College, 2010) 50. Morden indicates the sheer doubt surrounding Spurgeon's conversion account, particularly concerning the identity of the preacher. Already in the late nineteenth century, just after Spurgeon's death, a student of Pastor's College, named Danzy Sheen, published a study about Spurgeon's conversion in which he, supported by eyewitness' accounts, states that the preacher in question was indeed an ordained minister, namely, one Rev. Robert Eaglen.

[4] Spurgeon, *Autobiography*, 1:115.

"DUMB DOGS THAT CANNOT BARK": THE PURITAN ORIGINS OF PREACHING REVIVAL

Spurgeon's own experience and later ministry is a vivid testimony of a key element in revival history that also runs as a thread through the Baptist tradition: preaching the gospel as a means of conversion.[5] Direct and accessible sermons aimed to stir up faith among its audience, rather than bring mere doctrinal exposition. Spurgeon, like many revival preachers before him, perceived preaching as an actual "means of grace," bringing people face to face with the reality of the gospel. Already in his own time considered a Whitefield *redivivus*, he grew to be the supreme "prince" of revival preaching in the nineteenth century.[6] This was a trait he tried to press upon his students as well, as he writes in his posthumous *The Soul-Winner* (1895): "That is what you must do with your sermons, make them red-hot; never mind if men do say you are too enthusiastic, or even too fanatical, give them red-hot shot, there is nothing else half as good for the purpose you have in view."[7] To Spurgeon, it was "revival," not a university degree, which confirmed the true calling of a minister.[8] However, his revivalist view of preaching also brought him in conflict with the clerical establishment, who criticized Spurgeon for his lack of theological training and sophisticated speech.[9] Spurgeon, on his turn, could not but speak with contempt about academically trained ministers who lacked the communicative power to revive their audience, and more than once he identified them

---

[5] See David W. Bebbington, *Baptists Through the Centuries: A History of a Global People* (Waco: Baylor University Press, 2010) esp. 71–81, 277; William H. Brackney, *A Genetic History of Baptist Thought* (Macon: Mercer University Press, 2004) 531, 535–36; and Olof de Vries, *Gelovig gedoopt: 400 jaar baptisme, 150 jaar in Nederland* (Kampen: Kok, 2008) 66–76. For an account of revivalist preaching, see Jonathan Strom, "Pietism and Revival," in *Preaching, Sermon and Cultural Change in the Long Eighteenth Century*, ed. Joris van Eijnatten. *A New History of the Sermon*, no. 4; (Leiden: Brill, 2009) esp. 206–13.

[6] See David W. Bebbington, *The Dominance of Evangelicalism: The Age of Spurgeon and Moody* (Leicester: InterVarsity Press, 2005) 37–42. This is vol. 3 of the five-volume series *A History of Evangelicalism* (Leicester: InterVarsity Press).

[7] Charles H. Spurgeon, *The Soul-Winner: Or, How to Lead Sinners to the Saviour* (New York: Fleming H. Revell, 1895) 69.

[8] See Jan Martijn Abrahamse, "Staan we met lege handen? Charles Haddon Spurgeon en het geordineerde ambt," in *Van onderen! Op zoek naar een ambtstheologie voor een priesterschap van gelovigen*, Baptistica Reeks 7 (Amsterdam: Unie van Baptistengemeenten in Nederland, 2014) 95–113.

[9] See Bebbington, *Dominance of Evangelicalism*, 39; For Spurgeon's difficulty with academia, see David W. Bebbington, "Spurgeon and the Common Man," *Baptist Review of Theology* 5, no. 1 (1995): 63–75.

with the "dumb dogs that cannot bark" from Isaiah 56:10.[10] This is a rather harsh statement that, however, goes not without precedent but resounds the same critique of Elizabethan Puritans toward the inadequacy of many English clergymen who were unable to preach the Bible. After all, the Puritans were the "revivalist" kind of Protestants, who appeared within a few years after Elizabeth's ascension in 1558 to bring further reformation to the English church.[11] These dissenting minds took a firm stance against the prevailing practice of nonpreaching or reading ministers, which they—like Spurgeon would centuries later— taunted as "dumb dogs that cannot bark."[12]

This chapter aims to unravel the origins of Spurgeon's dissenting view of the preaching ministry, by returning to three significant transformations in the Elizabethan era that have laid the basis for revivalist preaching in the centuries that followed. The first is the reformation of the role of the parish minister. Instead of a ceremonial priest chiefly responsible for administrating the mass, ministers were to be educated as preachers, and thus required to be acquainted with Scripture. The second is the changing status of the sermon, here termed the "sacramentalization" of the sermon, which turned the sermon in a soteriological event. And third is the popularization of the sermon under influence of Ramist methodology, which changed the purpose of the sermon from mere instruction to persuasive exhortation. These three transformations

---

[10] "But, O! there are a great many among us Dissenters, and in the Church of England, too, that are dumb dogs. There are still plenty who do not know any thing about the gospel; who preach a vast deal about a great many things, but nothing about Jesus Christ; who buy their sermons cheap, and preach them at their ease; who ask God to tell them what to say, and then pull their manuscripts out of their pockets." Charles Spurgeon, "The Dumb Singing," in *Sermons of Rev. C .H. Spurgeon of London*, ser. 3 (New York: Robert Carter & Bros., 1883) 127.

[11] See Rosemary O'Day, *The English Clergy: The Emergence and Consolidation of a Profession 1558–1642* (Leicester: Leicester University Press, 1979) xii. For a recent attempt to define Puritanism, see Randall J. Pederson, *Unity in Diversity: English Puritans and the Puritan Reformation, 1603–1689*, Brill's Series in Church History 68 (Leiden: Brill, 2014).

[12] See also Patrick Collinson, *From Cranmer to Sancroft* (London: Hambledon Continuum, 2006) 47; and David M. Thompson, "Nonconformists and Polity," in *T&T Clark Companion to Nonconformity*, ed. Robert Pope (London: Bloomsbury, 2013) 89, 110n1. In the preparation of this paper I came across the excellent study of Arnold Hunt, in which he, in his closing paragraph, makes the same connection; see *The Art of Hearing: English Preachers and their Audiences, 1590–1640*, Cambridge Studies in Early Modern British History (Cambridge: Cambridge University Press, 2010], 401–2. My repeated references to his study in the following pages shows how my own reading of Elizabethan Puritanism resonates with his broader study of the late Elizabethan and Jacobean era.

form the structure of this chapter. Finally, some observations will be made regarding the character of ministry in the revivalist tradition.

The Reformation of the Ministry: From Priests to Preachers

The English Reformation, beginning during the reign of Henry VIII and affirmed by Elizabeth's *via media*, witnessed a tremendous turn around of the parochial ministry. Many clergy, and notably those of Puritan inclination, began to see themselves foremost as preachers.[13] As preaching became the principal duty of the minister, they needed to be able to read and exegete the scriptures. "Preaching accordingly required long years of training," writes Paul Seaver.[14] Suddenly universities became seminaries designated to bring forth able preachers. Rosemary O'Day, in her study *The English Clergy* (1979), speaks of a real "educational revolution."[15] This longing for better preachers was chiefly felt among Puritans. Several Puritan colleges (for example, Emmanuel College, Cambridge) were established where "emphasis was placed upon the cleric's pastoral duties, in accordance with the beliefs and practices of the reformed churches."[16] Consequently, instead of the priestly garment, these educated Puritan preachers preferred the black academic gown.[17]

Besides formal education at universities, the Puritan striving for better-educated preachers gave rise to extra-ecclesial phenomena: prophesyings, household seminaries, and the lecturers. The absence of skilled preachers in the Elizabethan church was the prime reason for the Puritan conferences, known as "prophesyings." This practice was adopted from continental reformers, such as Huldrych Zwingli's *prophetzei* in Zürich and notably John Calvin's

---

[13] See Hunt, *Art of Hearing*, 19–21, 30ff, 390.

[14] Paul S. Seaver, *The Puritan Lectureships: The Politics of Religious Dissent, 1560–1662* (Stanford: Stanford University Press, 1970) 6.

[15] O'Day, *English Clergy*, 2; Seaver, *Puritan Lectureships*, 6, 16, 43.

[16] O'Day, *English Clergy*, 2.

[17] See O'Day, *English Clergy*, 6; John Craig, "The Growth of English Puritanism," in *The Cambridge Companion to Puritanism*, ed. John Coffey and Paul C. H. Lim (Cambridge: Cambridge University Press, 2008) 36. For the controversy over the wearing of the priestly garments or vestments, see John H. Primus, *The Vestments Controversy: An Historical Study of the Earliest Tensions within the Church of England in the Reigns of Edward VI and Elizabeth* (Kampen: Kok, 1960).

company of pastors in Geneva.[18] Inspired by 1 Corinthians 14:29, pastors joined in biblical conferences to study and discuss scriptural passages in order to further their exegetical and preaching skills, and to further spiritual growth.[19] Though predominantly for pastors, interested laymen were also welcome to attend. As a consequence, these meetings became almost "a church in a church" beyond the control of church hierarchy. Hence, the heavy resistance from Elizabeth against these prophesyings, which eventually led to Archbishop Grindal's house arrest for his unwillingness to suppress them. A second and affiliated phenomenon is the so-called household seminary.[20] During the 1570s it became more and more common among Puritan ministers to take care of the next generation, as a sort of postgraduate seminary experience. This not only served to provide the practical divinity experience in preparation for the pastoral ministry still lacking at the universities, but also to constitute a collective Puritan identity. A significant example is the household seminary of Richard Greenham, who trained a number of men who grew to be eminent Puritan preachers: Joseph Hall, Richard Rogers, the famous preacher Henry "Silvertongued" Smith, Arthur Hildersham, and possibly Puritan's most elaborate theologian William Perkins.[21] In this way, future Separatist leader Robert Browne sought Richard Greenham's spiritual guidance

---

[18] For Calvin's "Company of Pastors," see Erik A. De Boer, *The Genevan School of the Prophets,* Travaux d'Humanisme et Renaissance 62 (Genève: Droz, 2012); Alexandre Ganoczy, "Calvin's Life," in *The Cambridge Companion to John Calvin,* ed. Donald K. McKim (Cambridge: Cambridge University Press, 2004) 16. For Zwingli, see C. A. Tukker, "Zwingli en de Nederlanden," in *Zwingli in vierderlei perspectief* (Utrecht: de Banier, 1984) 119–23.

[19] "Let the Prophetes speake two, or three, and let the other judge." Geneva Bible (1560). See further Patrick Collinson, *The Elizabethan Puritan Movement* (Oxford: Clarendon, 1967) esp. 167–76; idem, *The Religion of Protestants: The Church in English Society 1559–1625* (Oxford: Oxford University Press, 1982) 129–30, and *Elizabethan Essays* (London: Hambledon Press, 1994) 242.

[20] See Kenneth L. Parker, Eric J. Carlson, *"Practical Divinity": The Works and Life of Revd Richard Greenham*. St Andrews Studies in Reformation History (Aldershot: Ashgate, 1998) 43–47; Marshall M. Knappen *Tudor Puritanism: A Chapter in the History of Idealism* (Chicago: University of Chicago, 1939) 385–86; Collinson, *Religion of Protestants,* 118–19; John H. Primus, *Richard Greenham: The Portrait of an Elizabethan Pastor* (Macon: Mercer University Press, 1998) 42–45; Theodore Dwight Bozeman, *The Precisionist Strain: Disciplinary Religion & Antinomian Backlash in Puritanism to 1638* (Chapel Hill: University of North Carolina Press, 2004) 70–71; Tom Webster, "Early Stuart Puritanism," in *Cambridge Companion to Puritanism,* 52–53.

[21] See Parker and Carlson, *"Practical Divinity,"* 31, 95; Primus, *Richard Greenham,* 42–43; J. B. Jenkins, *Henry Smith: England's Silver-Tongued Preacher* (Macon: Mercer University Press,

"DUMB DOGS THAT CANNOT BARK": THE PURITAN ORIGINS OF PREACHING REVIVAL

and spent a number of months in his household, which, if we follow Browne's words, functioned like an Old Testament school of prophets.[22] However, the need for learned preachers became so urgent that alongside the parish ministry (and outside ecclesiastical hierarchy!) a new phenomenon appeared, known as the town lecturer. The lecturer was in fact a hired gun, often paid and installed by private Puritan laymen, usually gentry and nobility.[23] It offered a greater opportunity to preach the gospel freely, requiring less conformity to prescribed liturgy.[24] Seaver argues that the lectureship is one of the most conspicuous evidences of the Puritan laity's driving determination to obtain a godly preaching ministry.[25] It is no coincidence that "the first Baptist," John Smyth, started as the town lecturer of Lincoln for a period of time.[26]

It can be said that the English reformation generally changed the role of the parochial clergy from priests, predominantly ordained to administer the mass, to preachers who were educated to declare scripture. Yet, these examples illustrate how much the Puritans were willing to think outside the ecclesial lines to establish a preaching ministry. English nonconformity was largely born from the impatience with the prevailing lack of preaching ministers on a parochial level.

The Sacramentalization of the Sermon: From Seeing to Hearing

As the priest became a preacher, the sermon came to occupy, both theo-

---

1984) 11, 14–15; Lesley A. Rowe, *The Life and Times of Arthur Hildersham: Prince among Puritans* (Grand Rapids: Reformation Heritage Books, 2013). The suggestion that Perkins also attended Greenham's household seminary is made by Charles E. Hambrick-Stowe, "Practical Divinity and Spirituality," in *Cambridge Companion to Puritanism*, 193–94.

[22] "Wherefore, as those vvhich in ould tyme vvere called the prophetes & children of the prophetes & liued to gether, because of corruptiōs among others, so came he vnto him." Robert Browne, "A True and Short Declaration," in *The Writings of Robert Harrison and Robert Browne*, ed. Albert Peel and Leland H. Carlson, Elizabethan Nonconformist Texts 2 (London: George Allen & Unwin, 1953) 398.

[23] Seaver, *Puritan Lectureships*, 6–7. Of course, as Seaver shows, political motives also played a significant role in the establishment of the lecturer, as a means of mobilizing powers.

[24] See Seaver, *Puritan Lectureships*, 35.

[25] Seaver, *Puritan Lectureships*, 54.

[26] See, e.g.,, J. Bakker, *John Smyth: De stichter van het Baptisme* (Wageningen: H. Veenman & Zonen, n.d.) 27–36; Stephen Wright, *The Early English Baptists, 1603–1649* (Woodbridge: Boydell, 2006) 13–14.

logically and liturgically, a central place in the English church. Puritans heralded the sermon as the premier instrument of grace, a divine means of conversion ("to stir up faith"). Conversion from a Puritan point of view meant personal as well as social transformation.[27] Congruent with the Protestant emphasis on the personal conscience, a verbal address was required to counter sin, ignorance, and remnant popery.[28] As Paul Seaver comments, "the Puritans were certain that the effectual preaching of the Word and the diligent hearing of it were the ordinary means of salvation."[29] Where previously, in traditional religion, parishioners participated in a visible ceremony which had its climax in the elevation of the host,[30] the Reformation slowly altered the role of the laity from "seeing" into "hearing." Now the climax was the "inward experience" caused by the exposition of God's Word addressed to everyone's conscience.[31] Thus the spoken word outpaced "bread and wine" as the preeminent Protestant sacrament. Time and again, Puritans, like their continental precursors, referred to Romans 10:14b–15: "how shal they beleue in him, of whome they haue not heard and how shal they heare without a preacher? And how shal they preache, except they be sent as it is written."[32] As faith comes through hearing (*fides ex auditu*), "not listening" was sometimes viewed as a direct rejection of this Protestant premise. Puritans perceived human speech to be the vehicle of the Spirit, who placed the hearers in the realm of grace, as

---

[27] See Seaver, *Puritan Lectureships*, 5, 15, 20, 33, 40, 44, 46; also elaborately Christopher Hill, *Society and Puritanism in Pre-Revolutionary England* (London: Secker & Warburg, 1964) esp. 30–78; Hunt, *Art of Hearing*, esp. 19–59; Alec Ryrie, "Hearing God's Voice in the English and Scottish Reformations," *Reformation* 17 (2012): 50–51; Rosamund Oates, "Sermons and Sermon-Going in Early Modern England," *Reformation* 17 (2012): 201–7.

[28] Christopher Haigh, "Puritan Evangelism in the Reign of Elizabeth I," *English Historical Review* 92, no. 362 (1977): 30.

[29] Seaver, *Puritan Lectureships*, 5; Jan Martijn Abrahamse, "Een zaak van leven en dood: Hel en heil in Jonathan Edwards' *Sinners in the Hands of an Angry God*," *Soteria* 29, no. 3 (2012): 51–52. For an elaborate explanation see the study of Hunt, *Art of Hearing*, esp. 19–116. Of course, the "sacramentalization" of the sermon is already apparent in the theology of Martin Luther. See Fred W. Meuser, "Luther as Preacher of the Word of God," in *Cambridge Companion to Martin Luther*, ed. Donald K. McKim [Cambridge: Cambridge University Press, 2003], 136–48, esp. 137. Yet it is especially among the Puritans that preaching becomes the key to the reformation of the church.

[30] See Eamon Duffy, *The Stripping of the Altars: Traditional Religion in England 1400–1580*, 2nd ed. (New Haven: Yale University Press, 2005) esp. 91–107.

[31] Ryrie, "Hearing God's Voice," 52–53.

[32] *Geneva Bible* (1560); Hunt, *The Art of Hearing*, especially 22–27, 31.

people were personally confronted with the biblical message of Christ's salvation. Puritan minister Richard Greenham could therefore describe the preaching minister as the premier instrument to "bring men to Christ," and "the messenger of salvation."[33]

The soteriological emphasis on "lively preaching" among Puritans led to an outright confrontation between ecclesial and civil authorities over the practice of the "bare reading" of homilies. The reading of homilies (from Thomas Cranmer's *Book of Homilies*) was obligated shortly after the death of Henry VIII in 1547, to counter Catholic-minded priests leading ignorant laity astray.[34] Possibly intended as an *ad interim* solution, its practice continued well into Elizabeth's reign. Of course, there were also political reasons involved. Elizabeth resented the rising number of preachers, since the reading of homilies offered an easier way to control the religion of the masses.[35] Although a consensus on a clear definition of Puritanism seems far away, the refusal to accept the neglect of true preaching within the Church of England stands undisputed. The authors of *An Admonition to the Parliament* (1572), the first public manifesto of the Puritan side,[36] heavily criticized its survival by comparing the former practice against the "prescribed" manner in the book of Acts: "Then, as God gave utterance they preached the worde onely: now they read homilies, articles, injunctions, etc."[37] The famous Puritan front man Thomas Cartwright once wrote, "As the fire stirred giveth more heat, so the Word, as it were, blown by preaching, flameth more in the hearers, than when

---

[33] Parker and Carlson, *"Practical Divinity,"* 146–147. William Perkins, "A Golden Chain," *Works*, 1:71.

[34] See Eamon Duffy, *The Voices of Morebath: Reformation & Rebellion in an English Village* (New Haven: Yale University Press, 2001) 123; idem, *The Stripping of the Altars*, 447–48; T. H. L. Parker, ed. *English Reformers*, Library of Christian Classics (1966; Louisville: Westminster John Knox, 2006) 221–26, 255–59; Alexandra Walsham, *Catholic Reformation in Protestant Britain*, Catholic Christendom, 1300–1700 (Farnham: Ashgate, 2014) 235–85. See for the *Book of Homilies* (1547) Caroline Stacey, "Justification by Faith in the Two Books of Homilies (1547 and 1571)" *Anglican Theological Review* 83, no. 2 (2001): 255–79.

[35] See Seaver, *Puritan Lectureships*, 21–22; also Craig, "Growth of English Puritanism," 36.

[36] See Jan Martijn Abrahamse, "Robert Browne as an Unwanted Child: Explaining Separatism from the Nursery of Presbyterian Puritanism," *Perspectives in Religious Studies* 40, no. 4 (2013): 349–65.

[37] John Field and Thomas Wilcox, "An Admonition to the Parliament," in *Puritan Manifestoes: A Study of the Origin of the Puritan Revolt*, ed. W. H. Frere, C. E. Douglas (London: Society For Promoting Christian Knowledge, 1907) 11.

it is read."[38] James Kearney concludes, "True hearing was aligned with the movement of the Spirit in interpretation, while "bare reading" was aligned with the mechanical repetition of empty formulae that Protestants associated with the Catholic Mass."[39] Since the mere reading of set homilies lacked the required affectionate exhortation that sought to apply the message of scripture to the concrete situation of a local parish, reading could therefore not be considered preaching at all. As Arnold Hunt writes in his study of English preaching, reading of homilies "could not save souls, because it lacked the converting power of the spoken voice."[40]

The distinction between reading and preaching became a dividing line between conformists and Puritans.[41] The latter commonly referred to parish ministers who were unable to preach but read printed homilies as "dumb dogs."[42] The reference "dumb" or "dumb dogs" in the sense of being mute, is directly derived from Isaiah 56:10, where it says in the translation of the Geneva Bible (1560), "Their watchmen are all blinde: they haue no knowledge:

---

[38] Cited in Horton Davies, *The Worship of English Puritans* (1948; Morgan: Soli Doe Gloria Press, 1997) 186.

[39] James Kearney, *The Incarnate Text: Imagining the Book in Reformation England* (Philadelphia: University of Pennsylvania Press, 2009) 28; Oates, "Sermons and Sermon-Going," 203.

[40] Hunt, *Art of Hearing*, 10.

[41] See Hunt, *Art of Hearing*, 38.

[42] See Hill, *Society and Puritanism*, 48, 51, 54, 55, 60, 62, 68; Collinson, *Elizabethan Movement*, 42, 128–29; Horton Davies, "Elizabethan Puritan Preaching II," *Worship* 44, no. 2 (1970) 96–97; Craig, "Growth of English Puritanism," 38–40; and "Sermon Reception," in *Oxford Handbook of the Early Modern Sermon*, ed. Peter McCulloch, Hug Adlington, and Emma Rhatigan (Oxford: Oxford University Press, 2011) 178–97; Oates, "Sermons and Sermon-going in Early Modern England," 201, 203–205; and James S. Baumlin, *Theologies of Language in English Renaissance Literature: Reading Shakespeare, Donne, and Milton* (Lanham: Lexington Books, 2012) 168–71. The famous preacher Edward Dering once preached before Queen Elizabeth (February 25, 1569) saying, "To keep back the ignorant from the Ministerie, whom God hath not called to suche a function, take away your authoritie from the Bishops, let them not at their pleasure make Ministers in their Closset, whom so euer it pleaseth them. To stop the inconueniences that grow in the Ministerie by other, who say they are learned and can preach, and yet do not, that are as I said dum Dogs, and wil not barcke, bridle at the least their greedy appetites, pul out of their mouthes these poisoned bones that they so greedely gnaw vpon." Quoted in J.W. Blench, *Preaching in England in the Late Fifteenth and Sixteenth Centuries: A Study of English Sermons 1450– c. 1600* (Oxford: Blackwell, 1964) 301. See also Frere and Douglas, *Puritan Manifestoes*, 57, 110; *The Works of William Perkins*, ed. Ian Breward (Sutton Courtenay Press, 1970) 1:55 and 3:24; William Fulke, "A Brief and Plain Declaration," in *Elizabethan Puritanism*, ed. Leonard J. Trinterud (New York: Oxford University Press, 1971) 261, 263.

they are all domme dogs: they can not barke."[43] The text was used to portray the nonpreaching priests as dysfunctional "watchdogs" who could not do their task of warning the sheep of an approaching wolf.[44] The tolerance of these dumb ministers played a significant role in Robert Browne's separation from the English church, making him subsequently a pioneer of English Separatism and, hence, the Baptist tradition. In his catechesis *A Booke Which Sheweth the Life and Manners* (1583), he puts lively preaching over against bare reading to distinguish "popish" baptism from biblical baptism: "By preaching of the worde of Baptisme, we vnderstande not the blinde reading, or fruitles prating thereof at randome, but a due teaching by lawfull messengers, of our redemption, mortifying, and raysing with Christ."[45] Like his former tutor Richard Greenham, Browne typified preaching ministers in terms of "messengers." He writes in his autobiography, "faith is not Vvrought by reading."[46] Likewise the *Admonition* of 1572 rhymes, "Reading is not feeding."[47] Puritan divine William Fulke offers an insightful comment on the reading of homilies. According to Fulke the problem is not amiss of doctrinal orthodoxy, but that these homilies "are not applied to the proper circumstances of times, places, persons, and occasions."[48] If preaching is to be effective as an instrument of grace, it needs to be applied to its concrete audience, a point further discussed below. Ready-made sermons for a general audience lacked the necessary relevance for a particular parish. In conjunction with Romans 10:14, Puritans saw parish

---

[43] Geneva Bible (1560).

[44] See Patrick Collinson, *From Cranmer to Sancroft* (London: Hambledon Continuum, 2006) 47; Thompson, "Nonconformists and Polity," 89, 110n1.

[45] Robert Browne, "A Booke which sheweth the life and manners," in *Writings of Robert Harrison and Robert Browne*, 259; also Robert Browne, "A True and Short Declaration," 408–9. Browne later criticized Thomas Cartwright for his reluctance to separate from these "dumb ministers," see explicitly Robert Browne, "An answere to Master Cartwright," in *Writings of Robert Harrison and Robert Browne*, esp. 471–73. See Jan Martijn Abrahamse, "'To do the Lordes message': De sacramental turn, Robert Browne, en de zoektocht naar een ambtstheologie," in *Van onderen! Op zoek naar een ambtstheologie voor een priesterschap van gelovigen*, ed. Jan Martijn Abrahamse, en Wout Huizing, Baptistica Reeks 8 (Amsterdam: Unie van Baptistengemeenten, 2014) 128–46; and "'Is Smyth also among the Brownists?' A Confrontation Between John Smyth and His Predecessor Robert Browne," *Baptist Quarterly* 46, no. 3 (2015): 108–11.

[46] Browne, "A True and Short Declaration," 209. This is a significant difference between John Smyth and Browne; see Abrahamse, "'Is Smyth also among the Brownists?' 6–7.

[47] Field and Wilcox, "Admonition to the Parliament," 22.

[48] Fulke, "Brief and Plain Declaration," 240.

ministry as divinely ordained to do precisely that: bringing God's lively voice (*viva voce*) to a particular community.

As preaching became the church's most sacred sacrament, aimed at the conversion of people, it required a different method, a scheme which enabled preachers to bring the biblical text to its contextual application.

The Popularization of the Sermon: From Instruction to Exhortation

In the late 1560's a new phenomenon reached Cambridge, the methodological revolution of Peter Ramus.[49] His *Dialectica* became a popular textbook especially among Puritans. Peter Ramus (or Pierre de la Ramée, 1515–1572) was a typical offshoot of sixteenth-century Renaissance thought, who advocated a complete reform of the liberal arts.[50] Ramus based his revision on a restructuring and simplification of Aristotelian logic and rhetoric. Inspired by the work of Rudolphus Agricola (1444–1485),[51] Ramus considered the classical system too vague, confusing, and inconsistent. Ramus's reform existed in the bringing together of logic and rhetoric into one system of thought: logic became an instrument in finding truth, and rhetoric an instrument of the transmission of truth, to persuade an audience.[52] Another important difference is that Ramus's logical method does not deal in probabilities (syllogisms), like medieval scholasticism, but works with certainties (axioms). Axioms are

---

[49] Craig R. Thompson, *Universities in Tudor England* (Washington: Folger Shakespeare Library, 1959) 9–10; H. C. Porter, *Reformation and Reaction in Tudor Cambridge* (Cambridge: Cambridge University Press, 1958) 52.

[50] See Wilbur Samuel Howell, *Logic and Rhetoric in England, 1500–1700* (1956; New York: Russell & Russell, 1961) 8–10, 146–72; Lee A. Sonnino, *A Handbook to Sixteenth-Century Rhetoric* (London: Routledge & Kegan Paul, 1968) 1–10; Thomas M. Conley, *Rhetoric in the European Tradition* (1990; Chicago: University of Chicago Press, 1994) 124–50; Willem J. van Asselt, and Pieter L Rouwendal, "Distinguishing and Teaching: Constructing a Theological Argument," in *Introduction to Reformed Scholasticism*, ed. Willem van Asselt, Reformed Historical-Theological Studies (Grand Rapids: Reformation Heritage Books, 2011) 92–94; Howard Hotson, *Commonplace Learning: Ramism and its German Ramifications, 1543–1630*, Oxford-Warburg Studies (Oxford: Oxford University Press, 2007) esp. 3–37; and Steven J. Reid, and Emma Annette Watson, eds. *Ramus, Pedagogy and Liberal Arts: Ramism in Britain and the Wider World* (Farnham: Ashgate, 2011) esp. 7–23. See for Peter Ramus the work of Water J. Ong, *Ramus, Method, and the Decay of Dialogue* (1958; New York: Octagon, 1974); and *Ramus and Talon Inventory* (Cambridge, MA: Harvard University Press, 1958).

[51] Conley, *Rhetoric in the European Tradition*, 125–28.

[52] Conley, *Rhetoric in the European Tradition*, 130.

subsequently analyzed and divided into constitutive parts: from definition to division (dichotomies). Characteristic for Ramist logic is the use of large brackets, visualizing the arrangement of the concepts into large dichotomous tables, sometimes covering whole pages (resembling a genealogical tree), so that they could be memorized more easily.[53] Wilbur Howell, in his classic *Logic and Rhetoric in England* (1956), explains the Ramist reformation as an attempt to bring the theory of communication in harmony with the times, "seeking to bring learning into a closer relation with the practical needs."[54] In short, Ramist methodology was more focused on the communication of knowledge, which corresponded with an era that witnessed the rise of a middle class, and thus requested a new rhetoric to convince the commoner.[55]

Given Ramus's bridging of theory and praxis it is no surprise to see that his methodology gained substantial support among the Cambridge Puritans.[56] In Cambridge, Ramus was read prominently by Gabriel Harvey (1550–1631), who had to chance to buy a copy of Ramus's work in 1569.[57] Together with Laurence Chaderton (c. 1536–1640),[58]—who lectured on Ramus's *Ars Logica*. Harvey introduced Ramist rhetoric in the late 1560s and 1570s. Other adherents were William Temple, William Gouge of King's College, and of course,

---

[53] Possibly, Ramus borrowed the dichotomous division from his former mentor, Johannes Sturm, as particularly expressed in his 1529 lectures in Paris on Hermogenes of Tarsus (Cf. Conley, *Rhetoric in the European Tradition*, 131). For an example of a Ramist chart, see Sonnino, *Handbook to Sixteenth-Century Rhetoric*, 246.

[54] Howell, *Logic and Rhetoric in England*, 9; Van Asselt and Rouwendal, "Distinguishing and Teaching," 94.

[55] See Howell, *Logic and Rhetoric in England*, 10.

[56] See Howell, *Logic and Rhetoric in England*, 193, and Conley, *Rhetoric in the European Tradition*, 132–40. It was particularly the work of Perry Miller which first established Ramus's influence on English and American Puritans. See Miller, *The New England Mind: The Seventeenth Century* (Boston: Beacon Press (1939) 493–501. More recently, Sarah Knight explained Ramus's status as a Huegenot martyr as a possible reason for his sudden popularity among the younger generation Puritans in Cambridge. See "Flat Dichotomists and Learned Men: Ramism in Elizabethan Drama and Satire," in *Ramus, Pedagogy and Liberal Arts*, 47–68; Diane Parkin-Speer, "Robert Browne: Rhetorical Iconoclast," *Sixteenth Century Journal* 18, no. 4 (1987): 520.

[57] Howell, *Logic and Rhetoric in England*, 178; and John Charles Adams, "Gabriel Harvey's *Ciceronianus* and the Place of Peter Ramus' *Dialecticae libri duo* in the Curriculum," *Renaissance Quarterly* 43, no. 3 (1990): 551–69.

[58] See Porter, *Reformation and Reaction*, 51n1; and Knight, "Flat Dichotomists," 47–55. See for the life and works of Laurence Chaderton, Peter Lake, *Moderate Puritans and the Elizabethan Church* (Cambridge: Cambridge University Press, 1982) 1–15, 25–54.

Cambridge's most celebrated scholar, William Perkins (1558–1602).[59] Perkins used Ramistic dichotomous division pervasively in his classic on preaching, *The Arte of Prophesying* (Lt. 1592; Eng. 1606). Donald McKim, in his analysis of Perkins's use of Ramism, offers reasons why Puritans felt so attracted toward this practical methodology, of which three are notably relevant to this paper.[60]

First, Ramism maintained a dynamic unity between theology and ethics. Perkins explained theology in terms of good ethical behavior (*bene vivendi*). Right belief (doctrine) stood in a direct relation to right living (discipline). This connection became particularly apparent in Puritan preaching, where the "uses," or applications, were heavily emphasized: it prevented theology from becoming an academic enterprise with no practical value for the church. Second, its practicality provided a helpful three-part structure for preaching, known as "plain style" preaching: exegesis, doctrine and application.[61] Exegesis is usually quite brief, so that one stumbles very quickly into "what needs to be believed." The exposition of doctrine brought the content of the text in direct relation to the gospel. The third and last element, application, formed the climax of the sermon in which the preacher encouraged his audience to connect the practical implications of the sermon text to their daily lives.[62] So it is not that instruction was absent, but it served a higher purpose, namely, the reformation of life. To be concise, Ramist method served a theology that elevated the sermon as the primary means of the explanation of

---

[59] See Donald K. McKim, "The Functions of Ramism in William Perkins' Theology," *Sixteenth Century Journal* 16, no. 4 (1985): 503–17; and *Ramism in William Perkins' Theology*, American University Studies 15 (New York: Peter Lang, 1987). Of course, not all Puritans used Ramist methodology; for example, Edward Dering and John Knewstub. See Leonard J. Trinterud, *Elizabethan Puritanism* (Oxford: Oxford University Press, 1971) 136.

[60] See McKim, "Functions of Ramism ," 508–15.

[61] See. Blench, *Preaching in England*, 57–60; McKim, "Functions of Ramism," 511; Stephanie Sleeper, "Plain Style," in *Puritans and Puritanism in Europe and America: A Comprehensive Encyclopedia*, ed. Francis Bremer and Tom Webster (Santa Barbara: ABC-CLIO, 2006) 2:479–80; Ronald J. Allen, "Puritan Plain Style," in *Patterns of Preaching: A Sermon Sampler*, ed. Ronald J. Allen (St. Louis: Chalice Press, 1998) 7–13; and Randall J. Pederson, *Unity in Diversity: English Puritanism and the Puritan Reformation, 1603–1689*, Brill's Series in Church History 68 (Leiden: Brill, 2014) 32.

[62] See "it provided clergy with the theoretical framework by which they could stress in their sermons the need for changes in the lives and behavior of a congregation." McKim, "Functions of Ramism," 511.

God's Word, "by which the preacher could impart information as well as instruct and correct the lives of the hearers."[63] And third and last, Ramism formed a practical hermeneutical key as it approached scripture as a universal truth (an axiom) to be discovered and further distributed into parts.[64] In this way a scriptural passage could be exegeted and turned to several applications. Hence, it enabled Puritans to expose the natural and internal logic of scripture, seemingly without the need to submit the biblical text to a foreign philosophical scheme. Donald McKim concludes about Perkins's use of Ramism: "It provided the framework in which preaching was done to challenge the mind and stir the heart. Ramism produced a form by which discourse could be analyzed and easily memorized so the preacher might be even more effective."[65]

McKim's study has shown how the adoption of Ramist methodology coincided with the Puritan stress on preaching as the premier means of conversion. Plain style preaching facilitated the Protestant search for sincerity and simplicity required to redirect the focus of parishioners to internal reflection, instead of traditional religion, known for ceremony and ostentation, as Patrick Collinson observes.[66] Richard Greenham therefore pronounces his sorrow over the decay of preaching he observes in his day.[67] He welcomes eloquence as a helpful preaching tool, but warns to make its effect dependent "on carnal and mans wisdome" instead of "the power of the word" itself.[68] In similar wordings, Robert Browne refuted all forms of scriptural handling that neglected to bring scripture to its application: "But chiefly the applying must not be forgotten. For defaultes and erroures, must be improued by the scriptures, with rebuke, and iudgmentes, denounced as there is cause, and the truth must

---

[63] McKim, "Functions of Ramism," 511–12; John G. Rechtien, "The Ramist Style of John Udall: Audience and Pictorial Logic in Puritan Sermon and Controversy," *Oral Tradition* 2, no. 1 (1987): 199; Oates, "Sermons and sermon-going in early modern England," 205.

[64] McKim, "Functions of Ramism," 514.

[65] McKim, "Functions of Ramism," 516. "Ramus's *Dialectic* played a role in inculcating students with political and social values consistent with the interests of Puritan educators." See Adams, "Gabriel Harvey's *Ciceronianus*," 562.

[66] Collinson, *Elizabethan Puritan Movement*, 356–82. See for English traditional religion and liturgy, Duffy, *Stripping of the Altars*, 11–52, 89–106.

[67] See Parker and Carlson, *"Practical Divinity,"* 201, 206, 211–12, 249.

[68] Parker and Carlson, *"Practical Divinity,"* 200.

be proued....Exhortation also must be vsed with confirming and strengthninge of the weaker."⁶⁹ A sermon which does not result in application excludes the audience and prevents them from being edified.⁷⁰

Conclusion: Contesting Clergy

Spurgeon's firm dismissal of non-revivalist ministers with Isaiah's term "dumb dogs" did not fall from the sky, but has literally strong roots in Elizabethan Puritanism. Among these dissenting minds an explosive mix of traits was joined that could not but lead to a conflict with the established church. This oppositionist relation to the establishment would continue to characterize subsequent nonconformist traditions, among which Baptists have a rightful place. Of course, the importance of the preaching ministry already appeared in continental Protestantism. However, there is a significant difference, for Elizabethan Puritanism always remained a minority movement and devoid of official power. Puritans, at least not until Cromwell in the mid-seventeenth century, did not establish a new national church. And those who did separate (as Robert Browne did) remained a persecuted and scattered minority. In other words, unlike the continental reformation, preaching was arguably the most significant means for Elizabethan Puritans to bring further reformation, or revival, to the English church and its parishioners.⁷¹ To revive the established church Puritan preachers trusted the transforming power of the divine scriptures to bring people to faith (Rom. 10:14), and developed a fitting method of preaching that climaxed in the concrete application to people's lives. Consequently, those ministers who failed to bring the message for which they were sent were considered lapdogs of the state. Arnold Hunt, in his recent study, draws a similar conclusion, as he explains the preeminence of vivid preaching among Puritans, and the later revivalist tradition, was a consequence of a lack of "religious and political control."⁷² Revivalist preaching is

---

⁶⁹ Robert Browne, "A Treatise vpon the 23. of Matthewe," in *The Writings of Robert Harrison and Robert Browne*, ed. Albert Peel and Leland H. Carlson, Elizabethan Nonconformist Texts 2 (London: George Allen and Unwin, 1953) 172.

⁷⁰ See Browne, "A Treatise vpon the 23. of Matthewe," 174.

⁷¹ See Hunt, *Art of Hearing*, 4. Hunt even notes that in spite of previous thinking oral transmission even superseded printing "in terms of its popularity, its ability to reach the illiterate and its scope for active audience participation and the rapid dissemination of the preacher's message." Only from the 1620s this distinction slowly began to diminish and printed sermons gained a higher appreciation (12).

⁷² Hunt, *Art of Hearing*, 400.

never the means of those who have the power of coercion, but always of those who are destined to raise a prophetic voice, aimed to bring change in the entrenched routine of institutionalized religion. As such, Spurgeon's critique toward the English churches and particularly its ministry in the nineteenth century is no different. Nevertheless, a slight nuance is to be made. Where Elizabethan Puritans tried to supplement established academic training with practical ministerial formation to produce adequate preaching ministers, Spurgeon entirely rejected academic education. Still, though his nonconformity went clearly beyond his Puritan ancestors on this point, it was the same motivation that drove him: providing the church with preachers able to bring the message of the gospel to practical application.

The revivalist tradition exemplified by the Elizabethan Puritans and Baptist preacher Charles Spurgeon reveals a dissenting form of ministry, a "contesting clergy" not only in the sense of challenging the status quo of the role of the clerical office, but also in the sense of challenging the common church member.[73] For revivalist preaching simultaneously puts to question the sufficiency of academic training for church ministry, as the habitual church member who did not yet experience personal conversion. In this way, Baptists, together with Spurgeon, are real heirs of the Puritan revivalist tradition.

---

[73] This reference is a play on the title of Curtis W. Freeman's recent book *Contesting Catholicity: Theology for Other Baptists* (Waco: Baylor University Press, 2014).

19

Revival Among the Aliens: The Case of Lithuanian Baptists

Lina Toth (Andronoviene)

The story of Memel Baptist church (now Klaipeda) in Prussian Lithuania is not only a story of a local revival amongst predominantly German-speaking believers, but also is instrumental to the beginnings of the Baptist movement in Latvia and, through one particular person, Martin Kallweit, the Baptist beginnings in Russian Transcaucasia.[1] The role that Memel Baptists—at one point, the largest Baptist church by membership in continental Europe—have played in the European Baptist history is not widely known and deserves further exploration.[2] At the same time, as shown below, there has been no revival-like phenomenon amongst ethnic Lithuanians in the Roman Catholic context of Lithuania Proper.[3] This may have something important to say about the cultural, social, and political conditions in which other revivals have taken place, as well as our interpretation of what we call a revival.

---

[1] See, e.g., H. J. Coleman, "Baptist Beginnings in Russia and Ukraine," *Baptist History and Heritage* 42, no. 1 (2007): 24; Ian M. Randall, *Communities of Conviction: Baptist Beginnings in Europe* (Schwarzenfeld: Neufeld, 2009) 87–88.

[2] Randall, *Communities of Conviction*, 99.

[3] Perhaps the only episode that would come close to a religious revival has taken place rather recently and was related to the fall of the Soviet regime and the restoration of the independent Republic of Lithuania in 1990. Streikus, for example, describes it as "a few years of resurging enthusiasm for the Catholic faith," but notes that "soon the [Catholic] Church's prestige…evaporated." Arūnas Streikus, "The History of Religion in Lithuania since the Nineteenth Century," in *Religious Diversity in Post-Soviet Society: Ethnographies of Catholic Hegemony and the New Pluralism in Lithuania*, ed. Milda Ališauskienė and Ingo W. Schroeder (Farnham: Ashgate, 2012) 53. However, even at this point, as well as at other peak points for the Catholic church in Lithuania, religious revival was inseparable from, indeed was part and parcel of, the national revival.

REVIVAL AMONG THE ALIENS: THE CASE OF LITHUANIAN BAPTISTS

J. H. Rushbrooke's 1923 edition of *The Baptist Movement in the Continent of Europe*[4] provides short overviews of the origins and history of Baptists in different European countries, including those that had sprung up into an independent existence after 1918 (so after the earlier version of the book, published in 1915).[5] Thus, for example, chapter 11 consists of nine pages on Latvia, including accounts of settlers from the Baptist church of Memel (that is, Prussian Lithuania), and the baptism of the first Latvians, again in Memel.

The next chapter, on Lithuania, is only two and a half pages. The second half of the title gives a clue to the brevity: "A Barren Soil?" The chapter starts, however, with a short account of the Baptist church in Memel. Rushbrooke observes that whilst the church had reached Lithuanian Latvians (four churches at the time of Rushbrooke's writing), the church "failed to gain any considerable influence among the Lithuanians" in Lithuania Proper.[6] Rushbrooke mentions the German- and Russian-speaking Baptists in Kowno (Kaunas), the temporary capital of independent Lithuania, but he comments, "it is unfortunate that...there is as yet no Baptist preacher appealing directly to the masses in their own language."[7] Rushbrooke—or rather, Teodoras Gerikas (Theodor Gerik), the Lithuanian Baptist leader who had collected this information for Rushbrooke and later took up the ministry of preaching in Kaunas[8]—then mentions some twenty Lithuanians from a Reformed background in Lithuania Proper, near the Latvian border. Again, it is significant that these do not come from Catholic families. These, Rushbrooke notes, had "accepted Baptist principles,"[9] but more than half of them had since emigrated. I have not yet been able to discover any other source corroborating this emigration,[10] but in any case, we are discussing a handful of isolated Baptists

---

[4] J. H. Rushbrooke, *The Baptist Movement in the Continental Europe* (London: Kingsgate, 1923).

[5] J. H. Rushbrooke, ed., *The Baptist Movement in the Continental Europe: A Contribution to Modern History* (London: Carey Press/Kingsgate, 1915).

[6] Rushbrooke, *Baptist Movement* (1923) 117.

[7] Rushbrooke, *Baptist Movement* (1923) 117.

[8] Rushbrooke, *Baptist Movement* (1923) 207.

[9] Rushbrooke, *Baptist Movement* (1923) 118. Latužis suggests that this small grouping was a split from a Pentecostal-style group based in Biržai, in the northeast of the country. Albertas Latužis, *Po Jo Sparnais: Baptistų istorija Lietuvoje 1841–1990 [Under His Wings: Baptist History in Lithuania 1841–1990]* (Klaipėda: Eglė, 2009) 109–11.

[10] It is presumably related to the Latvian phenomenon of the "Brazilian revival" For the background on Latvian Baptist emigration to Brazil, see Olaf Bruvers, *The Revival in Latvia during 1920s and Subsequent Baptist Immigration to Brazil* (Riga: Amnis, 2009).

of Lithuanian ethnicity.

This study will fall into two parts. First, an analysis of the development and a remarkable growth of Baptists in Memel. As my interest is specifically Lithuanian-speaking Baptists, or Prussian Lithuanians, I will explore a particular feature of this region: a form of pietistic revival and the importance of this home-based, lay-led movement of prayer meetings that served as a soil which eventually grew a modest, but certainly much stronger group of Prussian Lithuanian Baptist churches compared to Lithuania Proper. I will then investigate the anaemic growth of the Baptists in Lithuania Proper, until 1940, which marks the annexation of Lithuania by the Soviet Union and a drastic disruption of the fragile Baptist beginnings in Lithuania. However, should the following years be investigated, the broad strokes of such investigation would first show the complete disappearance of German-speaking Baptists, including the Memel church, and the continuous struggle of Baptists in Soviet, and later post-Soviet, Lithuania, to find contextually appropriate ways of relating to the culturally Catholic population.[11]

Prussian Lithuania: The Fertile Protestant, Pietistic Soil

At this point, a brief introduction to the geopolitical and cultural context of Memel in particular, and Prussian Lithuania[12] in general, may be of help. The region around Memel, or Memelland as it was sometimes known, was the eastern part of the Prussian Kingdom and, from 1871, unified Germany. Founded by the Teutonic Knights, Memel, or Klaipeda, as it was and is called by the Lithuanian speakers, was situated on the northernmost tip of East Prussia. In 1923, under controversial circumstances, the region came under the jurisdiction of the new independent Republic of Lithuania, but retained considerable autonomy, not the least in religious matters.[13]

---

[11] At this point, I express my heartfelt thanks to Albertas Latužis, whose expertise in issues in Lithuanian Baptist history has been invaluable for this research, both through his book, *Po Jo Sparnais*, and his availability for personal conversations; and to Ruta Inkenaitė, who in many ways has become a research assistant for this project. Her help in locating important pieces of material from her personal archive, as well as in transcribing and/or translating some of the historical correspondence, has been invaluable.

[12] Prussian Lithuania is sometimes referred to as Lithuania Minor.

[13] For the general background to the region and its problematics in English, see Peter Thaler, "Fluid Identities in Central European Borderlands," *European History Quarterly* 31 (October 2001): particularly 528–33; Vygantas Vareikis, "Memellander/Klaipėdiškiai Identity and

Memel was deeply influenced by German culture and thus Lutheranism. The identity of Prussian Lithuanians was formed in this context, at times under the severe pressure of Germanization, and thus in some way was an expression of national revival. The religious-cultural context of Memel was cosmopolitan. The local population was largely Protestant, predominantly Lutheran, and, especially if one ventured into the surrounding villages, with a strong pietistic flavour.

Established in 1841, Memel church was the first Baptist church in East Prussia and one of the earliest amongst European Baptist churches.[14] The roots of Memel church lie in an "awakening," to use Rushbrooke's word,[15] begun by a local carpenter, Eduard Grimm. Lutheran by background, Grimm became an apprentice in Zurich. In 1830, Grimm met Samuel Fröhlich, the leader of Zurich's "Neutaueufer" group. Five years later, upon his profession of personal faith, he was baptised by Fröhlich by sprinkling. Having returned to Memel, Grimm kept his new faith to himself until, during Pentecost of 1839, he found himself unable to keep quiet any longer. There was some interest in his message, and Grimm soon baptised eleven people by sprinkling and encountered the first wave of persecution from city authorities.

Among the attendees of Grimm's rapidly growing group was an English sea captain and shipbroker,[16] Joseph Hague, a son of a Baptist minister who had served, before his death, in Scarborough.[17] It was Hague who pointed

German-Lithuanian Relations in Lithuania Minor in the Nineteenth and Twentieth Centuries," *Sociologija. Mintis ir veiksmas* 6, nos. 1–2 (2001): 54–65, accessed March 30, 2015, http://www.ku.lt/wp-content/uploads/2013/03/2001_nr_1–2.54–65.pdf.

[14] The history of Memel Baptist Church has been recorded, in great detail, by one of its later ministers, Otto Ekelmann, in *Gnadenwunder* [The Wonder of Grace] (Memel, 1928). Further documents have been uncovered, and further research performed at Das Zentrale Oncken-Archiv des Bundes Evangelisch-Freikirchlicher Gemeinden, Elstal, Germany, by Ruta Lysenkaite (Ambrasuniene) one of the graduates of the International Baptist Theological Seminary, Prague. Lysenkaite's research resulted in her master's thesis, "Baptist Beginnings in the Baltic Countries: The Case of the Church in Memel" (master's thesis, International Baptist Theological Seminary, Prague, 2001).

[15] J. H. Rushbrooke, *Some Chapters of European Baptist History* (London: Kingston, 1929) 72.

[16] In the context of the announcement of marriage of his daughter, Mary Ann, to "Mr. Geo. Nettleto of Bridlington," Hague is described as ship-broker. *Yorkshire Gazette*, April 9, 1853.

[17] "Extracts from the Journal of Mr. Oncken," *Baptist Missionary* magazine, vol. 22, Boston 1842, 272.

Grimm towards the theology of baptism by immersion, which, after studying the matter, Grimm came to accept. This was not true of Grimm's entire group; some left. It was also Hague who suggested contacting Gerhard Oncken of Hamburg as someone who could baptise them by immersion. Thus, Grimm wrote to Oncken with a request to come to Memel. It is important to note, therefore, that this contact between Grimm's group and Oncken was not the initiative of the latter; in fact, Oncken seems to have been rather suspicious at first, and sent one of his aides, A. F. Remmers, to investigate the "Memel circle."[18] Remmers's report was positive and, on October 5, 1841, *Memelschen Wochenblatt* reported that the "agent of the Bible Society, Oncken, has crossed the border."[19] Oncken baptised twenty-nine people on two consecutive nights, in order to avoid the intervention of city authorities. Memel Baptist congregation was officially constituted, and Grimm was ordained as pastor. One of those baptised was Joseph Hague; Oncken in his diary noted his hopes "that Mr. H. will soon commence a regular service on the Lord's day [for the English speakers]."[20]

The story of the years that followed involve both great growth and great difficulties, both from the outside—mostly by city authorities, Lutheran and Reformed pastors, and at times the mob—and from the inside. It took just over a month for the congregation to split. Grimm, who did not approve the application of rigorous discipline to the members, was removed from leadership and subsequently formed the "Second Baptist congregation" in Memel, whilst the "First Baptist congregation," supported by Oncken, came under the leadership of F. Engberg, the owner of the place where the congregation was gathering.[21] The two groups were reconciled and reunited in 1856, after Grimm left for the United States.[22] In 1851, the newly built "Kapelle" (chapel) was opened, with seating or standing capacity of 1,500.[23] "[F]or that time, in mainland Europe, a Baptist building of that size was a phenomenon. It was

---

[18] Ekelmann, *Gnadewunder*, 4.
[19] The list of aliens who have crossed the border is found in *Memelschen Wochenblatt*, October 5, 1841, reported in Ekelmann, *Gnadewunder*, 5.
[20] "Extracts from the journal of Mr. Oncken," *Baptist Missionary* magazine, vol. 22, Boston 1842, 273.
[21] Oncken's heavy hand is very notable, as it was he who installed the Memel ministers and preachers. Ekelmann, "Gnadewunder," *Die Gemeinde*, 19 (1968): 7.
[22] Latužis, *Po Jo Sparnais*, 45.
[23] Ekelmann, "Gnadewunder," 176.

larger than the Hamburg mother church."[24]

Mission-mindedness was an important feature of the Memel congregation; at one point the number of its mission stations had grown to thirty-three, including one in the capital of Czarist Russia, St. Petersburg.[25] A few of these later became independent congregations.[26] By 1875, the membership had reached 2,780; this included both the mother church and twenty-seven mission stations. The following year, in 1876, 1,242 members were transferred to the former mission points, now new independent Baptist churches.[27]

Another important episode in the congregation's life was the Great City Fire of 1854. With most schools and churches suddenly without buildings, the Memel Baptists opened their doors to a day school, a Lutheran community, and some of those who were left homeless. This engagement with the city signified a significant shift in the attitudes toward the Baptists in Memel.[28]

The Great Fire was also the beginning of the mission among Lithuanian speakers. Ferdinand Niemetz, the then pastor of Memel Baptist Church, wrote: "After the fire we could not keep away the Lithuanians. They came and prayed immediately at our services."[29] Soon there were more than 640 Lithuanians attending the Lithuanian services, which were started by Niemetz and another significant person who was set aside for the evangelisation of Lithuanians, Karl Albrecht.[30] Albrecht reports in the *American Baptist Missionary Journal*: "The work of grace which has for some time been strikingly going on among the Lithuanians is, I rejoice to say, progressing.... The people, naturally warm-hearted and frank, seem of later years to have been pre-

---

[24] Randall, *Communities of Conviction*, 102.

[25] Latužis, *Po Jo Sparnais*, 52.

[26] Albertas Latužis, personal interview, *Klaipeda*, 6 July 2015.

[27] Randall, *Communities of Conviction*, 99, 106.

[28] Here it is interesting to note a parallel story of the Great Fire of Hamburg of 1842, and a marked change in the attitude towards Oncken's Baptist church among citizens and authorities alike, as they were deeply impressed by the church's assistance provided to those devastated by the fire. See, e.g., Robert E. Johnson, *A Global Introduction to Baptist Churches* (New York: Cambridge University Press, 2010) 189.

[29] "Nachricht aus Memel," *Missionsblatt* 11 (1854): 45, quoted in and translated by Ruta Lysenkaite, "Baptist Beginnings in the Baltic Countries," 18.

[30] "Nachricht aus Memel," *Missionsblatt* 11 (1854): 45.

pared still more to receive the truth. Wherever I appear, great joy is manifested.... Often loud weeping and exclamations interrupted my speech; but there was never undue excitement."[31]

However, Albrecht's attempts to do mission work on the other side of the frontier (that is, Catholic Lithuania Proper) were—I quote Rushbrooke— "largely frustrated by the Roman Catholic clergy with the help of the Russian Government.... Thus it has come about that the largest group of Lithuanian Baptists is found in Memelland."[32]

Beside the work among Lithuanians by Memel's congregation (and a smaller Baptist congregation in Rusnė-Priekulė), there were three entirely Lithuanian Baptist congregations in Prussian Lithuania.[33] A considerable number of Prussian Lithuanians were also involved in the congregations south of Nemunas river.[34] Virtually all of these congregations were in villages; this is not surprising; German dominated in towns, but Lithuanian was more commonly spoken in the countryside. All these congregations were born in the context of Prussian Lutheran pietism.

Pietism in Prussian Lithuania

A key factor in the formation of the spirituality of Lithuanian speakers in Prussian Lithuania was their form of Lutheran pietistic revival: religious meetings at homes called *"surinkimai"– gatherings* is a loose English translation, *Die evangelische Gemeinschaftsbewegung* in German[35]—which were practiced up to the beginning of WWII. These meetings were led by "sayers of God's word" (*sakytojai*)—laymen who were recognised as able to understand and interpret the scripture with feeling and in a way that would be understandable for common people. The meetings were accompanied by much

---

[31] "Journal of C. Albrecht, Lithuania. "The Work in Lithuania," *American Baptist Missionary Magazine* 40 (1860): 36–37.

[32] Rushbrooke, *Some Chapters of European Baptist History*, 74. "Russian government" refers to the Czarist regime and thus the years prior to Lithuania's becoming independent country in 1918.

[33] Latužis, *Po Jo Sparnais*, 29.

[34] Latužis, *Po Jo Sparnais*, 63.

[35] There is no English equivalent of the term, whilst in German this has been translated as "Die evangelische Gemeinschaftsbewegung"; see, e.g., Wilhelm Gaigalat, *Die evangelische Gemeinschaftsbewegung unter den preußischen Litauern: Geschichtliches und Gegenwärtiges* (Königsberg: Ostpreußische Druckerei und Verlagsanstalt, 1904).

singing. They were conducted in Lithuanian and thus played an important role in supporting Lithuanian identity in the face of extensive Prussian colonisation policy and later, towards the end of nineteenth century, aggressive Germanization.[36]

The type of Prussian Lithuanian pietism can be traced to the beginning of the eighteenth century and was, to some extent, influenced by the Moravians, but especially by Zalzburg colonists who, after their expulsion from Zalzburg by Leopold von Firmian in 1731, were invited by Friedrich Wilhelm I, king of Prussia, to settle in many of the homesteads left empty after the Great Plague of 1709, with the guarantee of further material provisions. Many of these twenty thousand Zalzburgers ended up in East Prussia. The "revivalistic ways" of these foreigners created quite a "sensation," and this was especially true of Prussian Lithuanians.[37] "To the clergy it was a matter of astonishment that the Lithuanians frequently attended the Salzburger services, although they did not understand their language. But to see the devotion of these men and to hear their songs moved them."[38]

Thus, in spite of some initial clashes with the colonists,[39] by mid-eighteenth century Prussian Lithuanians were holding very similar gatherings. By the nineteenth century, at least 40 percent of adult Prussian Lithuanian speakers were taking part in the gatherings.[40] It should be noted that some of the gatherings had spread to the border region of Lithuania Proper, but again they were primarily operating among the people from Protestant backgrounds.[41] The practice continued until the arrival of the Nazis in 1939, when such meetings were banned.[42]

The revivalist spirit of Lithuanian Prussian gatherings plowed the soil

---

[36] Birute Zemaityte, "Pietizmas Mazojoje Lietuvoje" [Pietism in Lithuania Minor], accessed July 1, 2015, http://www.mazoji-lietuva.lt/pietizmas-mazojoje-lietuvoje/.

[37] W. R. Ward, *The Protestant Evangelical Awakening* (Cambridge: Cambridge University Press, 1992) 147. For a more detailed account of the Zalzburger immigration, see ibid., 93–115.

[38] W. Hubatsch, *Geschichte der Evangelischen Kirche Ostpreussens*, vol. 1 (Gottingen, 1968) 191, quoted in Ward, *The Protestant Evangelical Awakening*, 147. Some of the colonists also took it as their task to connect with the locals; Ward mentions that "Hofer, a Salzburger who had joined the Moravians, learned Lithuanian in order to hold meetings for that people in their own tongue." Ward, *The Protestant Evangelical Awakening*, 148.

[39] Zemaityte, "Pietizmas Mazojoje Lietuvoje."
[40] Zemaityte, "Pietizmas Mazojoje Lietuvoje."
[41] Burbulys, *Gyvoji Evangelija*, 90.
[42] Zemaityte, "Pietizmas Mazojoje Lietuvoje."

for the later emergence of the Baptists. However, it must also be noted that whilst a great part of the Lutheran church either tolerated or even supported the gatherings—as the participants typically continued as official members of the Lutheran church—the emergence of Baptists was frequently seen as a threat, as Baptists officially broke the links with the State Church. Thus, the strengthening of Lutheran parish life and building new churches was seen to be an important strategy in counteracting Baptist activities. To some person expressing concern regarding the growth of the Baptist activity, a Prussian Lithuanian pietistic periodical, the *Conservative Letter of Friendship*, notes: "Let him know that the soul which really knows its Saviour and...firmly believes that nothing else but 'the blood of Jesus Christ...cleanses us from all sins,' that soul will remain firm, even if fifty-five Baptists would beset that soul with their testimonies."[43] However, even with such occasional clashes between the Lutheran Pietists and Baptists, there was plenty of commonality and synergy. This was not the case, however, in Lithuania Proper.

Baptists in Lithuania Proper: "The Barren [Catholic] Soil"

The Story in Broad Strokes

Lithuanians in Lithuania Proper[44] spoke the same language as those in Prussian Lithuania, but otherwise their life could not have been more different. As late as 1929, Rushbrooke calls it a "Catholic and backward country."[45] The accusation of backwardness could be related to the fact that the Grand Duchy of Lithuania was the last pagan country in Europe, accepting baptism only in 1387, and had in many ways retained various pagan elements for centuries, which resulted in a somewhat syncretic form of catholicity.[46] There had been a brief period of Reformation, mostly promoted by the Lithuanian nobility, but due to a very successful Jesuit mission in Lithuania, not least by the establishment of Vilnius University, Lithuania was soon Catholic again, with the exception of small Reformed and Lutheran islands. Under the Czarist Russian hand—from 1795 to 1918—suppression of national consciousness

---

[43] *Konzervatyvų Draugystės laiškas* 75 (1901): n.p., quoted in Latužis, Po Jo Sparnais, 161.

[44] Lithuania Proper is sometimes also referred to as Lithuania Major.

[45] J. H. Rushbrooke, *Some Chapters of European Baptist History* (London: Kingston, 1929) 78.

[46] On the syncretism of the Balts, see Ward, *Protestant Evangelical Awakening*, 38. Whilst discussing Livonia primarily, Ward suggests that in the Baltic region "the penetration of Christianity of any kind was remarkably shallow" (38).

meant that the Catholic Church became an essential element for the preservation of Lithuanian identity. The key role of the Catholic Church, and some particular priests and bishops, in starting the national revival and nurturing it against the Czarist suppression of the Lithuanian language, is unquestionable. Thus by 1918, when Lithuania proclaimed its independence, Lithuanian identity and Catholicism were considered virtually inseparable, with the Catholic Church dominating the political and cultural life of the country.

In contrast to the emergence of national revival, one would be pressed hard to pinpoint a revival of religious nature in Lithuania Proper. In terms of the Baptist beginnings, we can turn back to Rushbrooke's description of 1923, corroborated by local records describing a handful of Lithuanian speaking Baptists, primarily from the Reformed background. Out of this handful, of particular importance is Teodoras Gerikas, an early orphaned son of a Latvian mother and a Lithuanian Catholic father, who became Baptist in a Latvian context. From 1908, he assisted the famous Latvian Baptist J. A. Frey as a colporteur, and soon started translating literature into Lithuanian.[47] Gerikas received his education in the Baptist seminary in Hamburg, and was enabled, by British Baptists and the American Baptist Foreign Mission Society (ABFMS), to work as a traveling missionary in order to encourage the Baptist movement in Lithuania Proper and thus prepare for the formation of a Baptist Union. As Rushbrooke notes, "The modesty, tact, and skill of Gerikas have within a few years won general recognition, and the earliest results of his labour are full of promise."[48] Most of the Lithuanian Baptist activities can be directly linked to the work of this remarkable person. Another person to mention is Jonas Inkenas, who, with Gerikas's encouragement, enrolled for theological studies in the Baptist seminary in Riga, Latvia (1925–1929) and, enabled by ABFMS, continued theological studies in Newton Theological Institution, Massachusetts, USA (1929–1932). Upon completing his bachelor in theology, Inkenas returned to Lithuania. He settled in Šiauliai, a centrally located Lithuanian town, and commenced a preaching ministry for several small, dispersed Baptist congregations. Another two Lithuanian Baptist women, Marija Variakojytė (from 1935, the wife of Jonas Inkenas) and Dorotėja Inkenaitė (a sister of Jonas Inkenas), were also supported by ABFMS

---

[47] Rushbrooke, *Some Chapters of European Baptist History*, 76.
[48] Rushbrooke, *Some Chapters of European Baptist History*, 78.

and acquired a master's degree in religious education at the Newton Theological Institution (1930-1933). Both became key workers in the ministry of translation and preparation of Christian literature, as well youth and children's work.

Ethnic Tensions and the Creation of the Unions
One of the marks of the progress in the Baptist cause in Lithuania was the building up of the new, fragile Baptist Union, with efforts put into encouraging the cooperation of non-Lithuanian Baptist congregations. These included a primarily German-speaking one in Kaunas,[49] in Polish-occupied Vilnius, which was a very multicultural congregation whose roots are at least partly Pashkovite,[50] but which did not have any Lithuanian speaking members,[51] and some Latvian congregations.

Although extensive, the ministry and mission of the Latvian churches had little impact upon the local Lithuanian speakers. As Latužis has suggested, "For Lithuanians, this 'Latvian faith' remained unacceptable, though attractive; they were happy to attend Baptist festivals, but only very few accepted the gospel."[52] In the Kaunas Baptist congregation, which was primarily German, a lay evangelist named Gustav Freidank promoted the work among Lithuanians.[53] A small group of Lithuanian speakers gathered together with Russian speakers. The services would take place in Russian, un-

---

[49] This congregation reached four hundred members at the height of its life. See Latužis, *Po Jo Sparnais*, 58.

[50] Pashkovites, also known as Radstockists, were a Russian evangelical movement born in the nobility salons of St. Petersburg in 1870s through the ministry of an English preacher, Lord Radstock and his first Russian convert, Madame Elizaveta I. Chertkova. Later known as "Evangelical Christians," the movement merged with Russian Baptists in 1944. For further details, see Andrey P. Puzynin, *The Tradition of the Gospel Christians: A Study of Their Identity and Theology during the Russian, Soviet, and Post-Soviet Periods* (Eugene, Oregon: Pickwick Publications, 2011).

[51] Latužis, *Po Jo Sparnais*, 59. The Pashkovite connection came through the Zass sisters, who belonged to Kargel's Evangelical Christian congregation in St. Petersburg and had moved to Vilnius in 1911.

[52] Latužis, *Po Jo Sparnais*, 90.

[53] Latužis, *Po Jo Sparnais*, 92–93. In 1930 Freidank was officially designated as a colporteur-evangelist by the Lithuanian Baptist mission conference.

til, in 1933, after Gerikas' strategic relocation to the temporary capital of Lithuania; a separate Lithuanian Baptist congregation was founded.[54] In 1938, this Lithuanian congregation had nineteen members, forty-five children in Sunday school, and twelve young people in the youth group.[55] A few other Lithuanian congregations emerged: Biržai (1918), Šiauliai (1923), Panevėžys (1918), Telšiai (1932) and Rokiškis (1938). Their membership was no more than fifteen in each, except for the Šiauliai congregation, which had twenty-eight members—the largest of all Lithuanian Baptist congregations![56]

The creation of the Baptist Union in Lithuania turned out to be an extremely difficult task. Here it is helpful to recall the situation that existed before the creation of independent Lithuania in 1918: Latvian-speaking congregations had belonged to the Latvian Baptist Union. Congregations in Prussian Lithuania—both German- and Lithuanian- speaking—were part of the East Prussian Baptist Union. Kaunas and all other tiny Baptist groupings were not officially linked to anybody else.[57] However, after 1918 and especially after 1923 when Memelland became part of the territory of the Republic of Lithuania, the question of a Union became a pressing one. The key person pushing this matter forward was the aforementioned Gerikas. He could speak Lithuanian, Latvian, German, Russian, and English; he was both competent and acceptable as a link-person for various parties.[58] One of his ideas was to unite small isolated groupings and individual Lithuanian speaking believers into a "virtual" Baptist congregation he called "Diaspora."[59] The intent was to create links and a sense of belonging, even though all the members of this Diaspora never gathered all in one place. Later, many of these members became ardent supporters of the idea of a Baptist Union.[60]

Support for the development of common links also came from some Memellander Germans and Prussian Lithuanians, particularly Jurgis Skvirblys, who organised a festival in 1923, the purpose of which was for the Baptists of the two different parts of the new country—Prussian Lithuania

---

[54] Latužis, *Po Jo Sparnais*, 94.
[55] Latužis, *Po Jo Sparnais*, 95.
[56] Latužis, *Po Jo Sparnais*, 109
[57] Latužis, *Po Jo Sparnais*, 121.
[58] Latužis, *Po Jo Sparnais*, 121.
[59] Latužis, *Po Jo Sparnais*, 123.
[60] Latužis, *Po Jo Sparnais*, 123.

and Lithuania Proper—to get to know each other. Quite aptly, this festival took place on Pentecost Sunday.[61]

Whilst reluctant to discuss the founding of a Baptist Union given their belonging to East Prussian Baptist Union, Prussian German Baptists were strong supporters of the idea of an alliance aimed at common work. Latvian congregations opposed the idea on the grounds that, as Germans would comprise the majority, they would dictate their terms to others.[62] Quite wisely, Gerikas acted slowly. In the meantime, he continued to cultivate informal links by visits and correspondence.[63]

In October 1923, a gathering of the representatives of these various congregations took place in Memel/Klaipeda. The outcome of the meeting was the creation not of the Baptist Union as such, but of Lithuanian Baptist Mission Work Union (LBMWU).[64] The dual purposes of this union were cultivating relationships between the Baptists and representing the Baptist causes at governmental offices.[65] Another decision made at this meeting was the agreement on the publication of a small magazine of an evangelistic nature, in Lithuanian—a monthly *Tiesos Draugas* [Friend of the Truth]—as well as other literature and the distribution of scripture in various languages of the country.[66] The LBMWU organised annual conferences. Providing an overview of the work of the Union in 1930, a minister of the German-speaking congregation in Šilutė-Priekulė reported: "in thirty-three locations, five [ordained] preachers and twenty-five of their helpers are preaching the Gospel. The membership is 1,160."[67] In 1933—ten years after the creation of LBMWU—the Baptist Union of Lithuania was officially founded.

However, ethnic tensions loomed in the background and would at times flare up, especially between the German and Lithuanian speakers. Here is a snippet, in an extract from a 1929 letter by Gerikas to Inkenas, who had just moved to the United States for his theological studies:

---

[61] Latužis, *Po Jo Sparnais*, 123.

[62] Latužis, *Po Jo Sparnais*, 124–25.

[63] Later, Lithuanian Latvian congregations adopted a much more positive attitude toward the union and provided regular financial contributions to its cause. Latužis, *Po Jo Sparnais*, 126.

[64] Latužis, *Po Jo Sparnais*, 125–26.

[65] Latužis, *Po Jo Sparnais*, 126.

[66] Latužis, *Po Jo Sparnais*, 126.

[67] *Der Wahrheitszeuge* 16 (1930) n.p., quoted in Latužis, *Po Jo Sparnais*, 128.

Kaunas congregation people are very angry for you not visiting them before your departure. It's difficult to explain to them the reasons. Brother Freutel [the minister of the congregation] does not want to have anything in common with me. He says:..."You have become a great Lithuanian patriot and do not consider the matters of the society." So I must listen to such reproaches. You know very well that I want to live in peace with everybody. But brother Freutel, it seems, is not happy to see Lithuanians moving. He would like them to consult the Germans in all matters.[68]

Thus, one of the challenging questions for this fledgling Lithuanian work was the issue of multiple identities and, particularly, the issue of "being a Baptist Lithuanian." Referring to the possible relocation of Anskis Klumbys, a Prussian Lithuanian, to Birzai (Lithuania Proper), Gerikas notes in a personal letter: "Let us see. He is too German, but perhaps he will improve."[69] It is likely that the need to work on preserving peace among different ethnic groups did mean sacrificing bolder, more intentional attempts of developing genuinely Lithuanian Baptist identity and mission.

On the other hand, it is also clear that virtually no Baptist work among Lithuanians would have been possible had it not been for the help of those from other nations—particularly, the American Baptist Foreign Mission Society and the Baptist World Alliance.

The Role of World Baptists in Supporting Lithuanian Baptist Beginnings

Researching this period in the Lithuanian Baptist life, I was amazed to discover the frequency of visits and the intensity of correspondence between the Lithuanian Baptist leaders and the Baptists abroad—particularly in relation to Walter O. Lewis, ABFMS Representative in Europe. In 1930, in a personal letter Gerikas wrote that Dr. Lewis—to whom Gerikas on more than one occasion privately, refers as "uncle Lewis"[70]—"gained a good impression [from his visit] in Lithuania.... He said that this was one of the most important mission fields. For us his visit brought great joy."[71]

---

[68] Gerikas, letter to Inkenas, November 13, 1929. The letters are in the personal archive of Ruta Inkenaite, Klaipeda, Lithuania.
[69] Gerikas, letter to Inkenas, February 18, 1930.
[70] Gerikas, letter to Inkenas, June 30, 1930.
[71] Gerikas, letter to Inkenas, June 30, 1930.

Here the role of Gerikas was crucial again, both in the efforts he had put into developing international relationships, and in his networking skills.[72] Gerikas's participation in the 1923 BWA Congress in Stockholm had laid the beginning for this relationship. Gerikas also took part in the 1928 Congress in Toronto and, in 1934, with another eleven representatives from Lithuania, in the Baptist Congress in Berlin.

ABFMS financially assisted Lithuanian Baptists in a variety of ways. This included the abovementioned full sponsorship of the education of three young Lithuanians at Newton Theological Institution.[73] Gerikas's own support was also almost solely dependent on AMFMS.[74] Both Rushbrooke and Lewis had visited Lithuania a number of times. Links were formed also with a handful of American Lithuanians, including those involved in a small Lithuanian Baptist congregation in Peabody, Massachusetts.

Opposition of the Catholic Church and Relations with the State

Yet even with all of the moral and financial support from abroad, the surviving reports, periodicals, and personal correspondence reveal a continuous struggle and a strong sense of "the harvest being great, but the labourers being few." In a private letter to Inkenas, Gerikas writes: "To tell you the truth, my dear brother, I feel I'm just not managing with all the work. Perhaps an observer would think: what is this Gerikas doing at all? But I think you will not think so." He then lists various tasks: correspondence with "brothers and supporters abroad," reports on the work of Baptist mission, matters to solve among Lithuanian, German, Latvian and Russian believers, acting as the Chairperson of the Union, fighting for Baptist rights in the country, relating to "truth seekers," writing articles for various newspapers, sermons, travels,

---

[72] Latužis, *Po Jo Sparnais*, 166.

[73] In order to help Inkenas secure a non-quota student visa, Lewis writes to the American Consul in Riga that the Foreign Mission Society "is guaranteeing the expenses of Mr. Inkenas while in the States." W. O. Lewis, letter to the American Consul, Riga, Latvia. August 6, 1929. Copy available through the author.

[74] In consulting Inkenas about the best way to fill in the annual report required by the Lithuanian government, Gerikas writes: "In terms of the office and persons from which I receive my salary, I report: "European Representative of American Baptist Foreign Mission Society, Dr W. O. Lewis, 48 Rue de Lille, Paris, France. Last year I reported that you receive your support from there too." Personal letter to Inkenas, February 1938.

hosting (in his own home) various guests, taking care of all civil registry, encouraging the translation of hymns and publication of a hymnal, editing Baptist periodical and Christian literature.... "And with all of that, there is a lack of true health."[75] At times, letters become very poignant: "It seems I will need to keep burning until I burn out, in [this] work."[76] Gerikas's health and all-consuming work were a continuous matter of concern for AMFMS. In 1931, Lewis wrote to Inkenas: "I am afraid that he is so far gone with tuberculosis that he will never be able to do hard work again. I hope that as soon as possible after you finish your work you will come back and do your best to help us establish our cause in Lithuania."[77]

Such an amount and range of work would have been challenging in any circumstances, but two factors deserve special if brief attention: relating to the state authorities and the pressure of the Catholic Church.

I have already referred to the importance of the Catholic Church, and the "Lithuanian Catholic faith," in reviving and sustaining Lithuanian identity under the Czarist regime. Lithuanian identity as necessarily Catholic, and indeed Lithuanian Catholic nationalism, continued to play a key part in the shaping of the national consciousness during the interwar period of Lithuania's independence. It is not surprising that in such a climate, particular persons within the Catholic Church could have exercised influence, in Rushbrooke's summary, "both by legal and extra-legal methods."[78] In one of his letters, Gerikas refers to the Telšiai bishopric. In his judgment, there were people in the town interested in the gospel—"but the wee bishop [who resides in Telšiai]...is very angered. The police keep confiscating the Bibles and other Christian literature, handing them over to the court, and calls it 'antireligious rubbish.'"[79] Gerikas also complained that in certain villages and towns, *Tiesos Draugas* was not passed to the subscribers, as a local priest or organist ran the post office.[80]

Another significant feature of the church-state relationship in interwar

---

[75] Gerikas, letter to Inkenas, February 18, 1930.
[76] Gerikas, letter to Inkenas, January 29, 1931.
[77] Lewis, letter to Inkenas. July 17, 1931.
[78] Rushbrooke, *Some Chapters of European Baptist History*, 78.
[79] Gerikas, letter to Inkenas, June 30, 1930.
[80] *Tiesos Draugas* 10 (1931): 4.

Lithuania was that, from the creation of the state in 1918 to the Soviet annexation of 1940, Lithuania Proper did not have a civil registry. Two main reasons typically named for this are the dominance of the Catholic Church and its opposition to the introduction of civil registry, and the silent agreement of the Catholic majority of the society.[81] Quite obviously, this created serious difficulties for those belonging to "unrecognised" religions as well as nonreligious persons, in terms of marrying, registering children, and burying the dead. Thus, one of the pressing matters of the Union—in whatever shape—was a legal recognition of the Baptist Registry Centre in Kaunas, established in 1931–32.[82] The Centre, run by Gerikas, had eased the situation for all Baptists in Lithuania Proper, but demanded a lot of Gerikas' time. "I have to write so many documents I am wet with sweat," wrote Gerikas in a letter in 1930.[83]

Beside civil registry matters, various other documents and permissions were required. An official permit from the Ministry of Education had to be obtained for organising larger gatherings such as annual meetings of the Lithuanian Baptist congregational delegates. The police then had to be provided with the text of the main address to be read during the gathering.[84]

Looking at the work of both pioneers, Gerikas and Inkenas, one is reminded of Rushbrooke's image of a dry, barren soil, and a tiring, often disappointing struggle of encouraging any seed to sprout. Only a few months after his return from theological studies in the United States, Inkenas wrote a letter to the foreign secretary of ABFMS, James H. Franklin, sharing with him how difficult he found the work to be. Franklin responded:

> [P]erhaps it is not strange that the adjustments now seem harder than they appeared immediately upon your return to your native country when the warmth of the welcome from family and friends was so reassuring. Now you are face to face with the hard conditions, and you will need such grace and strength as only the Lord can give…. In a very real sense you are one of the pioneers of Baptist work in Lithuania, and it is entirely possible that in the years that lie ahead some historian will know that a

---

[81] See, e.g., Regina Laukaityte, "Society Without a Civil Registry (1918–1940): Outcomes and Consequences," *Lithuanian Historical Studies* 18 (2013): 105–22.

[82] Latužis, *Po Jo Sparnais*, 137.

[83] Gerikas, letter to Inkenas, April 14, 1930.

[84] Gerikas, postcard to Inkenas, June 2, 1939.

few of the Baptists of this age in Lithuania worked so unselfishly and effectively that they laid the foundations of a great movement.[85]

Instead of the great movement, these fragile beginnings were soon to be cruelly interrupted. Hitler's invasion of Memelland in 1939 was one of the first clear signs that their world was about to end. On a postcard to Inkenas on 1 September 1939 Gerikas wrote:

> Solemn, serious events have really shaken the world. They will also painfully affect our work, because the links with abroad have been severed, but we must work, trusting in the Lord's provision.... Brother Rushbrooke sends a letter and asks to greet everybody. He does not know whether he will be able to connect with other countries in the future. Let us pray for the Lord to protect our beloved country from the storms of a war.[86]

The Lithuanian Baptist Union held their last convention on June 29, 1940. The world as they knew it was already crumbling. On June 15, 1940, the Soviet Union army had crossed the border into Lithuania, thus enacting the earlier secret agreements of Ribentrop and Molotov.[87] The world of Lithuanian Baptists was about to be turned upside down, with new, violently enforced ideology, deportations to Siberia, and nationalization of property. Less than a year later, on June 22, 1941, Nazi Germany occupied all the Lithuanian territory. For the next four years, the region was engulfed in war. The end of this war left nothing of the great Memel congregation except the building. Gerikas' health continued to deteriorate and he died upon returning to Lithuania at the end of war. Later, Jonas Inkenas, his wife, and their three daughters—my mother and my two aunts—were deported to Siberia. But that is a story for another occasion.

Conclusion

Thus we have two contrasting stories of Baptists in Lithuania. On the one hand, there is the Germanic revival in Memel: a local phenomenon which nevertheless had soon adopted Oncken's approach and structures and retained

---

[85] Franklin, letter to Inkenas, December 31, 1932.
[86] Gerikas, postcard to Inkenas, September 1, 1939.
[87] See, e.g., Bronis J. Kaslas, "The Lithuanian Strip in Soviet-German Secret Diplomacy, 1939–1941," *Journal of Baltic Studies* 4, no. 3 (1973): 211–25.

impressive numbers and influence. Other congregations in the region of Prussian Lithuania, having grown out of the Prussian pietistic soil, also enjoyed considerable growth and solidity. On the other hand, there is the story of the constant, tiring struggle and fragility in Catholic Lithuania, and no revival whatsoever. The first story ends right at the border with Lithuania Proper, and raises some important questions.

As demonstrated, revivals in Lithuania were an exclusively Protestant phenomenon, both in Prussian Lithuania and Lithuania Proper. The same would be true for the larger geographical region surrounding Lithuania. Whilst Prussian Lithuanians were drawn to Zalzburgers, and the Moravians significantly impacted Livonians and Estonians,[88] neither form of pietism— nor its later children such as the Baptists—had any bearing upon the religious and daily life of Catholic Lithuanians in Lithuania Proper. W. R. Ward notes "the evident power of [pietistic] revival in breaking old paganism of the Baltic lands,"[89] but no such revival touched Lithuania Proper. Ward does not discuss this omission, although the thesis in his work, *The Protestant Evangelical Awakening*, centres around the idea that the European revivals that swept much of Europe starting with eighteenth century were a Protestant product, relying on an interdependent, international Protestant culture. The two stories of two Lithuanias would seem to be an excellent corroboration of this thesis.

Perhaps with the exception of Catholic Ireland,[90] I struggle to think of any example, in Europe at least, of a revival amongst the Catholics—particularly in the contexts in which Catholics were enjoying considerable political and social freedom and power.[91] On the other hand, one must bear in mind the history of evangelical revivals in Slavic Orthodox contexts,[92] which would suggest, contra Ward, that a revival cannot be limited to a simply and solely

---

[88] On Moravians in Livonia and Estonia, see Ward, *Protestant Evangelical Awakening*, 149–55.

[89] Ward, *Protestant Evangelical Awakening*, 353.

[90] My thanks to David Bebbington for reminding me of the Irish phenomenon. It must be remembered, however, that the Irish Catholic revivals were inseparable from the "anti-English" sentiment, and thus rather different in nature from the European Protestant revivals.

[91] I am not here discussing the growth of Protestantism in some of the Catholic South American countries.

[92] See, for instance, Puzynin, *The Tradition of the Gospel Christians*, chap. 2.

Protestant phenomenon.[93] In any case, the history of the Lithuanian Baptist movement underlines the importance of the religio-cultural context for the interpretation of what we call a "revival."

---

[93] In this regard, some of the important issues to explore would be respect for the Bible, prominent in both Protestantism and Orthodoxy, and the honour given to the "holy people" within Orthodoxy, which may have parallels with the radical nature of revivalistic conversions.

20

Three Romanian Baptist Evangelists: Pitt Popovici, Liviu Olah, and Iosif Ton

George Hancock-Stefan

The purpose of this chapter is to look at spiritual revival in Romania during the twentieth century, centralized in the city of Oradea in the mid-seventies and the three evangelists (revivalists) intrinsically connected with it. To get a better understanding of this revival, the chapter first examines the definition of revival, the spiritual events that took place in the Romanian Eastern Orthodox Church, the development of the Baptist churches in Romania, and restrictions that came when Communism took over Romania.

For most historians, the definition of revival is closely intertwined with evangelism. In Psalm 85:6, the Psalmist prays for a revival, because the knowledge and instruction of God was received less frequently with the passing of time: "Will you not revive us again that your people may rejoice in you?" William P. Mackay penned the song "Revive Us Again" in 1863, which concludes with these words, "Revive us again fill each heart with Thy love / May each soul be rekindled with fire from above / Hallelujah! Thine the glory, Halleluiah, Amen / Hallelujah, Thine the glory, Revive us again." Another characteristic of revival is the addition of new people to the family of God through passionate evangelistic preaching and under various powerful manifestations of the Holy Spirit's presence. Thus, revival and evangelism are used interchangeably because whenever the church was revived, it became an evangelizing force.[1]

---

[1] Scholars have debated the definition of revival for a long time. In his lecture "Theology of Revival", Timothy K. Beougher asks, "Is there a distinction between revival and awakening?" and makes the following distinction: "Renewal—When God touches the heart of a single individual; Revival—when God touches a community of faith, and Awakening—when the wider society is impacted." See Tim K. Beougher, *James P. Boyce Society Lectures*, accessed on April 7, 2004, http://sbts.edu/resources/lectures/james-p-boyce-society-lectures/theologyofrevival.

THREE ROMANIAN BAPTIST EVANGELISTS: PITT POPOVICI,
LIVIU OLAH, AND IOSIF TON

According to Eastern Orthodox theology, one becomes a child of God through infant baptism. The Romanian nation practiced infant baptism, adding an element of nationalism to Orthodoxy, resulting in the entire nation being considered Christian. Iosif Trifa, an Orthodox priest, started a movement called the Lord's Army (organized in 1922), prompting a spiritual renewal within the Orthodox churches.[2] This revival started one Christmas evening when he was listening to drunk people pass his house using particularly foul swear words. He emphasized two points: (1) the Orthodox Church members needed to repent and be revived and (2) the Lord's Army was committed to staying in the Orthodox Church. Also, Dumitru Cornilescu translated the Bible because there had not been a new translation since 1874. The Romanian Orthodox Church rejected this translation and it became known as the Cornilescu translation (or the Protestant translation).[3]

Martyn Lloyd-Jones wrote that the main difference is that revival is primarily for the church, while evangelism is for those who are outside the church. See Martyn Lloyd-Jones, *Revival* (Wheaton, IL: Crossway,1987) 99–100. Some important information and debate on definition is found in William E. Allen's small book, *The History of Revivals of Religion* where he studies revivals from the time of Tertullian until the American Revival of 1857–58. For a description, see http://revival-library.org/index.php/catalogues-menu/general-histories/history-of-revivals-of-religion. This year, Richard McLaughlin wrote "The Essence of Revival," which studies the revivals that have taken place on the Wheaton College campus in 1936, 1943, 1950, 1970, 1995, and 2015. See Richard McLaughlin, "The Essence of Revival," *Wheaton Magazine* (Spring 2015): 14–19.

[2] In the book *Amintiri cu Sfinti* (Recollections (Living) of the Saints) Daniel Branzai has two articles—one summarizing the history of Oastea Domnului (The Lord's Army) written by Adolf Novak (last modified June 12, 2008, https://amintiricusfinti.wordpress.com/2008/06/12/oastea-domnhului-adolf-novak) and another where he reprints vignettes from Iosif Trifa's life in his own words. See "Iosif Trifa—Oastea Domnului," last modified June 14, 2008, https://amintiricusfinti.wordpress.com/2008/06/14/iosif-trifa-oastea-domnului. Some Romanian historians have made a comparison between Iosif Trifa, the founder of the Lord's Army (Oastea Domnului) and John Wesley, the founder of Methodism. Both men were used by God and wanted to stay in their own churches, but the church leaders rejected them. In the case of Iosif Trifa, they went so far as to not allow his body to be buried in priestly vestments.

[3] Some people make comparisons between Martin Luther, whose life changed as he read the Epistle of Paul to the Romans, and Dumitru Cornilescu, whose life was changed during the translation of the Epistle of Paul to Romans. A short story of his life can be found at http://www.crestinul.ro/cornil.htm. A more expanded version, written in a publication by a group of converted Eastern Orthodox priests, can be found at "Marturia intoarcerii preotului Dumitru Cornilescu," last accessed October 15, 2015, https://asociatiapreotilorconvertitisauld-intars.wordpress.com/2012/04/12/marturia-intoarcerii-preotului-dumitru-cornilescu. A critical assessment of his translation written by Bogdan Mateciuc is available in a publication called

BAPTISTS AND REVIVALS

Baptist churches were established in Romania towards the end of the nineteenth century and developed in the midst of one wave of persecution after another. The Romanian Baptist historians talk about the eight waves of persecution, the last of which lasted from 1942 to 1944 when no Baptist church was allowed to open. By the order of General Antonescu, all Baptist churches were closed and Baptist leaders were dispossessed of their rights. Even when they pleaded with the government and the Orthodox leaders to be allowed to open their churches to celebrate Easter, they were refused. One reason the Orthodox Church was so inimical to Baptist churches was that the Baptists sought to evangelize members of the Orthodox Church, who converted, left the Orthodox Church, and became members of Baptist churches.[4]

The Romanian Baptist churches were sown in suffering and developed under persecution, from the Romanian monarchs in the first part of the twentieth century and from the Communist dictators in the second half. From the late forties until the Communists came to complete power, the Communists sought the help of other persecuted groups in Romania. However, once they were firmly established, the Communists began purging the party of unwanted factions, including the very groups who had helped them. The Orthodox Church retained certain rights as the national church, while the Roman Catholic Church, Protestant (Lutheran, Reformed, Unitarian) and Neo-Protestant Churches (Baptist, Pentecostal, Plymouth Brethren) were systematically persecuted. The Lord's Army was also forbidden to meet and their leaders were imprisoned.

To understand what happened during the Communist regime in Romania, one must understand two concepts: The Department of Cults and "the empowered one" (*inputernicitul*). The Department of Cults was the state office that supervised and determined all the activities of the church—how many seminarians the denomination could have, how many hours they could hold worship services, who could be baptized, and when and where they could hold baptisms. The churches needed the approval of the department for any minor (or major) repairs. Licenses for preaching were granted and revoked through

---

Odaia de sus (*The Upper Room*) last accessed October 15, 2015, http://www.odaiadesus.ro/cornilescu.html.

[4]Alexa Popovici, *Istoria Baptistilor Din Romania* vol. 2, *1919–1944* (The History of the Romanian Baptists, vol. II2 1919–1944) (Chicago: Romanian Baptist Church, 1989) and Daniel Mitrofan, *Pigmei si Uriasi—file din istoria persecutarii baptistilor* (Dwarfs and Giants—Pages from the History of Baptist Persecutions) (Oradea: Christianus, 2007) 28–42.

this office. Announcements of effusive thanksgiving for the leadership of the party became a part of all church announcements. The empowered one was the person on-site representing the department. He would be present at all church meetings, take notes, and report back to the department. He saw and signed off on the list of people eligible for baptism, but would negatively pressure the candidates through their work place. The candidates would often remove their names from the list and not be baptized.[5]

This chapter focuses on one denomination—Romanian Baptist—and, within that denomination, on three Baptist pastors whose gift was evangelism. They evangelized first in their churches, then in their regions, and then throughout Romania. They were the denomination's evangelists and revivalists. Pitt Popovici started his ministry in Arad in 1945, moved to Timisoara in 1953, and concluded his Romanian ministry in 1967 when he was forced out of the country. Liviu Olah started his ministry in Timisoara in 1968 and lived in Oradea from 1972 to 1975, during the 1973 Romanian Awakening. Olah's pastor's license was revoked before a planned river baptism, so he returned to Timisoara in 1975 and stayed until 1978 when he was forced out of the country. Upon returning from his studies abroad in 1972, Iosif Ton became the pastor of the Baptist church in Ploiesti and professor at the Baptist Theological Seminary in Bucharest. When Olah's preaching license was revoked and he was forced from Oradea, Ton became the pastor in 1977. He continued as the pastor of the Oradea church until 1982 when he, too, was forced out of Romania.

This chapter has three subsections. First, concise biographies of the three evangelists are presented. Next, their methods, characteristics, commonalities, and accomplishments are described. Finally, several conclusions are offered concerning the nature of revival in Romania under these three Baptist evangelists.

Concise Biographies of the Three Romanian Baptist Evangelists

Pitt Popovici

Pitt Popovici was born on September 12, 1918, in Harrisburg, Pennsylvania. Three years later, the family returned to Romania, hoping the economy

---

[5]Iosif Ton, *Confruntari* (*Confrontations*) (Oradea: Editura Artea Crestina, 2009) is currently the best assessment of all the confrontations between the Romanian church and the Communists. See also Mitrofan, *Pigmei si Uriasi*, 55–96. There are more church histories being written at this time; in the future we will have more data about the work of the church.

had improved. At the age of twelve, Popovici gave his life to Christ and was punished by his school's Orthodox priest because he refused to make the sign of the cross. When he was nineteen years old, he started theological studies. During his theological studies at the Baptist Theological Seminary in Bucharest, he served as an evangelist in various parts of the country. During WWII, from February 1940 until May 1945, Popovici served in the Romanian Army because military service was required for every young man. He then worked as the pastor of Dragostea (Love) Baptist Church in Arad and became the editor of *The Baptist Beacon*. The church increased its membership threefold during this time.

On October 24, 1945, Popovici married Hortensia Cristea, and they were blessed with three daughters. Seven years later, he became the pastor of the First Baptist Church of Timisoara. In 1954, the Communist government pressured the Baptist churches to follow their rules, which would devastate local churches.[6] The Timisoara Baptist community, led by Popovici, boldly wrote a memorandum declaring that they did not accept the regulations. On November 15, 1959, Pastor Popovici was told that he would lose his preaching license unless he agreed. When he again refused, he was forbidden to preach or work as a pastor anywhere in the country. This was regarded as major turning point because a Baptist community refused to follow the laws of the Department of Cults and willingly suffered the consequences.

After five years of constant battles with the Communist regime that refused to restore him to the pastor's office, Popovici applied for an American visa. Meanwhile, in the fall of 1965, he was again recognized as pastor and served at the First Baptist Church of Timisoara until departing for the USA in September 1967. During his years at the church, membership grew from 172 to over 500 people. When Popovici arrived in the United States, he started broadcasting via the shortwave radio channel HCJB Quito, wrote several books, and started several churches on the West Coast and in the Atlanta

---

[6] The rules imposed on the churches include: Churches were limited to a single worship service on Sunday, which prohibited them having their usual two services, one in the morning and one in the evening. They were prohibited from having young people attend the Sunday morning Bible hour. They were prohibited from having various musical groups such as a band. Licensed pastors were prohibited from going to other churches.

area.⁷

Ioan Ciobota introduced Popovici to his radio audience on May 31, 2010, with the following statement, "In the days of his youth he committed his life to God and entered with all his energy in the work of evangelism. During the time of communism, he has been forced to leave Romania. He translated seven books and wrote twenty-seven. He preached the gospel through six radio stations worldwide and many have been touched and converted through the sermons of this man. He is of small stature but tall in the eyes of God and lives according to his will."⁸ Pitt Popovici currently resides in Atlanta and is looking forward to either celebrating his ninety-seventh birthday or going to be with the Lord. He heads an organization that supports evangelists/missionaries in what he calls the "forgotten" villages of Romania.

Liviu Olah

Liviu Olah was born on May 1934 in Oradea. In 1947, at the age of thirteen, he received Christ in his heart and committed his life to serving Him. He studied law and passed his bar exam in 1956. When asked why he studied law, he answered that his Christian brothers and sisters needed a defender in the Communist courts. That same year he entered the Baptist Theological Seminary in Bucharest, but was not allowed to complete his final year due to governmental pressures. Although Olah did not complete his seminary studies, Pitt Popovici called him to help at the First Baptist Church of Timisoara. On September 10, 1960, Olah married Eugenia Lupescu from the Timisoara church and they were blessed with one daughter. In 1968, after Popovici left for the United States, Olah was ordained as pastor at the First Baptist Church of Timisoara. The church grew by ninety people in a short time, and the authorities revoked his preacher's license. For close to three years, he supported his family by doing odd jobs.

---

⁷ Pitt Popovici is regarded as the patriarch of Romanian Baptist evangelists. The data presented here has been gathered from various articles and blogs on the internet or from direct conversations with him. The sources include: http://petrupopovici.com/; https://amintiricusfinti.wordpress.com/2009/02/15/petru-popovici-12/#more-344; https://dezvaluiri.wordpress.com/petru-popovici/; http://www.resursecrestine.ro/editoriale/59106/interviu-cu-petru-popovici; "A personal letter from Pitt Popovici," accessed October 15, 2015, https://cronicasezonovilor.wordpress.com/2013/10/12/autorul-alexa-popovici-in-istoria-baptistilor-1.

⁸ Ioan Ciobota interviewed Pitt Popovici on the radio in Australia. See "Interviu cu Petru Popovici," last accessed October 15, 2015, http://www.resursecrestine.ro/editoriale/59106/interviu-cu-petru-popovici.

In 1972, Olah was called to pastor the Emanuel Baptist Church of Oradea. Many regard 1973 as the year of the greatest spiritual awakening (or revival) in Romania. The Emanuel Church grew by hundreds, and Olah baptized over two thousand people in three years. The single largest baptism was for 149 people, but numbers regularly reached between fifty and eighty. People came from different parts of the country to hear him speak and churches were packed hours before he started preaching. His preaching license was revoked again in 1975 on the evening before he planned to baptize believers at a nearby river. After that, he returned for a short time to Timisoara. For three years, he preached without a pastor's license in the Baptist Church of Bujac, Arad. After constant threats and persecution, as well as numerous barriers placed on him and his family, Olah decided to immigrate to the United States in 1978. He served as pastor in Detroit and Los Angeles until he went to be with the Lord on July 4, 2008.[9]

Iosif Ton

Iosif Ton was born in 1934, the same year as Liviu Olah. Ton received Christ in March 1951 and was baptized at the First Baptist Church of Cluj on June 27, 1951. He graduated in 1955 from Cluj University with a degree in Romanian literature. He started seminary that same year, but during his studies, he became an atheist. Those were Ton's "wilderness years," in which he lived a worldly life and was an informer for four or five years. During this

---

[9]As yet, we do not have any official biography on Liviu Olah or a work on the revival that took place in Oradea. In the absence of these publications, we have hundreds—if not thousands—of testimonies about people who have been converted or who have attended evangelistic meetings where Liviu Olah preached. The testimonies are found at "Liviu Olah—'Jarul dragostei mântuitoare,'" last accessed on October 15, 2015, https://amintiricusfinti.wordpress.com/2013/03/04/liviu-olah-%E2%80%91-jarul-dragostei-mantuitoare and "Liviu Olah—marturia lui Paul Ghitea," last accessed on October 15, 2015, http://barzilaiendan.com/2008/07/17/liviu-olah-marturia-lui-paul-ghitea. Recently, Daniel Mitrafon published a book entitled *Pasi* (*Steps*) in which he has a summation of Olah's work with a well-known sermon entitled, "The Secret of the Jerusalem Church Success" in which Olah enumerates the principles that the church must follow in order to have the same spiritual vitality as the Jerusalem Church. These principles are: (1) holy living, (2) love, (3) unity, (4) being well-spoken, (5) walking with Jesus, (6) prayer, and (7) praising the Lord. The longest section of this sermon is spent on prayer. In a most recent correspondence with Mrs. Liviu Olah, I found that during his life Liviu Olah wrote a single book, *On Prayer*, and that she has published some of his sermons in a book.

time, he was a professor and a translator for tourists. Ton married his childhood sweetheart, Elizabeta Cosman, and God blessed them with a daughter. Ton came back to the Cluj Church in 1968 where he asked for forgiveness and was reintegrated into the church. The following year, he went to Oxford, England to complete his theological studies. He returned to Romania in 1972 and became a professor at the Baptist Seminary and the pastor of the Baptist Church in Ploiesti.

In the early seventies, Ton and other Baptist pastors wrote papers arguing against the Communist regime, highlighting all the practices that were used against the church with the intent of destroying them. In addition, Ton described the shortcomings of the Communist's concept of the "new man," which Ton argued could only be developed by Christ through new birth. In 1977, he became the pastor of Emanuel Oradea and stayed there until 1982 when he was forced to leave Romania. When he came to Oradea, he announced that his gift was teaching, not evangelism. The church prayed fervently for him to receive the gift of evangelism so he could continue the work that Liviu Olah started. Upon his exile in 1982, Ton became the president of the Romania Missionary Society (RMS). The RMS is an organization that does radio broadcasting over the BBC's Trans World Radio, translates a complete theological curriculum for the underground seminary, helps with orphans and the needy, and publishes many theological books. In 1990, he returned to Romania and founded Emmanuel Christian University, radio stations, and publishing houses. In 1996, he left Emmanuel and committed himself to a preaching and teaching ministry for the rest of his life. Ton is currently eighty-one years old and resides with his wife near Portland, Oregon.[10]

---

[10] The information about the life of Iosif Ton (Americanized as Joseph Tson) can be found in an unpublished manuscript entitled "My Life," about his life until the point he was forced out of Romania. When the Romanian communist government fell in December 1989, all the Secret Police files were opened. As a result of this event, Ton has written *Marturia complete a preotului Iosif Ton* (*The complete confession of Pastor Iosif Ton*) which was broadcast by BBC (https://dezvaluiri.wordpress.com/1–marturia-lui-iosif-tson). This was followed by a BBC interview which was published as "Pastorul Ton admite că a colaborat cu Securitatea," last accessed on October 15, 2015, http://www.bbc.co.uk/romanian/news/story/2007/10/071016_pastor_marturie.shtml. In his book *Confrontations*, we have Ton's detailed presentation of his confrontations with the Communist government until he was exiled. Since then, he has written books of sermons, history, and theology issues.

Romanian Baptist Methods, Characteristics, Commonalities, and Accomplishments

The High Calling of the Evangelist/Revivalist

The conversion of these three men was monumental in their lives. They converted in their early teen years and were aware of the high calling for ministry that God placed on their lives. Not only were they aware of that high calling, but God immediately took them through times of suffering. Each of them experienced countless hours with the Department of Cults and various agents of the Secret Police. In fact, each of them had special agents assigned to watch them twenty-four hours a day. Each one of them was confronted with the pivotal question: What is the worst thing that the Communists could do to me? They were willing to suffer ridicule, they were willing to have their preaching licenses revoked, they were willing to be questioned and tortured by the police, and they were willing to let their wives and children be partners in their suffering because they felt that God called them to be evangelists. They were willing to face death for the sake of Christ and His gospel.

Men of deep, Consistent, and Persuasive Prayer

Upon arriving at his first church in Arad, Popovici organized a prayer group. From within, he encountered a church that had been dallying with sin for many years and was struggling to move past it. From without, there was so much persecution that few people came to hear the gospel. However, an open confession by the church's members opened the floodgates of blessing.

During the time that he was waiting to be licensed, Olah prayed three to four hours every day for God to open Romania to the Word of God. When he arrived at the church of Oradea, he organized all the people—from children to church leaders—into groups for active systematic prayer.

Ton surrounded himself with pastors who spent hours each day for many years praying for specific things. Each piece of writing that was smuggled out of the country in the 1970's was bathed in prayer as it was written, as it waited for a person to take it out of the country, and as church members faced the results of the persecution that followed from its distribution.

Calling the Church to Holy Living by Pointing out the Sins that Enslaved Them

While each one of the three evangelists called the church to a higher standard, Olah was the most specific on this point. He pointed out sins that had become a regular part of society—especially stealing and drinking. People could not imagine living in a Communist society without stealing. They justified this sin because the Communist regime took their lands and their factories. They felt that they were simply reclaiming what was theirs. Many people in the church behaved exactly like those in the world. Yet in this climate, Olah had the church members sign a pledge that they would no longer steal. Once they did that, they had to pledge that they would abstain from alcoholic beverages. Oradea was in an area that had famous vineyards, but alcoholism had become a problem. Some church members wrote that once they made that commitment and confessed their sinfulness, the outpouring of the Holy Spirit started. [11]

A Sense of Union between These Men and the Holy Spirit
Popovici, Olah, and Ton would preach sermons that lasted close to one hour. They knew the scriptures from memory and were good orators. Iosif, who followed Liviu at Oradea, described him in these words:

> For those who did not live through the wonder of Oradea let me describe how Liviu preached. He would come to the pulpit and start simply with a certain topical discussion. After this regular beginning, one felt as though a sound of a storm was coming and one felt the presence and the power of God. Liviu's voice was changed suddenly and the voice that one heard was passionate and deep. One would not hear what the man was saying, but felt that they were in the presence of God and that now they had an encounter with God and that God was speaking directly to them. Something like this I have never witnessed by any pastor in the world. [12]

Immediate and Long Range Results
The immediate results of the three evangelists' work were evident in the groups of unconverted people who came in large throngs to the churches to hear their sermons. It was not uncommon for people to travel great distances

---

[11] Sammy Tippit, *God's Instrument in Revival*, last accessed October 15, 2015, http://www.heartcrysa.com/God's%20Instrument%20in%20Revival%20-%20Tippit.pdf

[12] Ton, *My Story*, 62. See the testimony of Iosif Ton about Liviu Olah in *Jarul dragostei mintuitoare*, found at Liviu Olah - "Jarul Dragostei mântuitoare," last accessed October 15, 2015, https://amintiricusfinti.wordpress.com/2013/03/04/liviu-olah-%E2%80%91-jarul-dragostei-mantuitoare.

to hear them preach. Many who came declared they were drawn by the Holy Spirit and went back to their homes converted and ready to serve the Lord. The size of churches grew, and new people aspired to leadership roles in the church. This result was totally unexpected by the Communists who expected Christianity to wither and disappear, yet it grew stronger before their own eyes. Popovici alone preached in 238 of Romania's churches as he crisscrossed the country. Since being forced out of Romania in 1967, he has preached in 102 churches in other nations.

The Importance of Music in Their Ministry
All three evangelists emphasized the importance of music in their churches. Whenever they traveled for evangelism, choirs and musical groups traveled with them. The music early in the service prepared people for the sermon, whereas the music after the sermon prepared thousands to accept the gift of salvation.

A Passion for Jesus
Each of the revivalists evidenced their love for Jesus and their fervent desire to make Him known to as many people as possible. They would talk freely about their love for Jesus, almost as the mystics before them had for centuries voiced their love for Jesus Christ.

A Vision for Their Country
What distinguishes a pastor from an evangelist or a revivalist is the range of their vision. When one talked with Popovici, Olah, or Ton, the conversation quickly changed from the local evangelism to their vision for the conversion of the whole country. Even while under the pressure of Communist restrictions, these three men envisioned that a time would come when they would preach from stadiums and Romania would have Christian radio stations and Christian schools.

Professional Background and Preaching Style
One could listen to Popovici as to a beloved brother who had something of eternal value to say to you. He was always amazed that in spite of his lack of superior education, God was using even him in such great ways. Olah was a meticulous lawyer who made sure that you were aware of every vestige of resistance to God in your life or that you saw new segments of God's glory.

Ton, as a professor of Romanian language and literature, demonstrated the beauty of the Romanian language by articulating theology clearly.

Adjusted to Life Outside of the Home Country

The thirty years that Olah spent in the United States never compared to the Himalayan heights reached during the Oradea Revival. He was the associate pastor and the senior pastor of various Romanian Baptist Churches in the United States. He was invited to speak at American churches and conventions, but he felt that the intensity of the revival that he experienced in Romania was seasonal and unrepeated. In contrast, Popovici's forty-eight years in the United States superseded his activity in Romania. He started twenty-three churches, either by himself or with others, broadcast on nine radio stations, and went on nineteen missionary trips. Even in his late nineties, he financially sponsors a group of evangelists in difficult areas of Romania. The only one who seems to have had an equal impact in both Romania and the Western world is Iosif Ton. He is presently celebrating his eighty-first birthday. As the head of the Romanian Missions Society, he spoke in some of the largest churches in the Western world, raised millions of dollars for radio broadcasts and book publications, wrote books that are being used in seminary classrooms, and was involved in underground seminary education. He also regularly speaks in Romania in churches, at retreats and pastors' meetings, and at contemporary Romanian cultural and religious events.

The Oradea Revival (1973–1975): The Epicenter of Romanian Revivals

There is a need for a book to be written devoted entirely to the Oradea Revival of 1973–1975. Romanian Baptists had revivals before Oradea and after it, but nothing compares with it. It is one of the few Romanian revivals that did not move in a charismatic direction. Olah was anti-charismatic and preached against glossolalia. [13] The effectiveness of all these in Romanian evangelists is evident. This revival had the greatest impact of any revival in Romanian Baptist history.

Conclusion

While studying spiritual revivals and looking specifically at the spiritual awakening in Romania, I came to several conclusions. First, that they were

---

[13] Daniel Mitrofan. *Pasi,* 129.

seasonal and regional. They were seasonal because of the intensity of the work of God. They were regional because they could not be exported to different parts of the country. The Romanian spiritual awakening impacted the whole country, but its center was the area of Timisoara, Oradea, and Arad. I believe that God used Pitt Popovici to create unthinkable resistance against the government that God used Liviu Olah in the midst of the revival, when seemingly impossible things were happening, and that God used Iosif Ton to bring to maturity the thousands converted in the revival. By the time that Ton was forced out of Romania, the revival had come to an end; God accomplished his work for that moment. The work can now continue, even without the people he once used.

The fruits of that revival continue. New leaders who came to Christ during the revival and were mentored or influenced by Popovici, Olah, or Ton came to the forefront during the following generation. The Communist government fell, and Christians became involved in politics and government. Christians built colleges, orphanages, and new churches while they waited for another outpouring of the Holy Spirit.

In the United States between 1720 and 1760, a new passion for God spread across the nation. Theodore Frelinghuysen, George Whitefield, and Jonathan Edwards led the Great Revival through their passionate sermons, concern for the eternal fate of their audiences, and willingness to sacrifice to further the gospel of the Lord. Pitt Popovici, Liviu Olah, and Josif Ton carried this godly tradition into twentieth-century Romania, and the work they did for the revival of their nation continues to have an effect on the believers of today.

Part 3

The Majority World

21

New Zealand Baptists and the Cultural Restraint of Revival

Martin Sutherland

Revivals, as David Bebbington has reminded us, have been a bit of a puzzle for historians. Too often we have lapsed into cynical contextual analysis, if only to avoid the uncritical triumphalism of insider versions of events. These are often, we suspect (cynically perhaps), marred by inflated estimates and resort too easily to supernaturalist explanations. The solution, as Bebbington characteristically suggests, is to do some actual history—to take seriously real events, in real places, in real time, involving real people. As it always does, this micro-history approach prevents us offering the too-frequent combinations of interpretation-driven data that sadly have bedeviled Christian history. His own series of local studies, embodied in his 2012 volume *Victorian Religious Revivals*[1] has enabled Bebbington to do what he does so well—moving seamlessly from analysis to modeling, from description to definition and differentiation.

Three of these contributions help us understand revival in the New Zealand context. They are worth summarizing.

First, Bebbington traces the development and suggests an evolution of "Patterns of Revival." This diachronic, macro-historical approach traces shifts in the dominant paradigm from the late seventeenth century to the twentieth century and successively identifies Presbyterian, Congregational, Methodist, Synthetic, and Modern patterns. In broad terms the movement starts with local, clergy-defined events, but culminates in the late-nineteenth-century "Modern" style, characterized by an increasingly urban focus, increasingly led by professional revivalists like Dwight Moody, and ultimately attaining massive reach in the long ministry of Billy Graham.

---

[1] David Bebbington, *Victorian Religious Revivals: Culture and Piety in Local and Global Contexts* (Oxford: Oxford University Press, 2012).

Second, we are called to recognize that "revivals have taken a variety of forms, spontaneous or planned, small scale or vast." Synchronic studies of local cases suggest that a crude grid can be constructed which portrays this diversity.

    A.   Planned and Large Scale
    B.   Planned and Small Scale
    C.   Spontaneous and Large Scale
    D.   Spontaneouos and Small Scale

Third, as well as different types of revival and various styles of revivalism, there is also a continuous evolution in approaches to the study and interpretation of revivals. Bebbington calls historians beyond the rather tired categories of religion and society, to the more dynamic realms of culture and piety. Each of these three elements in the Bebbington interpretation of revivals provides an instructive lens on the history of Baptists and revival in New Zealand.

Revivalisms

The significance of the historical evolution of approaches to revival is of obvious importance in understanding the New Zealand context. New Zealand was the scene of the last major British colonizing transfer of large numbers of people. Mass immigration did not commence until the 1840s and reached its first peaks in the 1870s. Thus, New Zealand was being colonized at the same time as the so-called Modern style of revivalism was coming to prominence. The earlier patterns, which flourished or had significant influence in Britain, the United States, and Canada and even in Australia (which was settled a full generation or two earlier), had little impact in this furthest outpost.

Baptists were among these shifting Victorian communities. Although there were one or two desultory efforts at organized emigration, Baptists largely "washed up" in family groups on New Zealand shores. Anglicans, Methodists, Presbyterians, and Catholics had well-established structures and denominational identities decades before the formation of the New Zealand Baptist Union in 1882.

Although largely from England, the new settlers brought with them few of the longstanding tensions within English Baptist life. Indeed, there are signs of a deliberate shedding of those assumptions, especially the Particular/General–Calvinist/Arminian divide. They most definitely were, however, missionary Baptists. There is no shyness about evangelism or mission. A New Zealand Baptist Missionary Society was set up—arguably too soon—within three years of the formation of the fledgling and already struggling Baptist

Union. The Canterbury Association, which predated the Union, was begun specifically to support evangelism; early criticism of the colony-wide Union was that it was failing on exactly that front.²

In terms of revival patterns, New Zealand Baptists clearly embraced the Modern style. Moody's activities were reported—regularly and consistently favorably—in the pages of the *N.Z. Baptist*. In an address to the Union Conference of 1884 (its third national conference), Rev. James Gilmore called for dedicated evangelists and deeper commitment to reaching the lost. However, it was clear that some methods were to be favored above others.

> Enthusiasm is always necessary and wherever seen is always beautiful: would that the Churches had more of it! Unfortunately, the thought in the minds of many is that there cannot be enthusiasm without excitement or sensationalism. Never was a greater mistake. Who has shown greater enthusiasm in the great work of preaching the Gospel than D. L. Moody? And let us listen to his own words after his recent mission in London, a mission which has been by far the most successful of any in which the great evangelist has been engaged. He says, 'I am never excited in my most exciting meetings. I can sleep like a top within three minutes of going into a meeting, and I can be sound asleep three minutes after leaving it. If I were to get into such a state of nervous excitement as General Booth, for instance, gets into when he addresses large meetings, I should have been dead long ago.... There is nothing in my work approaching to the exhaustion, nervous and physical, which the operations of the Booth family involve.'³

New Zealand Baptists sought a place at the main table of religious life. Many were wearied of the marginalized status they had endured in England. They made much, for instance, of their stability and the substantial nature of their church buildings. It was essential, on the other hand, that any hint of a reputation as wild-eyed fanatics be avoided. In general, as the quoted passage implies, New Zealand Baptists were suspicious of the Salvation Army. One of the revivals, at the southern settlement of Owaka, in 1880, thus presented problems, as it had been initiated by the preaching of two young Salvation Army women. Moody, on the other hand, fitted the need for respectability

---

² Martin Sutherland, *Conflict and Connection: Baptist Identity in New Zealand* (Auckland: Archer Press, 2011) 19–32.

³ *N.Z. Baptist*, November 1884, 167.

nicely. A month after Gilmore's address, Rev. W. C. Spencer reported favorably on the success of Moody's mission in San Francisco. The measure? Churches were revived and their debts paid off! You can't get more respectable than that.[4]

Moody's "Modern" approach was also attractive in more positive and compelling terms. It seemed to offer a successful method. In a postscript to his 1884 address, Gilmore made his admiration of modern methods even clearer:

> May I say that there is an intelligence department in the service of the Lord Jesus, and that it is the duty of every Christian worker to enter this branch of the service, to so study human nature, that we may better understand how to deal with each and every case. Read how Christ dealt with individual cases and you will see at once that He always shaped His treatment according to the peculiarities or exigencies of the case. See the marvelous wisdom Paul displayed at Athens: what a clear insight into human nature he displayed before King Agrippa. Anyone who has heard D. L. Moody must have been struck with his wonderful insight into human nature, the quickness with which he grasps the situation, and suits his subject. And is the same Spirit who actuated Paul, who actuates and guides D. L. Moody, not ours as well?[5]

Jesus, Paul, Moody—almost equal exemplars. Moody, indeed, attained a status second only to Charles Spurgeon in the popular New Zealand Baptist mind. A meeting between the two men in 1884 is reverently reported in the denominational newspaper as akin to a crown being passed to a successor.[6] This was of direct importance to New Zealand Baptists, as they were already claiming Charles's son, Thomas Spurgeon, as their own, due to his immensely successful ministry in Auckland. It was clearly of great importance to maintain that link. At the 1889 conference, Thomas Spurgeon, having resigned the pastorate in Auckland, was appointed Union Mission Preacher— a role clearly modeled on Moody. Spurgeon junior finally left New Zealand in 1893, after only mediocre success as Mission Preacher. Nonetheless, New Zealand Baptists were delighted to read his report that on his passing through Chicago in 1893 "Mr Moody took me under his kindly wing, and gave me opportunity of

---

[4] *N.Z. Baptist*, December 1884, 188.
[5] *N.Z. Baptist*, November 1884, 169.
[6] *N.Z. Baptist*, October 1884, 146.

speaking for Jesus."⁷ In the early 1890s there was even hope that Moody might conduct a mission in New Zealand.

From the outset, then, New Zealand Baptists were missionary minded, open to respectable modern methods, and willing to commit resources. As the decades unfolded, they participated enthusiastically in the mission of R. A. Torrey and C. M. Alexander in 1902, they embraced the revivalism of Joseph Kemp in the 1920s and 1930s and they were active participants in Billy Graham's visits, the Trans-Pacific Crusade in the 1960s, Tom Skinner in the 1970s and Luis Palau in the 1980s.

Yet, for all the enthusiasm for revivalism among New Zealand Baptists, there was a startling absence of revival to show for it.

Types of Revival

In his influential overview of religious history in Australasia till 1930, Hugh Jackson devoted a major chapter to revivalism. Jackson's study is especially helpful as it gives equal attention to pietist movements such as Keswick, and Roman Catholic missions along with conversionist movements such as those of Moody and Torrey. Jackson shows that the broader church world in Australasia displayed an interest in revivalist activity and methods at least equivalent to that of New Zealand Baptists. Yet, despite this, "there was no general revival." Indeed "there was never anything remotely comparable to the First and Second Great Awakenings in America which helped shape a culture and a society."⁸ Instead, there were pockets of awakening—local revivals such as that among Cornish miners in Moonta, South Australia, in 1875, to which David Bebbington also devotes a chapter.⁹ The closest to successful revivalism in New Zealand was the ministry of the Open Brethren preacher Gordon Forlong in Rangitikei in the 1880s. Crucially, in both Australia and New Zealand, revival success was essentially rural. Indeed, the efforts of "modern" revivalists achieved little in the towns.¹⁰

New Zealand, in an even more marked fashion than Australia, has been

---

⁷ *N.Z. Baptist*, September 1893, 138.

⁸ H. R. Jackson, *Churches and People in Australia and New Zealand, 1860–1930* (Wellington: Allen and Unwin, 1987) 49.

⁹ Jackson, *Churches and People*, 54–57, and Bebbington, *Victorian Religious Revivals*, 193–228.

¹⁰ Jackson, *Churches and People*, 58.

no hotbed of revival. Yet neither has it been devoid of them. Four useful examples can be plotted using the coordinates of David Bebbington's revival landscape

A. Planned and Large Scale: Billy Graham, 1959
B. Planned and Small Scale: Owaka timber workers, 1880s
C. Spontaneous and Large Scale: Maori Conversions, 1830s and 1840s; Charismatic Renewal 1970s & 1980s
D. Spontaneous and Small Scale

Other cases might be cited but these four are indicative of the history (or lack of history) of revival in New Zealand. It will be noted immediately that there is no exemplar for Type D: Spontaneous and Small Scale revival. Definitions and categories are a problem here. There are, of course, numerous instances of congregational growth and successful ministries. However, it is an intriguing aspect of the New Zealand story that such outbreaks, relatively common in such places as the American frontier, are effectively absent.

It is worth briefly considering the key features of each of the four exemplars chosen, this time in chronological order, especially noting the degree of Baptist involvement.

The conversion of Maori in the 1830s and 1840s has many of the hallmarks of a classic people movement. After twenty years of little apparent impact, the gospel seeds sown by Anglican, Methodist, and Catholic missions took hold from the mid-1830s. Rapid and widespread conversions, often facilitated by Maori evangelists, followed. The surge was halted by the rising tide of colonization and disputes with the British crown and settlers over land. Much Maori religious energy was diverted into indigenized versions of Judaeo-Christianity. Baptists came late to Maori mission. The one organized attempt to establish a work faltered after three years.[11]

Local Baptists, who had a strong tradition of evangelism, welcomed the small-scale revival in South Otago, in the timber camps of Owaka in 1880. Interestingly, however, the ministry of "two Salvation Army lasses," who had been invited by Baptist leaders to share the gospel, triggered the response. The revival was short-lived and ultimately faded as the working teams dispersed. Nevertheless, it provided enough impetus to enable a Baptist church to be established in 1887.

---

[11] R. F. Keam, *Dissolving Dream: The Improbable story of the First Baptist Maori Mission* (Auckland: n.p.: 2004).

The only true example of large-scale, planned revival along "modern" lines was the 1959 mission of Billy Graham, which also included Australia. Approximately a quarter of the New Zealand population heard Graham's message and upwards of 17,000 decisions were made for Christ. As was expected in these campaigns, the backing was ecumenical. Baptists played an active part and shared proportionately in the fruits of Graham's visit.[12]

The charismatic renewal of the 1970s and 1980s was a profound movement in New Zealand church life. Although arguably it led to few genuine new converts, it firmly qualifies at the revivifying end of revival. In New Zealand, it was remarkable for its spread across all denominational groups. Baptists were particularly affected. So much so, indeed, that the denomination can be characterized today as largely charismatic in style.

These exemplars are indicative of the peculiarities of Baptist experience of revival in New Zealand. Moreover, they are also reflective of the innermost dynamics of revival itself. With no part in Maori conversion and only the single local instance to cite, New Zealand Baptists have little to show on the revival ledger before World War II. This is in marked contrast to the Open Brethren, another sect-like group that might be expected to have displayed a similar pattern to the Baptists. As Jackson noted and Peter Lineham has extensively documented, the Brethren were at the center of several revival-like outbreaks. Associated with the preaching of men such as Gordon Forlong, C. H. Hinman, and E. Moyes, revivals can be identified in a number of places during the 1880s. Lineham notes that "by 1883 revivals were affecting districts up and down the west coast of the North Island...and it was [Brethren] assembly evangelists who were the preachers."[13] Other locations can be added: inland Taranaki, the remote east coast of the North Island, together with the Nelson district and South Canterbury in the South Island.[14]

There is no Baptist equivalent to this Brethren success. Indeed, the Open Brethren example represents a compelling comparison with the New Zealand Baptist experience of revival. The first point to note is the style of revivalism

---

[12] See B. Gilling, "Mass Evangelism in Mid Twentieth Century New Zealand" in *"Rescue the Perishing": Comparative Perspectives on Evangelism and Revivalism*, Waikato Studies in Religion 1, ed. Douglas Pratt (Auckland: College Communications, 1989) 43.

[13] Peter Lineham, *There We Found Brethren: A History of Assemblies of Brethren in New Zealand* (Palmerston North: G.P.H. Society, 1977) 62.

[14] Lineham, *There We Found Brethren*, 67–76.

that characterized the Brethren efforts. Forlong and others were decidedly not in the "modern" style that prominent Baptists had embraced. Their approach was closer to the Baptist adaptation of the "congregational" model, with elements of the "Methodist" approach.[15] It was this amalgam of more basic styles that gained success in the new colony.

This point is further emphasized when the geographic locations of the Brethren revival successes are considered. North Island west and east coasts, Nelson districts, South Canterbury, North Canterbury are all rural areas and all areas in which Baptists were barely represented. In New Zealand the Open Brethren were largely a rural movement. Baptists, by contrast, clustered in the towns. This more urban-like (although the term is barely valid for colonial New Zealand) focus makes sense of the embrace of "modern" revivalist methods. After all, it was in the cities that Moody and his contemporaries had their startling successes. However, Dunedin, Christchurch, Wellington, and Auckland were a far cry from London and New York. In this we reach a crucial element in the story of Baptists and revival, and revival in general in New Zealand. Outside the defined pockets of small rural communities, the essential conditions for revival did not exist until well into the twentieth century.

The Cultural Restraint of Revival

In his study of Victorian revivals, David Bebbington considers in depth a series of case studies. These studies from the Anglo worlds of Britain, the Americas, and Australia enable Bebbington to illustrate at once both the "local and global contexts" signaled in the subtitle of his book. In defending this microhistory approach to revivals, Bebbington counters the usual concerns about narrow studies being employed, however cautiously, for wider interpretation. In particular, parochial details—especially in source-rich Victorian cases—might overwhelm the wider narrative. "The local may eclipse the general."[16] Bebbington counters this with the number and variety of his examples. In any event, the local cases are illustrative, rather than generative of interpretative models.

The fundamental importance of this should not be missed. Local studies are significant, but not merely for detailed evidence. In his concomitant call for the recognition of *culture* as a key dimension of revival Bebbington lays

---

[15] See Bebbington, *Victorian Religious Revivals*, 6–11.
[16] Bebbington, *Victorian Religious Revivals*, 44.

claim to another, deeply embedded, logic. In this logic, the local is not merely significant; it is essential.

The nexus between culture and its local expression is the community. Bebbington cites Michael McClymond's dictum that "a revival should be understood as a communal event." Thus

> The topography of the places where awakenings took place ought to be a subject for enquiry because settlement patterns, communications systems, and locations of churches helped determine the cultural ambience of religious stirrings there. Towns and villages shaped the attitudes of their residents. Questions about the gender, age, occupation, and ethnic distribution of the converts must be placed within that context.[17]

Culture, of course, has many layers, but this local context is especially important for understanding revival. It is also, potentially, just as essential to an understanding of a lack of revival. If, as Bebbington trenchantly concludes, "awakenings rooted themselves in popular culture,"[18] then local communities, and especially the shared nuances of local popular culture, become ineradicable constitutive elements in revival history. High culture of course will play a role too. It might set the notation system and probably define the lyrics, but the music of revival draws fundamentally on the rhythm of community and the melodies of popular culture. Global in significance it might be, but revival cannot be unwound from its local settings. This is of immense significance in the New Zealand story of revivalism, and in particular the experience of Baptists in that narrative.

New Zealand Baptists from the start had both the means and motive for revival. They embraced modern models and genuinely sought a new prominence in the colony. Only one thing seems missing: actual Baptist revivals. Despite all the efforts, all the willingness, all the energy, it cannot with any accuracy be said that Baptists experienced "conversions on a significant scale in a short period of time" before World War II. The claim is much stronger for later decades. Billy Graham in 1959 and the charismatic renewal in 1970s and 1980s were important enough. There was nothing especially Baptist about them, but then that is in the nature of modern revivals. The point must not be missed that, in the century before 1959, for Baptists the Promised Land

---

[17] Bebbington, *Victorian Religious Revivals*, 46.
[18] Bebbington, *Victorian Religious Revivals*, 47.

was largely dry. In order to explain this, we need to return to models and definitions, and to the specifics and exigencies of colonial New Zealand.

British settlement in New Zealand did not seriously get under way until the 1840s. The population of colonists grew only slowly, not reaching the point of exceeding the Maori population until the 1880s. Moreover, in a segmented country, divided naturally by mountain ranges, steep hills, and dense bush, with almost no roads in 1850, settlement happened in pockets. The colony was in fact several mini-colonies, adjoined only by coastal shipping, each developing their own unique hinterlands.

Such an environment presents obstacles to revival. Revivals are community events. In a new colony, community faces many challenges. For a start, there is the sheer variety of backgrounds. With few mono-cultural, transplanted settlements, there is often little of popular culture that is instantly shared with those among whom one finds oneself. (Beyond immediate family of course, but then men especially often lacked even that. As much as half the adult male population in New Zealand was unmarried in the decades before 1890.) Add to that the difficulties of communication and the transience of the single male population in particular, and you have a unique set of issues that present intriguing questions for the social and cultural historian.

How did New Zealand society operate? How was community formed? Popular understandings of New Zealand history have for a long time been dominated by the nationalist histories offered first by William Pember Reeves at the end of the nineteenth century and then by Keith Sinclair in the middle of the twentieth century. A more nuanced approach, however, has long been available and more influential among historians. Sinclair was an Auckland historian who sought a unified story of a nation, a story read in Auckland dimensions. His contemporaries W. J. Gardner and W. H. Oliver, by contrast, were regional scholars who saw different patterns. Recognizing the inherent realities of distance and communication, they presented a colony characterized not by national structures but rather as a collection of isolated and insulated local communities. These communities were overwhelmingly rural. The larger towns were much harder to analyze. What cohesion existed in the towns was understood to be based less on shared institutions and activities than on class.

Gardner defined a genre of mid-twentieth century (often centennial) regional histories with his 1956 *The Amuri: A County History*. The Amuri district is in North Canterbury in the South Island where, Gardner suggested, remote both from Nelson, its political centre, and Christchurch, its commercial centre, homogeneous in being given over entirely to a dozen or so great sheep runs, the Amuri developed...a strong sense of community.... The coming of small-farm settlers and the development of better communications have changed the face and character of the county, but much of the old sense of unity persists. Amuri people, as a whole, are aware of a distinctive history.[19]

In 1969, Oliver presented a New Zealand historiography that found cohesion and interdependence at this local level. Common membership of local institutions such as clubs, churches, schools, lodges, and bands enabled integration and community.[20] A picture of an almost Arcadian idyll emerges, an image of a colonial society akin to rural Shropshire. This vision of a transplanted bucolic echo of England is explicit as late as the 1980s. Thus, Dunedin historian Erik Olssen could offer this summary, in the 1981 *Oxford History of New Zealand*.

> Until the late 1930s almost half the population still lived in towns under eight thousand or in the country. Parochial loyalties survived, traditional patterns of deference proved resilient, and kin, sex and religion provided the bonds within communities. In general, country people shared the same aspirations, the same values, belonged to the same clubs, sent their children to the same schools, played the same games, and belonged to a church.[21]

Among historians this regional and local communities model continues to hold considerable sway. However, in a seminal article in 1982, social historian Miles Fairburn, then of Massey but later at Canterbury University, challenged the evidence for even this level of social cohesion. Colonial society, he argued, was marked by degrees of mobility and transience the significance of which had hitherto been unrecognized. Far from replicated English villages,

---

[19] W. J. Gardner, *The Amuri: A County History* (Culverden: Amuri County Council, 1956) xxiv.

[20] W. H. Oliver, *Towards a New History? 1969 Hocken Lecture* (Dunedin: Hocken Library, 1971).

[21] E. Olssen, "Towards a New Society" in *Oxford History of New Zealand*, ed. W. H. Oliver and B. R. Williams (Oxford: Clarendon Press, 1981) 256. The paragraph survives largely unchanged in the revised version of this chapter in the 1992 second edition. See also Rollo Arnold, *The Farthest Promised Land: English Villagers, New Zealand Immigrants of the 1870s* (Wellington: Victoria University Press, 1981).

it was thus far more likely the case that most colonists lived with only an attenuated form of social cohesion.

> There was not only a good chance that the individual would live remote from the junctions of social activity. There was also the strong probability that the effects of geographical mobility would socially isolate him. If remoteness made frequent face-to-face contact seem strange, mobility made the faces seem those of strangers. Transiency undermined horizontal bonding by creating anonymity and by dissolving or loosening associations if it had not inhibited or prohibited them in the first place.[22]

As one female colonist wrote in 1887:

> In the Colonies there is little but little of the *home* feeling so strong and prevalent *at home*—no attachment to place, locality, or friends as in England.... there are no associations or memories of that kind in the Colonies, therefore there is not the same check or restraint there.[23]

Crucially, popular culture was prevented from developing into local nuances and regional expressions as, in Fairburn's words, "the incessant interchange of population between places homogenized mores and rituals."[24] But homogenization was a form of reduction. The dominant ideology of the colonist, the attitude above all else that was commonly held, was that of the "fair go," the accordance of space to each, so that they might pursue their claim to self-reliance and material improvement. This could have a direct impact on religious attitudes. In a remarkable account of New Zealand published in 1883, John Bradshaw JP devotes a chapter to the nature of religious conviction in the emerging colony.

> The colonist is for the most part a man enjoying a large share of individuality.... His conceptions of religion are likely to be influenced by the general tenor of his life. His religious views will probably not be irretrievably wedded to a narrow groove of a particular school, and, although a member of a church, he is almost certain to be an advocate for religious equality.[25]

---

[22] M. Fairburn, "Local Community or Atomized Society: The Social Structure of Nineteenth Century New Zealand," *New Zealand Journal of History* 16, no. 2 (1982) 158. These arguments were later expanded in M. Fairburn, *The Ideal Society and Its Enemies: The Foundations of Modern New Zealand Society 1850–1900* (Auckland: Auckland University Press, 1989).

[23] "Hopeful" cited by Fairburn, "Local Community or Atomized Society?" 159.

[24] Fairburn, "Local Community or Atomized Society?" 160.

[25] J. Bradshaw JP, *New Zealand As It Is*, 2nd ed. (London: Sampson, Low, 1883) 314–15.

Although the observer would find the denominations and sects of Britain ostensibly replicated in the new colony, the claims of "party" were weakened.

> The natural independence of the colonists, their separation from the restraints of hereditary customs, their school-boy regard for individual merit rather than for a well-filled purse, and the freedom which is enjoyed by all sects alike, have tended to make them more liberal towards diverging opinions than would otherwise have been the case.[26]

All should be given space to make their religious choice, to have a "fair go." This might make New Zealand colonists all sound like Baptists, but it makes them poor fodder for revivals.

Religious historians have challenged Fairburn's proposals on a number of fronts no less than others who are keen to demonstrate the importance of "ties that bind." Nevertheless, it remains an agenda-setting analysis, as much of the social evidence in rural areas remains ambivalent at best. My own studies of Baptists, in two contrasting colonial settings, tend to support Fairburn's basic thesis that dislocation and transience were more powerful factors than connection or tradition.[27]

In the towns the emerging picture, though with different forms, is no less atomized. The towns could replicate structures quickly, but their working-class populations were highly mobile and they had to weather the successive blows of land war conflict, economic downturn, imperial wars, epidemic, depression, and war again, before the forces of cohesion finally gained traction in the 1950s. It would, however, be too simplistic to assume that, even then, whole-city cultural identities emerged. Earlier impressions of a "Dunedin culture" or a "Christchurch way" are likely mirages generated by and confined to intellectual and artistic elites. Although Wellington and Auckland became the bureaucratic and commercial powerhouses of the country as demographic shifts from country to town and from south to north took hold, it was not at this level that cultural solidification seems to have taken place. The relatively low population meant that cities sprawled rather than developed compact forms. As late as the 1970s Auckland was described as suburbs "tied together

---

[26] Bradshaw, *New Zealand As It Is*, 311.

[27] Martin Sutherland, "Cohesion and Conflict in 1880s Cambridge," *New Zealand Journal of Baptist Research*, 4 (October 1999): 3–21, and "Baptist Development in Colonial New Zealand," *New Zealand Journal of Baptist Research*, 9 (October 2004): 3–22.

by a sewerage system."[28] "Urban communities also created subcultures…'settlement clusters' of emigrants with varying degrees of geographical and social exclusivity."[29]

Baptists and Revival

To the extent that Fairburn's proposals for the colonial period are fair (and, clearly, they are at least partly right) then we may gain some at least partly right insight into New Zealand Baptists and their lack of revivals. Indeed, the four revivals I have identified fit a pattern remarkably well, either directly or as exceptions that at least support the rule.

To this day the one truly great revival or mass conversion in New Zealand's history is the rapid conversion of Maori. Not a Baptist was to be seen in this, of course, but it is the standout exception to the rather sparse revival landscape of colonial New Zealand. In cultural and community terms the link is obvious. Maori, unlike the colonists, did have cohesive local communities and a shared popular culture. Recent studies of Maori-led evangelization in this period show beyond question that these local elements were the essential conduits of the gospel.[30]

What about Owaka in 1880, the mini-revival in which Baptists gained from the efforts of the Salvation Army? Crucially, Owaka was, at this time, a timber-milling center. The revival did not take place among the few local farmers or shopkeepers; it was among the Bushmen and millers. There was, then, likely to be found enough of a genuine community among these men who, unusually for the colony at that time, were a concentration of people working at a common task. This was, in fact, typical of the small-scale revivals in New Zealand, many of which were among timber working gangs, often with a common ethnicity. Indeed, there may have been a positive attraction

---

[28] Cited by G. Dunstall. "The Social Pattern" in *Oxford History of New Zealand*, 2nd ed., ed. G. Rice (Auckland: Oxford University Press, 1992) 456.

[29] Melanie Nolan, "Constantly on the Move, but Going Nowhere? Work, Community and Social Mobility" in *New Oxford History of New Zealand*, 382.

[30] See especially the examinations of conversion in relation to culture in *Mana Maoriand Christianity*, ed. Hugh Morrison, Lachy Patterson, Brett Knowles, and Murray Rae (Wellington: Huia Publications, 2012). Vincent O'Malley, *The Meeting Place: Maori and Pakeha Encounters, 1642–1840* (Auckland, Auckland University Press, 2012). Tony Ballantyne, *Entanglements of Empire: Missionaries, Maori and the Question of the Body* (Durham NC: Duke University Press, 2014).

to religious revival as a means of preserving that ethnic identity. As Peter Lineham points out "it is no accident that one of the strongest revivals in New Zealand was among Danish settlers in the [lower North Island] Seventy mile bush."[31]

Before World War II, what revivals there were, were among uniquely defined groups in rural areas. Baptists barely figured in revival success in this period by virtue of the demographic reality that they were concentrated in the towns and cities. Predominantly merchants and small business owners, they could sustain few causes in rural areas. This put Baptists at a disadvantage in relation to revival. The nascent cities of colonial New Zealand were not the fertile seedbed for revival that Moody found in Victorian centers in Britain and the USA. If they did not come of age as culture vessels until the 1950s, then there is little surprise that genuine revival success would also have to wait until then, with first Billy Graham, and then, later, a very different, charismatic renewal.

Conclusion

New Zealand was a late colony. Scholars of older societies can miss the significance of the undercapitalized, poorly defined structures and infrastructures, which persisted in New Zealand well into the 1930s and in some senses, shape the country still. The deep-seated alienation and sense of dislocation that this created is a feature of the New Zealand psyche that emerges frequently in reflections on its art and literature. This characteristic has been noted even by those closest. The Australian novelist Patrick White, commenting in 1963 on New Zealander Janet Frame's first novel, *Owls Do Cry*, reflected:

> I find this book particularly interesting because of my own New Zealand cousins. Although they are intellectuals and have a different social level from the family in the book there is the same despair and confusion under the simple, uncomplicated New Zealand surface.[32]

---

[31] Peter Lineham, "When the Roll is Called up Yonder, Who'll Be There?: An Analysis of Nineteenth Century Trans-Atlantic Revivalism in New Zealand and Canada" in *"Rescue the Perishing": Comparative Perspectives on Evangelism and Revivalism*, Waikato Studies in Religion 1, ed. D. Pratt (Auckland: College Communications, 1989) 9.

[32] Patrick White to Ben Heubsch, 17 February 1963 in *Patrick White: Letters*, ed. D. Marr (Sydney: Random House, 1994) 218-219.

The twin motifs, sometimes interlocking, of the "man alone" and of a sterile, repressive "puritanism," are standards of New Zealand literature that seek to capture the cultural dislocation which the former colony has barely thrown off even today.[33] The effect of this alienation reaches beyond letters. The present study suggests that its impact extends to religious phenomena as well. New Zealand Baptists who translated themselves to this strange new land were naïve to imagine that genuine communities could be created merely by wishing them so. It takes time. It takes history. If revivals are truly communal affairs, then perhaps even revival must tarry.

---

[33] The best studies of the literary engagement with the peculiarities of the New Zealand experience are L. Jones, *Picking Up the Traces: The Making of a New Zealand Literary Culture, 1932–1945* (Wellington: Victoria University Press, 2003) and F. Pound, *The Invention of New Zealand: Art and National Identity, 1930–1970* (Auckland: Auckland University Press, 2009). See also J. Belich *Paradise Reforged: A History of the New Zealanders from the 1880s to the Year 2000* (Auckland: Allan Lane / Penguin Press, 2001) 325–90.

22

Joseph Kemp, Revivalism, and the New Zealand Baptist Movement

John Tucker

In his annual report for 1920, the secretary of the Baptist Union of New Zealand announced with excitement, "The Rev J. W. Kemp, whose remarkable ministry...is known to very many of us, has come to the Auckland Tabernacle, where it is expected his special gifts will not only exercise a great influence in Auckland, but will be felt throughout the whole Dominion."[1] The note of excitement was understandable. Joseph Kemp was an internationally renowned pastor and evangelist. His reputation was established at Charlotte Chapel in Edinburgh where, during two remarkable seasons of revival, hundreds were converted and what had been an empty chapel became the largest Baptist church in Scotland. Kemp's international profile was further extended through his very popular Bible correspondence school and his speaking ministry in Keswick circles and at Second Advent conferences in the United States, where he was known as "the Scottish Spurgeon."[2]

Given his reputation, Kemp was immediately drawn into denominational leadership. Between his arrival in New Zealand in 1920 and his death in 1933, he was a regular speaker on Baptist Assembly platforms and a prolific contributor to the *New Zealand Baptist* magazine. He played a pivotal role in the establishment of the Baptist Theological College, serving on its board until his death,[3] and he was president of the Baptist Union of New Zealand in 1929. Beyond denominational affairs, he established a number of significant institutions: the Bible Training Institute (now Laidlaw College), the *Reaper*

---

[1] *New Zealand Baptist Handbook, 1920–1921*, 13.

[2] Winnie Kemp, *Joseph W. Kemp: The Record of a Spirit-Filled Life* (London: Marshall, Morgan & Scott, 1936) 115.

[3] Martin Sutherland and Laurie Guy, *An Unfolding Story: A History of Carey Baptist College* (Auckland: Archer Press, 2014) 16–20.

magazine, and a Keswick-styled Easter convention at Ngaruawahia in the Waikato. In a very short space of time, Kemp welded together a national alliance of evangelicals in a way that few other people in this country have ever done. He was one of the most influential leaders within the New Zealand Baptist Union in the first half of the twentieth century, and, arguably, one of the more influential leaders of any denomination in this country's history.

In recent years, Kemp's ministry in New Zealand has attracted considerable attention.[4] The existing historiography tends to view Kemp's ministry primarily through the lens of fundamentalism. According to Martin Sutherland, for example, Kemp was "a principal figure in the introduction of fundamentalist concerns to New Zealand."[5] Jane Simpson claims that Kemp, "More than any other ordained minister…mediated theological concerns of a specifically fundamentalist nature to a small but significant proportion of conservative Protestants in New Zealand."[6] She goes so far as to argue that, in regards to New Zealand, "Kemp's main significance is as the prime interpreter of American fundamentalism."[7] Kemp certainly leaned strongly towards fundamentalism. Through his earlier American ministry he had encountered firsthand the "dangers" of modern biblical scholarship, or higher criticism, and he did bring those concerns with him to New Zealand. Kemp was, for example, the first minister in New Zealand to plan and host an identifiably fundamentalist campaign: the "Conference of Christian Fundamentals."[8] Speaking in the Auckland Town Hall on the "The Mysteries and Menace of Modernism,"

---

[4] See, for example, G. R. Pound, "Reverend J. W. Kemp and the Baptist Tabernacle" (MA thesis, University of Auckland, 1978); Jane M. R. Simpson, "Joseph W. Kemp and the Impact of American Fundamentalism in New Zealand" (BA hons. diss., University of Waikato, 1987); Jane Simpson, "Joseph W. Kemp: Prime Interpreter of American Fundamentalism in New Zealand in the 1920's" in 'Rescue the Perishing': Comparative Perspectives on Evangelism and Revivalism, ed. Douglas Pratt (Auckland: College Communications 1989) 23–42; Martin P. Sutherland, "Joseph Kemp and the Establishment of the New Zealand Baptist College, 1922–33," New Zealand Journal of Baptist Research 8 (2003): 32–51; Peter Lineham, "The Foundation of the Bible Training Institute," in Gospel, Truth and Interpretation: Evangelical Identity in Aotearoa New Zealand, ed. Tim Meadowcroft and Myk Habets (Auckland: Archer Press, 2011) 49–67.

[5] Martin Sutherland, "The Basis of Union: New Zealand Baptists Forge a Denomination in the 1940s," Journal of Religious History 27, no. 1 (2003): 67–82, 69.

[6] Simpson, "Joseph W. Kemp: Prime Interpreter," 24.

[7] Jane Simpson, "Kemp, Joseph William," Dictionary of New Zealand Biography, accessed February 26, 2015, http://www.TeAra.govt.nz/en/biographies/4k8/kemp-joseph-william.

[8] New Zealand Baptist (NZB) (February 1922) 25.

he portrayed modernism as a parasite which was feeding on the life of the church and if not stopped would destroy the life on which it was feeding:

> I charge Modernism with being a menace to the whole work of God. It has attacked our mission stations. It has destroyed faith in the miraculous. It has banished God from the world. It denies worship to Christ. It has smitten the pulpit with the paralysis of unbelief. The churches have withered under its influence. It has lowered the standard of ethics. It has robbed us of our Bible. It has taken away my Lord and I know not where they have laid Him.[9]

Kemp's fear of liberalism in theology was matched by his concern about immorality in society. On his arrival in New Zealand he declared, "We are living in a world of change…We have now a new standard of morality. Men find it easier to sin now than formerly. The air seems to be filled with a strange and subtle incitement to impurity. Ghastly perils are threatening our young people."[10] The remedy, according to Kemp, was for the people of God to come out from the world and to be separate. Dancing, drinking, and gambling were "things of the world," which must be shunned.[11]

Kemp's Theology of Revival

In his attitudes to theology and culture, therefore, Kemp might be characterized as a fundamentalist. But the contention of this essay is that fundamentalism does not provide an adequate framework for understanding Kemp's ministry and influence within New Zealand and especially among Baptists in New Zealand. Kemp's ministry also needs to be seen through the lens of revivalism. At heart, Kemp was a revivalist. His primary objective, his guiding vision, was revival. Through his education at the Glasgow Bible Training Institute, a school which arose out of a Moody-Sankey mission and which was modeled on the Moody Bible Institute in Chicago, he had received a firm grounding in the transatlantic revival tradition of D. L. Moody. Through his personal experience of revival, both in Wales and then in his church in Edinburgh, he developed an insatiable appetite to see a similar movement of God

---

[9] *Reaper*, April 1929, 27–29.
[10] *NZB* (October 1920) 148.
[11] Pound, "Reverend J.W. Kemp," 41–46.

in each of the churches he later pastored.[12] And through his subsequent ministry in the United States he developed strong connections with some of the leading trans-Atlantic revivalists of his day and imbibed many of their convictions and emphases.[13] Charles Finney and his lectures on revival particularly influenced Kemp.[14] While he believed that revival was "a divinely spontaneous thing"[15] that could not be worked up, Kemp also came to believe that there were "divine laws" that controlled revival movements.[16] Obey those laws, Kemp told Baptists in New Zealand, and you can expect God to grant revival.

In an important article on the subject he argued that, besides the renewing work of the Holy Spirit, there were four laws or conditions that needed to be satisfied.[17] First, Kemp said, there must be an honest recognition of the need for revival: "[O]n the one hand the professing Church is rapidly losing her hold upon the world, and on the other hand the world is sinking deeper and deeper into heart breaking indifference. The Church makes loud pretensions and accomplishes so little; the while, the world looks on and laughs.... Church of God, recognize thy need and confess it before Him."[18] Secondly, there must be a return to the place of prayer—fervent and sustained prayer: "All history teaches us that revivals come by the way of intercession."[19] This was his experience at Charlotte Chapel: "Those who knew the inner spirit of those years of reviving know that it was the manifest work of the Holy Ghost. The Church of Christ needs the divine flame, and she can have it by prayer. This church has proved it so."[20] Thirdly, there must be a readiness to put away

---

[12] Pound, "Reverend J.W. Kemp," 4.

[13] *NZB* (January 1928) 17.

[14] Kemp, *Joseph W. Kemp*, 22.

[15] *NZB* (July 1922) 135–36; (September 1922) 167–68.

[16] Kemp's *Reaper* regularly stressed this point, running articles with titles like "Conditions of Revival" (July 1923) 144; "What is a Revival?" by Charles Finney, (August 1923) 172; "Revival and Its Necessary Conditions" (January 1924) 309; "How to Secure Revival" (February 1924) 317; "How to Begin a Revival" (January 1927) 294.

[17] "In Expectation of the Coming Revival," *NZB* (October 1922) 189. This paper is almost identical to one he published in Edinburgh: "Revival: Its Necessary Conditions," *Charlotte Chapel Record* (1913) 4–5.

[18] *NZB* (October 1922) 189.

[19] *NZB* (October 1922) 189.

[20] "When a Church Prayed for More than Revival: The Amazing Story of Charlotte Chapel, where for two years there was practically no preaching," *Sunday School Times*, June 19, 1915, 363. A copy of this article is located on the CD which accompanies Ian L. S. Balfour,

every evil thing. "We must," Kemp insisted, "separate ourselves from all that would weaken and prevent our being robust Christians." That included not just sin, but those behaviors that, though permissible, might serve to hinder or impede the Spirit's work in and through us.[21] Finally, there must be a restoration of the great biblical words and themes in preaching—there must be evangelism. The "old faith" must be proclaimed:

Not a little of the present spiritual declension may be attributed to defective preaching.... Sin, Incarnation, atonement, resurrection, Christ's intercession on high, and His promised return are obliterated from the preacher's list, and can it be wondered at that such sermons make no impression on the unsaved, and that the temperature of Church life registers low? The world is waiting for preachers with a message to deliver, a burning theme so uttered as to demand attention. Such preachers break in on the spirit of materialism and practical atheism with such a power of conviction as to arouse men from torpor and indifference.[22]

In Kemp's mind, these were the necessary conditions for revival. His ministry in New Zealand can be understood as a sustained attempt to fulfill each of these conditions. In his preaching and writing Kemp repeatedly drew attention, first, to the church's need for revival. He constantly kept the subject before his congregation, teaching on the history of revival, explaining the dynamics of revival, and reporting on the outbreak of revival in different countries.[23] At Bible conferences, at regional association meetings, and at the annual Assembly of the Baptist Union, he led sessions on revival, impressing on his colleagues that "revival should have a central place in the Christian ministry and in all our churches."[24] His articles in the *New Zealand Baptist* frequently declared that revival was the "supreme need" of a weak and struggling church. "Let us get back to Pentecostal methods, and we shall get Pentecostal

---

Revival in Rose Street: Charlotte Baptist Chapel, Edinburgh, 1808–2008 (Edinburgh: Rutherford House, 2007).

[21] *NZB* (October 1922) 189.
[22] *NZB* (October 1922) 189.
[23] *NZB* (March 1922) 55; (June 1922) 115; (July 1929) 215; (June 1931) 221.
[24] *NZB* (February 1922) 25; (January 1923) 3; (July 1927) 195.

results."²⁵ The *Reaper*, magazine, which Kemp founded and edited, also devoted columns in almost every issue to the subject. In all of this, Kemp was urging the church in New Zealand to recognize its need for revival.

The second characteristic feature of Kemp's ministry was its emphasis on prayer. Arthur Tucker, one of Kemp's elders in the 1920s, said that he would sometimes get a call from the minister with the simple command to be in the vestry at 7:00pm. He would arrive to find other officers assembled and "Kemp would say, 'Gentlemen, get down on your knees...our conversions have been down of late.' Sometimes it was for an hour, sometimes until midnight or until breakfast the next morning."²⁶ Under Kemp, prayer came to dominate the Tabernacle's calendar. Prayer meetings were scheduled for every night of the week when there was no public meeting. Soon every lunchtime in the week was also given over to prayer; special daylong prayer meetings from 8 a.m. to 10 p.m. were introduced. Beyond this, on Kemp's initiative, the ministers of different denominations in Auckland started meeting together every Tuesday morning to pray "until the fire falls."²⁷ At Kemp's suggestion Baptist ministers in Auckland—and around the country—also gathered on occasion to "pray down" a revival.²⁸

Through his speaking and writing Kemp constantly kept the need for prayer before his congregation and the denomination. In his annual report to the church each year Kemp routinely appealed for more prayer: "The long expected and much prayed for Revival still tarries, but the passion for it does not die, and we must earnestly continue in prayer that the heavens might rain copious showers of blessing upon God's thirsty heritage."²⁹ Kemp's articles in the *Baptist* frequently called for prayer:

> Human hands may repair the altar of the Lord that is broken down, and lays the victim on the wood; but if we try to organise a revival, to achieve by mere machinery that which belongs alone to the power of God, we shall be condemned to the helpless futility of the Baal priests of old. Let

---

²⁵ "In the Dawn of a New Revival," *NZB* (July 1922) 135–36; "In the Glow of Revival Enthusiasm," *NZB* (August 1922) 147–48; "In the Track of Revival Fires," *NZB* (September 1922) 167–68.

²⁶ Pound, "Reverend J.W. Kemp," 13.

²⁷ *NZB* (August,1924) 169.

²⁸ *NZB* (July 1927) 195; (August 1924) 169.

²⁹ Auckland Baptist Tabernacle Annual Report, 1925–1926, 3. Copy held in Auckland Baptist Tabernacle archives.

the prophet of the Most High but cry out with faith to the God that answereth by fire, and the fire of Jehovah will not tarry. Beyond all other duties and opportunities there lies now before the Church the call to instant and continued prayer....[30]

The *Reaper* magazine also carried articles with titles like, "How Prayer Brought Revival."[31] In his presidential letter to the denomination Kemp wrote, "We ministers must do more praying.... What would be thought of dividing the twelve hours of our day by giving six hours to prayer for the gospel, and six to the ministry of the Word?...Prayer and power are inseparably connected."[32] According to J. J. North, principal of the Baptist Theological College and an elder at the Tabernacle, Kemp "organised prayer on a larger scale and with a more persistent ardour" than any man he had ever met.[33]

Kemp's ministry was marked, thirdly, by a call to holiness and, therefore, separation from the world. Early on, when he discovered to his horror that young people at the Tabernacle had their own football club, and that it promoted "immorality" by holding a dance, he announced the club's closure. During his first major evangelistic campaign at the Tabernacle, Kemp made his stance abundantly clear with a series of lectures warning his people about the "The Delirium of the Dance," "The Menace of the Movies," "The Woes of the Winecup," and "The Curse of the Card Table." Two years later he and some businessmen from the Tabernacle went further and established an annual Easter convention to promote holiness and separation from the world. Through his preaching and writing, Kemp regularly called his fellow Baptists to what he called "Modern Puritanism."[34]

Kemp's Ministry as an Evangelist

Finally, Kemp's ministry was characterized by a policy of vigorous evangelism. In his Presidential address to the Baptist Assembly Kemp declared,

---

[30] NZB (August 1922) 147–48. See also, "Wanted! Men Who Can Pray," *NZB* (June 1923) 107; "Are We Men of Prayer?" *NZB* (August 1923) 164; "Prayer, Our Most Urgent Need," *NZB* (September 1923, 171–72.

[31] *Reaper*, November 1929, 215.

[32] *NZB* (February 1930) 48–49.

[33] *NZB* (May 1927) 133–34. In the estimate of the Tabernacle's secretary, Kemp "made prayer the basis of all his work." See *NZB* (October 1933) 299.

[34] *NZB* (July 1923) 138.

"Let the Church realise as its first responsibility and the first charge upon its strength, the duty of preaching the gospel of Jesus Christ, and there will be added to it revival." He believed that faithful proclamation of the "old gospel" would lead to revival and he gave himself to this as a matter of absolute primacy.[35] But while Kemp's evangelistic message might have been an old one, his methods—at least by New Zealand standards—were not. In 1920, the Auckland Tabernacle was not the thriving church it had been under Thomas Spurgeon, son of the famous Charles Spurgeon. So Kemp introduced a number of innovations designed to attract the unconverted.[36] The long-standing tradition of pew rents was abolished and a sign was erected in the vestibule assuring visitors that all seats were now free. In summer Kemp made good use of the Tabernacle's strategic location on a central city intersection and staged open-air rallies to attract crowds to evening services.[37] "Once inside the doors, 'strangers' were welcomed and put at ease by one of twenty-four young men of the newly formed Tabernacle Ushers Association. They were all hand-picked by Kemp for their courtesy and gentlemanly instincts, and they had all undergone Kemp's rigorous training course."[38] The Sunday evening worship service itself was popularized. Kemp introduced gospel hymns and choruses from the *Redemption* songbook. He personally preferred the better class of music but, he said, "we were out to catch the people" (and he had seen the important role than music had played in the revival in Wales).[39] During the winter of 1924, Kemp became the first minister in Auckland to broadcast church services on the radio, convincing his officers to install permanent broadcasting facilities in the church.[40]

The same innovation and planning were evident in the special evangelistic campaigns that Kemp launched from the Tabernacle. After a massive organizational overhaul, a rigorous training program, and several months of prayer, Kemp believed the church was ready to receive a big "ingathering of souls."[41] In May 1921 he launched his first major evangelistic campaign. And

---

[35] Pound, "Reverend J.W. Kemp," 9, 12.
[36] "Suggestions for Officebearers' Meeting," 20 October 1920, Auckland Baptist Tabernacle archives.
[37] *NZB* (April 1923) 77.
[38] G. R. Pound, "Kemp," *NZB* (June 1978) 8–9.
[39] Officers' Minutes, 20 October 1920, Auckland Baptist Tabernacle archives.
[40] Pound, "Reverend J.W. Kemp," 24.
[41] Pound, "Kemp ," *NZB* (September 1978) 13.

it was major. For thirteen weeks the Tabernacle was open every night. Kemp was the primary speaker, but he was assisted by an army of two hundred volunteers who distributed hundreds of invitation cards to people around the streets of the city. The well-drilled members of the Tabernacle Ushers Association welcomed visitors into meetings. A newly formed 120-voice chorus choir trained by Kemp assisted with the music. A group of soul-winners worked the inquiry room. Kemp also had teams of young people conducting simultaneous evangelistic missions in several suburban Baptist churches. After thirteen weeks, 160 "decisions" were recorded, with these converts fed into Kemp's newly organized church program. And reports of the campaign were, it seems, carefully circulated, with news about the "stirring times" at the Tabernacle appearing in local newspapers and the denominational magazine.[42]

Over the next ten years, Kemp ran a number of special evangelistic campaigns out of the Tabernacle. In addition, he initiated a series of interdenominational evangelistic campaigns. The famous evangelist Captain Gipsy Pat Smith headlined the first of these, in 1924. This interchurch cooperation continued at the end of the year when the Auckland churches ran a tent campaign during the summer holiday period. A large marquee was erected in the Civic Square in front of the Auckland Town Hall, where Kemp and other local evangelical ministers took turns preaching. The campaign, it appears, was highly successful, reaching people who would not normally darken the door of a church.[43] So, over the next decade, Kemp and his colleagues held a number of similar summer tent crusades.[44] Kemp was also active outside of Auckland. He led missions in a number of Baptist churches throughout New Zealand.[45] As President of the Baptist Union in 1929, he made a four-month evangelistic tour of every Baptist church in the country and conducted several campaigns in Australia. Kemp gave himself to evangelism—to preaching the old gospel—and he urged his denomination to follow suit. Evangelism was the church's "foremost duty," "her primary task."[46] In his presidential address he appealed to the churches: "I cannot stress too strongly my deep conviction

---

[42] "Stirring Times at the Auckland Tabernacle," *New Zealand Herald*, July 8, 1921, 9; *NZB* (May 1921) 62; (July 1921) 77, 83–4; (September 1921) 109.

[43] *NZB* (March 1929,) 87.

[44] *NZB* (March 1925,) 79; (February 1926) 31; (February 1928) 58; (March 1929) 87.

[45] *NZB* (October 1922) 201; *Reaper*, June 1923, 92; *NZB* (December 1924) 298.

[46] *NZB* (January 1928) 16–18.

that the time is opportune for a vigorous evangelism throughout all our churches, and if we are but obedient to the heavenly vision we may ere long be rejoicing together in a heaven-sent revival. Lord! Hasten the day."[47]

Understanding Kemp's Fundamentalism

The New Zealand ministry of Joseph Kemp can be seen as a sustained attempt to fulfill what he saw as the necessary conditions for revival. Viewing his ministry through the lens of revival enriches our understanding at several points. First, it helps us make sense of Kemp's separationist theology. Geoff Pound argues that Kemp attempted to turn the church into a haven from the world, a cultural enclave, to isolate and protect his people from the temptations rampant in a rapidly changing society.[48] But Kemp's primary concern was much more positive. He was motivated by a vision for evangelism and revival. In his first public address in New Zealand he declared, "We do not ignore the fact that the Church is not reaching the masses as she ought. Empty pews are a sad comment on our labours. Why is it? Is it because the Church has tried to be too much like the world from which she is called to be separate...?"[49] His primary concern, it seems, was revival. "If," he said, "the present and insistent cry of the Church for revival is to be answered we must return to the standards of holiness. It is useless to pray if we do not sanctify."[50]

This commitment to evangelism and revival also explains why Kemp campaigned so vigorously against theological modernism. Kemp feared that liberal theology, by stealing the church's confidence in scripture and the gospel, had "smitten the pulpit with the paralysis of unbelief."[51] It was an enemy of evangelism and, therefore, an obstacle to revival. In an address entitled "The Bible in the Billows," Kemp lamented:

A cold and chilling blizzard of skepticism has swept over the country spreading a deathlike spirit of indifference leading to a rejection of the supernatural and an open hostility to the great verities of Revelation. The Bible is treated with indifference and contempt. To this attitude to the Bible can be

---

[47] "Revivalism and Evangelism," NZB (November 1929) 319. Kemp devoted every one of his monthly presidential letters to the subject of evangelism.
[48] Pound, "Reverend J.W. Kemp," 48.
[49] *NZB* (October 1920) 149.
[50] *NZB* (January 1927) 14–15.
[51] "The Menace of Modernism," *Reaper*, April 1929, 27–29.

traced, I am confident, the stagnation so prominent in many quarters. There is a general complaint about the paucity of conversions and the spiritual apathy and deadness that prevails. All this arises largely out of the decadence of faith in the word of God.[52]

Kemp's commitment to evangelism and revival also explains why Kemp moderated his attacks on modernists. He never directly attacked the theological seminaries in New Zealand where liberal ideas were being taught, nor did he personally attack or confront the seminary teachers who were spreading these ideas. Why? Kemp was determined to maintain partnerships across the church for the sake of evangelism. This became clear when he returned from a trip to the United States in 1926. Kemp was deeply disturbed by the bitterness and suspicion that he witnessed between fundamentalists and modernists because it dreadfully weakened the work of evangelism.[53]

This emphasis on evangelism as a condition for revival also explains the relationship between Kemp and J. J. North, the other dominant leader within the New Zealand Baptist movement during the interwar period. Theologically, Kemp and North were miles apart. North believed that antimodernists were "nagging literalists,"[54] and that Baptist ministers should keep their "windows open to all the light which comes from every quarter."[55] He, himself, willingly embraced higher criticism and publicly declared his belief in theistic evolution. This was too much for many conservative Baptists, who labeled North a "modernist" and launched a vicious attack on him at the 1927 Baptist Assembly. Remarkably, Kemp leapt to his defense: "He resented very deeply aspersions that had been made against the 'soundness' of Principal North. He declared that if North was a modernist, so in the same sense was he. He did not always agree in details with his friend, but they stood together for the great evangelical verities, and he would not hesitate to place anyone for whom he cared under the Principal for theological training."[56] In other words, Kemp

---

[52] Manuscript for address given to Bible Training Institute 1927, MA202, J. J. North papers, New Zealand Baptist Research and Historical Archives.
[53] *NZB* (December 1926) 337.
[54] *NZB* (December 1942) 322.
[55] *NZB* (January 1927) 2.
[56] *NZB* (November 1927) 330.

recognized in North a "total commitment to evangelism and conversionism."[57] Revivalism trumped fundamentalism.

Understanding Kemp's Impact among New Zealand Baptists

Finally, a focus on revivalism also casts light on Kemp's impact among New Zealand Baptists. Kemp never saw in New Zealand the revival for which he longed,[58] but his ministry was exceedingly fruitful. At the end of his first year at the Tabernacle, the church Secretary declared that Kemp's coming had been "an epoch-making event in the history of the Tabernacle."[59] Over the next twelve years the church grew from 585 members to over a thousand. Hundreds more were baptized, and thirty were sent overseas on missionary service. Reports of Kemp's ministry circulated widely among New Zealand Baptists. The editor of the *Baptist* magazine declared, "No minister has ever done more continuously well in his church."[60] "[H]is church is the most outstanding illustration of the power of a scriptural and evangelical ministry that we know of."[61] Baptist ministers and congregations across New Zealand were inspired by Kemp's ministry and guided by his approach to revival and evangelism. At the annual Assembly of the Baptist Union, and at regional Baptist association meetings, Kemp was asked to provide instruction on the subject of revival. On one such occasion the *Baptist* magazine reported: "He has been greatly used of God to do the work of an evangelist. And his counsel to his ministerial brethren, and in open conference, will be influential in the direction of genuine revival."[62]

It certainly was. From their beginnings, New Zealand Baptists have talked about revival, read about revival, prayed for revival, and worked for revival. Allied with this, they have given themselves to evangelism, whether denominational evangelists at the local church level in the form of Sunday evening gospel services or at the denominational level through Easter Camps or

---

[57] Martin Sutherland, "'Baptist and Evangelical': Changing Perceptions of being Evangelical among New Zealand Baptists, 1926–1946," in *Gospel, Truth and Interpretation: Evangelical Identity in Aotearoa New Zealand*, ed. Tim Meadowcroft and Myk Habets (Auckland: Archer Press, 2011) 74–75.
[58] Kemp, *Joseph W. Kemp*, 96.
[59] *NZB* September 1978, 13.
[60] *NZB* November 1928, 324.
[61] *NZB* November 1929, 322.
[62] *NZB* November 1922, 208.

missions conduct that. Baptists were also enthusiastic supporters of larger interdenominational evangelistic campaigns, such as those led by R. A. Torrey in 1902 and Wilbur Chapman in 1912–13. During the 1920s and 1930s Baptist interest in revival lifted noticeably, recalling each of Kemp's laws of revival. During this period there was a growing recognition of the church's need for spiritual renewal. Regional associations, like the Otago and Southland Auxiliary, spent time discussing "The Greatest Need of the Church: Revival."[63] There was, secondly, a growing emphasis on prayer. Ministers in the provinces set up "Prayer and Revival Fellowships," with church members banding together to pray daily for the coming revival.[64] Churches hosted weekly all-night prayer vigils.[65] There was, thirdly, a growing commitment to holiness and separation from the world, particularly in Auckland, where a legalistic brand of piety took root under Kemp's influence, sometimes strangling interest in questions of social justice.[66] Finally, there was a growing engagement in evangelistic activity across the denomination. In 1932, for example, a large number of churches from Invercargill in the Deep South to Whangarei in the North conducted a series of tent missions. It was an extraordinary effort, something New Zealand Baptists had never done before.[67] And it bore a striking resemblance to Kemp's approach in Auckland, with the careful planning and promotion, the use of marquees, the large chorus choirs, the *Redemption* hymns, the inquiry tents, the involvement of local Baptist pastors, the prayers that evangelism would turn into revival. Kemp died in 1933 but this "rising tide of evangelistic effort" rolled on.[68] Between 1932 and 1936 the Baptist Union continued to organize evangelistic tent missions up and down the country. Revivalism flourished.

The same cannot be said for fundamentalism. Joseph Kemp may have been a primary agent in the transplantation of American fundamentalist concerns into New Zealand. Among Baptists, however, fundamentalism did not take deep root during the 1920s and 1930s. J. J. North's influence—and the

---

[63] *NZB* (July 1934) 204.
[64] *NZB* (April 1935) 99; May 1935, 163.
[65] *NZB* (July 1930,) 213.
[66] Simpson, "Joseph W. Kemp and the Impact of American Fundamentalism in New Zealand," 95–96; G.T. Beilby, *L.A. North: The Man and his Memoirs* (Wellington: New Zealand Baptist Historical Society, 1983) 22.
[67] *NZB* (March 1932) 65; (June 1932) 166.
[68] *NZB* (October 1932) 321.

more thoughtful, spacious evangelicalism of British Baptist life—would continue to prevail. It was not until after World War II, when New Zealand Baptists looked increasingly to conservative traditions in the United States, that fundamentalism really made itself felt.[69]

By viewing Kemp primarily through the lens of fundamentalism, New Zealand's religious historians have misunderstood him and his ministry in New Zealand. At heart, Kemp was a revivalist. His primary objective was revival, and his ministry can be seen as a sustained attempt to fulfill the conditions for revival. Viewed through that lens, we gain a much clearer picture of Kemp's separationist theology, his antimodernist posture, and his relationship with other evangelical leaders, and his impact within the New Zealand Baptist movement. Furthermore, this analysis suggests that fundamentalism itself can be misunderstood. Viewed through the lens of revival, we see that Joseph Kemp's fundamentalism was motivated less by a fearful, obscurantist reaction to modern life and thought, and more by a positive concern for the church to fulfill its role as an agent of transformation.

---

[69] On this see John Tucker, *A Braided River: New Zealand Baptists and Public Issues 1882–2000* (Bern: Peter Lang, 2013).

23

German Baptist Churches of Southeast Queensland and Revival

David Parker

Has there ever been revival in Australia? This is a tricky question about which opinions differ widely. If there was no full-scale revival, then were there localised revivals? American revivalist and prolific writer on the subject J. Edwin Orr certainly thought so, and gave anecdotal evidence for many examples in the South Seas generally including Australia.[1] The period of the Billy Graham crusades across Australia in 1959 is often regarded as the best example of something near to revival.[2] But the noted revival scholar Stuart Piggin is in no doubt. He affirmed with complete certainty that it was a "revival…and a great one,"[3] There have also been claims of revival amongst Aboriginal communities and in Pentecostal history.[4]

The answer to the question of whether there has been revival in New Zealand depends a great deal on what definition is used. After some detailed analysis, Piggin ends up focusing on three obvious factors as the key components: "revitalisation of the Church, the conversion of large numbers of unbelievers, and the diminution of sinful practices in the community."[5]

---

[1] J. Edwin Orr, *Evangelical Awakenings in the South Seas* (Minneapolis: Bethany Fellowship, 1976) chaps. 8, 15, 21.

[2] S. B. Babbage and I. Siggins, *Light beneath the Cross* (Kingswood: World's Work; 1960) 180f–81.

[3] Stuart Piggin, *Spirit, Word and World: Evangelical Christianity in Australia* (Brunswick East, Acorn Press, 2012) 171. This work appears under different titles: *Evangelical Christianity in Australia: Spirit, Word and World* (Melbourne: Oxford University Press, 1996) and *Spirit of a Nation: The Story of Australia's Christian Heritage* (Sydney: Strand Publishing, 2004).

[4] Piggin, *Spirit, Word and World*, 197–99.

[5] Piggin, *Spirit, Word and World*, 156.

On this basis, he lists sixty-nine places where revival took place in Australia between 1834 and 1905, but there is no documentation provided for these events.[6] The list includes only four in Queensland: Warwick 1873, Toowoomba 1877, Marburg 1881, and amongst the Kanakas in 1905 and 1906. Although Billy Graham was neither the first, nor the last, revivalist to visit this country, it seems that there has been nothing apart from Graham's crusade touching great sections of the nation in the way that many would expect from the celebrated revivals in other times and places, such as those in Wales, East Africa, Europe, and the so-called awakenings in USA. This is the mythology of revival in Australia.

There is little mention of Baptist churches experiencing revival in the sources cited; the most common denomination seems to be Methodist. In Queensland Baptist publications there are plenty of references to revival, but it is usually a matter of looking back longingly to historic examples in other countries and expressing earnest hope and fervent prayer for a repeat of revival in the future. This expression of hope for revival cuts out around 1990. Nevertheless, there are often reports of occasions when there were numerous converts from particular evangelistic efforts. Piggin observed that given their theology and traditions, Baptists more than any other denomination should have been able to benefit from the Billy Graham crusades; the percentage of Baptist decisions was five times higher than expected.[7]

German Baptists of Southeast Queensland

This leads us to consider the German Baptists of southeast Queensland and the possibility of revival in that community.[8] There is a well-known photograph taken in 1905 of a group of no fewer than fifty-two candidates for baptism, all dressed in white, lined up outside the Kalbar, previously known as Engelsburg, church; they were the fruit of a local evangelistic crusade. The question arises, whether this is the kind of occurrence that was in mind in the references to "revival" which are scattered throughout the literature of the

---

[6] Piggin, *Spirit, Word and World*, 40, 61.
[7] Piggin, Spirit, *Word and World*, 166.
[8] Ken R. Manley, *From Woolloomooloo to 'Eternity': A History of Australian Baptists* (Milton Keynes, UK: Paternoster, 2006) 170–76; *Queensland Baptist Jubilee Record*, vol. *1855–1905* (Brisbane: W.R. Smith, n.d.) 108–14; David Parker, ed., *Pressing on with the Gospel: The Story of Baptists in Queensland 1855–2005* (Brisbane: Baptist Historical Society of Queensland, 2005) 17–20.

German Baptists. There are other reports in the records of other German Baptist churches of sizeable numbers of baptisms such as fifty at Tarampa in 1881.

There is a report of the very first appearance of German Baptists in Queensland in the 1860s, which said they caused a stir within the small German community in Brisbane: "Lutheran ministers were induced to hold prayer meetings themselves, and there was a regular reformation of habits, if not a thorough revival among Germans."[9] There were many conversions as a result. It is interesting that the German Baptists grew from this initial group and organised themselves as an association several years before their English counterparts. At its peak, their largest church was much stronger than any of the English ones, apart from the founding Wharf Street church that was numerically anomalous.

The emergence of German Baptist churches in southeast Queensland was a development unique in Australia, arising out of an influx of German immigrants from the 1860s that were either Baptists before leaving their fatherland, or were converted after their arrival in the colony. They formed a series of churches in the rural West Moreton district, west and north of Ipswich, several of which have persisted to the present and whose members and their descendants have made a highly significant contribution to Baptist life in Queensland.

Although not numerically large in comparison with similar movements in North America, German migration to Queensland, mostly for economic reasons, was relatively large in local terms. In 1871, when the immigration rate was high, they comprised almost 8 percent of the population. Around 1890 they reached their maximum pre-war number of about 15,000, although the percentage was falling by then. The proportion of Germans in the population in areas where Baptists flourished was often very high—sometimes virtually 100 percent. Prior to World War I, Germans were the largest group of non-British, non-Irish immigrants and Queensland had the highest number in Australia.

When the English-speaking Baptist Association was formed in 1877, it

---

[9] *The Queensland Freeman*, June 1881, 83. In 1868 Pastor C. F. A. Schirmeister was pastor of St. Andreas on Wickham Terrace, North Brisbane, and Pastor G. Hampe was minister at a church in Cordelia Street, South Brisbane; Robin Kleinschmidt, email message to author, May 1, 2015.

consisted of eight churches with 618 members; by then the Germans numbered six churches with 320 members. Even at the time of the jubilee of English Baptist work in 1905, the German Baptist church membership was 471 while the English churches totalled 2,040.[10]

German Baptists in City and Country

The very first Christian witness by Germans in Queensland took place from 1838 when a group of families from the Gossner Mission were engaged by a visionary Presbyterian minister, Dr John Dunmore Lang, to evangelise indigenous people near Brisbane; their adherence to the Lutheran faith was mostly recognized as being loose. The mission itself was not a success and with its break-up, most of the personnel were gradually integrated into other churches, including the Baptists.

Legislation passed by the government of Queensland, which became a separate colony only in 1859, was designed to expand the population and economy by attracting new settlers to farming regions and resulted in large numbers of Germans arriving in the 1860s. Initially, they mostly lived in the Brisbane area, especially close to where the Gossner Mission had existed. Some of these began worshipping with the pioneer Wharf Street Baptist church, whose energetic pastor, Rev B. G. Wilson, welcomed them and actively evangelised amongst them.

Because of differences over the doctrine and practice of communion, the German group soon developed its own identity and separated from Wharf Street Baptist Church. It was this group, whose gospel preaching and vigorous witness to believer's baptism, that caused the reaction of the fledgling Lutheran community mentioned above.

As the new colonial government made land available under attractive terms for farming in the areas west of Ipswich, many of these Brisbane based Germans moved to this district. It is here that the German Baptist churches were set up, with the first ones appearing in the late 1860s at Vernor on the Brisbane River, at Mt Walker, and on the Bremer River. The areas of land, which the Germans occupied, were usually covered in extremely dense virgin scrub in remote locations and often in hilly and inaccessible areas. This meant that the conditions of farming and life generally were extremely harsh, but the new immigrants worked hard, and in time made a success of their newfound

---

[10] *Queensland Baptist Jubilee Record*, vol. 1855–1905, 133.

life.

Other Christians in these areas were mainly Lutheran but also included Roman Catholic and, after 1883, the Apostolic Church of Queensland, followed by the Churches of Christ, who often proselytised from the Baptists. As the German Baptists moved into a second generation, some of the younger families moved to other, more distant areas, including the South Burnett, but they did not form German-speaking churches there.

Characteristics of Revival: I. Church Growth

Turning to the question of revival and the German Baptist churches, the most obvious characteristic was the extraordinary growth. There is anecdotal evidence of rapid growth amongst these churches to be found in their published histories, newspaper reports, and conference documents, although firm statistics are not plentiful; nor is it possible to make precise comparisons with other churches.

The most common of these references are reports of large numbers of conversions and baptisms. The record for a single baptismal service for the Kalbar church was eighty-two baptisms in 1910. This was the result of the work of local evangelists.

For example, H. Moller reported to J. G. Oncken in a letter dated July 6, 1871, that at Normanby Reserve, "About four years ago our congregation consisted of five members, while now the number amounts to sixty, not counting those outside." This is possibly a reference to adherents or to those living in other places.[11] He mentioned a gathering at which twenty-five were converted and "the love of God surged through many poor sinners' hearts, which caused us to recall the Pentecost of Jerusalem."

Overall, the efforts by the Germans to establish churches, with modest but adequate buildings and many other activities, quite early after the establishment of the farms and communities indicate that they quickly garnered enough strength for this organisational development. As soon as they could, they replaced the original buildings with larger and much more elaborate ones—in fact, the church at Kalbar became the largest building in the entire district. Over nearly thirty years, they continued to establish churches and outstations in each new district that opened up to farming. Some of these churches grew to a considerable size, even when compared with the English

---

[11] Letter in collection of Baptist Church Archives, Queensland.

churches in the urban areas.

The case at Zillman's Waterholes may have been special, but perhaps it was not all that unusual—a sudden exodus of many members to the West Moreton area depleted this church near Brisbane in 1869. However, there were so many new converts immediately afterwards that within only two years they found it necessary to build a church to house the number attending services for which they thought meetings in their homes might have been sufficient.

Furthermore, they established a conference or association of German churches almost as quickly as the churches were formed. The first effort was in 1869, which covered both the West Moreton churches and one back in Brisbane. They worked in conjunction with the English-speaking Baptist church in Ipswich under its insightful pastor, Thomas Gerrard, to form a General Baptist Association in 1870 to provide a system for ordination of pastors in the interests of good church order. This took place some seven years before the English Baptists formed their association, even though the English churches preceded the German ones by more than a decade!

Although some of the growth that led to the establishment of these churches was based on Baptists who migrated from Germany, one report said that at Tarampa only thirty were Baptists on arrival, but by 1877 the membership was three hundred.[12]

Many of the converts were young people who needed careful nurturing, made more difficult because they were generally poorly educated; Sunday schools and youth groups formed to offset this problem were reported as being not very successful.[13] Similarly, the churches lacked good pastoral care as it was not until 1878 that a full-time ordained minister was available to serve them in the person of Rev. Hermann Windolf, an experienced pastor from Germany who had trained at Hamburg and was in close contact with J. G. Oncken. Previously they had to rely on lay leaders. However, gifted as some of them were, they were untrained theologically and administratively; they still had to work their farms as well as lead the churches, and as one report said dismally, these men "did their best, and that was in most cases very little" so

---

[12] Richard Scanlan and David Parker, *Tarampa Baptist Church* (Brisbane: Baptist Historical Society of Queensland, 2000) 7.

[13] *Queensland Baptist* (December 1881): 178.

it was no wonder that "the steam ran down!"[14]

Growth came from regular services and the pastoral interest of leaders and members and families; they were reported to be "indefatigable as bush missionaries."[15] There were often itinerant evangelists, frequently English speaking, who visited the churches over the entire period under review producing a steady flow of converts; there were "waves of revival" during a visit by one to Marburg in 1884.[16]

Some of the growth may have come from intermarriage with other denominations, but either side did generally not encourage this practice. What did cause some growth was the state of the Lutheran churches in the area at the time—they were poorly organised, fractious, did not have enough pastors, and often did not adhere strongly to their own confessional basis.[17] It is revealing that in the Logan District to the southeast, where the Lutheran cause was much tighter confessionally and better organised, Baptists made no inroads at all.[18]

Characteristics of Revival: II. Intense Spirituality

Visitors from the English-speaking Baptists often remarked on the intensity of spiritual life at German Baptist conventions and church services and the "festive" nature of the gatherings, plus the consumption of large amounts of food![19] This evaluation was also backed up by reports from the German Baptists themselves to the Baptist newspaper back home. In fact, the regular pattern for their conference sessions was business and fellowship during the day, usually with serious discussion papers on church life, an inspirational service in afternoon and evening followed by a long night of "revival," usually

---

[14] "German Baptists in Queensland," *Queensland Freeman*, June 1881, 83.

[15] *Queensland Times*, April 15, 1871.

[16] Richard Scanlan and David Parker, *Marburg Baptist Church* (Brisbane: Baptist Historical Society of Queensland, 2000) 7.

[17] F. Otto Theile, *One Hundred Years of the Lutheran Church in Queensland* (Brisbane: United Evangelical Lutheran Church in Australia, 1938) 15–16, accessed February 24, 2015, http://nla.gov.au/nla.obj-30585562. In later years, they also lost members to the Apostolic Church.

[18] I am indebted to Robin Kleinschmidt, email to author, February 16, 2015, for this insight.

[19] *Queensland Baptist*, May 11, 1902, 66.

extending to the early hours of the next morning.[20] There were similar kinds of gatherings at Easter and Whitsunday as well.

At least one report of a typical meeting strongly suggests something very close to revival: "Their services commenced at 11 a.m. on the 25th [December], and continued until half-past eight the following morning, during which time a good many cried for mercy and several found peace."[21] So these gatherings were highly important to the participants and they were usually well attended, even though traveling to attend them was likely to be extremely difficult.

Their first duty upon taking up their land was to clear the thick bush, build a simple home, and get their farm established. Although these were daunting and physically exhausting tasks, the people were quick to establish worship services; home devotions were vital as well. All this indicated that they placed high value on worship and fellowship as necessities for their spiritual life, which would have produced an intensity of fervour. They often had brass bands and choirs to support their worship and Ira Sankey's songbooks were not unknown, although with German words.[22] The occasional visits of itinerant preachers such as evangelists, ministers, and missionaries of the English Baptist Union were usually welcomed as ways of fostering devotion.

Unlike Lutherans, Baptists did not have to wait for ordained ministers to arrive but appointed local leaders. However, when Windolf arrived he soon found some "sore places" due to lack of training and experience of these lay pastors, not to mention the "drawbacks and malpractices," even "controversial elements [who were prone to] fight each other" resulting in "a paralysing influence."[23] Despite the "prolonged spiritual dryness," Windolf was soon able to report "the Lord in his grace has now blessed us in abundance [with a] blessed time of revival and progress." [24]

---

[20] Brian Kickbush, *Minden Baptist Church Centenary, 1882–1982* (Minden: Minden Baptist Church, n.d.) 3; *Queensland Times*, June 2, 1885.

[21] *Queensland Times*, December 31, 1874, referring to Vernor.

[22] William Higlett, "Sketches of Bush Work in Queensland," *Sword and Trowel* (October 1887): 538–541.

[23] Hermann Windolf reporting in *Der Wahrheitszeuge*, May 1879. The collected reports from this journal were prepared by Glenn Roberts; see "Recent Acquisitions for the Baptist Archives," in *Baptist Historical Society of Queensland Newsletter*, no 3, July 1985, 3.

[24] Hermann Windolf reporting in *Der Wahrheitszeuge*, September 1881.

The harsh conditions of daily life and the relative isolation and remoteness emphasised by their being migrants in a strange land with their own culture must have given added value and intensity to their Christian fellowship. Even so, there were often disagreements amongst people of such strong minds and wills. Factors of this kind no doubt contributed to the characteristic strictness of their church rules and administration of discipline, which often resulted in humble confessions and restorations.

Further evidences of their piety included regular prayer meetings and special periods of intense prayer; one church reported five consecutive nights of prayer for overseas missions.[25] It also included their support of evangelistic work locally and farther afield, as well as local and nearby church planting.

These Baptists had a keen interest in foreign missions, noted by Donald W. Dayton as a sure sign of revival.[26] Despite not being affluent, the conference appointed a treasurer for missions[27] so they could support financially as well as in prayer the fledgling Queensland Baptist Mission in Bengal and the Russian mission.[28] They regularly welcomed visiting missionaries to their meetings. There was even a Women's Missionary Society.[29] It was not surprising therefore that two of their women went overseas in missionary service—one to the German mission in Cameroon and another to a Queensland-based mission in India.

Even if the examples of intense spirituality amongst the German Baptists were not constant or widespread, there were enough to show that revival was in the air. Rev. Samuel Blum, who came to Queensland from the USA in 1900, certainly sensed it, and summed up the situation aptly:

> We believe that there is a great deal of genuine piety in the hearts of German Baptists. They hold a sharp separation from the world. The candidates for baptism are examined very carefully, and church discipline is frequent. In missionary enterprises they are up to date, but in doctrine they are as old-fashioned as the first church in Jerusalem. In contribution they are liberal, and firmly believe in the expansion of the Lord's Kingdom, even if their views of political expansion are narrow. It will take

---

[25] *Minden Baptist Church Centenary*, 14.
[26] Donald W. Dayton, *The New International Dictionary of the Christian Church*, ed. J. D. Douglas (Grand Rapids: Zondervan, 1978) s.v "Revivalism."
[27] *Minden Baptist Church Centenary*, 4.
[28] *Minden Baptist Church Centenary*, 10.
[29] *Queensland Times*, May 16, 1907.

some time before they accept views of some doctrines, which are common in our English Baptist churches. We must take the German as he is.[30]

These signs of revival could be attributed in measure to local factors. However, a significant group of the people had come from the Templin church in Germany where, in the few years prior to their departure, there had been revival with hundreds of conversions and baptisms.[31] There may also have been some lingering effects from the movement of German pietism, including occurrences of "enthusiasm" (*Schwaermerei*), which sometimes appeared amongst the Lutherans. However, there is apparently no record of the initial Gossner missionaries—often regarded as Moravian in orientation—making any contribution of this kind.

Characteristics of Revival: III. Community Impact

If the conversions and piety characteristic of the German Baptists point to the existence of revival in their midst, then there is some difficulty in the case of the third distinguishing feature: beneficial impact on the community, both in terms of the German Baptist community itself and the people around them.

Unfortunately, there do not appear to be any reports like those from elsewhere to suggest that "the hotels are empty and the churches are full."[32] But it is clear that the churches did hold together and grow for many years; some can report several generations of membership. Mostly the churches were well regarded by their community, and from time to time experienced good will in the form of practical assistance and support at difficult times.

There were often tensions within the Baptist German community, just as there were amongst their Lutheran counterparts, although perhaps not so chronic. The first Lutheran congregation was formed in 1858, but it took until

---

[30] *Queensland Baptist*, August 1901, 108.

[31] Laurie Wolter, *From the Fatherland to the Fassifern Scrub: Celebrating the 125th Anniversary of the Kalbar Baptist Church 1875–2000* (Kalbar: Kalbar Baptist Church, 2000).

[32] See *Der Wahrheitszeuge*, October 1883—a report about a revival of this kind in a town called Edenthal; this town cannot be identified positively, but it may be a district of that name located near Kingaroy in southeast Queensland where there was a large Lutheran population; if this is the case, then there is such a report related to German Baptists in the area.

1885 to establish functioning denominational organisations, and until 1921 for full denominational unity, whereas the Baptists had an organisation by 1869, albeit with many fluctuations in its effectiveness.

Admittedly, the first church at Vernor could not be built in 1870 as initially planned because of a disagreement, and it had to change its site as well.[33] The conference of German Baptists had many incarnations before it matured into an effective entity around 1900, especially under the leadership of the pastor-missionaries who came from USA. The first ordained minister, Hermann Windolf, did not enjoy harmonious relationships with his initial congregation, probably due largely to the transition from lay to ordained leadership and a different concept of church membership.[34] Upon his transfer to a second church (Marburg), there was an expulsion of twenty-nine members, although many were restored. As Samuel Blum conceded, "When we are face to face with a German, we are dealing with obstinate customers."[35]

There were usually good, albeit spasmodic, relationships with the English Baptist Union prior to the 1920s, and some of the German churches were in membership. In the case of Kalbar there was some movement in and out of the union over open membership issues. Good relations were maintained with church leaders in Germany and links were established with the German Baptists in the USA.

Perhaps the most notorious case of tension within the German Baptist community occurred at Marburg where on one occasion there were rival pastors conducting different services simultaneously in the same building! This resulted in physical violence, which came to the attention of the police and the law courts. Eventually, there were two Baptist churches in the same small

---

[33] *Brisbane Courier*, September 10, 1873.

[34] Manley, *From Woolloomooloo to 'Eternity,'* 174; Windolf probably shared the views of his mentor in Germany, J. G. Oncken, in opting for a more centralised form of church life, which would have clashed with the independence which was characteristic of the rural, lay-led churches he found in Queensland. He also felt that people were admitted to church membership "too lightly" and that the leaders were often "capable of unbridled ego" (quotations found in Ken R Manley, "'Planted in a New Land': German Baptists in Australia (c.1860–1914)" in *Gemeinschaft der Kirchen und gesellschaftliche Verantwortung. Die Würde des Anderen und das recht anders zu denken, Festschrift für Professor Dr. Erich Gelbach*, ed. L. Lybaek, K. Raiser, and S. Schardien (Münster: Lit Verlag, 2004) 108–23. (The main information in this paper is also found in Manley, *From Woolloomooloo to 'Eternity,'* 168–76).

[35] *Queensland Baptist*, August 1901, 108.

town, which for a time refused efforts at mediation. Eventually reconciliation took place and the church continued to witness faithfully for few more generations.[36]

The record of beneficial impact on the community and the reputation of the German Baptists for unity among themselves were not so good. Not surprisingly, times of "peace" were worth noting, and were sometimes followed by remarkable growth! The Bremer River fellowship rejoiced in an 1871 letter to Oncken reporting "we presently have peace and harmony in our midst and enjoy precious hours in our edification sessions." Windolf likewise rejoiced in 1883 when there was formal reconciliation between three churches with the hope of "precious fruit…and prosperity."[37]

The Heritage of Revival

By the 1920s, the days of strong growth were over and so were the days of revival—at least in some minds. The Kalbar historian said that after this date "there is very little spectacular to report—no mass conversions or baptisms as in the early years, not strong revival movement."[38]

This was a reference to the kind of event recalled by one old timer who said, "I remember revivals there that would have rejoiced the heart of any Salvationist—something like the Welsh Revival of some years ago in miniature. That was in the early seventies, when German Baptists were meeting in a slab place."[39]

By this time the German Baptists were losing their identity as a separate community. There were several factors at work, especially the cessation of immigration, which would not resume again until after World War II; but by then the old situation was well past. Then there was the impact of World War I on Germans in Australia, which, among other things, hastened German churches' adoption of the English language.[40] This signaled the integration of second and later generations more or less completely into the wider society.

---

[36] *Queensland Times*, January 20, 1887; *Brisbane Courier*, February 3, 1887; *Queenslander*, January 29, 1887.

[37] Hermann Windolf reporting in *Der Wahrheits*zeuge, January 1883.

[38] Kalbar Baptist Church, 1875–1975, 10.

[39] *Brisbane Courier*, May 13, 1922. "Slab place": a simple building construction using rough timber cut into slabs, not smooth-sawn timber planks, typical of the pioneer colonial period.

[40] Another striking impact was the forced change of names of the German towns (and the Baptist churches) to English names, sometimes with polemic overtones—Engelsburg to Kalbar: Marburg to Townshend; Minden to Frenchton.

This was coupled with better communications and other infrastructure, which meant that the German communities were now far less isolated than they had been sixty years earlier.

Another highly significant factor affecting the German churches was the change in rural economy on which they were largely based, resulting in many families moving out of the districts thus weakening the churches. Families also were much smaller.

By this time, the churches were appointing English-speaking Australian pastors (some of whom had German backgrounds) and they all became members of the Baptist Union of Queensland. The German Baptist Conference was rendered inactive and finally faded out of view around 1930. Over the eighty years since then, a few of the German churches have ceased to function, while the rest have continued to witness and serve, although sometimes finding it difficult to sustain themselves.

Nevertheless, in their fifty-year history as a separate group, they performed an important role of evangelising and caring for their own people. As Samuel Blum wisely pointed out:

> German Baptist churches must be looked at as a very important factor in evangelizing the people of Australia. If German Baptist churches are failures for the training of Christian characters, then the Baptist denomination as a whole is a failure. The time may come when German churches are no more wanted, but for the present we must have them. We believe that the German churches are organs for the slow assimilation of the Germans, and we ought to help them in their work.[41]

Their history of a strong and virile faith characterised by periods of remarkable growth and intense spiritual experiences is a heritage which cannot be taken from them. It ought to be remembered as a vital part of our story, even if it cannot be described as revival in the fullest sense of that term.

---

[41] *Queensland Baptist*, August 1901, 109.

24

A Hundred Years of Baptist Ministry in Bangladesh

Dennis Dilip Datta

The "Serampore Trio" headed by William Carey of India in West Bengal in 1796 initiated the Baptist ministry in Bengal/Bangladesh. Soon the mission expanded into East Bengal (Bangladesh). The result of expansion was rapid, but a great field still remained unexposed to the gospel due to the shortage of funds and personnel. The Baptist Missionary Society (BMS) decided to engage partners in order to reach the whole of Bengal with the gospel. One of their missionaries, Rev. John Chamberlain Page (1822–1894), visited Adelaide, South Australia, in 1864 and encouraged Dr. Silas Mead and the Flinders Street Baptist Church to become a missionary church. Subsequently, the South Australia Baptist Missionary Society as well as the Victoria and other regional missionary societies were formed and decided to extend their prayers, money, and missionaries to support work in East Bengal. In 1913, seven regional societies were united under one head, the Federation of Mission Society of Australia, which later took the name Australian Baptist Missionary Society (ABMS), now known as Global Interaction.

The ABMS started their ministry in what was called East Bengal in 1882 through the challenge and encouragement of Miss Ellen Arnold, the pioneer missionary of the region. The New Zealand Baptist Missionary Society (NZBMS) was formed in 1881, and in 1886 it also started a ministry in East Bengal and the princely state of Tipperah. The Southern Baptist Convention (SBC) came to East Pakistan in 1957. The Association of Baptists for World Evangelism (ABWE) started its ministry in 1958.

In Bangladesh, the churches planted by these five missions are now bound in fellowship under five associations: Bangladesh Baptist Church Sangha (BBCS) of BMS, Bangladesh Baptist Church Fellowship (BBCF) of ABMS, NZBM, and SBC, the Garo Baptist Convention (GBC) of ABMS, Bangladesh Tribal Association of Baptist Churches (BTABC) of ABWE, and Bangladesh Association of Baptist Church (BABC) of ABWE. From the very beginning, these five missions had a strong influence on the nationals in the churches. They controlled the churches, schools, training institutions, and so forth. Very seldom were the nationals consulted for advice regarding their churches. One mission agency even handed over their mission stations to another mission society and sold the mission properties to unidentified people. This kind of action demoralized the local churches.

The missions never built up young local leaders, as Paul did with Timothy. In Bangladesh, there was no theological institution to train ministers until 1967 when the College of Christian Theology Bangladesh (CCTB), an interdenominational theological school, was set up. It is very unfortunate that due to lack of expert hands like doctors and technicians, some of the best medical ministries had to close. After 1834, following the British Parliament's withdrawal of total restrictions on missionaries going to India, the missionaries faced strong opposition from the Hindu Religionists. First they protested, and then they reformed their theology. The conservative fundamentalist Hindus first started the "Ramakrishna Mission" aimed at attracting the Hindu lower cast. This group is now globally active. The second step was taken by the educated, both higher and lower caste, to join "Brahama Somaj" a Unitarian form of religion condemning the worship of idols and so forth; this group is no longer active.

After World War I, the global socio-political scenario was changing very rapidly. Nationals demanded more opportunity and participation in nation building. So it was that the church and the tiny Christian communities needed national leaders who could speak for them and make appropriate decisions for their safety and security. The Edinburgh Conference was held in 1910. From this conference the idea of mission and church integration quickly became very popular. It was hoped that the independent, indigenous churches would thereby be strengthened. In 1919, Rev. B. A. Nag of the Baptist Missionary Society (BMS) initiated a dialogue to bring the Baptists under one flag. Earlier, in 1890, the Garo Baptist churches had integrated as the Garo Baptist Union (GBU). The churches planted by the ABMS and the NZBMS decided with much prayer to form a church union. The result was the East Bengal Baptist Union (EBBU), which was formed in 1919. In 1922, the British Baptist Churches were united under Bengal Baptist Union (BBU). In 1952, the Assembly of BBU decided to form two unions: West Bengal BU and East Pakistan BU, the EPBU becoming Pakistan Baptist Sangha in 1955; following independence, it was renamed Bangladesh Baptist Sangha. It is very interesting to notice that BMS and BBU became one institution. The BMS, following the spirit of the Edinburgh Conference, handed over their churches, preaching points, schools, hospitals, and so forth to the Bengal Baptist Union with operational financial support. The ABMS, NZBMS, and SBC, however, allowed the churches to form a union, but the mission institutions retained control of the churches. They did not give any financial support for the operational expenses to the newly formed EBBU. In their policy of opening new mission stations or selling out mission station or properties, the national EBBU was still not consulted. Even in 1957, the AMBS handed over two mission stations to the Southern Baptist Convention, but the EBBU had no say in this change. The ABMS pioneer mission station Faridpur was an example of mission sales without national approval.

In 1939, a survey team was appointed by the then Bengal Christian Council (an ecumenical body) to examine the promising areas of missionary work in Sirajganj and the Garo area in the eastern part of Bengal. On this team were two expatriate missionaries and one national of BBU. The survey team recommended the Sirajganj area: "The survey committee is of opinion that there are definite indications of a movement towards Christianity in the Sirajganj area, and that it bears all the signs of a genuine spiritual movement in its early stages."[1] Sirajganj was an EBBU area, but the survey team did not consult the EBBU. The ABMS worked in the Sirajganj area from 1891 to 1948; after this time, the mission station was closed. This was again the scenario of mission policy: missionaries never involved the nationals in evangelism and church planting. Lay people or general members of the churches developed the idea that evangelism and church planting was the task of missionaries and their paid staff.

I belong to the Bangladesh Baptist Church Fellowship (EBBU>BBCF). Our church will celebrate its centenary in 2019. Earlier I shared our relationship with our three partner missions. The East Bengal Baptist Union was formed in 1919 with ten churches in the geographical area of East Bengal. We received the church buildings from the missions, but no financial grant

---

[1] Field Council Minutes, April 1939, 4013, quoted in *From Five Barley Loaves: Australian Baptist in Global Mission, 1864–2010*, ed. Tony Cupit, Ros Gooden, and Ken R. Manley (Preston, Australia: Mosaic Press, 2013) 72. The editors of *From Five Barley Loaves* note that the Field Council Minutes are held in Global Interaction (formerly Australian Baptist Missionary Society) Moore Potter House, 597 Burwood Road, Hawthorn VIC 3122.

was given for operational purposes. Nonetheless, our leaders took up the challenge to continue the ministry. From the third year, the EBBU became a mission, supporting evangelists, running schools, and facilitating medical clinics. Additionally, the EBBU assumed responsibility for two mission outreach efforts from the ABMS.

During this period, the political situation became increasingly volatile. The rise of Indian nationalism and the cry for an independent India created much confusion among missionaries concerning their presence and ministries. In 1885, the Indian National Congress was born. In 1919, Mahatma Gandhi started the nonviolent and the non-cooperation movement. On December 23, 1919, the British Parliament passed the Government of India Act. This act gave the Indian people limited responsibility to rule the country, make new laws, and hold elections. In 1930 Mahatma Gandhi launched the "Civil Disobedience Movement" against British rule in India. In 1942, he launched a vigorous program called "Quit India." Missionary societies became very alarmed that their work would be affected by new political realities.

On October 8, 1931, a meeting took place between Mahatma Gandhi and representatives of the British Missionary Societies at the Church Mission House in London. "The meeting was private, and chief concern in the minds of those present, doubtless, was the reported attitude of their guest towards the work of Christian missions in India."[2] The reason for holding this very private meeting was the prior gathering in India called "Delhi Unity Conference of Religious Freedom" (1929). To ease the tension, Mahatma Gandhi admitted that he had contributed a large part in drafting the resolution and representing his views. He told his host:

> Religion is a personal matter and I am not going to ask another man to become Hindu or a parsee [Zoroastrian]. I would be doing something contrary to my belief. You have amazing self-sacrifice; you are great organizers; you are good men. I want to multiply occasions for your service. I want to work closer with you, but I do not want you to get India to change her faith.[3]

During these years missionaries performed many outstanding social ministries and became the catalyst for social changes. Missionaries were awarded the high civil award called Kaiser-I-Hind (an award given for public service

---

[2] *Missionary Herald* (London: Baptist Missionary Society, 1931) 11.
[3] *Missionary Herald*, 11.

in India) by the Governor General of British-India government. The missionaries recognized were Miss Ellen Arnold and Dr. Cecil Mead of ABMS and Rev. B. N. Eade of NZBMS. Miss Arnold refused the award.

In 1947, India was partitioned and the British created two countries: India for Hindus and Pakistan for Muslims. Bengal was divided into two parts: Muslim East Bengal and Hindu West Bengal. This arrangement provided a homeland for both Hindus and Muslims, but what was to be done about the Hindu, Christian, Buddhist, and Sikh who were living in the new country of Pakistan? Mr. Nehru, the first prime minister of India (1947), declared that India would be a secular India.

Mohammad Ali Jinnah, the father of the newly created Pakistan, stated in his inaugural address to the Constituent Assembly of Pakistan on August 11, 1947, that, "In course of time Hindus would cease to be Hindus and Muslims would cease to be Muslim, not in the religious sense, because that is the personal faith of each individual, but in the political sense as citizens of the state."[4] He also said, "You are free, you are free to go to your temples, you are free to go to your mosques or to another place of worship in the state of Pakistan. You may belong to any religion or caste or creed—that has nothing to do with the business of the state."[5]

The assurance given by the leaders of India and Pakistan proved fruitless. The countries got involved in conflicts that resulted in chaos and confusion. Religious killings became rampant. People migrated from one country to another country. Almost all the key people of the Protestant community, including Baptists of East Bengal, migrated to India. In 1955, an education census was conducted by the ecumenical council and found only five college graduates and one preacher who had the bachelor of divinity (B.D.). In 1956, the East Bengal name was changed to East Pakistan, and the country became the Islamic Republic of Pakistan, the only Islamic country in the world. The birth of an Islamic Republic gave the fundamentalist and orthodox Muslims an opportunity to block the evangelistic activities of the missionaries and the nationals. Outdoor preaching was abandoned but "book rooms" were opened to attract the enquirers. Moreover, visas for missionaries were restricted. The Southern Baptists had to abandon their plan to start a hospital. Following the 1965 war between India and Pakistan, missionaries' movements on the India

---

[4] G. Allana, *Pakistan Movement Historical Documents* (Karachi: University of Karachi, Department of International Relations, n.d. [1969]) 407–11.

[5] Allana, *Pakistan Movement Historical Documents*.

border area were highly restricted. The Southern Baptists had to wait seven years to see their first convert, a Muslim. In this restriction, God worked in His own way. In 1963, Southern Baptists established their first church, Immanuel Baptist Church, in Dhaka, the capital city of East Pakistan. The BMS had planted their only church in Dhaka in 1829, located in the old part of the city. Until 1963 this BMS church was the only church in the provincial capital.

In 1966, we first heard about World Evangelization and cooperation among the Evangelicals to take the gospel to the all nations. It was the outcome of the Berlin Conference of 1966 and Singapore Conference of 1968. In our part of the world, the mission and the local denominations launched a joint program called "Purbo Pakistan Jaykta Prochar Abhijan" (East Pakistan Joint Preaching Movement), in 1969. This joint program created a very big impact among the churches, but it had to be cancelled because of the onset of the Bangladesh liberation war.

In the period 1919 to 1970, the EBBU>EPBU had self-trained or short-course-trained pastor/evangelists; even the chief executive officer of the union was an honorary position. The EBBU started with ten churches. By their twenty-fifth anniversary, the number of churches had risen to only thirteen. Between 1945 and1970, their golden jubilee, the number of churches had increased to eighteen. This slow growth was due to the reasons mentioned earlier: lack of trained national personnel, instability of missionary presence, and the socio-political situation. The country was ruled by martial law for about fifteen years, and for the rest of the time under a cantonment-backed, so-called democratic government. At the same time a political movement started in East Pakistan to seek independence for East Pakistan [later named Bangladesh]. Islam provided the spirit and charisma for the creation of Pakistan, but within twenty-four years, the spirit of Islam was no longer a force powerful enough to keep Pakistan united. In 1971, the eastern part of Pakistan (East Pakistan) became Bangladesh, an independent country. The country had four basic guiding principles: Nationalism, Socialism, Democracy, and Secularism. Unfortunately, in 1975 the country came under the rule of an army junta under which it remained until 1990 when the country became a democratic country with Westminster-type democracy restored. From 1975 to 1990, Islam was adopted as the official religion of Bangladesh, and Sunday was officially designated a working day. Ordinances were promulgated to "monitor" missionaries, churches, nongovernmental organizations' restriction on importing Bibles, NGO's bringing foreign funds, and so forth. A new Ministry of Religious Affairs was created. A bill called the Blasphemy Bill was placed in the Parliament on July 7,1992, but no action was taken.

In 1969, an international governmental organization was launched—the Organization of Islamic Cooperation (OIC). Initially it was an Islamic conference; now it is a forum for Islamic cooperation. "Judging by the structure of its organization, style of operation and functioning, procedural aspects, feature of its charter, and the nature of its membership, the OIC qualifies to be called an International Governmental Organization (IGO) like the UNO, the ASEAN, and the OAU."[6] The fifty-seven member OIC countries have a total population of 1.4 billion, and the total GDP is barely five trillion US dollars. The OIC has different structures and institutions at work. They indirectly fund measures to combat Christian activities. This is a big challenge for evangelical work in the OIC member states like Bangladesh.

Despite these challenges, the sharing of the Good News in Bangladesh was on its way. After Bangladesh independence, a group of new theological graduates returned from the Philippines; they brought a new vision and commitment based on the Declarations of Berlin (1966) and Lausanne (1974), organized by the Billy Graham Evangelistic Association (BGEA), "Let the Earth Hear His Voice," and they helped give the church a new direction. We invited a few church growth specialists like Dr. Donald McGovern and Dr. Cal Guy to come to Bangladesh and offer advice to us. They challenged us with a new idea that "He went to the people, lived with them, and shared His message with them." The missions and the churches closed the "Book Room" and went to the population groups. At the same time, more international Christian conferences such as "The Future of World Evangelization: Unreached People" of 1984 and the International Conference for Itinerant Evangelists in Amsterdam in 1983, 1986, and again in 2000, challenged us and gave a new impetus to evangelism. In 1980 BBCF adopted a new goal of 20 percent growth over the present church membership by 1990 then another 10 percent growth by 2000; let us look at the following tables.

---

[6] Noor Ahmed Baba, "Organization of Islamic Conference," *Theory and Practice of Pan-Islamic Cooperation* (Dhaka, Bangladesh: University Press, 1994) preface.

A HUNDRED YEARS OF BAPTIST MINISTRY IN BANGLADESH

Bangladesh Baptist Church Fellowship (BBCF)
Number of Churches: 1919–2014

Imperial Period 1919–1947	Pakistan Regime 1948–1971	Bangladesh Time 1972–2014	Total
10	8	478	496

Source: The BBCF Secretariat

Now BBCF has developed a strategic plan called Vision 20/20. By 2020, our church membership will reach 45,000 and the number of churches will be 530. Along with church planting we have a big socioeconomic development program for the new believers and for the nation. The Garo Baptist Convention belongs exclusively to the Garo ethnic community. They are identified as an ethnic language group of the Tibeto-Burman family. They live in the northeastern part of Bangladesh and in the plain of the Garo Hills area of the state of Meghalaya, India.

The Baptist Missionary Society (BMS) started the initial work among the Garos in 1868. The first Baptist church was planted in 1876, and the Garo Baptist Union >Garo Baptist Convention was organized in 1890. From the following tables, one can understand the growth of the GBC.

Garo Baptist Convention (GBC)
Number of Churches 1890–2014

Imperial Period 1890-1947	Pakistan Regime 1948-1971	Bangladesh Time 1972–2014	Total
88	36	33	157

Source: The BBCF Secretariat

Why such a comparatively poor showing? Possibly because we did not hear the prudence of wise men like W. E. French, who served in Bengal/Bangladesh from 1911 to 1950. I find him to be the first person to understand the situation; he said, "Our Baptist methods will never produce mass movement, for our emphasis is essentially on the personal salvation of individuals and the weeding out of the sheep from the goats."[7]

Donald McGovern and Cal Guy echoed the voice of Rev. French; both McGovern and Guy suggested we close the Book Room and go to people groups. The success of BBCF is due to our following the message to "go to people groups." Another observation by William Carey, the great grandson of Dr. William Carey, is relevant: he complained, "the mission...educated, employed, paid, and controlled its Indian agents without reference to the churches, thus withdrawing the natural leaders from the churches, and constituting them as a separate body of professional evangelists under a foreign organization."[8] Rev. Carey based his insightful assessment on living for thirty-five years (1884–1919) with the people of deep rural Bangladesh. These educated, employed, paid agents were the faithful helpers of the mission. The rural people called them *"Babu"*— a dignified man. They never lived with the people, ate with people, or shared the gospel in the people's language. They sat in a comfortable "book room" and waited for an inquirer to come to them and ask about Christianity. This was not a successful strategy.

The history of the Baptist church started in Bengal/Bangladesh in 1796, when Dr. William Carey planted the first Baptist church in Dinajpur, now Bangladesh. Thus, Baptists have a history of over 215 years in Bengal/Bangladesh. The church growth movement in BBCS is shown in the following table:

The Bangladesh Baptist Church Sangha (BBCS)
Number of Churches: 1796–2014

Imperial Period 1890-1947	Pakistan Regime 1948-1971	Bangladesh Time 1972–2014	Total
145	14	209	368

Source: The BBC Secretariat

We have already noted that the churches the Baptist Mission Society (BMS) planted were brought under a new umbrella in 1922 called Bengal Baptist Union>Bangladesh Baptist Church Sangha (BBCS). The BMS and

---

[7] W. E. French, *The Gospel in India* (London, 1946) 123, quoted in Brian Stanley, *The History of Baptist Missionary Society, 1792—1971* (Edinburgh: T&T Clark, 1992) 270.

[8] Stanley, *History*, 285.

BBCS were integrated in 1935 in a true sense of partnership. The national organization (BBCS) "took over all functions hitherto exercised by the mission, and act quite independently of it, subject to certain controls on finance and the location of foreign missionary personnel being retained by the mission."[9]

Another Baptist group, the Association of Baptists for World Evangelism (ABWE), arrived in 1958. They opened two ministries in Chittagong city and in Cox's Bazar. In Chittagong city, they started a literature ministry, and they built a hospital in Cox's Bazar. The ABWE was very evangelical, but non-cooperative; they were not even a member of the Baptist World Alliance. The ABWE founded two church groups: the Bangladesh Tribal Association of Baptist Churches (BTABC) and the Bangladesh Association of Baptist Churches (BABC). At present BTABC has 141 churches and the BABC has seventeen churches.

Five Baptist missionary societies labored in Bangladesh, but the result was not very successful. Today, all five missions have changed their strategies. Over the last twenty years BMS World Mission of the United Kingdom has had a lean period in Bangladesh due to visa issues and expanding work in other countries. Now they have a growing team in Bangladesh but continue to operate on a partnership basis. The ABMS has changed its name to Global International. The NBMS is now Tranzsend. The Southern Baptists are now engaged in clandestine ministry in Bangladesh.

After the liberation of Bangladesh, the mission societies ABMS, NZBMS, SBC, and ABWE, along with some other international proxy ministries, started to engage in Muslim evangelism in a clandestine way. They adopted the Muslim culture, language, dress, food habits, and so forth. This new movement was started, keeping the local churches in the dark regarding the new strategy. Islam is the majority religion, the religion of about 92 percent of the total population of 118 million. The BMS could not work independently because of the partnership structure; it continued to operate within the structures of BBCS. In the early 1900s Rev. William Goldsack, Rev. Bevan Jones, Dr. Samuel Zwemar, and Rev. John Tackle began to experiment with Muslim evangelism even as the Catholic Church had done in the seven-

---

[9] Gordon Soddy, "Baptists in Bangladesh," *National Council of Churches* (Dhaka, Bangladesh: Bangladesh, 1987) 203.

teenth century. The Catholic-converted Muslims are called "Occult Christians"; "they are occult because they have not the permission from the great mogor [Moghul Ruler in India] to make use of their liberty for changing their religion nor are we allowed, under pain of death for us and them, to admit them to the Law of Jesus Christ."[10]

We do not yet know the success of this clandestine movement; let us pray to the Lord of harvest. Within BBCS and in BBCF there has been a steady growth of people coming to faith from the majority population, known as Muslim Background Believers (MBBs). BBCF has thirty-five congregations, which include MBBs, and BBCS has around twenty such congregations. Both BBCF and BBCS have a strategy of placing evangelists/church planters in strategic locations with a view to establishing a church that engages with the local population.

John F Kennedy (1917–1963) said, "Ask not what your country can do for you. Ask what you can do for your country." We Christians in Bangladesh are not even 1 percent of the total population, yet we serve 20 percent of the population through our social ministry. We are grateful to the missions who brought the gospel to Bangladesh. Many of their people died without seeing fields ripen to gold and yield to the reaper. I thank God that I lived to see the day when:

There were streams in the desert
burning sands become pool, and
there were springs of water on the thirsty ground.
~Isaiah 35:7

---

[10] J. J. A. Campos, *History of Portuguese in Bengal* (Patna, India: Janki Prokashan, 1979) 267.

25

Baptists and Revival in Africa through Changing Scenes: The Nigerian Baptist Experience, 1850–2014

Simon Ademola Ajayi

Africa is a vast continent with great diversity of lands and peoples, made up of fifty-four countries. It is the second largest continent in the world, with an area of 30.3 million square kilometers (11.7 million square miles), which is roughly one-fifth of the earth's landmass. The northern part of the continent lies along the Mediterranean Sea, and below it is the vast Sahara desert, which is reputed to be the largest desert in the world.[1] Many distinct human populations of a great complexity of cultures occupy it.[2] As a matter of fact, the indigenous peoples of Africa are so culturally diverse that no single language, social organization, economy, custom, myth, or legend is common to all of them.[3] The diversity of the peoples and their cultures both within and between geographic regions and nation-state boundaries is quite obvious, details of which need not delay us here.

Meanwhile, it is significant to stress that the religious inclinations of the people are equally diverse, with Christianity, Islam, and African Traditional Religion (ATR) being the most dominant. Christian missionaries from both Europe and America brought the Christian faith into the continent, alongside Western education, literacy, and orthodox medical and healthcare facilities, as well as allied social services. Over time, the church in the continent has not only grown, but also developed. Today, that continent is one of the most fruitful fields for the spread of the gospel. It is significant that despite strong com-

---

[1] S. Ademola Ajayi, ed., *African Culture & Civilization* (Ibadan: Atlantis Books, in association with Ibadan Cultural Studies Group, 2005) 9.

[2] Ajayi, *African Culture & Civilization*, 9.

[3] William A. Shack, "Culture and Culture Areas [of Africa]," in *Encyclopaedia of Africa South of the Sahara*, ed. John Middleton, vol. 1 (New York: Simon & Schuster Macmillan, 1997) 384.

petition from Islam, which is visibly dominant in North Africa, with a modicum of strength in many countries in West and East Africa, Christianity is apparently a force to be reckoned with in Africa, south of the Sahara.

Baptist Beginnings in Africa

Baptists were among the pioneer Western missionaries that blazed the trail for the gospel in Africa, especially during the period of the reintroduction of Christianity into the continent in the nineteenth century. Among the first places to experience the presence of the Baptist denomination were Liberia and Nigeria. From the United States of America came the American Baptist Missionary Union and the Foreign Mission Board (FMB) of the Southern Baptist Convention to these two countries respectively. By the same token, early Baptist ventures took root among European settlers in South Africa.

The earliest Baptists ventured into Africa in 1822 when freed slaves from America settled in Liberia, a process which helped to facilitate close cultural, economic, and political ties with the USA Baptists (and Methodists). Before World War I, the most notable areas of Baptist missionary work in Africa, apart from Liberia and Nigeria were Cameroon, Congo (Zaire), Malawi, and South Africa. Significant Baptist expansion, growth, and continental spread have, however, occurred since World War II. The American Baptist Missionary Union, the Foreign Mission Board (FMB) of the Southern Baptist Convention, and the Foreign Mission Board of the National Baptist Convention came from the United States. From Europe came the Baptist Society of Great Britain and the Mission Society of the German Baptists.[4] Today, there are Baptists in at least forty-three of the fifty-four countries in the African continent. It should be noted, however, that very few Baptists live in North Africa, because of the strong hold and resilience of Islam, often aided by government restrictions, including prohibitions of missionaries and institutional ministries in that region of the continent. Only Egypt, in North Africa, has a significant Christian minority. At any rate, a number of the African countries are experiencing an explosion of growth, often with the fastest rates of increase of Baptists anywhere in the world. One such place is Nigeria, the country with the highest black population not only in Africa but also throughout the world.

Revival among Baptists in Africa has been quite dynamic. With fifty-

---

[4] "Africa," *Baptists Around the World: A Comprehensive History*, ed. Albert W. Wardin (Nashville: Broadman & Holman, 1995) 11.

four countries in Africa, it would be a herculean task to attempt a discourse on the entire continent. It would be easier for a camel to enter through the eye of a needle than for anyone to take a continental look at the subject without making unsubstantiated generalizations. This chapter concentrates on Nigeria. The choice of Nigeria is itself significant not only as the country with the largest black population in the continent but also because Nigeria has the highest concentration of Baptists in Africa and in the world.

In a nutshell, the purpose of this chapter to present in perspective the various identifiable epochs in the development, awakening, rekindling, and invigoration of Baptist work in Nigeria. The chapter is divided into subsections: the foundation of Baptist work in Nigeria in 1850; the rupture and Great Awakening of 1888; the 1914 reunion for greater and more accelerated exploits; Post-World-War-II decolonization and Nigerianization of Baptist leadership in Nigeria; the explosive era of Charismatic renewal of the 1980s and 1990s, which marked a critical turning point in Baptist revival in Nigeria; the twenty-first-century developments up to 2014, the terminal date in this presentation. Concluding remarks follow these.

Baptist Witness in Nigeria

Baptist growth in Nigeria has been remarkable. Baptist work was introduced into the country in 1850 by missionaries of the Foreign Mission Board of the Southern Baptist Convention, pioneered by Thomas Jefferson Bowen.[5] By the closing decade of the twentieth century, specifically at 1995, 80 percent of Baptists in the whole of West Africa lived in Nigeria.[6] Baptist expansion in Nigeria in the first four decades beginning from 1850 was rather slow for several reasons and challenging factors, which could be summed up as follows:
- Hostile climate and health hazards, culminating in the entire West African sub-region being tagged or designated with the frightening epithet, "The White Man's Grave"[7]

---

[5] Readers interested in the life and missionary venture of Thomas Jefferson Bowen in Nigeria will benefit from the fairly comprehensive account in S. Ademola Ajayi (with J. T. Okedara) *Thomas Jefferson Bowen: Pioneer Baptist Missionary to Nigeria, 1850–1856* (Ibadan: John Archers, 2004).

[6] *Baptists Around the World*, 67.

[7] For an insightful discourse on the high rate of mortality among early white missionaries from the Western world due to the menace of malaria and other tropical diseases, see L. J. Bruce-

- Poor transportation and grossly inadequate communication facilities, which made it difficult for the missionaries to do any expansive work
- Shortage of manpower in relation to the extensive mission field
- The controversial polygyny or polygamy problem
- The resilience of the traditional religion
- Hostility of some traditional rulers, as well as persecution of early converts
- Language barrier
- Civil wars and political upheavals in many areas where the missionaries initially established their mission fields, notably Yorubaland, southwestern Nigeria, which made it very dangerous for the missionaries to travel
- Civil war in the United States of America, the source of Baptist work in Nigeria, just when the mission work was finding its feet in the 1860s
- Lack of continuity in the work of many missionaries
- Financial constraints
- Culture shock
- Deprivations by the mission staff, as well as related challenges.[8]

All the challenging circumstances did not augur well for the growth of early Baptist work in the country as they made far-reaching expansion difficult. Given its numerous challenges, it is surprising that the mustard seed planted by the pioneer Baptist missionaries even germinated or blossomed. Ironically, that was at a time when, as Professor Emmanuel Ayandele rightly asserts, "the Anglicans and Methodists were already counting their votaries in thousands."[9] It is significant that the Wesleyan Methodists and the Church Missionary Society (the missionary wing of the Anglican Church) had certain

---

Chwatt and Joan M. Bruce-Chwatt, "Malaria and Yellow Fever: The Mortality of British Expatriates in Colonial West Africa" in *Health in Tropical Africa during the Colonial Period*, ed. E. E. Sabben-Clare, D. J. Bradley, and K. Kirkwood (Oxford: Clarendon Press, 1980) 43–59; Also useful is R. E. Dummet "The Campaign Against Malaria and the Expansion of Scientific Medical and Sanitary Services in British West Africa, 1898–1910," *African Historical Studies* 1 (1968): 153–97; For more on the state of health during the beginning of colonialism, see Raph Scrahm, *A History of the Nigerian Health Services* (Ibadan: Ibadan University Press, 1971).

[8] Readers interested in a fairly detailed account of the challenges faced by the early Baptist missionaries in Nigeria will benefit from the comprehensive account in S. Ademola Ajayi, *Baptist Work in Nigeria, 1850–2005: A Comprehensive History* (Ibadan: BookWright Publishers, 2010) chap. 5.

[9] E. A. Ayandele, "New Introduction" in T. J. Bowen, *Central Africa: Adventures and Missionary Labors in Several Countries in the Interior of Africa, 1849–1856*, ed. E. A. Ayandele (London: Frank Cass, 1968) vii–viii.

advantages over the Baptists. These sister missions came from Europe, geographically closer to Africa.

Thus, Baptist work in Nigeria during its first three to four decades showed a marked declension from the early zeal conveyed by the pioneer missionaries and the mission boards that sponsored those missionaries. Admittedly, the mission took momentous steps in realizing its objectives; yet, measured against the effort that was invested and the cost both in terms of human and material resources, the result of Baptist venture in this early period was not impressive. In spite of this reality, one should still emphasize that all the early sporadic attempts at Baptist enterprise, despite the slow pace of growth, were not altogether a complete waste of effort. At least, a spiritual mustard seed had been planted which would bear important political, economic, social, and allied fruits.

Meanwhile, the Baptists of Nigeria have, at various epochs in their denominational history, witnessed significant landmarks in their crusading zeal, renewal, and reawakening in the life of the church congregation—in short, its pursuits of spiritual and religious enthusiasm. Some of the most salient landmarks are here identified and highlighted.

Rupture and the Great Awakening of 1888

The period spanning the 1860s and 1870s was, in many respects, a critical period in the history of Baptist work in Nigeria. Partly as a result of the ripple effects of the American Civil War (1860–1865) and allied challenges, the Southern Baptist Convention mission field in Nigeria was, for about seven years between 1868 and 1875, left with no American missionary on the ground. With the possible exception of Ogbomosho, Baptists in the country during that early period were neither numerically nor socially a powerful community in any of the towns where they were established. Some members of the church, foremost of whom was Babalola Barika, had hoped still for the return of the missionaries.[10] Even when he arrived in Ogbomosho in 1875, William Joshua David, the new missionary, described the congregation there as "disorganised, dispirited, and dying,"[11]

In June 1875, as a result of the more favorable post-war economic climate

---

[10] See W. J. David Diary: Entry for August 30, 1876, where, according to David, Barika was especially happy for his (David's) arrival, glorifying God for answering the prayers of the little congregation. He received David with wild demonstration of joy and enthusiasm.

[11] W. J. David Diary: Entry for September 3, 1876.

in America, Rev. William J. David was sent by the Foreign Mission Board to revive Baptist work, which had suffered a temporary neglect for almost a decade. On arrival, David went to Lagos, and in a short while, he visited deserted stations in Abeokuta, Oyo, and Ogbomosho. At each place, he was able to find some converts who had remained faithful throughout the years of neglect.

Right from 1850, when the Southern Baptists arrived in Nigeria, up to the late 1880s, the American missionaries had virtually been the sole propagators of the gospel in the country. From the mid-1870s, however, the spirit of nationalism had enveloped the Baptist church in Nigeria. Since there was no American Baptist missionary on the Nigerian field from 1868 to 1975, the indigenous Baptists had kept the Baptist faith alive in Lagos and Ogbomosho. They had developed what Travis Collins describes as a psychological independence.[12] They had been compelled by the circumstances of the period to take some local initiative for the spread of the gospel. The American Civil War had freed the black slaves in America, while back in the Nigerian field, the years of absence of missionaries had encouraged the spirit of self-reliance as they took responsibility for running the few existing Baptist churches and schools in Nigeria.

In 1888, there was a major revival in the Baptist denomination in Nigeria, which affected the country's only viable Baptist Church—the First Baptist Church, Lagos. At that time, young Nigerian Baptist men and women in their prime developed fervor for evangelization, even though they could not achieve their goals all alone. They clamored for a "national" or independent church. They resolved to pursue this goal with every resource at their disposal, especially through the promotion of the Nigerian languages and culture, including African music and drumming and the like. Those young converts of the revival were spurred by the American Baptist missionaries' rejection of their ideas of how best to produce a national Christianity. For example, among many other social standards, "trousers were required for church but when he wore them the African discovered he was accused of 'aping.' If he attempted to straddle two cultures he was termed half-civilized."[13]

By 1886, that is, two years before the explosion, the bitterness had got to an alarming proportion. In that year, a group of Africans styling themselves

---

[12] Travis Collins, *The Baptist Mission of Nigeria, 1850–1993* (Ibadan: Oluseyi, 1993) 21.

[13] J. B. Webster, "The African Churches" in *Nigeria Magazine*, no. 79, December 1963, 257.

"Paul, Silas, and others" were reported to have advocated in a letter for the establishment of an African or West African Church, crying "Secession! Secession!! Secession!!!."[14] Their nationalist urge could be glaringly discerned in the speeches and writings of some of the secessionist leaders and congregations not long after the historic breakaway. In 1900, for instance, barely twelve years after the historic division, the Native Baptist Church published an advertisement in a Lagos newspaper, which stated inter alia:

> The Native Baptist Church stands for individuality of race, congregational independence, self-support and self-government in Native Churches, simplicity of worship, temperance, the retention of native names, native dress, healthful native costumes and habits, and the use of the native language in religious worship.[15]

In the same vein, Dr. Mojola Agbebi, one of the secessionist leaders, in maintaining his ideological stance of "boycotting the boycottables" in the Western culture, had previously discarded his English name of David Brown Vincent as "denationalizing."[16] True to his word in his Africanist affirmation, Agbebi refused to appear in Episcopal robes of the hood and cassock while simultaneously abandoning his European costumes for native ones. By the same token, other emerging, young, indigenous Baptist leaders such as Lewis Stone took the name Lewis Fadipe while Lajide Mills became Lajide Tubi. These national churchmen apparently challenged the racial pretensions that Western missionaries had established in the churches. In short, there was tension between African cultural values and those of the West, which eventually snowballed into a division in the Lagos church. This division also prompted a scheme of reinvigoration for church growth and development within the Baptist orbit. Meanwhile, the movement for self-determination spread into places such as Ogbomosho in the interior of Yorubaland, southwestern Nigeria. In 1903, just a few years later, the Native Baptist Church in Lagos also experienced another division. Churches of the independent Baptist movement in Lagos, that is, Ebenezer and Araromi, consequent upon their breakaway from American Baptists, asserted a degree of self-government surpassing anything previously achieved in the country, especially among the mission-

---

[14] *Lagos Observer* (newspaper) February 1, 1886.
[15] *Lagos Standard*, April 4, 1990.
[16] See the text of the sermon delivered by Dr. Mojola Agbebi on the occasion of the first anniversary of the founding of the African Bethel Church, Lagos on December 21, 1902, published in the *Lagos Weekly Record*, April 4, 1903.

affiliated churches, in the following three decades or so. Henceforth, they were no longer dependent for all their needs and ideas upon the headquarters of the Southern Baptist Convention mission in America.

The division of the denomination into two bodies—American Mission Baptists and Native Baptists—though apparently undesirable, greatly helped the extension of Baptist orbit especially in later years. The two native Baptist churches extended their arms into many new areas and grew much faster than the American mission churches. Louis Mayfield Duval, one of the missionaries who arrived in Nigeria in 1901, in analyzing the effects of the Historic Schism of 1888 on the growth of Baptist work in Nigeria, remarked:

> This was apparently a heavy blow to our mission, not only in Lagos but also in the whole country. But that which in the eyes of men is a calamity is often used of God for the extension of His kingdom; and thus it proved in this case. This was the beginning of a movement that spread over the whole country, including the other denominations that suffered more than we; for our people continued true to the doctrine of the Baptists, and we were eventually reunited in the convention some years later.[17]

The painful division of the Baptists helped to invigorate both the Native Baptists and their American mentors. There was a mass appeal to an increasingly nationalistic-minded people of a purely African-controlled church, while missionaries and mission-founded churches also adapted to local realities. The result was that, while there existed only four surviving Baptist churches from the first four decades of Baptist work in Nigeria, the post-schismatic period invigorated the work such that by 1914 when the two bodies reunited, the number of Baptist churches that had been established had increased astronomically to over eighty.

The 1914 Reunion and Reinvigoration for Greater Evangelistic Exploits

The year 1914 marked a period of great awakening in the Baptist body in Nigeria. In that year, the Nigerian Baptist Convention emerged as a national entity when the two hitherto independent Baptist groups reunited under the umbrella of the Yoruba Baptist Association drawing together members of the American Mission Baptists and the Native Baptists. They joined spiritual forces for organized efforts in a more vigorous way. The union started in

---

[17] L. M. Duval, *Baptist Missions in Nigeria* (Richmond, VA.: Southern Baptist Convention, 1928) 188.

1914 under the name Yoruba Baptist Association because, up to 1914, Baptist work in Nigeria was largely restricted to the Yoruba ethnic group of Southwestern Nigeria. In 1919, however, the Yoruba Baptist Association changed its name to the Nigerian Baptist Convention, to bear a national cognomen as a result of Baptist penetration into other parts of the country. Following the formation of the Nigerian Baptist Convention, the Baptist movement in Nigeria suddenly began to grow more rapidly throughout the country—from the Niger Delta in the South to the Northern regions of Nigeria.

The Post-World-War-II Reawakening and Explosion

After 1945, there were dramatic changes in all areas of human endeavor in Africa, including the religious sphere. Henceforth, the winds of change that began to blow in the political realm through the process of decolonization became equally noticeable in Christian circles. The Southern Baptist missionaries in the Nigerian field had helped to facilitate the provision of Western education for Nigerian youths by establishing primary, secondary, and teacher training institutions in several parts of the country. Moreover, through collaboration with the Nigerian Baptist Convention, scholarships were given to young men who demonstrated great promise and potential to acquire specialized training and tertiary level education outside the country, notably in America, Europe, and Sierra Leone. By the mid-1940s, a number of beneficiaries of the scholarship programs had started to arrive in the country to take up leadership positions in churches and educational institutions, as well as key areas of the Nigerian Baptist Convention life. After World War II, therefore, indigenous Baptists in Nigeria began to assume greater responsibility for the expansion of Baptist work in the country. These leaders included the likes of James Tanimola Ayorinde, who served as the first indigenous General Secretary, and Aremu M. Laosebikan, who was the first indigenous Education Secretary. By 1947, all Baptist schools, except the theological seminary in Ogbomoso, were placed under the proprietorship of the Nigerian Baptist Convention. The political transition witnessed at the state level during the Africanization years reverberated in the church. From then onwards, foreign missionaries of the Southern Baptist Convention who had been working in the Nigerian field moved from their erstwhile supervisory roles to the role of advisers and supporters.[18] The tempo of change accelerated from 1960 onward

---

[18] Ajayi, *Baptist Work in Nigeria, 1850–2005*, 188.

when even more Nigerians began to reposition themselves for their responsibility of more vibrant contributions to the growth of Baptist witness in Nigeria. It is notable that the years following political independence in Nigeria (1963) produced larger numbers of converts than during the preceding era.

The Explosive Era of Charismatic Revival in the 1980s and 90s

The 1980s and '90s was an era of charismatic renewal; it was a period of great reawakening, increased spiritual interest, and vibrancy in the life of the Nigerian Baptist polity. It was a new era during which the Baptist denomination in Nigeria, like its Protestant counterparts, began to witness a major upheaval. There was, for instance, the growing influence of the Charismatic Renewal movement in the congregations. These Christians placed much emphasis on "baptism of the Holy Spirit." On the other hand, the traditional Baptists perceived this development as a direct threat to the age-long tradition of the Baptist Church. The infiltration of what was perceived as "unbaptistic practices" into the Nigerian Baptist Convention as a result of the growing influence of Pentecostalism, especially among the youth, caused great apprehension and controversy between youths and church or Convention leaders during this revolutionary phase.

Doctrinal conflicts resulting in a growing dichotomy between youths and adults became quite common in most Baptist churches in Nigeria during this new era. Among the former were found the group of charismatic Christians while the majority of the latter belonged to the group branded "traditional Baptists." More often than not, neither of the two categorizations was ever always willing to bow to the claim of supremacy by the other on doctrinal issues. While the youths yearned for, and sometimes exhibited, charismatic fervors in the liturgy of worship and praying, most adults, especially the traditional ones, saw such actions as "excessive" and "unbaptistic." This development resulted in a few cases of schism as well as mass exodus of youths from Baptist churches to churches of other denominations, especially the new generation charismatic and "Prosperity" churches.[19] It is significant that many new Pentecostal Christian denominations or Ministries in Nigeria today took

---

[19] For a fairly detailed discussion on the Prosperity Churches see, S. Ademola Ajayi, "The Prosperity Churches in Nigeria: A New Phenomenon in a Depressed Economic Setting" in *Money Struggle & City Life: Devaluation in Ibadan and Other Urban Centres in Southern Nigeria 1986–1996*, ed. Jane J. Guyer, LaRay Denzer, and Adigun Agbaje (Ibadan: BookBuilders, 2003) 259–69.

their roots from the Baptist Church. The following neo-Pentecostal church founders or ministers, for instance, are all of Nigerian Baptist origin: Gbile Akanni of Living Seed, Peace House, in Gboko, Benue State of Nigeria; Pastor Tunde Bakare of Latter Rain Assembly, Lagos; Bishop Francis Wale Oke of Christ Life Church, also known as Sword of the Spirit Ministries; Dr. Uzodinma Obed of Glory Tabernacle Ministry, Ibadan; Pastor Olubi Johnson of Scripture Pasture Christian Centre; Evangelist Sunday Popoola of Word Communications Ministries; Rev. Alex Adegboye of Stone Church; and Dr. Sola Kolade of Vine Branch Church, Ibadan, Nigeria. Today, although they are no longer Baptists, they remain useful instruments in promoting gospel growth. Moreover, in the Redeemed Christian Church of God (RCCG) in Nigeria, with branches all over the world, many of the renowned pastors are formerly from the Baptist ministry.

The trend of what happened during this phase was in itself a sign of the growth and vitality of the Baptist Church in Nigeria after a seemingly catastrophic transition. And, the relative understanding and peace currently experienced between the two generations of Baptists in the country is clear evidence of maturity through a developmental process. One must admit, however, that there has been an overwhelming temptation to shape liturgy to fit consumer demands and inject dynamism through ecumenical contact. The fact that currently the charismatic and ecumenical movements have influenced many Baptist churches—a trend that has led to a wide variety of practices and preferences—can, therefore, not be denied. Consequently, there is now a wide variety of practice, from liturgical formality to charismatic exuberance, from reformed traditionalism to ecumenical and Pentecostal experiment. The effects of charismatic renewal are seen most obviously in the increasing informality of worship and hymns. Many young pastors of today who are apparently well trained and more widely exposed to current trends than their predecessors, go the Pentecostal way. Shouting, "Halleluiah," which was anathema or "unbaptistic" in the past, is now common practice. Unlike the former stereotyped order of services, the modes of worship have been broadened to manifest exuberant praise services in which a number of praise choruses are sung. There is increasing accommodation or "toleration" of charismatic prayer sessions, including all-night or prayer vigils, and a deeper and more aggressive Bible Study, coupled with allied programs to meet the spiritual appetite of the growing number of youths and young adults. In many Nigerian Baptist churches, the first three days of the month are devoted to fasting and praying. In sum, the extent of the revolution is such that the lukewarm Baptist of old has, to a large extent, given way to Pentecostalism these days. Today, it is not uncommon to find many "Baptist" Churches who are caught up in "contemporary" Pentecostal styles of worship. To those who appreciate novelty, all this is welcome. To others, it is disturbing. To some churches have come freshness and vitality, to others restlessness and dissention. A fact that cannot be denied in the light of recent developments, however, is that some Baptist churches today are in danger of becoming part of a generic evangelicalism with few or any denominational distinctions.

By the same token, a quiet change began to appear in the profile of the Nigerian Baptist ministerial personnel during the new phase. During the 1980s the inflow of the new cadre of students flowed into the theological training institutions of the denomination in preparation for pastoral ministry. These students were university graduates; some of them even held higher degrees before enlistment for theological training. Admittedly, a few university graduates had passed through the Baptist seminaries in Ogbomosho and Kaduna in the past; this class of pastoral trainees increasingly began to gain admission into the theological schools in the 1980s. By the time they graduated and accepted calls into the pastorate of churches at the end of the 1980s, the ground was well watered for leadership positions that would not rubber-stamp the status quo. As the number of highly educated persons continued to increase in the local congregations and especially among the pastoral teams, the number of young people acceding to the faith continued to rise. What followed in the closing decade of the twentieth century was the questioning of denominational policies on existing sensitive issues.[20] The era experienced the birth of the "Stand-Up-for-Jesus Baptist Movement" among the young ministers from Lagos, one of the country's major cities and former capital. What are some of the common things these young pastors shared? They had a passion for Jesus; they had a vision for the Nigerian Baptist Convention; they had great energy; their academic and spiritual backgrounds created their style.

Members of the "Stand-Up-For-Jesus Movement" spearheaded a major revival not only in their churches but also within the umbrella Nigerian Baptist Convention. During this revolutionary phase, therefore, many areas of the

---

[20] Solomon A. Ishola "Defining Congregational Government in the 21st Century—The Nigerian (African) Experience." Paper presented at the Baptist World Alliance Annual Gathering and General Council Session, 2007, hosted by the Ghana Baptist Convention, Accra, July 2–7, 2007, 3.

status quo were greatly overhauled. Certain elements of charismatic fervor, which were hitherto regarded as "unbaptistic," were increasingly accommodated, giving way to a new revival in worship. During this phase, Baptist work became more unprecedentedly vibrant and extended to hitherto unreached areas in the country. On the international scene, Nigerian Baptists continued to exert considerable influence in Africa and at the global level.

The New Century and a More Aggressive Crusading and Revivalist Zeal

The new century has focused more on consolidating existing work and breaking new ground. Like their counterparts in other parts of the globe, Baptists of Nigeria are wholly dependent on evangelism for their existence and growth. Towards ensuring an accelerated expansion of the gospel, a nationwide campaign, tagged Operation Reach All (ORA) by A.D. 2000, was launched in 1990. The program was a special emphasis of the Convention, the aim of which was to create increased awareness in the churches, reach the unreached people of Nigeria, and spread the Christian gospel to every nook and cranny of the country by A.D. 2000. That operation called for a more vigorous establishment of preaching stations and the founding of new churches by older, established ones, as well as intensifying the spread of the gospel message to the unreached peoples. From the inception of ORA, new, innovative strategies were adopted to reach restricted areas of the country. It was indeed a bold mission thrust of the Nigerian Baptist Convention that involved all of its departments, churches, institutions, and organizations. It is significant that by the close of the 1990s and the commencement of a new millennium, ORA 2000 recorded the planting of thousands of new churches.

A new force of change that is worthy of attention is that from the beginning of the new century also, the annual gatherings of the Nigerian Baptist Convention have been more of a spiritual retreat than a time of business. And, as a rider, the annual sessions, which had hitherto been characterized by deep fissures, became considerably less combative.

In furtherance of the quest for the advancement of spiritual emphasis, a new revivalist program tagged Baptist Night of Wonders has been introduced under the current administration. This is a quarterly, all-night program introduced under the leadership of the current President of the Convention, Dr. Supo Ayokunle, which brings together all Baptists throughout Nigeria to lift up their voices in worship and corporate prayers unto God. It serves as a channel for further proclaiming the Good News and reaching out to more people in Nigeria and Africa, as part of the Convention's challenging task of fulfilling the mandate of the Great Commission. Through these avenues, among others, many more lives are touched, encouraged, and strengthened through the ministry of the Nigerian Baptist Convention.

Revival sometimes comes in times of crises and persecutions. We have seen earlier how the 1888 crisis led to schism and accelerated the advancement and spread of the Baptist church. The fruits of that revival continued for a considerable length of time. Meanwhile, the Nigerian Baptist Convention family has, for some decades now, been a victim of a spate of religious crises in some parts of the country, especially in Northern Nigeria.[21]

In February 2000, for instance, Islamic fundamentalists struck in Kaduna in a renewed, politically motivated religious riot. The attack was in the wake of the introduction of the Sharia legal system in Northern Nigeria. The introduction started in Zamfara State and was later embraced by a number of states such as Niger, Sokoto, and Kano. Under the guise of the then raging Sharia controversy in Kaduna State, Muslim youths unleashed terror on the Christian community in the town. Several houses and churches belonging to Christians were destroyed in the process. This time around, Baptists were among the worst hit. Twenty-three Baptist churches were burnt down in the state, fifteen of which were located in Kaduna Township. The Mission houses and Pastoriums were not spared. And worse still, the Baptist Theological Seminary in Kaduna was almost completely destroyed. The human casualty figure indicated that five Baptist pastors, including three student pastors of the seminary and two full-time pastors, lost their lives.[22] It was one of the most harrowing experiences ever witnessed in the history of Baptist work in Northern Nigeria. Apart from the psychological effect of widespread insecurity that pervaded the entire Christian community, many of the victims, especially those of Southern Nigeria origin, folded up their businesses while others relocated to their hometowns or states or at least moved their families. Many pastors and their families were forced to relocate. The trend has now been worsened by the current menace of the fundamentalist Islamic sect, *Jama'atu Ahlissunnah Lidda'awati Wal-Jihad*, otherwise known as Boko Haram, under the cover of religion, in several parts of Northern Nigeria. The sect, whose name, Boko

---

[21] For a fairly detailed discourse on the spate of ethno–religious conflicts in Northern Nigeria, see S. Ajayi, *Baptist Work in Nigeria, 1850–2005*, 309–12.

[22] See the closing remarks of the General Secretary, Nigerian Baptist Convention, to the 87th Annual Session of the NBC, 15–20 April 2000, 4.

Haram, means, "Western Education is heresy" has killed hundreds of people and destroyed several properties, including churches, in the past two years. There was the pathetic case of a Baptist pastor and wife from one of the states in Southern Nigeria, whose only child, a grown up son, was killed in one of the states in Northern Nigeria where the pastor was serving as a gospel minister, thus leaving the couple childless.

From the closing years of the first decade of this century, the threat of the Boko Haram extremists in northeast Nigeria, especially aimed at Christians, has been obvious enough. Consequently, a new passion for ecumenism has spread across the nation. The concern and brotherly awakening about the fate of Baptists and other Christians in the northern part of Nigeria is impacting the whole Christian community in Nigeria, including Baptists.

Concluding Remarks

The Baptist Church in Nigeria, as in some other countries in Africa, is so obviously vibrant and growing, physically and spiritually, throughout all regions of the country and beyond. As highlighted above, the Baptist denomination was introduced into Nigeria in 1850, while the Nigerian Baptist Convention, the umbrella body of all Nigerian Baptists, came into being in 1914. Only last year (2014), the Convention celebrated its centenary anniversary, by which time giant strides had been made. As at that date, the convention had grown to over ten thousand churches with about three million baptized believers and up to six and half million nonbaptized members spread across the nation.[23] As a matter of fact, the Nigerian Baptist Convention is currently the second largest Baptist Convention affiliating with the Baptist World Alliance (a fellowship of 228 Conventions and Unions in 121 countries) and the largest Baptist assemblage in the world after the Southern Baptist Convention, USA, and the National Baptist Convention, also in the United States.[24] The Baptist presence is ubiquitous throughout the nation. It is significant that apart from the churches cooperating with the mainstream Nigerian Baptist Convention, there are a number of small, independent churches, some of which are defi-

---

[23] S. Olasupo A. Ayokunle, introductory remarks, "A Century of Nigerian Baptist Convention Life: A Call for Celebration and Renewal" in *A Centenary of Nigerian Baptist Convention: A Call for Celebration and Renewal* (Ogbomosho: Nigerian Baptist Theological Seminary, 2014) 29.

[24] http://www.nigerianbaptist.org accessed on July 13, 2014.

nitely growing, though not at such a successful or phenomenal rate as the Nigerian Baptist Convention. Baptist presence in Africa in general and Nigeria in particular presents a vital presence.

Index

Aalders, Cynthia, 202–3, 211–12
Abbots Creek Church, 40–41
Aberdeen, lay-led revival, 237–38
ABFMS (American Baptist Foreign Mission Society), 313, 317–18
ability, distinguished from inability, 15–16, 23
abolitionism, 63
Abrahamse, Jan Martijn, 6
Adegboye, Alex, 403
African-Americans, 82, 87, 100
African Baptists, 7, 393–408
African Bethel Church, Lagos, 399n16
Agbebi, Mojola, 399
Aitsan, Lucius, 132
Ajayi, Simon Ademola, 8
Akanni, Gbile, 403
Albrecht, Karl, 309–10
Alexander, C. M., 343
Allen, Jimmy, 111
Alline, Henry, 116
Allison, Neil, 6, 113n1
altar calls. *See* invitation
America
    Baptists in, 18, 33
    Edwards's influence on, 18–26
    Great Awakenings in, 2, 32, 218–19
    the South and revivalism, x–x
American Baptist Foreign Mission Society (ABFMS), 313, 317–18
American Baptist Missionary Union, 394
American Baptist Telugu Mission, 78
AMFMS, 318
Anderson, Allen, 263
Anderson, Benedict, 125
Anderson, Christopher, 245
Anderson, Robert Mapes, 70
Andrew Fuller
depression of, 143–50
Anglican Church, 231, 279
Anglican Church Missionary Society, 142n5, 399
antinomianism, 13, 116
Apostolic Mission, of William Seymour, 70, 76
Araromi Baptist Church, Nigeria, 399

Aristotelianism, and Ramism, 298
Arminianism, 16, 23, 240, 254
Arnold, Ellen, 382, 386
Ash, John, 177, 204
Ashley, W. A, 272
Asia Baptists, 7
Assemblies of God, 71, 83–84, 264
Association of Baptist Churches (Ireland), 5, 231n25
Association of Baptists for World Evangelism (ABWE), 382
assurance, of salvation, 148, 153–57, 242–43
atheism/atheists, Iosif Ton, 330
atomic bombs, and spiritual distress, 108
Aukland Baptist Tabernacle, 355, 360–62, 366
Australia: Baptist missions in: English, 380–81; German, 370–73, 380–81; development of, and church construction, 7, 373–74, 376, 381
Australian Baptist Missionary Society (ABMS), 382, 386, 391
awakening, defined, 324n1
Ayandele, Emmanuel, 396
Ayokunle, Supo, 406
Ayorinde, James Tanimola, 401
Azusa Street Revival, 64–66, 68–69, 73, 78–82

Backus, Isaac, 20–21, 23
Bakare, Tunde, 403
Baker, BO, 99–100, 106n33, 107n41
Baker, Daniel J., 60–61
Baker, Dick, 100–101
Bangladesh Association of Baptist Churches (BABC), 382–92
Bangladesh Baptist Church Fellowship (BBCF), 382, 384, 389 (table), 392
Bangladesh Baptist Church Sangha (BBCS), 382, 391–92
Bangladesh Baptist Sangha, 384
Bangladesh Tribal Association of Baptist Churches (BTABC), 382, 391
baptism/s believers', 19, 21, 243, 247; at camp meetings, 53; by country: Australia, 370–71, 373; Romania, 330;

Scotland, 247, 250; decline of, 56–57; Eastern Orthodox, 325; of individuals: of Isabel Crawford, 4; John Collett Ryland, 185; Lucius Aitsan and wife, 132; infant, 21, 34–35, 237, 325; and Lord's Supper, 21–22; modes of: immersion, 245, 250, 308; sprinkling, 307; and mysterious sun sign, 54–55; and preaching, 297; prerequisites for, 129–30; proper subjects for, 22; and salvation, 136; second, 65; in Second Great Awakening, 48–49, 221; of the Spirit, 64–65, 71, 83, 264
Baptist Association (Australia), 371–72
Baptist Church in Ploiesti, Romania, 331
Baptist Church of Bujac, Arad, Romanis, 330
Baptist Congress, Berlin, 318
Baptist Education Society, 175–76
Baptist General Convention of Texas, 99n2
Baptist Highland Mission, 245
Baptist Home Missionary Society of Scotland, 245
Baptist Irish Society, 230
Baptist Missionary Society (BMS), x, 18, 246, 382–83, 389
Baptist Registry Centre, Kaunas, 320
Baptists. *See also* Free Will Baptists; Missionary Baptists; Northern Baptists; Particular Baptists; Regular Baptists; Separate Baptists; Arminian/Calvinistic union for revival, 240; and Azusa Street Revival, 78–82; in British military, 275, 280–81; and Calvinism, 29–30, 161–62, 189–90; censorship of, in Lithuania, 320–21;chaplaincy, in WWI, 275–76; and church budgeting, 91–92; congregational government of, 46–47; by country/region: Australia, 7, 370–74; Bangladesh, 2, 382–92; Canada, 4, 243; Cornwallis Twp., N.S., 116; East Bengal, 386; England, 215–16ff., 297; Ireland, 5, 231n25; Lithuania, 304ff., 312–14, 317–18, 321; New Zealand, 340–48, 350–54; Nigeria, 395–408; Romania, 326, 332–35; Sandy Creek, 37; Scotland, 239–40, 242–44, 249–50, 252–57; South Carolina, 3, 44ff., 45–47; Southern America, 32–33, 47; Wales, 263–66; decline of, 6, 161–62, 190n50; European history of, 304ff; and evangelical awakening, 216–20, 307

as "full gospel," 64, 83–84
growth of, 197, 215, 232
holiness-fundamentalists, 75–76
and Jonathan Edwards, 12–18, 31
and just war, 274–75, 279
and non-Baptist converts, 48n14
as Nonconformists, 301
and Pentecostalism, 75, 78, 86, 345
persecution of, 7
and Second Great Awakening, 214ff.
Seventh Day, 246
and stewardship campaigns, 94
and WWI, 265, 276
Baptist Society of Great Britain, 394
Baptist Student Union (BSU), 99
Baptist Unions
of England, 5, 215, 233, 257n18
of Great Britain and Ireland (BUGBI), 275, 277
in Ireland, 6
of Lithuania, 314–15, 3160317
of New Zealand, 355
of Scotland, 5, 215, 233, 239, 270, 272
Baptist World Alliance, 317, 407
Barika, Babalola, 397
Barnes, Elizabeth, 119
Bartleman, Frank, 67
Baylor Religious Hour (BRH), 99, 104
Baylor University, 98–111
BBC Trans World Radio, 331
Beaufort, South Carolina, 60
Bebbington, David, 16, 26, 31, 65, 203, 214–15, 280n42, 339–40, 344, 346–47
Beck, Rosalie, 2
Beddome, Benjamin, 178, 183–84, 200n2
Bell, E. N., 71
Bellamy, Joseph, *True Religion Delineated*, 20, 25
Benander, C. E., 80
Benedict, David, 20, 47
Bengal. *See* Bangladesh Baptists
Bengal Baptist Union (BBU), 383
Bengal Christian Council, 384
Benskin, Frederick George, 277
Benson, Louis F., 201, 204
Beougher, Timothy K., 324n1
Berg, Virginia Lee, 84n88
Beruldsen, Christina, 264
Beruldsen, Eilif, 264
Bethel Association, and Second Great Awakening, 48–49

INDEX

Bible
   Cornilescu/Protestant translation of, 325
   exegesis/application of, 301
   as foundation of hymns, 203
   and higher criticism, 271, 356, 365–66
   Bible Missionary Society, 80–81
   biblicism, 151, 166
Big Stephen's Creek Church, 52, 56
Billy Graham Evangelistic Association, x, 1, 369, 388. *See also* Graham, Billy
Birrell, C. M., 219
Black, C. M., 266
Black Swamp Church, 49
Blair, Ann, 123
Blum, Samuel, 377, 381
Blundell, Thomas, 171
BMS (Society for Propagating the Gospel among the Heathen), 142, 151–52, 156, 158–59, 171–72
Boardman, George, 117
Boddy, A. B., 264
Boggs, Frank, 109
Booth, Abraham, 175–76, 341
Bow, J. G., 81n75
Bowen, Thomas Jefferson, 395
Bradford Academy, 25
Bradshaw, John, 350
Brahama Somaj religion, 383
Brainerd, David, 117–18
Brantly, William, "Animating Scenes in Zion," 53
Brethren Church, 234–35
Briggs, John, 197
Brighton Street Evangelical Union Church, 237
Brine, John, 161, 190–91
Bristol Education Society, 165, 167–72
Britain. *See* Great Britain
British Empire, and missionaries, 124–28
British Missionary Societies, and Mahatma Gandhi, 385
Broadmead Baptist Church, Bristol, 277
Brookes, Iveson, 52
Brooks, Thomas, 148
Broome, J. R., 201–2, 208
Brown, C. C., 93
Brown, John Newton, 24
Browne, Robert, 292–93, 297, 297n45, 301–2
Bruce, William, 268
Brushy Creek Church, 57–62

Bull, Josiah, 182
Bunyan, John, *Grace Abounding to the Chief of Sinners*, 148
Burma, 16, 121, 126
Butler, Jon, 32–33, 38
Butt, Howard, 104–7, 107n41, 109

Cairns, David, *Army and Religion* committee, 284
Cairns, D. S., 265
Caldwell, Robert, *Theologies of the American Revivalists*, 23, 23n39, 26, 30–31
Calvin, John, and Company of Pastors, 291–92
Calvinism. *See also* High Calvinism; Hyper-Calvinism; New Calvinism; and decline of churches, 161–62, 189–90
   Edwardsean, 13, 18, 23n42, 28–29
   Evangelical, 149, 162, 179, 181ff., 189–98, 192n61, 197–98
   five points of, 190, 195
   of George Whitefield, 33
   and John Ryland Jr, 197–98
   of Methodist minister, 232n32
   and the Modern Question, 166, 190
   and Particular Baptists, 4–5
   revival of, 30
   Ryland's characterization of, 196
   and "subjective warrant," 15
Cameron, Duncan, 247
Campbell, John, 243
camp meetings, 48–53
Canadian Literary Institute, 13
Canterbury Baptist Association, 341
Carey, William (the elder)
   An Enquiry Into the Obligations of Christians ..., 16
   "attempt great things; expect great things" phrase of, 18
   and Calvinism, 194
   as cross-cultural missionary, 142
   influences the Judsons, 24
   as multilingual, 171–72
   in Scotland, 242
   and Serampore Trio, 178
Carey, William (the younger), 382, 390
Carlyle, Thomas, 182n7
Carmichael, Joseph, 5
Carrubbers' Close Mission, 236–38
Carter, Terry, 5
Carter, William, 219–20
Cartwright, Peter, 75

411

Cartwright, Thomas, 295, 297n45
Casper, Scott, 118
Catholic Church, in Lithuania, 313
Catholics/Catholic Church
  by country/region: in Australia, 373; Lithuania, 6–7, 310, 319; New Zealand, 340; Romania, 326
  and homilies, 295
  and Muslims, 391–92
  and paganism, 312
  sociopolitical power of, 322–23
  censorship, of Lithuanian Baptists, 320–21
Chaderton, Laurence, 299
Chambers, Oswald, 276–77
Champion, Leonard G., 194, 203
chaplaincy
  for ANSAC troops, 282
  in British Expeditionary Force (BEF), 283
  in England, 6
  history of, 284–86
  Jewish, 278n30
  in U.S. military, 275–76
  Welsh, 281
  in WWI, 6, 275–77, 278n26, 279–80
Chapman, Wilbur, 367
charismatic renewal. *See* Pentecostalsm
charity, as student mission, 103
Charleston Association of Baptists, 18, 46, 50–51
Charleston Baptist Church, 46
Charlotte Baptist Chapel, Edinburgh, 257–59, 263–64, 270n82, 355, 358
Charlton, Thomas, 99n3
Charnwood Road Baptist Church, 181
Charteris, William Cramb, 276, 280, 282, 296
Child, James, 40n3
Cho, Nancy, 203
Christian and Missionary Alliance church, 83
Christian Brethren, 268
Christian Endeavor societies, 263
Christian history, 339
Christianity
  in Great Britain, 278
  in sub-Saharan Africa, 394ff.
Christ Life Church (Sword of the Spirit Ministries), 403
Chun, Chris, 2, 31
church discipline, 93–94, 95n16, 377
church histories, 223–25

Church Lads' Brigade, 275
Church of England. *See* Anglican Church
church officers
  deacons, 70
Church of God in Christ (Pentecostal), 70
Church of Scotland, 234
Ciobota, Ioan, 329
Clark, Fred, 269
Clements, K. W., 274
clergy education, 47, 52, 62, 116, 131, 161–64, 167, 173–74
Cline, Eva, 137
Cody, Bill, 107n39
Collins, Arch, 71
Collins, Hercules, 160
Collins, Travis, 398
Collins, William, 177
colonization
  and Burma, 126–27
  and class, 348
  and empire, 115
  and missions, 124–28
  in New Zealand, 344, 348–52
  and white settlers, 127n59
  Zalzburg settlers, 311
Colonsay island, 245
Columbian College, 178
Communion. *See* Lord's Supper
Communists/Communism, and Romanian Baptists, 326–28
Company of Pastors (Calvin), 291–92
Concert of Prayer, 17n20
Condie, Maggie, 262–63
Conference of Christian Fundamentals, 356
confessions of faith
  Baptist Faith and Message, 25
  Calvinistic, 201
  London Baptist Confession, 31
  New Hampshire Confession, 24; and free will, 24–25
  of Philadelphia Baptist Association, 36
  Philadelphia Baptist Confession of Faith, 18, 23, 36
  Second London Confession, 18, 36, 201, 203
  Westminster Confession of Faith, 23
Congregational church, 249, 268, 275–76
Congregationalists
  Jonathan Edwards, x
  and New England revivals, x
  New Light movement, 19–20, 22
  Separate, 35

INDEX

and Separate Baptists, 19
conversions
   in Australia, 370, 373–75
   and Hyper-Calvinism, 15
   of individuals: of Charles Haddon Spurgeon, 288–89; of John Ryland Jr., 183–86
   of Kiowas, 132–33
   in Nigeria, after independence, 402
   and peer pressure, 106n36
   at revival meetings, 103, 107, 111–12
   in Scotland, 243, 250
   in Second Great Awakening, 219–20
   at student prayer meetings, 103
   and "the Jesus road," 133
   Whitefield's understanding of, 34
Cook, L. Katherine, 99n3
Cook, Paul E. G., 197
Cooper, Thomas, 219
Cooperative Program. *See* Southern Baptist Convention (SBC)
Cordoiner, David, 268
Cornilescu, Dumitru, 325, 325n3
Cotton Famine, 220–21
Couper, W. J., 243
covetousness, and church discipline, 95n16
Cowper, William, 200
Cox, F. A., 197
Craig, Lewis, 40n3
Crawford, Isabel, 4, 129ff., 134–35, 137
Crawford, John, 131
Crocker, Chris, 4
Crosby, Thomas, 177
Cross, Anthony, 4
Croy, James, 243n3
culture
   and Baptist mission in Nigeria, 398–99
   and revivalism, 5, 262–63, 346–52
   of sensibility, 117–20

Dagg, John L., 19
Dallas Morning News, 108
Darnton, Robert, 120, 128
Datta, Dennis Dilap, 7–8
David, William Joshua, 397–98
Davies, Gwen, 113n1
Davis, Elnathan, 39–40
Davis, James, 58–59
Davis, Jonathan, 58–59
Dayton, Donald W., 377
deacons, as church leaders, 70
Declaration of Berlin, 388

Declaration of Lausanne, 388
Delhi Unity Conference of Religious Freedom, 385
Denny, Bob, 101, 104–5
Denver Bible Institute, 85
Dering, Edward, 296n42
Dever, Mark, 28n57, 30
discipleship/sanctification, and Cooperative Program, 94–95
disease/illness
   of Andrew Fuller, 157–58
   of Anne Steele, 202
   cholera outbreak, Scotland, 246
   and divine healing, and Worrell, 75
   influenza pandemic, 287
   in Nigeria, 395–96
   smallpox, 248
   WWI attrition, 286–87
Dissenters, 290n10
Dixon, Arthur Cecil, 75–78, 80, 277
   Speaking with Tongues, 76
Dobbins, Gaines, 92
Dowie, Alexander, 76
Downie, Dr. and Mrs. David, 78
Downs, Pvt. J., 282–83
Dragostea (Love) Baptist Church, Romania, 327
Drummond, R. J., 269
Dunbar, Duncan, 246
Durham, William H., 71, 78
Duval, Louis Mayfield, 400

Eade, B. N., 386
Eaglen, Robert, 288n3
East Bengal. *See* East Pakistan
East Bengal Baptist Union (EBBU), 383–85
Eastern Europe, 6–7
Eastern Orthodox soteriology, 325
East Pakistan, becomes Islamic Republic, 386
East Pakistan Baptist Union, 383
East Pakistan Joint Preaching Movement, 387
East Prussian Baptist Union, 315–16
Eaton, T. T., 80n69, 81n75
Ebenezer Baptist Church, Nigeria, 399
economic depression, and revival, 221–22
Edgefield, South Carolina, 51–53, 55–56
Edgefield Baptist Association, 56–57, 61–62
Edgefield Female Academy, 52n29, 54
Edgefield Village Church, 52–53, 56
Edinburgh Conference, 383–84

education
- for biblical languages, 164
- and catechisms, 177–78
- of clergy, 47, 52, 62, 116, 131, 161–64, 167, 173–74
- dissenters' schools, 176–79
- household seminaries, 291–93
- of indigenous ministers, 179
- and Isabel Crawford, 129–30
- lacking: in Australia Baptists, 373–74; in Greenville Village area, 57
- Manning's view of, 116
- of missionaries, 178
- Northern Education Society, 173
- for Particular Baptists, 162–64
- pastor/evangelist training in Pakistan, 387
- and "prophesyings," 291
- and Ramism, 298–301
- and revival, 3–4, 98, 100
- by SBC, in Nigeria, 401–2
- scholarships, in Nigeria, 401
- Separate Baptists' view of, 47
- spread by evangelical Baptists, 176–79
- Spurgeon's view of, 289–90
- and teaching, as spiritual gift, 33
- theological, 165–68, 170, 172, 179–80
- Western, in Nigeria, 401

educational institutions
- Acadia University, 117
- of Baptist General Convention of Texas, 99n2
- Baptist Missionary Training School (Chicago), 131
- Baptist seminaries: in Nigeria, 404; in Riga, 313
- Baptist Theological College, New Zealand, 355
- Bible school of Isabel Crawford, 136–37
- Bible Training Institute (now Laidlaw College), 355
- Bradford Academy, 25
- Bristol Baptist Academy, 11, 13, 165–66
- Bristol Education Society, 168
- Calabar College in Jamaica, 179
- closed to Dissenters, 176
- Colby College, 117
- College of Christian Theology Bangladesh (CCTB), 383
- East Texas Baptist College, 99n2
- Emmanuel Christian University, 331
- Emmanuel College, Cambridge, 291
- Furman Academy and Theological Institution, 52, 55, 60, 62
- George Washington University, 178
- Glasgow Bible Training Institute, 357
- Hardin-Simmons College, 99n2
- Howard Payne College, 99n2
- Mary Hardin Baylor College, 99n2
- Newton Theological Institution (Massachusetts), 313–14, 318
- Philadelphia Theological Institute, 178
- Prairie College, 131
- Prairie College, Manitoba, 131
- rise of seminaries, 291
- Rochester Theological Seminary, 83
- Southwestern Baptist Theological Seminary, 90
- Spurgeon's pastors college, 68
- underground seminary, Romania, 331
- University of Cambridge, 176
- University of Oxford, 176
- Vilnius University, 312
- Wayland College, 99n2
- Yale University, 29
- Yale University, and Edwards conferences, 29

Edwards, Jonathan
- academic conferences on, 29
- as American revivalist, 336
- and assurance, 154
- biography of, by Miller, 27
- ecclesiology of, 21n33
- on emotionalism, 77
- eschatology of, 17
- and evangelical Calvinism, 149
- and infant baptism, 22
- influence of, 2, 12–31, 195
- and John Ryland Jr, 189
- on natural and moral ability, 23
- and revivalism, x, 11
- writings of: *An Humble Attempt*, 2, 16–17, 183, 194; *A Divine and Supernatural Light*, 12; *Enquiry into the Freedom of the Will*, 2, 15–16; *Freedom of the Will*, 24; *Gospel of Christ Worthy of All Acceptation*, 15; *A History of the Work of Redemption*, 25; *Life of David Brainerd*, 25, 114, 192; preface to Bellamy's *True Religion*, 20; "Sinners in the Hands of an Angry God," 26–28

Edwards, Morgan, 22, 38–40, 42, 61

Edwards at 300 conference proceedings, 29

INDEX

Edwardsean Calvinism, of Isaac Backus, 23
egalitarianism, following revival, 60
Egyptian Christians, 394
Ekelmann, Otto, *Gnadenwunder,* 307n14
Elim Pentecostal movement, 264
Elizabeth I, opposed to preachers, 295
Elliott, Stephen, 61
Emanuel Baptist Church of Oradea, 330–31
emotionalism
   of Andrew Fuller, 143–50
   and Baptist-Pentecostal interaction, 86–87
   of camp meetings, 49–50
   and community, 128n60
   criticism of, 75–78
   of Edward Manning, 117–21
   of evangelists, 75
   and Great Southern Revival, 33–34
   and imperialism, 125–26
   and Pentecostalism, 69–70, 74–75
   and piety, 4
   and reading, 114, 119–20
   and Scottish revival, 269
   and sentimentalism, 120–21
   and Separate Baptists, 38–39
   of women, 77
empire. *See* colonization
Engberg, F., 308
Engelsburg Baptist Church, 370
Engelsing, Rolf, 122–23
England
   Baptist Union, 5
   chaplaincy in, 6
   Reformation, and the ministry, 291–93
   Second Great Awakening, 214ff.
English Baptist Union (Australia), 376
Enlightenment Age, 151n44
Episcopal Church, 55, 61
Erskine, John, 193
eschatology
   and Baptist Missionary Society (BMS), 18
   and fishermen's revival, 269–70
   and full gospel preaching, 84
   and global events, 127–128
   and missions, 126
   and Modern Missionary Movement, 17–18
   and Pentecostalism, 69, 75–76
   and reading revolution, 123–24
   Worrell's view of, 74
ethics, and theology, in Ramism, 300

ethnic tensions, and creation of unions, 314–17
Evangelical Alliance (England), 216
Evangelical Awakening. *See* Second Great Awakening
evangelicalism. *See also* Great Awakening; Second Great Awakening
   among elite, 61
   of Andrew Fuller, 151
   and assurance, 154–55
   and Baptists, 115
   and Bristol Academy, 165–66
   components of, 166
   defined, 195, 280n42
   and Edward Manning, 117
   and Enlightenment, 11
   and hymnody, 203, 205
   of Joseph Kemp, 362–63
   and Particular Baptists, 141n2
   of Pitt Popovici, 329n7
   and print culture, 121–24
   and revival, 324
   in Scotland, 233–34, 236
   and Steele's hymns, 211–12
   supersedes fundamentalism, 367–68
evangelism
   of Aimee Semple McPherson, 84–86
   in Bangladesh, 384
   and Calvinism, 191
   of Charleston Baptists, 50
   of children, 236n54
   as class-based, 238–39
   high calling of, 332–35
   of Isabel Crawford, 132–36
   itinerant, 71–75
   of Joseph Kemp, 355–68
   Maori, 344
   in New Zealand, 366–67
   and Nigerian Baptists, 405–8
   and preaching style, 6
   qualities of evangelists, 333–35
   results of, 333–34
   and revival, 359
   and speaking in tongues, 76–77
   as spiritual gift, 33ˋ
   and stewardship, 91–92, 94
   in Stirling, Scotland, 262
   of Worrell, 71–75
evangelization
   International Conference for Itinerant Evangelists, 388
   in Lithuania, 311n38

and Maori of New Zealand, 352–54
of Muslims, 391–92
Evans, Caleb, 13, 165, 168–69, 204
An Address to the Serious and Candid Professors of Christianity, 13n7
Evans, Hugh, 13, 168–69
Evans, Rees, 177

Fadipe, Lewis (aka Lewis Stone), 399
Fairburn, Miles, 349–52
Faith Mission Conference, Edinburgh, 264
Fanning, Buckner, 104, 107–8
Farquharson, John, 243, 247
Fawcett, John, 172–73, 200n2
Federation of Mission Society of Australia, 382
Ferguson, Angus, 248
Findlater, Robert, 243–44
Finney, Charles, 75, 229, 237–38, 358
Firmian, Leopold von, 311
First Baptist Church, Cluj, Romania, 330
First Baptist Church, Lagos, Nigeria, 398
First Baptist Church, Timisoara, Romania, 328–29
First Church in Charleston, 18
First Church of San Jose, 84
First New Testament Church of Los Angeles, 68–70
Fish, Roy, 229
Fisher, Elmer Kirk, 70, 70n25, 86
Fisher, John, 251
fisherman's revival, in Scotland, 6, 267–73
Flinders Street Baptist Church, 382
foreign missions, and eschatology, 17
Forlong, Gordon, 343, 345–46
Foskett, Barnard, 13, 165
Foster, John, 172
Foster Hill Road Cemetery, and military casualties, 287
Fowler, Clifton, *Grace and Truth* journal, 85
Fowler, Le Ray, 106n33
Frame, Janet, *Owls Do Cry*, 353–54
Francis, Benjamin, 167, 200n2
Franklin, James H., 320
Fraser, William, 247–48
Fraserburgh, Scotland, revivalism, 269–70
Fraserburgh Baptist Church, 270–71
Free Church of Scotland, 234
Free Will Baptists, 24–25
Frelinghuysen, Theodore, 22, 336
French, W. E., 389
French Revolution, and eschatology, 17

Frey, Eleanor Mae, and Holiness movement, 83–84
Frey, J. A., 313
Friedrich Wilhelm I, 311
Frölich, Samuel, 307
Fulke, William, 207
Fuller, Andrew
and Calvinism, 14, 194–95
as diarist, 142–43
Edwards's impact on, 2, 13n7, 14–18
and eschatology, 17–18
evangelical spirituality of, 150–52
Gospel of Christ Worthy of All Acceptation, 13n7, 15, 149
grief at death of daughter, 146–47
health decline of, 157–58
and John Ryland, 14n11
on natural and moral ability, 23–24
reshaping of, 159
and Scottish Baptists, 242
spiritual struggle of, 5, 145–50
as theologian, 16
Fuller, Henry, 223
Fuller, Richard, 61
Fundamentalism
and A. C. Dixon, 75–78
and Joseph Kemp, 7, 356, 364–66, 368
as superseded by evangelicalism, 367–68
and William B. Riley, 75–78
fund raising. *See* stewardship
Furman, James C., 44, 55
Furman, Richard, 18, 46, 47n11, 50–51

Gaelic Schools Society, 245, 249
Galashiels, Scotland, 260–62
Gale, John, 177n89
Gall, James, 238
Gandhi, Mahatma, 385
Gano, John, 42
Gardner, W. J., *The Amuri: A County History*, 348–49
Garo Baptist Convention (GBC) of Bangladesh, 382, 389
Garo Baptist Union (GBU), 383
Gee, Donald, 264
gender, and sentiment, 120–21
General Baptists, 12–13, 222–23, 233
General Convention of Foreign Missions. *See* Triennial Baptist Convention
General Missionary Convention, 50
George, Timothy, 178
Georgia revival, 63

416

INDEX

Gerikas, Teodoras (Theodor Gerik), 305, 313, 315–21
German Baptist Association, 374
German Baptists, 7, 370–80, 394
Gerrard, Thomas, 374
Gibson, William, 230
Gill, John, 185n25, 190–91
Gillisonville, South Carolina, 60
Gilmore, James, 341–42
Gilmour, William, 268, 271
Glasgow, Scotland, 259–60
Global Interaction organization, 382
Global International, 391
Glory Tabernacle Ministry, Nigeria, 403
glossolalia
   and cessationist view, 82
   church withdrawal from, 265
   critics of, 75–78
   in early Pentecostalism, 65, 73
   in Edinburgh, 264
   explanations for, 77–78
   and infallibility, 82
   as spiritual gift, 74, 78–79
   in Sweden, 80–81
   and xenolalia, 66, 74, 77, 79, 81
Goldsack, William, 391
Gordon, Grant, 194
Gospel Mission Movement, 69n20
Gouge, William, 299
Gould, J. R., 276
Govan, Scotland, 259–60
Graham, Billy, 101, 339, 343. *See also* Billy Graham Evangelistic Association
   and Bangladesh, 7–8
   and Edwards's sermon, 27–28
   and evangelicalism, 28
   and New Zealand, 345, 353
   ordained as Southern Baptist, 27
Graham, B. J. W., *Christian Index* newspaper, 89
Graham, Ruth, 27
Grahamville, South Carolina, 60
Grant, Hay Mcdowall, 238–39
Grant, Keith, 4
Grant, Peter, 246
Great Awakening. *See also* Second Great Awakening
   in America, 2
   and Enlightenment, 11
   First, 32, 45n3
   impetus for, 12
   in Nigeria, 400–401

   and paedobaptists, 22–23
   time spans of, 45n3
Great Britain, 2, 4, 6
   as Christian, 277–78
   colonization of New Zealand, 348–52
   Day of Intercession, in WWI, 266n58
   emigration, to New Zealand, 340
   and India, 385
Great City Fire in Memel, 309
Great Revival. *See* Second Great Awakening
Great Southern Revival, 33, 37
Great War. *See* World War I
Greenham, Richard, 292–93, 295, 297, 301
grief, and depression, 143–50
Griffith, H. P., 58–59
Griffith, W. P., 60
Grimm, Eduard, 307–8
Grindal, Edmund, 292
Grossner Mission, Australia, 372
Guttery, A. T., 276
Guy, Cal, 388, 390
Guy, William, 181

Hague, Joseph, 307–8
Haldane missionaries, 5, 243–44, 250
Half-Way Covenant, 21
Hall, John, 269
Hall, Joseph, 292
Hall, Robert, Jr., 158
Hall, Robert, Sr., 15, 149, 171
Help to Zion's Travellers, 170
Hammond, Edward Payson, 236n54
Hampe, G., 371n9
Hancock-Stefan, George, 8
Hankins, Barry, 22
Hansen, Collin, "Young, Restless, Reformed," 30
Harper, John, 259–60
Harper Memorial Baptist Church, 260
Hart, Oliver, 46
Hartwell, Jesse, 55
Harvey, Gabriel, 299
Haverton, Dick, 105
Haykin, Michael, 30, 197
Heading, William, 287
Heath, Gord, 113n1
Hebridean islands, 247
Helensburgh Baptist Church, 277
Helm, Paul, 23n42
Henry Luce Foundation, 29
Herndon, T. V., 92

High Calvinism. *See also* predestination
and Andrew Fuller, 148–49
and Baptist decline, 189–90
compared with Puritanism, 149–50
as false, 191
and John Brine, 161
and John Ryland Jr., 187–88
and lack of assurance, 153–54
liberating theology of, 13n7
and the Modern Question, 190
as non-missionary, 161
and Northamptonshire, 194
and vanity, 187–88
view of revival, 161
of the West Country, 191n60
Hildersham, Arthur, 292
Hiley, David John, 280
Hill, Ron, 102–3, 103n17
Hill, Rowland, 185n25
Hindmarsh, Bruce D., 145, 194
Hindu Religionists, 383
Hinman, C. H., 345
history/historiography
  Christian, 339
  and Joseph Kemp, 355–56
  of New Zealand, 348
  of Victorian revivals, 346–51
Holifield, E., 23
holiness-fundamentalists, 75–76, 360–61
Holiness tradition. *See* Pentecostalism
Holmes, Stephen, 31
Holy Club, 12n4
Holy Spirit
  baptism of, 65
  and Baptists, 86
  and emotionalism, 33–34
  and India revival, 78–79
  and Keswick teaching, 72
  in Philadelphia Confession, 36
  and preaching, 333
  and revival/evangelism, 161, 182, 324, 358
  and Stearns's theology, 35
Hombury, Mervyn, 174
Hoover, J. N., 64–65
Hopkins, Samuel, 25
Hornuong, E.W., 284
Hoshizaki, Reiji, 99, 101, 106n33
Hosken, C. H., 221
Howard, Wilbur Forrester, 101n13, 110
Howe, George, 61

Howell, Wilbur, *Logic and Rhetoric in England*, 299
Hudson, Lemuel J., 57, 60
Hull, Bill, 109
Humphrey, Frederick James Harry, 280, 286
Hunt, Arnold, 290n12, 296, 302
Huskins, Bonnie, 113n1
Hutchison, William, 246
hymns/hymnals. *See also* singing
  in Australia, 376
  "Blest Be the Tie that Binds," 119n24
  Bristol Collection, 204
  Christocentric, of Watts/Steele, 208–9
  as devotional and spiritual, 206
  effect of punctuation/grammar, 212
  organization of hymnals, 206–7
  Redemption songbook, 361
  "Revive Us Again," 324
  sung at revivals, 5, 219, 244
  and theological convictions, 203–4
Hyper-Calvinism, 13, 15, 196n86

illness/disease, 145–47
Immanuel Baptist Church (East Pakistan), 387
imperialism, and missionaries, 128, 128n60
India, 24, 78, 386
India (1903), Baptist Missionary Society (BMS) in, x
Indian National Congress, 385
Inkenaitė, Dorotėja, 313–14
Inkenaitė, Ruta, 306n11
Inkenas, Jonas, 313, 316, 320
International Conference for Itinerant Evangelists, 388
invitation
  at conclusion of sermon, 38n28, 283
  omitted from student revival, 106
  to Tidence Lane, 39
Ireland
  Baptist Union, 6
Islam
  in North Africa, 394
  as official religion of Bangladesh, 387
  Sharia law, in Northern Nigeria, 406
Islamic Republic of East Pakistan, 386
Ivimey, Joseph, 163

Jackson, Fillmore, 136–37
Jackson, Hugh, 343, 345
Jamaica, 167n35, 179

INDEX

Jamaica Baptist Missionary Society, 179n99
Jeffreys, George, 264
Jeffreys, Stephen, 264
Jenson, Robert, 12
Jesuits, in Lithuania, 312
Jews, in Great Britain, 278n30
Johnson, Olubi, 403
Johnson, William Bullein, 3, 19, 49, 52–53, 55–57, 63
Johnstone, Thomas, 268
Johnston Stearns, Sarah, 34n8
John Street Methodist Church, 237
Jones, Bevan, 391
Jones, Humphrey, 232
Jones, R. B., and Welsh Revival, x
Jones, R. Tudur, 281
Jones, Thomas, 281, 286
Joshua, Seth, 264
Judson, Adoniram, 24
Judson, Ann
    An Account of the American Baptist Mission to the Burman Empire, 26
    Burmese catechism of, 26
    and Edwards's *History of the Work of Redemption*, 25
    as first intercontinental missionary, 23–24

Kalbar Baptist Church, 370, 373, 378–79
Kallweit, Martin, 304
Kaunas (Kowno), Lithuania, 305, 315
Keach, Benjamin, 203–4
Kearney, James, 295
Kellison, Kim, 3
Kemp, John, 7
Kemp, Joseph, 257–59, 343, 355–68
Kendall, George, "The Revival at the Front," *Baptist Times*, 283
Keswick holiness influence, 66, 68, 70, 72, 76–78, 263n47, 355
Kidd, Thomas, 23
Kimber, Isaac, 177n89
King, Gerald, 84
King, Willie, 137
Kiokee Church, 40–41
Kirk, John, 237
Kirtland, Charles, 231
Kitchener's Army and Pals Battalions, 275
Kitchner, First Earl Herbert, 275n6
Klaipeda, Lithuania. *See* Memel, Lithuania
Kleinschmidt, Robin, 375n18
Klumbys, Anskis, 317
Knibb, William, 167

Knight, Sarah, 299n56
Knowles, James, 25
Kolade, Sola, 403
Kowno (Kaunas), Lithuania, 305, 315
Kuykendall, Michael, 75

laity
    in Australia, 374–76
    evangelization of, 236
    in Lithuania, 310–11
    and prayer meetings, 238
    as Puritan town lecturers, 293
    and revivalism, 5, 232n33, 237–38, 244
    in Scotland, 237–38, 249
    and transatlantic revival, 229–30
Landmarkism, 69n20. *See also* Worrell, Adolphus Spalding
Lane, Hannah, 113n1
Lane, Tidence, 39–40
Lang, John Dunmore, 371
Langley, Ralph, 105, 106n33
Lanphier, Jeremiah, 228
Laosebikan, Aremu M., 401
Latham Springs encampment, 101
Latter Rain Assembly, Nigeria, 403
Latužis, Albertas, *Po Jo Sparnais*, 306n11
Latvia, Baptists in, 304–5
Latvian Baptist Union, 315
Lay Revivals (1857–62), 1
Ledbetter, Henry, 41
Lennie, Tom, 251
Lewis, Walter O., 317
Liberia, and Baptists, 394
Library of Congress, and Edwards conferences, 29
Liddell, Eric, 270
Lilly Endowment, and Edwards conferences, 29
Lincoln, Heman, 117
Lineham, Peter, 345, 353
literacy, and reading revolution, 123–24
literature. *See also* periodicals
    and Baptist piety, 113ff.
    biographies, 27, 117–18
    as escapist, 120
    Fuller's diary, 142ff.
    Janet Frame, *Owls Do Cry*, 353
    Manning's diary, 115–17
    as ministry in Bangladesh, 391
    missionary, 121
    multilingual, in Lithuania, 316
    new genres of, 114–15

of New Zealand, 353–54
novels, 119
and piety, 113–15
The Power of Sympathy, 119
reading aloud, 121
sentimental, 119–21
textual and emotional communities, 128n60
translated to Lithuanian, 313
Lithuania, 2, 6–7
  Baptist revival in, 304ff.
  Baptist struggles in, 320–22
  Baptist unions, 314–17, 321
Lithuanian Baptist church (Peabody, Mass.), 318
Lithuanian Baptist Mission Work Union (LBMWU), 316
Lithuanian Baptist Union, 321
Little Stephen's Creek Church, 56
Living Seed, Peace House, Nigeria, 403
Liviu, Olah, 324ff.
Llewellyn, Thomas, 167
Lloyd-Jones, Martyn, 325n`
London Missionary Society, 142n5
Lone Wolf, Kiowa chief, 133
Lord's Army revival, 325
Lord's Supper
  and administration controversy, 134n13
  as converting agent, 252n2
  differences over, 372
  elements of, 261
  and Half-Way Covenant, 21
  hymns for, 209–10
  and revivals, in Scotland, 249, 252
Love, J. F., 93
Low Country Baptists, 47, 49, 52, 60
Lucas, J. E., 95n16
Luther, Martin, and primacy of the sermon, 294n29
Lutherans
  in Australia, 372–73, 375, 378–79
  and Lithuanian revivalism, 312
  pietistic revival, 310–12
  in Prussian Lithuania, 307
  in Romania, 326
Luther King House, x
Lysenkaite (Ambrasuniene), Ruta, 307n14

MacArthur, Donald, 245–46
MacDougal, Duncan, 249–50
MacFarlane, Duncan, 250
MacFarlane, James, 250
MacFarlane, John, 250
MacFarlane, Robert, 250
Mackay, William P., "Revive Us Again" hymn, 324
Mackenzie, William, 243n3
Mackintosh, Lachlan, 245
Macleod, Roderick, 249
MacLeod, Samuel, 248
MacQueen, James, 248–49
MacRae, Alexander, 244
Mancke, Elizabeth, 113n1
Manley, Ken R., 205, 212–13
Manly, Basil, 51–52
Manly, Basil, Sr., 19
Manning, Edward, 4, 113, 115–21
Maori (New Zealand) revivals, 7, 344, 352
Marsden, George, 29
Marshall, Daniel, 3, 34, 36, 36n13, 36n15, 40–41, 47
Marshall, Hannah Drake, 36
Marshall, Martha Stearns, 3, 36, 36n13, 40, 40n36, 42
Marshman, 178
Martin, Donald, 247
Martin, William, 238
Martinez, Angel, 106n33
Mason, C. H., 71
Massachusetts, New Light Congregationalists, 19
Masters, V. I., 96
Matheson, Duncan, 236, 239
Matthews, Gethin, 285
McClure, William, 230
McClymond, Michael, 347
McGovern, Donald, 388, 390
McGready, James, 48
McGregor, A. Y., 262
McIver, Bruce, 104, 106, 107n41, 111
McKim, Donald, 300–301
McLaren, Annie, 263
McLean, Archibald, 242
McLean, John, 262
McLoughlin, William, 19
McPherson, Aimee Semple, 84–86
Mead, Cecil, 386
Mead, Silas, 382
Medhurst, T. W., 251
Meek, Donald, 244–46, 250
Memel Baptist Church, 19, 305, 307–9
Memel/Memelland, Lithuania, 304ff., 309, 316
Mencken, H. L., 26–27

Mercer, Jessie, 23
Methodists
  in Australia, 370
  converts join, 55
  definition of revival, 65
  and Great Southern Revival, 42–43
  in Nigeria, 396
  revivalism in colonial America, x, 2
  and Second Great Awakening, 48
  Welsh Calvinistic (1904–5), x
Metropolitan Tabernacle, London, 232
Middleditch, C. J, 218, 230
Miller, Perry, 27–28, 30, 299n56
Mills, Lajide (aka Lajide Tubi), 399
Minkema, Kenneth, 21
Missionary Baptists, 45–46, 340
missions/missionaries
  after WWII, 107
  Alexander Stewart, 243
  and Ann Judson writings, 26
  Australian interest in, 377, 382
  in Bangladesh, 392
  Bristol Education Society, 165, 167–72
  in Cameroon, 377
  as catalyst for social change, 385–86
  and colonial subjects, 126–27
  criticisms of, 68
  Ellen Arnold, 382
  foreign movement of, 50
  home missions, 166–67
  and imperialism, 124–28
  in India, 245, 377
  in Jamaica, 167n35
  John Farquharson (Breadalbane), 243
  in Lithuania, 313–14, 317–18
  of Memel church, 309
  in Nigeria, 398–408
  and periodicals, 121–22, 125
  Queensland Baptist Mission in Bengal, 377
  as racially superior, 127–28
  Russian, from Australia, 377
  in Scotland, 243–46
  and Second Great Revival, 62
  and speaking in tongues, 76–77
  Student Summer Mission Program, 109–11
  and Western/non-Western relations, 142
  WMU fund raising for, 96–97
Mizo Baptists, x
Modernism, and Kemp's fundamentalism, 356–57, 364–66

Modern Missionary Movement, and Fuller, 16
Modern Question. *See under* Calvinism
Mohler, Albert, 30
Moller, H., 373
Moody, Dwight Lyman, 4–5, 66, 77, 131, 250, 252–53, 339, 341–43, 357
Moody, Jess, 104, 107n41
Moody, Josh, 31
Moody Church, Chicago, 76
Moore, Mark, 107n41
morality, as lacking in New Zealand, 357
Moravians, and Lithuanian pietism, 311
Morden, Peter, 31, 194
Morgan, Abraham Rees, 282
Morgan, David, 232
Morgan, G. Campbell, 255n13, 277
Morris, John Webster, 146, 152
Morse, John, 35
Mountain Creek Church, 56
Moyes, E., 345
Mt. Moriah Church, 56
Mulkey, Phillip, 47
Mullins, E. Y., 95n16
Munro, Donald, 247
Murray, Derek, 113n1, 119n24, 244
Murray, Iain, 29
Murray, Morris, 284
music, 106, 107n41, 334. *See also* singing
Muslim Background Believers (MBBs), 392
Muslims, 8, 386–87, 392

Nag, B. A., 383
National Baptist Convention Foreign Mission Board, 394
National Conference for Desiring God, 29
Native Americans
  Cattaraugus reservation, 135
  and Isabel Crawford, 132–33
  Kiowas, 132–33
  and the Marshalls, 36n15
  in New York, 134–35
  in Oklahoma, 132–34
  Onnaqaggy tribe, 36
  Seminoles, 137
  Tonawanda reservation, 135
  Tuscaroras, 135
  in Washington state, 4
Native Baptist Church, Lagos, Nigeria, 399–400
Nazareth Church in Spartansburg, 48
Neo-Protestantism, in Romania, 326

Nettles, Tom, 19
New Birth. *See* conversion
New Calvinism, 29–30. *See also* Calvinism; Hyper-Calvinism
New Connection General Baptists, 222–23
New Divinity school, 20, 20n30, 26
New Light Congregationalists, 19–20, 22, 116
New Park Street Chapel, 281
Newton, John, 145, 186–87, 187n37, 188, 200
New Zealand, 2, 6–7, 339–54, 372
New Zealand Baptist Missionary Society (NZBMS), 340–41, 382
New Zealand Baptist Union, 340–41, 356
Niemetz, Ferdinand, 309
Nigeria, 2, 8, 393–408. *See also* Africa
Nigerian Baptist Convention, 400–401, 404–8
Noel, Baptist, 216, 231–32
Noll, Mark, 28–29, 194, 197
Nonconformists, in British military, 279
North, Brownlow, 238
North, J. J., 361, 365
Northamptonshire Association, 11, 13–14, 170, 193–94
Northamptonshire Association of Particular Baptist Churches, 153
North Carolina, 3, 109
Northern Baptists, 70, 83
Northern Education Society, 172–73
North Frederick Street Church, 235, 251

Oates, M. D., 101, 106n33
Obed, Uzodinma, 403
O'Brien, Brandon, 21
O'Day, Rosemary, *The English Clergy*, 291
Oke, Francis Wale, 403
Olah, Eugenia Lupescu, 329
Olah, Liviu, 324ff., 329–30
Oliver, W. H., 348
Olsen, Erik, *Oxford History of New Zealand*, 349
Oncken, Johann Gerhard, 307, 321–22, 373–74
Open Brethren denomination, 345
Oradea, Romania, 324ff.
ordinances. *See* baptism; Lord's Supper
ordination
  of Aimee Semple McPherson, 84–85
  of Eleanor Mae Frey, 83
  of Shubal Stearns, 35

Organization of Islamic Cooperation (OIC), 388
Orr, J. Edwin, 5, 197, 214–15, 225–26, 229, 369
Orthodox churches, 322, 324–26
Overend, Frederick, 223
Owen, John, 156

Packer, J. I., 29
paganism, in Lithuania, 312
Page, John Chamberlain, 382
Pakistan, as secular, 386
Pakistan Baptist Sangha, 383
Palau, Luis, 343
Palmer, Phoebe, 237
Palmer, Waitstill, 35
Parham, Charles, 66
Parker, David, 7
Particular Baptists
  in America, 18
  and Andrew Fuller, 141ff.
  and Anne Steele's hymns, 2–9, 212–13
  Calvinistic heritage of, 198–99
  Confession of Faith (1689), 201
  decline and renewal of, 12–13
  defined, 141n1
  and education of clergy, 162–64
  and Edwardsean Calvinism, 18, 149
  and Edwards's *Freedom of the Will*, 16
  and Edwards's *Humble Attempt*, 16
  and evangelical Calvinism, 181ff
  and High Calvinism, 148–49
  hymns of, 200ff., 201–7
  and Jonathan Edwards, 11–12
  and revivalism, 4–5, 160ff.
  and Rippon's hymns, 205
  as Separate Baptists in America, 18
  and support of clergy, 163–64
  and unity proposal, 233
Pasadena, California, 64
pastoral care, in Australia, 373–74
Paternoster Press, 31
Paterson, W. P., 269–70
Payne, Ernest, 197
Pearce, Samuel, 118, 171
Pentecostalism
  1920s revival, 83
  and African-Americans, 70–71, 82, 87, 402–4
  and Aimee Semple McPherson, 84–85
  and A.S. Worrell, 70–75
  as Christian renewal, 3, 402

INDEX

Elim movement, 264
  in Europe, 263n47
  failures of, 80
  former Baptists as leaders of, 70
  of New Zealand Baptists, 345
  of Nigerian Baptists, 404
  periodical reporting of, 77–79
  and revivalism, 6, 64ff.
  in Scotland, 264
  and Welsh revival, 67–68, 263–66
periodicals. *See also* literature
  abundance of, 115, 122–23
  American Baptist Missionary Journal, 309
  American Baptist Missionary Magazine, 121, 124
  Apostolic Faith magazine, 72–73
  Army and Religion Report, 265
  Baptist Argus (Louisville), 73–74, 79–81
  The Baptist Beacon (Romania), 328
  Baptist magazine, 366
  Baptist Magazine, 215, 217, 221
  Baptist Messenger, 221
  Baptist and Reflector, 93
  Baptist Reporter, 215, 217–20
  Baptist Times, 283
  Boston Traveler, 217
  British Baptist Reporter, 221
  Charlotte Chapel Record, 262
  Christian Index, 53, 89
  Christianity Today magazine, 30
  Conservative Letter of Friendship, 312
  Freeman, 218, 232–33, 235, 237–38
  General Baptist Magazine, 233
  Gospel Herald or Poor Christian's Magazine, 221
  Irish Chronicle, 217–18
  Memelschen Wochenblatt, 307
  New York Examiner, 217
  New York Independent, 217
  New York Protestant Churchman, 217
  New York Tribune, 217
  New Zealand Baptist magazine, 341, 355, 359–60
  Presbyterian Magazine, 228
  Primitive Church (or Baptist) Magazine, 221
  Reaper magazine, 355–56, 360–61
  Revival, 214, 216, 238
  Revival magazine, 220
  Scottish Baptist Magazine, 255–56, 260
  Scottish Guardian, 233, 237

Tesos Draugas (Friend of the Truth), 316, 319
Time magazine, 29–30
Time magazine, 29–30
Voice of Truth or Baptist Record, 221
Watchman, The, 78–79
Western Recorder (Kentucky), 73, 81–82
Word and Work, 79
Wynd Journal, 238
Perkins, William, 292, 293n21
  The Arte of Prophesying, 300
  on Ramism, 301
persecution of Baptists, 7, 40n37, 326, 328, 330, 332–34, 406–7
Pew Charitable Trusts, 29
Pewtress, Thomas, 230
Philadelphia Baptist Association, 18, 36, 42
Philadelphia Education Society, 178
pietism, 271, 307, 310–12, 322
piety/pietism. *See also* church discipline
  in Australia, 377
  and conversion, 34n5
  and emotionalism, 4
  and Lithuania, 307, 322
  and New Calvinism, 30, 116–17
  and New Light Congregationalists, 116
  in Prussian Lithuania, 310–12
  and Scottish revival, 271
Piggin, Stuart, 369
Piggott, John, 160
Piper, John, 29–30
Pitts, William, 3
pity *vs.* sympathy, 126
Platt, David, 30
polity
  autocratic "Spirit-led," 68–69, 82
  congregational, 19–20, 22, 46–47, 82
  exclusion of Pentecostalists, 70
Popoola, Sunday, 403
Popovici, Hortensia Cristea, 328
Popovici, Pitt, 324ff., 327–29, 335
Post, Ansel Howard, 64, 64n3, 65, 70
Pound, Geoff, 364
poverty
  and decline of fishing industry, 267, 270–71
  in Scotland, 259, 259n26
  unaffected by revival, 271–72
Prather, Scott, 8
prayer
  of Aimee Semple McPherson, 85–86
  at Baptist Night of Wonder, 406

423

charismatic, in Nigeria, 404
in Charlotte Chapel, 258
and Concert of Prayer, 17n20
and confession, 332
as essential for revival, 358
and fasting, in Nigeria, 404
Kemp's emphasis on, 360–61
of Liviu Olah, 332
of Iosef Ton, 332
WWI Day of Prayer, 265–66
Prayer Call, 193–94, 193n73, 197
prayer meetings
by children, 251n46
and confessions of sin, 102–3
and conversions, 103
interdenominational, 232, 235
led by laity, 238
ninety days of, 107
and revivalism, 5, 68, 216, 221, 360, 367
in Scotland, 243, 246, 264
at Smale's church, 72
for student-led revival, 102
for working men, 228
preaching/preachers. *See also* chaplaincy; sermons
centrality of, 6, 280
in English reformation, 293
and exhortation, 301–2
as focus of Pentecost story, 76
homilies *vs.* sermons, 295–98
Moody and Arminianism, 254
Pitt Popovici, 327–29, 329n7, 334–35
plain style of, 300–302
from priests to preachers, 291–93
and revival, 324
sacramentalization of, 293–98
and seminaries, 291
Spurgeon's ministry, 290ff.
Stearns's style of, 39
by students, 100, 103–6
town lecturers, 293
predestination. *See also* High Calvinists/Calvinism
and assurance, 148
in confessions of faith, 24
and election, 24
and Holy Spirit, 182n9
Presbyterians
in Australia, 372
converts join, 55
Evangelical, 229–30
and revival, 60–61

of Scotland, x, 234, 244, 254
and Second Great Awakening, 48–49
Prestridge, J. N., 80n69
Primitive Baptists, 45–46, 153–55, 275–76
Princeton University, 28
prophecy, of Lewis Rector, for revival, 58
Protestants/Protestantism
in Great Britain, 278
mid-eighteenth-century establishment of, 2
in New Zealand, 340
in Romania, 326
Prussia, 6–7, 310
Prussian Lithuania. *See* Lithuania
Purbo Pakistan Jaykta Prochar Abhijan, 387
Puritans/Puritanism
in 19th and 20th centuries, 26–27
An Admonition to the Parliament, 295
and Andrew Fuller, 147–48
and English Reformation, 291
and High Calvinism, 149n38
as minority movement, 302
and preaching, 6, 292, 302
and Ramism, 299–300
and revivalism, 5–6, 289
sermon as sacramental, 294–95
vs. Spurgeon, 303
and vestments, 291

Queen St. Baptist Chapel, 216

race, and revivals, 63, 82, 87, 100
racial superiority of missionaries, 127
Radcliffe, Mr (lay revivalist), 238
radio broadcasting, 328, 362
Ramakrishna Mission (Hindu), 383
Ramism
elevation of the sermon, 300–301
and popularization of the sermon, 290–91
Ramsbottom, B. A., 204
Ramus, Peter (Pierre de la Ramée), *Dialectia*, 298
Randall, Ian, 66
rationalism, 81, 262
Rector, Lewis, 58
Redeemed Christian Church of God (RCCG), 403
Reese, Joseph, 47, 50
Reeves, William Pember, 348
Reformation, English, and the ministry, 291–93
Reformation Today (RT) magazine, 31

INDEX

Reformed Church, and working men's prayer meetings, 228
Regular Baptists, 12
  in America, 18–19
  Marshall family, 36
  vs. Separate Baptists, 41
Remmers, A. F., 308
renewal, defined, 324n1
restorationism, 68, 79, 86
revivals/revivalism
  absent in WWI, 266
  in Africa, 394–95
  in America, 217–18; Dallas, Texas, 108–9
  analyses of, 218–19, 251
  in Australia, 369ff., 370, 376
  Baptist Night of Wonders, 406
  Baptists and Puritan revivalism, 303
  at Baylor University, 3–4, 98, 100
  and case studies of, 346–52
  characteristics of, 378–80
  charismatic, in Nigeria, 402–5
  and Charles Haddon Spurgeon, 288ff., 303
  city-wide crusades, 108–10
  and community spirit, 54
  conditions for (Kemp), 358–59, 364–66
  and confession of sin, 333
  by country/region: Connecticut Valley, 12, 19, 34; East Anglia, 267–73
  and cultural restraint, 346–52
  defined, 182, 182n8, 251, 324–25, 324n1, 325n1, 344–46
  in England, 214–17, 220–21
  and Enlightenment Age, 11
  as evangelical, 141n2, 324
  and First Great Awakening, 32n1
  fishermen's, 268
  four types of, 344
  in France, 218
  geographic range of, 2
  and geography, 348–50
  in Great Britain, 218
  as high calling, 332–35
  High Calvinist view of, 161
  historical evolution of, 340–43
  histories of, by J. Edwin Orr, 214
  and hymnody, 205
  hymnody of, 219
  in India, 78
  interdenominational, 230–31
  in Ireland, 217–18
  and Isabel Crawford, 129
  of John Kemp, 7
  Joseph Kemp's theology of, 357–61
  Kemp's laws of, 367
  lay-led, 237–38
  in Lithuania, 322
  and Lithuanian nationalism, 304n3
  Lord's Army, in Romania, 325
  in Low Country, 49
  major issues addressed, 1
  and membership increases, 54–56
  in the military, 287
  in military units, 277–78
  and missionaries, 273
  Modern style of, 340–43
  Moody's "Modern" approach to, 342
  in New Zealand, 340–41, 344–46, 352–54, 363, 367, 369
  Nigerian zeal in 21st century, 405–8
  as nondenominational, 347–48
  in Northampton, 185–86
  opposed by Anglicans, 231
  in Oradea, Romania, 335
  and Particular Baptists, 4–5, 141–42
  patterns/styles of, 339–40, 345–46
  and Pentecostalism, 65
  and periodicals, 217–20
  and personal renewal, 152
  and piety, 377–3789
  and planned campaigns, 251
  and preaching, 302–3
  in Prussian Lithuania, 311–12
  Reformed pattern of, 228ff.
  renunciation of worldly things, 271
  in Romania, 324ff., 329, 335–36
  of Saluda Association, 58–59
  in Scotland, 233–34, 242–44, 248–49, 252ff., 258–70
  at Sheepshead Church, 181–82
  and singing, 5
  on Skye Island, 249–50
  in Slavic Orthodox context, 322–23
  and social class discrimination, 238
  sociocultural context of, 347–52
  and solar eclipse, 58
  in South Carolina (1830s), 53–61
  and speaking in tongues, 264
  spiritual principles for, 330n9
  and stewardship, 88–92
  student-led, at Baylor, 101–4
  in Sweden, 218
  tent crusades: in Waco, 102
  theology of (Joseph Kemp), 357–61

425

training for youth-led meetings, 110–11
as transatlantic, 228–30, 239–41
Trans-Pacific Crusade, 343
two Baylor events, 105–8
types/styles of, 340, 343–46
varieties of, x, 2
Waco Youth for Christ, 105–8
in Wales, 254–55, 258, 281
Welsh, 263–66
as widespread in 1850s, 227–28
in WWI, 285–86
youth revivals, 3–4, 55–56, 106–11
Revolutionary War, and First Great Awakening, 32
Rhett, Robert Barnwell, 61, 61n59
Rhode Island, Baptist arrival in, 18
Rice, Luther, 24
Ridgecrest Baptist Assembly, 109
Riley, William B., 75–78
    Speaking in Tongues, 76
Rippon, John, 169
    A Selection of Hymns ..., 5, 204–6, 206n32
Roberts, Evan, 255, 261, 264, 282
Roberts, R. Philip, 161
Robertson, A. T., 95
Robinson, Jackie, 100, 103–4, 107n41, 109
Robinson, Robert, 178
Rogal, Samuel J., 203
Rogers, Richard, 292
Romania, 2, 7, 325ff.
    persecution of churches, 327–28, 328n6
Romania Missionary Society (RMS), 331
Ross, Donald, 238
Ross, Murdoch, 248
Rothschild, Emma, 115
Roxburgh, Ken, 6
Rushbrooke, J. H., 312, 318–19
    The Baptist Movement in the Continent of Europe, 302
Russia, Transcaucasia, 304
Ryland, Jane Beddome, 183
Ryland, J. E., 194
Ryland, John, Jr.
    academic circle of, 194–95
    and Andrew Fuller, 144, 149, 195
    at Bristol Academy, 13
    career of, 198nn92–94
    considerable usefulness of, 183
    conversion and revival experience of, 183–86
    as Edwards's apostle, 195
    esteems Jonathan Edwards, 14

and evangelical Calvinism, 166, 181ff.
as founder of BMS, 171
and Fuller and Sutcliff, 14n11, 16–17
and Great Evangelical Revival, 198
and High Calvinism, 190–91
as High Calvinist, 196
as hymn writer, 200n2
influence of, 194
mentors of, 186–89, 193, 193n72
ordination sermon to Thomas, 174–75
Serious Remarks II, 191
and Sutcliff, 195
teaches Hebrew, 172
theology of, 193
vanity of, 187–88
Ryland, John Collett, 181n1

Sabbath Day, and Sunday working in WWI, 266
Sabbath school, 220, 222, 246
    as mission, 130–31
Sabbath schools, in Australia, 374
sacraments. *See* baptism; Lord's Supper
sermons as, 293–98
Saddle Mountain mission, 132–33
Saffery, John, 167
Salem Witchcraft Trials, 26
Saluda Baptist Association, 58–62
Salvation Army, 84, 268, 341
Samford University, 99n3
sanctification
    and Cooperative Program, 95n16
    and fundamentalism, 364–66
Sandemanianism, and Particular Baptists, 13
Sandy Creek Baptist Association, 3, 22–23, 37–38
Sandy Creek Baptists, and Arminianism, 23
Sandy Creek Church, 37–41
Sankey, Ira D., 5, 250
Sardis Church, 53–54, 56
Satan/the devil, 77
    as counterfeiting spiritual gifts, 73–74
    and Pentecostalism, 74
Savannah River Association, 61–62
SBC. *See* Southern Baptist Convention (SBC)
Scarborough, L. R., 90–91, 94
Schirmeister, C. F. A., 371n9
scholarship
    Edwards studies, 30–31
    higher criticism, 271, 356, 365–66

INDEX

scholasticism, syllogisms and axioms of, 298–99
Schweitzer, Richard, 266, 277–78
Scotch Itinerant Society, 245
Scotland
  Baptist Missionary Society (BMS) in, 246
  Baptists and revival in 19th century, 242ff.
  Baptist Union, 5, 239, 270, 272
  chaplaincy in, 6
  decline of Baptists in, 6
  decline of religious life in, 267
  emigration to America, 248, 250, 272
  fishermen's' revival in, 267–73
  revivalism in, 5–6, 233, 251, 257n19
  social upheaval of, 244
  temperance, and No License debate, 281
  and Welsh revival, 263–66
Scottish Baptist Association (SBA), 239–41, 243
Scottish Brethren, 234–35, 237
Scottish revivalism
  and Haldane missionaries, 5, 243–44, 250
Scott, W. Major, 269
Scripture Pasture Christian Center, 403
Scroggie, W. Graham, 270n82
Seaver, Paul, 291, 293
Second Advent conferences, 355
Second Great Awakening, 3, 45n3
  and Baptists, 214ff.
  four main points of, 61–62
  and interdenominational camp meetings, 48–53
  results of, 62–63
  in South Carolina, 49–50
self-examination, and assurance, 155–56
Semaphore Trio, 382
Semple, Robert, 38
Separate Baptists, 12, 297
  in America, 18–20
  biblicism of, 47
  contrasted with Low Country Baptists, 47
  development of, 19
  geographical spread of, 40–41
  gradual decline of, 47
  and Great Awakening, 22–23, 33
  and Holy Spirit, 34n5, 40
  and Jonathan Edwards, 20
  Marshall family, 2–3, 36, 40–41
  nine ordinances of, 41n41
  ordinances of, 41n41
  vs. Regular Baptists, 41
  of Sandy Creek, 37–38
  and Sandy Creek Baptist Association, 37–38
  in the South, 22
  in South Carolina, 45–48
  and Southern revivals, 63
  spread to South Carolina, 45
  Stearns family, 2–3, 35
  of Up-country (South Carolina), 46–47
  and Whitefield's preaching style, 34
  and women's preaching, 47
Separate Congregationalists, 35
Serampore College, 178
sermons. *See also* preaching/preachers.
  elevation of, in Ramism, 300–301
  and homilies, 295
  popularization of, 298–301
  and Ramist methodology, 290–91, 300–301
  sacramentalization of, 293–98
  of student revivals, 106–7
Seventh and James Baptist Church, 103
Seventh Day Baptists, 246
Seventy-Five Million Campaign, 88ff.
Seymour, William J., 66, 69–70
Seymour A. J., and Azusa Street Revival, 66
Shakespeare, John Howard, 6, 275–76
Shearer, John, 260
Sheen, Danzy, 288n3
Sheepshead Baptist Church, 181–82
Shetland Islands Baptists, 246
Shurden, Walter, 18
Šilutė-Priekulė congregation, 316
Simeon, Charles, 242
Simpson, Jane, 356
sin, and confession, 333
Sinclair, Dugald, 245
Sinclair, Keith, 348
singing. *See also* hymns; music
  among British troops, 283
  and language preservation, 311
  praise choruses, in Nigeria, 403–4
  and revival culture, 5, 262–63
  in tongues, 264
Skinner, Tom, 343
Skvirblys, Jurgis, 315–16
Skye Island, 249
slaves, at revivals, 33, 57, 60, 62
Smale, Joseph, 67–69, 70n25, 74–75, 86
Smalley, John, 189, 193
Smith, Adam, 233
Smith, Andrew, 3
Smith, Gypsy Pat, 363

Smith, Henry "Silvertongued," 292
Smyth, John, 293, 297n45
Snape, Michael, 266
 God and the British Soldier, 285–86
Society for Propagating the Gospel among the Heathen (BMS), 142, 151–52, 156, 158–59, 171–72
Society for Propagating the Gospel at Home (SPGH), 243
Society of Baptist Union of Great Britain and Ireland, 6
Socinians, 12
solar eclipse, and Saluda Association meeting, 58–59
soteriology
 and assurance, 153–57, 242–43
 Eastern Orthodox, 325
 and primacy of the sermon, 290, 295
 and sovereign grace, 148–49, 195–96
South Africa, European Baptists in, 394
South Australia Baptist Missionary Society, 382
South Carolina
 and Baptist framework, 62–63
 Baptist unification in, 45–48
 political tensions in, 61n59, 63
 revivalism in (1830s), 53–61
 and Second Great Awakening, 3
 South Carolina Baptist State Convention, 52
Southern Baptist Convention (SBC)
 American Baptist Missionary Union, 394
 in Bangladesh, 384, 391
 and Baptist Faith and Message, 25
 and Billy Graham, 27
 Cooperative Program, 3; and discipleship/sanctification, 94–95
 in East Pakistan, 382, 386–87
 and Edwards's reformed thoughts, 18
 Foreign Mission Board (FMB), 394–95
 formation of, 62–63
 and fund raising, 3, 88ff.
 and Jonathan Edwards, 19
 Seventy-Five Million Campaign, 88ff.
 and Women's Baptist Home Mission Society, 132
Sparks, Johns, 38
speaking in tongues. *See* glossolalia
Spencer, W. C., 342
Spinks, W. H., 277
spiritual gifts. *See* glossolalia
spirituality
 of Andrew Fuller, 143–45, 150–52
 and anxiety/depression, 143–50
 and assurance, 153
 as characteristic of revival, 373–78
 as experiential, 149–50
 High Calvinistic, 149–50
 of Nigerian Baptist Convention, 405–6
 and pietism in Prussian Lithuania, 310–12
 and Puritan introspection, 149–50
Sprange, Harry, 5
Spurgeon, Charles Haddon
 Autobiography of, 6
 conversion of, 288–89
 pastor's college of, 68
 vs. Puritanism, 303
 and revival, 215–16, 229, 232
 The Soul-Winner, 289
Spurgeon, Thomas, 342–43, 362
Spurr, F. C., 283, 286
Stanley, Brian, 142
Staughton, William, 171, 178
Steadman, William, 167, 173–74
Stearns, Martha, 3, 36, 36n13, 40, 40n36, 42
Stearns, Sarah Johnston, 34n8
Stearns, Shubal, 2, 22, 47, 63
 and Calvinism, 23n40
 influence of, 39–40
 new birth of, 34
 ordains Daniel Marshall, 41
 and South Carolina Baptists, 47
Stearns family, 35
Steele, Anne, 5, 200ff., 202, 205, 207–12
Steele, Henry, 201
Steele, William, 201
Stennett, Joseph, 177, 200n2, 204
Stennett, Samuel, 200n2
Stepney Academy, 175
Stevens, Laura, 126
stewardship
 as Baptist doctrine, 90
 and eternal damnation, 93
 and evangelism, 91
 and founding of Cooperative Program, 94
 and revivalism, 89
Stewart, Alexander (1), 242
Stewart, Alexander (2), 243
Stewart, James, "Why Be Christian?," 104
Stewart, John, 39
Stinton, Benjamin, 177–78
Stirling, Scotland, revival in, 262, 264–65

INDEX

Stoddard, Solomon, and halfway covenant, 21
Stokes, Claudia, 115
Stokes, Katy Jennings, 99n3
Stone, Lewis (aka Lewis Fadipe), 399
Stone Church, Nigeria, 403
Stout, Harry, 11–12
Stratton, John Roach, 85
Sturm, Johannes, 299n53
subjective warrant and Calvinism, 15
Sunday, Billy, 4, 134
Sunday school, 374
Sutcliff, John, 13, 13n7, 14, 16–17, 149, 171–72, 193n73
Sutherland, Martin, 7, 113n1, 356
Sweden, and Azusa Revival, 80
Sweeney, Douglas, 21
Sweet, William Warren, 42
sympathy, 118–21, 126, 126 –127

Tackle, John, 391
Talbot, Brian, 5
Tate, Nahum, 204
Tattersall, Thomas Newell, 278–79, 281, 286
Taylor, Dan, 12
Taylor, Steve, 247
tears. *See* emotionalism
temperance, and No License debate, 271
Temple, William, 299
Templin Baptist Church, Germany, 378
Tennent, Gilbert, 2
Terrill, Edward, 165
testimonies, at Baylor revival, 105–6
Texas Baptist Department of Student Work, 111
Theodosia (pseudonym for Anne Steele [q.v.]), 201
theology
  of Anne Steele's hymns, 210–13
  confessional, of Particular Baptists, 203
  and ethics, in Ramism, 300
  of High Calvinism, 192–93
  and higher criticism, 271, 356, 365–66
  and hymnal arrangement, 206–7
  Moody's impact on, 253–54
  Reformed, of Sandy Creek Church covenant, 23
  and revivalism, 5
  of revivalism (Kemp), 357–61
  separationist, 368
Thomas, J. J., 258

Thomas, John, 144–45, 156
Thomas, Micah, 174, 174n73, 175
Thomas, Thomas, 175
Thompson, C. M., 81n75
Thomson, D. P., 270
Thomson, Sinclair, 246
Thorne, Susan, 125
Thornton, Guy, *With the Anzacs in Cairo*, 282, 286
Tidwell, J. B., 90
Ton, Elisabetta Cosman, 331
Ton, Iosif, 324ff., 330–31, 335
Toplady, Augustus, 185n25
Torrey, R. A., 66, 72, 343, 367
Toth, Lina, 6–7
Towner, William, 84
Townsend, Leah, 49, 62
Transzend (formerly NBMS), 391
Triennial Baptist Convention, 18, 23–24, 50–51
Trifa, Iosif, 325, 325n2
Trinity, in Anne Steele's hymns, 209
Troup, John, 268
Truett, George W., 92–93
Tson, Joseph. *See* Ton, Iosf
Tubi, Lajide, 399
Tucker, John, 7
Tulloch, William (1), 240–41
Tulloch, William (2), 250
Turner, Daniel, 177
Turner, James, 239
Twain, Mark, 27
twentieth century, progressivism and jazz age, 26

United Free Church, Scotland, 265–66, 269–70
United Methodist Church, 275–76
United Navy and Army Board (U.B.), and military chaplaincy, 275–76
United Presbyterian Church, Scotland, 234
United States. *See* America
Utley, Uldine, 84n88

Van Engen, Abram, 115
Variakojytė, Marija, 313
vestments, of Puritan preachers, 291
Victoria Missionary Society, 382
Vincent, David Brown, 399
Vine Branch Church, Nigeria, 403
Virginia Regular Baptists, 36

Wacker, Grant, 27, 86
  America's Pastor, 38
Waco, Texas, 98–111
Waggoner, Earl, 22
Wales, x, 1, 6, 67–68, 254–55, 260–61, 263–65. *See also* Welsh Revivals
Walker, Arthur, 109
Waller, John, 40n3
Wallin, Benjamin, 200n2
Walter, Dr., 237
Walworth Road Baptist Church, London, 260
war, 274, 285
Ward, John, 177, 177n89, 178
Ward, William, 172
Ward, W. R., *The Protestant Evangelical Awakening,* 322
Ward Road Congregational Church, 269
Warrender Park United Free Church, 269
Washington state, Native American conversion, 4
Watson, Ernest Lodge, 283, 286
Watson, J. R., 207–8, 212
Watt, James, 242
Watts, Isaac, 200, 202, 204–5, 207–12
Wearmouth, Robert F., 278n26
Weaver, C. Douglas, 3, 219
Weaver, Frank, 263
Weaver, Richard, 239
Welch, Timothy, 67–68
Wellborn, Charles, 100, 103, 106n34, 109
Welsh Neck Church, 47
Welsh Revivals, x, 1, 6, 67–68, 263–65, 280–81. *See also* Wales
Wesley, Charles, 12n4, 75, 200
Wesley, John, 12n4, 75, 77, 156–57, 325n2
Wesleyan Methodists, in Nigeria, 396
Wesleyans, and sanctification, 66
Wesley brothers, 13
West Bengal Baptist Union, 383
Wharf Street Baptist Church, 371–72
White, Patrick, 353
Whitefield, George, 2, 12–13, 75, 336
  assurance and activism of, 156–57
  and believers' baptism, 19
  and First Great Awakening, 32
  and Great Southern Revival, 33–34
  and paedobaptism, 22
  preaches at Castle Hill, 185
Whitely, Marilyn Färdig, 4
White Memorial Free Church, 260
Whitley, W. T., 215

Whitsitt, W. H., 80n69
Wilberforce, William, 117
Williams, John, 230, 235, 237
Wilson, B. G., 372
Wilson, Grady, 27, 27n55
Wilson, Linda, 113n1
Wilson, Samuel, 170, 177n89
Windolf, Hermann, 374, 376
Winter, Ralph, 16
Wolffe, John, 286
women. *See also* McPherson, Amee Semple
  in congregational meeting, 130
  emotionalism of, as unbiblical, 77
  evangelists: Annie McLaren, 263; Miss Condie, 262–63; Miss Davis, 262
  leadership roles of, 6
  ministry of, among Separates, 42, 47
  opposition to, 237n57, 341
  and Pentecostalism, 77n57
  preachers, 42, 341, 344
  role of, in revival, 262–63
  as Salvation Army preachers, 344
  in Scottish revivals, 262–63
  of Separate Baptists, 47
  as threats, 87
Women's Baptist Home Mission Society, 132
Women's Missionary Society (Australia), 377
Women's Missionary Union (WMU), 3, 89, 95
Woodfin, Leta, 107n39
Woodruff Church in Greenville, 48–49
Woodstock, Ontario, 130
Word Communications Ministries, Nigeria, 403
World Evangelization, and Pakistan, 387
worldliness, and lack of revival, 358–59, 361
World War I
  and Christian casualties, 286–87
  and revivalism, 6, 265–66, 274–87
  supported by Baptists, 274
World War II, and Lithuania, 321
Worrell, Adolphus Spalding, 3, 70–75, 86
  and Azusa Street Revival, 73
  Full Gospel Text-Book, 72
  Gospel Witness journal, 71
  language of equipment, 72n37

YMCA (Young Men's Christian Association), 276–77
Yoruba Baptist Association, 400–401

Young, Walter E., 277
Youth for Christ rally, 101
youth-led revivals, 3–4, 55–56, 98, 100–111
Yuille, Mr., 262

Zalzburg colonists, 311
Zwemar, Samuel, 391
Zwingli, Huldrych, 291

www.ingramcontent.com/pod-product-compliance
Lightning Source LLC
Chambersburg PA
CBHW030601230426
43661CB00053B/1793